Oxford Biblical Studies Online

FREE 6-month subscription with purchase of a new book—a $180 value!

Oxford Biblical Studies Online provides unrivalled access to six essential Oxford editions of the Bible alongside commentary and annotations from study Bibles, seamlessly combined with reference material and primary texts.

Online access to the finest scholarship in Biblical Studies includes . . .

- Nearly 5,000 A–Z articles, from Abel to Zion, including exclusive content from the forthcoming *Oxford Encyclopaedia of the Bible*, integrated with chapter-based scholarly works

- Maps and illustrations

- Interactive timelines and bibliography

- Tools and resources are available to aid research at any level

D0022093

To activate your FREE 6-month subscription to Oxford Biblical Studies Online, go to https://ams.oup.com/order/OBSO4TEXTBKSCRIP and follow the instructions for entering your activation code, printed in the box on the right.

JY18726660924301

For customers outside the Americas, please go to https://subscriberservices.sams.oup.com/token to enter this code.

Please note that your subscription will start as soon as the activation code is entered.

This offer expires December 15, 2019.

www.oxfordbiblicalstudies.com

OXFORD
UNIVERSITY PRESS

A BRIEF INTRODUCTION
TO THE OLD TESTAMENT

A BRIEF INTRODUCTION
TO THE OLD TESTAMENT

The Hebrew Bible in Its Context
THIRD EDITION

MICHAEL D. COOGAN

with

CYNTHIA R. CHAPMAN

New York   Oxford

OXFORD UNIVERSITY PRESS

Oxford University Press is a department of the University of Oxford.
It furthers the University's objective of excellence in research,
scholarship, and education by publishing worldwide.

Oxford   New York
Auckland   Cape Town   Dar es Salaam   Hong Kong   Karachi
Kuala Lumpur   Madrid   Melbourne   Mexico City   Nairobi
New Delhi   Shanghai   Taipei   Toronto

With offices in
Argentina   Austria   Brazil   Chile   Czech Republic   France   Greece
Guatemala   Hungary   Italy   Japan   Poland   Portugal   Singapore
South Korea   Switzerland   Thailand   Turkey   Ukraine   Vietnam

For titles covered by Section 112 of the US Higher Education
Opportunity Act, please visit www.oup.com/us/he for the
latest information about pricing and alternate formats.

Published by Oxford University Press
198 Madison Avenue, New York, New York 10016
http://www.oup.com

Library of Congress Cataloging-in-Publication Data
Coogan, Michael David, author.
   A brief introduction to the Old Testament: the Hebrew Bible in its context/Michael D. Coogan
with Cynthia R. Chapman.—Third edition.
      pages cm
   Includes bibliographical references and index.
   ISBN 978-0-19-023859-9 (alk. paper)
   1. Bible. Old Testament—History of Biblical events. 2. Bible. Old Testament—Criticism,
interpretation, etc. 3. Bible. Old Testament—Language, style. I. Chapman, Cynthia R.,
1964-co-author. II. Title.
   BS1197.C56 2015
   221.6'1—dc23
                                                        2015004123

Printing number: 9 8 7 6 5 4 3 2

Printed in the United States of America
on acid-free paper

Brief Contents

Contents

Color plate section follows page 218

Preface

The title of this text indicates its scope. It covers all of the books that form the Bible for Jews and the Old Testament for Christians. The text opens with an introduction to the Bible in general, to the contents and order of its several canons, and to issues of interpretation, including textual criticism and translation. This is followed by a chapter on the Bible's geographical and historical background. Then, beginning in Chapter 3, I follow a chronological order. From Genesis through 2 Kings, I follow the Bible's narrative chronology; for the sixth century BCE and later I follow a historical chronology. Within this chronological framework, generally I discuss books as they are dated by internal evidence or by scholarly consensus. Thus, Amos and Hosea are discussed in Chapter 17, which deals with the northern kingdom of Israel in the eighth century BCE; Jeremiah is covered in Chapter 19, which deals with the southern kingdom of Judah in the seventh and early sixth centuries; and so on.

Moreover, so as not to privilege any book or period, I have attempted for the most part to make the discussion proportionate to the length of the individual books. The main exception is in Chapters 3 and 4, where I deal with a relatively small amount of material to introduce students inductively to new ways of interpreting what is familiar to many of them.

In my own teaching, I stress the primacy of the Bible over this textbook. I require students to read the biblical material being discussed before looking at the textbook, and encourage them to reread it after they have read the text and the material has been discussed in class.

Each chapter begins with a **short introduction** connecting it with what has preceded and providing a preview of the material it covers. Each chapter concludes with "**A Look Back and Ahead**," summarizing the material just discussed and linking it with what comes in the next chapter. At the end of each chapter is a list of **important names and terms** that have been highlighted in the chapter; these terms are defined in the **glossary** at the end of the book. There is also a short list of **questions for review**, followed by a **brief bibliography**. I have selected these suggestions for further reading to provide significant and recent treatments of material covered in the chapter and, over the course of the entire book, to acquaint students with major resources for the study of the Bible. Since the purpose of the book is to introduce students to the Bible itself and to strategies for interpreting it, rather than to the history of scholarship, the text does not often cover the views of individual scholars. At the end of the book is a more **general bibliography**; the works listed there give ample references to fuller treatments.

The primary translation used is the New Revised Standard Version (NRSV), although I have modified it when a more literal or, in my view, more correct translation is relevant to the discussion. I have also followed the NRSV in the numbering of chapters and verses. Hebrew words are transliterated using a simplified system that will be clear to those familiar with the language.

For this new edition, I have been immensely fortunate to have Professor Cindy Chapman of Oberlin College as my collaborator. She brought to the revision not just a fresh perspective, but also expertise in gender theory and anthropological approaches to the study of the Bible and immense pedagogical skill. We both reviewed the entire text, and then spent many hours discussing ways to improve it. Many of the changes described below are the result of this truly joint effort.

NEW TO THIS EDITION

- Updates and revisions throughout the text ensure that it presents the most recent scholarship with the greatest clarity, accuracy, and accessibility.
- The sections dealing with women have been more fully integrated into the larger contexts.
- In chapters discussing the Torah/Pentateuch, I have decreased the emphasis on the Documentary Hypothesis and increased discussion of other interpretive strategies and methodologies.
- In the discussion of Second Temple literature, I have rearranged the material so that wisdom literature (the books of Proverbs, Job, and Ecclesiastes) and the Song of Solomon are dealt with together in Chapter 24, "The Wisdom of the Sages."
- This enabled me to devote a separate chapter to Chronicles and Psalms, now titled "Retelling the Story of David."
- The last chapter has been reorganized to cover novellas of various types, in the books of Ruth (which has been moved from Chapter 12), Jonah, Esther, and Daniel.
- To help students develop Bible literacy, I have added important names to the list of terms at the end of each chapter.

- Translations of nonbiblical ancient texts, bibliographies, timelines, and maps have been revised to reflect the latest scholarship.
- New images have been added.

A variety of supplemental materials are available to accompany the book. An Instructor's Manual with chapter summaries, pedagogical suggestions, additional readings, and multiple-choice, true/false, fill-in-the-blank, and essay questions is available on the book's Ancillary Resource Center (ARC) along with PowerPoint lecture outlines, downloadable art from the book, and a computerized test bank. A companion website for students (www.oup.com/us/coogan) contains the following study resources: a glossary, web links to further resources, and self-assessment quizzes automated to reveal the answers as students work through the questions. For more information, please contact your Oxford University Press representative or call 1-800-280-0280.

In preparing this third edition, I have profited from comments from many colleagues and students, and I thank them all, especially Mira Balberg, Northwestern University; Peggy L. Day, University of Winnipeg; Martien Halvorson-Taylor, University of Virginia; John Harris, East Texas Baptist University; Karina Hogan, Fordham University; Richard Warren Johnson, East Texas Baptist University; Micah Kiel, St. Ambrose University; Eve Mroczek, Indiana University; James R. Mueller, University of Florida; Andrea Ng'Weshemi, Lane College; and Robert Stoops, Western Washington University.

As always, I am immensely grateful to my editor at Oxford University Press, Robert Miller, and his assistant Alyssa Palazzo, for their continuing support, patience, and advice.

Abbreviations

Acts	Acts of the Apostles	Josh	Joshua
Am	Amos	Judg	Judges
Bar	Baruch	KJV	King James Version
BCE	Before the Common Era (used in dates instead of BC)	Lam	Lamentations
		Lev	Leviticus
CE	Common Era (used in dates instead of AD)	Lk	Luke
		Macc	Maccabees
chap(s).	chapter(s)	Mal	Malachi
Chr	Chronicles	Mic	Micah
Cor	Corinthians	Mk	Mark
Dan	Daniel	Mt	Matthew
Deut	Deuteronomy	Nah	Nahum
Eccl	Ecclesiastes	Neh	Nehemiah
Esth	Esther	NRSV	New Revised Standard Version
Ex	Exodus	Num	Numbers
Ezek	Ezekiel	Prov	Proverbs
Gen	Genesis	Ps(s)	Psalm(s)
Hab	Habakkuk	Rev	Revelation
Heb	(The Letter to the) Hebrews	Rom	Romans
Hebr.	Hebrew	Sam	Samuel
Hos	Hosea	Sir	Sirach
Isa	Isaiah	Tim	Timothy
Jas	James	v(v).	verse(s)
Jer	Jeremiah	Wis	Wisdom of Solomon
Jn	John	Zech	Zechariah
Jon	Jonah	Zeph	Zephaniah

Credits

PART ONE

INTRODUCTORY

What Is the Old Testament?

For more than two thousand years, the Old Testament has been sacred scripture for Jews and Christians and has had a profound impact on their lives, beliefs, and worship, as well as on their art and literature. In its pages, we meet familiar figures such as Adam and Eve, Abraham and Sarah, David and Solomon, and many other memorable kings, queens, prophets, and heroes. The Old Testament is also, even preeminently, the biblical writers' account of how God interacted with the world and particularly with his people Israel.

But the Old Testament as a whole is not a continuous narrative. Rather, it is an anthology, a collection of writings produced and assembled in stages over more than a thousand years. The anthology consists of what are called books, and those books are further subdivided into chapters and verses (see Box 1.1).

Like every anthology, the Old Testament is a selection. The ancient Israelites produced many other writings, some of which are mentioned in the Bible but have not survived, such as "the Book of the Wars of the Lord" (Num 21.14). Unlike anthologies of other literatures, however, the Old Testament is arranged not according to when the books were written but by several other systems, the first of which is a narrative chronology. Thus, the first dozen or so books recount events from the creation of the world to the early sixth century BCE* (see Box 1.3); this does not mean, however, that this is the order in which they were written. As we will see, the opening chapter of Genesis, the first book of the Bible, was written much later than many of the chapters and books that follow it. The rest of the anthology that is the Old Testament is organized more or less thematically. Different religious communities, however, differ in how they arrange its books and about which books to include. The technical term for the official list of books comprising the Bible is a **canon**. The Greek word *kanōn* means a rod, often used for measuring, like a ruler or yardstick, and thus has the extended meaning of something fixed, by rule as it were. In biblical studies "canon" has the specialized meaning of a closed list of writings that are considered sacred scripture and hence authoritative. The religious communities for whom the Bible is authoritative do not entirely agree about which books they include in their respective canons, the form of those books, or the

---

* In this book we follow frequent scholarly practice by using BCE (Before the Common Era) and CE (Common Era) instead of the more explicitly Christian terminology BC (Before Christ) and AD (Latin Anno Domini, "the year of the Lord").

Box 1.1 CHAPTER AND VERSE

Since ancient times, the Bible has been separated into books. In the late Middle Ages, each book was divided for easy reference into larger units, or chapters; a few centuries later the chapters were further divided into smaller units, or verses. Modern printing convention usually puts a period or colon between the numbers designating the chapters and the verses, so that Genesis 1.2 (or 1:2) means the book of Genesis, the first chapter, the second verse. That is the system used in all Bibles, and it is the one we will use in this book.

The chapter and verse numbers used in this book follow the New Revised Standard Version (NRSV). Other translations occasionally have some variation in numbering.

---

order in which those books occur; this is because the processes that led to the formation of the various canons of the Bible were complex and extended over many centuries.

THE JEWISH CANON

In Jewish tradition, the Bible has three parts—the Torah, the Prophets, and the Writings; from the first letters of the Hebrew words for these parts (*Torah*, *Neviim*, and *Ketuvim*, respectively) comes the frequently used acronym **Tanakh** (Tanak). For Jews, Tanakh is simply the Bible; scholars often refer to it as the **Hebrew Bible**, in preference to the Christian term **Old Testament**, which is a somewhat different canon in terms of both content and order of the books (see pages 7–8).

The Torah

The first part of the Bible to be considered authoritative or canonical was its opening five books—Genesis, Exodus, Leviticus, Numbers, and Deuteronomy—known as the **Torah**. These books are linked by a continuous narrative chronology, from creation at the beginning of Genesis to the death of Moses at the end of Deuteronomy.

The Hebrew word *torah* means "teaching" or "law." Until modern times these five books were considered the "teaching of Moses," and Moses was traditionally believed to be their author; few scholars today accept that in its literal sense (see further pages 46–47).

The Prophets

The second part of the canon in Jewish tradition is the **Prophets**, which has two divisions. The **Former Prophets** consist of the books of Joshua, Judges, Samuel, and Kings, which continue the narrative chronology of the Torah. They begin immediately after the death of Moses, with the divine appointment of Joshua as his successor, and recount the history of the Israelites in the Promised Land, from their entry into it under Joshua's leadership to their loss of it to the Babylonians in 586 BCE. The **Latter Prophets** are the books named after individual prophets; these are sometimes divided into the **Major Prophets**—the longer books of Isaiah, Jeremiah, and Ezekiel—and the **Minor Prophets**—the twelve shorter books from Hosea through Malachi.

The label "Prophets" links historical narratives with prophecy, indicating that these narratives serve the purpose of communicating the divine will as it relates to the historical context of the prophet. Prophetic books therefore include interpretation, specifically from a divine perspective, communicated through divinely informed interpreters or prophets.

The Writings

The third division of the Jewish canon, the **Writings**, contains a variety of books in different genres. There is historical narrative: The books of Chronicles cover the same chronological span as the Torah and Former Prophets and conclude with the return from exile in Babylon in the second half of the sixth century BCE; the books of Ezra and Nehemiah continue this narrative, relating the history of the Jews in the late sixth and fifth centuries. The Writings also include what modern scholars identify as historical fiction, the books of Ruth, Esther, and Daniel; the poetical books of Psalms, Proverbs, Song of Solomon, and Lamentations; and reflections on the human condition in the books of Job, also mostly in poetry, and Ecclesiastes.

The Process of Canonization

Because of their association with Moses, the five books of the Torah had a special authority, and they were the first to be given canonical status; this may have occurred as early as the fifth century BCE, as suggested by the description of Ezra as "a scribe skilled in the law (*torah*) of Moses that the LORD the God of Israel had given" (Ezra 7.6). Because of their narrative chronology, the order of the books of the Torah never varies.

By the second century BCE, the Prophets also had canonical status; a late second-century BCE source, the prologue to the book of Sirach, refers to "the Law and the Prophets." We find the same terminology in other Jewish works of that period and later, in the New Testament. The traditional order of the Major Prophets is chronological—Isaiah, Jeremiah, Ezekiel—but this varies; in some manuscripts, Isaiah comes after Jeremiah or after Ezekiel. The order of the twelve Minor Prophets varies even more in different manuscripts.

The Writings were the last part of the Jewish canon to be collected and designated as authoritative, although this process apparently was not complete until at least the second century CE. After "the Law and the Prophets," the prologue to Sirach mentions "other books," without specifying their content; similarly, Luke 24.44 refers to "the law of Moses, the prophets, and the psalms." As these fairly vague designations of the third part of the Jewish canon imply, its contents were somewhat fluid, as was the order of the books in it.

Several overlapping criteria were used in including a work in the canon. One criterion was date: For a book to be included, it should have been written before the fourth century BCE or attributed to an author who had lived before then. Another criterion was language: For a book to be included, it should have been written in Hebrew; although some parts of Ezra and Daniel were written in Aramaic (see Box 22.2 on pages 350–51), they were largely in Hebrew, and so this did not count against them. A third criterion was extent of use. The last criterion also could affect the order of books; thus, the books of Song of Solomon, Ruth, Lamentations, Ecclesiastes, and Esther, collectively known as the five *megillot*, or "scrolls," frequently (although not always) occur in that order because of their being read on a specific holy day in the liturgical cycle: Song of Solomon at Passover, Ruth at Shavuot (Weeks or Pentecost), Lamentations at Tisha B'Av (the ninth day of the month of Av, when the Temple in Jerusalem was destroyed), Ecclesiastes at Sukkot (Booths), and Esther at Purim.

Jewish writers of the Hellenistic and Roman periods produced a large variety of writings in many genres. In some communities, some of these books had the status of scripture. But in the aftermath of the unsuccessful Jewish revolts against the Romans that ended in 70 and 135 CE, most of these books were excluded from the developing Jewish canon. Similarly, although different forms of scriptural books were in circulation in different Jewish communities, eventually this textual diversity stabilized, as one form, known ultimately as the Masoretic Text, became standard.

Box 1.2 THE DEAD SEA SCROLLS

In 1947, a Bedouin shepherd discovered jars containing scrolls in a cave near the Dead Sea, close to a site called Qumran. Subsequent discoveries by the Bedouin themselves, and later by archaeologists, uncovered several hundred mostly fragmentary documents, known as the Dead Sea Scrolls.

The scrolls are written in Hebrew, Aramaic, and Greek, and are of several different types. Many are biblical manuscripts, and their discovery provided Hebrew texts more than a thousand years older than the manuscripts of the traditional Jewish text of the Bible, the Masoretic text. Every book of the Hebrew Bible except Esther is represented at least in fragmentary form in the scrolls, and by and large these texts do not differ significantly from the medieval Masoretic texts. There are, however, many minor differences even among multiple copies of the same biblical text. The picture that emerges from this collection of manuscripts is of an evolving rather than fixed canon, a more fluid stage in the establishment of the books of the Bible. A second

FIGURE 1.1   Part of a scroll containing the book of Isaiah. One of the Dead Sea Scrolls, it is the oldest manuscript of a complete book of the Bible, dating to the second century BCE. The scroll has fifty-four columns, each about 10 in (25 cm) high; the one shown contains Isaiah 1.26–2.21.

major category of writing within the scrolls is works produced by the community, including collections of hymns and commentaries on various books of the Bible.

The group for whom these scrolls were a kind of library is generally identified as the Essenes mentioned in the first-century CE historian Josephus and other later sources. The community apparently hid the scrolls in caves during the First Jewish Revolt against the Romans in 66–73 CE, but the total victory of the Romans effectively wiped out the Essenes and the scrolls remained unknown until the twentieth century.

THE CHRISTIAN CANONS

As a religious movement that began within Judaism, early Christianity naturally adopted the Jewish scriptures as sacred texts. Almost every book of the New Testament contains many quotations from and allusions to the Jewish scriptures, which illustrates their authoritative status.

Contents

The Christian canon of what in the late second century CE came to be called the Old Testament included all the books of the Jewish canon. It also included about a dozen books that were not part of the Jewish canon as it had developed. Many of these authentic Jewish religious writings of the third century BCE to the first century CE were excluded from the Jewish canon because they were composed in Greek rather than Hebrew or because of their relatively late date. Nevertheless, some Jewish communities did consider them authoritative scripture.

These books were included by the early Christians in their canon of scripture, in part because they were preserved in manuscripts of the translation of the Hebrew scriptures into Greek known as the Septuagint. Among Greek-speaking Jews of the eastern Mediterranean world, the Septuagint was their scripture, and since most early Christians were also Greek-speaking, the Septuagint became their primary Bible as well. Moreover, several of these books were alluded to in the developing canon of the New Testament and thus seemed to have a kind of scriptural warrant.

These additional books are in several different genres, including:

- Historical narratives, in the books of Maccabees and 1 Esdras
- Historical fiction, in the books of Tobit and Judith
- Additions to and revisions of the books of Daniel and Esther

- Longer poetical works, the Wisdom of Solomon and the Wisdom of Jesus, Son of Sirach (also called Sirach, Ben Sira, and Ecclesiasticus)
- Other works, such as the book of Baruch and the Letter of Jeremiah

Also included in many modern study Bibles are 2 Esdras (also known as 3 Esdras and 4 Esdras), the Prayer of Manasseh, and Psalm 151.

Eventually these books and different versions of books were designated "Deuterocanonical"— that is, belonging to a second canon—because they were not included in the Jewish canon; they have also often been called **Apocrypha**, a misleading term that means "hidden (books)," although there was never anything hidden about them.

Another category of Jewish writings of the Hellenistic and Roman periods is known as the Pseudepigrapha because most of them, although written in the Hellenistic and Roman periods, are attributed to much earlier biblical characters such as Adam, Enoch, Abraham, Joseph, Jacob, and Job. None of the Pseudepigrapha are canonical, although many were widely known among both Jews and Christians in antiquity; they provide further evidence of the rich diversity of Jewish and in some cases Christian literary activity based on the Bible.

Order

Christians also rearranged the order of the books of the developing Jewish canon into three slightly different divisions. The first division contained what were considered the historical writings and included the Torah and the Former Prophets in the same order as in the Jewish canon. The book of Ruth, part of the Jewish collection of Writings, was placed after the book of Judges because it is set "in the days when the judges ruled" (Ruth 1.1). This first division also added other books from the Writings because they were viewed as historical: 1 and 2 Chronicles, Ezra, Nehemiah, and Esther. With them were included other apparently historical works: Tobit, Judith, and 1 and 2 (and sometimes 3) Maccabees.

This grouping of historical writings was then followed by a second division, often called the poetical and wisdom books, in which were placed other works taken from the Writings: Job, Psalms, Proverbs, Ecclesiastes, and Song of Solomon; to them were added Wisdom of Solomon and Sirach.

The third division of the developing Christian canon contained the Latter Prophets of the Jewish canon augmented by several books from the Writings as well as some of the Deuterocanonical books that had prophetic associations. The book of Daniel belonged to the Writings in the Tanakh, but the New Testament book of Matthew considered him a prophet (Mt 24.15), so the book that bears his name was placed according to its narrative chronology after the book of Ezekiel. The book of Lamentations was placed just after the book of Jeremiah because it was traditionally thought to have been written by the prophet Jeremiah. The same focus on prophetic authorship governed the inclusion of the books of Baruch and Letter of Jeremiah.

The result in the Christian canon is an arrangement of books with their own distinct rationale. First come the historical books, those dealing with the past. These are followed by books that may be understood as dealing with the present. Finally come the books interpreted as dealing with the future. The result is that the prophetic books come immediately before the New Testament, the events of which they are traditionally interpreted as predicting.

Further Revision

These changes resulted by the fifth century CE in the Christian canon, which then remained relatively stable for more than a thousand years. In the sixteenth century, however, another significant change occurred. Martin Luther and other Protestant reformers argued that within the Old Testament, only those books written in Hebrew should be considered authoritative, and so the Apocrypha—the books of Tobit, Judith, Maccabees, Wisdom of Solomon, Sirach, Baruch, Letter of Jeremiah, along with the Additions to Daniel and Esther—were no longer considered canonical and so were not included in Protestant Bibles.

After removing these Greek works, the Protestant Old Testament became identical in content to the Jewish Tanakh, but because the Protestants retained the Christian ordering of the books, the two canons are distinct.

In response, the Roman Catholic Church at the Council of Trent in 1546 decreed that all forty-six books of the Old Testament, including the Apocrypha, were canonical and equally authoritative. Thus we find division among Christians concerning the contents of the canon of the Old Testament. All the books of the Jewish canon are accepted as canonical by all Christian communities, although in a different order from that in the Tanakh. Protestants consider only the books of the Jewish canon to be canonical, whereas Roman Catholics and Eastern Orthodox Christians also consider the Apocrypha to be canonical. Christians agree, however, on the order in which the books that they include occur.

In modern Roman Catholic Bibles, the Deuterocanonical or Apocryphal books are inserted among the books of the Jewish canon. Modern Protestant Bibles, especially study Bibles, frequently include the Apocrypha in a separate section between the Old Testament and the New Testament.

The result of all of these processes is a complicated list, as Box 1.3 shows.

THE STUDY OF THE BIBLE

Textual Criticism

Before the printing of the first book—the Bible—by Johannes Gutenberg in the fifteenth century CE, all books were written and reproduced by hand. These hand copies are called "manuscripts" (from the Latin words for "hand" and "writing"). We have no original manuscripts for any of the books of the Bible. The earliest New Testament manuscripts date to the second century CE, at least several decades after the books were written. For the Old Testament, our earliest, mostly fragmentary copies are from the Dead Sea Scrolls (see Box 1.2); they date from the

Box 1.3 THE CANONS OF THE HEBREW BIBLE/OLD TESTAMENT

JUDAISM	CHRISTIANITY		
Hebrew Bible (Tanakh)	*Old Testament*		
	PROTESTANT	**ROMAN CATHOLIC**	**EASTERN ORTHODOX**
Torah	**[Pentateuch]**		
Genesis	Genesis	Genesis	Genesis
Exodus	Exodus	Exodus	Exodus
Leviticus	Leviticus	Leviticus	Leviticus
Numbers	Numbers	Numbers	Numbers
Deuteronomy	Deuteronomy	Deuteronomy	Deuteronomy
Prophets (Neviim)			
Former Prophets	**[Historical Books]**		
Joshua	Joshua	Joshua	Joshua
Judges	Judges	Judges	Judges
1 & 2 Samuel	Ruth	Ruth	Ruth
1 & 2 Kings	1 & 2 Samuel	1 & 2 Samuel	1 & 2 Samuel
Latter Prophets	1 & 2 Kings	1 & 2 Kings	1 & 2 Kings
Isaiah	1 & 2 Chronicles	1 & 2 Chronicles	1 & 2 Chronicles
Jeremiah	Ezra	Ezra	Ezra
Ezekiel	Nehemiah	Nehemiah	1 Esdras
The Twelve	Esther	Tobit	2 Esdras
Hosea		Judith	Nehemiah
Joel		Esther	Tobit
Amos		1 Maccabees	Judith
Obadiah		2 Maccabees	Esther
Jonah			1 Maccabees
Micah			2 Maccabees
Nahum			3 Maccabees
Habakkuk	**[Poetical Books]**		
Zephaniah	Job	Job	Job
Haggai	Psalms	Psalms	Psalms
Zechariah			Psalm 151
Malachi			Prayer of Manasseh
Writings (Ketuvim)	Proverbs	Proverbs	Proverbs
Psalms	Ecclesiastes	Ecclesiastes	Ecclesiastes
Proverbs	Song of Solomon	Song of Solomon	Song of Solomon
Job		Wisdom of Solomon	Wisdom of Solomon
		Sirach (Ecclesiasticus)	Sirach (Ecclesiasticus)
Five Scrolls			
Song of Solomon	**[Prophets]**		
Ruth	Isaiah	Isaiah	Isaiah
Lamentations	Jeremiah	Jeremiah	Jeremiah

Box 1.3 *continued*

Ecclesiastes	Lamentations	Lamentations	Lamentations
Esther	Baruch	Baruch	Baruch
Daniel			Letter of Jeremiah
Ezra-Nehemiah	Ezekiel	Ezekiel	Ezekiel
1 & 2 Chronicles	Daniel	Daniel	Daniel
		Additions to Daniel	Additions to Daniel
	Hosea	Hosea	Hosea
	Joel	Joel	Joel
	Amos	Amos	Amos
	Obadiah	Obadiah	Obadiah
	Jonah	Jonah	Jonah
	Micah	Micah	Micah
	Nahum	Nahum	Nahum
	Habakkuk	Habakkuk	Habakkuk
	Zephaniah	Zephaniah	Zephaniah
	Haggai	Haggai	Haggai
	Zechariah	Zechariah	Zechariah
	Malachi	Malachi	Malachi
			(4 Maccabees)

third century BCE to the first century CE, in most cases centuries after the books were first written.

Even though the scribes who copied the manuscripts intended to copy exactly what was in front of them and usually did so, they could make mistakes, as we all do when copying. Sometimes words were misspelled, sometimes a line or even a paragraph was inadvertently skipped. Sometimes, too, scribes made deliberate changes, correcting what they thought were earlier errors, adding material familiar to them from other manuscripts, and even changing what in their view was factually or theologically incorrect.

Our English translations of the Bible, therefore, are several steps removed from a long-lost set of early Hebrew originals. The task of tracing manuscript clues back to a reconstructed original is known as **textual criticism**. This scholarly method involves assessing the evidence from multiple ancient manuscripts in order to make judgments about which textual traditions are earliest and which represent later divergences from a presumed original. This is immensely difficult, because thousands of manuscripts need to be compared.

Moreover, even before the Jewish canon was established, many of the books that eventually ended up in it were being translated into other languages, so that those who no longer understood Hebrew could still read the sacred texts. The earliest of these ancient translations is in Greek, and is known as the Septuagint, from the Greek word for "seventy," because according to legend some seventy translators of the Torah independently produced identical translations, thereby proving that the translation was as inspired as the original. We should assume that, like the scribes who copied Hebrew manuscripts, the Septuagint translators wanted to be as faithful as possible to the text in front of them. So studying ancient translations like the Septuagint is another path to the original. Again, however, we no longer have the first Septuagint manuscript but only copies, so these, too, must be compared, both with one another and with Hebrew manuscripts. Besides, translation involves interpretation, not just copying, and Hebrew and Greek words often have different nuances, so it is often uncertain what the Hebrew behind the Greek was. All this is also true of translations into other ancient languages, such as Aramaic and Latin. The textual critic examines all of the evidence in order to determine what the earliest form of a text may have been.

English Translations

The Bible was originally written in Hebrew, Aramaic, and Greek. Since antiquity, translations have enabled readers who do not know those languages to read it. Translators have to know the original languages, and they also must use textual criticism in deciding exactly what to translate. Throughout history, some individuals have undertaken the monumental task of translating the entire Bible by themselves; notable examples are Jerome's translation into Latin in the late fourth and early fifth centuries CE, and Martin Luther's translation into German in the sixteenth century. More frequently, however, translation has been carried out by committees or groups of scholars.

That is the case for the most important translation of the Bible into English, the **King James Version** (also called the Authorized Version), published in 1611 under the patronage of King James I of England. Drawing on earlier translations into English but correcting them against the original languages, several dozen scholars worked for seven years to produce it. Because of its superb style as well as its accuracy, it became the most widely used English translation of the Bible.

As the English language changed, however, and as scholars' expertise in biblical languages and in textual criticism increased, it was eventually thought important to revise the venerable King James Version. The first revision, the Revised Version, completed in England in 1885, was followed by the American Standard Version of 1901, the Revised Standard Version of 1952, and the New Revised Standard Version of 1989. All of these used the King James Version as their basis, but modernized the English and corrected its translation when new evidence required it. In some Protestant circles, these revisions were considered too liberal, and other more theologically conservative versions also were produced, including the New King James Version (1982) and the New

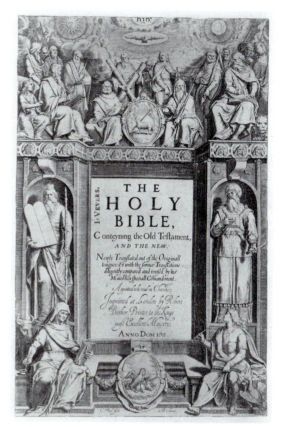

FIGURE 1.2 The title page of the first edition of the King James Version.

International Version (1978, 1984), and its most recent revision, Today's New International Version (2005). Other important modern English translations of the Bible include the Jewish Publication Society's *Tanakh* (1985), The New American Bible (revised edition, 2011), under Roman Catholic auspices, and The Common English Bible (2011).

Readers of the Bible who do not know Hebrew, Aramaic, and Greek can often gain insight into the original meanings of the text by comparing translations, especially when studying a passage in detail.

Redaction Criticism

While text criticism seeks to peel off layers of additions and errors in order to recover a more original version of the biblical text, another scholarly methodology known as **redaction criticism** endeavors to uncover and chart the development of a biblical text from its earliest written form to its final canonical form. Many books of the Bible went through several editions, over the course of several centuries, editions that sometimes included major revisions, expansions, and rearrangement. The book of Jeremiah, for example, tells us that the prophet originally dictated his prophecies or "oracles" to his scribe Baruch, who wrote them down (Jer 36:1–4, 32). So, in theory at least, there was an original. But that original was expanded by stories about the prophet, told in the third person and therefore not by the prophet himself. The result of these accumulated expansions that date to different time periods is a very different set of versions for the book of Jeremiah. The traditional Hebrew Masoretic Text is roughly fifteen percent longer than that found in the Septuagint and in some manuscripts among the Dead Sea Scrolls, and the order of some of the chapters also differs. The redaction critic's task is to compare manuscripts of biblical books like the book of Jeremiah and to account for the editorial processes that produced the current versions.

Other Approaches

Textual criticism and redaction criticism were just two of the methods developed by biblical scholars in the nineteenth and early twentieth centuries. They were enhanced by cross-fertilization from other academic disciplines, including anthropology, sociology, linguistics, folkloristics, and literary criticism. Since the later twentieth century, the number of approaches has increased dramatically, especially in types of what is called ideological criticism. These include feminist and other gender-related approaches, ethnic (e.g., African and African American, Asian and Asian American, and Latino/a), postcolonialist, and the like. Interest has also increased in the history of interpretation of the Bible over the ages by scholars and theologians, and in what is called reception history—how creative artists such as writers, painters, sculptors, choreographers, and composers incorporated biblical characters and themes into their works.

As the subtitle of this book indicates, in the chapters that follow our primary goal will be to understand the Bible in its original historical contexts. At the same time, we will sample other methods that have been developed from the time the books of the Bible were first written to the present.

A LOOK BACK AND AHEAD

Although the word "Bible" originally meant "book," it is not one book but a collection of many books, written by many authors over many centuries. Jews and Christians have their own versions of the collection and different names for it as well. Jews and Protestants agree on the contents of what they call the Tanakh (the Hebrew Bible, or simply the Bible) and the Old Testament, respectively, but those contents are arranged differently. Roman Catholics and Orthodox Christians include in their Old Testament additional ancient Jewish books interspersed among the others. This diversity has more than a superficial significance, for it indicates that the Bible was not sent down from heaven as a complete unit but resulted from decisions made over many centuries by leaders of different religious groups.

For many reasons, including its complicated history, interpreting the Bible is challenging, involving a seemingly endless array of interpretive strategies, often as bewildering to biblical scholars as to beginning students. For both, however, all methods may be viewed as means to an end: greater understanding and appreciation of one of the most important books ever produced.

We will start our study of the Old Testament with the first book of the Bible, the book of Genesis. But before doing so, in the next chapter we will survey the geographical and historical contexts in which the books of the Old Testament were written.

IMPORTANT NAMES AND TERMS

Each name or term is defined briefly in the Glossary. Its first significant occurrence in this chapter appears in **boldface** type.

Apocrypha	Latter Prophets	redaction criticism
canon	Major Prophets	Tanakh
Former Prophets	Minor Prophets	textual criticism
Hebrew Bible	Old Testament	Torah
King James Version	Prophets	Writings

QUESTIONS FOR REVIEW

1. What are some of the differences between Jewish and Christian canons of the Bible, and how can they be explained?

2. What are the theological or religious implications of the complicated processes by which the Bible was shaped?

BIBLIOGRAPHY

For an introduction to the development of the canon, see Marc Zvi Brettler, "The Canonization of the Bible," pp. 2153–58 in *The Jewish Study Bible* (ed. A. Berlin and M. Z. Brettler; New York: Oxford University Press, 2d ed., 2014; available in Oxford Biblical Studies Online). For fuller treatments, see Lee Martin McDonald, "Canon," pp. 778–809 in *The Oxford Handbook of Biblical Studies* (ed. J. W. Rogerson and J. M. Lieu; Oxford: Oxford University Press, 2006; available in Oxford Biblical Studies Online); and Julio Trebolle, "Canon of the Old Testament," in *The New Interpreter's Dictionary of the Bible* (ed. K. D. Sakenfeld; Nashville, TN: Abingdon, 2006), 1:548–63.

On the interpretation of the Bible in general, see Steven L. McKenzie, ed., *The Oxford Encyclopedia of Biblical Interpretation* (New York: Oxford University Press, 2013; available in Oxford Biblical Studies Online). For textual criticism, see P. Kyle McCarter, "Text Criticism: Hebrew Bible," pp. 369–83 in *The Oxford Encyclopedia of the Books of the Bible*, vol. 2, ed. M. D. Coogan (New York: Oxford University Press, 2011; available in Oxford Biblical Studies Online).

For translations into English, see Gerrit J. van Steenbergen, "Translations, English," pp. 435–49 in *The Oxford Encyclopedia of the Books of the Bible*, vol. 2, ed. M. D. Coogan (New York: Oxford University Press, 2011; available in Oxford Biblical Studies Online).

The Promised Land: Geography, History, and Importance

Before turning to the biblical narrative, we will look at the setting of much of that narrative, the land of Israel. This is the territory God promised to give to Abraham and to his descendants forever, and thus this "**Promised Land**" is a central focus of the entire Bible and remains so for Judaism. As part of this initial examination, we need to analyze the central term "Israel," as its meaning shifts over time and across genres and reflects the development of ancient Israelite self-understanding.

GEOGRAPHY

Terminology

Since antiquity, a variety of terms have been used both for the larger region of which ancient Israel was a part and for ancient Israel itself. For the larger region, that is, the lands near the eastern Mediterranean Sea and beyond, scholarly convention uses the term "Near East." Like its older synonym "Orient" and similar terms like "Levant" and "Middle East," it is Eurocentric, that is, from the geographical perspective of those living in the West; but as there are no convenient alternatives,

we will use it in this book. For the lands adjacent to the Mediterranean Sea, that is, the western part of the Near East between modern Turkey and Egypt, we will use "**Levant**."

Modern politics also complicates terminology for our primary focus, ancient Israel. In this book, unless explicitly stated, terms such as "Israel," "Syria," and "Palestine" refer to ancient entities rather than to the modern ones that have the same names. Also, following ordinary usage, the term "Israelites" means the ancient inhabitants of Israel ("Israelis" is generally used for the modern inhabitants).

For most of its history, the Promised Land was not called Israel. Prior to the emergence of a political entity that called itself Israel in the late second millennium BCE, this region formed part of what its frequent overlords, the Egyptians, called **Canaan**. That is how the Bible itself uses the term: The "land of Canaan" is the usual designation for the territory promised to Abraham, and the Bible uses this designation especially in narratives describing the period before ancient Israel came into existence. Modern scholars often use the term "Canaanite" in a broader sense to designate the culture shared by the ancient inhabitants of the Levant, now comprising modern Israel, Jordan, Palestine, Lebanon, and western Syria.

The principal territory of the ancient Israelites extended from Dan in the far north to Beer-sheba in the south, and from the Mediterranean Sea in the west to the Jordan River in the east (see Figure 2.3). In some periods, the Israelites controlled more territory, and in many, far less. When describing geography, we will use the term "Israel" for this territory. Modern scholars often also use the term "Palestine" as a general designation for the geographic region to the south of Lebanon and Syria and to the northeast of Egypt, and we will use it occasionally also, especially to avoid confusion with the political entities that were called "Israel" in ancient times. The word "Palestine" is derived from the word for "Philistines," another group of ancient inhabitants of the land, especially on its southern Mediterranean coast, and is first attested in Greek historians of the fifth century BCE.

The meaning of the term "**Israel**," however, shifts within the Bible itself, depending on the historical time period and the perspective represented. We can chart the development of this term through the historical books in the Bible and into the prophetic books as well. In Genesis, we meet Jacob, the foundational ancestor of the nation of Israel. One night, while sleeping outdoors on his journey to the Promised Land, Jacob wrestled with an angel who renamed him "Israel." This Jacob became the father of twelve sons, and in the books of Joshua and Judges, these "sons of Jacob," now "sons of Israel," become the twelve tribes of Israel, collectively known as "Israel." Moving forward in the Bible's historical narrative, the books of 1 and 2 Samuel describe the establishment of the "kingdom of Israel" under King David, a united kingdom made up of the same twelve tribes who claimed descent from Jacob. This United Kingdom, however, fractured after only two generations. Ten northern tribes broke away from the dynasty of David and continued to be known as the kingdom of Israel. David's own tribe of Judah became the southern kingdom of Judah. At this point, the biblical authors have narrated around five hundred years of ancient Israel's national story (approximately 1400-900 BCE), and the word "Israel" has designated a revered ancestor, a nation, a united kingdom of twelve tribes, and a northern kingdom composed of only ten tribes.

In 722 BCE, the northern kingdom of Israel fell to the powerful empire of Assyria, and the conquered population was scattered in exile. So on one level, this conquest marks the end of the "kingdom of Israel." Within the Bible, however, the surviving southern kingdom of Judah comes to see itself as the sole remnant of the original house of Israel. Judeans become the memory holders for the history of "all Israel," and they claim the title "sons of Israel" or "Israelites." This rapid summary of the biblical story in no way covers all of the intricacies of the history of ancient Israel, but it demonstrates the shifting nature of the term Israel and the need to define this term in relationship to successive periods within an evolving national story.

The term "**Judah**" has a similarly complex history and range of definitions. After the conquest of the northern kingdom of Israel, the kingdom of Judah continued to exist for over a hundred years until its conquest by the Babylonians in the early sixth century BCE. While the people of Judah gradually came to see themselves as the remnant of the house of Israel, they also continued to use the terms "Judah" and "Judeans." In the Persian empire, which succeeded that of the Babylonians in the late sixth century BCE, Judah became known as Yehud, a Persian province, and still later as Judea, a Greek and subsequently a Roman province.

It is from the name "Judah" that the words "Judaism" and "Jew" come. Many scholars make a historical distinction between ancient Israel and Judaism, considering the latter as beginning no earlier than the sixth century BCE, after the end of Israelite autonomy and the dispersion of Judeans outside their land; that is the terminology we will use in this book. Others, however, correctly remind us that such a distinction fails to recognize the many continuities between ancient Israel and later Judaism, continuities that are a central facet of Judaism itself.

Other terms that we will use are "**Mesopotamia**," the Greek designation of the land "in the middle of the rivers," the fertile floodplain of the Tigris and Euphrates Rivers comprising modern Iraq and northeastern Syria; "Transjordan," the region to the east of the Jordan River valley in modern Jordan; and "Asia Minor," for the land mass roughly the same as that now forming Turkey in northwestern Asia.

The Larger Setting

The lands of the Bible include the regions bordering the eastern Mediterranean Sea and to their east, comprising the modern countries of Turkey, Syria, Lebanon, Israel, Palestine, Jordan, Saudi Arabia, Egypt, Iraq, and Iran. In the late biblical periods, Greece and Italy also came into play, and other lands, such as Arabia, Ethiopia, and Libya, are occasionally mentioned in the Bible. (See Figures 2.1 and 2.2.)

Ancient Israel was located on the southwestern portion of a wide band of arable land that

extended from the Persian Gulf in the east, northward through Mesopotamia, then westward, bordering the Syrian desert, and southward into Palestine. This region, known as **the Fertile Crescent**, was linked by shared culture, by related languages, and, during the first millennium BCE when ancient Israel existed as a kingdom and later a province, by imperial control by various powers. Immediately south of the western arm of the Fertile Crescent was Egypt, which often exercised considerable influence beyond its borders. On the eastern side of the Fertile Crescent, we find a series of imperial powers that controlled the arc of the crescent into the Levant: Assyria (ninth to seventh centuries BCE); Babylonia (late seventh to sixth centuries BCE); Persia (sixth to fourth centuries BCE).

Since the nineteenth century CE, explorations and excavations have greatly increased our knowledge of the history, languages, literatures, religions,

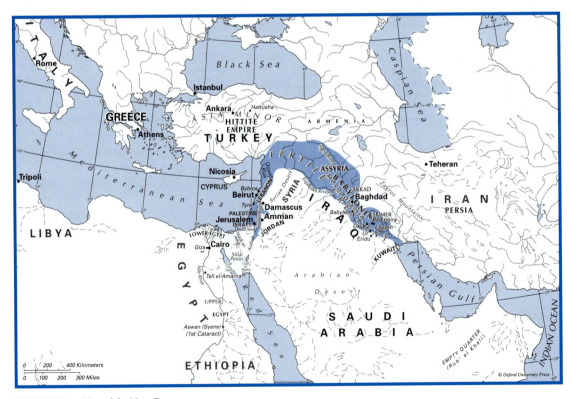

FIGURE 2.1   Map of the Near East.

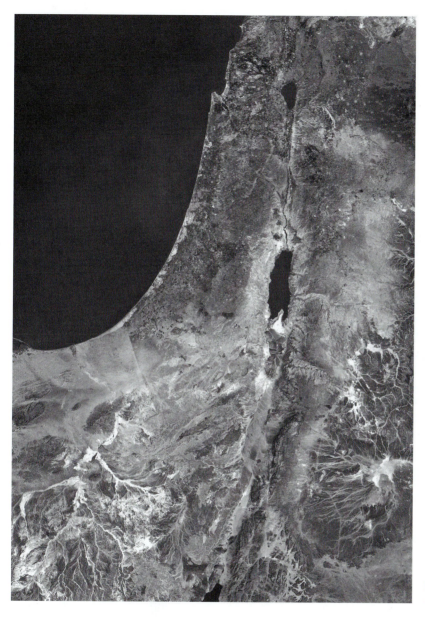

FIGURE 2.2   Satellite photo of the Levant.

and cultures of the ancient Near East, and this has been extremely important for modern interpretation of the Bible. The biblical writers and their neighbors shared myths, legal traditions, literary genres, and similar understandings of institutions such as prophecy and kingship, and of divinity as well.

Topography

The area occupied by ancient Israel even at its greatest extent was relatively small, about 9,000 mi^2 (23,000 km^2), roughly the size of Belgium or the state of Vermont. Despite its small size, however, it has six dramatically distinct geographical regions (see Figure 2.3). The flat coastal plain of the

FIGURE 2.3   Map of principal geographical divisions and road systems of ancient Palestine.

Mediterranean contained the principal north-south road in antiquity. The land strip to its east, known as the Shephelah or "the lower part," consists of foothills that form the transition between the coastal plain and the central hill country to the east. Running through the land from north to south like a spine is the hill country, subdivided by the biblical writers into districts, including the hill country of Ephraim and the hill country of Judah. Immediately to the east of the hill country is a dramatic drop in elevation into the Rift Valley, a geological feature that extends from southern Turkey into Africa. Several important bodies of water along this rift form a natural boundary between Israel and the regions to the east. In the north we find the Sea (or Lake) of Galilee (also called Chinnereth), from which flows the Jordan River. This river meanders southward for 70 miles (110 km; its actual length is about 135 miles [220 km]) to the Dead Sea (see Figure 2.4). At nearly 1,400

FIGURE 2.4   A view of the Jordan River as it flows into the Sea of Galilee, looking south.

ft (425 m) below sea level, the **Dead Sea** is the lowest point on the land mass of the earth. Because of its low elevation, temperatures in the Dead Sea basin are extraordinarily high, resulting in continuous evaporation and increased salinity; its name in the Bible is the Salt Sea. On the eastern side of the Jordan River and the Dead Sea is the Transjordanian plateau where three kingdoms closely related to Israel are found: Ammon, Moab, and Edom.

Climate and Rainfall

For the last ten thousand years or so, the region's climate has been relatively stable. It is temperate, without extremes of cold or heat except for high temperatures in the lower Rift Valley and the Sinai. Jerusalem is representative, with a mean low temperature in the winter of about 40°F (5°C) and a mean high temperature in the summer of 86°F (30°C).

As in much of the Mediterranean basin, there are essentially two seasons, a rainy one, extending from late fall to early spring, and a dry one, from late spring to early fall. The rain in the winter months is abundant; in Jerusalem, for example, rainfall averages about 22 in (550 mm) per year, about the same as in San Francisco and London.

Because of the topography described earlier, the rainfall diminishes to the east. As the moisture-filled clouds proceed eastward from the Mediterranean, the elevation of the hill country forces them upward, causing much of the Rift Valley to be in a rain shadow, so that, for example, Jericho, just north of the Dead Sea, averages less than 6 in (150 mm) of rain annually. The moisture that remains in the clouds is deposited on the western part of the Transjordanian plateau; to its east, as the rainfall diminishes, begins the great desert that extends from northern Syria into the Arabian peninsula, the desert framed by the Fertile Crescent.

For some biblical writers, this was an ideal climate, providentially given:

> For the land that you are about to enter to occupy is not like the land of Egypt, from which you have come, where you sow your seed and irrigate by foot like a vegetable garden. But the land that you are crossing over to occupy is a land of hills and valleys, watered by rain from the sky, a land that the LORD your God looks after (Deut 11.10–12).

From the perspective of the Israelites, the climate of Egypt was labor-intensive. The Egyptians had a different view. From their perspective, the annual flooding of the Nile in summer regularly provided both water in a generally rainless terrain and also fresh topsoil; for those of other lands, who depended on rain—in the Egyptian view, whose Nile was in the sky—life was more difficult:

> The vile Asiatic is miserable because of the place wherein he is: shortage of water, lack of many trees, and the paths thereof difficult because of the mountains.*

Even for some biblical writers, Egypt was paradisiacal—like Eden, the garden of the LORD (Gen 13.10), where cucumbers, melons, leeks, onions, garlic, and fish were abundant (Num 11.5).

Produce

Like many of the lands that border the Mediterranean, ancient Israel had a fairly rugged terrain, but its soil was eminently suitable for growing grain, olives, and grapes without irrigation, and for raising sheep and goats. At many periods in its history, it not only grew enough food for its own population, but also exported commodities to other regions, notably wine and olive oil to Egypt, where the climate is less suitable for growing grapes and olives.

For ancient Israelite farmers, the "early rain" in the late fall softened the soil that had baked in the summer sun, enabling it to be plowed and the first crop of wheat or barley to be planted. This was harvested in the spring. Grapes, olives, and other fruits and vegetables were harvested in the late summer.

For the biblical writers, Israel was "a land flowing with milk and honey" (Ex 3.8). The "milk" was usually from sheep or goats rather than cows, since much of the land is not ideal for raising larger cattle, and was generally eaten as yogurt or

---

* Trans. V. A. Tobin, p. 161 in *The Literature of Ancient Egypt* (ed. W. K. Simpson; 3d ed.; New Haven, CT: Yale University Press, 2003).

cheese. The honey was probably not bees' honey; rather, it was a thick molasses-like syrup, made by boiling and straining grapes or dates. The phrase "flowing with milk and honey" thus both indicates the land's productivity and accurately names some of its principal products.

As in other ancient religions, the prosperity of the nation was inextricably linked to its patron deity. For Israel, this was its god, whose name was Yahweh, traditionally translated "the LORD" (see Box 3.4 on page 38):

> For the LORD your God is bringing you into a good land, a land with flowing streams, with springs and underground waters welling up in valleys and hills, a land of wheat and barley, of vines and fig trees and pomegranates, a land of olive trees and honey, a land where you may eat bread without scarcity, where you will lack nothing, a land whose stones are iron and from whose hills you may mine copper. You shall eat your fill and bless the LORD your God for the good land that he has given you. (Deut 8.7–10)

Road Systems

The topography affected the location of major roads. There were two major north-south routes. One was along the eastern edge of the coastal plain from Egypt northward; the southern part of this route is called "the way of the land of the Philistines" (Ex 13.7). Just south of the Carmel promontory it moved to the interior through the great Valley of Jezreel (later called the Esdraelon Valley), and then up the Rift Valley to Hazor and Damascus. The other major international route was the "King's Highway" (Num 20.17), just east of the Rift Valley on the Transjordanian plateau, connecting Arabia with Damascus; a subsidiary route across the northern Sinai Peninsula connected the King's Highway with Egypt. These two international routes were used by troops, traders, and travelers, and hence were guarded by major cities and forts along their lengths.

Subsidiary north-south roads went through the central hill country and through the Jordan Valley. Many smaller roads also connected places in the hill country.

The Boundaries of the Land

Different biblical sources give different boundaries for the land of Israel. The maximum boundaries are given in detail in several texts, of which the following passage is typical: "Your territory shall extend from the wilderness to the Lebanon and from the River, the river Euphrates, to the Western Sea" (Deut 11.24). This summarizes a highly idealized view of the extent of Israel's territory. It encompasses the entire Levant, from the Euphrates River in northern Syria to the "wilderness" (the Negeb) in the far south. Paralleling the Euphrates as the northern boundary, some texts give as the corresponding southern boundary the "river of Egypt" or the "wadi of Egypt." This is probably not the Nile but one of the major rain-dependent watercourses (wadis) northeast of Egypt, the Wadi el-Arish or the Wadi Besor. These maximal territorial descriptions contrast to the narrower, and in most periods more realistic, definition "from Dan to Beer-sheba."

An example of the shifting boundaries of the land, reflecting degrees of actual control, is the status of Transjordan. For brief periods, the Israelites controlled some territory in Transjordan north of the Arnon, but later texts give the Rift Valley as the eastern border of the territory controlled by Israel.

HISTORY

Because the Bible is an anthology whose contents were written over the course of more than a thousand years, analysis of any part of the Bible requires knowledge of the historical context in which it was written. Moreover, many parts of the Bible are explicitly historiographic: They present themselves as an account of what happened to the people of Israel and to groups and individuals within it. Thus, before turning to the biblical narrative, it is important to be familiar with the broad outlines of the history of ancient Israel. As we examine the biblical traditions, we will return to this history in more detail.

For the first ten or so books of the Bible, it is difficult to speak of history in any verifiable sense, since there are no records apart from the Bible itself of the individuals and events that those books contain. But as we move further into the Bible, as the narrative deals with events described as taking place in the first millennium BCE, we find more and more correlations between the Bible and nonbiblical ancient sources.

Archaeologists have traced how culture developed from prehistoric hunter-gatherer societies to urban centers, a process that took many thousands of years. By the end of the fourth millennium BCE, cities had emerged in the great river valleys of Egypt and Mesopotamia, and, in part to deal with the complexity of life in those cities, writing had also been invented. Many ancient texts have survived, especially in the media of baked clay tablets from Mesopotamia and papyri from Egypt. Using these texts, along with other archaeological evidence and the writings of ancient historians, it is possible to establish a chronology of the ancient Near East and to reconstruct in considerable detail the lives both of kings and queens and of ordinary men and women who lived there.

Following the rise of urban centers in Egypt and Mesopotamia is the period known in the Levant as the Bronze Age, subdivided into three eras: the Early Bronze Age, ca. 3300–2000 BCE; the Middle Bronze Age, ca. 2000–1550; and the Late Bronze Age, ca. 1550–1200. In Egypt, relatively stable rule over the entire Nile Valley had been established by the beginning of the third millennium BCE, inaugurating the Early Dynastic Period. Not long thereafter, the region immediately to the northeast of Egypt, Canaan, became part of the Egyptian ambit and was often under its direct control. In the Early Bronze Age this international contact included not only trade but at times also some Egyptian colonization of the region in the form of trading outposts, military garrisons, and administrative centers.

In Mesopotamia likewise, urban civilization had been established by about 3000 BCE, and southern Mesopotamia was dominated by the Sumerians from their southern city-states. Around 2300, the Sumerians were overtaken by Semitic-speaking Akkadians, but they regained control for the last century of the millennium under the leadership of the cities of Ur and later Isin.

At the end of the third millennium, a period of instability ensued for several centuries in both Egypt and Mesopotamia. In Egypt, this "First Intermediate Period" was followed by the Middle Kingdom, which lasted until the mid-second millennium, a time for the most part of prosperity and international influence. In Mesopotamia, the history is more complicated, but eventually in the eighteenth century BCE, the **Babylonians** from the south succeeded in controlling much of Mesopotamia and northern Syria for several centuries, including the homeland of the Assyrians to the north of Babylonia proper. In Palestine, this was the Middle Bronze Age, a period of prosperity and wealth, enhanced by trade with Egypt.

By the mid-second millennium, the stability of the previous centuries was breaking down. In Egypt, a "Second Intermediate Period" of about a century was followed by rule by dynasties of foreign origin (the Hyksos), which lasted from 1650 to 1550 BCE. In Mesopotamia, Babylon itself was captured in 1595 by the Hittites, an Indo-European people from Asia Minor (modern Turkey) who would become a major force in the Near East for several centuries; although the Hittites withdrew from Mesopotamia, no centralized local control existed in Mesopotamia itself for several centuries. The balance of power in the northern Levant shifted to the Hittites, who from their homeland vied with Egypt for control of the coastal region between them, and with another new power, Mitanni, for control of northern Mesopotamia.

The expulsion of the Hyksos from Egypt in the mid-sixteenth century provides a convenient date for the beginning of the Late Bronze Age, a period of renascence that would culminate in Egyptian imperial control over much of the Levant. This "New Kingdom" was the apex of Egypt's power in antiquity. Egypt's rival for control of the Levant was the kingdom of Hatti, the home of the Hittites, but after a series of costly battles in northern Syria in the early thirteenth century BCE, the two superpowers made peace, and both flourished for another century.

Box 2.1 TIMELINE

Date	Egypt	Canaan	Syria	Mesopotamia
ca. 3300–2000 BCE	Early Dynastic Period and Old Kingdom	Early Bronze Age	Early Bronze Age	Sumerian city-states
		Under Egyptian influence and control	Under Mesopotamian influence and control	
ca. 2300–2000	First Intermediate Period			
ca. 2000–1550	Middle Kingdom	Middle Bronze Age	Middle Bronze Age	Rise of Babylon
ca. 1650–1550	Second Intermediate (Hyksos) Period			Rise of Hittites
ca. 1550–1200	New Kingdom	Late Bronze Age	Late Bronze Age	
			Hittite control of northern Levant, Egyptian control of southern Levant	
ca. 1200–539	Collapse of power			Collapse of power
		Iron Age		Rise of Assyrians
		Rise of smaller nation-states in Palestine and Syria		
ca. 1005–928		Rule of David and Solomon in Israel		
ca. 928		Separate kingdoms of Israel and Judah		
ca. 722		Fall of Israel to Assyria		
ca. 715–687		Rule of Hezekiah in Judah		
ca. 640–609		Rule of Josiah in Judah		
ca. 600–539		Neo-Babylonian Period		Rise of Babylon
ca. 586			Fall of Judah to Babylon and destruction of the First Temple	
ca. 539–332		Persian Period		Rise of Persia
ca. 332–63 BCE		Hellenistic Period		
ca. 63 BCE–330 CE		Roman Period		
ca. 70 CE			Fall of Jerusalem and destruction of the Second Temple	

Note: More detailed chronologies can be found in individual chapters and on pages 428–33.

No direct connections have been found between the abundant documentary evidence from the ancient Near East for the second millennium and the biblical narrative of Israel's ancestors and origins found in the first seven books of the Bible. As a result, it is impossible to determine whether or not the individuals and events described in those books existed, and, if they did, when they lived. Among scholars who find a historical kernel to the narratives, proposed dates for Israel's ancestors span the entire second millennium BCE. A convergence of possibilities makes a date in the first half of the millennium, during the Middle Bronze Age, not unreasonable. This connects the migration of Jacob and his family to Egypt, described at the end of Genesis, with the Hyksos period. Scholars are also divided on the historicity of the Exodus from Egypt. Many but by no means all scholars would date it to the reign of the Egyptian pharaoh Rameses II in the mid-thirteenth century BCE. This is based in part on the first occurrence of a biblical entity in a nonbiblical source, the mention of Israel in a list of defeated foes in a victory hymn of Rameses II's successor Merneptah at the end of that century.

At the end of the Late Bronze Age and the beginning of the succeeding Iron Age, in the late thirteenth and early twelfth centuries BCE, political and socioeconomic upheaval occurred throughout most lands bordering the eastern Mediterranean, and as part of this, both the Egyptian and Hittite empires collapsed. In the power vacuum that resulted, several groups rose to prominence in Palestine. The Philistines were part of a group of Sea Peoples who had unsuccessfully attacked Egypt and had settled on the southeast coast of the Mediterranean. There they flourished and began to extend their territory to the north and east, coming into conflict with Israel, which was slowly increasing its own territory. Eventually, what had been a loose confederation of tribes in Israel became a monarchy, under Saul in the late eleventh century BCE and then David and Solomon in the tenth. These rulers were able to defeat the Philistines and to exercise some control over other neighboring states. Although the Bible remains our primary documentation for most of

these events, archaeological data provide important supplementary evidence.

At Solomon's death, what had been a united monarchy split into two separate kingdoms, the northern kingdom of Israel and the southern kingdom of Judah. In the northern kingdom, whose capital for most of its history was the newly established city of Samaria, a series of dynasties enjoyed prosperity for some time. In the less prosperous southern kingdom of Judah, the dynasty descended from King David continued to rule from its capital in Jerusalem. But by the late tenth century BCE, the Egyptians had begun to recover some power and to extend their control beyond their own borders. Under the pharaoh Shishak, Egypt invaded Palestine about 924 BCE. This campaign is mentioned in the Bible and in Egyptian sources and has left traces in the archaeological record. From this point on, we find more and more direct correlations of the Bible with nonbiblical texts and with archaeological evidence.

Meanwhile, in northern Mesopotamia the **Assyrians** had begun to expand into the Levant, and their incursion affected the smaller states. In a battle in 853 BCE, at Qarqar in northwest Syria, a regional coalition that included Ahab, the king of Israel, was able to check the Assyrians' advance; but by the late eighth century, their march toward imperial domination of the entire region had resumed. They captured Samaria in 722, making the former northern kingdom of Israel an Assyrian province, and they subdued the southern kingdom of Judah, laying siege to Jerusalem in 701 and forcing King Hezekiah's submission. With no more obstacles in their path, they proceeded to move into Egypt, eventually capturing its capital of Memphis in 671 BCE.

Assyrian control of Egypt, however, was tenuous, and the Assyrian empire was overextended. By the mid-seventh century BCE, the Babylonians in southern Mesopotamia had begun to assert themselves, and by the end of that century they had replaced the Assyrians as rulers of the Near East, having captured and destroyed the Assyrian capital of Nineveh in 612 BCE. Judah was caught up in these events and, despite moments of autonomy, eventually succumbed to the

Babylonians. Jerusalem was besieged in 597 by the army of the Babylonian king Nebuchadrezzar (also spelled Nebuchadnezzar) who forced its surrender and deported the king and some of the ruling class. The new king he installed, however, proved disloyal, and so in 586, after a long siege, the Babylonians destroyed the city of Jerusalem, including the Temple that Solomon had built, and brought to an end the dynasty founded by Solomon's father David in the tenth century BCE. A significant part of the population was deported to Babylon, and others fled to Egypt and elsewhere; this was the beginning of the Diaspora, or dispersion, of the Jewish people.

Babylonian control of the Near East was relatively short-lived. By the mid-sixth century BCE, Babylon was threatened by the **Persians** to the east, who under Cyrus the Great captured Babylon itself in 539 BCE. Cyrus also allowed deportees to return to their native lands, among whom were the Judeans, or Jews, in Babylonia. Some did return, and they rebuilt the Temple in Jerusalem in the late sixth century. Persian control lasted for some two hundred years. For Judah, now the Persian province of Yehud, it was a relatively peaceful time.

As the Persians expanded to the west, they came into conflict with the Greek city-states and were eventually defeated by them in the latter part of the fourth century BCE. Under Alexander the Great, the Greeks took over the Persian empire, including the Levant and Egypt. When Alexander died prematurely in 323, his generals divided his vast territories into three parts: Greece proper, taken by Antigonus; Egypt, taken by Ptolemy; and Syria and Mesopotamia, taken by Seleucus. The latter two were rivals for control of Palestine, but eventually the successors of Seleucus prevailed. For some time the Jews in Jerusalem were left relatively free to practice their religion, but in the early second century, one of the Seleucids, Antiochus IV Epiphanes, tried to restrict the practice of Judaism and to impose Greek religion and culture on the Jews. Under the Maccabees, a successful revolt was launched, and a semiautonomous kingdom was established in the region now called Judea.

Meanwhile, farther to the west, the Roman republic was expanding its control into the eastern Mediterranean, and it captured Jerusalem in 63 BCE. By the end of the first century BCE, the Roman republic had become an empire, and it exercised unparalleled control over much of Europe, north Africa including Egypt, and western Asia. Under Roman rule Judea at first flourished, but internal dissent among the Jews exacerbated by inept administration by Roman provincial governors led the Romans to destroy the Temple and Jerusalem in 70 CE.

That year marks the end of any form of Jewish autonomy in the Promised Land in antiquity and is a suitable concluding point for this survey of the historical contexts in which the Old Testament was formed.

Archaeology and the Bible

Since the nineteenth century CE, discoveries of texts and of artifacts have greatly enhanced our understanding of the Bible's historical and cultural background. Serious exploration of the Levant began with extensive mapping and with the identification of places mentioned in the Bible with actual sites. By the early twentieth century, European and American archaeologists were excavating major sites throughout the Near East and Egypt. In Palestine, attention focused on the major cites of ancient Israel, as Jerusalem, Samaria, Megiddo, Shechem, Jericho, Taanach, and Gezer were all partially uncovered. A preoccupation of many of these early excavators was historical, even apologetic: to confirm, by independent data, the factual accuracy of biblical traditions.

In the 1920s and 1930s, many more projects were begun, and excavation techniques improved. Greater accuracy in dating excavated remains was made possible through the refinement of ceramic typology. Using this method, archaeologists could date the ubiquitous pottery fragments and, more important, the layers or strata that contained them. But very little of the vast amount of material that was excavated and published could be related directly to the Bible, and debates often ensued about how to synthesize biblical and archaeological data.

When work resumed after World War II, new projects were undertaken, and many sites that had been excavated previously (and fortunately only partially) were redug with more sophisticated methods. The result, by the late twentieth century, was a vast amount of excavated material that is still being interpreted and synthesized. In part because of the flood of material from periods long before and after biblical times or with little direct relevance to the Bible, archaeology began to develop as an independent discipline, as had already happened with the study of ancient Greece and Rome. More attention was given to the material culture of the region, and in some circles, a theoretical tension developed between archaeology and biblical studies. Many earlier archaeologists were also biblical scholars. Now, more and more archaeologists were acquiring interest and expertise in periods and regions not directly pertinent to biblical history. Many archaeologists have lacked sufficient expertise to connect what they excavated with written sources, especially the Bible, and many biblical scholars have simply ignored the potential contributions of archaeology to the interpretation of the Bible.

Among the most important discoveries of the last century and a half are ancient texts from the entire ancient Near East, including Egypt. From a historical perspective, the repeated references, especially from the Iron Age onward, to individuals and events mentioned in the Bible made it possible to construct a detailed and accurate chronology of biblical times. But for the most part, connections between ancient texts and the Bible are indirect. Moreover, like the Bible, other ancient texts also need to be interpreted, and also like the Bible, they cannot be taken at face value. For example, a ruler may claim a victory in a battle that other sources make clear ended in a stalemate or even a defeat. The nontextual discoveries, the material culture of the ancient inhabitants, are even more in need of interpretation, not just in terms of date but also in terms of function and significance.

Yet despite undeniable chronological and geographical discontinuities, the literary, religious, and institutional traditions of the Levant, including ancient Israel, are best understood as part of a cultural continuum that, allowing for local particularities, was consistent and pervasive. It is thus impossible to interpret the Bible without taking into account both archaeological remains and ancient nonbiblical texts, and that is why we will refer frequently to them throughout this book. Reading the Bible without reference to all of the data that have been recovered is like reading the text of a play: Nonbiblical evidence, both archaeological and textual, often supplies the setting, the staging, and the costumes, as it were, enabling a much richer understanding and appreciation.

IMPORTANCE

Because the Bible is an anthology, its writers have different views of the land and of Israel's relationship to it. One view, found in biblical texts from various periods, is that the land belongs to Yahweh, who has given it to the Israelites; similar views of divine grants of territory by gods to their worshipers are found in other ancient Near Eastern religions. Because of its connection with Yahweh, the land also has a sacred character; it is a "holy land" (Zech 2.12), and by contrast other lands are "unclean" (Am 7.17). In the land, the capital city Jerusalem, also called Zion, has a special status. It is Yahweh's home in which he has chosen to dwell, and it is called "the navel of the world" (Ezek 38.12), "the center of the nations" (Ezek 5.5), and "the joy of all the earth" (Ps 48.2).

Yahweh is not just the owner of the land, however; he is also its lover. The fullest elaboration of this metaphor is found in Isaiah 62.4–5:

> You shall no more be termed Forsaken,
>   and your land shall no more be termed Desolate;
> but you shall be called My Delight Is in Her,
>   and your land Married;
> for the LORD delights in you,
>   and your land shall be married.
> For as a young man marries a young woman,
>   so shall your builder marry you,
> and as the bridegroom rejoices over the bride,
>   so shall your God rejoice over you.

This "land of Yahweh" (Hos 9.3) has been given to the Israelites as their possession. In some texts, the promise of the land is made without conditions. Yahweh promises that the land will belong to

Abraham and his descendants forever; it is an outright gift, not explicitly subject to being revoked.

In other passages, the Israelites' control of the land is dependent on their observance of its owner's requirements: "Honor your father and your mother, so that your days may be long in the land that the LORD your God is giving you" (Ex 20.12; Deut 5.16). In this view, if the Israelites break the commands of Yahweh, they will be punished. Their successes and failures in the Promised Land are directly related to their relationship with Yahweh.

A LOOK BACK AND AHEAD

Israel's relationship to the land is a central theme of biblical literature, and that relationship was characterized as much by absence as by presence. The themes of exile and of return pervade the book of Genesis, to which we will now turn. In its opening chapters, the man and the woman are expelled from the Garden of Eden in punishment for their disobedience to divine command; Cain, as a punishment for having killed his brother Abel, also has to move "east of Eden" (4.16); and the inhabitants of Babel are scattered by Yahweh over all the earth (11.9).

These episodes anticipate the narratives that follow, in which the geographical focus is the land of Canaan. There the ancestors of Israel lived, from there they journeyed to other lands, and there they ultimately returned. Their story is also the story of the nation as a whole, a story of presence and absence, of exile and return, of promise and fulfillment.

IMPORTANT NAMES AND TERMS

Each name or term is defined briefly in the Glossary. Its first significant occurrence in this chapter appears in **boldface** type.

Assyria	**Fertile Crescent**	**Mesopotamia**
Babylon	**Israel**	**Persia**
Canaan	**Judah**	**Promised Land**
Dead Sea	**Levant**	

BIBLIOGRAPHY

For a brief summary of the geography, history, and archaeology of ancient Israel, see *The New Oxford Annotated Bible* (4th ed.; ed. M. D. Coogan; New York: Oxford University Press, 2010; available in Oxford Biblical Studies Online), pp. 2224–26 and 2236–47, from which some of the material in this chapter is adapted; for the geography, see also M. D. Coogan, *The Oxford History of the Biblical World* (New York: Oxford University Press, 1998; available in Oxford Biblical Studies online), Chap. 1, "In the Beginning." A fuller summary of the history and geography may be found in B. S. J. Isserlin, *The Israelites* (Minneapolis: Fortress, 2001 [1998]), pp. 21–92.

For surveys of the archaeology of ancient Israel, see the works listed in the General Bibliography, page 435.

PART TWO

COSMIC ORIGINS

Creations

Genesis 1–3

THE BOOK OF GENESIS

The Bible begins with the book of Genesis, an originally Greek word that means "beginning" and hence "birth." The book of Genesis is a narrative about beginnings: of the world as the ancients understood it, of the first humans, and especially of the ancestors of Israel. The entire narrative is tied together by a series of genealogies, or births, beginning with the "generations of the heavens and the earth" (Gen 2.4) and continuing through Abraham, Isaac, and Jacob to Jacob's sons.

Genesis can be divided into two major sections. Chapters 1–11 consist of accounts of cosmic origins, including accounts of the creation of the world, the garden of Eden, and the first humans until after the Flood. Linked to these chapters by genealogies, chapters 12–50 contain the beginnings of the story of the Bible's principal focus, that of ancient Israel; in them we read of Israel's ancestors Abraham and Sarah; Isaac and Rebekah; and Jacob and Leah, Rachel, Zilpah, and Bilhah and their children.

Like most of the books of the Bible, Genesis is a complex work. It was compiled over many centuries by ancient writers who made use of all sorts of historical and literary materials; it was given its final form during the second half of the first millennium BCE, long after the occurrence of the events it narrates. A major accomplishment of modern biblical scholarship has been the identification of many stages of this development. Because of its importance and its complexity, Genesis will be treated in the next three chapters.

In this chapter, we will examine two accounts in Genesis 1–3 about the very beginnings of the cosmos, about how in the views of ancient people the world came to be. We will also see how in these accounts, the biblical writers adopted, adapted, and sometimes rejected myths from the rest of the ancient Near East.

GENESIS 1 AND THE SABBATH

The first account of creation, with which the Bible opens, is in Genesis 1.1–2.4a, that is, the first chapter and the first few verses of the second. It begins:

> When God began to create the heavens and the earth—the earth was a formless void, and darkness was on the face of Deep and a wind from God was swooping over the face of the waters—then God said, "Let there be light!" and there was light.

The more familiar translation of the opening words—"In the beginning God created"—is influenced by the beginning of the Fourth Gospel (Jn 1.1: "In the beginning was the word") but it is incorrect according to a strict grammatical interpretation of the original Hebrew, which should be translated "When God began to create" or, more literally, "In the beginning of God's creating." The verse thus does not describe "creation out of nothing," a later theological notion, nor does it address such abstract issues as the ultimate origins of matter; rather, it deals with the formation of a cosmos, an ordered universe, out of preexisting but chaotic matter—an unformed earth and an unruly sea over which a wind from God swoops like a large bird.

The process of creation begins with the divine command "Let there be light!," a command that is immediately fulfilled—"and there was light." God separates the light from the darkness and names them "Day" and "Night." Thus ends the first day. The process of creation continues, with a kind of liturgical rhythm, through six days in all.

The sequence of events can be outlined as follows:

Day 1	light	Day 4	heavenly bodies
Day 2	dome	Day 5	aquatic creatures and birds
Day 3	land plants	Day 6	land animals humans

This is a literary arrangement, with creations on each of the first three days paralleled by successive creations on each of the next three. Thus, corresponding to the creation on the first day of undifferentiated light is the creation on the fourth day of the heavenly bodies that produce light; corresponding to the creation on the second day of the dome that keeps back the waters is the creation on the fifth day of those creatures that inhabit the regions nearest the dome, the sea creatures and birds; and corresponding to the creation on the third day of land and plants is the creation on the sixth day of animals and humans, who live on the land and eat the plants.

Each act of creation is described by a formula: "God said . . . it was so (or God created) . . . God saw that it was good." As the repetition of the formula on the third and sixth days indicates, on each of them are two separate acts of creation. This may be a literary device, or it may indicate that an eight-act scheme has been fitted into a six-day chronology to highlight the seventh day (see Box 3.1).

The last act of creation is that of humans, made "in the image of God," whose role in the universe is to be its rulers—to "fill the earth and subdue it; and have dominion over . . . every living thing" (1.27–28). But that is not the conclusion of the narrative. Rather, it ends with the divine rest on the seventh day, and thus one of its purposes is to highlight the **sabbath**, the day of rest (see Box 3.2).

Enuma Elish

Several ancient texts have similarities to the Genesis account. One is **Enuma Elish**, a work in seven tablets that describes how the god **Marduk** became the king of the gods and the chief god of Babylon. Although often called "the Babylonian creation epic," *Enuma Elish* is actually a hymn in praise of Marduk, probably written in the second millennium BCE.

The poem opens with a description of the world before creation:

> When skies above were not yet named,
> nor earth below pronounced by name.

The first two words are also the conventional title of the poem, for *enuma elish* means "when above." Then, we are told, two primeval realities, Apsu, the god of the fresh water, and **Tiamat**, the goddess of the salt waters, "mixed their waters together," and from their union the first generation of gods was born; among these were earth and sky. The myth thus explains how, in southern Mesopotamia, the land and hence the horizon, the sky, came into being where the fresh waters of the Tigris and Euphrates Rivers flow into the salt water of the Persian Gulf, forming a delta.

Subsequent generations of gods were born, and their noisy gatherings disturbed Apsu, who, despite Tiamat's objections, decided to kill the younger gods. They, however, learned of the plan and killed

Box 3.1 GENESIS AND SCIENCE

Ever since the Bible came to be considered authoritative, the description of creation in six days in the opening chapter of Genesis has often been taken as a scientifically accurate account of the beginnings of our universe. Taking biblical chronology literally, earlier scholars calculated that the world was created from October 18 to 24 in 4004 BCE. As scientific understanding advanced, astronomers, geologists, paleontologists, and other scientists were frequently denounced because their discoveries were inconsistent with the biblical account.

The Bible was written by men (and, probably, women) whose knowledge was that of their times, not ours. In their understanding, like that of their contemporaries, the earth was the center of the universe, and the heavenly bodies revolved around the

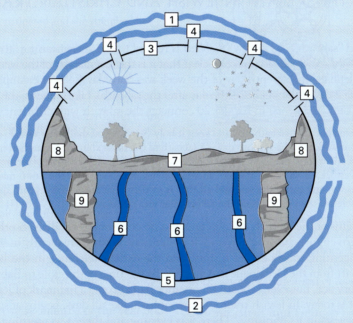

FIGURE 3.1   The ancient Israelite view of the world as described in Genesis 1. In this view, which was shared by many ancient Near Eastern and Mediterranean peoples, surrounding the world is water, shown here as the waters above the earth (1) and the waters below the earth (2). The waters are kept in place by a double "dome" or "firmament." In the upper dome (3), the sky, are "windows" (4) through which rain is released, and from the lower dome (5) springs and rivers (6) flow upward to the earth (7). Into the upper dome are set the heavenly bodies, which rise in the east and set in the west. According to other biblical passages, "pillars" or mountains (8) support the upper dome, and other pillars (9) support the earth.

and there were also turbulent waters; creation was the process by which these already existing realities were transformed into an orderly cosmos.

The second verse of Genesis alludes to the main characters found in *Enuma Elish's* battle—the storm-god and the primeval sea—but in place of a violent battle we find quiet divine control: "Darkness was on the face of Deep and a wind from God was swooping over the face of the waters." The Hebrew word for "deep," *tehom*, is linguistically related to the name of the goddess Tiamat, and in the Bible *tehom* never occurs with the definite article; thus it should literally be translated as a proper name, "Deep," rather than "the deep" wherever it occurs. Genesis 1.2 thus seems to be setting the stage for a retelling of the battle, but instead of dispatching violent winds and shooting arrows, God simply spoke.

The notion that the word of a deity was creative and powerful is not confined to Genesis: It is found elsewhere in the Bible; in an Egyptian creation myth in which the god Ptah created other gods "through what the heart thought and the tongue commanded"; in a hymn to the Mesopotamian moon-god Nanna, whose creative and fruitful word is praised; and in *Enuma Elish* itself, where Marduk's command can both create and destroy (4.25).

The act of creation in both accounts occurs through division and organization of existing materials. In *Enuma Elish* Marduk splits the body of Tiamat in order to create a dome in the sky to hold back her waters. He then organizes the celestial beings, apportioning to each one month of the year. In Genesis 1, God "separates the light from the darkness" and used a dome to "separate the waters from the waters."

We also find a similarity in the plurality of divine beings that is involved in the decision to create humanity. In the last act of creation in Genesis, the formula by which God creates human beings varies significantly from that used for earlier creations: "God said: 'Let us make humans, in our image, according to our likeness' " (Gen 1.26). The use of the plural here, as elsewhere in the early chapters of Genesis (3.22; 11.7), probably refers to the **divine council**, the assembly of the gods, which is invoked here for the final and most significant act of creation. In *Enuma Elish* the assembly of the gods also ratifies Marduk's decision to execute Qingu and to make humans from his blood. The biblical writers shared the widespread concept of a supreme deity presiding over the other gods, and the Bible contains frequent references to the divine council (for example, Job 1.6; Ps 82.1; Jer 23.18).

Finally, like *Enuma Elish*, the Bible begins with a series of births. This first account of creation ends with the summary phrase, "These are the generations of the heavens and the earth" (2.4). The word translated "generations" means something like "genealogy," but etymologically it has to do with giving birth or begetting. The same word is used throughout Genesis to introduce lists of descendants, beginning in 5.1: "These are the generations of Adam."

The first account of creation in Genesis both employs and alludes to mythical concepts and phrasing, but at the same time it also adapts, transforms, and rejects them. (See Box 3.3.) Thus, while in *Enuma Elish* and other ancient Near Eastern myths such realities as the sun, the moon, constellations, and even the primeval sea are deities, in Genesis there is only one god, and the Bible's first creation story daringly asserts that it is this singular god who creates what for other cultures are divine. To avoid even the hint that these other deities are present, the authors of Genesis 1 use circumlocution to designate the sun and the moon—"the greater light to rule the day and the lesser light to rule the night" (1.16), although "sun" and "moon" are common words elsewhere in the Bible.

Moreover, in *Enuma Elish* and other ancient Near Eastern cosmologies, human beings were created to do the work that the gods had previously been doing for themselves—it was now humans who would build the gods' houses (their temples) and grow and prepare their food (sacrifices), so that the gods would have a life of ease. In this understanding, humans were essentially the slaves of the powers that control the cosmos, but in Genesis 1 human beings are its rulers, given dominion over every living thing (1.28; see also Ps 8.5–8).

Box 3.3 MYTH AND THE BIBLE

Ancient cultures were as intrigued as we are by beginnings, and they constructed elaborate **myths**—narratives in which the principal characters are gods—to explain how the world as they understood it came to be. The creator deity is usually the principal god or goddess of the city or region in which a myth was written. Like their ancient Near Eastern neighbors, biblical writers made use of myths to explain the origins of their world.

The early chapters of Genesis deal with prehistory, and are largely mythical. In these Israelite expressions of the origins of the world, of society, and of civilization, the principal agent is the god of Israel. Although presented as a prologue to the larger historical narrative that follows in Genesis and beyond, these chapters are not historical in any modern sense.

Thus, while alluding to older mythic traditions, the first account of creation in Genesis also challenges and upends some features within those traditions. As we will see, this account probably dates to the time of the exile in Babylon in the sixth century BCE. Its authors are in effect giving an alternative to the account found in *Enuma Elish*, which according to other Babylonian texts, also of the sixth century, was recited annually during the spring new year festival in Babylon. At the end of that new year festival, Marduk would be crowned and proclaimed king of the gods once again through the recitation of his fifty names. At the close of the Genesis creation story, it is the sabbath that is metaphorically enthroned when God creates it, blesses it, and declares it holy. For the Judean exiles in Babylonia, the observance of this religious rite from their homeland punctuated their week, creating a sense of order and community.

The Battle before Creation Elsewhere in the Bible

Although the first account of creation in Genesis 1, while alluding to the battle between the storm-god and the sea that preceded creation,

also partially rejects that mythic motif, other biblical passages from different periods retain the mythological language. Psalm 74 is typical:

> God my King is from of old,
> working salvation in the earth.
> It was you who drove back Sea by your might;
> who broke the heads of the dragons in the waters.
> It was you who crushed the heads of Leviathan;
> who gave him as food for the creatures of the
> wilderness.
> It was you who cut openings for springs and torrents;
> it was you who dried up ever-flowing streams.
> Yours is the day, yours also the night;
> it was you who established the luminaries and the sun.
> It was you who fixed all the bounds of the earth;
> it was you who made summer and winter. (vv. 12–17)

Here the primeval chaotic sea—also called a multi-headed dragon and Leviathan (see Box 24.3 on page 394)—is defeated by the creator before he begins his work of creation. Similar language is used in Job 38.8–11; Psalm 104; and Psalm 89.5– 12, in which the primeval watery adversary of the deity is also given the name Rahab, as in Isaiah 51.9–10.

Thus, in other parts of the Bible, not only is there often no reference to the six days of creation, but we do find much more explicit mythology that the biblical writers shared with their ancient Near yet with a touch of annoyance: "This one, this time, is bone of my bone and flesh of my flesh" (Gen 2.23). In one of the several examples of wordplay that are used in this second account, she is called "woman" (*ishshah*) because she came from "man" (*ish*). That is why, the narrator tells us, "a man leaves his father and mother and clings to his wife and they become one flesh." Because the woman was originally a part of the man, the two have been trying to get back together ever since their separation. This is the explanation for the power of heterosexual attraction.

The first human is called *adam* because he is formed, as by a potter, from the *adamah*, the reddish soil that characterizes the Levant. Generally in the Hebrew Bible, the word *adam* means humankind, the human species in general; an individual male is called *ish*. Beginning in Genesis 4.25, and in the genealogy that follows in 5.1–5, *adam* is the personal name of the first human, hence **Adam**.

The fashioning of humans from the soil is a well-attested motif in the ancient Near East. In one Egyptian myth, the god Khnum formed animals and humans from clay on a potter's wheel; and in the Mesopotamian myth of *Atrahasis*, humans are made by the birth-goddess from a mixture of clay and the blood of a slain god, so that, as in *Enuma Elish*, the gods will no longer have to work. The biblical narrative shares this widespread notion of the divine origin of all things and the related idea that humans alone have a uniquely divine component: Thus, only the human creature, among all the Lord God's clay-made creatures, is brought to life by the breath of the Lord God.

Two trees are singled out as of special importance in the garden, the **tree of life** and the **tree of the knowledge of good and evil**. The tree of life is a motif found in many cultures, something that will give immortality and even eternal youth. It is frequently depicted in art (see Figure 3.3), and the

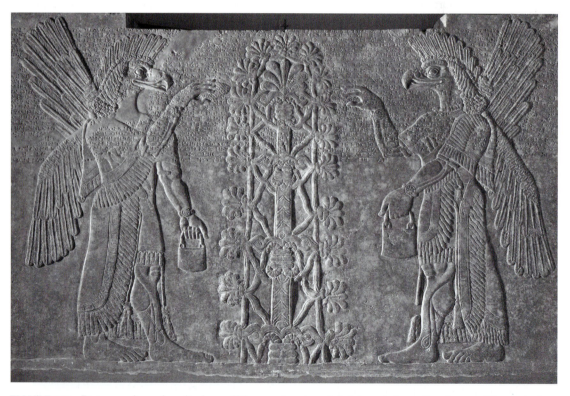

FIGURE 3.3   Divine guardians of a stylized tree of life on an Assyrian relief of the early first millennium BCE. The tree is about 4.5 ft (1.4 m) high.

seven-branched candlestick of Jewish tradition, the menorah, is probably a stylized representation of the tree of life. We will return to the other tree in a moment, but first we will consider an ancient Near Eastern text that sheds some light on the narrative as a whole.

Gilgamesh

The questions implicitly asked in the second account of creation and the language used for the answers to them are unique to the Bible. A clustering of similar motifs is found in the epic of *Gilgamesh*, one of the oldest and most popular tales in the ancient Near East.

The epic is named for its hero, **Gilgamesh**, a legendary ruler of the central Mesopotamian city of Uruk. Whether or not he was a historical figure is debated, but if he was, his literary character has embellished the historical record greatly. As the epic opens, we are introduced to Gilgamesh as an unpopular king, one who forced his soldiers to participate in athletic contests and who also insisted that it was his right to sleep with brides on their wedding night. The citizens of Uruk complained to the gods, and their response was a complicated plan. The mother-goddess Aruru made a new creature out of clay named **Enkidu**. Enkidu lived on the fringes of civilization, naked and with hair uncut:

His locks of hair grew luxuriant like grain.
He knew neither people nor country; he was dressed as cattle are.
With gazelles he eats vegetation,
with cattle he quenches his thirst at the watering place.
with the wild beasts he presses forward for water.

As time passed, a hunter glimpsed the creature and discovered that he had been freeing the animals that the hunter had trapped. He went to Uruk for Gilgamesh's help, and Gilgamesh sent back with him a prostitute, Shamhat. Following the instructions given her, the prostitute seduced Enkidu:

Shamhat spread open her garments, and he lay upon her.
She did for him, the primitive man, as women do.
His love-making he lavished upon her

for six days and seven nights. . . .
When he was sated with her charms,
he set his face toward the open country of his beasts.
The gazelles saw Enkidu and scattered,
the cattle of the open country kept away from his body.

Enkidu returned to Shamhat, and she addressed him:

You have become wise Enkidu, you have become like a god.
Why should you roam open country with wild beasts?
Come, let me take you to Uruk.

She then clothed him with part of her clothing and led him back toward Uruk, where they met Gilgamesh at a house where a wedding had just occurred, and Gilgamesh was about to exercise his royal prerogative of sleeping with the bride. Shocked, Enkidu blocked the door of the house, and he and Gilgamesh fought. The fight, which Gilgamesh won, distracted him from his purpose, and he and Enkidu embraced and became friends.

Gilgamesh and Enkidu then set out on a series of adventures together. At one point in their journeys, the goddess Ishtar attempted to seduce Gilgamesh, but he rudely rejected her advances, and in punishment, it was decreed that Enkidu must perish. Afflicted with a terrible disease, Enkidu finally died, and Gilgamesh was grief-stricken.

Enkidu's death caused Gilgamesh to focus on and fear his own death, and so he set out on a quest for immortality. His journey eventually led him across the ocean and beyond the waters of death to the only humans whom the gods had made immortal, the hero Utnapishtim and his wife. Gilgamesh inquired how they had achieved such status, and Utnapishtim replied with the long story of the Flood, which takes up the entire eleventh tablet of the epic's twelve tablets in its best known ancient edition. We will return to the close relationship between this account of the Flood and that found in Genesis 6–9 on pages 60–61. Here we will note by way of summary that although the gods had decided to destroy all humans

FIGURE 3.4   A gold pendant from Ras Shamra (ancient Ugarit), dating to the fourteenth or thirteenth century BCE. It depicts a nude fertility-goddess flanked by snakes, standing just over 2 in (5 cm) high, on a lion, and holding ibexes in her hands. The background probably represents a starry sky.

knowing good and evil," the man and the woman are expelled from the garden of Eden and are barred access to the tree of life, which would give them immortality and make them fully divine.

A LOOK BACK AND AHEAD

The first three chapters of Genesis introduce themes that will be developed as the narrative of Genesis and the rest of the Bible proceeds. Among these themes are the divinely established order of the cosmos, the observance of the sabbath, the importance of strict obedience to divine commands, and the experience of exile.

The interpretation of these chapters also provides a sample of some of the interpretive strategies or methodologies that will be used throughout this book. Two are especially important. First, to understand the meanings of a word or concept in a particular biblical passage, it is necessary to examine how it is used elsewhere in the Bible. Second, because the biblical authors did not live in a vacuum, it is essential to look at other writings from the ancient Near East, which will often provide parallels and sometimes contrasts with the biblical text.

The opening chapters of Genesis have also introduced us to the presence of repetition, inconsistency, and contradiction within the Bible. In the next chapter, we will begin to examine how modern scholars have explained these phenomena.

IMPORTANT NAMES AND TERMS

Each name or term is defined briefly in the Glossary. Its first significant occurrence in this chapter appears in **boldface** type.

Adam	*elohim*	**garden of Eden**
anthropomorphic	**Enkidu**	**Gilgamesh**
cosmology	*Enuma Elish*	**Marduk**
divine council	**Eve**	**myth**

sabbath

Tiamat

tree of life

tree of the knowledge
of good and evil

Yahweh

QUESTIONS FOR REVIEW

1. What levels of meaning can be found in Genesis 1.1–2.4a?

2. What are the similarities and differences between the biblical and the Babylonian presentations of cosmic beginnings?

3. What levels of meaning can be found in Genesis 2.4b–3.24?

4. Compare the two accounts of creation in Genesis 1–3. What are the differences in order, style, and vocabulary?

5. How did the biblical writers make use of ancient Near Eastern mythology in their accounts of creation?

BIBLIOGRAPHY

An excellent short commentary on Genesis is John S. Kselman, "Genesis," pp. 83–188 in *The HarperCollins Bible Commentary* (ed. J. L. Mays; San Francisco: HarperSanFrancisco, 2000).

The most detailed modern commentary on Genesis in English is Claus Westermann, *Genesis* (trans. John J. Scullion; Minneapolis: Augsburg, 1984–86). There is also an abridged version of this three-volume work: *Genesis: A Practical Commentary* (Grand Rapids, MI: Eerdmans, 1987).

Among the many translations of ancient myths, including *Enuma Elish* and *Gilgamesh*, the following are especially recommended: Stephanie Dalley, *Myths from Mesopotamia* (Oxford: Oxford University Press, rev. ed., 2000)—the translations in this chapter from *Enuma Elish* ("The Epic of Creation") and Gilgamesh are adapted from this work; Andrew George, *The Epic of*

Gilgamesh (New York: Penguin, 2003); and Benjamin Foster, *The Epic of Gilgamesh* (New York: Norton, 2001).

Comprehensive anthologies of ancient Near Eastern and Egyptian texts, including these myths, are William W. Hallo, ed., *The Context of Scripture* (3 vols.; Leiden: Brill, 1997–2002); James B. Pritchard, ed., *Ancient Near Eastern Texts Relating to the Old Testament* (3d ed.; Princeton, NJ: Princeton University Press, 1969)—there is also an abridged version, *The Ancient Near East: An Anthology of Texts and Pictures* (Princeton, NJ: Princeton University Press, rev. ed., 2011); and Michael D. Coogan, *A Reader of Ancient Near Eastern Texts: Sources for the Study of the Old Testament* (New York: Oxford University Press, 2012).

An insightful discussion of these myths is Richard J. Clifford, *Creation Accounts in the Ancient Near East and in the Bible* (Washington, DC: Catholic Biblical Association, 1994).

A SUMMARY OF THE DOCUMENTARY HYPOTHESIS

The original basis for separating strands or documents in the Pentateuch was the different names used for God. In one source, J (or the Yahwist), the beginning of the worship of the god of Israel as Yahweh is placed back in the primeval age: "It was then that the name Yahweh was first invoked" (Gen 4.26). In this source in Genesis the deity is known as Yahweh by Noah (8.20), Abraham (12.8; 15.7; 24.6), Isaac (25.21), Jacob (27.20; 28.13), and others. But according to other sources, this was not the case. In P, throughout Genesis, God is known as God (*elohim*) or by titles such as God Almighty (*el shadday*; see further pages 77–79), but it was not until the time of Moses that the divine name Yahweh was revealed: "God [*elohim*] spoke to Moses and said to him: 'I am the LORD [*yahweh*]. I appeared to Abraham, Isaac, and Jacob as God Almighty [*el shadday*], but by my name "The LORD [*yahweh*]" I did not make myself known to them'" (Ex 6.2–3). In the E source, the revelation of God's personal name Yahweh is also set in the time of Moses:

> God [*elohim*] said to Moses . . . "Thus you shall say to the Israelites, 'The LORD [*yahweh*], the God of your ancestors, the God of Abraham, the God of Isaac, and the God of Jacob, has sent me to you':
>
> This is my name forever,
>   and this is my title for all generations." (Ex 3.14–15)

This inconsistency about whether God was known as Yahweh before the time of Moses made it possible to isolate different sources in Genesis. Then other characteristics of the sources could be identified apart from which divine name they used, and they could be further differentiated in the last four books of the Pentateuch, where they all regularly use Yahweh.

Here is a summary of the main characteristics of each source.

J

The J, or Yahwist, source, is identified in Genesis first by its consistent use of the divine name Yahweh (spelled *Jahwe* in German; hence "J").

In the passages where that name is used, Yahweh is described with vivid anthropomorphisms, that is, in very humanlike ways. Thus, in the narrative of the garden of Eden (Gen 2.4b–3.24), he forms the first human from clay like a potter and breathes life into him; he walks in the garden; and he makes clothes for the man and the woman. In subsequent J passages, he shuts the door of the ark after all have boarded (Gen 7.16); he smells the odor of the sacrifice that Noah offers after the Flood (8.21); he goes down to view the Tower of Babel (11.5); he visits Abraham for a meal (18.1–8) and bargains directly with him (18.22–33); and he meets Moses and tries to kill him (Ex 4.24).

In J, the geographical location of many of the narratives concerning the ancestors of Israel (Gen 12–50) is in the territory of Judah, which was the dominant southern tribe and later the name of the kingdom ruled by the dynasty founded by David. Jacob's son Judah, the ancestor of the tribe that bears his name, also features prominently in the ancestral narratives in J.

In J, the father-in-law of Moses is named Reuel (Ex 2.18), and the mountain on which Moses receives the law is called by its familiar name, Sinai (Ex 19.18).

The J source has a principal theme of a threefold promise to Abraham of land, descendants, and blessing. The boundaries of the Promised Land in J, "from the river of Egypt to the great river, the river Euphrates" (Gen 15.18), match the territorial claims ascribed to David and Solomon, kings of Israel in the tenth century BCE. This is one reason that many scholars have dated J to the tenth century, although others have opted for a ninth-century date (as did Wellhausen), and others prefer still later dates. In this book, we will assume a tenth-century date.

The J source is the fullest of the four sources; when isolated from the others, it can be read as a fairly continuous narrative.

E

The E, or Elohist, source gets its name from its consistent use of the divine title *elohim* ("God") in Genesis and until the revelation of the name Yahweh to Moses in Exodus 3. Because the original version of E was probably truncated when it was combined with J (see page 50), E is fragmentary throughout the Pentateuch. It may begin as early as Genesis 15, although it can more easily be identified from Genesis 20 onward.

In E, the deity is more remote than in J, typically revealing himself indirectly, through dreams (for example, Gen 20.3; 28.12), divine messengers ("angels"; Gen 21.17; 22.11; Ex 3.2), and prophets. Only in E is Abraham called a prophet (Gen 20.7), and the same is true of Miriam (Ex 15.20).

In E, the mountain of revelation to Moses is called Horeb (Ex 3.1; 33.6), and Moses's father-in-law is named Jethro (Ex 3.1; 18.1).

In Genesis 12–50, the geographical setting of E narratives is often in the northern part of Israel, which from the late tenth to the late eighth century BCE was a separate kingdom, somewhat confusingly also called Israel. In poetic texts, this northern kingdom is often named for its dominant tribe, Ephraim, and so E is focused on Ephraim as J is focused on Judah (a coincidence that may serve as an additional memory aid). This focus on the north, and also the emphasis on prophecy, suggests that E originated in the northern kingdom, probably in the ninth century, but perhaps in the eighth (the date given by Wellhausen).

Because of its fragmentary nature, some scholars have questioned whether E actually existed as a separate source. Others prefer simply to speak of JE, recognizing that while there may have been originally distinct sources, they cannot easily be separated.

D

The D, or Deuteronomic, source is found entirely, or almost entirely, in the book of Deuteronomy. According to a scholarly consensus developed in the nineteenth century by Wellhausen's predecessors, the core of Deuteronomy is the book that was discovered in the Temple during the reign of Josiah, the king of Judah, in the late seventh century BCE (see 2 Kings 22.8). As we will see, Deuteronomy has its own complicated history, and it apparently uses traditions that are older than the seventh century. There are some connections between D and E; like E, D uses Horeb (Deut 1.2; 5.2)

as the name of the mountain of revelation rather than Sinai, and D also emphasizes prophecy (Deut 13.1–5; 18.15–22). Like E, it probably also originated in the northern kingdom of Israel. (For further discussion of the particulars of D, and the Deuteronomic school for which it was a primary text, see pages 154–55.)

P

The P, or Priestly, source is so named because of its emphasis on matters of religious observance and ritual. Thus, in Genesis, the first account of creation, which is P, concludes with the account of divine rest and hence of the sabbath observance (Gen 2.2–3). P is also concerned with details of dietary law (for example, Gen 9.4–6), and, in the ancestral narratives, the command to Abraham to practice circumcision appears in P (Gen 17.9–14).

In P, as in E, the deity is often called *elohim* until the revelation of the divine name to Moses (Ex 6.2–3). Unlike E, however, P preserves other designations of the deity, such as *el shadday* and other combinations with *el*; we will discuss these further on pages 77–79. In P, the deity is even more remote and transcendent than in the other sources, never appearing directly, as in J, or even indirectly through dreams and messengers, as in E. For P, especially beginning in Exodus, the deity is typically manifest in his "glory." This is a concrete image that means a light-filled cloud that both indirectly reveals the divine presence and simultaneously conceals it.

While J has a covenant with Abraham (Gen 15.18–21), and J and E also describe the covenant at Sinai/Horeb, in P a thematic series of covenants occurs. The first is the covenant with Noah and his descendants, whose sign is the bow in the sky (Gen 9.12–17). The second is the covenant with Abraham, whose sign is circumcision (Gen 17.11). The third is the covenant between God and Israel, whose sign is the sabbath (Ex 31.12–17); this covenant is mediated by Moses on Mount Sinai, which is P's name for the mountain of revelation.

Because P was the final editor of the already existing sources, the first chapter of the Pentateuch (Gen 1) is P, and its last chapter (Deut 34) is also largely P; P has thus framed the Torah. In Genesis,

Several more recent methodological approaches take as their starting point the final form not just of the Torah but of the Bible as a whole. One approach shows how later biblical texts are in conversation with earlier biblical texts, commenting upon them and sometimes even reversing earlier-held beliefs. This approach, known as "inner-biblical exegesis," demonstrates that the earliest interpretations of the Bible are to be found within the Bible itself, and these "inner-biblical" interpretations give us a glimpse of how some ancient readers understood the texts in front of them. A second and closely related approach is what is called "canonical criticism," which likewise attempts to look at the entire Bible as a complete text with its own intrinsic unity.

As we look more closely at the books of the Pentateuch in the following chapters, we will explore these and other methods.

PRIMEVAL HISTORY

We return now to the biblical text in the rest of the introductory chapters of Genesis, which contain a variety of mythic and other materials about early human history after creation until the birth of Abraham. We will look closely at the two sources, J and P, that are found in Genesis 4–11. First we will consider episodes where the two sources are distinct; then we will look at the Flood narrative, where they are combined. As in the accounts of creation in Genesis 1–3, both sources freely borrow and adapt material from the cultures and literatures of their neighbors, and our understanding of the biblical sources is greatly enhanced by examining parallel materials from the ancient Near East.

J (THE YAHWIST SOURCE)

In the J source in Genesis 4–11, three interrelated themes can be identified: the deteriorating relationship between humans and the soil, the

divinely ordained separation of the divine from the human realms, and the progressive corruption of humanity.

Humans and the Soil

The close relationship between humans and the soil was established in the J account of creation (Gen 2.4b–3.24), in which the first human is called *adam* because he is taken from the soil (*adamah*). That originally harmonious relationship was broken by the disobedience of the man and the woman: One of the punishments that the man was given was that "the soil (*adamah*) is cursed because of you, with toil you shall eat from it all the days of your life" (3.17). Nevertheless, at death, he will return to the soil, in burial: "For out of it you were taken; you are dust, and to dust you shall return" (3.19).

The relationship between humans and the soil further deteriorates with the pollution of the soil by the blood of Abel; his murderer, his brother Cain, is also "cursed from the soil" and is told that the soil will no longer produce for him. Hence he is to become a wanderer on the earth; his expulsion "east of Eden" (4.14, 16) parallels that of his parents (3.24). (See Box 4.1.)

An apparent restoration of the original harmony between humans and the soil seemed possible when Noah was born: "Out of the soil that the LORD has cursed this one shall bring us relief from our work and from the toil of our hands" (Gen 5.29). Noah was a "man of the soil" (Gen 9.20), but after the Flood, Noah's agriculture led to trouble. He was the first to plant a vineyard and to make wine from its grapes. The wine made him drunk, and the events that followed eventually resulted in the cursing of his grandson (see further Box 4.2). Once again, J implies, the soil and human corruption are linked.

The Boundary between the Divine and the Human

The J source highlights the boundary between the divine and the human realms: Any attempt to cross it is a violation of the divinely imposed order,

Box 4.1 CAIN AND ABEL

The short narrative of **Cain** and **Abel** in Genesis 4 raises puzzling issues. One is why Yahweh preferred Abel's offering to Cain's. Although postbiblical tradition attempted to fill in the blanks with a moralizing expansion, such as that Abel gave the best he had but Cain gave a lesser offering, the text itself is silent. In the Bible, God often chooses a younger son over his older brother; for example, Isaac is preferred to Ishmael and Jacob to Esau, and David, the divinely chosen king, is the youngest of eight brothers. The theme of rival brothers is common in world literature, including that of the ancient Near East. Both Egyptian and Mesopotamian texts tell of such sibling conflict, often with deadly consequences. The Bible contains other accounts of sibling rivalry. In Genesis, examples include Noah's sons (Gen 9.22–27; see Box 4.2 on page 54), Isaac's twin sons Jacob and Esau (see, for example, Gen 27), and Joseph and the other sons of Jacob (for example, Gen 37). The narrative of David's court describes a struggle for succession among his sons: Absalom killed Amnon, only to be killed himself (2 Sam 13.28–29; 18.14–15), and Solomon succeeded to the throne instead of his older brother Adonijah, whom Solomon eventually had killed (1 Kings 1.1–2.25). Other themes in the Cain and Abel narrative found in many literatures include divine vengeance on a murderer and the soil being made infertile by blood that has been shed violently.

Another issue is who Cain's wife was. If the narrative is understood as continuous, then she must have been his sister because Adam and Eve were the only ones who could have been her parents. In this case, Cain and his wife would have committed incest. Again, however, this apparently did not concern the Yahwist; the building of the first city by Cain's son Enoch comes immediately after the narrative of Cain and Abel, implying that there was already a large population.

Finally, we may note that among Cain's descendants is the first metalsmith, Tubalcain. One of several puns on Cain's name in the text is the word for "smith" (*qayin*); the same word is also the root of the name of the Kenites (*qenim*), a nomadic group whose activities included metallurgy and who often interacted with the Israelites. Implicitly connecting the Kenites with their murderous ancestor Cain, who was divinely cursed to be a wanderer, both explains their itinerant lifestyle and expresses Israelite superiority over these neighbors. This kind of putdown of others by an account of their ancestor's reprehensible conduct is a motif often found in J in Genesis.

and Yahweh moves quickly to stop it. Thus, in the garden of Eden story, by eating the forbidden fruit the man and the woman became like gods (Gen 3.22). One of their punishments was being banished from the garden so that they could no longer have access to the tree of life and become immortal and thus fully divine. Likewise, the sexual union of the sons of God with human women (Gen 6.1–4; see Box 4.3) violated the boundary, and Yahweh imposed a limit on the life span of their offspring. The same theme is also found in the story of the Tower of Babel (Gen 11.1–9; see Box 4.4), which relates how humans tried to reach the divine home in the sky.

clean animals and birds and two pairs of the unclean. Noah did so, and "the LORD shut him in" (Gen 7.16); that is, in a typically vivid anthropomorphism, we are to visualize Yahweh closing the door of the ark after all had boarded. The Flood is caused by rain and lasts forty days and forty nights. After the Flood, Noah released three doves in succession; the first two returned to the ark, but when the third did not, Noah knew that it was safe to disembark. He immediately built an altar to Yahweh and sacrificed some of the clean animals and birds; when Yahweh, in another anthropomorphism, smelled the odor of the sacrifice burning, he said that he would never again curse the ground, despite human wickedness.

The P Version

Throughout the P account of the Flood, readers will easily identify much of the same terminology that was used in the P account of creation (Gen 1.1–2.4a). In J, the Flood is caused by rain, but in P it results from an undoing of creation: "All the fountains of great Deep burst forth, and the windows of the heavens were opened" (Gen 7.11). According to P's chronology, the Flood lasted for a full year. It ended in a kind of renewal of creation, when, as in the opening of the P creation account, "God made a wind blow over the earth" (8.1; compare 1.2). Then Noah released a raven, not a series of doves as in J; when it failed to return, he left the ark with all his family and the animals. God blessed Noah and his sons, the new ancestors of humankind, in language again suggesting a second creation: "Be fruitful and multiply, and fill the earth" (9.1; compare 1.28). In contrast to the vegetarian diet decreed in Genesis 1, now humans are permitted to eat meat, but they are prohibited from eating blood or taking the life of another, "for in his own image God made humankind" (9.6; compare 1.26–30).

P gives the same basic reason for the Flood as J: the annoyance of God (*elohim*) at human corruption and violence. Noah is given detailed instructions about the construction of the ark, almost a blueprint, and is told to bring into it his extended family and two of every kind of animal, male and female. In J, Noah offers a sacrifice after the Flood, and therefore needs extra pairs of the clean animals, those permissible for sacrificial use, so as not to cause their extinction. But in P, no sacrifices occur before the time of Moses, so only a pair of each species of animals is required.

The Priestly source concludes its version of the Flood narrative with God making a covenant with Noah, as representative of the human species and of all creation. In this covenant, God promises never again to destroy the world by a flood. This is the first of the three covenants that punctuate P's version of the Torah. Like the succeeding covenants with Abraham (Gen 17.11) and with Israel on Mount Sinai (Ex 30.16–17), this covenant too has a sign, "the bow in the clouds" (Gen 9.12–13).

Ancient Near Eastern Parallels

As we have seen, part of the *Gilgamesh* epic is an account of the Flood, as told by **Utnapishtim** to Gilgamesh in the eleventh tablet of the epic (see pages 41–42). This tablet was one of the first ancient Near Eastern texts to be deciphered, by George Smith in 1872; it immediately attracted wide attention (see Figure 4.4). Some argued that

FIGURE 4.4 Tablet XI of the standard version of the *Gilgamesh* epic. It contains the story of the Flood as told by its hero, Utnapishtim. Deciphered in 1872, it was one of the first modern discoveries to provide a close parallel to biblical traditions.

the text proved that the Bible was true, for the Babylonians had simply copied the biblical account of the Flood. But subsequent discoveries made it clear that the Flood story was widespread in the ancient Near East, and although the Babylonian version deciphered by Smith was contemporary with some biblical writers, and therefore theoretically the Babylonians could have known of Genesis, other versions of the tale were written many centuries before biblical Israel existed.

In any case, close connections are found between the biblical and the nonbiblical accounts. In both, there is divine anger; the hero is warned by a god of a Flood about to occur; he is given detailed instructions about building and caulking a boat; and he is instructed to take on board his family and animals. After the Flood, the boat comes to rest on a mountain, and the hero releases three birds. Here is the version in *Gilgamesh*:

> When the seventh day arrived,
> I put out and released a dove.
> The dove went; it came back,
> for no perching place was visible to it, and it
>   turned round.
> I put out and released a swallow.
> The swallow went; it came back,
> for no perching place was visible to it, and it
>   turned round.
> I put out and released a raven.
> The raven went, and saw the waters receding.
> And it ate, preened, lifted its tail, and did not
>   turn round.
> Then I put everything out to the four winds, and
>   I made a sacrifice. . . .
> The gods smelled the fragrance,
> the gods smelt the pleasant fragrance,
> the gods like flies gathered over the sacrifice.

Clearly the biblical writers were drawing on an ancient and widespread tradition when they included the Flood story in their account of primeval history.

Conclusion

As the parallels with other ancient Near Eastern texts make clear, the accounts of the Flood belong to the genre of myth, like the other narratives in Genesis 1–11. Although devastating floods have occurred in many parts of the world at various times, no geological evidence has been found for a worldwide deluge such as that described in Genesis and in *Gilgamesh* and other ancient texts. This mythic dimension continues in the conclusion to the Flood in P.

The sign of the covenant between God and Noah and every living creature is "the bow in the clouds" (Gen 9.13). This refers to the rainbow, which will remind God of his promise. But the bow also has mythological significance. The word for "bow" is same as the one used for the weapon that propels arrows. The storm-god, whose wind blew over the earth after the Flood as at the first creation, has set his terrible weapon in the clouds—he has, as it were, permanently stored it there, so that it will not be used again. The conclusion of the Flood story thus reminds us of the beginning of Genesis 1, with its allusion to the battle between the storm-god and the primeval chaotic sea.

A LOOK BACK AND AHEAD

The presence of two different accounts of creation in the opening chapters of Genesis has led us to consider how this might have occurred. In this chapter, we have examined an important scholarly explanation, the Documentary Hypothesis. Although over the last century individual scholars have often modified, supplemented, and corrected the classic formulation given by Wellhausen, the Documentary Hypothesis has been where scholars begin, and we will continue to refer to it in the next several chapters along with other methods to interpret the biblical text.

The first eleven chapters of Genesis are a kind of prologue or overture. Like other ancient Near Eastern peoples, the ancient Israelites developed myths of the origins of the cosmos and of the human condition. In retelling these myths, the biblical writers introduce themes that will be developed as the narrative continues; among these are a mysterious deity who can be both unpredictable and generous, the phenomenon of sibling rivalry, and the experience of exile.

In P's schematic history, the genealogies link creation to Abraham. The primeval history ends

Box 5.3 CIRCUMCISION

In Genesis 17, **circumcision**, the removal of the foreskin, is required of all the male descendants of Abraham on the eighth day after birth. It is presented as a practice originating with Abraham and distinctive to his group. Thus, circumcision is characteristically practiced by Jews, and also by Muslims, who regard themselves as related to Abraham through Ishmael (see further Box 5.5).

But circumcision was not an exclusively Israelite procedure. Most of the nations that bordered Israel practiced circumcision, except the Philistines, who are often called "uncircumcised." The Babylonians also were uncircumcised, and so P, writing from or in light of the Babylonian exile, emphasizes circumcision as a mark of identity in the covenant community, a ritual of belonging that could be carried out anywhere. Other ancient and modern cultures have also practiced circumcision, probably going back to prehistoric times.

Comparative anthropological data, along with an Egyptian depiction of the procedure (see Figure 5.2), suggest that circumcision originated as a rite of passage at puberty, when a boy became an adult and, in traditional societies, was allowed to marry. There are traces of this in the Bible. In the account of the rape of Jacob's daughter Dinah in Genesis 34, circumcision is insisted upon by her brothers as a precondition of marriage

FIGURE 5.2   An Egyptian relief from about 2200 BCE, showing circumcision being performed on young men.

with their sister (Gen 34.14–17), and in Exodus 4.26 we find the phrase "a bridegroom of blood by circumcision" also associating marriage with circumcision (see further page 85). The only references to circumcision on the eighth day after birth elsewhere in the Bible are Genesis 21.4 and Leviticus 12.3, like Genesis 17 also P and therefore relatively late. But it is impossible to determine when, or why, the time when the procedure was performed was changed from puberty to the eighth day after birth.

The sequencing of events leading up to and following the covenant of circumcision in Gen 17 is significant. P places this covenantal mark on the male generative organ just after the birth of Ishmael and prior to the begetting of Isaac. P thus communicates that Isaac not Ishmael was conceived within the covenant.

In the New Testament, many in the early Jesus movement continued to consider circumcision a mark of covenantal identity. Paul had to develop an argument to clear gentile Christians of the obligation to become circumcised. He does this through an appeal to Gen 15:6, where God reckons Abraham as "righteous" prior to his circumcision in Gen 17. Based on the sequencing of the narrative, Paul concludes that circumcision is not necessary for salvation, and Christians are not obliged to be circumcised (Rom 4.1–12). While this view was fiercely disputed in the early decades of Christianity, Paul's interpretation eventually prevailed.

had responsible excavation. This revealed that at Shechem, a major religious area in the city had been in use throughout much of the second millennium BCE. Because the name Bethel means "house of El" [NRSV "house of God"], it also presumably had a permanent religious structure.

The repetition of these narratives suggests that each originated at a particular shrine, and only later was attached to one or more of the patriarchs. This may also mean that the tribal groups associated with Abraham, Isaac, and Jacob were originally distinct and united only later, a union expressed artificially by the genealogy, which makes Abraham the father of Isaac and Isaac the father of Jacob. This would mean that the original narratives are earlier than the genealogies, perhaps even much earlier.

Etiological narratives are also associated with personal names. The change of Abram's name to Abraham is explained in Genesis 17.5 (see further Box 5.1), and the meanings of the names of Ishmael, Isaac, Jacob, and Jacob's twelve sons are each explained by narratives associated with their conception or birth. In the case of Isaac, several narratives play with the root meaning of his name, "to laugh."

The Documentary Hypothesis accounts for two similar narratives by assigning them to separate source documents that originated at different times and in different communities. Form criticism attempts to account for a different kind of repetition or similarity between stories. Several plot elements, for example, are found repeatedly in the ancestral narratives: the birth of twin boys in which the younger shows his superiority to his brother (Jacob and Esau, Perez and Zerah), the childless woman (Sarah, Rebekah, Rachel, Tamar), the matriarch in danger in a foreign land (Sarah, twice, and Rebekah), the founding of a sanctuary or shrine (see above), and the acquisition of rights to a well (Abraham, Isaac). These shared plotlines and character types were likely popular story features that circulated orally within multiple groups. Compilers of the Bible might have preserved these well-known literary tropes because they spoke to a long-standing oral tradition. One example of the sustained use of a popular literary trope is the use of clothing as a means of deception in the cycle of stories concerning Jacob: Jacob wears a disguise so that his blind and aged father Isaac will think that he is his older brother Esau and give him the inheritance. Later, in ironic reversals, Jacob himself is deceived, by the substitution of Leah for Rachel at his wedding, possible because the bride was veiled, and by the presentation to him of Joseph's famous coat, stained with goat's blood so that Jacob will think that Joseph has been killed by a wild animal. Likewise, Jacob's son Judah is deceived by his daughter-in-law Tamar, disguised as a prostitute, and Joseph's garment, left behind in his would-be seducer's hand, becomes the evidence that sends him to prison.

ANCIENT NEAR EASTERN PARALLELS

Many of the plot elements in Genesis 12–50 are found in other ancient texts. One of the most significant is the epic of **Kirta** (also called Keret),

partially preserved on three clay tablets found at Ugarit (see Box 5.4). As the first surviving tablet begins, we are introduced to its hero, a king called Kirta, whose children have died and whose wife has left him. In a dream at night, the god **El** (see pages 77–79) appears to him and gives him lengthy instructions for preparing an expedition to another city, where he will obtain a wife. When he awakes, Kirta carries out the instructions. In the course of his journey, he stops at a shrine, where he vows to the goddess Asherah that he will present her with substantial amounts of gold and silver if the journey is successful. It is, and Kirta returns to his home with a new wife. The marriage is blessed by the gods, and she soon produces sons and daughters.

As in the *Kirta* epic, in the ancestral narratives in Genesis we have childless ancestors; divine promise of offspring, sometimes in a dream; a

Box 5.4 THE UGARITIC TEXTS

In 1928, a Syrian farmer plowing his field near the Mediterranean coast uncovered a tomb that contained ancient pottery. Further digging in the field uncovered more such tombs, and the French archaeologist Claude Schaeffer began to excavate the cemetery and then a large nearby tell known as Ras Shamra. Within weeks he had begun to expose the ruins of a once-flourishing city.

This city had been occupied, with interruptions, since about 6500 BCE. In the latest level of occupation, which is dated to the end of the Late Bronze Age about 1200 BCE, Schaeffer found many clay tablets, some inscribed with a previously unknown writing system. These tablets were quickly deciphered, and they revealed that the name of the site in antiquity was Ugarit; the language of the newly deciphered texts was thus called **Ugaritic**. Eventually, many thousands of texts were recovered in the ongoing excavations at Ras Shamra and in its vicinity. Several dozen of them, written in Ugaritic and found in the vicinity of the city's temples, were myths, notably about the gods El and Baal, and epics, concerning the legendary founder of the royal house of Ugarit, Kirta, and another ancient hero, Danel (mentioned in Ezek 14.14).

This discovery was one of the most important of the twentieth century for illuminating the larger context in which the Hebrew Bible was written. Knowledge of Canaanite religion and culture, of which the texts from Ugarit are an exemplar, was vastly enhanced, and the understanding of the religion of ancient Israel was transformed.

journey for a wife; in the course of the journey a stop at a shrine where a vow is made; and ultimately the birth of children. While these plot elements in *Kirta* do not occur in the same order in Genesis, nor are all found in connection with every patriarch, a remarkable clustering of similar elements is found, and it is likely that both the Canaanites of Ugarit and the ancient Israelites used a common set of motifs when telling the story of an ancestral founder.

THE JOSEPH NARRATIVE

Some scholars have identified the cycle of stories concerning Jacob's favorite son **Joseph** in Genesis 37–50 as an originally independent literary composition, a kind of novella or short work of historical fiction, not just a composite of traditions like the preceding ancestral narratives. As such, it is an artfully constructed story about only one of the sons of Jacob, Joseph, and is not a complete account of his life but rather focuses on his fraternal relationships and his life in Egypt.

Although set in Egypt, little in the narrative has a distinctive Egyptian coloring, and few details can be correlated with Egyptian sources. Thus, no internal clues exist as to the original date of the Joseph story, and several periods from the tenth century BCE onward have been proposed. Moreover, no mention of Joseph son of Jacob as an Egyptian official is found in any Egyptian records as we might expect, because he is described as the most important official in Egypt after the pharaoh himself. If there is some historical kernel underlying the narrative, then a plausible setting for the rise to power of a Semite in largely xenophobic and nationalistic Egypt is the period from the mid-seventeenth to the mid-sixteenth centuries BCE, called the "Hyksos Period," when for a brief time Egypt was ruled by dynasties originally of Semitic origin.

The hero of the narrative is Joseph, Jacob's favorite son. Like fictional heroes of later biblical times, he manages to survive in exile in a foreign court, overcoming all sorts of obstacles with divine assistance, and eventually saving his family.

In contrast to the earlier ancestral narratives, no direct divine revelation comes to Joseph, and women are for the most part absent from the Joseph story. At the same time, the Joseph story has been integrated carefully into its larger narrative context. Most of the major characters in the Joseph story have already been introduced, especially Jacob and his many sons. Moreover, similarities of plot exist, especially the rivalry between brothers. Other themes familiar from previous chapters in Genesis include dreams, famine, danger to the hero, journey to Egypt, and deception. Clothing is especially important: The "coat of many colors" (Gen 37.3) shows his father Jacob's preference for Joseph, as the older son of Rachel, Jacob's favorite wife. He is stripped of this coat (37.23), and then it is stained with goat's blood by his brothers to deceive Jacob into thinking that Joseph has been killed. This distinctive garment was probably a special robe worn by royalty; it thus anticipates Joseph's rise to power in Egypt, where he became second only to the pharaoh himself; the exact phrase is used elsewhere only of the robe worn by King David's daughter Tamar (2 Sam 13.18–19). Joseph is stripped of his clothing again when he is falsely accused of rape. When he rises to power in Egypt, Joseph is clothed with appropriate Egyptian garb and, in an ironic reversal, gives his brothers fine garments as a gift.

In some ways Joseph is incidental to the main narrative—the god of the ancestors is the god of Abraham, Isaac, and Jacob. Yet his travels mirror those of the Israelites as a group. He is the first of Jacob's family to go to Egypt from Canaan, and his body, properly mummified in Egyptian manner, will accompany the Israelites on their journey out of Egypt and will eventually be laid to rest in Canaan. The story of Judah and Tamar (Gen 38) is a digression from the story of Joseph, and may not be part of the original novella. It does, however, contain themes found both in the main narrative and the Joseph story, including deception by clothing, and especially the birth of twins, in which the younger supersedes the older.

THE ANCESTORS OF ISRAEL

Genesis is the story of origin for what ultimately became the nation of Israel and the kingdoms of Israel and Judah. In the ancestral narratives, ancient Israelites and later Judeans remembered and celebrated their founding heroes. Abraham is presented as an ideal figure, obeying every divine command. Although a modern reader might question his willingness to deceive, as when he tells Sarah to say that she is his sister (Gen 12.11–13) and when he conceals his intention of sacrificing Isaac both from his servants and from Isaac himself (22.5, 8), it is unlikely that many ancient readers would have viewed such episodes negatively. Rather, Abraham is a model believer, which is how he is remembered by Jews, Christians, and Muslims (see Box 5.5). His wife Sarah is also a complex figure. She attempts to solve the problem of her own barrenness by offering her slave woman Hagar to Abraham as a wife. Later, when Sarah is able to bear her own son, she regards both Hagar and her son Ishmael as a threat and convinces Abraham to send both away.

Isaac is the least developed of the three male ancestors, appearing in only a few episodes as a major character, and even then, he is often the passive victim. All of the Isaac-related episodes are set in the south, and for this reason many scholars have proposed that Isaac was originally the ancestor of a relatively minor southern tribe that eventually joined Israel and was connected with the other tribes by genealogical link with Abraham and Jacob.

Rebekah, on the other hand, provides dramatic examples of how the matriarchs are active participants in the narratives. After agreeing to her marriage to Isaac, she, like Abraham, travels from Haran to the Promised Land. While pregnant, she receives a revelation from Yahweh about her sons, and later in life, she initiates the scheme to get the inheritance for her favorite son Jacob at the expense of his older twin brother Esau. Using language that replicates Abraham's call, Rebekah responds to a "call" to "go" from "her country," "her kindred," and "her father's house" (Gen 12.1; 24.2–4, 28). She receives a blessing that echoes part of the blessing to Abraham:

> May you, our sister, become thousands of myriads;
> may your descendants gain possession of the
> gates of their enemies. (Gen 24.60; see 22.17)

Like the patriarchs and distinct from the other matriarchs, Rebekah is introduced with a birth

---

Box 5.5 ABRAHAM, FATHER OF BELIEVERS

Abraham has a dominant role in the three monotheistic religions—Judaism, Christianity, and Islam—so much so that they are often called the "Abrahamic" religions. For all three, Abraham is both a progenitor and the "friend" of God (2 Chr 20.7; Isa 41.8; Jas 2.23; Qur'an 4.125).

For Jews, Abraham is their ancestor, through Isaac and Jacob, and also a model believer. Because Jesus was a Jew, he too was a descendant of Abraham (Mt 1.1; Lk 3.34). For Christians in general, Abraham is a model of faith (Rom 4.16–22), whose righteousness was approved by God before he was commanded to practice circumcision. Muslims trace their connection to Abraham through Ishmael, Abraham's son by Hagar, and Ishmael's descendants include the prophet Muhammad, born in Arabia in the late sixth century CE. Thus for Muslims too, Abraham is the father of believers, and he is considered the first Muslim, a word that literally means "one who surrenders" (to God).

notification and full genealogy (Gen 22.20–24; 24.15, 24). When she is pregnant, she inquires directly of Yahweh concerning her difficult pregnancy, and she receives a special revelation that is not shared with her husband Isaac (Gen 25.22–28). Finally, Rebekah's favored son Jacob inherits her skills in trickery and deception and uses these traits to achieve the favored position of heir in his father's house. Because of the relative weakness of Isaac as a character in the ancestral narratives and the comparative complexity of Rebekah, some scholars have suggested that Rebekah is the primary genealogical link between Abraham and Jacob.

Jacob is the most complex of the three patriarchs. A trickster and a deceiver from birth, he himself is also ironically the victim of treachery and deception. Despite Jacob's flaws of character, however, God works through him, and ultimately transforms him, when he sees God face to face and is renamed Israel (Gen 32.28–30). Jacob's household, which comes to represent symbolically the "house of Israel," includes his two primary wives, **Leah** and **Rachel**, and his two secondary wives, Bilhah and Zilpah, and twelve sons and a daughter. Among his wives, Rachel is the one he loved and the one who, like Sarah and Rebekah before her, struggled with barrenness. Eventually, Rachel bears two sons, but dies in childbirth with the second. The matriarchs' struggles with infertility and this example of maternal death likely reflect common experiences among ancient Israelite women. Theologically, overcoming infertility became a sign of divine favor and marked the son as divinely chosen.

The Sons of Jacob

The narratives about the sons of Jacob are a kind of personalized history of the tribes whose supposed ancestors they were. Eventually the dominant tribes were Judah in the south and the Joseph tribe of Ephraim in the north, and the prominence of those two tribes is evident both in the stories of their ancestors and in the positive poetic characterizations of them in the tribal catalogue in Genesis 49, an early Israelite poem.

Reuben, the firstborn of Jacob's sons, loses that status because he sleeps with Bilhah, his father's concubine. The next oldest, Simeon and Levi, are punished for their violence in the affair of the rape of Jacob's daughter Dinah. Of the sons of Leah, that makes Judah the heir of Jacob, and Joseph, the older of the two sons of Rachel, is his counterpart.

The ancestors of the tribes that were geographically on the periphery, Dan and Naphtali, and Gad and Asher, are sons of the secondary wives of Jacob, Zilpah the maid of Leah and Bilhah the maid of Rachel. As such, they are given only perfunctory attention both in the narrative and in Genesis 49.

Genealogies

One social convention that recurs in the ancestral narratives is **endogamy**, marriage within one's ethnic, cultural, or religious community. For the survival of the community's identity, and for keeping its property within the group, endogamy was essential. In Genesis, as in much of the rest of the Bible, exogamy, or marriage outside the group, was frowned upon.

Although he had moved some distance from his ancestral home in northern Mesopotamia, Abraham sent his servant back there to get a wife for his son Isaac from among his kin. Isaac urged Jacob to do the same, unlike his brother Esau, who had married Canaanite women. Figure 5.3 shows the intricate network of relationships by marriage and descent in the extended family of Terah, Abraham's father.

Despite the cultural preference for endogamy, however, the patriarchs often married outside the group. Abraham fathered children through Hagar, an Egyptian, and through Keturah, probably also a foreigner (Gen 25.1–5); Esau "took his wives from among the Canaanites," both a Hittite woman and a Hivite woman (Gen 36.2), as well as Ishmael's daughter; Judah married Shua, also a Canaanite; Joseph married Asenath, also an Egyptian. The issue of intermarriage was one that continued to divide the Israelites and subsequently Judaism. Despite the recognition that marriage outside the group threatened the preservation of its identity,

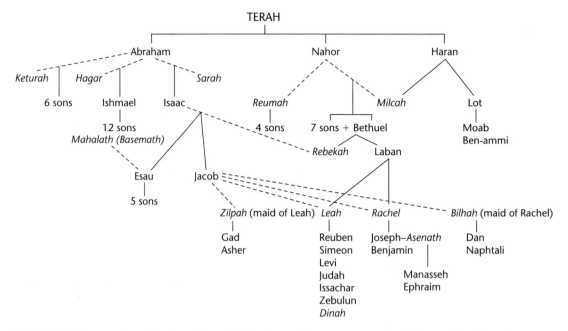

FIGURE 5.3   The genealogy of the descendants of Terah, showing their intermarriages and offspring. Note: Women's names are in italics. Solid lines indicate descent; dotted lines indicate marriage.

especially its religious identity, individuals continued to do so, like Moses, whose wife Zipporah was the daughter of a priest of Midian. Other major biblical figures were acknowledged as born from such "mixed" marriages—most notably David, whose great-grandmother, Ruth, was a Moabite.

The genealogy in Figure 5.3 shows an ancient recognition of kinship among various groups. Thus, while the genealogies can exalt one group at the expense of another, they also recognize close connections among tribal and national entities in the Levant, as their related languages and shared cultural features illustrate. One of the latter is the organization of tribal groups by multiples of six or twelve: Abraham had six sons by his third wife, Keturah, and Nahor, Ishmael, and Jacob each had twelve.

The narratives attached to the genealogies, and the poetic catalogue of tribes in Genesis 49, elaborate on the relationships. Thus, for example, the tribe of Levi's eventual loss of land inheritance (Num 18.23–24) is connected to its ancestor's role in the violent retaliation for the rape of Dinah (Gen 49.5–7). With Levi removed from the list, in

order to maintain the number twelve another had to be added, and so the Joseph tribe was subdivided into Manasseh and Ephraim, who alone among his grandsons were blessed by Jacob. But Jacob reversed the birth order and gave the blessing to Ephraim, the younger son (Gen 48.14–20). Hence, at the close of Genesis, we are left with two dominant tribes—Judah in the south and Ephraim in the north with Ephraim as the presumptive heir.

The genealogies thus are expressions of relationships between groups. They explain how one group became more powerful than another, but by attributing kinship to originally distinct groups, they support political and social interaction and even unity.

HISTORY AND THE ANCESTORS OF ISRAEL

The further removed biblical writers are from the events they describe, the less secure are modern scholars' attempts to determine whether those events actually happened. With regard to Abraham and Sarah, Isaac and Rebekah, and Jacob and his family, we are for the most part in the realm of legend, and it is extremely difficult to determine if any of the traditions concerning them have a historical basis.

The quest for historicity is complicated by several factors. First, biblical chronology for this period is unreliable; note especially the long life spans attributed to the ancestors. Second, because so many stages of composition and editing have shaped the narratives, they often contain anachronisms, since each generation of storytellers, writers, and editors added details from their own times. Third, because of the use of different sources in the final form of the narrative, many inconsistencies are found.

For example, the ancestral homeland of the ancestors is northern Mesopotamia, in the vicinity of Haran. There Terah had lived (Gen 11.31) and Abraham was born (24.4); from there Abraham had left for the land of Canaan (12.4); and from the extended family in that region wives were arranged for Isaac (24.10) and Jacob (29.4). Only twice in Genesis (11.28–31; 15.7) is the place of origin of Terah and Abraham given as "Ur of the Chaldeans," a difficult phrase. There was a major city in southern Mesopotamia called Ur, occupied from the fifth to the mid-first millennium BCE. The term "Chaldeans" is often a synonym for Babylonians, but it is unattested in nonbiblical sources until the early first millennium. The identification of Abraham's original home as Ur may be an anachronism, perhaps to be connected with the exile in Babylon in the sixth century BCE. Details such as this, then, come from the times of the writers and editors of the narratives and cannot be considered historical.

The ancestors of Israel are for the most part described as itinerant herders with flocks of small cattle, moving about the land but never settling in one place. They resemble the seminomads who have existed in the Middle East from earliest historical times to the present, interacting and sometimes in tension with the more settled farmers, but primarily subsisting on the fringes of the latters' lands. As such, they would have been insignificant to the established societies of their day, extras, as it were, on the set of world history. Thus, it is not surprising that in the extensive written records we have from the entire second millennium BCE, no mention is made of any of the characters in Genesis. In the one case where we have what appears to be a historiographic account, the story of the conflict between two groups of kings (Gen 14), none of the nine kings named in the narrative, nor Melchizedek, king of (Jeru)Salem (14.18), can be identified in nonbiblical sources. Conversely, no mention can be found in Genesis of any known historical figures. The writers of Genesis are usually vague, not naming, for example, the pharaohs who interacted with Abraham and Joseph.

Given this lack of nonbiblical correlations, it is not surprising that modern scholars have dated the period in which Israel's ancestors lived from as early as the mid-third millennium BCE to as late as the early first, and some scholars think that the entire narrative is a historical fiction written late in the biblical period.

Although parallels in other ancient texts have shed light on the Genesis narratives, they have not been able to provide conclusive evidence for dating the earliest traditions within them. This much can be said: Many of the details of lifestyle and social custom embedded in the narrative are not inconsistent with a second-millennium BCE setting. At the same time, because the narratives were edited and reedited over the course of much of the first half of the first millennium BCE, they also contain many details that fit best in that period. But one body of data may be significant, concerning the deity worshiped by the ancestors, "the god of the fathers."

THE RELIGION OF THE ANCESTORS

As we have seen, in the J source, the name Yahweh is used from the time of Adam onward. But in both E and P, that name is not revealed until the time of Moses. Both of the latter sources use the Hebrew word *elohim* for the deity until that point, but P also uses other titles. The P account of the call of Moses summarizes its understanding as follows:

> God . . . spoke to Moses and said to him: "I am Yahweh. I appeared to Abraham, Isaac, and Jacob as El Shadday [NRSV: God Almighty], but by my name 'Yahweh' I did not make myself known to them." (Ex 6.2–3)

Not only does P here disagree with J, asserting that God was not known to the ancestors as Yahweh, but P uses an ancient title for the deity, "El Shadday." This title occurs five times in the P narrative in Genesis (17.1; 28.3; 35.11; 43.14; 48.3) and consists of two parts: the divine name El and the epithet "Shadday," which probably means "the one of the mountain." The same divine name El is used in other combinations in Genesis, including "El Elyon" ("El the most high"), "El Olam" ("El the eternal"), "El Roi" ("El the one who appears" [or "the one who sees"]), "El Bethel" ("El of Bethel"), and especially in the phrase "El, the god of Abraham/my father/Isaac/etc."

The word "El" is a common Semitic word meaning "god." It can be used of any deity and occurs in a related form in Arabic, "Allah." It is also the name of the chief god of the Canaanite pantheon, known principally from the texts discovered at ancient Ugarit (see Box 5.4). In the *Kirta* epic (see page 72) and in another epic called *Aqhat*, the ruler of the gods is El, who presides over the council of the gods, in his tent, on his sacred mountain. His epithets characterize him: He is the king, the father of years, the eternal father, the creator of creatures, the bull, and the kind and compassionate one. In *Kirta* and *Aqhat*, he is the guider of ancestral destinies who reveals himself in dreams, protects the protagonists of the epics, and guarantees that they will have progeny.

This same El, the Canaanite high god, was the god of Abraham, Isaac, and Jacob. When Melchizedek, the king of Salem and high priest of its deity El Elyon, blesses Abram, Abraham accepts the blessing (Gen 14.18–20). Moreover, several proper names in Genesis 12–50 are formed with the noun "el" (Ishmael, Israel, Bethel, Penuel), and no personal names in those chapters include a form of the divine name Yahweh, which is the most frequent element in Israelite names in the first millennium BCE.

Later, in the time of Moses according to P, the ancestral deity El was identified as Yahweh. Yahweh

FIGURE 5.4 The Canaanite god El seated on his throne, blessing a worshiper or king standing to the left. This stone stela from ancient Ugarit dates to the thirteenth century BCE and is about 18 in (47 cm) high.

retains many of the characteristics of El. El is called "the kind, the compassionate," and the same qualities are attributed to Yahweh, notably in the ancient formula in Exodus 34.6, which can be literally translated "Yahweh, Yahweh, [is] El the loving and merciful." Like El, he is a paternal and creator deity and a king, and he also can be called "the bull" (Gen 49.24). So, remarkably, the latest source in Genesis, P, preserves a memory of a distant past, when the god of Abraham, Isaac, and Jacob was not Yahweh but El.

A related question is whether or not the ancestors of Israel were monotheists. Postbiblical Jewish tradition gives a positive answer, elaborating as it often does on the silences in the biblical text. Why did Abraham have to leave Mesopotamia? Because in his zeal for the worship of the one true god, he antagonized his neighbors, who threatened his life. But the authors of Genesis make no such claim; for them, the god of the ancestors is

FIGURE 5.5 A caravan of Canaanite traders arriving in Egypt, depicted in an Egyptian tomb painting of the nineteenth century BCE.

one among many. Note, for example, Jacob's instructions to his family:

> "Put away the foreign gods that are among you, and purify yourselves, and change your clothes; then come, let us go up to Bethel, that I may make an altar there to the god who answered me in the day of my distress and has been with me wherever I have gone." So they gave to Jacob all the foreign gods that they had. (Gen 35.2–4)

Unlike later reformers, Jacob did not destroy the images of the other gods; he simply ordered them buried, so that when his family returned from worshiping the god whose temple is called "house of El" (for that is what "Bethel" means), they could retrieve them.

Genesis thus preserves very ancient memories of the time before Moses, when Israel's ancestors worshiped not Yahweh but the Canaanite god El. As we will see in the next chapter, however, sometime after about 1500 BCE, El was replaced as the principal deity of Ugarit by Baal. Thus, dating the ancestors to the first half of the second millennium, the Middle Bronze Age, is at least plausible.

A LOOK BACK AND AHEAD

One of the principal themes of the ancestral narrative in Genesis is that of exile and return under divine guidance and protection. In Genesis 12.10–20, Abram goes down to Egypt, where Sarai is taken into the pharaoh's harem and Abram is enriched. In response, Yahweh afflicts the pharaoh with plagues, and the pharaoh orders Abram to leave. This is an anticipatory summary of the journey to Egypt by Jacob and his sons that dominates the end of Genesis (chaps. 37–50) and of the escape from Egypt that is the subject of Exodus 1–15.

Throughout Genesis 12–50, many of the major characters leave the Promised Land of Canaan and go to a foreign land, but they also return there. In several cases the land to which they go is Egypt: first Abraham and, in the Joseph narrative, Joseph himself, then his ten brothers, then his ten brothers and Benjamin, his full brother, and finally Jacob along with his extended family. But the movement is often in the reverse direction as well—from Egypt back to Canaan, as in the cases of Abraham at the beginning of the ancestral narrative (13.1) and, at its end, Jacob himself, whose mummified body is brought back to Canaan for burial in the ancestral tomb at Hebron (50.13). Yet as Genesis concludes, the rest of Jacob's family—"the sons of Israel"—are still in Egypt. The story of their emigration—their exodus—from Egypt back to Canaan is the subject of the books that follow.

One other character is also in Egypt. According to E, God himself will accompany Jacob and his family into Egypt and out again: "I am God, the god of your father; do not be afraid to go down to Egypt, for . . . I myself will go down with you to Egypt, and I will also bring you up again" (Gen 46.3–4). The same idea is expressed in more liturgical language in Deuteronomy:

> A fugitive Aramean was my father; he went down into Egypt and lived there as an alien, few in number, and there he became a great nation, mighty and populous. When the Egyptians treated us harshly and afflicted us . . . the LORD heard our voice and . . . brought us out of Egypt . . . and gave us this land, a land flowing with milk and honey. (Deut 26.5–9)

This is the story of Jacob, anticipated in that of Abraham, of northern Mesopotamian origin, whose tenuous existence leads him from Canaan to Egypt. Its opening words are a good summary of the narrative of Genesis, which is ultimately a prologue to the story of the Exodus that follows.

IMPORTANT NAMES AND TERMS

Each name or term is defined briefly in the Glossary. Its first significant occurrence in this chapter appears in **boldface** type.

Abraham	Hagar	Rachel
circumcision	Isaac	Rebekah
El	Ishmael	Sarah
endogamy	Jacob	tell
Esau	Joseph	Ugaritic
form criticism	*Kirta*	
Gunkel	Leah	

QUESTIONS FOR REVIEW

1. How do the promises of Genesis 12:1–3 create tensions in the ancestral narratives?

2. Does the Documentary Hypothesis fully explain the existence of similar stories in Genesis 12–50? Why or why not?

3. What other kinds of analysis can be used to further understanding of these passages and their relationships to each other?

4. What historical clues do we have for dating the earliest forms of the ancestral narratives?

5. Discuss the importance of the Ugaritic texts for understanding both the ancestral narratives and the religion of the ancestors.

6. Discuss the theme of exile and return in the book of Genesis.

BIBLIOGRAPHY

For commentaries on Genesis, see the bibliography to Chapter 3.

Among the most important scholarly discussions of the history of the ancestral traditions is Martin Noth, *A History of Pentateuchal Traditions* (trans. B. W. Anderson; Englewood Cliffs, NJ: Prentice-Hall, 1972). A recent discussion is Ronald Hendel, *Remembering Abraham: Culture, Memory, and History in the Hebrew Bible* (New York: Oxford University Press, 2005).

For an introduction to the discoveries from Ugarit and their significance, see Peter C. Craigie, *Ugarit and the Old Testament* (Grand Rapids, MI: Eerdmans, 1983).

For translations of the Ugaritic texts into English, see especially Michael D. Coogan and Mark S. Smith,

Stories from Ancient Canaan, 2d ed. (Louisville, KY: Westminster John Knox, 2012), and Dennis Pardee and others, "West Semitic Canonical Compositions," pp. 237–375 in W. W. Hallo, ed., *The Context of Scripture*, Vol. 1: *Canonical Compositions from the Biblical World* (Leiden: Brill, 1997).

For discussions of the problem of the historicity of the ancestral narratives, see B. J. Isserlin, *The Israelites* (Minneapolis: Fortress, 2001 [1998]) pp. 48–50; and R. S. Hendel, "Genesis, Book of: The Patriarchs and History," *Anchor Bible Dictionary* (ed. D. N. Freedman; New York: Doubleday, 1992) 2. 937–38.

CHAPTER 6

Escape from Egypt

Exodus 1–15

THE BOOK OF EXODUS

The next four books of the Bible—Exodus, Leviticus, Numbers, and Deuteronomy— recount the story of two generations, the one that experienced the Exodus and their immediate offspring, and, within the first generation, the life of one individual in particular, **Moses**. The beginning of the book of Exodus narrates his birth, and the end of Deuteronomy his death. More space is given to this period and to Moses than to any other period or individual in the rest of the Hebrew Bible. That narrow focus indicates the importance the ancient Israelites placed on the time of Moses, a period when Israel itself came into existence, and that set the patterns for Israel's beliefs and practices.

The word "exodus" comes from Greek and literally means "a going out," an appropriate title for the book that narrates how under the leadership of Moses, the Israelites escaped from Egyptian persecution and began their journey back to the Promised Land. The book of Exodus, called "Names" (Hebr. *Shemot*) in Jewish tradition from its opening words ("These are the names," 1.1), continues the narrative of Genesis, describing how the initial prosperity of the family of Jacob in Egypt was replaced by official persecution and even attempts at extermination. This is the context for the divine choice of Moses to lead the Israelites out of Egypt and back to the Promised Land. After the escape from Egypt, they arrive at the mountain of God (**Sinai**, also called Horeb), where God gives them a series of laws, including the Ten Commandments, and instructions about religious rituals and ritual objects. These divine directives are set in a narrative context of repeated rebellion, including the episode of the golden calf. When the book concludes, the Israelites are still at Sinai, having constructed the ark of the covenant and the tabernacle following divine specifications. Because of the importance and the complexity of the material in the book of Exodus, we will discuss it in three chapters, beginning with the escape from Egypt in Exodus 1–15.

As is the case for the rest of the Pentateuch/Torah (see pages 46–47), Moses was traditionally viewed as the author of the book of Exodus. Modern critical scholarship, however, sees Exodus as a composite, shaped by Priestly writers from several earlier sources, principally J, but also others.

EXODUS 1–15

The Narrative

The book of Genesis ends with a paradox: The descendants of Abraham through Isaac and Jacob are not in the Promised Land of Canaan, but in Egypt. The first fifteen chapters of the book of Exodus describe their escape from Egypt and the beginning of their journey back to Canaan, both under Moses's leadership.

Packed into Exodus 1–15 are many smaller units, in a variety of forms or genres, which have been combined into a relatively coherent narrative by the final Priestly editors. These include:

- The birth narrative of Moses (Ex 2.1–10)
- An extended **theophany**, in which God appears to Moses (3.1–4.17) and calls him to lead Israel out of Egypt
- Fragments of folklore, such as the account of a divine attack on Moses (4.24–26)
- Brief genealogies, of Moses and especially of Aaron (6.14–25)
- The contest narrative between Moses and Pharaoh (chaps. 7–11), into which the narrative of the plagues is set
- Legislation concerning the Passover ritual (chaps. 12–13)
- Fragments of the first stages of an itinerary from Egypt to Mount Sinai (12.37; 13.18, 20; 14.2; 15.22–23, 27)
- The hymn in Exodus 15.1–18, one of the oldest parts of the Bible, called "The Song of the Sea" or "The Song of Miriam"

The Early Life of Moses

Legendary material tends to accumulate around the early lives of important religious and political leaders. We have such a legend for Moses, the story of his rescue as a newborn.

The pharaoh, the king of Egypt, alarmed at the rapid growth of the population of the Hebrews, ordered the Hebrew midwives Shiphrah and Puah to kill all newborn boys, but they disobeyed the royal command. Women characters are often unnamed in the Bible, but these heroic women are named, given speaking roles that show their ingenuity, and ultimately, God rewards them with families of their own. Pharaoh then ordered his own people to throw every newborn boy into the Nile. Moses's mother hid him as long as she could, but finally she put him in the hands of providence, setting him adrift in a papyrus boat on the Nile. His cries attracted the attention of Pharaoh's daughter, who was bathing, and she rescued him. Moses's sister then suggested that she get a Hebrew woman, Moses's own mother, to breastfeed him. When he was weaned, Pharaoh's daughter adopted him and named him. Throughout this story of Moses's infancy, women act as his saviors.

This birth legend, which resembles other ancient traditions (see Box 6.1), serves several functions. It is an etiology, giving a folk etymology for Moses's name (Hebrew *Mosheh*), erroneously connecting it with a similar sounding (but rare) Hebrew verb meaning to draw out (*mashah*). In fact, the name is a common Egyptian word, meaning "to be born," found in the names of pharaohs such as Thutmoses and Rameses. The legend also connects Moses with Noah, for the Hebrew word for the papyrus boat occurs elsewhere in the Bible only for Noah's ark, and, like Noah's boat, the makeshift vessel into which Moses was placed was also smeared with pitch to make it waterproof. Moses's role as savior of his people thus is deliberately paralleled with Noah's role as the savior of the entire human species.

These observations, and parallels in nonbiblical sources, suggest that the story of Moses's escape from death as an infant is not historical, a conclusion reinforced by the failure of the story to explain why Aaron and other males of Moses's generation who took part in the Exodus were not killed.

Only one other event in Moses's life before his call is described, his murder of an Egyptian who was beating one of Moses's countrymen. As a result, Moses was forced to flee and settled down in Midian, where he married Zipporah, the daughter of the local priest, and they had a son.

Box 6.1 LEGENDS OF RESCUE

The legend of the hero saved from apparently certain death as an infant is widespread in world cultures. Notable examples are Dionysus, Heracles, and Oedipus in Greece; Cyrus and Zarathustra in Persia; Romulus in Rome; and Jesus in Christianity.

The closest parallel to the story of Moses's rescue is a first-millennium BCE autobiographical legend of the late third-millennium Mesopotamian king Sargon the Great, in which Sargon describes his origins as follows:

> I am Sargon the great king, the king of Agade.
> My mother was a high priestess, I did not know my father. . . .
> My mother, the high priestess, conceived me, she bore me in secret.
> She placed me in a reed basket, she sealed my hatch with pitch.
> She left me to the river, whence I could not come up.
> The river carried me off, it brought me to Aqqi, drawer of water
> Aqqi, drawer of water, brought me up as he dipped his bucket.
> Aqqi, drawer of water, raised me as his adopted son.*

While many details are strikingly similar to the story of Moses's rescue, there need not be a direct literary connection between the two texts. Rather, we have here another example of the genre of rescue narratives concerning important political and religious leaders. These legends show that they are divinely protected from birth, and thus designated for a special role.

The rescue of the infant Moses from death at Pharaoh's hands is the principal source for the account of the infant Jesus's escape from Herod the Great's decree of death in Matthew 2 and forms part of that Gospel's thematic connection of Jesus with Moses. When Herod died, it was revealed to Joseph that "those who were seeking the child's life are dead" (Mt 2.20), echoing Exodus 4.19.

---

* Transl. Benjamin R. Foster, p. 912 in *Before the Muses: An Anthology of Akkadian Literature* (Bethesda, MD: CDL, 3d ed., 2005).

The Call of Moses

We find two accounts of the call of Moses to be the leader of the Hebrews in their exodus from Egypt. The first, in Exodus 3–4 is more complete. In it, God appears to Moses in a burning bush, revealing himself as the god of his ancestors.

In the first of a series of objections to the divine commission to secure the Israelites' release from Pharaoh, Moses asks God what his name is. God replies three times, with a slightly different answer in each (Ex 3.13–15). In the first, "I am who I am" (NRSV), or perhaps better "I will be who [or "what"] I will be," God appears to be evasive, in effect refusing to tell Moses his name. Divine figures show reluctance to give their names elsewhere in the Bible (Gen 32.29; Judg 13.17–18) and in other literatures, for naming suggests control, and knowing a deity's name would allow the deity to be manipulated.

This is immediately followed by two further responses. The first of these abbreviates the sentence

Box 6.2 THE DIVINE NAME YAHWEH

The etymology of the divine name is unclear; the three different responses to Moses's question (Ex 3.14–15) may reflect some confusion in ancient Israel itself about exactly what the divine name meant. Most scholars identify it as a form of the verb "to be," meaning either "he who is" or "he who causes [something] to exist." The latter translation is especially compelling, in part because of the frequent phrase *Yahweh seba'ot* (NRSV: "LORD of hosts"), which would identify the god of Israel as "(the one) who causes the heavenly armies to exist"; note also *Yahweh shalom* (NRSV: "The LORD is peace"; Judg 6.24). The name would thus originally have been a kind of title or epithet, identifying the deity as creator.

just given as "I am," and the second gives the deity's proper, personal name, **Yahweh** (see Box 6.2). From this point onward, Yahweh will be used regularly in all sources.

The narrative continues with further objections by Moses, each countered by an increasingly impatient deity. Moses is given almost magical signs of his divinely bestowed authority: He can change his staff into a snake, his hand from healthy to diseased, and the Nile's water into blood. But Moses is still unsatisfied, claiming that his inability to speak will prevent him from being Yahweh's spokesperson, his prophet. Yahweh responds angrily, announcing that Aaron will serve as Moses's "mouth" (Ex 4.16), and Moses wisely stops objecting.

Moses's reluctance to accept the divine summons is typical of the genre of the call of a prophet or leader. Like Moses, Jeremiah is a reluctant prophet who is given divine reassurances (Jer 1.6–10); similarly, Gideon is a reluctant judge, who is given signs of divine presence and protection (Judg 6.15–24, 36–40).

The second account of the call of Moses, in Exodus 6.2–7.7, which is P, is set after Moses's return to Egypt and repeats much of the material found earlier, including the revelation of the divine name, discussion of Moses's speech impediment, the appointment of Aaron as Moses's spokesperson, and the announcement of the

plagues. It also contains some characteristic P themes, especially the genealogy in 6.14–25 and a greater role for Aaron. **Aaron** is important for P because he was the ancestor of the priests who officiated in the Temple in Jerusalem—they are called "the sons of Aaron" (Lev 1.7; etc.)—and who eventually produced the P source. Thus, beginning in Exodus 7.1, in P, Aaron's role is emphasized, sometimes even at Moses's expense. It is Aaron, for example, who should "tell Pharaoh to let the Israelites go" (Ex 7.2; contrast 4.22), and it is Aaron's staff that turns into a snake (7.9–10; contrast 4.2–5).

We also find an important historical note in P: "I am Yahweh. I appeared to Abraham, Isaac, and Jacob as El Shadday, but by my name Yahweh I did not make myself known to them. I also established my covenant with them, to give them the land of Canaan" (Ex 6.2–4). This passage introduces a lengthy speech in which Yahweh reiterates his covenant promise to Abraham, Isaac, and Jacob to give the Israelites the land of Canaan, establishing continuity between the ancestral period and the time of Moses. At the same time, while preserving a very ancient tradition, P also stresses discontinuity: The ancestors did not know Yahweh by his personal name. This enhances the importance of Moses as the one through whom the full revelation of God was made to Israel, and at the same time recognizes that historically something new had happened. (See also pages 77–79 and 93–95.)

Divine Attack on Moses

Following the narrative of the call of Moses in chapters 3.1–4.17 is a short passage (4.24–26) oddly inconsistent with the larger plot. Moses has finally acceded to the divine command to return to Egypt and to secure the Hebrews' release from Pharaoh, yet one night, while Moses is on the way back, Yahweh tries to kill him. The scene is reminiscent of Genesis 32.22–32, in which a divine adversary attacks Jacob at night, and it anticipates the divine attack on the Egyptians, also at night (Ex 12.29–32).

The narrative, which has folklore motifs and was probably originally more detailed, is compressed and therefore difficult to interpret. What is clear is that Moses's wife Zipporah averts the threat by circumcising her son and touching "his feet" with the foreskin. The term "feet," as often in the Bible, is a euphemism for the genitals, but whose "feet" are being touched is unclear. A likely interpretation is that of the NRSV, which specifies the pronoun "his" by translating "Moses's." Thus, neither Moses's son nor Moses himself had been circumcised, which may be why Yahweh attacked Moses. Zipporah takes action, circumcising her son. By touching the bloody skin to Moses's genitals, she makes it appear that Moses too had just been circumcised, thus tricking Yahweh into leaving Moses alone. Once again, Moses is saved by a woman. (On circumcision, see Box 5.3 on pages 70–71.)

The Plagues

In its present form, the account of the plagues is a complex blending of the Pentateuchal sources, like the Flood story (Gen 6–9). Each has its own themes and emphases, but they have been combined into a relatively smoothly flowing narrative. In this final form there are ten plagues—the Nile turned to blood, frogs, gnats, flies, cattle disease, boils, hail, locusts, darkness, and death of the firstborn. We also find accounts of the plagues in Psalms 78.44–51 and 105.28–36. In these poetic treatments, synonymous parallelism links plagues that are separate in Exodus (for example, flies and gnats in Ps 105.31), and neither the order nor the number nor even the identification of the plagues is the same as in the final text of Exodus. Clearly the story of the plagues circulated widely in ancient Israel, with considerable variations in the retellings.

The plague narrative also introduces the characters of the Egyptian "magicians," more accurately "priests," like Moses and especially Aaron. The contest between the two sides, each representing their own deities (see Ex 12.12: "I will punish the gods of Egypt"), has a comic dimension. In the prelude to the account of the plagues themselves, both Aaron and the Egyptian priests are able to turn a staff into a serpent—any good magician knows that trick! Likewise, the Egyptian priests are able to duplicate the first two plagues, those of the Nile being changed into blood and the frogs. When it comes to the third plague, "the magicians tried to produce gnats by their secret arts, but they could not" (Ex 8.18). And the later plague of the boils affects the magicians as well as the rest of the Egyptians. Moses and Aaron have won the contest!

The initial ability of the Egyptian magicians to duplicate the feats of Aaron is one indication of genre: The account of the plagues is a contest narrative, like those found in the story of Joseph (Gen 41) in the story of Elijah and the prophets of Baal (1 Kings 18.20–40), and in the book of Daniel (chaps. 1–6). In all of these tales, the Israelite heroes prove themselves superior to their polytheistic rivals because God is on their side.

Throughout the ages, many suggestions have been made to identify the plagues with natural phenomena. Thus, it has been proposed that in its annual summer flooding the Nile carried in suspension particles of reddish soil, or perhaps algae, which made it look like blood; darkness has been supposed to refer to a solar eclipse or a sandstorm; cattle plagues, hail, and locusts are frequent disasters in an agricultural economy; and so on. Although plausible, these rationalizations ignore the primary point of the plague narrative: The plagues

Box 6.3 THE HARDENING OF PHARAOH'S HEART

For modern readers the repeated "hardening" of Pharaoh's heart is troublesome, especially when it is the LORD himself who is explicitly responsible for the hardening. Instead of a God who is supposed to "do what is right" (Gen 18.25), God is described as deliberately making Pharaoh stubborn so that he will refuse to let the Hebrews go.

The poetic tradition states it bluntly:

> And Yahweh made his people very fruitful, and made them stronger than
>   their foes,
> whose hearts he then turned to hate his people, to deal craftily with his
>   servants. (Ps 105.24–25)

The result is enormous suffering for the Egyptians, culminating with the killing of their firstborn, "from the firstborn of Pharaoh who sits on his throne to the firstborn of the female slave who is behind the handmill, and all the firstborn of the livestock" (Ex 11.5; see also 12.29).

The same idiom is also used of the conquest of the land of Canaan: "It was Yahweh's doing to harden their hearts so that they would come against Israel in battle, in order that they might be utterly destroyed, and might receive no mercy, but be exterminated" (Josh 11.20).

For both the plagues in Egypt and the conquest of Canaan, it is probably a mistake to look for profound divine ethics. Rather, in a simplistic division, only two groups exist, the Israelites and their enemies. Yahweh is the god of Israel and is on the side of his people: Their enemies are his enemies, and whatever he and they do to these enemies is justifiable.

At the same time, we may observe some discomfort in the text with the divinely caused stubbornness in Pharaoh that results in greater suffering. Alongside the most frequent expression that "Yahweh hardened Pharaoh's heart," we also find "Pharaoh hardened his own heart" and "Pharaoh's heart was hardened," both alternatives subtly suggesting that it was Pharaoh rather than Yahweh who was to blame.

---

are *not* natural phenomena but are caused by direct divine action; Deuteronomy calls them "great and awesome signs and wonders" (6.22). While it is true that in ancient times, even natural phenomena were perceived as the result of divine activity, the plagues are more than natural, as the immunity of the Israelites from the cattle plague, the hail, and the darkness indicates. The last plague is clearly an extraordinary event caused by God directly: All the firstborn in Egypt die, but only the firstborn, and again not the Israelites' firstborn. The ability of the Egyptian magicians to replicate the first two plagues also shows that we should not take them literally: How could the Nile be changed into blood twice, or frogs cover the land of Egypt twice?

In the end, as Yahweh's representatives, Moses and Aaron have shown themselves to be superior to Pharaoh and his magicians, and, on the divine level, Yahweh has defeated the gods of Egypt.

Passover

The last plague is the killing of the firstborn of the Egyptians, in specific retaliation for Pharaoh's treatment of Israel, Yahweh's "firstborn son" (Ex 4.22). Closely associated with this terrible catastrophe is the celebration of the **Passover**. The legislation concerning this ancient ritual in Exodus 12.1–27 is primarily P; P has also incorporated another tradition in 13.1–16. As earlier in the P narrative with the legislation concerning the blood prohibition (Gen 9.4–6) and circumcision (Gen 17), the Passover is integrally related to the plot in which it is imbedded.

Underlying the Passover appear to be two distinct springtime rituals: one agricultural in origin, called the "festival of unleavened bread," and another probably pastoral in origin, of the sacrifice of the firstborn lamb. The most ancient biblical law collections mention only the Festival of Unleavened Bread (Ex 23.15; 34.18), showing that it was originally distinct. It occurred at the time of the barley harvest, in the early spring; the alternate name for Nisan, the month in which the Passover occurs, is Abib, which means freshly ripened grain (see further Box 8.4 on page 121). In this ritual, farmers would offer to their deity bread made from the new harvest, with the flour unadulterated by "leaven," that is, sourdough from flour made from a previous harvest. The sacrifice of the newly born lamb, also occurring in the

Box 6.4 THE DEVELOPMENT OF THE PASSOVER CELEBRATION

According to the earliest traditions, Passover was originally a pilgrimage festival. The pilgrimage would presumably have been made to a local sanctuary. In the later Judean monarchy and subsequently, however, Passover became a national festival, during which all worshipers were required or at least urged to go to Jerusalem for the celebration. During the time of the monarchy, the celebration of the Passover in Jerusalem is implied in Deuteronomic legislation: "You are not permitted to offer the passover sacrifice within any of your towns that Yahweh your God is giving you. But at the place that Yahweh your God will choose as a dwelling for his name, only there shall you offer the passover sacrifice" (Deut 16.5–6).

According to the historical books of the Bible, national celebration of the Passover was part of the religious reforms of two kings, Hezekiah in the late eighth century BCE (2 Chr 30) and Josiah in the late seventh (2 Kings 23.21–23; 2 Chr 35.1–19). The Jerusalem-centered observance is also found in later sources, including the New Testament, in which Jesus goes to Jerusalem to celebrate the Passover, and the first-century CE historian Josephus, who reports that as many as three million people were in the city for the Passover celebrated in 65 CE. The same Jerusalem orientation is retained in the prayer near the end of the modern Passover service: "Next year in Jerusalem."

Over the course of time, and in different cultural contexts, the "order" (*seder*) of the Passover changed. In P (Ex 12.3), because of the changed circumstances of the community after 586 BCE, with the Temple destroyed and many in exile in Babylon, the Passover became a family celebration, as it is in Judaism today. By the second century BCE, wine was added to the celebration. The Last Supper of Jesus, incorporating the elements of unleavened bread and wine, was a Passover meal.

spring, would have been the shepherds' expression of gratitude to their deity for the fertility of their flocks, as well as a petition for continued fertility.

These separate spring rituals were joined as part of the process of Israel's emergence in Canaan, in which disparate groups, including farmers and shepherds, joined to form a new entity (see further pages 187–88). The rituals were also historicized, becoming linked with the Exodus event. Thus, the eating of unleavened bread is explained by the haste with which the Israelites had to flee Egypt (Ex 12.34, 39). Likewise, the eating of the lamb recalls the slaughter of the lambs whose blood was smeared on the doorposts of the houses of the Israelites in Egypt. As in the narrative of the sacrifice of Isaac, the lamb is a substitution for the firstborn (Gen 22.13). Finally, the "bitter herbs" (Ex 12.8), probably a type of lettuce, are associated with the bitterness of the oppression suffered by the Hebrews (Ex 1.14).

The Passover celebration is described as taking place in "the first month of the year" (Ex 12.2). The calendar of the ancient Israelites is not fully understood, and evidence exists both for a spring new year, as here, and a fall new year, as in later Jewish tradition, where Rosh Hashanah occurs in September or October (although there is little evidence for the celebration of the New Year as such in biblical times). P's emphasis on the Passover as occurring at the beginning of the year is consistent with its portrayal of the entire Exodus complex as marking a new beginning, even a new creation.

The Event at the Sea

As with other aspects of the Exodus traditions, as the event at the sea was told and retold, written and rewritten, it too was magnified. It should be remembered that these amplifications were motivated in part by the desire to praise Yahweh, who had brought Israel out of Egypt. Three versions of the event can be identified.

The P account of the event at the sea is the most detailed and the most dramatic. Found in Exodus 14 (vv. 1–4, 15–18, 21–23, 26–29, although other sources are also present here), it features the sea split as Moses lifted his staff: "The waters were divided. The Israelites went into the sea on dry ground, the waters forming a wall for them on their right and on their left" (14.21–22). The Egyptians followed, and when the Israelites reached the other side, Moses lifted his staff again, and the returning waters engulfed the Egyptians.

In the final composite narrative, P implies that the event at the sea is a new creation: As in the accounts of creation (Gen 1.2, 9) and its renewal after the Flood (Gen 8.1, 14), the wind blew, the waters were divided, and the dry land appeared (Ex 14.21). What is being created here, however, is not the cosmos but rather Israel itself, by Yahweh, the one who causes everything to exist (see Box 6.2).

Embedded in P's narrative is another version of the event at the sea:

> At the morning watch Yahweh in the pillar of fire and cloud looked down upon the Egyptian army, and threw the Egyptian army into panic. He clogged their chariot wheels so that they turned with difficulty. The Egyptians said, "Let us flee from the Israelites, for Yahweh is fighting for them against Egypt." (Ex 14.24–25)

According to this account, which is probably J, Yahweh caused the Egyptians to panic when their chariots got stuck in the mud.

Yet a third version of the event is found in Exodus 15, one of the oldest poems in the Bible. This poem, "the Song of the Sea," is attributed both to Moses (Ex 15.1) and to **Miriam**, who is called a prophet (15.20–21). She leads the Israelite women in a victory song and dance, as women often did (see Judg 5.1; 11.34; 1 Sam 18.6–7), and she may have originally been given credit for the Song, later transferred to Moses. (See further Box 9.1 on page 140.)

The Song of the Sea relates how when Yahweh blew with his nostrils, the sea became churned up, and

> Pharaoh's chariots and his army he cast into the sea;
>   his picked officers were sunk in the Reed Sea.
> The floods covered them;
>   they went down into the depths like a stone. . . .
> You blew with your wind, the sea covered them;
>   they sank like lead in the mighty waters.
>   (Ex 15.4–5, 10)

According to this account, the Egyptians, apparently in ships or barges, were swamped by a storm at sea and sank to the sea's bottom.

These three versions of the event are incompatible. If the Egyptians were already on the floor of the sea, as in P, then they could not sink like a stone or lead. If they were on the sea's surface, as Exodus 15 suggests, their chariots are irrelevant. But here as elsewhere, the final Priestly editors of the Pentateuch were less concerned with a superficial consistency than with preservation of traditions, and one of those traditions, the account of the Egyptians' chariots getting stuck in the swamp, provides a clue to what may have occurred. A possible reconstruction is as follows. Under the leadership of Moses, a small group of Hebrew slaves (perhaps a few hundred at most; see page 92) escaped from their forced labor in the eastern Nile delta. They headed for one of the swamps or wetlands (the "Reed Sea"; see page 92) in the vicinity, pursued by their guards. Because they were on foot, the escapees were able to make their way through the swamp, but the Egyptians, in chariots, got bogged down and gave up the pursuit, so the Hebrews got away. This event would have been relatively inconsequential to the Egyptians, but for those who escaped, it was miraculous.

THE EXODUS AND HISTORY

As with the ancestral narratives in Genesis 12–50, no direct correlation exists between any person or event found in Exodus 1–15 and nonbiblical sources. Once again, the Bible is remarkably vague: Neither the pharaoh who begins the persecution of the Hebrews nor his successor, the pharaoh of the Exodus itself, is named, and their characters lack particulars by which we might be able to identify them. If the biblical writers had given us the names of these pharaohs, we would know at least approximately when those writers thought the events took place. Moreover, the considerable documentation from ancient Egypt makes no mention of the Hebrews, Moses, Aaron, the plagues, or the defeat at the sea.

This lack of correlation has led some scholars to be skeptical that anything like the Exodus ever occurred. The view of a majority of scholars, however, is that the biblical traditions, although containing anachronisms and signs of later editing, do preserve authentic historical memory.

First, the escape from slavery in Egypt under the leadership of Moses is a constant in biblical tradition, found in a variety of forms in all sources from the earliest to the latest. It is deeply imbedded in Israel's legal traditions, including the most ancient, such as the Ten Commandments (Ex 20.2), and in the earliest biblical poems, such as Exodus 15, Deuteronomy 33 (vv. 2–4), and Judges 5 (vv. 4–5). And the Exodus continues to be a major theme in Israel's literature, especially the historical books, the prophets, and the psalms.

Closely related to the pervasive importance of the Exodus in the Bible is the presence of indisputably Egyptian elements in the accounts of the Exodus. The names of Moses, Aaron, Phinehas, and others of the generation associated with the Exodus are of Egyptian origin. The cities Pithom and Rameses (Ex 1.11) have tentatively been identified with specific sites in the eastern Nile Delta (see Figure 6.1), and the time of their construction coincides with the most likely date for the Exodus (see the following section).

Although the Bible does lack specifics, nothing in the Exodus narrative is inconsistent with what is known about ancient Egypt. A convergence of evidence thus exists, and the most likely reconstruction based on that evidence is that an Exodus (or, according to some scholars, more than one) did take place. That is more reasonable than the hypothesis that the Exodus never occurred.

THE DATE OF THE EXODUS

When the Exodus might have occurred is uncertain, and several times between the sixteenth and the thirteenth centuries BCE have been proposed. Biblical tradition dates the Exodus in relation to other events. According to 1 Kings 6.1, it took place

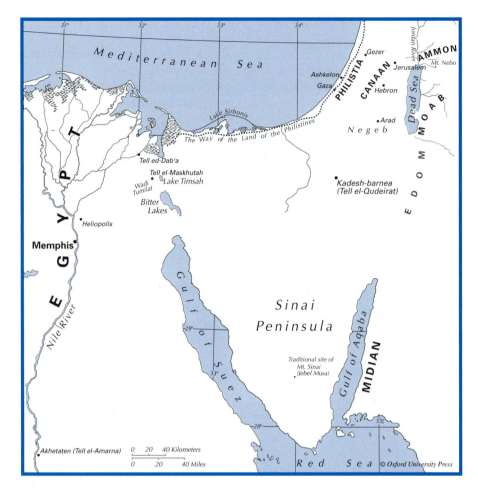

FIGURE 6.1   Map of the Nile Delta and the Sinai Peninsula. Tell el-Maskhutah and Tell ed-Dab'a have been identified as the cities of Pithom and Rameses (Ex 1.11). Jebel Musa in the southern Sinai Peninsula is the traditional identification of Mount Sinai, but that is questioned by most scholars.

480 years before the building of the Temple by Solomon. That occurred, according to the chronology used in this book, about 965 BCE, which would place the Exodus in the mid-fifteenth century BCE. But the figure of 480 years is suspicious: It is the product of twelve, the number of the tribes, times forty, the typical length of a generation. The authors of the books of Kings understandably wanted to provide a symbolic link between Moses and the construction of the Temple under Solomon.

Some scholars connect the Exodus with the expulsion of the foreign Hyksos rulers from Egypt,

which took place in the mid-sixteenth century BCE (see page 73). There are, however, problems with such an early Exodus. It leaves a relatively long span of time, the entire Late Bronze Age (1550–1200 BCE) and beyond, covered only in the book of Judges. Moreover, although this was a period when Egypt controlled all of Canaan, no hint of Egyptian presence there can be found in the narratives of the book of Judges. Rather, the land is populated by groups whose existence is attested only at the end of the Late Bronze Age and especially at the beginning of the succeeding Iron

Age, such as the Moabites, the Ammonites, and the Philistines. The Amarna Letters, an important collection of diplomatic correspondence with the Egyptian pharaoh Akhenaten dating from the fourteenth century BCE, give us a detailed view of Canaan in the Late Bronze Age. The correspondence includes letters from the kings of such city-states as Ashkelon, Shechem, Gezer, and Jerusalem, but there is no mention of any individual or group that could plausibly be identified with Israel, which would be expected if Israel had been a presence in the land for several centuries.

The principal alternative is to date the Exodus sometime in the thirteenth century BCE. This date is derived in part from the occurrence of Israel in a hymn on a victory stele erected by Pharaoh Merneptah (1213–1203 BCE) after a campaign in Syria and Palestine early in his reign (see Figure 6.2). It reads in part:

> The princes are prostrate, saying: "Shalom [peace]!"
> Not one of the Nine Bows lifts his head:
> Tehenu is pacified, Hatti at peace,
> Canaan is captive with all woe.
> Ashkelon is conquered, Gezer seized,
> Yanoam is made nonexistent;
> Israel is wasted, bare of seed,
> Hurru is become a widow for Egypt.
> All who roamed have been subdued
> by the King of Upper and Lower Egypt, Banere-
>   meramun,
> son of Re, Merneptah, Content with Maat,
> given life like Re every day.*

This extremely important text—it contains the earliest reference in a nonbiblical ancient Near Eastern source of any person, entity, or event mentioned in the Bible—testifies to the presence of a group called "Israel" in the land of Canaan toward the end of the thirteenth century BCE and thus provides a date before which the Exodus must have occurred. The other entities mentioned are geographical regions and cities; Israel is identified in the original hieroglyphic text as a people. According to the biblical chronology, it took some forty years for the escaped Hebrew slaves to enter the Promised Land. Accepting that figure

FIGURE 6.2 The stela of Pharaoh Merneptah, which contains the first mention of Israel in a nonbiblical source.

as approximately accurate, then a mid-thirteenth century Exodus and an entry into Canaan by the Exodus group some time thereafter, but before Merneptah's campaign, would allow for a group called Israel to become sufficiently established by the time of Merneptah so as to be mentioned in his victory hymn. This would make Merneptah's father, Rameses II (1279–1213) (see Figure 6.3), the pharaoh of the Exodus, and his father, Seti I (1294–1279), the pharaoh who began the persecution of

---

* Trans. M. Lichtheim, *Ancient Egyptian Literature* (Berkeley: University of California Press, 1976; 2006), 2.77.

FIGURE 6.3   Pharaoh Rameses II shown in his chariot in battle with his enemies the Hittites, in a copy of a relief from Karnak.

the Hebrews. This is the view held by most, but by no means all, biblical scholars.

The Embellishment of the Story

As the story of the Exodus was passed on, both orally and in writing, details were modified and often exaggerated. The tendency to embellish what had originally occurred is evident in differences among the accounts of this central event. For example, how many people escaped from Egypt? Exodus 12.37–38 tells us that the number of the Israelites was "about six hundred thousand men on foot, besides children. A mixed crowd also went up with them, and livestock in great numbers, both flocks and herds." Allowing, conservatively, one wife for each man and two children for each couple, that adds up to a group of well over two million

people, along with their sheep and goats ("flocks") and cattle ("herds"). This number is impossibly high, greater than reasonable estimates of the entire population of ancient Egypt. Furthermore, that many people and animals would have left discernible traces in the landscape of the Sinai peninsula, but no evidence has been found of a substantial population living in that arid region at any time.

Significantly, another biblical tradition suggests a much smaller number of people. In a traditional culture, where women married soon after menarche and were repeatedly pregnant throughout their reproductive years, two midwives could serve only a relatively small number of women of reproductive age—no more than several hundred and probably fewer. We thus have a population of an entirely different order of magnitude than that given in Exodus 12.37–38, and the number given there must be an exaggeration. If the number of the Hebrews was relatively small, the lack of mention in Egyptian sources of their escape from work-slavery is unsurprising.

A later example of the same tendency to aggrandize the tradition is the identification of the body of water crossed by the escapees with the Red Sea. The Hebrew term used throughout the Bible is *yam sûf*. Although this can occasionally refer to either of the two northern arms of the Red Sea, the Gulf of Suez (Num 33.11) and the Gulf of Aqaba/Eilat (Num 14.25; 1 Kings 9.26), it literally means "sea of reeds," and the most likely geography of the Exodus locates it just east of the region where the Hebrews lived (see Figure 6.1 on page 90). Several shallow bodies of water are possible identifications for this "**Reed Sea**," including the Bitter Lakes and Lake Timsah, lying between the Gulf of Suez and the Mediterranean Sea, and Lake Sirbonis, on the Mediterranean coast just east of the Nile Delta. The ancient Greek translation of the Hebrew Bible (the Septuagint), dating to the third century BCE, translates *yam sûf* as "Red Sea," a much more dramatic setting than a wetland for the miracle of the splitting of the sea.

THE EXODUS AND THE HISTORY OF RELIGIONS

During the Late Bronze Age (1550–1200 BCE), a shift occurred in the pantheons of much of the ancient world: Rule over the gods passed from an older to a younger god. This transfer of power is evident in the myths of several different groups. In Babylon, *Enuma Elish* recounts how Marduk, the god of the storm, is chosen as king of the gods when the older generation of gods, led by Anu ("sky"), is unable to counter the threat posed by the primeval goddess of the sea, Tiamat (see further pages 32–35). In Greek myth, the older god Cronus is supplanted as supreme deity by his son Zeus, perhaps originally a sky-god but better known as the "cloud gatherer" whose weapon is the thunderbolt. Variants of the myth are found in Hittite and Indic mythology.

The same shift in power is also found in Ugaritic myth (see Box 5.4 on page 72), in many

ways the closest to the biblical traditions. In the Ugaritic Baal cycle, Prince Sea (also called by the parallel term Judge River) threatens the storm-god **Baal**, apparently with the support of the high god El, but Baal defeats Prince Sea and is acclaimed as king of the gods, who build him a suitable palace on Mount Zaphon, made of cedar as well as silver, gold, and precious stones. As his epithet "rider on the clouds" shows, Baal is the storm-god, providing the essential rains of winter. When he "sounds his voice in the clouds, flashes his lightning to the earth . . . the earth's high places shake" (see Figure 6.4 on page 94).

Traces of this widespread shift in power in the pantheon are also found in ancient Israel. At the time when the Exodus from Egypt most likely occurred, toward the end of the Late Bronze Age, biblical sources describe a new revelation. As P reports in Exodus 6.2–3, during the ancestral period the god of Abraham, Isaac, and Jacob was El (see pages 74–75). Yahweh identifies himself as this deity, but in biblical literature, Yahweh also has characteristics of a storm-god. Like Baal, he "rides upon the clouds" (Ps 68.4), and his voice is thunder:

> The voice of Yahweh is over the waters;
> the God of glory thunders,
> Yahweh, over mighty waters.
> The voice of Yahweh is powerful;
> the voice of Yahweh is full of majesty.
> The voice of Yahweh breaks the cedars;
> Yahweh breaks the cedars of Lebanon. . . .
> The voice of Yahweh flashes forth flames of fire.
> The voice of Yahweh shakes the wilderness.
> (Ps 29.3–8; compare Judg 5.4–5)

Like Baal, Yahweh reveals himself on a mountain in the midst of a storm (Ex 19.16–18), and, like Baal, he will eventually acquire a temple, "a house of cedar" (2 Sam 7.2; see also 1 Kings 6.14–18).

Often the storm-god is described as victorious over the forces of chaos, sometimes depicted in serpent form; an example is the myth of Marduk and Tiamat in Mesopotamia, in which the creation of the world follows the victory. No detailed account of creation has been discovered at Ugarit, but the Bible provides numerous examples of a sequence in which the storm-god of Israel defeats the primeval waters and then creates the world. In addition to

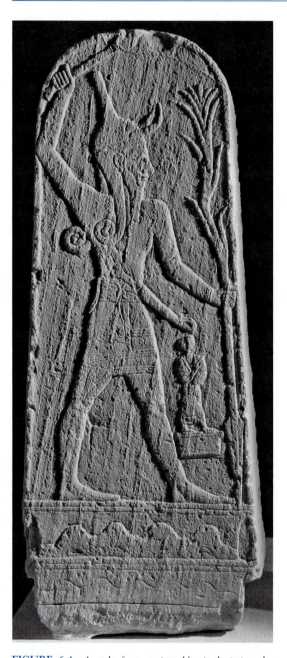

FIGURE 6.4 A stela from ancient Ugarit depicting the Canaanite god Baal. He holds a stylized lightning bolt in his left hand, illustrating his status as storm-god. The stela is about 4.7 ft (1.42 m) high and dates to the mid-second millennium BCE.

examples given on pages 37–38, note especially Psalm 89:

> Let the heavens praise your wonders, O Yahweh,
> your faithfulness in the assembly of the holy ones.
> For who in the skies can be compared to Yahweh?
> Who among the gods is like Yahweh,
> a god feared in the council of the holy ones,
> great and awesome above all those around him?
> O Yahweh God of hosts,
> who is as mighty as you, O Yahweh?
> Your faithfulness surrounds you.
> You rule the surging of the sea;
> when its waves rise, you still them.
> You crushed Rahab* like a carcass;
> you scattered your enemies with your mighty arm.
> The heavens are yours, the earth also is yours;
> the world and all that is in it—you have founded them. (Ps 89.5–11)

This mythic pattern is applied to the Exodus event, especially in Exodus 15. As storm-god, Yahweh uses his wind, blown through his nostrils, and causes the sea to churn. But the myth is historicized: The enemy of the storm-god is not the sea itself but Pharaoh and his army, and the sea is merely a weapon used by the deity to defeat the Egyptian forces. Moreover, the event takes place in historical time. So in appropriating the myth of the storm-god and the sea, Exodus 15 partially demythologizes it. Yet some mythic elements remain, including the acclamation of Yahweh as the supreme deity and his enthronement in a new home:

> Who is like you, O Yahweh, among the gods?
> Who is like you, majestic in holiness,
> awesome in splendor, doing wonders? . . .
> You brought them in and planted them on the mountain of your own possession,
> the place, O Yahweh, that you made your abode,
> the sanctuary, O Yahweh, that your hands have established.
> Yahweh will rule forever and ever. (Ex 15.11, 17–18)

The same mythic motif is found in other biblical texts, as in Psalm 114:

> When Israel went out from Egypt,
> the house of Jacob from a people of strange language,

---

*   Rahab is one of the names used in the Bible for the primeval sea.

Judah became God's sanctuary,
    Israel his dominion.
The sea looked and fled;
    the Jordan turned back. (Ps 114.1–3)

Here the narrative chronology of the books of Exodus through Joshua is collapsed. Those books relate sequentially how the Israelites came out of Egypt, wandered in the wilderness for forty years, and then under the leadership of Joshua crossed the Jordan River and took possession of the Promised Land. The crossings of two bodies of water bracket this formative period, and the accounts of the crossing of the Sea of Reeds at its beginning (Ex 14–15) and of the Jordan River at its end (Josh 3) are deliberately paralleled: In both events, the waters stand up in a heap (Ex 15.8; Josh 3.16), and the Israelites cross "on dry ground" (Ex 14.22; Josh 3.17; 4.22). But in Psalm 114, although the two bodies of water are again actual places—the (Reed) Sea and the Jordan (River)—they are personified and linked; this recalls the parallel titles of Baal's adversary, Prince Sea and Judge River.

Likewise, in the book of Isaiah's appeal to Yahweh to act as he has in the past, the defeat of the primeval waters is linked with the event at the Reed Sea:

Awake, awake, put on strength,
    O arm of Yahweh!
Awake, as in days of old,
    the generations of long ago!
Was it not you who cut Rahab in pieces,
    who pierced the dragon?
Was it not you who dried up the sea,
    the waters of great deep;
who made the depths of the sea a way
    for the redeemed to cross over? (Isa 51.9–10)

As elsewhere in the ancient world, then, toward the end of the Late Bronze Age Israel began to worship a new deity, or a new manifestation of the ancestral deity. From the perspective of the history of religions, Yahweh can be understood as the Israelite manifestation of the storm-god, who throughout the ancient Near East and elsewhere became the dominant deity toward the end of the Late Bronze Age.

The origins of the name and identity of Yahweh as a distinct deity are lost in the mists of history. Some nonbiblical texts locate the use of this name in the territory of Midian, east of the Red Sea, toward the end of the Late Bronze Age, precisely where the Bible has the name revealed to Moses, and it is possible that Moses adopted the worship of Yahweh from his father-in-law Jethro, the priest of Midian. (See further Box 7.2 on page 99.)

At the same time, the sources J and P both emphasize continuity rather than discontinuity. In J, Yahweh has been worshiped since the time of Adam (Gen 4.26), and in P, the deity who reveals himself to Moses as Yahweh identifies himself as the god of Israel's ancestors (Ex 3.15; 6.2–3). For the biblical writers, it is Yahweh who has been worshiped all along. Modern historians of religion correctly observe that change has occurred here, and they are able to do so in part because P also recognizes discontinuity: Something new happened in the time of Moses and the Exodus, with, appropriately, a new revelation and an event of mythic dimensions.

A LOOK BACK AND AHEAD

The narrative of the escape from Egypt is the linchpin of the Pentateuch, the organizing principle that informs it from beginning to end. The many occurrences of the motif of exile and of return that recur throughout Genesis, from the narrative of the garden of Eden through the wanderings of Abraham and Sarah, of Hagar and Ishmael, of Isaac and Rebekah, and of Jacob and his extended family, have been in a sense preparation for the beginning of the narrative of the return of Israel to the Promised Land. That journey home—that exodus—is led by Moses. His character and his presence will continue to dominate the Pentateuch, which ends with his death in Deuteronomy 34, with the Israelites poised to reenter the land of Canaan.

As the interconnected stories of the Exodus and of Moses are retold, they continue to speak to new audiences and have relevance for new contexts. For example, Moses's encounters with Pharaoh anticipate and provide a literary model for later encounters between prophets and kings, and the celebration of the Passover continually recalls for Israel its origin as a people freed from slavery by a merciful and compassionate deity.

In the next chapters, we will also observe how in the rest of the Pentateuch legal and ritual traditions from many different periods are attached to Moses and the events associated with him, beginning with the Exodus and continuing with the revelation at Sinai.

IMPORTANT NAMES AND TERMS

Each name or term is defined briefly in the Glossary. Its first significant occurrence in this chapter appears in **boldface** type.

Aaron	Moses	Sinai
Baal	Passover	theophany
Miriam	Reed Sea	Yahweh

QUESTIONS FOR REVIEW

1. Compare the narrative of the plagues in Exodus with the hymnic summaries in Psalm 78.42–55 and Psalm 105.26–45. Be prepared to discuss the significance of the similarities and differences for understanding the history of traditions.

2. The description of the first Passover in Exodus 12 probably reflects the way the feast was celebrated during the monarchy. What earlier elements can be isolated in this chapter? How can the union of originally distinct agricultural and pastoral rituals be explained?

3. Compare Exodus 14 and 15. How do the prose and poetic accounts of the event at the Re(e)d Sea differ?

4. What are the issues involved in determining the historicity and the date of the Exodus?

5. How did the biblical writers make use of ancient Near Eastern mythology in their accounts of the Exodus?

BIBLIOGRAPHY

A good commentary on Exodus is Carol Meyers, *Exodus* (Cambridge: Cambridge University Press, 2005). For a shorter commentary, see P. K. McCarter, Jr., "Exodus," pp. 119–44 in *The HarperCollins Bible Commentary* (ed. J. L. Mays; San Francisco: HarperSanFrancisco, 2000). An important older commentary is B. S. Childs, *The Book of Exodus: A Critical, Theological Commentary* (Philadelphia: Westminster, 1974).

An excellent summary of the historical issues connected with the Exodus is C. A. Redmount, "Bitter Lives: Israel in and out of Egypt," Chap. 2 in *The Oxford History of the Biblical World* (ed. M. D. Coogan; New York: Oxford University Press, 1998; available in Oxford Biblical Studies Online).

For a summary of the use of the Exodus motif in biblical and later traditions, see M. D. Coogan, "Exodus, The," pp. 209–12 in *The Oxford Companion to the Bible* (New York: Oxford University Press, 1993; available in Oxford Biblical Studies Online).

For translations of the Ugaritic myths concerning Baal, see the bibliography to Chapter 5.

CHAPTER 7

From Egypt to Sinai

Exodus 16–20 and 24

Once the Israelites have left Egypt, everything that follows in the Torah is set in the context of their journey toward the Promised Land. That journey is interrupted, however, by a lengthy stay at Mount Sinai, where God gives Moses the Ten Commandments, along with many other laws and detailed instructions concerning religious ceremonies, the priesthood, sacred objects, and the like. The sojourn at Sinai begins in Exodus 19, and the Israelites do not leave there until Numbers 10.12. The intervening material comprises about one-third of the entire Pentateuch, indicating its importance.

In this chapter, we will examine the narrative of the first stage of the journey, from Egypt to Sinai, the making of the covenant at Sinai, and the first collection of laws embedded in the Sinai narrative, the Ten Commandments.

ITINERARIES

At intervals in the narrative from Egypt to Mount Sinai, and then later from Mount Sinai to Moab on the eastern border of Canaan, the Priestly source (P) records the stages of the journey. These itineraries serve to organize the narrative and to move it along, as did the genealogies in Genesis. The itineraries are then brought together in Numbers 33 at the end of the journey, as a kind of summary, in a document that may in fact be the original from which various segments were inserted into the narrative at appropriate points. Few of the places named in the itineraries can be identified with certainty.

INCIDENTS ON THE JOURNEY

Interspersed among the itineraries are narratives attached to particular places. Thus, on the journey from Egypt to Sinai, we find accounts of the divine provision of **manna** (see Box 7.1) and quails for the Israelites in Exodus 16, and of the miraculous production of water from a rock in Exodus 17.1–7. Alternate versions of these events are reported on the journey from Sinai to Canaan, manna and quails in Numbers 11 and water from a rock in Numbers 20. The final editors of the Pentateuch have thus bracketed the stay at Sinai with parallel episodes.

Another example of bracketing occurs with the next episode, concerning the delegation of Moses's authority. In Exodus 18, Moses's father-in-law Jethro,

FIGURE 7.1 Jebel Musa, the traditional identification of Mount Sinai. As imposing as this mountain is (elevation 7,497 ft [2,285 m]), no ancient evidence connects it with the biblical mountain of revelation, and many scholars prefer another location, in southern Jordan or northern Saudi Arabia.

holy nation" (Ex 19.5–6). This obscure phrasing, probably very ancient, declares Israel's special status, collectively set apart from other nations as priests are from ordinary persons. Following Moses's instructions, the people prepared for a divine revelation, in which Yahweh with all of the manifestations of the storm—cloud, thunder, lightning, earthquake—descended on the mountain to make a covenant with the Israelites.

COVENANT

The concept of covenant is central to the Bible. Its significance is indicated by its thematic importance in P, which is organized around three covenants, those between God and Noah, God and Abraham, and God and Israel. On a broader level, the two principal divisions of the Bible in Christianity are called the Old Covenant ("Testament") and the New Covenant. As the word "testament" suggests, covenant is a legal term.

The Hebrew word for covenant, *berît*, has an uncertain etymology, perhaps meaning a bond or mutual agreement. In the Bible, *berît* means something like "contract," and it is used for legal agreements such as marriage, debt-slavery, solemn friendship, and especially treaties. On several occasions in the Bible, we are told of treaties between rulers. These are of two types: a parity treaty, in which the two parties are equals, and a **suzerainty treaty**, in which one party, the suzerain, is superior to the other, the vassal, to use medieval terms.

The Treaty Form

One of the most influential examples of form criticism in biblical interpretation (see pages 68–70) is the analysis of the structure of ancient Near Eastern treaties, especially suzerainty treaties and its application to the biblical concept of the covenant between God and Israel. Two groups of suzerainty treaties are especially important. The first is a series of treaties between the kings of the Hittites in Asia Minor, Egypt's rivals for control of the Levant in the latter part of the second millennium BCE, and their vassals, smaller states that were subject to them. Another group, between the kings of Assyria and their vassals, comes from the seventh century BCE. We will look more closely at these Assyrian treaties on page 155; here we will focus on the Hittite treaties.

The Hittite treaties, of which several dozen examples are known, have the following structure:

I. *Identification* of the suzerain.

II. *History* of the relationship between the two groups, with emphasis on the benevolent actions of the suzerain toward the vassal.

III. *Stipulations*: the obligations imposed on the vassal. He must show absolute loyalty to the suzerain and thus have no independent relationships with other powers; he may not attack another vassal of the suzerain; he must respond to a call to assistance from the suzerain; he must submit disputes with another vassal to the suzerain; and he must pay tribute.

IV. *Provision for deposit of copies of the treaty in the temples of the principal gods of the two parties*, and often for its periodic public reading.

V. *Divine witnesses to the treaty*: lengthy lists of the national deities of both parties who are summoned as witnesses to the treaty; these typically conclude with the invocation of the oldest generations of the gods, "the mountains, the rivers, the springs, the great sea, heaven and earth, the winds, the clouds."

VI. *Blessings* for observance of the treaty and *curses* for violations of it, to be carried out by the gods who were its ultimate guarantors.

While not all of the treaties contain all of the elements, their occurrence is sufficiently well attested to make this outline a standard pattern.

Elements of the treaty form are found in the Bible in passages that concern covenant. We will examine in more detail on page 104 the light that the form sheds on the Ten Commandments; here are some examples from other texts:

- The identification of the suzerain (I) and the historical prologue (II) are found in the covenant renewal ceremony in Joshua 24.2–13.

- The Covenant Code (Ex 20.22–23.33; see further pages 111–13) may be understood as a lengthy list of stipulations (III).

- Corresponding to the placement of copies of the treaty in the temples of the two parties (IV) is the placement of the tablets of the law in the ark of the covenant (Deut 10.1–5), from which they are taken, as in the treaties, for periodic reading (Deut 31.10–13). The existence of two tablets of the text of the covenant (Ex 31.18; 34.29) may be derived from the practice of making copies of treaties and other contracts for each party.

- We also find allusions to the divine witnesses (V). In Deuteronomy, heaven and earth are invoked as witnesses (Deut 4.26; 31.28), and in one instance, as in the treaties, these are associated with blessings and curses: "I call heaven and earth to witness against you today that I have set before you life and death, blessings and curses" (Deut 30.19).

In prophetic literature, one of the genres that the prophets use is the "covenant lawsuit," in which Yahweh as suzerain sues Israel for breach of contract. In a typical lawsuit passage, the most ancient divine witnesses to the treaties are also invoked:

> Hear what Yahweh says:
> Rise, plead your case before the mountains,
>   and let the hills hear your voice.
> Hear, you mountains, the lawsuit of Yahweh,
>   and you enduring foundations of the earth;
> for Yahweh has a lawsuit with his people,
>   and he will contend with Israel. (Mic 6.1–2)

BIBLIOGRAPHY

For commentaries on Exodus, see the bibliography to Chapter 6.

A good summary of the classic view of the relationship between treaty and covenant is George E. Mendenhall and Gary A. Herion, "Covenant," pp. 1179–202 in *Anchor Bible Dictionary*, vol. 1 (ed. D. N. Freedman; New York: Doubleday, 1992).

A selection of Hittite treaties is found in Gary Beckman, *Hittite Diplomatic Texts* (2d ed.; Atlanta: Scholars, 1999).

For a summary of scholarly views on the Ten Commandments, see Patrick D. Miller, "Ten Commandments," pp. 517–22 in *The New Interpreter's Dictionary of the Bible*, vol. 5 (ed. K. D. Sakenfeld; Nashville, TN: Abingdon, 2009). For a discussion of the interpretation of the Ten Commandments and their significance, see Michael Coogan, *The Ten Commandments: A Short History of an Ancient Text* (New Haven and London: Yale University Press, 2014).

Law, Ritual, and Holiness

Exodus 20.22–23.33 and 25–40 and Leviticus

As the book of Exodus continues, many more divine instructions are given to Moses, so much so that the narrative itself becomes almost a framework for materials inserted into it. That in fact is the conclusion of critical scholarship: The final Priestly editors of the Pentateuch inserted into an older narrative legal and ritual traditions of different origins and dates, in part to provide them with a special authority by associating them with Moses and the revelations at Sinai. In this chapter, we will examine several collections of laws, those known as the Covenant Code, the Ritual Decalogue, and the Holiness Code, as well as the framework in which they are embedded in the books of Exodus and Leviticus. It is from collections such as these that the Pentateuch gets its reputation as a law book. Yet in it, as we have seen, law and narrative are intertwined, and in many respects, law is a response to divine action, especially the Exodus. We will begin with a look at ancient Near Eastern law collections.

LAW IN THE ANCIENT NEAR EAST

The several collections of biblical laws, like many other genres found in the Bible, are paralleled elsewhere in the ancient Near East. About a dozen complete or virtually complete law collections are known, principally from ancient Mesopotamia and Asia Minor. The earliest are from ancient Sumer, dating to the late third millennium BCE, and the latest, from Babylonia, are from the seventh century BCE. In addition, hundreds of thousands of contracts and records of lawsuits and other court cases show how legal principles functioned in ordinary life.

One of the very first of the ancient law codes to be discovered was the **Code of Hammurapi** (a more correct spelling than the traditional "Hammurabi"), engraved on a monumental basalt stela dating to the reign of the Babylonian king for which it is named, who ruled in the first half of the eighteenth century BCE (see Figure 8.1). Because it is one of the most complete of the law collections that has survived, and because of its importance in the history of interpretation, we will take it as representative of the others.

In the Code of Hammurapi, the "code" proper is nearly three hundred laws, all in the form of particular cases and circumstances, dealing with such topics as perjury, theft, medical malpractice, real estate, banking, marriage (the longest section), and similar topics that are concerns of all complex societies (see Box 8.1 on page 111).

FIGURE 8.2   A circular altar from the mid-third millennium BCE at Megiddo, about 30 ft (9 m) in diameter. Like the altar described in Exodus 20.25–26, this Canaanite altar is made of unhewn stones, but it also has steps, which is forbidden in Exodus.

The Code of Hammurapi and similar nonbiblical collections contain both criminal and civil laws. The Covenant Code, like other biblical collections, differs from these by including among the laws dealing with criminal and civil matters regulations concerning worship (see Figure 8.2). In the Covenant Code, perhaps to emphasize the sacred character of the entire collection, the laws concerning worship frame the criminal and civil cases.

The complex character of the Covenant Code is evident from the assortment of topics it addresses, the different forms of laws that it includes, and the inconsistency in the way that it refers to the deity: Sometimes, especially in the opening and closing sections, the deity is speaking, but elsewhere he is generally spoken about.

The central section of the Covenant Code is the cases in Exodus 21.1–22.17, which deal with slaves, personal injuries, damages by and to animals, and loss of property. As is true of all laws, the Covenant Code gives us a window into the organization and values of the society that produced it. Like the Ten Commandments, the Covenant Code reflects an agrarian society, one with grain fields, vineyards, and houses (see, for example, Ex 22.5–7). It was also a society in which slavery was an accepted institution and women were considered property. (For further discussion of the status of women in Israelite law and ritual, see page 130.)

Like the Code of Hammurapi, the Covenant Code sets the laws in an explicitly religious context. In both, it is the deity who is ultimately the source of legal authority, and in both there is a human intermediary, Hammurapi and Moses, respectively. Thus, as in most other aspects of life in the ancient world, the distinction between sacred and secular was not nearly as sharp as it is in much of the modern world. In both codes, violation of the law is ultimately an offense against the deity.

The laws that frame the case laws in the Covenant Code are more specifically religious and also more specifically Israelite. An example is the law concerning the sabbath: "Six days you shall do your work, but on the seventh day you shall rest, so that your ox and your donkey may have relief, and your homeborn slave and the resident alien may be refreshed" (Ex 23.12). Unlike the P version of the sabbath commandment (Ex 20.11), the motivation for the sabbath observance here is humanitarian, extending even to animals. This same humanitarian motive is found in the version of the sabbath commandment found in the Decalogue in Deuteronomy (Deut 5.14–15), as well as in other laws in the Covenant Code.

Some of the values in the Covenant Code are often different from our own. For example, one of the laws concerning property is the case of a virgin who was seduced: "When a man seduces a virgin who is not engaged to be married, and lies with her, he shall give the bride-price for her and make her his wife. But if her father refuses to give her to him, he shall pay an amount equal to the bride-price for virgins" (Ex 22.16–17). Because the wronged daughter is the father's property and her value has been diminished by her loss of virginity, the one who has seduced her must make restitution to the father by paying the full bridewealth ("bride-price"), even if he does not marry her.

A second example concerns the institution of slavery: "When a slaveowner strikes a male or female slave with a rod and the slave dies immediately, the owner shall be punished. But if the slave survives a day or two, there is no punishment; for the slave is the owner's property" (Ex 21.20–21; see further 21.2–11). The principle of retributive justice (see Box 8.2 on page 114) does not apply in the case of injury to a slave because the slave does not have the rights of a free Israelite male.

At the same time, the Covenant Code also gives expression to principles that are still valid. As in the Decalogue, the mother is put on the same level as the father (Ex 21.15, 17; compare 20.12). Moreover, members of lesser social classes are to be the objects of special concern: "You shall not wrong or oppress a resident alien, for you were aliens in the land of Egypt. You shall not abuse any widow or orphan" (Ex 22.21–22). The appeal to the Exodus experience is significant, for it instructs the Israelites to remember what it was like to be members of an underprivileged social class, and to treat the less powerful and less fortunate as God had treated them.

THE ARK, THE TABERNACLE, AND THE PRIESTLY VESTMENTS AND ORDINATION

In Yahweh's commands to Moses in Exodus 25–31, and Moses's carrying out of those commands in Exodus 35–40, the Priestly tradition (P) gives lovingly detailed descriptions of objects and institutions having to do with ritual. The context in which P originated was the Temple in Jerusalem, constructed in the tenth century BCE and destroyed in the early sixth, and P's descriptions clearly are informed by the architecture, ritual objects, and practices of the Temple in Jerusalem. But are they simply idealized retrojections of the Temple and its rituals, with some modifications to suit the period of the Exodus and wandering in the wilderness, or do they have a historical basis in the period before the Temple was functioning? Some scholars have argued that the descriptions of the tabernacle (also called "the tent of meeting") preserve earlier traditions from the premonarchic period in the twelfth and eleventh centuries, when the ark of the covenant was a moveable sanctuary housed in a tent.

The Ark of the Covenant

Among the detailed instructions given to Moses are those concerning the construction of the divine throne, which had two parts. First is the ark proper, 2.5 cubits (about 4 ft [1.1 m]) long and 1.5 cubits (about 2.5 ft [.7 m]) wide and high, made of acacia, a hard wood that is insect resistant and found throughout the desert regions. The ark was overlaid with gold and was carried on poles through rings attached to each side. The

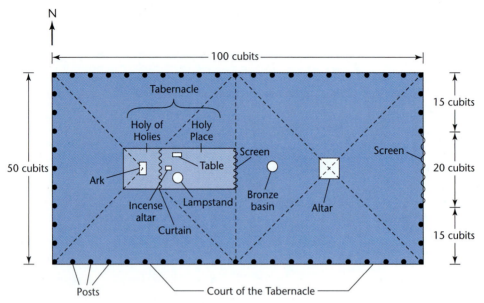

FIGURE 8.4   Plan of the tabernacle as described in Exodus 25–27.

P for the wilderness period (see Figure 8.4). It is also called the "tent of meeting" because it was the place where Yahweh "met" with Moses and the Israelites (Ex 29.42–43). In the ancient Near Eastern understanding of temples, the earthly structure was a copy of the true divine home in the heavens; thus, later tradition observes, the tent that Moses constructs was "a sanctuary that is a sketch and shadow of the heavenly one" (Heb 8.5), "a copy of the holy tent that you prepared from the beginning" (Wis 9.8). That Yahweh's heavenly home was a tent is therefore presumed and is consistent with the relationship of Yahweh to the Canaanite high god El (see pages 77–79), who also lived in a tent. P appropriately incorporates a tent-shrine into its description of the fully developed worship of Yahweh that began at Sinai, during the journey from Egypt to Canaan: a movable shrine for a people on the move.

The court of the tabernacle was made of intricately woven curtains set on a frame of acacia wood. The entire structure could be dismantled for travel. Its plan was bipartite, with a total enclosed area of 50 by 100 cubits (about 75 by 150 ft [22 by 45 m]),

consisting of an open courtyard, divided in half. On one side of this courtyard, which all the Israelites were permitted to enter, was a bronze basin used for purification rituals, and in the center of this half was the principal altar of sacrifice. The other half contained the tabernacle itself, consisting of another enclosed area, "the holy place" (Ex 26.33), which only the priests were permitted to enter. Within it were an offering table, an incense altar, and an ornate, perpetually burning seven-branched lampstand. Attached to this inner enclosure was a room, "the holy of holies" (Ex 26.34), the most sacred place, separated from the rest by an especially intricately woven curtain. Only the high priest (Aaron and his successors) could enter this space, and only on the Day of Atonement, for it contained the ark (see Lev 16.2–3).

The Priestly Vestments and Ordination

Exodus 28 gives detailed instructions for the priestly vestments, which, like the tabernacle curtains, were woven of multicolored yarns. The details are rich with symbolism, but difficult to picture. We may highlight as examples the ephod and the Urim and Thummim attached to it. The ephod, a kind of apron, was blue, with ornamental pomegranates and golden bells decorating its hem. Attached to the shoulder straps of the ephod were two semiprecious stones, each engraved with the names of six of the twelve tribes of Israel. Hanging from the shoulder straps was a "breastpiece of judgment," ornamented with twelve semiprecious stones, each also engraved with the name of a tribe. This was a kind of pouch that held the Urim and Thummim, stones used in rendering oracular judgments (see further pages 243–44). The bells served as a kind of warning, because the chief priest was "Holy to the LORD," the words engraved on a rosette ornamenting the priestly headgear. The ordination ceremony of the priests—Aaron and his sons—is also described in detail. The carrying out of these instructions, however, does not occur in the book of Exodus but in Leviticus 8–9.

THE GOLDEN CALF

Between the accounts of the divine blueprints for the ark, the tabernacle, and other ritual objects in Exodus 25–31 and of their manufacture in Exodus 35–40 is an interruption: the episode of the golden calf and its sequel. The narrative of the golden calf (Ex 32) is extraordinarily complex, comprising several different sources that are difficult to disentangle.

At first reading, the narrative is straightforward. During Moses's absence of forty days and forty nights (see Box 8.3) on top of Mount Sinai, the Israelites at the base of the mountain became restive. They persuaded Aaron to make a gold statue of a young bull, which they worshiped. Yahweh told Moses what had happened, and Moses came down from the mountain, broke the tablets of the testimony in his anger, and punished the guilty parties.

Box 8.3 FORTY DAYS AND FORTY NIGHTS

In the history of biblical interpretation, many numbers found in the Bible have often been interpreted symbolically. While such interpretations are frequently fanciful, sometimes numerical symbolism is present. We have seen some examples in the genealogy in Genesis 5 (see page 58); another is the frequent use of the number forty in measuring time. Often a period of forty days (and nights) or forty years serves as a transitional marker, separating two distinct epochs in biblical narrative. Thus, the Flood lasts for forty days and forty nights (Gen 7.12), and it marks a new beginning. Likewise, in their journey from Egypt to Canaan, the Israelites spend forty years in the wilderness (Num 14.33; Deut 2.7; 29.5), and Moses twice spends forty days and forty nights on top of Mount Sinai (Ex 24.18; 34.28). Several of the judges have terms of forty years (Judg 3.11; 5.31; 8.28; 1 Sam 4.18), and that is also the span of the reigns of David (1 Kings 2.11) and Solomon (1 Kings 11.42). In some of the latter cases, the numbers either may be accurate or may simply be round numbers.

This symbolism is picked up in the New Testament, where before his ministry begins, Jesus is in the wilderness for forty days (Mk 1.13), a period that in Luke is paralleled by the forty days between his being raised from the dead and taken up to heaven (Lk 4.2; Acts 1.3).

the Bible thought it important to incorporate diverse traditions even if they were inconsistent.

The Ritual Decalogue has two major emphases. One is that the worship of Yahweh is not to be corrupted by the practices of the Canaanites, and hence intermarriage is forbidden. The second is the establishment of regular holy days. In both the Covenant Code (Ex 23.14–17) and the Ritual Decalogue (Ex 34.18, 22–23, 25–26), three festivals are mentioned. They were pilgrimage festivals, celebrated at a regional sanctuary and linked to the agricultural cycle (see Box 8.4): the harvest of the barley in the early spring, of the wheat in the late spring, and of fruits such as grapes and olives in the fall. Moreover, as with the Decalogue, this suggests a date of origin sometime after the Exodus, when the Israelites were already settled in the land with a primarily agricultural economy.

The early spring observance, connected with the barley harvest, is called the "festival of unleavened bread" in both the Covenant Code (Ex 23.15) and the Ritual Decalogue (34.18), and although it is linked with the Exodus, no mention is made of the Passover lamb. The late spring observance, called the "festival of harvest" and connected with the harvest of the winter wheat ("the first fruits"; Ex 23.16; Num 28.26), is also called the "festival of weeks" because it occurs seven weeks and one day after the first (see Lev 23.15–16). This amounts to fifty days; hence the later term "Pentecost" (from Greek, meaning "fiftieth"). The fall observance, the "festival of ingathering," is later called the "festival of booths" (Deut 16.13), a name recalling the practice of camping out in the fields during the labor-intensive fall harvest, but in later sources, it is also linked with the Exodus: "You shall live in booths for seven days; all that are citizens in Israel shall live in booths, so that your generations may know that I made the people of Israel live in booths when I brought them out of the land of Egypt" (Lev 23.42–43).

Because the three agricultural festivals were timed to the natural climate of the region, they likely originated with the Canaanites and were continued and adapted by the Israelites, especially by connecting them with the Exodus from Egypt, as with the fall festival of Booths, and also the early spring festival of unleavened bread. The latter was also united with the spring ritual of the sacrifice of a newborn animal (see further pages 87–88). Thus, in the calendar in Deuteronomy, the Passover, the Exodus, the animal sacrifice, and the unleavened bread are combined (Deut 16.1–3).

SEQUEL

While Moses was up on Mount Sinai getting a replacement set for the broken tablets, he experienced a special divine revelation:

> The LORD descended in the cloud and stood with him there, and proclaimed the name, "The LORD." The LORD passed before him, and proclaimed,
>
> "The LORD, the LORD,
> a God merciful and gracious,
> slow to anger,
> and abounding in steadfast love and faithfulness."
> (Ex 34.5–7)

Then, at the end of Exodus 34, Moses came down from Mount Sinai. When he returned, he first gave the sabbath command (Ex 35.2–3), the sign of the covenant at Sinai. Then the instructions given to Moses in Exodus 25–31 are repeated virtually verbatim in the narrative account of their being carried out in Exodus 35–40.

So, following Moses's commands, the people contributed the materials and the artisans Bezalel and Oholiab made the tabernacle, the ark, and the vestments and Moses consecrated them. When all was complete, "the cloud covered the tent of meeting, and the glory of the LORD filled the tabernacle" (Ex 40.34). Even though the Israelites will be at Sinai until Numbers 10.11, Moses never ascends the mountain again. During the rest of the stay at Sinai and thereafter, Moses will usually receive divine instruction and guidance in the tabernacle, for that is where the deity now manifests himself.

Box 8.4 AN ANCIENT HEBREW AGRICULTURAL CALENDAR

An ancient Hebrew calendar divides the months of the year as follows:

Two months gathering	[September–October]
Two months planting	[November–December]
Two months late sowing	[January–February]
A month cutting flax	[March]
A month reaping barley	[April]
A month reaping and measuring (grain)	[May]
Two months pruning	[June–July]
A month summer fruit	[August]

The twelve-month calendar begins in the fall, perhaps indicating a fall new year celebration, as in Judaism today, where the New Year (Rosh Hashanah) occurs in September or October. The dominant pattern in the Bible, however, is that the New Year was celebrated in the spring; thus, the Passover is celebrated in the first month of the year (Abib or Nisan; for example, Ex 12.2; Lev 23.5). But evidence exists that a fall new year was also observed at some times in ancient Israel; for example, the festival of ingathering is said to take place at the "end of the year" (Ex 23.16; called "the turn of the year" in 34.22).

The three pilgrimage festivals in Exodus 34.22–23 correspond to the three principal harvests, which the Gezer calendar calls "reaping barley" (early April), "reaping and measuring grain" (late May), and "gathering" (September); the same Hebrew words for "reaping" and "gathering" occur with reference to the same times of year both in the Gezer calendar and in Exodus 34.22.

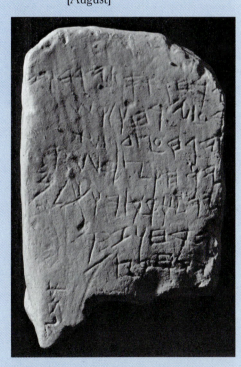

FIGURE 8.6 A limestone tablet from Gezer dating to the tenth century BCE, measuring about 3 by 4.5 in (8 by 11.5 cm). On it is an agricultural calendar written in an early form of the Hebrew alphabet.

THE BOOK OF LEVITICUS

Following the construction of the tabernacle at the end of the book of Exodus, the next book, Leviticus, continues the narrative of the stay at Sinai with more divine instructions given to Moses and Aaron. These instructions are concerned largely with ritual matters, and the entire book in its present form was shaped by the Priestly writers. They included in their compilation detailed rubrics about types of sacrifices to be offered to Yahweh and regulations about ritual purity; they also incorporated into the final version of the book an independent source, the Holiness Code, which, as its name suggests, has as a central theme the separation between the sacred and the profane. The book includes only a few chapters of narrative, which are connected closely with the ritual instructions. The Hebrew name of the book of Leviticus is (way)yiqra, its first word, "(and) he [the LORD] called"; the conventional English name, derived from ancient Greek manuscripts, is inaccurate, since the focus of the book is not the Levites, who are mentioned only in 25.32–33. The outline of the book makes its contents clear:

Chapters 1–7 Instructions concerning sacrifices

8–10 Narratives describing the consecration of the tabernacle, the altar, and the priests, and the offering of illicit fire and its consequences

11–15 Instructions concerning purity and impurity

16 Instructions concerning the Day of Atonement

17–26 The Holiness Code: a separate collection of regulations concerning sacrifices, purity, ethical conduct, and sacred times, which includes one narrative section (24.10–23) concerning blasphemy and concludes with an extended series of blessings and curses (chap. 26)

27 Additional instructions concerning vows and offerings

In its final form in the context of the entire Pentateuch, which was shaped by P, Leviticus fits into its narrative context, as occasional references to Egypt as past and Canaan as future indicate—for example, "You shall not do as they do in the land of Egypt, where you lived, and you shall not do as they do in the land of Canaan, to which I am bringing you" (18.3).

SACRIFICES (LEV 1–7)

The Sacrificial System

Sacrifice, the offering of something of value to a deity, was an important part of ancient Israel's religious life, as is evident from the repeated references to it throughout the Bible and parallels in other ancient Near Eastern sources to many of the details of the Bible's sacrificial system. This system can be understood on several levels, of which we will focus on two.

On one level, sacrifice can be understood as a gift to a god. One of the Hebrew words for sacrifice is *minhah*. In the Bible, this word has the general meaning of a gift from an inferior to a superior and can have the nuance of tribute from a vassal to a suzerain or part of an effort to curry favor with someone more powerful. In religious contexts, a *minhah* is thus a gift to God as superior from the offering individual or community. As a gift, the sacrifice, whether an animal or other commodity, could have several functions, including appeasing an angry deity, thanking a supportive deity, or motivating a deity to help the offerer. On an even more anthropomorphic level, the sacrificial animals and other offerings were a meal for the deity, presented on the altar, which served as a table. In some types of sacrifice, the roasted meat was shared between deity and worshiper, in effect a kind of "communion." Some sacrifices can thus be understood as a shared meal, a ritual of uniting.

On another level, sacrifice can be understood as a collection and distribution system for agricultural products, both animals and crops—in other words, as a form of taxation. It is significant that the three primary pilgrimage festivals (see pages 119–20) are set at the time of the three principal harvests in early spring, early summer, and early fall. At this time, the priests would collect a portion of the harvested crops, which would then be stored in temple treasuries, for distribution to the needy in times of famine or before the next harvest had ripened. During the time of the monarchy, from the tenth to the sixth centuries BCE, when priests were often under direct royal control, the sacrificial collection system would help centralize the monarchy's power. In addition to agricultural products, on occasion an offering could be real estate or even personal labor, as in the dedication of nonpriests to temporary or permanent sanctuary service as Nazirites.

Tithing had a similar function. According to Leviticus 27.30–33, all agricultural produce and livestock were subject to the **tithe:** That is, ten percent of these commodities were considered as belonging to Yahweh; the Hebrew word usually translated "tithe" literally means "a tenth." In a religious sense, this can be understood as a kind of rent from a tenant to a landlord, for according to Leviticus 25.23, the land itself belonged to Yahweh. Functionally, the tithe was a kind of universal taxation, which paid for the maintenance of the clergy and ultimately of the monarchy itself.

Leviticus mentions tithing only in a brief note in the concluding appendix (27.30–33), but it also occurs in Numbers 18.21–32, where it is explicitly designated for the Levites, and in other sources dating from almost all periods in the formation of the biblical traditions. One passage is especially informative. In Samuel's speech describing the negative consequences of the monarchy, a Deuteronomistic composition, he asserts that the king "will take one-tenth of your grain and of your vineyards and give it to his officers and his courtiers. . . . [And he] will take one-tenth of your flocks, and you shall be his slaves" (1 Sam 8.15–17). This, along with evidence from elsewhere in the ancient Near East, suggests that the tithe was a civic as well as a religious obligation, like the *minhah* (see page 122). In a monarchic system where the king controlled the priesthood, as was the case in Jerusalem, the crown and the Temple were linked.

Types of Sacrifices

Leviticus 1–7 elaborates four principal types of sacrifices:

- The *burnt offering* or *holocaust*: An animal sacrifice, in which the whole animal (a bull, ram, male goat, or bird) was slaughtered, its blood splashed on the altar, and the entire animal burned. (See Figure 8.7.)

- The *grain offering*: An offering of flour mixed with oil and incense. A "token portion" of the offering was consumed by the fire on the altar, and the rest was given to the priests.

- The *sacrifice of well-being* is similar to the burnt offering, in that the blood of the animal was sprinkled on the altar, but in this type only the fatty portions of the animal were burned, and the rest was shared by the worshiper and the priests.

- The *sin offering* and the *guilt offering*: In these offerings, a sacrificial animal served as a kind of substitute for an offender. Its blood was sprinkled on the altar and the fatty portions were burned, but the rest of the carcass was either discarded as profane and burned outside the sanctuary, or, in some cases, given to the priest who performed the ritual. The purpose of the offering was to remove an offerer's guilt, which was due either to advertent or inadvertent sin or to impurity.

FIGURE 8.7 A restored altar from Beer-sheba, dated to the eighth or seventh century BCE. The four projections on the top are called "horns" in the Bible; these symbolized strength and also could have been used to hold a grate on which offerings were placed to be burned. The altar is about 5.25 ft (1.6 m) high.

Both in Leviticus and elsewhere in the Bible, other types of sacrifices are also prescribed; one of the most frequently mentioned is incense offerings. Incense is made from spices and local and imported gum resins that when burned emit a pleasant odor. Incense served several functions, both practical and symbolic. On a mundane level, the burning incense would have masked what must have been a terrible stench from the slaughtering and burning of the animals being sacrificed. It also repelled flies and other insects that would have been attracted to the sacrificial precinct. At the same time, because incense was an expensive import, its use would have demonstrated the wealth and prestige of the offerer. Its smoke also symbolized the ascent of the offerer's prayers into the heavenly realm.

THE CONSECRATION CEREMONIES AND THEIR AFTERMATH (LEV 8–10)

In Leviticus the divine instructions are twice interrupted by narrative. First comes the completion of the fulfillment of the divine commands given in Exodus concerning the priesthood (Lev 8–9). In Exodus, all of the ritual objects had been made, and the most sacred objects and places had been consecrated; what remained was the ordination of the priests, which is now described. The entire ritual lasted eight days, and Moses himself officiated at its beginning, but once Aaron and his sons had been ordained, they assumed the priestly functions. The sacrifices they offered are the first sacrifices narrated by P in the Pentateuch, and at their conclusion, the divine approval is apparent: "The glory of the LORD appeared to all the people. Fire came out from the LORD and consumed the burnt offering and the fat on the altar" (Lev 9.23–24). The second episode, in Leviticus 10, is another example of priestly rivalry, similar to that in the episode of the golden calf (Ex 32). Two of Aaron's four sons made an incense offering of "strange fire" (NRSV "unholy fire"), probably meaning that they

performed an illegitimate ritual. As punishment in kind, they were destroyed when "fire came out from the LORD and consumed them" (10.2). When their bodies had been disposed of, by those not in the direct priestly line (to avoid contamination, as is prescribed in Lev 21.1–5, 10–11), and they had been mourned, Moses gave further instructions to Aaron concerning the priests' conduct, including prohibiting them from drinking alcoholic beverages prior to performing their sacred duties.

PURITY AND IMPURITY (LEV 11–15)

A large part of Leviticus is devoted to instructions concerning the pure and the impure. The traditional translations "clean" and "unclean" are misleading, for the categories do not deal with either hygiene or cleanliness. Rather, according to the definitions of Leviticus, the "clean" is what is pure, that is, suitable for human use and in some cases, required for continued membership in Israel's covenantal community, described as Yahweh's "holy nation" (Exod 19.6). The unclean, on the other hand, is impure, and either unsuitable for human use or forbidden for Israelites. For example, Leviticus 11 lists those animals that may be eaten and those that may not, and Leviticus 12–15 deals with conditions that cause impurity in persons and in objects.

Several theories have been proposed to explain these categories; probably they stem from a combination of overlapping factors, including the following:

- *Health*: Some animals may not have been eaten because they were recognized as carriers of disease; among these we can include those that eat other dead animals, such as vultures. Likewise, it may have been observed that people whose diet included pork or shellfish became ill more frequently. Some types of bodily emissions also made a person impure. These include abnormal genital discharges in both males and females and skin diseases. Early peoples probably recognized that these may have been contagious, and so an impure or unclean person was not only prohibited from participating in rituals, but also sometimes quarantined, to prevent spread of the condition to others.

- *Cultural differentiation*: One of the ways that cultures distinguish themselves from others is diet. Thus, for some, animals such as cow, horse, dog, and cat are part of the diet; for others, they are taboo and are never eaten. The pig is a good example. In the late second millennium BCE, when Israel was beginning to emerge in the land of Canaan, another group, the Philistines, had emigrated there from their homelands in the Aegean (see further Box 12.4 on pages 184–85). The Philistines, unlike the Israelites and most of their neighbors, did not practice circumcision, and they also included the pig as a part of their diet. Pig was not generally eaten by the Israelites or the Canaanites, and so both circumcision and avoidance of pig in the diet became cultural markers that distinguished the Israelites from the Philistines. Thus, even though the prohibition against eating pork is found in texts dating from the first millennium, it probably originated earlier, when the Israelites and Philistines were competing for control of the same region. Its preservation into and beyond the period of the Babylonian Exile is likely related to the fact that Babylonians, like the Philistines, ate pork and did not practice circumcision. The dietary laws and the practice of circumcision are retained in Judaism and Islam where they continue to mark communal boundaries.

- *A sense of order*: In her influential book, *Purity and Danger: An Analysis of the Concepts of Pollution and Taboo* (1966), the British anthropologist Mary Douglas argued that the difference between pure (or "clean") and impure (or "unclean") is based on a theoretical order in which distinct categories must be kept separate to be pure. With regard to food, this applies, for example, to fish, which are suited to their environment because of their fins and scales; but other aquatic creatures, such as lobsters, are not, because they have legs that would be more appropriate for a land animal. Likewise, animals that chew the cud and have divided hooves (such as cows) are permissible, but those that were thought to chew the cud but do not have divided hooves (such as camels and hares) or that have divided hooves but do not chew the cud (such as pigs) are not. This aversion to mixing of categories extends to clothing—the Israelites were not to wear clothes made from two different materials, nor were men to wear women's clothing or vice versa—and to agriculture—a field was not to be sown with two different crops, nor were two different kinds of animals to be bred together or used together to pull a plow.

- *Relationship to sex and death*: In ancient Israel, as in most cultures, taboos existed concerning death and sex. A person became impure by contact with a corpse or a dead animal that was not to be eaten; by skin disease, which can be understood as mimicking the decay that occurs after death; and by loss of fluids considered essential to life, such as semen and blood, especially menstrual blood. Some animals were prohibited because they are connected with death, especially those that eat other dead animals, and the consumption of blood was strictly prohibited.

But taking these explanations into account does not explain all prohibitions and taboos, and those found in Leviticus and elsewhere in the Bible do not form a comprehensive system. Moreover, only a few of the animals that humans were permitted to eat were considered suitable for sacrifice, because of the greater degree of holiness required for the most immediate contact with the divine (see pages 127–29). For similar reasons, although ordinary Israelites were permitted to bury their dead, the high priest was prohibited from any contact with a corpse, even of a member of his immediate family, and from the traditional signs of mourning.

Those who had contact with impure persons also became impure themselves, and so, for example, when a man had sexual intercourse with a menstruating woman, he too became impure. The impurity caused by contact with an impure person or object, such as a corpse or a dead animal, also affected objects that had contact with them.

Leviticus 13 discusses skin conditions that made a person impure. The descriptions do not enable precise diagnoses, but it is clear that the traditional translation of the Hebrew word *saraat* as "leprosy" is misleading. Rather, the Hebrew word is more general, referring to several conditions, including boils and other eruptions, psoriasis, and fungal infections. The identification of these conditions was made by priests, because they concerned ritual fitness, and also because in Israel as in much of the rest of the ancient world, priests often functioned as medical practitioners. One reason for this is that disease was often considered divinely caused as a punishment for sin. For some conditions, the afflicted person was also quarantined for a period, to prevent others from becoming impure by contact (as well as to prevent contagion) and to allow the condition to heal. Likewise, just as skin disease made a person impure, so its equivalent, such as mildew, made clothing and houses impure.

Leviticus 15 concerns impurity or uncleanness caused by genital discharges. Males become impure both because of abnormal discharges and by normal seminal ejaculation. For the first, which is a medical condition, a period of impurity lasts for seven days after the emission stops, followed by a purification offering. For the second, the impurity lasts for one day, and only a ritual washing is prescribed.

Women are impure for seven days during normal menstrual discharge, although later rabbinic tradition understood the seven-day period to begin after the bleeding had stopped. That is certainly the case with nonmenstrual vaginal bleeding; after the bleeding has stopped, the woman is impure for seven days, after which there as a purification ritual, as for males with abnormal discharges.

All of this detail is somewhat alien to modern readers, encompassing as it does both practical and religious dimensions. Yet for the biblical writers, the details of purity were part of a comprehensive way of life that marked the Israelites as a distinct people, chosen by God who himself was considered the author of the regulations. That distinctiveness was expressed in the concept of holiness: "For I am the LORD who brought you up from the land of Egypt, to be your God; you shall be holy, for I am holy" (Lev 11.45). This notion dominates the Holiness Code, which we will consider soon, but first Leviticus discusses another set of rituals, those of the Day of Atonement.

THE DAY OF ATONEMENT (LEV 16)

Following the instructions concerning purity and impurity, Leviticus 16 is devoted to what has become the most solemn observance in the Jewish calendar, that of Yom Kippur, the **Day of Atonement**. The ritual serves to purify the priest, the sanctuary, and the people. It is to take place annually on the tenth day of the seventh month, that is, in the fall according to a spring new year. It is called a "sabbath of sabbaths" (16.31; NRSV: "sabbath of complete rest"); in addition to refraining from work, the Israelites are also to "deny themselves" (16.29), which is later understood to mean a complete fast and perhaps also abstinence from sexual intercourse.

On the Day of Atonement, in addition to sacrificing a bull as a sin offering for Aaron, two goats are also provided, and lots are cast for them. One is dedicated as a sin offering "for Yahweh"; the other is designated as "for Azazel," an obscure term probably referring to some sort of demon, often translated as the "**scapegoat**." The sins of the community are symbolically transferred to this goat, which is then released in the wilderness.

For all of its importance in later Judaism, however, both the Day of Atonement itself and the rituals associated with it are given little attention elsewhere in the Bible.

THE HOLINESS CODE (LEV 17–26)

Since the late nineteenth century, scholars have identified chapters 17–26 of Leviticus as a separate source, named the **Holiness Code** because of its repeated use of words having to do with holiness. This source (often abbreviated as "H") is comparable to other collections of biblical law, especially the Covenant Code (see pages 111–13) and the Deuteronomic Code (see pages 149–52). The Holiness Code, while later than the other two collections, is earlier than P, which included it in its final edition of the Pentateuch; a generally accepted date is sometime in the seventh century BCE. It is, however, from the same larger priestly school as P, and thus presumably originated among priests in the Temple in Jerusalem. More recently, some scholars have argued that the Holiness Code is later than most of the rest of P in the Pentateuch and that the editors of the Holiness Code may have been responsible for a revision of P and thus for the final formation of the Pentateuch itself. Agreement remains, however, that the two sources (P and H) are distinct, in part because they are not entirely consistent.

Important evidence for the date of the Holiness Code is the close parallels in vocabulary and theme between it and the book of Ezekiel, named for the prophet Ezekiel who was also a priest in the Jerusalem Temple before his exile to Babylonia in 597 BCE. These parallels have led many scholars to conclude that the Holiness Code in some form preceded Ezekiel, although it is also possible that both were independently drawing on established priestly traditions. (See further page 325.)

Like the other collections of laws, the Holiness Code has its own complicated literary history. It has no obvious principle of arrangement and includes both apodictic and casuistic laws. It also contains some repetitions and inconsistencies. The Holiness Code ends with blessings and curses, already familiar to us from their use in ancient Near Eastern treaties (see pages 101–02). At times the curses seem to reflect the experience of exile in the sixth century BCE. For example, Yahweh declares as punishment for disobedience to his commands:

> I will scatter you among the nations, and I will unsheathe the sword against you; your land shall be a desolation, and your cities a waste. Then the land shall enjoy its sabbath years as long as it lies desolate, while you are in the land of your enemies; then the land shall rest, and enjoy its sabbath years. (Lev 26.33–34)

This warning may be understood as a prediction after the fact, based on what actually occurred

when the Israelites lost control of their land and were taken captive to Babylon. Nevertheless, Yahweh continues, the ancient covenant with Abraham, Isaac, and Jacob will not be revoked:

> When they are in the land of their enemies, I will not spurn them, or abhor them so as to destroy them utterly and break my covenant with them; for I am the LORD their God; but I will remember in their favor the covenant with their ancestors whom I brought out of the land of Egypt in the sight of the nations, to be their God. (Lev 26.44–45)

The Concept of Holiness

Central to the Holiness Code is the concept of holiness itself, as in the phrase "You shall be holy, for I Yahweh your god am holy" (Lev 19.2) and its many variations (20.7, 8, 26; 21.6, 8, 15, 23; 22.9, 16, 32). Words containing the consonants of the root for "holy" (Hebr. q-d-sh) occur more than twice as many times in the ten chapters of the Holiness Code as in the other seventeen chapters of the book of Leviticus; English translations obscure this frequency, since words like "sanctuary," "sanctify," "hallow," "consecrate," "dedicate," and "sacred" are all renderings of Hebrew words containing this root.

The primary meaning of the Hebrew word translated "holiness" (qodesh) is separation. The holy is that which is separate from the profane, the impure, the ordinary. Thus, for example, Israel is holy because it has been separated by Yahweh from other nations: "You shall be holy to me; for I the LORD am holy, and I have separated you from the other peoples to be mine" (Lev 20.26). As a consequence, to maintain its holiness, Israel must separate itself from the practices of other nations: "You shall not do as they do in the land of Egypt, where you lived, and you shall not do as they do in the land of Canaan, to which I am bringing you. You shall not follow their statutes" (Lev 18.3; see also 18.24).

Varying degrees of separation may be categorized according to persons, spaces, and times and visualized as a series of concentric circles (see Figure 8.8).

With regard to persons, in the center is Yahweh himself, who is holy. Nearest to Yahweh are the

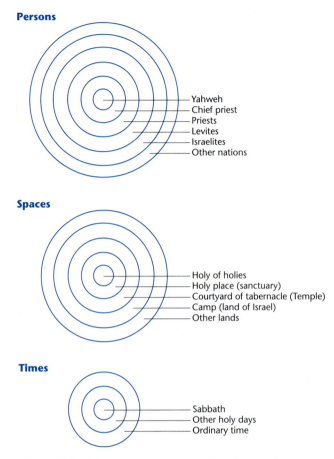

Persons

- Yahweh
- Chief priest
- Priests
- Levites
- Israelites
- Other nations

Spaces

- Holy of holies
- Holy place (sanctuary)
- Courtyard of tabernacle (Temple)
- Camp (land of Israel)
- Other lands

Times

- Sabbath
- Other holy days
- Ordinary time

FIGURE 8.8   Schematic representation of the degrees of holiness as applied to persons, spaces, and times.

priests, who have the closest contact with Yahweh. The highest-ranking priest during the time of Moses was Aaron, "the priest who is greater than his brothers, on whose head the anointing oil has been poured and who has been ordained to wear the vestments" (Lev 21.10). The successors of Aaron as preeminent priest were called "the great priest," "the chief priest," and later, "the high priest." Only this priest was permitted to enter the holy of holies, the innermost sanctum of the tabernacle, and later of the Temple. Next are the Levites, who, although they are not prominent in the book of Leviticus, in other sources are a class of minor clergy. The rest of the Israelites form the next group, and they too are holy; in P and in the Holiness Code, resident aliens

are included among them. Finally come other nations, who are least holy or even not holy at all, especially the Canaanites.

The degrees of holiness of space mirror those of persons. The "holy of holies" in the center of the sanctuary was where the divine presence dwelled. Only the high priest had access to the holy of holies, and only priests could enter the sanctuary. Within the larger structure of the tabernacle was the courtyard, which the Israelites were permitted to enter. The tabernacle itself was in the camp, but constituted a separate zone. When the Temple was built, these divisions were applied to the holy of holies, its innermost chamber, then the rest of the Temple, the Temple courtyard, and finally the land of Israel, which corresponds to the camp. The land of Israel itself was a "holy land" (Zech 2.12; Wis 12.3) in the midst of other nations; ultimately, it belonged to Yahweh and if the Israelites profaned it they would be expelled from it.

The same model can also be used to explain sacred time. At the center is the sabbath. According to P, the origins of the sabbath lay in the divine rest at creation. The land, which belonged to Yahweh, also needed its sabbaths. Less sacred than the sabbath are the "appointed festivals" (23.4–44), and less sacred still is what we might call ordinary time.

Prohibited Sexual Relationships

In the Holiness Code, Leviticus 18 and 20 are devoted to prohibited sexual relationships. Chapter 18 is introduced by a general statement about how the Israelites were to act differently from both the Egyptians and the Canaanites, implying that such forbidden practices were acceptable among those peoples, although little evidence supports that. The only specific references to non-Israelite rituals are

the offering of children to Molech (18.21; 20.1–5), a form of child-sacrifice only partially understood, and necromancy (consulting the dead; 20.6, 27).

The persons with whom sexual intercourse ("uncovering the nakedness of ") was prohibited include one's father or mother, father's wife (other than mother), sister, half-sister, stepsister, aunt, and daughter-in-law. Also banned was sex with the sister, daughter, or granddaughter of a sexual partner or with a menstruating woman. Male homosexual intercourse was also forbidden, as was bestiality. For violating these sexual taboos, the penalty was either expulsion from the community or, in some cases, death. (See Box 8.5.)

These lists are not entirely comprehensive, since some obvious omissions exist, such as father-daughter. Moreover, prohibitions mostly concern sexual activity by men with female relatives or relatives-in-law; although male homosexual relations are prohibited, female homosexual relations are not mentioned. Finally, not all of the prohibitions in Leviticus were always in force in ancient Israel, as biblical narratives attest.

Box 8.5 CAPITAL PUNISHMENT

In biblical law the penalty for a wide variety of crimes is capital punishment, which is divinely decreed. The modern argument that capital punishment is wrong because the Fifth Commandment states "Thou shalt not kill" is both a misinterpretation of that commandment, which refers to premeditated murder, and a selective disregard of the repeated use of capital punishment throughout the Bible.

On the other hand, the contrary argument that capital punishment is divinely ordained and should continue to be employed is also flawed. It, too, is selective, since few today would apply it to all cases in which it is prescribed in the Bible, such as for cursing or striking a parent (Ex 21.15, 17; Lev 20.9), violation of the sabbath (Ex 31.15), or prohibited sexual relationships (Lev 20.10–16).

The usual method of capital punishment was stoning. All members of the community participated, thus instilling a sense of collective responsibility for the carrying out of the death penalty. According to Deuteronomy 17.7, the first stones were to be thrown by the accusing witnesses. Burning is more rarely prescribed, for a man's sexual relationship with both his wife and her mother (Lev 20.14), and sometimes for adultery and prostitution (Gen 38.24; Lev 21.9).

WOMEN IN ISRAELITE RITUAL AND LAW

In the sections of Exodus and Leviticus concerning ritual, it is not surprising that women are mentioned only infrequently. The Israelite priesthood was patrilineal, passing from father to son. Women therefore had a much less significant part in Israelite temple or shrine-centered ritual than men; their roles were at best peripheral. We find mention of women "who served at the entrance to the tent of meeting" (Ex 38.8; 1 Sam 2.22) and of women who were singers and dancers in liturgical contexts (e.g., Ps 68.25). Still, women were not required to participate in the three pilgrimage festivals, presumably because of their reproductive and domestic functions. When we do hear of women's religious activity, it is often outside of the ritual spaces controlled by priests. Women performed ritual roles celebrating military victories or mourning the dead. In the story of Jephthah's daughter, we have evidence for a women's ritual pilgrimage to a mountain. (Judg 11.37-40). Women were also engaged in ritual activity in household shrines, as is suggested by the story of Micah's mother consecrating silver to Yahweh and commissioning an idol for the family's household shrine (Judg 17.1-6).

This subsidiary status of women in Israelite ritual is paralleled by their subordinate legal status. As we have seen, in Israel's earliest systems, women generally were considered property. The Tenth Commandment (Ex 20.17) lists the neighbor's wife between his house and his slaves and animals as property that is not to be coveted. Other laws describe how daughters were under the control of their fathers, who received bridewealth at the time of their marriage from the groom's family.

The sexual relationships prohibited to Israelite males included a large number that concerned women who were under the control of and therefore implicitly the property of another man. This is clear from the formulation "A man who lies with his father's wife has uncovered his father's nakedness" (Lev 20.11; see also 18.7-8)—the father's wife, whether or not she is the mother of the individual who sleeps with her, is the father's property, and it is his rights that have been infringed upon.

Because Israel was a patriarchal society, property passed from father to sons. Women could inherit only in exceptional circumstances (see Num 27.1–11; Job 42.15).

The subordinate status of women is illustrated further in the regulations concerning purity. Thus, after the birth of a boy, a woman is impure for seven days, until the boy's circumcision; but after the birth of a girl, she is impure for fourteen days (Lev 12.2–5). Impurity resulting from menstruation is a special case. As we have seen on page 125, many of the regulations concerning purity of individuals have to do with reproductive functions, so the existence of regulations concerning menstruation is not surprising. It is difficult to determine the degree to which women's activities were restricted by menstruation and other forms of vaginal bleeding. On the one hand, early marriage, frequent pregnancies, and years of breastfeeding would reduce the number of periods a woman would experience in her lifetime. On the other hand, without the benefits of modern medicine and surgery, miscarriages and transitions into menopause could result in prolonged periods of bleeding, rendering some women impure for weeks or even years. It remains unclear why ritually pure women were excluded from performing ritual functions in public worship.

These laws, then, reflect the ethos of the society that produced them. It was a patriarchal society in which women were under the control of males and could be considered their property. Only partially countering this essentially patriarchal view is the repeated mention of both father and mother as those who are to be honored (Ex 20.12; see also Ex 21.15, 17; Lev 19.3; 20.9).

THE ETHICS OF LEVITICUS

Despite its many details about sacrifices and purity, and also despite its reinforcement of women's subordinate status, Leviticus, like other biblical collections of laws, does include a profound humanitarian ethic. Reference to the Exodus experience invites the Israelites to model the divine action in freeing them:

> When an alien resides with you in your land, you shall not oppress the alien. The alien who resides with you shall be to you as the citizen among you; you shall love the alien as yourself, for you were aliens in the land of Egypt: I am the LORD your God. (Lev 19.33–34)

In fact, according to Leviticus, the resident alien, the stranger, was a full member of the community for ritual participation. Within the community special attention was to be taken so that the poor and the needy could subsist:

> When you reap the harvest of your land, you shall not reap to the very edges of your field, or gather the gleanings of your harvest. You shall not strip your vineyard bare, or gather the fallen grapes of your vineyard; you shall leave them for the poor and the alien: I am the LORD your God. (Lev 19.9–10)

Finally, Leviticus also includes what Jewish tradition will identify as one of most important commandments in the Torah: "You shall not take vengeance or bear a grudge against any of your people, but you shall love your neighbor as yourself: I am the LORD" (Lev 19.18). For the authors of Leviticus, as for later thinkers, love of neighbor summarized a wide-ranging social justice: When he was in need, one's neighbor, a fellow Israelite, was not to be cheated, not to be charged interest, and not to be made a debt-slave. Jesus is reported to have characterized this law as one of the two primary commandments (Mk 12.31). Loving one's neighbor as oneself, in effect, was to imitate what has been called the divine preferential option for the poor as manifested in the Exodus itself.

A LOOK BACK AND AHEAD

The stay at Sinai is the centerpiece of the Pentateuch, and into that context have been inserted legal and liturgical traditions from a variety of sources. In this chapter, we have seen both some of the earliest, such as the Covenant Code, an Israelite collection of laws that may have a non-Israelite origin, and some of the latest, such as the elaborate description of the equipment and personnel used in the worship of Yahweh.

Leviticus immerses us in an elaborate system of ritual and ritual purity that encompasses all aspects of life. It stems from a culture very different from our own, with its own codes and values, some of which we no longer find necessary or acceptable, although parts of Leviticus, for better and for worse, continue to be cited in contemporary ethical discussions. It is unclear to what extent the regulations in Leviticus preserve actual Israelite practices, and to what extent they are a utopian program for the community that P wished to reestablish following the return from exile in Babylon in the sixth century BCE.

In the next chapter, we will examine the book of Numbers, in which the Israelites leave Sinai and resume their journey toward the Promised Land.

IMPORTANT NAMES AND TERMS

Each name or term is defined briefly in the Glossary. Its first significant occurrence in this chapter appears in **boldface** type.

apodictic law	Covenant Code	scapegoat
ark of the covenant	Day of Atonement	tabernacle
casuistic law	golden calf	tithe
cherubim	Holiness Code	
Code of Hammurapi	Ritual Decalogue	

QUESTIONS FOR REVIEW

1. What are some similarities and differences between ancient Near Eastern laws and Israelite laws? What is their significance?

2. What are the different types of laws found in the book of Exodus? What subjects do they deal with?

3. What were the functions of the ark of the covenant?

4. What is the connection between the principal religious festivals in ancient Israel and the agricultural cycle?

5. What are the religious and social dimensions of sacrifice?

6. Discuss some theories that help explain the concepts of purity and impurity.

7. What is the primary meaning of "holiness"? How does the concept of holiness apply to person, places, and time?

BIBLIOGRAPHY

For commentaries on Exodus, see Bibliography to Chapter 6.

A good collection of law codes from the Ancient Near East is Martha T. Roth, *Law Collections from Mesopotamia and Asia Minor* (Atlanta: Scholars Press, 2d ed., 1997). See also James B. Pritchard, ed., *Ancient Near Eastern Texts Relating to the Old Testament* (Princeton, NJ: Princeton University Press, 3d ed., 1969); and William W. Hallo, ed., *The Context of Scripture*, Volume 2, *Monumental Inscriptions from the Biblical World* (Leiden: Brill, 2003).

A brief introduction to ancient Israelite law is C. S. Ehrlich, "Israelite Law," *Oxford Companion to the Bible* (New York: Oxford University Press, 1993; available in Oxford Biblical Studies Online), 421–23.

On the ark of the covenant, see Bruce C. Birch, "Ark of the Covenant," pp. 263–69 in *The New Interpreter's Dictionary of the Bible*, vol. 1 (ed. K. D. Sakenfeld; Nashville: Abingdon, 2006).

For an introduction to Leviticus, see Jeffrey Stackert, "Leviticus," pp. 573–81 in *The Oxford Encyclopedia of the Books of the Bible*, ed. M. D. Coogan, vol. 1 (New York: Oxford University Press, 2011; available in Oxford

Biblical Studies Online). A good commentary is Baruch A. Levine, *Leviticus* (Philadelphia: Jewish Publication Society, 1989).

For a survey of the interpretation of the sacrificial system, see Frank H. Gorman, "Sacrifices and Offerings," pp. 20–32 in *The New Interpreter's Dictionary of the Bible*, ed. K. D. Sakenfeld, vol. 5 (Nashville, TN: Abingdon, 2009).

For discussion of the concepts of purity and impurity, see Hannah K. Harrington, "Clean and Unclean," pp. 681–89 in *The New Interpreter's Dictionary of the Bible*, ed. K. D. Sakenfeld, vol. 1 (Nashville, TN: Abingdon, 2006).

For discussion of the status of women, see Carol Meyers, "Women's Religious Life in Ancient Israel," pp. 354–61 in *Women's Bible Commentary*, ed. C. A. Newsom, S. H. Ringe, and J. E. Lapsley (Louisville, KY: Westminster John Knox, 3d ed., 2012); and also a more general collection of essays by Phyllis A. Bird, *Missing Persons and Mistaken Identities: Women and Gender in Ancient Israel* (Minneapolis: Fortress, 1997), which includes her important essay "The Place of Women in the Israelite Cultus," originally published in 1987.

In the Wilderness

Numbers

In the book of Numbers, we return to the primary narrative theme of the Pentateuch, the journey from Egypt to the Promised Land of Canaan. In the context of the final stage of the journey in Numbers, we also return to some familiar subthemes: a rebellious people, an angry but eventually forgiving deity, and Moses as the intermediary between them. Interspersed in the account of the journey, as elsewhere in the Pentateuch, are divinely given laws and ritual instructions.

appendixes gives final instructions by Moses and by Yahweh for the imminent entry into the land.

Within this framework, however, the book is a hodgepodge of disparate, sometimes contradictory material, only loosely held together by narrative and by chronology. In addition to the sources of the Documentary Hypothesis, it also has material from other sources, such as independent poems at least some of which are very ancient. Because Numbers contains such disparate material, we will discuss it thematically.

THE BOOK OF NUMBERS

Numbers is the most complicated book of the entire Pentateuch, in terms of both its content and its sources. It takes its name from the censuses at its beginning (chaps. 1; 3–4) and near its end (chap. 26); its Hebrew title is taken from one of its opening words, *bemidbar*, meaning "in the wilderness," an accurate designation of the book's narrative setting. After the census and other preparations, in Numbers 10.10 the Israelites leave Mount Sinai and head toward the Promised Land. The central portion of the book, chapters 11–25, describes incidents on their journey, and finally a series of

PREPARATIONS FOR THE JOURNEY

The Census

At the beginning and end of the book of Numbers appears a census list of the Israelites, the first (chap. 1) of the generation that had come out of Egypt and the second (chap. 26) of those who had been born since the Exodus. The numbers given for males twenty years old and over, that is, of an age suitable for military service, are 603,550 in the first census and 601,730 in the second. These are of the same order of magnitude as that given for the male participants in the Exodus in Exodus 12.37, 600,000, but like it (see page 92), the numbers are impossibly high. No convincing interpretation has been given for the precision of the numbers, their origins, or why P included them in its narrative. Perhaps the best we can say is that P has incorporated numbers from earlier traditions, which implicitly confirm the divine promise to the ancestors that they would be fruitful and multiply.

Twelve tribes are counted in each census. Because the tribe of Levi had no inheritance, the tribe of Joseph was subdivided into Ephraim and Manasseh to maintain the number twelve (see further page 76). Supplementing the census of the twelve tribes is a separate census of the Levites (Num 3–4; 26.57–62), who number 23,000. Included in the census of the Levites is a description of the ritual duties of each Levitical clan.

The Arrangement of the Camp

With the census complete, instructions are given for the organization of the camp (Num 2) (see Figure 9.1). This is a schematic idealization of P's view of ancient Israel with little relationship to actual geography. The tent of meeting is in the center, with the priestly houses and then the tribes arranged around it, according to their respective degrees of holiness (see pages 127–29). The Temple built by Solomon in the tenth century BCE

(see pages 227–29) had its entrance on the east, and so in P's arrangement, the east side is the most prestigious. On this side are the highest priests, the sons of Aaron. Adjacent to them is the tribe of Judah, the dominant tribe in Israel's later history as the kingdom of Judah, flanked by Zebulun and Issachar, Judah's younger brothers according to the traditional genealogy. The other priestly houses and tribes are assigned positions on the other three sides. This arrangement expresses the priestly ideal of a temple-centered community in which the Aaronide priests have the highest authority and the Davidic king, represented by the tribe of Judah, answers to [or "takes instructions from"] the priests.

With all of the arrangements made, the Israelites break camp and follow divine guidance in the cloud on their journey to the Promised Land.

LAW, RITUAL, AND PURITY

Interspersed throughout Numbers, as in Exodus, are numerous divinely given regulations. Many of them duplicate or supplement those already found in earlier books and for the most part have been discussed in the preceding chapters in this book. These variant traditions concern the Passover (Num 9.1–14) and the ritual calendar in general (28–29); various types of sacrifices (5.5–10; 15); the rights and responsibilities of the priests and

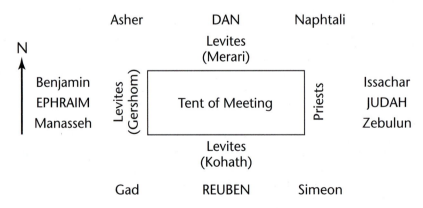

FIGURE 9.1   Plan of the camp of the Israelites as described in Numbers 2.

the Levites (18); ritual objects, such as the lamp-stand (8.1–4) and the silver trumpets (10.1–10); purity (5.1–4; 19.10–22); and an expanded description of the "glory of the LORD," the cloud that covered the tabernacle (9.15–23). Some new material also appears, most of which is P.

Law

The Wife Accused of Adultery

The longest case law in the Pentateuch concerns a woman suspected by her husband of being unfaithful (Num 5.11–31). Since "she was not caught in the act," the only recourse is to leave the decision up to the deity, and a complicated trial by ordeal takes place in the tabernacle.

We find parallels to the use of an ordeal in cases of suspected adultery in other ancient Near Eastern sources. The biblical case is unusually detailed, and the solution of the case has a magical dimension. If the woman is guilty, then she is supposed to become infertile (the precise meaning of the terms used in Num 5.21 is unclear). This divinely caused punishment is less severe than the death penalty, the punishment for adultery that has been witnessed rather than merely suspected (Lev 20.10; Deut 22.22). The ritual also includes the use of writing as a form of magical power. The priest writes out the curses that will be activated against the woman if she is guilty, and he then mixes the written curses into the "water of bitterness" that the woman will drink. In the ancient world, writing was often rare and therefore associated with magic, mystery, and divine power. Some scholars have argued that the entire procedure is a kind of sham in which nothing really happens to the woman, but the husband's suspicions are allayed.

Cities of Refuge

Numbers 35 assigns forty-eight cities to the Levites as their possession, since they have no tribal territory. Among these are six "**cities of refuge**," three on each side of the Jordan valley. The function of these cities is to provide asylum for someone who has taken another's life, until the matter of guilt can be resolved. If "the congregation" decides that the death was unintentional, then the killer is

allowed to live in the city of refuge and is protected from blood vengeance by the victim's "**avenger of blood**" (Hebr. *goel*, often translated "redeemer"), that is, his nearest male relative who has legal responsibilities toward the deceased. If the killer leaves the city, he may be killed by the avenger. This situation prevails until the death of the incumbent high priest; after that, the killer is free to return home and vengeance cannot be taken. If the killing was intentional, that is, was a murder, the murderer is to be executed, provided that at least two witnesses testify to his guilt.

This legal convention is P, and a variant tradition appears in Deuteronomy 19.1–11. Its implementation is described in Joshua 20, in which the six cities are named, but we find no examples in the Bible of any of the cities functioning in the way that the legal traditions describe.

Inheritance in the Absence of Male Descendants: The Case of the Daughters of Zelophehad

In ancient Israel as elsewhere in the ancient Near East, inheritance was patrilineal, that is, land, name, and property transferred from father to sons, with the oldest son getting twice as much as his brothers. But what if a man died without male offspring? That is the issue in the story of the daughters of Zelophehad in Numbers 27.1–11 and its sequel in 36.1–12. During Moses's division of the land (see pages 144–45), a problem is reported. The head of one of the clans of the tribe of Manasseh, Zelophehad, had no sons but five daughters. They protest that if they are not given an inheritance, then their family would die out: "Why should the name of our father be taken away from his clan because he had no son?" (27.4). The divinely given decision is that each daughter is to receive an inheritance equal to that of a male descendant of Manasseh. But the women must marry within their tribe, so that inalienable tribal property would not be transferred to another tribe by marriage.

Despite the prominence of the women in the narrative, what is at issue here is essentially an adjustment of the patrilineal system of inheritance in a special circumstance: The daughters' inheritance is only temporary, until they too produce sons.

Ritual

Vows

Two chapters of Numbers are devoted to the details of vows, solemn promises made to the deity. In Numbers 6, regulations are given for the nazirites. These were men or women who dedicated themselves to the deity, usually for a set period, during which they abstained from alcoholic beverages, left their hair uncut, and, like priests, avoided any contact with a corpse.

The topic of vows also comes up in Numbers 30, which states that vows made by a woman can be nullified by her father or, if she is married, by her husband, provided that he does so in a timely fashion. Since the property that would be offered in sacrifice to fulfill the vow belonged to the father or husband, he would have a material interest in the vow. Divorced or widowed women, who controlled their own property, had no such restriction.

The Priestly Blessing

Added as a kind of appendix to the regulations concerning the nazirites is the blessing to be given to the Israelites by the priests. Literally translated, it reads:

> May Yahweh bless you and may he protect you;
> May Yahweh make his face shine to you,
>   and may he be gracious to you;
> May Yahweh raise his face to you,
>   and may he give you peace. (Num 6.24–26)

This ancient prayer (see also Mal 1.9; Pss 4.6; 67.1) is still widely used in Jewish and Christian worship. (See also Figure 9.2.)

Priests

Much of the material concerning the priesthood in Numbers, as in Exodus and Leviticus, is P, which continues to emphasize the privileged status of the priests descended from Aaron and the subordinate status of the Levites. This privilege is evident in the unusual revelations made directly to Aaron: "The LORD spoke [or said] to Aaron" occurs three times in Numbers (18.1, 8, 20), and only twice elsewhere (Ex 4.27; Lev 10.8). To the earlier material, Numbers adds several significant bits of information. One of the most intriguing is the "covenant of salt" that guarantees the priests their share of the offerings

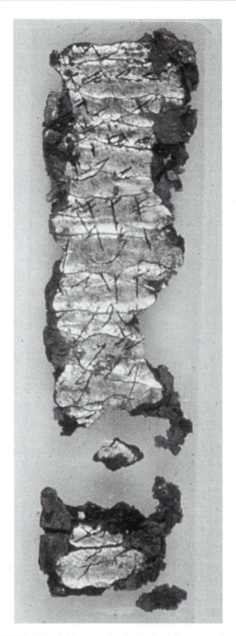

FIGURE 9.2   A silver amulet from a burial cave on the outskirts of Jerusalem, found along with hundreds of pieces of pottery, jewelry, and other artifacts. Unrolled, as shown here, it measures about 0.5 by 1.5 in (1 by 4 cm). It contains a form of the "Priestly Blessing," written in late seventh-century BCE script: "May Yahweh bless you; may he keep you; may Yahweh make his face shine upon you and may he give you peace" (see Num 6.24–26). This text is evidence that the blessing was current in ancient Israel; it was incorporated into the book of Numbers in a slightly different form.

(Num 18.19). The phrase seems to be the equivalent of "eternal covenant," probably because of the use of salt as a preservative. Another divine covenant with the priesthood is found in the conclusion to the story of Baal Peor (see page 142), in which Aaron's grandson Phinehas is rewarded for his actions with "a covenant of peace . . . a covenant of perpetual priesthood" (Num 25.12–13). For P, then, the status of priests was part of a divinely given blueprint for society, and within the priesthood, the descendants of Aaron were preeminent.

Purity

The Red Cow

The ashes to be used in the rituals of purification for those who have had contact with a corpse are produced by the elaborate process described in the first part of Numbers 19. It instructs that a red cow (the traditional translation "red heifer" is inaccurate) is to be slaughtered "outside the camp," and after some of its blood has been sprinkled toward the camp, its carcass is to be burned together with cedar, hyssop, and crimson material. The ashes are to be gathered for mixture with "water of purification."

This is an ancient ritual, rich in primal symbolism, which seems to have been secondarily incorporated into the sacrificial system, much like the "goat for Azazel" of the Day of Atonement (see page 126). Like the "goat for Azazel" and also the Passover lamb, the cow becomes a kind of substitute for the human: Its death is the means for preserving life. It is to be "red," probably representing blood, the same color as the crimson material and perhaps also the cedar with which it is burned. This obscure ritual is not mentioned elsewhere in the Bible.

THE CHRONOLOGY AND GEOGRAPHY OF THE WANDERINGS

From the return of Moses from Midian to Egypt early in the book of Exodus until the departure of the Israelites from Sinai, a little more than a year elapsed according to the narrative chronology of P,

the final editors of the Pentateuch. In the book of Numbers, the pace of the chronology increases. Because of the divine decree that none of the generation of the Exodus would be allowed to enter Canaan (see page 139), the Israelites had to wander in the wilderness for forty years (see Box 8.3 on page 117). During that time, Miriam and Aaron both died, as did most of the rest of the generation that had experienced the Exodus. Those forty years are the chronological framework of Numbers, and the wandering itself provides the geographical framework.

But the primary sources, J and P, differ on both chronology and geography. According to the summary of this period in Deuteronomy 2.14, the Israelites were at Kadesh (see following) only briefly, and they wandered in the wilderness some thirty-eight years before they reached the Wadi Zered, the southern boundary of Moab. This chronology, which also is adopted implicitly by J in Numbers, is at odds with that found in P, according to which most of the forty-year period was spent at Kadesh.

As we have seen, one of the organizing devices used by P to advance the narrative of the journey from Egypt to Canaan is the use of an itinerary, in which the places at which they stopped are given; near the end of the book of Numbers, P gives a summary of the entire itinerary (chap. 33). Identification of most of the places named is very difficult, however; to some extent they are locations that were familiar to P in the mid-first millennium BCE. Moreover, P's itinerary is not entirely consistent with that found in J or the book of Deuteronomy.

The location of **Kadesh** is a good example of the problems. Scholars generally agree that Kadesh, also called Kadesh-barnea, was thought by J to be the impressive site of Tell el-Qudeirat at an oasis in the northern Sinai Peninsula. Excavations at that site have shown that it was a major fortification from the tenth to the sixth centuries BCE, but that there was no settlement prior to that (see Figure 9.3). Obviously this creates problems for any association of Moses and the Exodus generation with the site, no matter when the Exodus is dated. We should also note that the name Kadesh (Hebr. *qadesh*) was a common one, meaning "holy (place)," and is used of several sites, both in the Bible in the variant form Kedesh (*Qedesh*) and elsewhere in the ancient Near East.

FIGURE 9.3   View of Tell el-Qudeirat in the northeast Sinai Peninsula, traditionally identified as Kadesh-barnea, where the Israelites camped on their journey from Egypt to Canaan. Four springs in the vicinity create an oasis in an otherwise arid environment, and the Arabic name of one of them, Ain Qadis, may preserve part of the site's original Hebrew name. On the right are the remains of a fortress built in the first half of the first millennium BCE.

REBELLIONS IN THE WILDERNESS

The narrative in the book of Numbers is punctuated by a series of rebellions against both Moses and Yahweh. Some of these are variants of narratives found before the Sinai sojourn, such as those about the water from the rock and the manna. In Numbers, however, the theme of rebellion is more prominent than in Exodus.

The rebellions begin immediately following the departure from Sinai:

> Now when the people complained in the hearing of the LORD about their misfortunes, the LORD heard it and his anger was kindled. Then the fire of the LORD burned against them, and consumed some outlying parts of the camp. But the people cried out to Moses; and Moses prayed to the LORD, and the fire abated. (Num 11.1–2)

This brief summary continues a pattern already established in the book of Exodus, one that will be repeated during the journey from Sinai to Canaan.

That rebellion is immediately followed by another, concerning the manna and quail: In a nostalgic longing for "the flesh pots" of Egypt (the evocative translation of the KJV in Ex 16.3),

> the riffraff among them had a strong craving; and the Israelites also wept again, and said, "If only we had meat to eat! We remember the fish we used to eat in Egypt for nothing, the cucumbers, the melons, the leeks, the onions, and the garlic; but now our strength is dried up, and there is nothing at all but this manna to look at." (Num 11.4–6)

The divine response was typically angry, and Moses had to intercede with Yahweh on the people's behalf, as he had in the episode of the golden calf and elsewhere, and will continue to do.

Rebellion by Miriam and Aaron (Num 12)

Numbers 12, a short chapter largely if not entirely belonging to E in the classic source analysis, contains an account of a revolt against the leadership of Moses, surprisingly by Miriam and Aaron. They are described as using as a pretext Moses's marriage to a non-Israelite (called here a Cushite woman; see Box 7.2 on page 99) and claiming that they too had been recipients of divine revelation.

In response, Yahweh declared that Moses had a special status. While other prophets receive authentic revelations in dreams and visions that can be difficult to interpret, the revelation given to Moses is direct—"face to face," or, more literally, "mouth to mouth" (Num 12.8). Thus, although Moses is a prophet, he is superior to all other prophets (see Deut 34.10).

The episode ends with Miriam being punished by affliction with a skin disease. After Moses prayed for her, she was healed, but had to be quarantined for seven days. As in the episode of the golden calf (Ex 32), Aaron was not punished, even though he too was guilty; also, as in Exodus 34, Moses is once again revealed as the preeminent divinely chosen leader. (See Box 9.1 on page 140.)

The Episode of the Spies (Num 13–14)

The account of Miriam and Aaron's attempted revolt is followed immediately by another story of rebellion, in which J and P are combined. Moses sent out twelve spies, one from each tribe, to see if the land of Canaan could be entered directly from the south. The spies penetrated as far north as Hebron and returned with grapes, pomegranates, and figs: It was a bountiful land! But the spies' report was mixed. A majority advised that the cities were too well fortified and their inhabitants too strong for the Israelites to defeat them. Only Caleb (in J; in P both Caleb and Joshua) argued that the land should be invaded because the Lord would give them victory. The people, however, followed the view of the spies whose report was unfavorable, and proposed to get a new leader who would bring them back to Egypt. Yahweh threatened to annihilate all the Israelites and to start anew with Moses. Moses again intervened, appealing to Yahweh's concern for his reputation and to his character as a merciful deity. Yahweh relented, but then decreed that none of the generation that had escaped Egypt would be allowed to enter the Promised Land; they would have to wander in the wilderness for forty years—the spies had spent forty days on their mission—until all had died. When the people heard this decree, they acknowledged their sin and decided to invade the land after all. Ominously, however, the ark of the covenant and Moses remained in the camp, and the Israelites suffered a major defeat. Beginning with this episode, each rebellion that follows results in more deaths, eventually eliminating the generation that had experienced the Exodus.

The episode has several literary functions. It explains, by an extended etiological narrative, why it took the Israelites so long to get from Egypt to Canaan. It also explains the dominance in southern Judah of the descendants of Caleb, who was of Kenizzite, not Israelite, stock (Num 32.12; Josh 14.6). P alters this genealogy and makes Caleb a member of the tribe of Judah (Num 13.6; 34.19). Finally, it prepares the way for Joshua to assume the leadership of the Israelites as Moses's divinely designated successor. Historically, the narrative may preserve a memory of an earlier occupation of Canaan from the south by one or more groups.

The entire episode is reminiscent of the story of the golden calf (Ex 32). Both share the themes of the rejection of Moses's leadership, a divine threat of extermination averted by Moses's intercession, and punishment by death of the guilty parties.

Rebellions by Priests (Num 16–17)

The narrative of rebellions in the wilderness continues in Numbers 16 with a revolt led by priests

Box 9.1 MIRIAM

Numbers 12 is the last episode in which **Miriam** plays a role; her death later is given only brief mention (Num 20.1). Nevertheless, she is a constant if minor presence throughout the Exodus narrative. Like Moses, Miriam is called a prophet (Ex 15.20), and on one occasion, in the story of her and Aaron's revolt against Moses, she is a direct recipient of divine revelation. Exodus 15.20–21 attributes to her the victory song celebrating the defeat of the pharaoh's army, a song taken up by Moses and the other Israelites (Ex 15.1). Traditionally Miriam has also been identified as the unnamed sister who arranged for the infant Moses to be nursed by his mother after the pharaoh's daughter found him in the reeds.

Miriam's relationship to Aaron and Moses is not consistently presented. In Exodus 15.20, she is called "sister of Aaron." According to Exodus 6.20, Moses and Aaron were brothers, which would make Miriam Moses's sister as well, a relationship made explicit in Numbers 26.59 and 1 Chronicles 6.3. In the conflict story of Numbers 12, no sibling relationship between Miriam, Aaron, and Moses is stated, and it is tempting to see behind this narrative three independent leaders, sometimes collaborators, sometimes rivals, who together were the human agents of the Israelites' escape from Egypt, as the prophet Micah recalls:

> For I brought you up from the land of Egypt,
>   and redeemed you from the house of slavery;
> and I sent before you Moses,
>   Aaron, and Miriam. (Mic 6.4)

against Moses and Aaron. The core narrative is P, which has somewhat clumsily incorporated an account of another revolt from J.

In J, the instigators are Dathan and Abiram, both of the tribe of Reuben. They refused to obey Moses and rejected his leadership:

> Is it too little that you have brought us up out of a land flowing with milk and honey to kill us in the wilderness, that you must also lord it over us? It is clear you have not brought us into a land flowing with milk and honey, or given us an inheritance of fields and vineyards. Would you put out the eyes of these men? We will not come! (Num 16.13–14)

Moses, they asserted, had failed—he made their lives worse by bringing them to this wilderness from Egypt, which they characterize as like the

Promised Land, flowing with milk and honey—but he still insisted on his position. The rebels were punished by being swallowed up by a chasm in the earth with their families and descending alive to the underworld, Sheol. Although on one level this is another story of rebellion with disastrous consequences, on another, it is an etiology for the decline of the tribe of Reuben, a repeated theme in the Pentateuch.

The revolt of Korah, combined by P with that of Dathan and Abiram, is another episode of priestly rivalry. A group of Levites led by Korah claimed that since the entire people of Yahweh was a holy people, the special status of Moses and Aaron was unjustified. Moses proposed a test: They should bring incense to the sanctuary, and if

Yahweh answered with fire, then they too would be considered chosen. But when the fire from Yahweh came, they and their supporters were burned to death. The next day, when the Israelites complained about this violent retribution, Yahweh sent a plague on the people, which was halted by burning incense only after some 14,700 had died. The entire Exodus generation is gradually being eliminated.

In the sequel in Numbers 17, the status of Aaron was reaffirmed on the very next day: Only his staff produced shoots, blossoms, and almonds (an example of a tree of life). The episode is followed in chapter 18 by an elaboration of the duties of various levels of the hierarchy and their compensation. The priests get a share of the sacrificial offerings, which are elaborated, while the Levites get the tithes. The tithes of the Levites, however, are also tithed, and this "tithe of the tithe" (Num 18.26) is to be given to the priests. (See further page XXX.)

The episode of Korah's revolt is related thematically to other narratives that show tension between priestly houses, including those of the golden calf (Ex 32), the strange fire (Lev 10), and the revolt of Aaron and Miriam (Num 12). For P, all of these narratives serve to legitimate the line of priests who claimed Aaron as their ancestral founder.

The Waters of Meribah (Num 20)

Numbers 20.2–13 is a second version of the miracle of water from the rock, bracketing the earlier account of the same event before Sinai (Ex 17.1–7). Like the earlier episode, it is on one level an etiology of a place name. In Exodus, that was Massa ("test"); here it is Meribah ("quarrel"; see v. 3: "The people quarreled with Moses"). Although water comes from the rock as it had in the earlier episode, Moses loses his temper, and both Moses and Aaron are condemned by Yahweh: "Because you did not trust in me, to show my holiness before the eyes of the Israelites, therefore you shall not bring this assembly into the land that I have given them" (Num 20.12). This punishment, hardly proportionate to the offense, is probably an attempt by P to rationalize why Moses, the divinely chosen leader, did not himself complete the journey from Egypt to Canaan; this is only one of several explanations given for that puzzling detail (see page 123).

Numbers 20 begins with the death of Miriam at Kadesh and ends with the death and burial of Aaron on Mount Hor, after his successor, his son Eliezer, had been robed with his father's priestly vestments. Aaron's death, explained by reference to the Meribah episode, continues the account of the elimination of the generation of the Exodus. The death of Moses will not be reported until the end of Deuteronomy, but it is anticipated in the Meribah narrative.

The Bronze Snake (Num 21.4–9)

Another episode of complaint, again about the "miserable bread" (the manna), leads to another divine punishment: "Then Yahweh sent fiery serpents [Hebr. *nehashim seraphim*] among the people, and they bit the people, so that many Israelites died" (Num 21.6). After the people's admission of guilt, Yahweh instructs Moses to make a "seraph" and to place it on a standard or pole, so "Moses made a bronze snake . . . and whenever a snake bit someone, that person would look at the bronze snake and live" (Num 21.9). The bronze snake was thus a kind of sympathetic magic that prevented death by snakebite.

The "fiery serpents" have a mythological background; these *seraphim* are winged serpents, like the winged cobras represented in Egyptian art. This narrative may be an etiology for the ritual use of a bronze snake in the Temple constructed by Solomon in Jerusalem, which legitimates it by connecting it with Moses. According to 2 Kings 18.4, this bronze snake (*nahash nehoshet*) was called Nehushtan, and incense was offered to it. We find no hint of condemnation of the ritual use of the snake in Numbers, nor any suggestion that this sacred object in any way violates the Second Commandment, which prohibits the making of graven images. But its questionable orthodoxy in some circles is indicated by its destruction by the Judean king Hezekiah during his religious reform in the late eighth century BCE (2 Kings 18.4).

Baal Peor (Num 25)

Following the episode of the prophet Balaam (Num 22–24; see page 143), the Israelites camped at Shittim, on the northern border of Moab, their last stop before the entry into the land. There they had sexual relations with Moabite women, and they ate the sacrifices and bowed down to their deity, Baal of Peor, a regional manifestation of the Canaanite deity Baal at Mount Peor (Num 23.28).

Both J and P have versions of this incident, and they differ in many details. In J (Num 25.1–5), the "people" were promiscuous with Moabite women, at whose invitation "Israel yoked itself to Baal-Peor," probably meaning that it engaged in a covenantal relationship with that deity. Yahweh became angry and commanded Moses to execute the participants.

In the P version (25.6–18), the apostasy is restricted to an Israelite man and a high-ranking Midianite woman, both of whom, while in the "tent" (a rare word probably signifying a religious shrine), were killed with a single spear thrust "through the belly" by Aaron's grandson Phinehas. This stopped the plague that was afflicting the Israelites, in which 24,000 had died. Because of his actions, Phinehas was rewarded with an eternal "covenant of peace" for his descendants in the line of chief priests. Thus, the episode provides yet another example of the divine choice of the line of Aaron as chief priests.

OPPOSITION ON THE JOURNEY

In addition to the battle with the Canaanites and Amalekites in the episode of the spies, we are told of other brief encounters with inhabitants of the territories through which the Israelites wish to pass on their journey to Canaan. These narratives follow a pattern: The ruler of the territory through which the Israelites wished to pass refused to allow them to do so; with divine assistance, they defeated him even though he was more powerful. Thus, in fairly rapid succession, the Canaanites living in Arad (21.1–3), the Amorites under the leadership of Sihon (21.21–32), Og the king of

Bashan (21.33–35), and the Midianites (31) were defeated; an encounter (but not a battle) also occurs with the Edomites (20.14–21).

These encounters seem to be another set of insertions into the time of Moses of events later in Israel's history, dating from its struggles for control of the Promised Land in the late second millennium to events in the first half of the first millennium BCE. At the same time, the groups with whom the Israelites have dealings fit the geography of the narrative; that is, they are largely in southern Transjordan, and no mention is made of other later enemies of the Israelites, such as the Philistines and the Arameans.

In constructing these narratives of opposition, the biblical writers made use of a variety of sources, some of which are fragments of ancient poems. The sources for two of these poems are given by the biblical writers as a kind of footnote. The defeat of the Moabites, the "people of Chemosh" (their national deity), is celebrated in a poem that is attributed to the "balladeers" (Num 21.27–30); neither the victors nor the balladeers were necessarily Israelites. The traditional boundary between Israel and Moab also is given in poetic form, from a source called "the book of the wars of Yahweh" (Num 21.14–15).

Numbers also describes the defeat of Sihon, the king of the Amorites (21.21–32), and Og, the king of Bashan in northern Transjordan (21.33–35). In biblical tradition, these two legendary kings become the prototypical enemies of the Israelites in their journey to Canaan. One of the legendary characteristics of Og was his great size: "Now only King Og of Bashan was left of the remnant of the Rephaim. In fact his bed, an iron bed, can still be seen in Rabbah of the Ammonites. By the common cubit it is nine cubits long and four cubits wide" (Deut 3.11). Like other pre-Israelite inhabitants of the land (see Num 13.32–33), Og was a giant; his iron bed, or perhaps his sarcophagus, was enormous—about 13 ft (4 m) long. He is also called one of the Rephaim, another group that dwelt in the land (Gen 15.20; Deut 2.20–21). In other sources, both biblical and nonbiblical, the term is used for the deified dead (on beliefs in life after death, see further pages 399–401).

Balaam the Seer (Num 22–24)

One of the strangest passages in the Pentateuch, and also one of the most difficult to analyze, is Numbers 22–24. The chapters feature humor, a talking animal, ironic reversals, and a non-Israelite prophet who was inspired by Yahweh.

A foreign seer, **Balaam**, the son of Beor, was hired by Balak, the king of Moab, to curse the Israelites, who were camped on the Moabite border. Warned at night by God that the Israelites were blessed, Balaam at first refused, but eventually, with divine approval, he went to Moab. At this point, God became angry and sent an angel to block the way. Balaam's donkey saw the divine messenger, but Balaam did not, and he beat the donkey to compel it to move forward. The donkey addressed Balaam, reproaching him, and finally Balaam saw the messenger and was allowed to proceed, with instructions to deliver a divinely received message.

Having finally arrived in Moab, Balaam ordered that a sacrifice be prepared, and after it had been offered, he was given his message by God, an oracle of blessing for Israel. But a blessing was not what Balak had ordered, and at his request, Balaam tried again to curse the Israelites, but repeatedly blessed them in several more divinely revealed oracles, which contain some memorable lines. Among these are:

> God [El], who brought them out of Egypt,
>   is like the horns of a wild ox for them.
> Surely there is no enchantment against Jacob,
>   no divination against Israel;
> now it shall be said of Jacob and Israel,
>   "See what God [El] has done!" (Num 23.22–23)

In the King James Version, the last phrase was translated "What hath God wrought!" and was used by Samuel Morse for the first message by telegraph in 1844.

These chapters have been the subject of much scholarly discussion, and no consensus exists on their origin or date. The main narrative describes the exchanges between Balak, the king of Moab, and Balaam, the seer who blessed Israel; imbedded in it is the satirical episode with the talking donkey who can see what the seer cannot. The poems themselves seem to be independent of each other—each has its own introduction—as well as often of their surrounding context. They were probably originally separate compositions, according to some scholars of an early date, which were put into the mouth of Balaam by the biblical writers.

Balaam the son of Beor is also known from an important if obscure nonbiblical source, a group of texts discovered in 1967. They are written in a language closely related to Hebrew on plastered walls at the site of Deir Alla in the eastern Jordan Valley and date to the late eighth century BCE. In these texts, Balaam is described as the "seer of the gods," who receives a revelation of doom (see Box 9.2 on page 144). Biblical writers seem to have appropriated the character of this Transjordanian seer and made him the proclaimer of a pro-Israelite and anti-Transjordanian message, in effect turning the words of a local visionary against his own people. (For further discussion of the phenomenon of prophecy in the ancient Near East, see pages 243–45.)

The Midianites (Num 31)

At the end of the episode of Baal Peor, Yahweh commanded Moses to "Harass the Midianites, and defeat them" (Num 25.17). That command is carried out in Numbers 31, which describes a major military encounter between the Israelites and the **Midianites**. As we have seen (in Box 7.2 on page 99), Midian was in the northeast part of Arabia, the likely location of Mount Sinai. Early relations between Midianites and Israelites seem to have been friendly. Moses was married to a Midianite, Zipporah, and in Numbers 10.29, he invited Midianites to join the Israelites in their journey to the Promised Land. By the end of the second millennium BCE, however, these camel-riding nomads were attacking the Israelites in raids, and in Judges 6–7, they are defeated by the judge Gideon. That defeat, later called "the day of Midian" (Isa 9.4), is a quintessential example of Yahweh's military victories on behalf of Israel. The defeat of Midian in Judges is anticipated in Numbers 31, which describes a total rout, the slaughter of all Midianite males, including Balaam, and the capture of their women and children and a great deal of spoil.

Box 9.2 EXCERPT FROM THE DEIR ALLA TEXTS

This excerpt from the Deir Alla texts shows both their fragmentary state and their evocative links with many biblical traditions:

> The account of Balaam son of Beor who was a seer of the gods. The gods came to him in the night, and he saw a vision like an oracle of El. Then they said to Balaam son of Beor: Thus he will do . . . hereafter, which. . . . And Balaam arose the next day . . . but he was not able to . . . and he wept grievously. And his people came up to him and said to him: Balaam, son of Beor, why are you crying? And he said to them: Sit down! I will tell you what the Shaddayin have done. Now, come, see the works of the gods! The gods gathered together; the Shaddayin took their places in the assembly. And they said . . . : Sew up, bolt up the heavens in your cloud, ordaining darkness instead of eternal light! And put the dark . . . seal on your bolt, and do not remove it forever! For the swift reproaches the griffin-vulture and the voice of vultures sings out. . . . The whelps of the fox . . . laughs at the wise. And the poor woman prepares myrrh while . . . for the prince a tattered loincloth. The respected one now respects others and the one who gave respect is now respected. The deaf hear from afar . . . and a fool sees visions.*

Among themes familiar from the Bible are the divine reversal of ordinary expectations, the idea of a divine assembly or council of the gods, the prophet as witness to the proceedings of that assembly (see page 248), and the title "Shadday," here applied to all of the gods.

---

* Adapted from J. A. Hackett, *The Balaam Text from Deir 'Alla̅* (Chico, CA: Scholars, 1980), p. 29.

PREPARATIONS FOR THE ENTRY INTO THE LAND

The last several chapters of the book of Numbers describe the final preparations for the entry of the Israelites into the Promised Land, the primary theme of the Pentateuch. At the same time, as in the rest of the book, the narrative does not entirely unify the chapters, which include material that is only tangentially relevant, especially more prescriptions concerning law and ritual.

The second census in Numbers 26 sets the stage. After it has been taken and the issue of the daughters of Zelophehad has been resolved (see page 135), Joshua is designated as Moses's successor, although his authority is subject to that of the priests (27.12–23); here P is clearly aware of the importance of Joshua in the book that bears his name (see page 163).

The status and obligations of the tribes of Reuben, Gad, and eastern Manasseh, traditionally viewed as having settled in Transjordan, are the subject of Numbers 32. According to this chapter, Reuben and Gad decided that Transjordan was suited to raising their numerous cattle and asked Moses to be allowed to settle there. Moses agreed, provided that they commit themselves to assisting the other tribes in their conquest of Canaan proper. The tribe of Machir, one of Manasseh's sons, was given land to their north, in the region known as Gilead. During the late second millennium BCE, then, Israel apparently included some groups east of the Jordan. When the independent kingdoms of the Moabites, Ammonites, Edomites, and Arameans, emerged there, as did that of Israel west of the Jordan, the territory of the Transjordanian Israelites came under non-Israelite control. In the genealogical narratives, this is explained by the loss of inheritance, especially in the case of Reuben. But the memory of Israelite control of Transjordanian territory survived, and the loss of some of that territory, notably Gilead, continued to rankle (see 1 Kings 22.3; Am 1.3). Like other narratives in the Pentateuch, then, the distribution of some land east of the Jordan to Reuben, Gad, and part of Manasseh reflects historical realities later than the narrative chronology but still relatively early in the development of Israel as a distinct political entity.

The account of the wanderings in the wilderness concludes in chapter 33 with a summary of the Israelites' itinerary from Egypt to the plains of Moab. Then in chapter 34, the boundaries of the Promised Land are given, followed by provision of forty-eight cities for the Levites, including the six cities of refuge (see page 135), because they had no inheritance of their own. Finally comes a further discussion of the problem of the daughters of Zelophehad.

A LOOK BACK AND AHEAD

At the end of Numbers, the Israelites have arrived at the border of the Promised Land—"in the plains of Moab by the Jordan at Jericho" (Num 36.13). According to the narrative structure of the Pentateuch presented by P, their religious, legal, and social structures were in place, provided by Yahweh, the same deity who despite their rebellions had guided them from Egypt through the wilderness to this point. For P, these structures are also a blueprint for the community that would return from exile in Babylon in the sixth century BCE.

At the same time, as the book of Numbers reiterates, the Israelites had been a rebellious community, and the divinely imposed punishment for one of its rebellions, the episode of the spies, was that all who had experienced the Exodus would have to die before the nation could enter the Promised Land. Hence they wandered in the wilderness for some forty years, until the entire Exodus generation died, including Aaron and Miriam. Only three individuals who experienced the Exodus were still alive: Caleb and Joshua, the good spies, and Moses himself. Joshua will replace Moses as the leader of the Israelites, for even Moses will die before entering the land, as a punishment for his role in the incident of the waters at Meribah. Before his death, however, he will give a lengthy farewell address, which is in essence the book of Deuteronomy and which we will consider in the next chapter.

IMPORTANT NAMES AND TERMS

Each name or term is defined briefly in the Glossary. Its first significant occurrence in this chapter appears in **boldface** type.

avenger of blood

Balaam

cities of refuge

Kadesh(-barnea)

Midianites

Miriam

QUESTIONS FOR REVIEW

1. Compare the narratives of Israel's wilderness sojourn in Numbers with the summary presentations in Psalms 78 and 106.

2. What messages are conveyed by the accounts of rebellions in Numbers?

BIBLIOGRAPHY

A good short commentary on the book of Numbers is Terence A. Fretheim, pp. 110–34 in *The Oxford Bible Commentary* (ed. J. Barton and J. Muddiman; Oxford: Oxford University Press, 2001; available in Oxford Biblical Studies Online). For a fuller commentary, see Baruch A. Levine, *Numbers 1–20* (New York: Doubleday, 1993) and *Numbers 21–36* (New York: Double day, 2000).

CHAPTER 10

The End of the Journey to the Promised Land

Deuteronomy

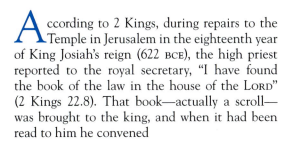

According to 2 Kings, during repairs to the Temple in Jerusalem in the eighteenth year of King Josiah's reign (622 BCE), the high priest reported to the royal secretary, "I have found the book of the law in the house of the LORD" (2 Kings 22.8). That book—actually a scroll—was brought to the king, and when it had been read to him he convened

> all the people of Judah, all the inhabitants of Jerusalem, the priests, the prophets, and all the people, both small and great; he read in their hearing all the words of the book of the covenant that had been found in the house of the LORD. The king stood by the pillar and made a covenant before the LORD, to follow the LORD, keeping his commandments, his decrees, and his statutes, with all his heart and all his soul, to perform the words of this covenant that were written in this book. All the people joined in the covenant. (2 Kings 23.2–3)

The king then inaugurated a major reform, destroying shrines to other gods throughout the country and all places of worship of Yahweh except in Jerusalem, and presiding over a national celebration of Passover there. Beginning in late antiquity, many have suggested that the "book of the law" that was found in the Temple was the biblical book of Deuteronomy, or at least a major portion of it.

THE BOOK OF DEUTERONOMY

Deuteronomy is the fifth and final book of the Torah/Pentateuch; its name, which is Greek in origin, means "second law" and succinctly summarizes its contents. (The book's Hebrew name, "*Debarim*," means "Words," from 1.1: "These are the words that Moses spoke . . .") Although it is set in the context of the last stage of the journey from Egypt to Canaan, Deuteronomy contains very little narrative. It is rather a lengthy speech given by Moses shortly before his death. In the course of the speech, which resembles a sermon, Moses summarizes the earlier history of Israel, including the promises to the ancestors, the escape from Egypt, the wanderings in the wilderness, the revelation at Horeb (the alternate name for Sinai used by Deuteronomy), and subsequent events. Most of the book, however, is devoted to another collection of laws. Not only do we find a third version of the Ten Commandments (Deut 5.6–21), but chapters 12–26 especially contain Israelite laws concerning criminal, civil, and religious matters, often paralleling or modifying laws found earlier in the Pentateuch.

According to the Documentary Hypothesis, most of Deuteronomy constitutes the Pentateuchal source called D, and D is probably not found outside of Deuteronomy. Precritical tradition identified Moses himself as the author of the book, but for several reasons, that is impossible. The framework narrative itself is set in the third person ("These are the words that Moses spoke to all Israel beyond the Jordan" [1.1]), and the narrator of those words is living on the west side of the Jordan River, in Israel, not east of the Jordan, where Moses died. Moreover, Moses's death and burial are described (chap. 34) and are unlikely to have been written by Moses himself, as some premodern commentators recognized. Finally, there is evidence that Deuteronomy dates from the eighth century BCE and later in Israel's history, as we will see.

Genre, Style, and Contents

The book of Deuteronomy on its surface is a distinct genre: It is a farewell address, in which a notable leader speaks to his constituents shortly before his death. Similar speeches are attributed in the Bible to Jacob (Gen 49), Joshua (Josh 23–24), Samuel (1 Sam 12), and David (2 Sam 23.1–7; 1 Kings 2.1–9). The authors of the book of Deuteronomy have taken this genre and have given its fullest exemplar, appropriately, to Moses, the most important human character in the Hebrew Bible.

Deuteronomy's style is best described as rhetorical. It is intended to persuade, and it does so by repeated use of the same phrases and concepts, which are italicized in the following summary: The *law* that Moses proclaims consists of *commandments*, *statutes*, *ordinances*, and *decrees*; in it the Israelites are urged to *love* God *with all their heart and all their soul*. He *chose* them from *all the nations*, rescued them from Egypt with his *mighty hand and outstretched arm*, because he *loved* them. Therefore, the Israelites are to *worship* him *alone*, and not *other gods*, so that he will *bless* them and their *days will be long* in the *land which he is giving them*, which they are *entering to possess*. For it is in this land that he will also *choose a place for his name to dwell*, and it is there that they are to *assemble* regularly for specified *festivals* at which this law will be *read*.

The law that is to be read, however, differs in an important way from that given at Mount Sinai,

found earlier in the Pentateuch in the books of Exodus, Leviticus, and Numbers. At Sinai, God spoke; in the book of Deuteronomy, it is Moses who speaks. Deuteronomy thus is an early stage in the continuing process of interpretation. By having Moses promulgate a "second law," the authors of Deuteronomy implicitly recognized that scripture needs interpretation, as well as adaptation to different historical contexts. That interpretative movement is evident in the complicated literary history of Deuteronomy itself.

Close analysis shows that Deuteronomy consists of not one, but several speeches of Moses, to which are added other materials:

Moses's first speech: 1.1–4.43 (narrator's introduction 1.1–5; narrative appendix concerning the cities of refuge in Transjordan 4.41–43)

Moses's second speech: 4.44–11.32 (narrator's introduction 4.44–5.1)

Moses's reproclamation of the divinely given law: chaps. 12–26

Moses's instruction concerning the covenant renewal at Shechem: chaps. 27–28

Moses's third speech: chaps. 29–30 (narrator's introduction: 29.1–2)

Supplementary material: narrative (chaps. 31; 32.45–52), poetry (the "Song of Moses," 32.1–44, and the "Blessing of Moses," chap. 33), and the account in chapter 34 of the death of Moses

In analyzing this composite structure, scholars have dated the sections to different periods. The earliest part, it is generally agreed, is the collection of laws in chapters 12–26, which may be as early as the eighth century BCE, although it shows signs of later editing. This collection has been incorporated into the framework of a speech by Moses, consisting of chapters 5–11 and 28 and dating to the eighth or seventh century. To this was added the material at the beginning and end of the book. The opening chapters (1.1–4.43) are a second introductory speech dating to the sixth century, reflecting the experience of the exile in Babylon after Jerusalem's destruction in 586 BCE.

The final stage in the composition of Deuteronomy was by the Priestly editors of the entire

Box 10.1 THE SHEMA

Deuteronomy 6.4–9 is one of the most important texts in Judaism:

> Hear, O Israel: The LORD is our God, the LORD alone. You shall love the LORD your God with all your heart, and with all your soul, and with all your might. Keep these words that I am commanding you today in your heart. Recite them to your children and talk about them when you are at home and when you are away, when you lie down and when you rise. Bind them as a sign on your hand, fix them as an emblem on your forehead, and write them on the doorposts of your house and on your gates.

Known as the "**Shema**," after the opening Hebrew word, which means "hear," this passage, in combination with Deuteronomy 11.13–21 and Numbers 15.37–41, became a frequently used Jewish prayer. It expresses the Deuteronomic and subsequent Jewish commitment to the teaching of Moses, a commitment expressed by repeated daily recitation of the words themselves, by instruction of subsequent generations, and by visual reminders in the form of phylacteries and mezuzahs, in which the words themselves, written on tiny scrolls, are attached to the arms and head during prayer and to the door of the home, respectively.

These practices, like the elevation of the Shema itself to the status of something like a creed in Judaism, are attested in the Second Temple period; note that Jesus is reported to have called Deuteronomy 6.5 "the greatest and first commandment" (Mt 22.37–38).

Torah, also during the sixth century BCE. Just as the book of Genesis begins with the Priestly account of creation (Gen 1.1–2.4a), so the final book of the Torah ends with Priestly additions to the book of Deuteronomy, describing the death of Moses (chap. 34).

The literary history of the book of Deuteronomy is thus further evidence of the process of interpretation: At several different stages in the nation's history the teaching ("torah"; see Box 10.2 on page 154) of Moses was reinterpreted for a new generation living in a different context.

The Deuteronomic Code

The core of Deuteronomy is the laws found in chapters 12–26. Like the collections of laws found earlier in the Pentateuch (notably the Covenant Code, Ex 20.22–23.33), the **Deuteronomic Code** deals with a variety of topics, including religious ceremonies and ritual purity, civil and criminal law, and the conduct of war. Like those collections, too, it is not comprehensive. Some of what any society would need for its legal system is absent, and the laws found in it do not deal with all possible circumstances, but are representative examples.

Date and Origin

The date of these laws is uncertain, as are their origins. Most likely they stem from earlier collections of laws, like the Covenant Code (Ex 20.22–23.33) and the Ritual Decalogue (Ex 34.10–26). In fact, some of the laws found in Deuteronomy are exact duplicates or nearly so of laws found in Exodus, such as "You shall not boil a kid in its mother's milk" (Ex 23.19; 34.26; Deut 14.21). Others, however, show considerable variation. It is thus not clear whether the laws in Deuteronomy are modifications of these biblical laws or whether they derive from other collections. In any case, the Deuteronomists have selected, modified, and added to their sources in line with their own perspectives. Special attention is given to one central sanctuary as the only permissible place where ordinary sacrifices are to be offered and pilgrimage festivals are to be celebrated. Likewise, a great many of the laws deal with the elimination of worship of other gods and the execution of those who support such worship. Finally, the laws in the Deuteronomic Code are frequently supplemented by references to the narrative setting: Moses's farewell address at the end of Israel's journey to the Promised Land.

Social Organization and Values

The Deuteronomic Code appears to represent a utopian society more than an actual one. If, as suggested above, Deuteronomy dates to the eighth century BCE and later, the Deuteronomic Code reflects on an idealized premonarchic period in order to offer something of a populist program for both monarchic and later exilic Israel.

At the same time, the Deuteronomists had to take historical realities into account. Although the society they wished to establish was a monarchy, like the society in which they lived, in their program the king's power was limited (see page 151). Thus, justice was to be administered on the local level, rather than by the king (16.18). Likewise, in the discussion of warfare, the king is not mentioned, although priests, civil officials, and military commanders are. Moreover, the true leader in warfare was Yahweh himself, and warfare was thus a kind of holy war.

One feature of this holy war is the "ban," which called for the total extermination both of Canaanites in the land (Deut 20.16–18) and of Israelite towns where idolaters were found (13.12–16). By the Deuteronomists' times, of course, there were no longer any Canaanites as such in the land who posed any sort of a threat either militarily or religiously. Thus, with reference to the Canaanites at least, the "ban" illustrates the Deuteronomists' insistence on exclusive and undefiled worship of Yahweh but does not necessarily indicate actual practice.

Humanitarian Concerns

The Deuteronomic Code in general has a more humanitarian cast than the Covenant Code. That earlier collection offered divine action on behalf of the Israelites in Egypt as a model that should inform their relationships with others in similar circumstances, especially "strangers" (NRSV "resident aliens"; see Ex 22.21; 23.9). In Deuteronomy, this appeal to Israel's own experience is emphasized by repetition and by extension.

Examples of this humanitarian emphasis are found in modifications made to laws in other collections. For example, the law concerning the release of a slave in the Covenant Code stipulates that a male slave who has served six years should be released free of debt (Ex 21.2). The Deuteronomic Code applies this law to male and female slaves and adds that the released slave should leave with abundant gifts that represent a share of the household's wealth. The Deuteronomic version of the law also situates the ethical impetus for the release of the slave in Israel's own experience of slavery: "Remember that you were a slave in the land of Egypt" (Deut 15.12–17). Likewise, in Deuteronomy's version of the Ten Commandments, the observance of the sabbath is motivated not by imitation of the divine rest after creation, as in Exodus 20.11, but by concern for slaves (Deut 5.12–15).

In some cases, however, Deuteronomy is more restrictive. Thus, the law concerning lost or fallen animals in Exodus 23.4–5 specifies animals belonging to the enemy, whereas the equivalent in Deuteronomy mentions only the "brother" (22.1–4; NRSV "neighbor").

Priests and Levites

One of the significant differences between the Deuteronomic Code and the Priestly traditions involves a different valuing and labeling of priests. Deuteronomy emphasizes **"Levites"** (also called the "levitical priests" and "the priests, the Levites") and associates this group with Moses. The Priestly traditions in Exodus, Leviticus, and Numbers focus on a group called "priests," which is then further specified as "the sons of Aaron." The evidence for these two classes of priests is difficult to disentangle, in part because of the different stages in the formation of Deuteronomy and the priestly material.

The general principle is that the entire tribe of Levi is a priestly tribe, and according to Exod 6.16-20, Moses and Aaron are brothers who descend from Levi. The legislation concerning priests in Exodus through Numbers is concerned almost exclusively with priests who are "the sons of Aaron." They are ordained, clothed in sacred vestments, and charged with carrying out rituals associated with sacrifice. When Deuteronomy refers to priests, on the other hand, they are specified as "levitical priests," and they are charged with the responsibility for the ark of the covenant (Deut 10.8–9) and administering judgments (Deut 17.8-12). The exalted status of the Levites in Deuteronomy may indicate their participation in the early Deuteronomic school (see pages 154–55).

The Levites, however, are also those who have no land inheritance, so Deuteronomy often portrays them as a needy and protected class, often grouped with slaves, strangers, orphans, and widows. This reduced status can be explained in part because of the Deuteronomic reform, in which all worship of Yahweh was to take place at one central sanctuary. During the time of the monarchy, this central sanctuary was the Jerusalem Temple where the priests who traced their lineage back to Aaron maintained hierarchical supremacy. Many Levites who had earned their livelihood by officiating at local shrines were left unemployed. The Deuteronomists' attempt to provide the Levites with an elevated status as designated teachers and interpreters of the law may be compensating for their reduced status in other realms.

The Law of the King
The Deuteronomic Code contains several noteworthy additions to earlier biblical collections. One, in Deuteronomy 17.14–20, concerns the institution of kingship. The king is to be divinely chosen, an Israelite and not a foreigner. He is forbidden from acquiring large amounts of three different sorts of possessions: horses, presumably for military purposes, especially by trade with the Egyptians; many wives, lest his heart be turned away from the exclusive worship of Yahweh; and silver and gold.

This "law of the king" seems to have been written with specific kings in mind, especially as they are described in the books of Kings. The extravagant acquisition of horses and gold and an enormous harem especially coincides with the description of Solomon's reign (see 1 Kings 3.1; 4.26; 9.28; 10.14–11.8), but trade and alliances with Egypt are mentioned of other kings, and a harem was an ordinary part of the royal establishment.

For the authors of Deuteronomy, first writing during the period of the monarchy, although kingship was a divinely sanctioned institution, it was to be severely limited. God's blessing for the people depended not on the king but on the entire nation's observance of its covenant with God. The Deuteronomists, in other words, advocated a reform in which the ideals of the premonarchic period would be combined with the realities of the monarchy. Like many of the prophets, they were reactionaries, but their nostalgia for the past was translated into a detailed program for the present and future.

Prophets
Another innovation in the Deuteronomic version of earlier laws is legislation concerning prophecy. In two unconnected passages, Deuteronomy discusses the issue of false prophets. This reflects the Deuteronomists' own close connections with the prophetic movement (see pages 152–53), and also addresses what must have been a chronic problem in ancient Israel: How could one distinguish between true and false prophets?

In the context of the promise of continued revelation to prophets like Moses, Deuteronomy asks the apt question: "How may we recognize a word that the LORD has not spoken?" (18.21), and answers it: "If a prophet speaks in the name of the LORD but the thing does not take place or prove true, it is a word that the LORD has not spoken" (18.22).

That seems clear enough, but earlier in the book a more complicated, and more realistic, criterion is provided:

> If prophets or those who divine by dreams appear among you and promise you omens or portents, and the omens or the portents declared by them take place, and they say, "Let us follow other gods" (whom

you have not known) "and let us serve them," you must not heed the words of those prophets or those who divine by dreams, for the LORD your God is testing you, to know whether you indeed love the LORD your God with all your heart and soul. (13.1–3)

Even a false prophet, the passage suggests, may be sent by Yahweh for his own purposes. Deuteronomy thus does not entirely resolve the issue of false prophecy.

Women in the Deuteronomic Code

The treatment of women in Deuteronomy is sometimes less restrictive than in other biblical legislation. As noted above, Deuteronomy's version of the law for releasing a slave treats male and female slaves equally (Deut 15.17). In the case of adultery, both Leviticus and Deuteronomy stipulate the death penalty for the man and the woman. Deuteronomy, however, draws a line of distinction based on the location of the adulterous act: If it takes place outside the city "in the open country," the woman is presumed to be innocent, since her cries for help would not have been heard (Deut 22.25–27).

At the same time, it must be recognized that these modifications do not substantially mitigate the essentially patriarchal ethos of ancient Israel, which also characterizes Deuteronomy. The Deuteronomic version of the Tenth Commandment (Deut 5.21) still designates the wife as property, along with real estate, slaves, and livestock. Moreover, several of the laws concerning family and warfare are directed only to men and men's concerns (see Deut 13.6–11; 20.10–14; 21.10–17; 22.13–21). While many of the laws can be read to apply to both men and women, none of the laws are addressed only to women.

THE ORIGINS OF DEUTERONOMY

Although an early form of the book of Deuteronomy may have served as the inspiration for King Josiah's reform, which mandated centralized worship at the Temple in Jerusalem, Jerusalem itself is not mentioned in Deuteronomy. The only place explicitly identified as a place of Israel's worship in the book is Shechem, an important tribal center during the premonarchic period and one of the principal cities of the northern kingdom of Israel after the death of Solomon in the late tenth century BCE (see Box 11.1 on pages 171–72). It is there that the tribes are directed to gather for the covenant renewal (Deut 11.29; 27.4, 13). Moreover, the laws concerning kingship in particular, and the book as a whole, make no explicit reference to the Davidic dynasty that ruled in Jerusalem.

Our reconstruction is that Deuteronomy was the work of a Deuteronomic school that originated in the northern kingdom of Israel prior to its fall to the Assyrians in 722 BCE. This school (see pages 154–55) insisted that Israel had to return to its original ideals, as expressed in the covenant mediated by Moses—united in worship of Yahweh alone at a single national shrine, and faithful to the laws promulgated by Moses.

When the northern kingdom fell to Assyria, some northerners escaped deportation and fled south to Judah. We see evidence for this migration in the increase in Jerusalem's population and settled area in the late eighth to seventh centuries BCE. The Deuteronomists would have been one segment of this transplanted northern population, and they would have brought with them their traditions in written form. In Jerusalem they established links with scribal and priestly groups, and probably had some influence on the reform and independence movement of King Hezekiah (715–687 BCE; see pages 271–72). It is quite possible, therefore, that the Deuteronomists' version of Israel's early legal traditions, the core of the book of Deuteronomy, ended up in the Temple library, where it was reportedly discovered during Josiah's reform nearly a century later.

This hypothesis of northern origins is supported by further evidence. Like the Pentateuchal source E, also likely of northern origin, Deuteronomy calls the mountain of revelation Horeb, rather than Sinai, its name in J and P. Also like E, Deuteronomy has an interest in prophecy (see page 151). Especially close connections exist between Deuteronomy and the book of Hosea, a prophet of the northern kingdom. Both speak of the divine love for Israel and insist on the exclusive worship of Yahweh; both also stress the importance of covenant and the need for religious and social reform.

The repeated references to the Levites and their relatively high status as "teachers" in the book of Deuteronomy suggest that they may have participated in the early stages of the Deuteronomic school. Since the priests who identified as "sons of Aaron" held the highest positions in the Temple in Jerusalem, Deuteronomy's portrait of highly respected Levite priests provides further evidence of a northern origin for the early core of this book.

Deuteronomy and Assyrian Rule

The book of Deuteronomy appears to originate from a time when Assyrian influence and domination of the Near East was at its height. One of the legal analogues for the concept of the covenant between Yahweh and Israel is the international suzerainty treaty. Such treaties were used widely in the Near East from the Late Bronze Age onward, and the language used in them pervades biblical tradition. In addition to the Hittite treaties from the late second millennium, another important group of treaties dates from the time of Assyrian domination of the Near East in the first half of the first millennium. The best-preserved and most extensive treaties are by the Assyrian king Esar-haddon (681–669 BCE), which were first discovered in 1956.

Under Esar-haddon, Assyria was at the zenith of its imperial reach, extending its control even to Egypt. Within the Assyrian empire, smaller entities that were loyal subjects (unlike the northern kingdom of Israel, which had rebelled) were allowed to maintain a quasi-independence, as long as they stayed loyal and paid the requisite tribute. In 672 BCE, arranging for the succession of his son Ashurbanipal after his death, Esar-haddon required his vassals to swear allegiance to the designated heir. Like the earlier Hittite treaties, these vassal treaties, of which several copies have been found, include the identification of the suzerain, a list of divine witnesses, a list of stipulations, and a lengthy

catalogue of curses that will fall on those who break the terms of the treaty. Unlike the Hittite treaties, the vassal treaties of Esar-haddon do not include blessings alongside the curses; Deuteronomy includes both blessings and curses, but the curses are four times longer than the blessings, paralleling the prominence of the curses in the Assyrian texts. The curses in the treaties of Esar-haddon are strikingly similar to those found in Deuteronomy 28.

These parallels and others, especially of vocabulary, suggest that the authors of Deuteronomy deliberately made use of the Assyrian treaty genre. They would certainly have been familiar with it because of the repeated submissions of kings of both Israel and Judah to Assyrian kings from the mid-ninth century BCE well into the seventh. The Deuteronomists' use of this genre can be viewed as subversive: They were asserting that Israel's authentic status was as vassal not of the king of Assyria but of Yahweh, a relationship solemnized by covenant (for which the Hebrew word is berît, which can also mean treaty). To Yahweh was owed exclusive allegiance, and failure to provide it would result in divinely imposed punishments just as severe as those found in the Assyrian vassal treaties.

Several historical contexts from the eighth century BCE on would have been likely times for this message to be proclaimed and reproclaimed. In the mid-eighth century the prophet Hosea, whose message was similar to that of Deuteronomy, proclaimed a lawsuit against Israel for its breach of covenant, in part because their foreign alliances implied a rejection of Yahweh's protection; see, for example, Hosea 11.12–12.1. Most significant are the two assertions of independence from Assyria by kings of Judah: Hezekiah in the late eighth century BCE and Josiah in the late seventh. In both cases severing ties to Assyrian imperial control was accompanied by religious reform, which reestablished the exclusive worship of Yahweh by means of a covenant renewal. It is precisely in these three contexts that we have proposed that principal preexilic stages of the formation of Deuteronomy occurred: the beginnings of the Deuteronomic school in northern Israel in the mid-eighth century, probably in association with the prophetic movement; its first full formulation

Box 10.2 THE MEANINGS OF "TORAH"

One of the characteristic terms used by the latest editors of the book of Deuteronomy to refer to its content of the book of Deuteronomy is as the "**torah**" given by Moses. Apart from three uses in chapter 17 (verses 11, 18, 19), the word "torah" is found mainly in chapters 1, 4, and 31–33, all sections that are generally thought to have come from the latest stage of composition in the exilic period.

The word "torah" itself occurs more than two hundred times in the Hebrew Bible, and it has a variety of meanings. In its ordinary sense "torah" means teaching or instruction. It is especially used of divine teaching or instruction throughout the Pentateuch and Deuteronomic literature, and occasionally in the prophets. It can have a more specific nuance of precise instructions, or rubrics, as in the legislation concerning sacrifices (for example, Lev 6.9). By the end of the monarchic period, however, it came to signify something more: a divinely revealed body of teaching mediated through Moses—hence, the "torah" of Moses, the teaching or law of Moses.

By the postexilic period, that "torah" was in "book" (that is, scroll) form (Ezra 6.18; Neh 8.19) and was essentially the same as the first five books of the Bible, the Pentateuch, known in Jewish tradition as the Torah. This is what is called "the Law" in the earliest descriptions of the Jewish scriptures. By extension the term "Torah" is then used to refer to the entire body of revelation, including not just the whole Bible but also the "oral teaching" that in Jewish tradition was also revealed to Moses on Sinai, the authoritative interpretation of the written law eventually set down by rabbinical sages.

and adaptation in the southern kingdom of Judah during Hezekiah's reform; and its reformulation during Josiah's reform.

THE DEUTERONOMIC SCHOOL

The original authors of Deuteronomy were also the founders of an intellectual movement that had an extraordinary and lengthy influence in the history of ancient Israel and in the development of its literature. This "school" is similar to that which produced the book of Isaiah over several centuries (see page 274) and is analogous to Greek philosophical schools such as Platonism.

The **Deuteronomic school**, as we have seen, had early northern connections with both the Levitical priesthood and the prophets. It continued to revise its core text, the book of Deuteronomy, as Israel's circumstances changed from autonomous kingdom in the north, to a vassal kingdom in the south, and ultimately to a conquered people living in exile in Babylonia. It also produced the Deuteronomistic History, the interpretive narrative of Israel's history in the Promised Land based on the ideals of the book of Deuteronomy, an extended work comprising the books of Joshua, Judges, Samuel, and Kings. This Deuteronomistic History was itself revised several times, much like the book of Deuteronomy (see further pages 161–63).

The Deuteronomic school is also responsible for editing the oracles and autobiographical and biographical reports of several prophets, including Isaiah of Jerusalem ("First Isaiah"), Hosea, Amos, Micah, and Zephaniah. The prophetic book with the closest connection to the Deuteronomists is that of Jeremiah, who himself may have belonged to the Deuteronomic school or been heavily influenced by it. Jeremiah's prophetic career began toward the end of the seventh century, during the reign of Josiah, whose reforms were both inspired by and modeled on the core of the book of Deuteronomy. (See further pages 302–3.)

This Deuteronomic school maintained its central message of fidelity to the teaching ("torah") of Moses, and adapted it to changing circumstances, from the period of Assyrian domination in the late eighth and early seventh centuries BCE to that of the exile. The exilic Deuteronomists interpreted the catastrophe of Jerusalem's destruction in 586 BCE and Israel's loss of autonomy as a deserved punishment for the nation's failure to observe the requirements of the teaching of Moses, the fulfillment of the curses for covenant violation.

MOSES IN THE PENTATEUCH

Moses dominates the narrative of the final four books of the Pentateuch. Moreover, Moses and the events associated with him—the Exodus from Egypt, the making of the covenant, the revelation of the divine name, the wandering through the wilderness—were so central to ancient Israel's self-definition that they were continually appealed to in the historical and prophetic books as preeminent authority and paradigm. It is thus not surprising that until the modern period Moses himself was considered the author of the entire Pentateuch.

Modern scholars, however, have analyzed the Pentateuch as composed of different sources from different periods, which in the books of Exodus through Deuteronomy not surprisingly contain inconsistencies and contradictions concerning Moses. One has to do with the relationship between Moses and Aaron. In general, the earlier the source, the more important is Moses in relation to Aaron. Conversely, in the latest source, P, the role of Aaron, the ancestor of the Jerusalem priesthood, is more

significant and Moses's role is diminished. Although Moses occasionally functions as a priest, in the final form of the Pentateuch Aaron is the priest par excellence. Still, even in P, Moses is primary. It is he who receives instructions from Yahweh concerning the priesthood and its rituals and who ordains Aaron as the first high priest.

Another inconsistency concerns Moses's communication with God. A widespread biblical tradition is that no one can see the "face of God" and live; this axiom is generally appealed to on occasions when it is broken (for example, Gen 32.30). In the case of Moses, it is not surprising that given his unique position, according to some biblical writers he had a special form of communication with God:

> When there are prophets among you,
>   I the Lord make myself known to them in visions;
>   I speak to them in dreams.
> Not so with my servant Moses;
>   he is entrusted with all my house.
> With him I speak face to face—clearly, not in
>   riddles;and he beholds the form of the LORD.
>   (Num 12.6–8)

Yet when it comes to describing Moses's actual encounter with God we find some reticence. In Exodus 33, Moses asks Yahweh, "Show me your glory" (v. 18). Yahweh replies, "I will make all my goodness pass before you, and will proclaim before you the name 'Yahweh' . . . but you cannot see my face; for no one can see me and live." Then follows a vivid yet restrained anthropomorphism:

> "See, there is a place by me where you shall stand on the rock; and while my glory passes by I will put you in a cleft of the rock, and I will cover you with my hand until I have passed by; then I will take away my hand, and you shall see my back; but my face shall not be seen." (33.21–23)

Moses will be prevented from seeing Yahweh's face by the divine hand, but he will be allowed to see Yahweh's back. The account of the theophany that follows in Exodus 34.5–9 omits this poignant detail. Still, as the conclusion to the theophany shows, Moses's experience was unique: "The skin of his face shone because he had been talking with God," so that he had to cover his face with a veil (34.29–35). Earlier translators misunderstood

FIGURE 10.1   Michelangelo's Moses. As often in art, Moses is depicted with horns, a misinterpretation of Exodus 34.29.

the Hebrew of this passage to mean that Moses had "horns," and he is often represented with them in art (see Figure 10.1).

In biblical narrative, Moses emerges as a complex character. Although a stutterer (Ex 4.10), he was also a prophet (Deut 34.10) and even more than a prophet (Num 12.6–8). He stands alone as

mediator between the people and Yahweh, yet one with considerable ambivalence about his role, a characteristic that is introduced at the time of his call (Ex 3–4) and repeatedly shown thereafter.

The cumulative portrait we get of Moses in biblical tradition is of a reluctant but gifted leader. While we have no independent corroboration of

FIGURE 10.2   What Moses saw from Mount Nebo (Deut 34:1–3).

Moses's existence, his dominating presence in multiple strands of biblical tradition points to the likelihood that he existed. Moreover, the presentation of Moses is not that of a model character. He has an Egyptian name and is married to a non-Israelite woman; he may even not have been circumcised at birth (see page 85). His leadership was often challenged, and his anger is often noted, as is Yahweh's anger with him. Biblical writers were capable of presenting an ideal type of leader: as we will see, in the book of the Bible that follows Deuteronomy, Joshua is such a character, as is David in the book of Chronicles. But Moses has complexity and depth, weaknesses as well as strengths.

Underlying the traditions about Moses, then, is probably a historical person. More than any other single individual, this Moses was the human founder of the religion of ancient Israel, whose basis is the idea that Israel was the people of Yahweh. Their relationship is expressed in terms of covenant, with Yahweh metaphorically understood as suzerain, husband, and parent. Israel's covenant obligations are codified in the Decalogue, in which the divine action in delivering Israel out of Egypt becomes the motive for the exclusive worship of Yahweh and the model for treatment of one's "neighbor."

Moses's Failure to Reach the Promised Land

According to Deuteronomy 34, Moses died before the Israelites entered the Promised Land. For the biblical writers this posed something of a problem: Why would God not allow his faithful servant to complete his mission? That the people who had escaped from Egypt were denied entry into the land seems deserved because of their repeated rebellions and disobedience, but we do find exceptions—Caleb and Joshua (Num 32.12)—so why not Moses also?

Several explanations are given to explain this paradox. One is that Moses himself must have done something wrong. Yahweh was a just judge, and if Moses had died, that must have been a punishment, as it was for the other Israelites. But a

punishment for what? According to P, it had something to do with the incident at Meribah. In Numbers 20.1–13, Moses and Aaron are both condemned for having failed to trust in God and to show his holiness to the Israelites. According to the P version of this episode (summarized in Deut 32.51, also P), the Israelites complain of thirst, so Yahweh instructs Moses and Aaron to take the staff and to command the rock to yield its water. Moses was angry that the Israelites once again expressed regret at having left Egypt, so he calls them "rebels" and then strikes the rock twice with his staff. The water flows, yet somewhat inexplicably Yahweh decrees that Moses and Aaron will not be allowed to bring the people into the Promised Land because they had not fully trusted in his power. Rabbinic interpreters explain this abrupt punishment by suggesting that Moses had sinned both by failing to verbally "command" the rock and in his independent choice to use the staff to strike the rock and bring forth water. Both of these interpretations seem desperate to preserve the divine reputation for justice.

Deuteronomy offers a different explanation, one followed by Psalm 106.32–33. According to it, Moses is being punished vicariously for the people's sin in the spies episode (see Num 13–14), when the people were reluctant to attack the land: "Even with me the LORD was angry on your account, saying, 'You also shall not enter there'" (Deut 1.37). As a result, despite his repeated requests, Yahweh refuses to allow Moses to enter the land.

The Death and Burial of Moses

Deuteronomy 34, the concluding chapter to the Pentateuch, describes the death and burial of Moses. As Yahweh had decreed, Moses would not enter the Promised Land, but he would be able to see it. So he climbs Mount Nebo, just a few miles east of the outlet of the Jordan River into the Dead Sea, and from there

> The LORD showed him the whole land: Gilead as far as Dan, all Naphtali, the land of Ephraim and Manasseh,

all the land of Judah as far as the Western Sea, the Negeb, and the Plain—that is, the valley of Jericho, the city of palm trees—as far as Zoar. The LORD said to him, "This is the land of which I swore to Abraham, to Isaac, and to Jacob, saying, 'I will give it to your descendants'; I have let you see it with your eyes, but you shall not cross over there." (Deut 34.1–4)

And then Moses dies, "at the LORD's command"; the Hebrew literally means "at the mouth of Yahweh," recalling the special intimate knowledge that Moses had of the deity: He knew him "mouth to mouth" (Num 12.8; see Deut 34.10; NRSV: "face to face"). In rabbinic tradition, this was interpreted literally: Moses died when God kissed him.

Then, the text says literally, "he buried him" (Deut 34.6). Although the Hebrew could also have the sense "he was buried," the burial of Moses by Yahweh himself is an appropriate conclusion to their long and intimate relationship. And, since Yahweh himself buried his servant, the exact location of his grave is unknown.

Dr. Martin Luther King, Jr., in what would be his final sermon, alluded to Moses's view of the promised land from the peak of Mount Nebo. King closed this sermon titled "I've been to the Mountaintop," saying, "Like anybody, I would like to live a long life. Longevity has its place. But I'm not concerned about that now. I just want to do God's will. And He's allowed me to go up to the mountain. And I've looked over. And I've seen the promised land. I may not get there with you. But I want you to know tonight, that we, as a people, will get to the promised land!"* King was assassinated the following day.

A LOOK BACK AND AHEAD

At the end of Deuteronomy, Israel is poised to return to the Promised Land. The book's stirring rhetorical style has an inspiring message: God's love of Israel, expressed in covenant and proven through history, will continue as long as the people are faithful to the teaching of Moses. That is the dominant theme that the Deuteronomists will use to organize the historical narrative that follows in the books of Joshua, Judges, Samuel, and Kings. At the same time, Deuteronomy concludes the Pentateuch, in which later Jewish tradition will enumerate a total of 613 commandments given by God through Moses, the traditional author of the Pentateuch. Obedience to these commandments will form the essence of Jewish tradition—the way of Torah.

In biblical narrative, the end of Deuteronomy is obviously not the end of the story: The promises to the ancestors have not yet been fulfilled, and the Israelites are not yet in the "land flowing with milk and honey." That fulfillment will take place in the book of Joshua. Yet in another sense, with Deuteronomy we reach what later tradition identified as the end of the primary divine instructions. When the Priestly editors of Israel's earlier traditions concluded the Torah with Deuteronomy, they deliberately established a paradigm for the community in exile: The necessary condition for survival as a people was fidelity to the teaching of Moses. And, since its compilation took place during the period of exile in the sixth century BCE, it is understandable that the Pentateuch ends with Israel still outside the Promised Land. One of the principal themes of the Pentateuch is the theme of exile and return. This theme pervades the book of Genesis, from the expulsion from the garden of Eden in Genesis 3 through the wanderings of Israel's ancestors in and out of the Promised Land. The remaining four books of the Pentateuch, Exodus through Deuteronomy, are essentially one long journey home, a journey that for the Priestly writers of the exilic period and for others foreshadowed the return from the captivity in Babylon.

---

* From a sermon delivered at Mason Temple in Memphis, Tennessee, on April 3, 1968, quoted from J. M. Washington, ed., *A Testament of Hope: The Essential Writings of Martin Luther King, Jr.* (San Francisco: Harper & Row, 1986), p. 286.

IMPORTANT NAMES AND TERMS

Each name or term is defined briefly in the Glossary. Its first significant occurrence in this chapter appears in **boldface** type.

Deuteronomic Code   **Levites**   **torah**
Deuteronomic school   **Shema**

QUESTIONS FOR REVIEW

1. What is the relationship of the book of Deuteronomy to the preceding four books of the Pentateuch? What is its relationship to the books that follow?

2. How do the laws in Deuteronomy differ from those found earlier in the Pentateuch? How can these differences be explained?

3. What are the core messages of the book of Deuteronomy?

BIBLIOGRAPHY

For a general introduction to Deuteronomy, see S. Dean McBride, "Deuteronomy," pp. 108–17 in *The New Interpreter's Dictionary of the Bible* (ed. K. D. Sakenfeld; Nashville, TN: Abingdon, 2007), Vol. 2.

Three good commentaries on Deuteronomy are Richard Clifford, *Deuteronomy* (Wilmington, DE: Michael Glazier, 1982); Richard D. Nelson, *Deuteronomy: A Commentary* (Louisville, KY: Westminster John Knox, 2002); and Jeffrey A. Tigay, *Deuteronomy: The JPS Torah Commentary* (Philadelphia: Jewish Publication Society, 1996).

For an excellent discussion of the significance of Deuteronomy as a form of interpretation, see Bernard M. Levinson, *Deuteronomy and the Hermeneutics of Legal Innovation* (New York: Oxford University Press, 1997).

For the status of women in Deuteronomy, see Carolyn Pressler, "Deuteronomy," pp. 88–102 in *Women's Bible Commentary*, ed. C. A. Newsom, S. H. Ringe, and J. E. Lapsley (Louisville, KY: Westminster John Knox, 3d ed., 2012).

For translations of the Assyrian treaties discussed on page 153, see E. Reiner, "The Vassal Treaties of Esarhaddon," pp. 534–41 in *Ancient Near Eastern Texts Relating to the Old Testament* (ed. J. B. Pritchard; Princeton, NJ: Princeton University Press, 3d ed., 1969); and S. Parpola and K. Watanabe, *Neo-Assyrian Treaties and Loyalty Oaths* (Helsinki: Helsinki University Press, 1988).

CHAPTER 11

Joshua and the Conquest of the Land of Canaan

Joshua

THE DEUTERONOMISTIC HISTORY

The Pentateuch ends with Moses dead and Israel camped on the eastern border of the land of Canaan. The promise that Israel will possess that land will be fulfilled in the book of Joshua. But the language, style, themes, and theological perspective of that book are distinctly different from those of the Pentateuchal sources J and P. It does share themes and language with the book of Deuteronomy, however, and so since the mid-twentieth century, most scholars have followed the proposal of the German biblical scholar Martin Noth that the books of Joshua, Judges, Samuel, and Kings (the Former Prophets of Jewish tradition; see page 4) comprise a larger work, called the "**Deuteronomistic History**" because of its close connections with the book of Deuteronomy. Deuteronomy itself, in the canonical arrangement, can thus be understood not just as a conclusion to the Pentateuch, but also as a kind of theological and thematic preface to the historical work that follows it.

That work is the second of three chronologically sequential histories in the Hebrew Bible. It picks up the story where the first, the Pentateuch, ends and continues until the Babylonian captivity in the sixth century BCE. The third is the book of Chronicles, which begins with the genealogy of Adam and, as the latest of the three, concludes with the return of the exiles from Babylon in the late sixth century BCE (see further pages 367–73).

This Deuteronomistic History had several editions. The latest is a product of Judeans who experienced exile in Babylonia and understood the entire history of Israel in the land as one of apostasy. This exilic edition of the Deuteronomistic History interprets the destructions of Samaria, the capital of the northern kingdom of Israel, by the Assyrians in the eighth century BCE, and of Jerusalem, the capital of the southern kingdom of Judah, by the Babylonians in the sixth, as deserved punishments from God for that apostasy. Traces of this southern Judean exilic perspective can be found throughout the work.

But there were also earlier editions. One is to be associated with the reign of the Judean King Josiah in the late seventh century BCE. His rule is prophesied in 1 Kings 13.2: "A son shall be born to the house of David, Josiah by name," and he, it is predicted, would defile the altar on which Jeroboam, the first ruler of the northern kingdom of Israel in the late tenth century, was offering incense, in clear violation of the Deuteronomic doctrine of worship at only one sanctuary. When Josiah does become king, the Deuteronomistic

Historians introduce his reign with unalloyed praise: "He did what was right in the eyes of the LORD, and walked in all the way of his father David; he did not turn aside to the right or to the left" (2 Kings 22.2). Moreover, the Deuteronomistic Historians present Josiah as the king during whose reign the "book of the law" was discovered during the repairs to the Temple, and who, inspired by it, inaugurated a sweeping reform to bring the nation into compliance with that book, which was likely an early form of Deuteronomy. There thus was an edition of the Deuteronomistic History associated with the reign of Josiah.

But Josiah is not the only king of the Davidic dynasty to be given such praise. His predecessor, King Hezekiah, who ruled in the late eighth and early seventh centuries BCE, is given even more unqualified approval:

> He did what was right in the sight of the LORD just as his ancestor David had done. . . . He trusted in the LORD the God of Israel; so that there was no one like him among all the kings of Judah after him, or among those who were before him. For he held fast to the LORD; he did not depart from following him but kept the commandments that the LORD commanded Moses. The LORD was with him; wherever he went, he prospered. (2 Kings 18.3–7)

As we have seen on pages 152–53, the circles responsible for Deuteronomy likely had northern origins, and after the destruction of the northern kingdom in 722 BCE some members of this group—which we have called a "school" analogous to schools of philosophy in ancient Greece—had moved south to Jerusalem. There they may have become engaged in King Hezekiah's religious reform (see 2 Kings 18.4; 2 Chr 29–31), and during his reign may have produced an earlier edition of the Deuteronomistic History. In this way, the Deuteronomistic History preserves stories that originated in the northern kingdom, but presents these stories with a decidedly southern Judean bias.

Two themes of Deuteronomy are prominent in the Deuteronomistic History. One is the exclusive worship of Yahweh as a prerequisite for Israel's continued possession of and prosperity in the Promised Land. Worship of other gods will inevitably result in divine punishment, as the curses in

Deuteronomy 28 detail. A second theme is worship should occur only at "the place that the LORD your God will choose" (Deut 12.5); for the Deuteronomistic Historians, writing from a Judean perspective, once the ark of the covenant was moved to Jerusalem by David (2 Sam 6) and installed in the Temple by Solomon (1 Kings 8.1–10), that "place" was the Jerusalem Temple exclusively. A third theme, introduced in the Deuteronomistic History, is that of a covenant made by Yahweh with the dynasty founded by David. We find some tension in the presentation of this theme, for the very institution of kingship is one about which ambivalence is repeatedly expressed.

The subject of the Deuteronomistic History is the history of the Israelites in the Promised Land of Canaan, from their entry into it under Joshua to their loss of it in the early sixth century BCE. In writing that history, the Deuteronomistic Historians made use of earlier sources, some of which they mention but no longer exist. These include "the Book of Jashar" (Josh 10.13; 2 Sam 1.18), "the Book of the Acts of Solomon" (1 Kings 11.41), "the Book of the Annals of the Kings of Israel" (1 Kings 14.19; etc.), and "the book of the Annals of the Kings of Judah" (1 Kings 14.29; etc.). In using these named and many other unnamed sources, which not infrequently present very different views, the Deuteronomistic Historians were more interested in setting down the traditions found in their sources than in a superficial consistency. Thus, they were in a very real sense responsible historians, preserving contradictory traditions despite their own ideological perspective.

That perspective is expressed in speeches by God and by key human characters. These speeches are compositions of the Deuteronomistic Historians, a technique employed by other ancient historians, such as the Greek writer Thucydides. In the earlier parts of the Deuteronomistic History, God often speaks directly to individuals, such as Joshua and Samuel. In the later books, for the most part, God speaks indirectly through prophets. These prophetic speeches function as an ongoing commentary on the narrative.

Covering Israel's history for over six centuries, the Deuteronomistic History is the earliest extended historical narrative known from antiquity, and it is a complex and subtle document.

THE BOOK OF JOSHUA

The Deuteronomistic History begins with the book of Joshua. Traditionally, Joshua himself was thought to be the author of the book that bears his name. Only the verses at the end of the book, which describe his death, were thought not to have been written by Joshua, but by Eleazar the priest, just as Joshua himself was sometimes credited with the last few verses of Deuteronomy, which describe Moses's death. And the last verse of the book of Joshua, which in turn describes Eleazar's death, was attributed to his son Phinehas. In the late nineteenth and early twentieth centuries, some scholars found in the book of Joshua the Pentateuchal sources J, E, D, and P, identified in the Documentary Hypothesis (see pages 48–50), and spoke of a "Hexateuch" ("six books") rather than a Pentateuch ("five books"). The recognition of the existence of the Deuteronomistic History, however, has made it clear that the book of Joshua belongs to that larger work, sharing its characteristic vocabulary, themes, and perspectives.

The broad outline of the narrative of the book of Joshua is straightforward. Yahweh appoints **Joshua** to be Moses's successor, and under Joshua's leadership the Israelites cross the Jordan and capture the entire Promised Land in a series of battles in which Yahweh fights for them. Several chapters are devoted to events in a relatively restricted region—at Gilgal, Jericho, Ai, and Gibeon. Then come more abbreviated accounts of victories over coalitions of southern and northern kings, followed by several summaries. With the land captured, Joshua proceeds to divide it among the tribes, first the land east of the Jordan River to the tribes of Reuben, Gad, and half of Manasseh, and then the territory in Canaan proper to the remaining nine and a half tribes. Cities of refuge and Levitical cities are established, and a dispute concerning an altar constructed by the Transjordanian tribes is resolved. Finally, Joshua gathers the tribes together for a farewell address and renews the covenant at Shechem.

As the beginning of the Deuteronomistic History, the book of Joshua appropriately presents a paradigm of how Israel was to live in the land: twelve tribes, with a divinely designated leader, united by covenant in warfare and in worship of Yahweh alone at a single sanctuary—all in obedience to the commands of Moses as found in Deuteronomy. The fulfillment of these commands is the principal theme of the book, as its opening makes clear. As part of his commission to Joshua, Yahweh instructs him:

> Be strong and very courageous, being careful to act in accordance with all the law that my servant Moses commanded you; do not turn from it to the right or to the left, so that you may be successful wherever you go. This book of the law shall not depart out of your mouth; you shall meditate on it day and night, so that you may be careful to act in accordance with all that is written in it. For then you shall make your way prosperous, and then you shall be successful. (Josh 1.7–8)

The book of Joshua ends with a final reference to "the book of the law of God" (24.26), at the conclusion of the covenant ceremony at Shechem; thus the entire book is framed by the theme of the law of Moses.

Sources

The book of Joshua is not just an ideological program, however. It is also a carefully constructed historical narrative, which incorporates into its final form a variety of older sources.

Etiological Narratives

Throughout the book of Joshua, as in other biblical narratives about the more distant past, are etiologies: short narratives that explain the origins of religious rituals, topographical features, genealogical relationships, and other aspects of ancient Israelite life. The book of Joshua includes more of these etiological narratives than any other book of the Bible—twelve of them containing the phrase "to this day." This phrase shows the chronological perspective of the narrator, writing later than the events being related.

As in the ancestral narratives in the book of Genesis, these etiological narratives were probably originally independent legends, and the explanations and etymologies that they contain are usually not historically accurate. In Joshua, they most frequently concern features of the landscape and the origins of the ethnic diversity of Israel. Thus, after the defeat of the Canaanite city of Ai, "Joshua burned Ai, and made it forever a heap of ruins, as it is to this day" (8.28), and then, over the body of the king of Ai, who had been executed, they "raised . . . a heap of stones, which stands there to this day" (8.29). This conclusion to Ai's conquest shows that the narrative originates as an explanation of the impressive ruins of Ai, which archaeological investigation has shown to be the result of the city's destruction in the mid-third millennium BCE (see Figure 11.1), long before the time of Joshua. The etiological narrative also explains the large mass of stones at the former gateway to the city, and implicitly the name of Ai itself, which means "the ruin." The story of Ai's destruction thus answers the questions: "How did these ruins get here?" and "How did Ai get its

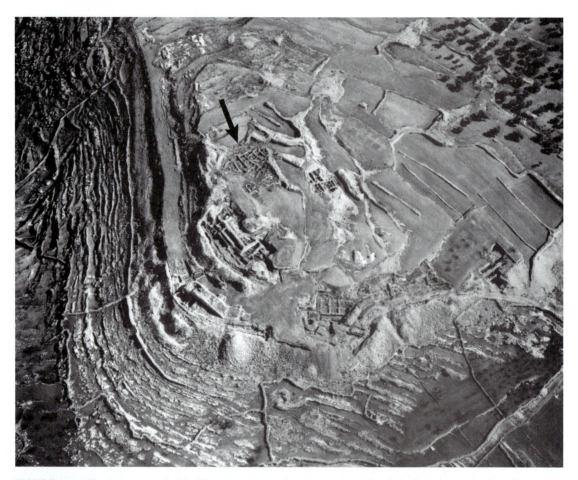

FIGURE 11.1   The ancient mound of Ai. The arrow points to the remains of an unfortified village dating to early in the Iron Age (twelfth century BCE). Below it are the ruins of a large temple from the Early Bronze Age (ca. 2500 BCE), and below that is a large defensive wall of the same period. Between the Early Bronze Age and the Iron Age the site was unoccupied. The account of the city's destruction in Joshua 8 thus is historically unlikely.

name?" It is likely that this etiological legend first existed independently and was connected with Joshua only secondarily.

Another etiological legend is associated with **Rahab**, the prostitute of Jericho who had sheltered the spies sent by Joshua across the Jordan ahead of the Israelites. According to Joshua 6.25, "Rahab the prostitute, with her father's house and all who belonged to her, Joshua spared. She has lived in Israel to this day. For she hid the messengers whom Joshua sent to spy out Jericho." This conclusion suggests that the entire Rahab story originated as an answer to the question of how a Canaanite group became part of Israel. Like the similar incorporation into Israel of the Gibeonites (chap. 9) and other non-Israelites (see 13.13; 16.10; Ruth), it is inconsistent with the Deuteronomic injunction to kill all Canaanites and not to intermarry with them (Deut 20.16–18; 7.1–4). The Deuteronomistic Historians were not entirely comfortable with this inconsistency, as is shown in the case of Rahab by their locating her and her extended family "outside the camp of Israel" (Josh 6.23) and in the case of the Gibeonites by their being made temple servants or slaves (9.21, 27).

These two examples illustrate how etiological narratives functioned. They were incorporated into the book of Joshua and contributed to the portrayal of Joshua as the central figure in the story of the conquest of the land. It is more likely, however, as we will see on pages 167–68, that he was originally only a local hero.

Boundary and City Lists

The central section of the book of Joshua (chaps. 13–19) consists of lists of boundaries of the territories of the twelve tribes and of cities contained within those territories (see Figures 11.2 and 12.1), as the land just captured is divided up by Joshua. To modern readers, these lists, like the genealogies in Genesis and Chronicles, and similar lists in the Bible and other ancient literature, often seem dry and unimportant. Yet for the ancient audience of Joshua, the lists were clearly of interest. The geographical information they contain is a record of local history and, taken as a whole, forms a kind of map in prose form. More generally, the

lists also demonstrate the importance attached to the land of Israel in the Deuteronomistic History in particular, and in the Bible as a whole (see further pages 26–27).

Several things are notable about these lists. The territories assigned to the tribes are not all described in the same detail. In general, that of the tribe of Judah (chap. 15) is the most detailed, and the farther removed from Judah a tribe's territory is, the more perfunctory is its geographical description. This suggests that the lists were compiled in Judah itself. Moreover, archaeological evidence for some of the places named indicates that they were not settled before the late seventh century BCE, suggesting a date for the lists as a whole during the reign of King Josiah, when they would have been incorporated into a preexilic edition of the Deuteronomistic History.

The boundary descriptions and city lists are followed by two other ancient geographical lists, those of the cities of refuge (chap. 20) and the Levitical cities. The establishment of the cities of refuge is an example of Joshua carrying out the commands that God had given to Moses (Num 35.9–15) and that Moses had given to Israel (Deut 19.1–13). Six cities are set apart as places to which someone who has killed another unintentionally may flee and be safe from vengeance on the part of the victim's family until the facts of the case have been adjudicated. Three cities are on each side of the Jordan, roughly equidistant, making them relatively accessible throughout Israel (see Figure 11.2).

The list of the cities of refuge shows signs of later reworking, including the addition of some priestly elements (see following), and it is questionable if they ever functioned as places of refuge in ancient Israel. Rather than being an actual ancient record, the list is more likely an example of how the later editors of the book of Joshua used other scriptural traditions as a source. Their primary function is to show how Joshua consistently carried out the commands that God had given to Moses (see 20.2) and to provide an example of how life in the land was to be lived.

Chapter 21 is a list of cities (and their surrounding territory) assigned to the members of

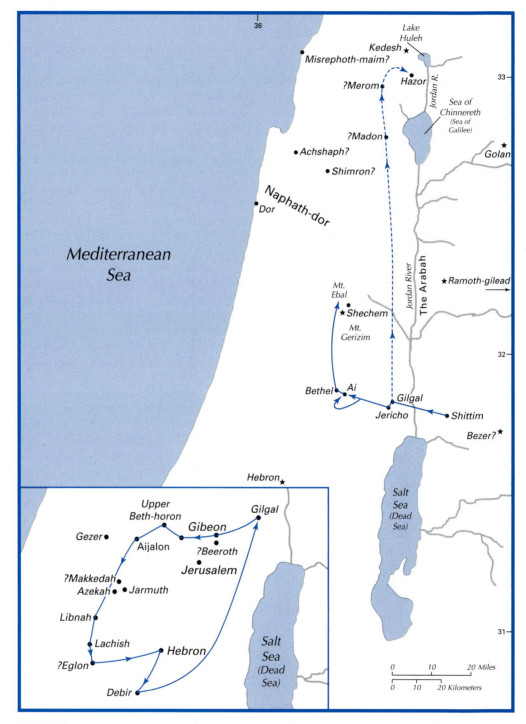

FIGURE 11.2   Map showing the principal sites mentioned in the account of the conquest of the land of Canaan in the book of Joshua. In the main map, the solid line locates the events in chapters 1–8, the dotted line those in chapter 11. The cities of refuge in chapter 20 are starred. The inset locates the events in chapters 9–10.

the tribe of Levi, who had become dispossessed early in Israel's history in the land. Like the cities of refuge, these Levitical cities may also have been an ideal rather than a reality, and the entire chapter also shows signs of priestly reworking. In establishing them, Joshua is again carrying out a command of Moses (Num 35.1–8).

Priestly Material

The final edition of the book of Joshua also includes material that originated in priestly circles. The mention of the high priest (20.6), for example, and the elaboration of various rituals and frequent references to "the congregation" suggest a priestly reworking of the Deuteronomistic History. Since the priestly source of the Pentateuch postdates the Deuteronomistic History, the priestly material in Joshua may represent an early written source produced by the same school that eventually produced the P edition of the Pentateuch.

The Characters

Joshua

Joshua is a minor figure in the Pentateuch, figuring in the narrative of the spies (Num 13–14) and in a few passages in which he is Moses's assistant and designated successor; these prepare for his role in the book of Joshua.

In the book of Joshua itself, Joshua is the main character, yet he is one-dimensional. He is consistently presented as the ideal successor to Moses, although he lacks Moses's complexity. Rather, Joshua's career is patterned on that of his predecessor: Moses himself is mentioned more than fifty times in the book of Joshua, and his life serves as the model for the Deuteronomistic Historians' presentation of Joshua. Note these parallels, following the order of events in Joshua:

- Joshua sent spies to scout out the land near Jericho (Josh 2), just as Moses had sent spies from the wilderness to scout out the Promised Land (Num 13; Deut 1.19–25).
- Joshua led the Israelites out of the wilderness into the Promised Land through the waters of the Jordan River (see Figure 11.3), which they crossed as if on dry ground, just as Moses led

the Israelites out of Egypt through the Reed Sea, which they crossed as if on dry ground because the water "stood up in a heap" (Ex 14.22; 15.8; Josh 3.16–17).

- After crossing the Jordan, the Israelites celebrated the Passover (Josh 5.10–12), just as they had done immediately before the Exodus (Ex 12).
- Joshua's vision of the "commander of Yahweh's army" (5.13–15) echoes the divine revelation to Moses in the burning bush (Ex 3.1–6).
- When Yahweh was angry with the people for their failure to observe the "ban" fully (see pages XXX–XX), Joshua successfully interceded with him (Josh 7.7–10), just as Moses had repeatedly persuaded God not to punish the people (see Ex 32.11–14; Num 11.2; 14.13–19).
- Obeying divine instructions, Joshua extended his sword, and the Israelites defeated the inhabitants of Ai (Josh 8.18), just as they had defeated the Amalekites as long as Moses stretched out his hand that held the "staff of God" (Ex 17.8–13).
- Joshua was the mediator of the renewed covenant between Yahweh and Israel at Shechem (Josh 8.30–35; 24), just as Moses was the mediator of the covenant at Mount Sinai/Horeb.
- Before their deaths, both Moses and Joshua delivered farewell addresses to the Israelites (the book of Deuteronomy and Joshua 23–24, respectively).

These parallels, and others like them, make it difficult to say much about the "historical Joshua." As we might expect from the closing of the book of Genesis with Joseph as the chosen son, and his son Ephraim blessed by the right hand of Jacob (Gen 48.13–20), Joshua is an Ephraimite (Num 13.8, 16). His grave is located in the tribal territory of Ephraim (Josh 24.30), and the events described in the most detail, those at Gilgal, Jericho, Ai, and Gibeon, take place in a relatively small region just to the south of Ephraim (see Figure 11.2, inset). It is probable, then, that Joshua was a local hero, like those in the book of Judges (see page 179), who was magnified and idealized by the Deuteronomistic Historians as the prototype for the ideal ruler of Israel, under whom the nation is united in warfare and in exclusive worship of Yahweh at a central

FIGURE 11.3   A view of the Jordan River near Jericho. The Jordan can be as wide as 100 ft (30 m) and as deep as 11 ft (3.4 m) in the spring, the season when the Israelites are described as having crossed it. Modern diversion of water from the river and its sources has considerably reduced its flow.

sanctuary and who fully obeys the requirements of the law of Moses.

Rahab

The only other individual who has any significant role in the narrative is **Rahab**, the prostitute of Jericho. Her importance is immediately suggested by her being named, unlike many other women in the Bible, and also unlike the spies who visit her. For the Deuteronomistic Historians, she is a model believer, even though she is a Canaanite. She hides the Israelite spies from her own people and deceives the king of Jericho, who wants to apprehend them. She later explains to the spies, "I know that Yahweh has given the land to you" (Josh 2.9). For the Deuteronomistic Historians, her fidelity to Yahweh serves to legitimate the inclusion of her family into the community of Israel. Later tradition attempts to bring her into the Israelite family more fully by having her marry an Israelite man. In the New Testament genealogy of Jesus, Rahab is the wife of Salmon and mother of Boaz (Matt 1.5), while the Talmud has her married to Joshua. In modern postcolonial readings of Rahab, she has become a decidedly negative figure, an indigenous woman who sells out her own people to military conquerors in order to secure the safety of her own family.

The Gibeonites

Another group of foreigners features in the narrative: the Gibeonites, who successfully deceive the Israelites by making them think that the Gibeonites are from "a very far country" (Josh 9.9; compare Deut 20:15), even though they live nearby.

The Israelites make a covenant with them, which Joshua insists be kept, even when it is learned that they lived nearby. They are spared from death but are to work as woodcutters and water carriers for the sanctuary.

The entire narrative (Josh 9) is an etiology, constructed to explain both the inclusion of another Canaanite group into Israel and also their inferior status. Like Rahab, the Gibeonite emissaries express their belief in the power of Yahweh.

History and the Book of Joshua

For much of the history of its interpretation, the narrative of the conquest of the land of Canaan by Joshua and the Israelites was accepted as an accurate account of what had actually taken place. That view, however, was irrevocably altered by modern study of the book and its biblical context, and by archaeological evidence.

The total conquest of the land and the extermination of the people living there are contradicted in the Bible itself. In the summary of the conquest, we are told that "Joshua took the whole land . . . and gave it for an inheritance to Israel" (Josh 11.23). Yet shortly thereafter, Yahweh informs Joshua that "very much of the land still remains to be possessed" (Josh 13.1), and the first chapter of the book of Judges describes in detail how several of the tribes failed to drive out the inhabitants of the land, who thus lived alongside the Israelites. Careful analysis of the biblical traditions themselves, then, suggests that the account of the conquest in Joshua 1–12 is not to be taken at face value. As we have seen, it is likely that Joshua was originally a hero of the tribe of Ephraim, and as such may have been involved in local victories over Canaanite opponents. But just as Joshua's role has been magnified by the Deuteronomistic Historians, so too their account of the conquest of the land of Canaan as described in the book of Joshua is not historically accurate. That conclusion is confirmed by archaeological data.

For much of the twentieth century, scholars were inclined to interpret the accounts of Joshua more literally and thought that they could relate them to the archaeological record. Thus, ignoring the statement that Israel had burned none of the cities in Canaan except for Hazor (Josh 11.13), it was proposed that the extensive destruction layers at sites through Canaan were caused by the Israelite conquest, especially Jericho (Josh 6; see Figure 11.4), Lachish (10.31–32), and Hazor (11.10–13). But subsequent investigation of those sites and others mentioned in the narrative has made it clear that no easy correlation between archaeological data and the biblical text can be made. This is especially true of the principal locales of the extended narratives of the book of Joshua in chapters 2–9. Gilgal has not been identified, but the cities of Jericho, Ai, and

FIGURE 11.4 An aerial view of Tell es-Sultan ("Old Testament Jericho"), showing the disruption of the ancient ruins by erosion and by several archaeological expeditions since 1868. Excavators have found no evidence of occupation at the ten-acre site during the latter part of the Late Bronze Age, the period when the events narrated in the book of Joshua likely occurred.

Gibeon were uninhabited at the end of the thirteenth century BCE, which is when a majority of scholars would place the time of Joshua (see page 91). Hazor and Lachish were destroyed at about that time, but almost a century apart.

Shechem is a special case (see Box 11.1). It was continuously occupied during the thirteenth and twelfth centuries BCE and suffered extensive destruction only at the end of the twelfth century, which is too late for Joshua and is probably to be associated with the events described in Judges 9. Moreover, Shechem is not listed among the cities defeated by the Israelites in Joshua 12.9–24, nor do they ever attack it in the book. Yet Shechem is the locale of the covenant renewal in Joshua 24 (and 8.30–35). If the association of Joshua with Shechem has any historical basis, and is not merely an example of the Deuteronomistic Historians' showing Joshua carrying out the commands of Moses in Deuteronomy, then the Israelites were present at Shechem without having to capture it.

How then are we to understand the account of the conquest in the book of Joshua? One way is to see the book itself as a kind of extended etiology, written several centuries after the events it describes in order to answer the question: How did Israel get control of the Promised Land? The answer is simple: Yahweh did it, with Joshua as the principal human leader. Their victories, moreover, explain the prominent mounds of ruined cities, like Jericho, Ai, and Hazor. The account of the conquest, then, like other etiologies, is a kind of fiction, and its message is theological rather than historical: Yahweh gave Israel the land, and its continued possession requires obedience to the law of Moses, like that shown by Joshua and the Israelites in the book of Joshua.

Military activity was almost certainly part of the process by which Israel gained control of the land, and it is possible that some of the victories described in Joshua may have occurred—the destruction of Hazor is the one that is frequently claimed. As we will see in the next chapter, however, the emergence of Israel in Canaan was slow and complicated, also involving the peaceful incorporation of some Canaanites into Israel, and control of the

entire Promised Land was not achieved until the end of the eleventh century BCE.

Institutions

The Ban and Holy War

One of the most troubling issues in the book of Joshua is the extermination of indigenous populations—"men and women, young and old" (Josh 6.21)—by the invading Israelites at Yahweh's command. The Hebrew word translated "devoted to destruction" (Josh 6.17 [NRSV]) or "**ban**" is *herem*, which literally means something prohibited. (The word "harem," the place where women were segregated in traditional Muslim society, is from the same root.) Referring to the spoils of war, it means that which is set apart for Yahweh as exclusively his, and therefore prohibited for any other use. It applies to all spoils, including animals and human beings, as well as inanimate objects. As an institution, the "ban" was also practiced by Israel's neighbors, the Moabites.

According to the book of Deuteronomy, the ban is to be applied to all cities of the land of Canaan. Moses instructs the Israelites that when they defeat the inhabitants of the Promised Land, they "must utterly destroy them" (Deut 7.2; the verb used here is from the same root as *herem*), not letting "anything that breathes remain alive" (20.16). The motivation was to avoid the risk of apostasy, because for the Deuteronomists, Israel was always in danger of corrupting its worship of Yahweh with Canaanite practices. Preservation of Israel's religious and cultural identity was essential, which also explains frequent biblical opposition to marriage with non-Israelites. In the oversimplification of the biblical writers, non-Israelites were the enemy, and they fully deserved the punishments that were divinely imposed on them. Thus, as with Pharaoh in the accounts of the plagues in Exodus, Yahweh also "hardened the hearts" of the Canaanites "in order that they might be utterly destroyed" (Josh 11.20; see further Box 6.3 on page 86).

The ban is one feature of what has been called "holy war," a phrase not used in the Hebrew Bible, although it does refer to the "wars [or "battles"] of

Box 11.1 SHECHEM IN BIBLICAL TRADITION

The ongoing importance of Shechem in ancient Israel is evident in its recurrence in a variety of sources set in different periods. It is associated with Abraham (Gen 12.6–8) and Jacob (Gen 33.20), both of whom are said to have built altars there. Jacob is also reported to have bought land at Shechem (Gen 33.19), and this plot was the site of the burial of Joseph according to Joshua 24.32. In Genesis 34, Shechem is the locale of the rape of Jacob's daughter Dinah and its aftermath.

Both its archaeological history and nonbiblical sources make it clear that Shechem was an important religious and political center during most of the second and first millennia BCE. Excavations at Shechem have uncovered a sanctuary that was in almost continuous use from the mid-seventeenth to the late twelfth centuries BCE, and it is tempting to identify some phase of it with the temple of El-berith, or Baal-berith ("El of the covenant," or "Baal of the covenant"; see Judg 8.33; 9.4, 46; the names are variant traditions).

Several biblical passages mention a large evergreen oak or terebinth as one of the dominant features of the city's sanctuary. This is "the diviners' oak" in Judges 9.37, a term connected with the "oak of Moreh" (literally, "oak of the teacher") in Genesis 12.6, where

FIGURE 11.5   The ancient site of Shechem (see arrow) is strategically located in the pass between Mount Ebal (on the right) and Mount Gerizim (on the left). It was here, according to Joshua 8.30–35 and 24, that the covenant renewal ceremony took place.

Box 11.1 *continued*

it is said to be near the altar that Abraham built, and Deuteronomy 11.30. In Genesis 35.1–4, Jacob, still residing at Shechem, was about to return to Bethel to fulfill the vow he had made when fleeing from Esau. In preparation for that religious act, he instructed his family: "Put away the foreign gods that are among you," and "so they gave to Jacob all the foreign gods that they had, and the rings that were in their ears; and Jacob hid them under the oak that was near Shechem."

A direct connection with earlier Shechem traditions is made in Joshua 24 by the almost verbatim repetition of the phrase "Put away the foreign gods that are in your midst" (v. 23), by the mention of "the oak in the sanctuary of the LORD" (v. 26), and by the mention of the burial of Joseph's mummified remains (v. 32).

Shechem's continuing importance is evident when Rehoboam, Solomon's successor as king of Judah, goes to Shechem to be accepted by the northern tribes as their king also (1 Kings 12.1). That mission ended in disaster with the secession of the northern tribes, and the first king of the northern kingdom of Israel, Jeroboam I, made Shechem his first capital (1 Kings 12.25). In the Hellenistic period the Samaritans identified Mount Gerizim as the only legitimate place of worship (see Jn 4.20) and constructed a temple there (see Box 23.1 on page 370).

Yahweh" (Num 21.14; 1 Sam 18.17; 25.28). The war was "holy" because Yahweh himself was present, invisibly enthroned on the ark, and he fought for Israel. Setting aside the spoils for Yahweh recognizes Yahweh's role in delivering the enemy into the Israelites' hand. As disturbing as it is to modern readers, it seems to have been an ideal rarely if ever carried out. In the Deuteronomistic History outside the book of Joshua, it figures only in the accounts of the Benjaminite war (Judg 21.11) and of the defeat of the Amalekites (1 Sam 15), where it was not observed.

The Ark and Ritual Procession

Because the book of Joshua was composed late in the monarchy, many of its details concerning institutions and rituals likely date to the time of its composition. Several aspects of worship, however, may preserve traditions from the premonarchic or early monarchic periods.

The ark of the covenant (see pages 113–15) is prominent in the narratives of the crossing of the Jordan in chapters 3–4 and of the capture of Jericho in chapter 6. In both episodes it is the central sacred object in a ritual procession, which is remarkable because this does not reflect the view of the book of Deuteronomy. Moreover, once the ark was brought to Jerusalem by David in the tenth century, it is seldom mentioned in the descriptions of worship in the Temple in Jerusalem (see page 230). The detailed accounts of the rituals in which the ark is central, then, although like the rest of the book of Joshua heavily edited by the Deuteronomistic Historians, probably preserve memories of early Israelite processions in which the ark was involved.

One setting for these rituals would have been military. This is most clear in the account of the capture of Jericho, in which seven priests blowing on seven horns precede the ark and the army in a procession around the enemy city. They march around it once a day for six days, and then seven times on the seventh day. The ark is also mentioned in other battle narratives (see 1 Sam 4; 2 Sam 11.11; also Num 14.44–45).

This use of the ark in warfare informs the interpretation of the account of the crossing of the Jordan in Joshua 3–4. Again there is a procession, led by the priests carrying the ark, but there are also military overtones. Although in the highly stylized narrative of the Deuteronomistic Historians we find none of the personification of the Divine Warrior found in the related Exodus account or in Psalm 114, the ark is the visible symbol of the presence of Yahweh, who leads the way across the Jordan into the Promised Land and who guarantees victory.

The Sanctuary at Gilgal

Another example of earlier religious traditions in the book of Joshua concerns the sanctuary at Gilgal. The Deuteronomistic Historians preserve the memory of an installation of sacred stones there (Josh 4), the celebration of the Passover (5.10–12), and probably the ritual of circumcision (5.2–9). These references in Joshua, like those in Judges (3.19) and 1 Samuel (7.16; 10.8; etc.), are entirely positive; only in eighth-century BCE prophets is the worship at Gilgal described

negatively (Hos 4.15; 9.15; 12.11; Am 4.4; 5.5). Gilgal was therefore an important place of worship and assembly during the premonarchic period, where some of the most important festivals of the tribal confederation took place, but it is impossible to reconstruct those rituals with any certainty.

An important feature of the sanctuary at Gilgal was the twelve stones that had been erected there (see Figure 11.6). Its very name is derived from the "circle" (Hebr. *gilgal*) formed by the stones. Like so many other features of early Israelite tradition in the book of Joshua, the installation of the stones is attributed to Joshua himself. But they were only a memory by the time of the final edition of the book of Joshua, when they, and the sanctuary in which they were a prominent feature, had fallen into oblivion. To reconcile the earlier tradition with the fact that the

FIGURE 11.6   An example of a monument of standing stones at Gezer, from the Middle Bronze Age (ca. 1650 BCE); compare Joshua 4.

stones were no longer visible, the final editor placed the stones not at Gilgal itself, but in the bed of the Jordan under its waters (Josh 4.9).

A LOOK BACK AND AHEAD

Coming in the Deuteronomistic History as it does immediately after the programmatic book of Deuteronomy, the book of Joshua presents a model of how ancient Israel was to live and be governed. Its constitution, as it were, was the teaching of Moses as found in Deuteronomy. Israel was to be a nation governed by one divinely chosen leader, under whose direction the nation should worship Yahweh, and Yahweh alone, and should live its life in strict accordance with the requirements of the laws taught by Moses.

This message is presented in an artificial narrative, in which disparate ancient sources have been shaped into a kind of theological fiction. The paradigm presented by Joshua is one that will serve the Deuteronomistic Historians in their presentation of the history that follows, a history that shows how, for the most part, Israel fell short of that paradigm. A principal exception is King Josiah, whose adherence to the law of Moses contributed to the portrait of Joshua in the book that bears his name.

In the next book, the book of Judges, the Deuteronomistic Historians present a dramatic contrast, showing how Israel in the premonarchic period repeatedly failed to live up to the model set by the book of Joshua.

IMPORTANT NAMES AND TERMS

Each name or term is defined briefly in the Glossary. Its first significant occurrence in this chapter appears in **boldface** type.

ban	Joshua	Shechem
Deuteronomistic History	Rahab	

QUESTIONS FOR REVIEW

1. How is the book of Deuteronomy related to the books that precede and follow it?

2. Define the Deuteronomistic History, and describe its principal themes.

3. What are the functions of the etiologies and the geographical lists in the book of Joshua?

4. In the book of Joshua, how is Joshua presented as the successor of Moses? Compare Deuteronomy 27 with Joshua 8.30–35.

5. How is the account of the fall of Jericho in Joshua 6 inconsistent with other details in the book and with the archaeological evidence?

6. How is the book of Joshua's account of the conquest of the land of Canaan to be interpreted?

BIBLIOGRAPHY

On the Deuteronomistic History, see the essays collected in Gary N. Knoppers and J. Gordon McConville, eds., *Reconsidering Israel and Judah: Recent Studies on the Deuteronomistic History* (Winona Lake, IN: Eisenbrauns, 2000); and Thomas Römer, *The So-Called Deuteronomistic History: A Sociological, Historical, and Literary Introduction* (London: T & T Clark, 2005).

An excellent commentary on the book of Joshua is Richard D. Nelson, *Joshua: A Commentary* (Louisville, KY: Westminster John Knox, 1997).

For a discussion of the problem of the historicity of the book of Joshua, see B. S. J. Isserlin, *The Israelites* (Minneapolis: Fortress, 2001), pp. 53–64; and Michael D. Coogan, "Archaeology and Biblical Studies: The Book of Joshua," pp. 19–32 in *The Hebrew Bible and Its Interpreters* (ed. W. H. Propp et al.; Winona Lake, IN: Eisenbrauns, 1990).

The Emergence of Israel in the Land of Canaan

Judges

The book of Judges continues the Deuteronomistic Historians' presentation of Israel's history in the Promised Land of Canaan. In the book of Joshua, they presented the ideal: Israel united in worship of Yahweh alone, and united under the leadership of a divinely designated successor to Moses in fighting against their enemies. Immediately following this programmatic presentation, however, the book of Judges gives a sobering and even appalling presentation of the reality, relating how the Israelites repeatedly failed to live up to the ideal by worshiping other gods, by refusing to come to each other's assistance, and by intertribal warfare. At the same time, it provides valuable data for reconstructing the processes by which Israel gradually established its own identity and extended its territorial control.

THE BOOK OF JUDGES

The book of Judges begins with a summary of the successes and, mostly, failures of individual tribes to extend their control over Canaan (chap. 1) and reports the death of Joshua (Judg 2.8–9 is repeated from Josh 24.29–30). Then follow narratives of the judges themselves (chaps. 3–16). The book concludes with two narratives of the

Israelites' failures to observe the religious and social obligations of their covenant with Yahweh (chaps. 17–18 and 19–21).

Jewish tradition identifies Samuel as the author of the book of Judges, but that is due to the ancient tendency to attribute anonymous works to well-known figures. Modern scholars consider the book to be the work of the Deuteronomistic Historians (see pages 161–63). The framework they give for the premonarchic period of the judges is one of repeated apostasy—"the Israelites did what was evil in the eyes of the LORD and worshiped the Baals" (Judg 2.11), followed by inevitable divine punishment, which leads to repentance and finally deliverance. The deliverance is provided by divinely inspired "judges," originally local heroes whose stories have been set into this framework.

In addition to their focus on the consequences of worshiping other gods, another interest of the Deuteronomistic Historians in the book of Judges is kingship. In the earlier part of the book, kingship is twice attempted and divinely rejected, reflecting an antimonarchic strand repeatedly found in the Deuteronomistic History. Yahweh was Israel's king, as the legal metaphor of covenant implied. In the book of Judges, the first attempt to establish human kingship is refused—"I will not rule over you, and my son will not rule over you; the LORD will rule over you" (8.23)—and the second, the short reign of Abimelech (chap. 9), ends in disaster.

The Deuteronomistic Historians' critique of kingship, however, seems to shift in the final chapters of the book, where a series of horrific stories are punctuated four times by the refrain: "In those days there was no king in Israel; every man did what was right in his own eyes" (17.6; 18.1; 19.1; 21.25). While this refrain is somewhat ambiguous, it seems to imply that the absence of centralized monarchic control resulted in constant threats from neighboring entities and internal disunity. Moreover, what "every man" did was often not right "in the eyes of Yahweh" (2.11; 3.7, 12; 4.1; 6.1; 10.6; 13.1). Especially at the end of the book of Judges, in the narrative of the rape and dismemberment of the Levite's concubine, resulting in civil war, the Deuteronomistic Historians present the fragility of the tribal confederacy (chaps. 19–21). If the book of Joshua was marked by "all Israel" conquering the land together, the book of Judges closes with all Israel receiving the dismembered pieces of a concubine's body and rallying against one of its own, the tribe of Benjamin. As readers we look for the strong moralistic judgment of the Deuteronomistic Historians, but instead, the book closes with what could be read as a final shaking of the head: "In those days there was no king in Israel; every man did what was right in his own eyes." By now, this refrain sounds like a drumbeat, setting the stage for the transformation of Israel's system of government that will be the topic of the books of Samuel that follow.

Sources

The Deuteronomistic Historians incorporated a variety of previously existing sources into their narrative of life in early Israel:

- Folk legends of originally local heroes (the "judges")
- Etiologies of place names
- Early poetry, including both a lengthy victory hymn, the "Song of Deborah" (chap. 5), and short riddles in verse in the Samson cycle (14.14, 18; 15.16)

The Narrative

The book of Judges opens with a double introduction or prologue. The first (1.1–2.5) is a summary of the successes and failures of several tribes, beginning with Judah. Most of them, we are told, were unable to defeat the Canaanites who lived in the land, and so they coexisted with them. That summary focuses on individual tribes, moving from south to north. This is followed by a second introductory section (2.6–3.6), which reports the death of Joshua and provides a kind of overture to the stories of the judges that follow.

Chapters 3.7–16.31 are the stories of the judges themselves, and they are presented sequentially, as if one judge followed another. If this were the case, the period of the judges would span more than four centuries, rather than the roughly two centuries between the Exodus in the mid-thirteenth century BCE and the rule of Saul, Israel's first king, which began about 1025. The accuracy of the apparently sequential chronology is also undercut by the formulaic character of many of the judges' terms of office: We are told that after Othniel's defeat of Aram, the land had rest for forty years; likewise, after Ehud eighty years, after Deborah forty years, and after Gideon forty years. Samson is said to have judged Israel for twenty years and Eli for forty (1 Sam 4.18). These numbers are conventional rather than precise. (See further Box 8.3 on page 117.)

Moreover, although in the framework of the Deuteronomistic Historians the hostility of neighboring entities is directed against all Israel, the judges seem to have been primarily local leaders, and their victories regional rather than national. Except for Jair (Judg 10.3) and Jephthah (11.1), both of whom are from Gilead, no two judges are from the same tribe or region. Overlapping periods of "judging" and of the peace that followed the defeat of an enemy are consistent with this interpretation. Like the summary in chapter 1, the narratives have been organized in part according to a geographical pattern from south to north (see Figure 12.1). The first judge, Othniel, is from Judah, and then, with some omissions, we have Ehud from Benjamin, Deborah from Ephraim, Gideon from Manasseh, Tola from Issachar, and Jair and

title "judge" is also applied to deities, including Yahweh and the Canaanite gods Baal and Sea.

The early twentieth-century sociologist Max Weber dubbed the judges "charismatic leaders," meaning those who arose in times of emergency and were selected because of their ability rather than their lineage or status. This selection is sometimes expressed by the phrase the "spirit of Yahweh came upon" them; the same phrase is used to describe Israel's first kings, Saul and David. In some cases, the same individuals and deities who are called "judges" are also called "saviors" or "deliverers," that is, those who were successful in battle.

The depiction of the judges is not always one of unqualified approval. Some, like Ehud, and Jael, are presented simply as one-dimensional heroic characters. But others, like Gideon and Samson, are more complex, having both good and bad qualities. All succeed, however, by using their wits to defeat an apparently stronger adversary.

Ehud

The first of the major judges whose story is told in detail is Ehud. He was from the tribe of Benjamin, a name literally meaning "son of the right hand," but somewhat comically he was left-handed. This trait enabled him to trick the Moabite king Eglon into thinking that he was unarmed and to assassinate him as he was presenting the tribute that had been imposed on the Israelites.

The brief narrative includes crude humor, involving Eglon's obesity, his bathroom habits, and the stupidity of his courtiers—all contrasted with the clever hero Ehud, who manages to trick his adversaries and then to rally the Israelites so that they defeat the Moabites (see Box 12.2).

Deborah and Jael

Only three women are named in the extended narratives in the book of Judges, Deborah, Jael, and Delilah, and two of them occur in the account

Box 12.2 THE MOABITES AND THE AMMONITES

Just east of the Jordan River and the Dead Sea lay the kingdoms of Ammon and Moab, parts of whose territory were assigned to the tribes of Gad and Reuben. Both the **Moabites** and the **Ammonites** are sporadically mentioned in the Bible and in nonbiblical texts from the first half of the first millennium BCE. According to the genealogy at the end of the book of Ruth (4.17; see pages 407–8), King David had a Moabite ancestor.

The Moabite and Ammonite languages are known from a few inscriptions, the most important of which is a stela erected by the Moabite king Mesha (see 2 Kings 3.4 and Figure 16.4) in the mid-ninth century BCE. Both languages are very closely related to each other and to Hebrew. We also know from the Mesha stela that the Moabites shared with the Israelites such institutions as the "ban" (see pages 170–72), and the view that the ups and downs of their history were a result of the favor or displeasure of their national god. Biblical tradition recognizes these cultural connections by making both the Ammonites and the Moabites descendants of Abraham's nephew Lot (Gen 19.36–38).

It is unclear whether the stories of Ehud's defeat of the Moabites (Judg 3.12–30) and Jephthah's defeat of the Ammonites (11.1–33) have any historical basis. It is likely, however, that the emerging nation-states on both sides of the Jordan were frequently in conflict, and the narratives in Judges may reflect that situation.

Box 12.3 THE SONG OF DEBORAH

The Song of Deborah (Judg 5.2–31) is a stirring account of a victory of some of the northern tribes over the Canaanites, and it has long been recognized as one of the oldest parts of the Bible. Because of its grammar and content, it probably dates to the twelfth century BCE, roughly contemporary with the events that it describes. This early date accounts for the Song's many obscurities, but despite them it is an important witness to early Israel's beliefs and organization.

The song is a victory hymn, incorporating elements found in other early biblical poetry, but combining them with specific details of an actual event. With a somewhat disjointed structure, the song celebrates how some of the tribes of Israel defeated their Canaanite adversaries. That is attributed first of all to Yahweh himself and his heavenly army—the stars of verse 20—and to human agents—Barak and two women: Deborah herself, and Jael, who killed the fleeing Canaanite general Sisera. The center of the poem, verses 14–18, is an account of how six of the ten northern tribes (the southern tribes Judah and Simeon are not mentioned) responded positively to the call to arms, but four did not. Both the names of the tribes and the order in which they are given differ somewhat from the other poetic tribal catalogues (Gen 49 and Deut 33). The poem ends with another woman, Sisera's mother, looking out from the city in vain for her son's return in victory, like Hecuba on the walls of Troy waiting for Hector.

of Deborah's judgeship. The first is **Deborah** herself. We find two accounts of her activities: a prose account from the Deuteronomistic Historians in chapter 4 and an older poem in chapter 5, the "Song of Deborah" (see Box 12.3).

Deborah's status as a woman is not highlighted by the biblical writers. Rather, her roles as judge, prophet, and military leader are presented matter-of-factly, without attention being given to her gender. Still, Deborah's status contrasts with other women in the book of Judges, who are frequently unnamed and generally dependent on fathers and husbands, sometimes, as with Jephthah's daughter and the Levite's concubine, tragically so.

The second named woman in this account is Jael. She too is an outsider, a member of the Kenite clan. The Kenites were a group of itinerant metal smiths—Jael lives in a tent. According to some traditions, they had close connections with the Israelites. As with Deborah, in the earliest form of the

tradition (Judg 5) Jael's role in the Israelite victory is stated simply, without her being a woman noted as unusual; she is simply a hero, paired in verse 6 with one of the judges, Shamgar. She entices the fleeing Canaanite general Sisera into her tent, offers him a refreshing drink, and when he collapses "between her feet," kills him by hammering a tent peg through his temple. There is a suggestion of seduction here, for the term "feet" is often a euphemism in the Bible for the genitals.

For the Deuteronomistic Historians, who recast the ancient poem in prose, that Jael is a woman is a further sign that Yahweh ultimately is responsible for the victory: The mighty Canaanite general Sisera will be "sold" by Yahweh "into the hand of a woman" (Judg 4.9)—the ultimate degradation.

Gideon and Abimelech

One of the longer narratives about the major judges tells of Gideon and his family in chapters 6–9.

It begins with an account of raids deep into Israelite territory by the camel-riding Midianites and their allies, both from the east and the south; Israel's earlier link with the Midianites (see page 143) has turned into overt hostility. For the Deuteronomistic Historians, this is a central episode in the premonarchic period, as is indicated by the appearance of a prophet in Judges 6.7–10, who condemns the Israelites for their worship of the "gods of the Amorites" in violation of the covenant made at Shechem (Josh 24.14–15). Gideon's given name was Jerubbaal, which literally means "Let Baal contend" and shows his father's devotion to that Canaanite deity (6.25); the name is reinterpreted to mean "one who contends with Baal" (6.32). The name "Gideon," meaning "hacker," is apparently a nickname, based on his military prowess, reinterpreted as "the one who cuts down forbidden ritual objects."

The prophet's oracle is followed immediately by the appearance of a divine messenger, who announces to a reluctant Gideon that through him Yahweh will deliver Israel. The divine role will be evident because Gideon is a nobody, an insignificant member of an insignificant clan in Manasseh and the youngest in his family. As a further sign of divine assurance, fire miraculously consumes the meal, or sacrifice, that Gideon offers the messenger. As the narrative proceeds, the divine presence continues to be demonstrated by signs, like those given to a similarly reluctant Moses in his initial theophany (Ex 4.1–17). Gideon thus is implicitly placed in the line of Moses and Joshua, as a divinely chosen leader who achieves victories with divine assistance, and he acknowledges the divine rule over Israel by refusing to become a king and the founder of a dynasty (8.22–23).

With cunning strategy Gideon defeats the Midianites, and then ruthlessly punishes those Israelites in Transjordan who had refused him aid. After this, however, Gideon and his family cease being model leaders. Gideon himself manufactures an idol from the Midianite earrings taken as spoils of war, recalling both the episode of the golden calf (Ex 32.2–4) and Achan's appropriation of spoils in holy war (Josh 7). Then, when Gideon dies, his

son Abimelech kills his many brothers and has himself crowned king at the old sanctuary at Shechem (see Box 11.1 on pages 171–72). This brief experiment with kingship ends in disaster, with Abimelech killed and the tower of Shechem destroyed by fire; all this is caused by an "evil spirit" from Yahweh (9.23)—a dramatic contrast to the "spirit of Yahweh" that had "clothed" Gideon himself (6.34) and inspired other judges.

From the perspective of the Deuteronomistic Historians, this episode has several morals: Yahweh alone must be worshiped; he alone is Israel's king who fights on its behalf; and if a human ruler is to be chosen, it is by divine rather than human initiative. Like so many of the Bible's heroes, Gideon is a complex character. He is a shrewd and successful military leader and a Yahwistic religious reformer, but in the end he is guilty of religious apostasy, and his family legacy is one of violence.

Jephthah and His Daughter

One of the saddest tales in the book of Judges is that of Jephthah and his vow (11.1–12.7). Jephthah is another outsider, the illegitimate son of a Gileadite with a prostitute. Expelled from his family, he becomes a successful bandit, so successful that when the Ammonites (see Box 12.2) threaten Gilead, the Gileadites turn to Jephthah for help, and make him their leader. In an initial negotiation, Jephthah details the history of the relationship between Israel and Ammon, summarizing the narrative of the wanderings before Israel entered Canaan, but that fails to allay the Ammonite king's hostility.

Jephthah's defeat of the Ammonites is described briefly. The narrator is much more interested in Jephthah's rash vow and its consequences. Before the battle, he had promised that if he were successful, he would sacrifice to Yahweh "whoever [or "whatever"—the Hebrew is not specific] comes out of the doors of my house to meet me" (Judg 11.31). When he did return victorious, his daughter came to meet him in the traditional women's victory dance.

Although like many other women in the Bible **Jephthah's daughter** is unnamed, the story now becomes hers. She agrees with her regretful father that he must keep his vow, but asks for a respite to lament her unfulfilled life as wife and mother—her "virginity"—with her companions (11.37). It is difficult not to be horrified by the piety that requires the death of a young woman. Jephthah himself is dismayed at what he must do, as in Greek tradition are, in close parallels, Idomeneus, when after a similar vow he must sacrifice his son, who is the first creature to greet him when he returns from the Trojan War, and Agamemnon, when he sacrifices his and Clytemnestra's daughter Iphigenia. In later retellings of the Greek tales, both Idomeneus's son and Iphigenia miraculously escape death at their fathers' hands, but there is no escape for Jephthah's daughter. Were biblical writers and audiences similarly horrified? Perhaps—they seem reticent to narrate the sacrifice in explicit terms: Jephthah "did with her according to the vow he had made" (Judg 11:39). Her fate was also commemorated in an otherwise unknown ritual: "For four days every year the daughters of Israel would go out to lament the daughter of Jephthah the Gileadite" (Judg 11.40).

Samson and His Women

The last of the judges is **Samson**, but he is not a typical judge. He is divinely chosen before his birth, rather than as a divine response to Israelite pleas for help in an immediate crisis. In the pattern of Sarah (Gen 11.30; 16.1), Rebekah (Gen 25.21), Rachel (Gen 29.31), and Hannah (1 Sam 1.2), Samson's mother, who is not named, is unable to have children, but a divine messenger announces to her (and not to her husband, Manoah) that she will conceive and that her son "will begin to deliver Israel from the hand of the Philistines." Moreover, he is to be a "nazirite," bound by vow not to cut his hair. These traditional elements form a prologue to the folktales that follow, in which Samson repeatedly will wreak havoc on the Philistines, but will ultimately be undone by his hair being cut. The note that Samson will begin to deliver Israel from the Philistines anticipates that the conflict between the Israelites and the Philistines will be a long

one and prepares for the encounters between them described in 1 and 2 Samuel (see Box 12.4).

Unlike the other judges, who fight for other Israelites, Samson's encounters with the Philistines are personal. He fights alone and never leads the Israelites in battle. For most of the Samson cycle, those solitary encounters have a comic quality. Samson is a preternaturally strong man, like Heracles or Paul Bunyan, and, like them, his strength is more impressive than his common sense, especially in his dealings with women. At the same time, he has a kind of naïve shrewdness, which enables him to repeatedly take advantage of the Philistines both by acts of violence and by outwitting them with riddles.

He is so strong that he can kill a lion with his bare hands. He can take three hundred foxes, tie them together in pairs by their tails, put torches between the tails, and release the foxes so that the Philistines' grain fields are set ablaze. He can kill thirty men in an outburst of violence—or even a thousand. After spending several hours with a prostitute in Gaza, he is able to wrench the city's gate from its foundations and carry it some forty miles beginning at sea level and ascending over three thousand feet (one thousand meters) to Hebron (see Figure 12.2). And, at the end of his life, he is able to cause the roof of the temple of the Philistine god Dagon to collapse by pushing down its supporting pillars.

In editing these folktales, the Deuteronomistic Historians are careful to explain that Samson is endowed with "the spirit of the LORD" (Judg 13.25; 14.6, 19; 15.14)—he is not just a lusty, amoral giant, but a hero who is both divinely chosen and flawed, like other judges. But the Deuteronomistic Historians also tell us of Samson's major weakness, his involvements with non-Israelite women. A subtheme of the edited cycle of legends is that such involvement inevitably leads to disaster. The first woman with whom Samson is connected is his unnamed Philistine wife, whom he marries over his parents' objections. The second is the prostitute of Gaza, presumably also a Philistine. The third is **Delilah**, and although she is not identified as a Philistine, her close connection with the Philistine

FIGURE 12.2.   Discovered in 2013, this part of a mosaic floor of a fourth-to-fifth century CE Galilean synagogue shows Samson carrying the city gate of Gaza (Judges 16:3).

Box 12.4 THE PHILISTINES

One of the groups of Sea Peoples who had menaced the coast of Egypt during the twelfth century BCE (see page 186), the **Philistines** settled on the southeast coast of the Mediterranean, where five cities, Gaza, Ashkelon, Ashdod, Gath, and Ekron (see Figure 12.1), became the centers of their power. By the eleventh century they had expanded eastward into Israelite territory. The first tribe affected by this expansion was Dan, which was forced to move far to the north (see Judg 18). Eventually, as described in 1 Samuel, the Philistines came into direct conflict with the Israelites, as both groups vied for control of the territory west of the Jordan River.

Our knowledge of the Philistines comes from three different sources. As one of the Sea Peoples, they are mentioned in Egyptian texts and depicted in Egyptian reliefs of the late second millennium BCE. Archaeologists have uncovered their material culture, one that is distinct from that of the Canaanites and Israelites, with very different ceramic styles, architectural traditions, and dietary habits. Our principal written source, however, which helps interpret the Egyptian and the archaeological data, is the Bible, especially the Samson narratives and those in 1 Samuel.

The Philistines had a centralized political organization, a kind of pentapolis. The rulers of their five principal cities formed a collaborative alliance and are described as acting in accord. They also seem to have had a standing army, probably augmented by mercenary groups such as that led by David (1 Sam 27.2), and a superior metallurgical technology (see 1 Sam 13.19–22), which gave them a further strategic advantage. Unlike most of their contemporaries in the region, their diet included pig as a principal source of protein, and they did not practice circumcision. We noted above (Box 12.2) that biblical writers reflected the close cultural and linguistic ties among the Israelites, Moabites, and Ammonites through the genealogical linkage of Abraham and his nephew Lot. The otherness and non-related status of the Philistines is communicated bibli-

FIGURE 12.3   Captive Philistine warriors, on a relief of Pharaoh Rameses III (1184–1153 BCE).

cally through repeatedly labeling them "the uncircumcised" and tracing the genealogical split with the Philistines and Israelites to a much earlier generation; the Philistines are considered descendants of Ham, the cursed son of Noah (Gen 10:6–14).

According to the book of Judges, the Philistines had consolidated their position along the coast, and had moved to the north and east. Samson's Philistine wife is from Timnah, in the Shephelah on the border with Israelite territory; excavations at the site of Timnah (Tel Batash) have uncovered Philistine occupation there during the late twelfth and eleventh centuries BCE. The relationships between Philistines and the Israelites seem to have been generally peaceful during the early period of their interaction as described in Judges; Samson moved freely between his own territory and Philistia. Only in the second half of the eleventh century did the two groups come into repeated armed conflict, as described in 1 Samuel. It was probably during this period that the Samson cycle originated, the Philistines having become such a threat that tales featuring an Israelite hero repeatedly outwitting them became popular.

rulers suggests that she is one as well. Within the larger context of Judges, Samson's ultimate undoing in Delilah's chamber ironically recalls Sisera's murder in Jael's tent (Judges 4–5).

Samson's victories over the Philistines, although personal, foreshadow those of the Israelites in 1 and 2 Samuel. Samson dies by bringing down the temple of the Philistine deity Dagon on thousands of worshipers and on himself. As in the Exodus narrative (see Ex 12.12), the god of Israel—and his representative—is more powerful than the gods of other nations. This will be later demonstrated dramatically when Yahweh himself, invisibly enthroned over the ark, will shatter the statue of Dagon (1 Sam 5.1–5).

HISTORY AND THE ISRAELITE CONFEDERATION

The latter part of the thirteenth century BCE and the beginning of the twelfth was a period of major upheaval throughout the regions bordering the eastern Mediterranean. The account of the Trojan War in the Homeric poems preserves a memory of part of this process. In what was to become Greece, the Mycenaean empire collapsed and its major cities were destroyed. In Asia Minor, the Hittite empire came to an end, and its major cities, including the capital Hattusha, were also destroyed. Similarly, in northern Mesopotamia, the Hurrian kingdom of Mitanni collapsed; and in Cyprus, many urban centers were devastated. Egyptian sources of the late thirteenth and early twelfth centuries BCE document one cause of this upheaval: invaders known as the Sea Peoples, of Aegean origin and comprised of several different groups, including the biblical Philistines. The Egyptian pharaoh Rameses III (1184–1153 BCE) effectively blocked the Sea Peoples from gaining control of Egypt, but the effort exhausted the Egyptians. They lost control of their empire in Palestine and a prolonged interval of weakness and internal strife followed.

Within the land called Canaan, where ancient Israel would ultimately emerge, we see a similar pattern of the collapse of old established powers coinciding with the arrival of the Sea Peoples. Around 1200 BCE major Canaanite cities, including Megiddo, Bethel, Hazor, Gezer, Aphek, Ashdod, Beth-shan, Beth-shemesh, and Lachish were destroyed, several probably at the hands of the Sea Peoples. Egyptian weakness allowed the Philistines to settle on the southeastern coast of the Mediterranean, in the area known today as the Gaza Strip. Many local urban centers of authority ceased to function, while hundreds of new agricultural villages emerged, largely in previously unsettled areas such as the highlands on both sides of the Jordan River. These mostly unfortified highland villages show some cultural innovations, but also considerable continuity with the preceding Canaanite culture. The shift in population centers from lowland Canaanite cities to rural highland villages paired with the continuity between the Canaanite material culture and that of the new highland settlements suggests a migration of people from the cities to the highlands. Among these resettled peoples in the highlands, we can locate an entity called "Israel." Although not all of the new settlements can be assigned to the Israelites, the Merneptah stela demonstrates that "Israel" was clearly part of this highland landscape (see page 91).

In many respects, the premonarchic Israelites were indistinguishable from others living in Canaan. The Israelites' material culture—especially their pottery, house plans, agricultural practices, and settlement patterns—was the same as that of their contemporaries on both sides of the Jordan, with the exception of the Philistines. Because of this, it is difficult to define precisely the political and social structure of ancient Israel in this early premonarchic period, two centuries before the establishment of dynastic kingship in the late eleventh century BCE. Scholars have used several terms, including "amphictyony," "league," and "confederation" to describe early Israel as a loosely knit confederation of tribes. What distinguished them from their contemporaries was the shared commitment, under the mechanism of the "covenant" or contract, to worship only Yahweh, the god of the confederation, and to provide mutual support and defense to each other. Passages in Deuteronomy (especially 27.1–29.1) and Joshua (8.30–35; 24) give a stylized version of the Israelites' shared commitment to their national god in the form of a covenant renewal ceremony. The tribes gathered at a central location such as Shechem, and there, before the ark of the covenant, they committed themselves to love Yahweh and Yahweh alone, and to love their neighbors, their fellow Israelites.

Perhaps because of some association with the twelve months of the lunar calendar, the number of twelve tribes was constant in Israel, although the names and order of the tribes changed as their historical circumstances altered. The tribal structure was geographical as well as ethnic. Most tribes had their own fairly stable territory, although this could change, as in the case of Dan, which was forced to move from the southern coast to northern Galilee because of Philistine expansion. Levi is a special case. Its territory was lost at a very early stage; when this occurred, the Joseph tribe was subdivided into Ephraim and Manasseh to preserve the number twelve. The separate geographical tribal entities, which probably also corresponded with extended kinship ties within each tribe, were linked by the developing myth of a common ancestor, Jacob, renamed Israel, whose twelve sons were identified as the ancestors of the individual tribes.

The composition of the Israelite confederation was complex, likely containing a mix of people with different histories. One major component of the group that called itself Israel was the group (or groups) that had come out of Egypt. They eventually made their way into Transjordan and from there into Canaan. As they settled there, they joined with other groups, some of whom were related by kinship and some not, to form a confederation. Evidence of this composite nature is found in a variety of sources. In the Exodus narratives, the number of the Israelites is augmented by a large group of foreigners (Ex 12.38; NRSV: "mixed crowd"). This recognizes, retrospectively, that "Israel" was always a complex entity, defined by more than kinship. Complicated kinship links existed among different components of Israel, as expressed by the four different mothers for the twelve sons of Jacob, a probably fictional genealogy recognizing the complexity of the confederation formed by the "descendants" of those sons.

Another group that contributes to the mix of what constituted early Israel comes from within Canaan. Early in the chronology of biblical narrative, Israel's ancestors are associated with key political and religious centers known to be influential during the period of the Canaanite city-states:

Jerusalem, Shechem, Hebron, and Bethel. While there is no reason to accept the ancestral narratives as straightforward history, the incorporation of these ancient Canaanite centers into Israel's story suggests a complex process of Canaanite to Israelite assimilation and syncretism.

The authors both of Deuteronomy and of the Deuteronomistic History repeatedly recognize the composite nature of Israel; for example, the membership of "all Israel" at the covenant ceremony in Joshua 8.33 includes "alien as well as native-born" (see also Josh 8.35), and the words of Deuteronomy 27.9—"this day you have become the people of the LORD your god"—imply the addition of new members. The book of Joshua also provides two etiological narratives that explain the inclusion of Canaanite groups within Israel: the family of Rahab, the prostitute of Jericho (Josh 2; 6.22–25), and the Gibeonites (Josh 9).

Other evidence for the composite nature of Israel includes the Passover festival, which combines originally distinct agricultural (the unleavened bread) and pastoral (the lamb) elements (see pages 87–88). Furthermore, although no Canaanite law collections have yet been discovered, given parallels between the biblical laws and other ancient Near Eastern law codes (see pages 109–12), Canaanite legal traditions may have been the source of some early biblical laws, such as parts of the Covenant Code which regulate life in an agrarian society. In other words, when the Exodus group joined with Canaanites to form the Israelite confederation, the Canaanites may have supplied its civil and criminal legal framework. Narrative confirmation of this occurs in the account of how Moses's father-in-law, the Midianite priest Jethro, instructed Moses about the establishment of a judicial system (Ex 18.13–27). In other sources, the institution of the judiciary is attributed either to God himself (Num 11.16–17) or to Moses (Deut 1.9–18); these differences imply some embarrassment over the "foreign" origin of the judiciary.

If the Canaanite members of the confederation contributed the legal system, those who experienced the Exodus added a concern for the enslaved, the oppressed, and the foreigner: "You shall not oppress a resident alien; you know the heart of an alien, for you were aliens in the land of Egypt" (Ex 23.9). Another important innovation was the concept of egalitarianism, in which all free Israelite males were equal before the law, at least in theory.

The cumulative evidence, then, suggests that the Israelite confederation was composed of groups of disparate origin, including Canaanites. What would have motivated such groups to join Israel? One factor could have been the persuasive power of the story of the victories of Yahweh, the god who had rescued Hebrew slaves from Egypt and led them through southern Transjordan into Canaan. Another may have been the political, military, social, and economic benefits of belonging to the confederation. The principle of mutual support ("love of neighbor") would have provided a strong incentive for highland villagers at risk from more powerful groups. The egalitarianism of early Israel may also have proved attractive to individuals or groups who had found the feudalism of the Late Bronze Age Canaanite city-states oppressive. Finally, the inclusiveness of the confederation would have provided a haven for survivors of the collapse of many of those same city-states.

The Canaanite membership of the Israelite confederation explains the material cultural continuities not only between early Israel and its neighbors but also between the Early Iron Age and the preceding Late Bronze Age. Had we only the archaeological record, we would be hard pressed to posit the existence of Israel as a culturally distinct group in the region—a significant contrast with the Philistines, with their very different material culture.

The unifying symbol of the confederation was the ark of the covenant, which served as the divine footstool and over which the deity was invisibly enthroned on the cherubim (see Figure 12.4). The ark was housed in a tent, which suggests that it was a moveable shrine, not attached to one sanctuary. It may have moved from one tribal center to another on a regular basis, accompanied by its officiating clergy, the Levites.

We also see evidence that the ark functioned as a religious symbol in war, representing the invisible presence of Yahweh as divine warrior fighting on behalf of Israel (see further page 115). As the book of Judges suggests, many of these wars were local rather than superregional, as different groups competed with individual tribes of Israel for control over their territory. In such encounters, the confederation would sometimes have been victorious, extending its reach by military means. This long and complex process is collapsed into the swift conquest of the land in the book of Joshua.

In the end, however, the confederation proved inadequate as a form of government. It was essentially decentralized, without continuity of leadership through dynastic succession. Moreover, the theory of mutual support was not always operative, as the failure of some tribes to join Deborah shows. Finally, the professional army of the Philistines proved superior to the volunteer militia of

FIGURE 12.4 A carved ivory knife handle or plaque from Megiddo, dating to the end of the Late Bronze Age (thirteenth–twelfth centuries BCE); it measures 2.2 in (5.7 cm) high. In the first scene, on the right, a Canaanite king returns from battle, with his chariot led by nude captives. In the second, on the left, the king is sitting on his throne whose sides are winged sphinxes, with his feet on a footstool. The throne and footstool are reminiscent of descriptions of the ark of the covenant and the associated cherubim throne of Yahweh. (See also Figure 8.3 on page 115.)

the Israelites, in which the farmers of the settlements, like those of Lexington and Concord in the American Revolution, took up arms only when necessary.

Folly in Israel

The closing three chapters of the book of Judges begin and end with the phrase "in those days there was no king in Israel" suggesting that the chapters bookended by this phrase capture a time of anarchy that only the rule of a king might resolve. Chapter 19 tells the story of the Levite's concubine, a horrific tale of violence and depravity. Chapters 20 and 21 follow with civil war and the reconstitution of the tribal confederacy. Unlike the stories that precede these chapters, the story of the Levite's concubine and the civil war with Benjamin that ensues encompass a nexus of important territories within ancient Israel. Place names and tribal affiliations from north and south seem to forecast the drama of kingship that will unfold between the Benjaminite house of Saul and the Judean house of David in the books of 1 and 2 Samuel that follow. The one who ultimately unites "all Israel" is a Judean concubine of a Levite man. These are the two tribes that represent the shared royal and priestly leadership of a resettled, postexilic Judah. The hometown of the Judean concubine is Bethlehem, the birthplace of King David (1 Sam 16.1, 18), and her father's house is associated with abundant hospitality. Her Levite husband is from the "hill country of Ephraim," a geographic tag for early tribal Israel and for the northern kingdom of Israel. Jerusalem, the future capital of a United Kingdom under David, is noted and bypassed, meaning the foreigners of Jerusalem play no role in the dissolution of the tribal confederacy. Instead, the enemy that successfully unites "all Israel" is Benjamin, but not just Benjamin; Gibeah, the hometown of Saul and the place where Saul's kingship is confirmed, when God possesses Saul and he enters a prophetic frenzy (1 Sam 10.10, 26). The house in Gibeah where the Levite and his concubine spend the night recalls the house of Lot, repeating the story of violence, sexual transgression, and hospitality gone awry.

According to the narrative, the concubine (i.e., a secondary wife) of an unnamed Levite left him and returned to her father's house in Bethlehem. After an interval, he followed her there, and after a few days in Bethlehem set out for his home to the north in Ephraim with his concubine and his servant. Because they left late in the day, they did not get far, reaching only Jerusalem, some six miles (ten kilometers) north of Bethlehem, as evening was approaching. But when the servant suggested to the Levite that they spend the night there, the Levite refused: "We will not turn aside into a city of foreigners, who do not belong to the people of Israel; but we will continue on to Gibeah" (19.12). Gibeah was a little farther to the north The geography is important, as is the terminology. Here, within a distance of about ten miles (sixteen kilometers) on the main north-south road through the Judean hill country, are three cities. Two of them, Bethlehem and Gibeah, "belong to the people of Israel," but Jerusalem, between them, is "a city of foreigners" (see Figure 12.1 on page 178). The material culture of these three settlements would have been the same. What distinguished them was not material but spiritual, not physical but metaphysical. "Belonging to Israel" meant worship of Yahweh alone and special obligations to fellow Israelites.

As the story continues, the inhabitants of Gibeah failed to live up to their obligations, violating the principles of hospitality and brutally raping the concubine. When the Levite discovered his wife's body with her hands on the threshold of the house where he was staying, he brought her home and dismembered her, sending one part to each of the twelve tribes. This reminder of the actual ceremony of covenant making (compare 1 Sam 11.7, and see further pages 102–3) stirred the tribes to action, and they united to enforce the punishment—the curse of the covenant ceremony—on the guilty tribe of Benjamin. It is one of the many ironies of the book of Judges that the only time that all the tribes of Israel are reported to have united in warfare (the ideal in the book of Joshua) is not to attack an enemy that threatens them but to punish one of their own.

For the Deuteronomistic Historians, this concluding episode in the book of Judges portrays the

interplay of human personalities and politics but from the actions of the divine covenant partner, who either rewarded or punished Israel in accordance with its observance of the law given to Moses.

1 SAMUEL

Sources

The presence of independent traditions is especially clear in 1 Samuel because of passages that are inconsistent. Thus we find three different accounts of how Saul was chosen as the first king of Israel: in a private meeting between himself and Samuel (1 Sam 9.1–10.16), in a selection by lot at a public ceremony over which Samuel presided (1 Sam 10.17–27), and as a popular choice following Saul's victory over the Ammonites (1 Sam 11). We also see two accounts of David's introduction to Saul: In 1 Sam 16.14–23, he is a skilled musician whose playing relieves Saul when "an evil spirit from God" comes over him; in the very next chapter, he comes from Bethlehem to the court as an apparent stranger (see 1 Sam 17.55–56) and defeats Goliath. Likewise, after Saul has turned against David, he twice tries to kill him with a spear (1 Sam 18.10–12; 19.10). Finally, toward the end of the book, which is dominated by the narrative of David and Saul's rivalry, David twice spares Saul's life (1 Sam 24; 26).

Scholars have also identified longer independent sources in 1 Samuel. Like the Pentateuchal sources (see pages 48–50), these are not explicitly marked in the text, and their existence is thus hypothetical. They include:

- *The Birth Story of Samuel and "Hannah's Song"* (1 Sam 1, 2): Both of these chapters likely originated as independent narratives and were attached to the figures of Hannah and Samuel only secondarily (see pages 197–98).
- *The Ark Narrative* (1 Sam 4.1b–7.1 and 2 Sam 6): the story of the ark of the covenant (see pages 113–15) in this era—its capture by the Philistines, its return to Israelite territory, and its eventual transfer to Jerusalem by David. Samuel

himself is not mentioned in the first section of this narrative, in contrast with the surrounding material; this is one reason for considering it a separate source.

- *The History of Saul's Rise* (mainly in 1 Sam 9–14): The Deuteronomistic Historians also probably used an originally independent account of Saul's career, evident especially in passages that treat Saul favorably in contrast to the final negative presentation of him.
- *The History of David's Rise* (embedded in 1 Sam 16–2 Sam 5): a pro-David account of how David became the divinely designated ruler of Israel, replacing Saul. In this source Saul is almost always depicted negatively.

Underlying this collage of sources is a clear narrative development, one that effectively recounts how **Saul** became Israel's first king but proved to be unworthy and how **David** emerged as the divine choice to succeed Saul.

The Narrative

The birth narrative that opens the book, now connected with Samuel rather than Saul, is followed by an account of Samuel's youth, in which he is shown to be the only leader in Israel acceptable to God. The nation itself suffers from internal problems and external threats. Eli's sons, the priests at Shiloh, are corrupt, and the capture of the ark by the Philistines appears to be a divinely sent punishment. According to the Deuteronomistic Historians' rhetoric, as in the period of the judges Israel has been worshiping gods other than Yahweh, and the Philistines are the agents of his anger.

At first the situation stabilizes: After their repentance, the Israelites defeat the Philistines, recover the territory that had been captured, and control them during Samuel's life. But Samuel's sons are as corrupt as Eli's had been, and the Israelites request a king from Samuel. Although Samuel opposes this request, Yahweh begrudgingly agrees, and Saul is anointed by Samuel. Saul shows his prowess as a leader by defeating the Ammonites, who have been menacing the Israelite city of Jabesh-gilead across the Jordan. The kingship is "renewed" (1 Sam 11.14) at Gilgal. A long and important speech by Samuel follows, in which he warns the people of the inevitable bad effects of kingship; and Saul's reign officially begins with an excerpt from an official record in 1 Samuel 13.1.

The Philistines continue to expand, and much of Saul's early career is devoted to keeping them in check. It is at this point that David appears on the scene. From the moment David is introduced, Saul's stature diminishes. We see the shift from Saul to David in the transfer of "the spirit of the Lord." Early in Saul's career, the "spirit of the Lord" possessed him, and he was able to achieve great victories. Then in 1 Sam 16, we learn that the spirit of Lord had "departed from Saul," and in its place, there was "an evil spirit from Lord." At the same time, Samuel had secretly anointed David as king, and the spirit of Lord "came mightily upon David." David rapidly rises to eminence in Saul's court and marries one of his daughters. As David's reputation grows, so does Saul's suspicion of him. Much of the latter part of the book recounts Saul's repeated attempts to eliminate David, whom he now perceives as a rival. David, forced to flee from Saul, establishes himself as a kind of bandit leader in southern Judah, working for the Philistines but against other enemies of the Israelites.

The book of 1 Samuel ends near the same place where the battle between Israelites and Philistines had taken place in chapter 4. Once again the outcome is defeat for Israel. Saul has failed in the primary task for which he was appointed as king in the first place: the containment, if not the defeat, of the Philistines. And once again, Israel's survival is threatened. How that crisis will be resolved is the subject of 2 Samuel.

The Characters

Hannah

First Samuel opens with the story of **Hannah**, who in the final form of the narrative is Samuel's mother and one of two wives of Elkanah. Following a familiar motif, Hannah is the loved one who, like Sarah, Rebekah, Rachel, and Samson's mother, is unable to have children. Elkanah's other wife, Peninnah, has several children and

taunts Hannah. In her distress, Hannah prays directly to Yahweh at the sanctuary in Shiloh and makes a vow, asking for a son. After returning home, Yahweh "remembers her" and allows her to conceive, and when her child is born, she names him Samuel. As in the earlier cases, this motif highlights the son as divinely designated for an important role. After Samuel has been weaned, Hannah takes him to the sanctuary at Shiloh and in accordance with her vow dedicates him to the service of Yahweh, giving him to the priest Eli.

This birth narrative of Samuel, however, contains several clues that show the Deuteronomistic Historians at work. In its present form, 1 Samuel 1 presents Hannah's longed-for Samuel as a transitional figure between the confederation and the monarchy. But the details of the birth narrative fit Samuel poorly. His name is explained as derived from Hannah's recognition of his origin: "I have asked him of the LORD" (1 Sam 1.20). The Hebrew root used here is *sha'al*, and it occurs some seven times in the chapter, once in the form *sha'ul* (v. 28), which is the same as Saul's name in Hebrew. It is likely, then, that this was originally Saul's birth-narrative and that it has been transferred to Samuel because, as we will see, the figure of Samuel is central to the purposes of the Deuteronomistic Historians.

Immediately following the dedication of her son at the temple, Hannah sings a song of thanksgiving, known as the "Song of Hannah" (1 Samuel 2.1–10). This song is likely another originally independent tradition. The hymn includes the anachronistic prayer that Yahweh "give strength to his king, and exalt the power of his anointed" (v. 10). As the book of Judges repeatedly puts it, however, "in those days there was no king in Israel," and so the hymn must date not from Samuel's childhood, before the monarchy had been established, but later, from the time of the monarchy itself. It has been inserted here not only because of an appropriate reference to the reversal of the status of the "barren woman" (v. 5), but also because of its emphasis on divine power. For the original author of the hymn, God exercises control over the nation and the lives of individuals, including "his king . . . his anointed." By incorporating the hymn at the beginning of their account of the monarchy, the Deuteronomistic Historians are telling us, in effect, that the outcome of the following story will be positive, both for kings and for those most in need.

Samuel

Like Joshua, Samuel is an idealized figure. He held three principal offices in ancient Israel—priest, judge, and prophet—and is presented as the individual who presided over the transition between Israel as a tribal confederation and Israel as a monarchy. We find occasional glimpses of Samuel's personality in the narrative—frightened when a boy by a divine revelation at night (1 Sam 3.15), angry when the people's demand for a king appears to be a personal rejection of him (1 Sam 8.4–6), and grieving when Saul is rejected by Yahweh (1 Sam 15.35). For the most part, however, the Deuteronomistic Historians' portrait of Samuel is of an ideal figure who is larger than life.

Samuel was first of all a priest, although not a member of the traditional priestly tribe of Levi. But as a child, he was consecrated to the divine service in the shrine at Shiloh, under the tutelage of Eli, who became his surrogate father. As a priest, Samuel is repeatedly described as offering sacrifices, and when Saul usurped that prerogative, Samuel strenuously objected.

Samuel was also a judge, both in the sense of a local military leader like the heroes of the book of Judges, and also as one who exercised typical judicial functions. 1 Samuel 12.6–17 is a set speech composed by the Deuteronomistic Historians, comparable to the addresses of other leaders on critical occasions in Israel's history. In this speech, Samuel lists himself alongside Jerubbaal, Barak, and Jephthah (1 Sam 12.11; some ancient traditions read "Samson" for "Samuel" here) as one divinely sent to deliver Israel from its enemies. And this is one of his functions: Under Samuel's leadership, "the hand of the LORD was against the Philistines all the days of Samuel" (1 Sam 7.13). Later events in the narrative, however, make that implausible. Even if occasional Israelite victories in battle occurred under Samuel's leadership, the war was far from over: Conflict between Israel and the Philistines continues in the latter part of 1 Samuel,

and the Philistine threat to Israel's existence was not ended until well into David's reign.

Samuel is also described as one who "judged Israel all the days of his life" (1 Sam 7.15). His activities as a magistrate, however, as the next verses make clear, were restricted to a limited region in Ephraim and Benjamin: "He went on a circuit year by year to Bethel, Gilgal, and Mizpeh; and he judged Israel in all these places. Then he would come back to Ramah, for his home was there; he judged Israel there" (1 Sam 7.16–17). These towns are within an eight-mile (thirteen-kilometer) radius, suggesting a local rather than national jurisdiction for Samuel, as with the earlier judges.

The conclusion that Samuel was originally a local leader is reinforced by accounts of his activity as a prophet. The Deuteronomistic Historians have preserved traditions that Samuel was a local "seer" (1 Sam 9.6–20), one who was connected with if not the head of a group of ecstatic prophets encountered by Saul. Yet in the Deuteronomistic Historians' own perspective, Samuel was the first of many prophets in the period of the monarchy to articulate the Deuteronomistic Historians' view of the failure of Israel to live up to its covenant with God. As such, for the Deuteronomistic Historians, Samuel's activity extended to all Israel; they assert that he was recognized as the recipient of the word of the Lord "from Dan to Beer-sheba" (1 Sam 3.20), the traditional northern and southern limits of Israelite territory. As a prophet, he relayed the divine judgment on the corrupt priesthood at Shiloh, on the king, and on the nation as a whole. Moreover, as a prophet, like the later prophets Nathan, Elisha, and Isaiah, Samuel is presented as crucial for kingship, functioning both as king-maker, anointing first Saul and then David, and as king-breaker, in the case of Saul.

For the Deuteronomistic Historians, Samuel recalls Moses—also priest, judge, and prophet— the idealized leader of early Israel when Yahweh was its king. In the pattern of Moses, he intercedes with God for the people and relays the divine word to them. Samuel thus represents both continuity with the past and innovation, even if that innovation was one over which he only reluctantly presided. An antimonarchical slant is present in the narrative and in the depiction of Samuel: The old system of divinely chosen leaders had been sufficient, and the establishment of the monarchy was another example of Israel's rebellion against divine rule.

We may conclude cautiously that Samuel, like Joshua, was an important local leader who was pivotal in the change in Israel's system of government. His authority was such that his sanction provided both Saul and David with apparently necessary legitimation. For the Deuteronomistic Historians, he was one in a continuous line of prophets beginning with Moses who functioned as intermediaries between Yahweh and the people, and this idealized role has largely obscured the historical Samuel.

Saul

Saul is a complex and ultimately tragic figure. Although he began his career as a successful military leader, he died during a rout of his army by the Philistines. Initially selected by God as king in response to the people's request, God eventually rejected Saul in favor of David. Saul's daughter Michal and his son and designated successor Jonathan also sided with David against their father.

Saul's choice as military leader and king results from his victory over the Ammonites besieging Jabesh-gilead. As with the judges of old, "the spirit of God came upon Saul" (1 Sam 11.6). In a symbolic act that recalls the much more gruesome dismemberment of the Levite's concubine, Saul slaughtered and divided an animal to remind the people of their mutual obligations under the covenant (see pages 102–4). As was the case at the end of book of Judges, Saul's delivery of the animal sacrifice united the Israelites militarily: They responded to his military call-up, and he led them in a rout of the Ammonites. He was then crowned king at the ancient sanctuary at Gilgal. This initial success was followed by important victories: "Against Moab, against the Ammonites, against Edom, against the kings of Zobah, and against the Philistines" (1 Sam 14.47). Even if this summary contains hyperbole, it attests to Saul's frequent successes in battle and must stem from the pro-Saul source called "The History of Saul's Rise."

Because of his personal qualities and his military successes, Saul was a popular leader. When he had been chosen by lot, the people shouted

"Long live the king" (1 Sam 10.24), and when he returned victorious from battle with the Philistines, the women of Israel danced and sang, for he brought them security as well as spoil.

Saul was also a shrewd leader. For Israel to survive its numerous external threats, especially that posed by the Philistines, it needed a regular fighting force. So Saul created an army. Among his troops were several sons of a Bethlehemite, Jesse, including David. As David's popularity increased, Saul, correctly as it turns out, began to view David as a potential danger to his ambition to establish a dynasty.

Saul's enmity toward David became, the narrators imply, obsessive. Saul, it appears, would go to any lengths to track David down, and even killed David's supporters, notably the priests of Nob, of whom we are told some eighty-five were slaughtered and their city razed.

Once David enters the narrative, the Deuteronomistic Historians' presentation of Saul is overwhelmingly negative. From their perspective, Saul ultimately failed because of divine rejection, expressed in Samuel's condemnation. The "evil spirit from the LORD" (1 Sam 16.14) that now possessed Saul results in increasingly erratic and homicidal behavior, and the object of his paranoia and violence is David. Modern readers have attempted to diagnose Saul's malady: Was it epilepsy or paranoid schizophrenia? For the Deuteronomistic Historians, no natural explanation is needed: God rejected Saul.

Historically, we may conclude that Saul failed because he was unable to deal with the Philistine threat decisively. He died on the battlefield, and although it was by his own hand, heroically. But for the Deuteronomistic Historians, Saul's failure to deal with the Philistines was only symptomatic of a deeper reason: Saul failed because God had rejected him, and nothing he could do would reverse the divine judgment. (See Box 13.1 on page 200.)

David

In 1 Samuel, David is almost without exception a heroic figure. Following a familiar pattern, David is introduced as Jesse's youngest son whom Yahweh chose without regard for the traditionally dominant

Box 13.1 POSITIVE ASSESSMENTS OF SAUL

The portrait of Saul in the final form of 1 Samuel is decidedly negative. That judgment is echoed in the summary of Saul's death by the Chronicler:

> So Saul died for his unfaithfulness; he was unfaithful to the LORD in that he did not keep the command of the LORD; moreover, he had consulted a medium, seeking guidance, and did not seek guidance from the LORD. Therefore he put him to death and turned the kingdom over to David son of Jesse. (1 Chr 10.13–14)

That this assessment is not entirely valid historically is indicated by the earlier traditions that depict Saul positively, of which two at the end of his life stand out.

Saul had begun his career with a victory over the Ammonites on behalf of the beleaguered inhabitants of Jabesh-gilead east of the Jordan River (1 Sam 11.1–11). According to 1 Samuel 31.11–13, when news of Saul's death and the ignominious display of his body and those of his sons on the walls of Beth-shan reached Jabesh-gilead, men from that city, in a daring night expedition, retrieved the bodies and gave them an unusual although apparently proper burial. That such loyalty to Saul endured some twenty years after the event that motivated it, is eloquent testimony to his reputation in his own time.

Another is found in David's lament over Saul and Jonathan, in 2 Samuel 1.19–27. In this lyrical eulogy, Saul's heroism is remembered, and along with Jonathan he is given unqualified praise:

> Saul and Jonathan, beloved and lovely!
> In life and in death they were not separated.
> They were swifter than eagles,
> they were stronger than lions. . . .
> How the warriors have fallen,
> and the weapons of war have perished. (2 Sam 1.23, 27)

This supports the presentation of David both as one who loved and respected Saul, as well as the one who benefited from his death for which David was not responsible. In any case, its attitude toward Saul is more positive than that of the Deuteronomistic Historians' presentation in the final form of 1 Samuel.

---

status of the firstborn son, as he had earlier chosen Isaac over Ishmael and Jacob over Esau. Like Saul, David was revealed to Samuel as the one to be anointed. But whereas Deuteronomistic Historians describe Samuel as reluctant to anoint Saul as king, there is no such reluctance in the case of David. Once anointed, the spirit of the Lord came upon David, as it had come earlier upon the judges and on Saul himself.

The dual narratives of David's introduction to the court of Saul continue the theme of divine favor and promote David as a hero of legendary status. In 1 Samuel 16.14–23, Saul's servants seek someone skillful in playing the lyre whose music might provide relief to Saul when he is tormented by "an evil spirit from the LORD." One of the servants then reports, "I have seen a son of Jesse the Bethlehemite who is skillful in playing," indicating that David has the sought-after musical ability. The narrative draws on the tradition of David as a talented poet and musician, "the sweet psalmist of Israel" (2 Sam 23.1 [KJV]; see Box 14.1 on page 210). The servant's description, however, continues, describing David as "a man of valor, a warrior, prudent in speech, and a man of good presence, and the LORD is with him." This lengthy introduction goes far beyond the musical talents that Saul seeks and instead provides the résumé of a king. This is one of many places in the David narrative where irony and foreshadowing are clearly evident. Upon hearing this description, Saul should have rejected the son of Jesse and chosen a simple musician instead. First Samuel 17 introduces David into Saul's presence in a different manner, describing how a young David, relying on his wits and piety, dispatches the Philistine champion **Goliath** with nothing more than a slingshot (see Figure 13.1).

Within Saul's entourage, David quickly rose to prominence. His military successes against the Philistines matched those of Saul, provoking Saul's anger and arousing his suspicions of David's ambition. To Saul's dismay, David formed a close relationship with **Jonathan**, Saul's oldest son and presumed successor. When Saul finally kept his promise to allow David to marry his daughter Michal for having killed Goliath, she too sided with her husband rather than her father. His popularity with the people also grew; in a statement anticipating David's eventual rule over both the northern and the southern tribes, we are told in 1 Samuel 18.16 that "all Israel and Judah loved David."

In part because of what is presented as the divine plan, Saul turned against David. For the narrators, David had done nothing to provoke Saul's hostility. Modest and pious, he was the king's loyal servant, who could scarcely believe that the king wished him dead. He fled for his life, and twice when given the chance to kill Saul, he nobly refused. He established a power base for himself in southern Judah, attacking enemies of Israel while nominally serving as a Philistine vassal.

David's marriages were politically advantageous, and in some cases even politically motivated. His

FIGURE 13.1 The story of David killing Goliath with a sling (1 Sam 17) is a legend that illustrates David's military ability. Ancient Near Eastern armies often included slingers, as in this detail from reliefs showing the Assyrian siege of the Judean city of Lachish in 701 BCE. The sling worked by centrifugal force. A leather or cloth pad had thongs attached to it on two sides. The slinger placed the sling stone in the pad, and, holding the two thongs in his hand, whirled the sling around his head, releasing one of the thongs when the sling had achieved sufficient momentum. Skilled slingers were accurate at long distances, as was David when he killed Goliath. (For other scenes from these reliefs, see Figs. 18.3 and 18.4.)

marriage to Saul's daughter Michal made him a member of the royal family and provided some legitimacy to his later becoming king. His marriage to Nabal's widow Abigail linked him to the powerful Calebite clan in southern Judah around Hebron, the city that became his first capital, and his marriage to Ahinoam of Jezreel strengthened his connections with the same region.

The portrait of David in 1 Samuel, then, contains hints of what is to follow. But his hour had not yet come.

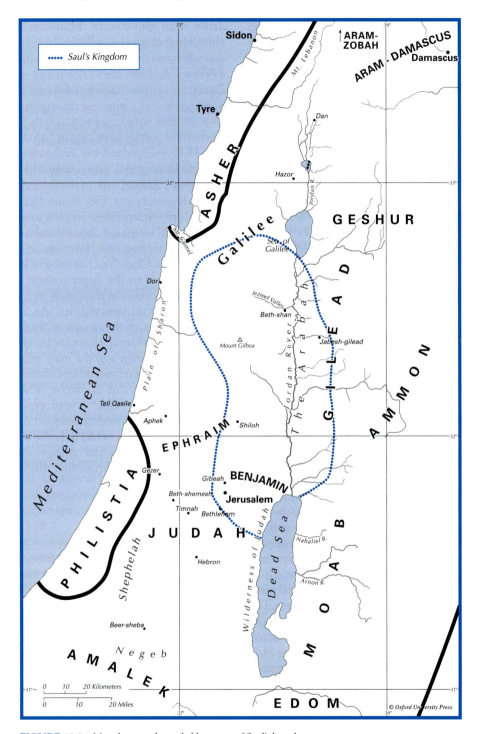

FIGURE 13.2   Map showing the probable extent of Saul's kingdom.

when he sent the spoils of war with the Amalekites to "the elders of Judah" (1 Sam 30.26).

Within the household, the father was the head and ruler of his domestic domain, exercising control over the means of sustenance and over sons, wives, daughters, and servants and slaves. A wife's primary function was to bear children, but as in the time of the confederation, she also played a critical economic role within the household, producing bread, cloth, and beer.

Succession

Within the family, according to ancient traditions, the oldest son was the primary heir. The same principle of patrilineal succession also prevailed in the larger society, modeled on the family. The priesthood was hereditary, as was the office of magistrate ("judge"), at least in the case of Samuel's sons (1 Sam 8.1). The resistance to such succession expressed in the book of Judges by Gideon (Judg 8.22–23) is exceptional, if not an ideological bias on the part of the Deuteronomistic Historians, who insist that it was God who ultimately chose leaders and that the divine choice was not dependent on patrilineal descent or other human conventions.

This principle of succession was naturally extended by Saul to his oldest son Jonathan, whom Saul intended to become king after him. When Jonathan was killed in the battle at Mount Gilboa that closes 1 Samuel, another of Saul's sons was recognized as his successor by the northern tribes (2 Sam 2.8–10). Widespread social change was thus not a feature of Saul's rule.

The Army

The major innovation of the early monarchy was the army. One of the weaknesses of the tribal confederation was its lack of a permanent, professional military. According to the book of Judges, individual tribes and groups of tribes relied on a volunteer militia. But this militia proved unable to deal with the Philistine threat, as Saul recognized. Soon after having assumed power as king, he established a standing army: the first observation that the Deuteronomistic Historians make after the accounts of Saul's accession is that he "chose three thousand out of Israel" (1 Sam 13.2).

Some of these troops were under Saul's personal command, and others were under his son Jonathan and his cousin Abner; the leadership of the army was thus controlled by Saul through his family. Although poorly equipped (1 Sam 13.22), they formed the nucleus of a fighting force that would have been supplemented as occasion required by volunteers. Conscription was probably not yet institutionalized.

This army's primary loyalty was to the king rather than to Israel more generally, and the troops were called "the servants of Saul" (18.5, 30; 22.17). They were paid for their services by exemption from taxes and apparently by land grants. They also received some of the spoils taken from defeated enemies. The army was comprised of different groups, one of which is called the "runners" (22.17; NRSV: "guard"), also a term used for a contingent of David's army. Some of these soldiers functioned as the king's personal bodyguards.

David followed Saul's example, forming a cadre of soldiers, including mercenaries, whose loyalty was to him personally rather than to some larger entity. They apparently subsisted by a kind of banditry. Later he hired himself and his private army to the Philistines, which shows their military worth. In employing David, the Philistines were perhaps also motivated by a desire to keep this unpredictable outlaw under their oversight. The statement that the Philistines employed David and his men is a detail that has the ring of fact, since it is one of the few negative notes about David in 1 Samuel and is unlikely to have been invented by the Deuteronomistic Historians. They go to some lengths to insist that David's raids were directed only against Israel's enemies rather than at parts of Israel itself, and that David did not join the Philistines against Israel in the battle in which Saul died. Apparently David's activity as a mercenary for the Philistines was something of an embarrassment, but it was a well-known tradition that the Deuteronomistic Historians could not ignore.

Religion

As in the period of the judges, the principal places of worship were local shrines, each presided over by its own priesthood. Only Shiloh seems to have

QUESTIONS FOR REVIEW

1. How do the Deuteronomistic Historians incorporate different and even inconsistent traditions into their work, and how does this contribute to their presentation of the period of the early monarchy?

2. What factors led to the establishment of the monarchy in ancient Israel? What were the reasons for opposition to it?

3. How do the depictions of the characters of Samuel, Saul, and David reveal the perspectives of the Deuteronomistic Historians?

4. What is the theological problem that arose with the establishment of kingship in Israel?

BIBLIOGRAPHY

Good commentaries on 1 Samuel include Robert L. Cohn, "1 Samuel," pp. 245–61 in *HarperCollins Bible Commentary* (ed. J. L. Mays; San Francisco: Harper & Row, 2000); Jo Ann Hackett, "1 and 2 Samuel," pp. 150–63 in *Women's Bible Commentary* (ed. C. A. Newsom, S. H. Ringe, and J. E. Lapsley; Louisville, KY: Westminster John Knox, 3d ed., 2012); and P. Kyle McCarter, Jr., *I Samuel* (Garden City, NY: Doubleday, 1980).

For a careful survey of the historical context, see Carol Meyers, "From Kinship to Kingship: The Early Monarchy," Chap. 5 in *The Oxford History of the Biblical World* (ed. M. D. Coogan; New York: Oxford University Press, 1998; available in Oxford Biblical Studies Online).

For summaries of the career of Saul, see Steven L. McKenzie, "Saul, Son of Kish," pp. 116–20 in *The New*

Interpreter's Dictionary of the Bible, Vol. 5 (ed. K. D. Sakenfeld; Nashville, TN: Abingdon, 2009); and David M. Gunn, "Saul," pp. 673–81 in *The Oxford Companion to the Bible* (ed. B. M. Metzger and M. D. Coogan; New York: Oxford University Press, 1993; available in Oxford Biblical Studies Online).

For reconstructions of the life of David, see Steven L. McKenzie, *King David: A Biography* (New York: Oxford University Press, 2000); Joel Baden, *The Historical David: The Real Life of an Invented Hero* (New York: HarperCollins, 2013); and Jacob L. Wright, *David, King of Israel, and Caleb in Biblical Memory* (New York: Cambridge University Press, 2014).

CHAPTER 14

The Reign of David

2 Samuel and 1 Kings 1–2

The book of 1 Samuel ends with the death of Saul. Now the focus shifts to David, who will soon become Saul's successor. Because of its importance, the material pertaining to the **United Monarchy**, the reigns of David and his son Solomon, which lasted for most of the tenth century BCE, is covered in both this chapter and the next.

2 SAMUEL

Second Samuel continues the narrative of 1 Samuel without interruption because the two books were originally one (see page 195). Still, the death of Saul at the end of 1 Samuel is a logical place for the division that was eventually made, and David's reign is the exclusive focus of 2 Samuel. David's death, however, does not occur until 1 Kings 2. This shows that the books of Samuel and Kings also were divided only later.

As the narrative develops, the complexity of David's character that had only been hinted at in 1 Samuel is laid out clearly. He is the divinely chosen king, yet he comes to power as the result of carefully calculated political and military moves. The Lord is with him, yet he repeatedly incurs divine wrath. And most strikingly, having been presented in 1 Samuel as a heroic figure, in this material David is almost an antihero—often absent from the battlefield, duped by his son, forced into exile, and, at the end of his life, impotent and senile.

Sources

As in 1 Samuel, the Deuteronomistic Historians made use of a variety of sources in composing the narrative of David's reign in 2 Samuel. Chapters 1–5 continue "The History of David's Rise," culminating in his becoming king over both Judah and Israel. The Ark Narrative is concluded in 2 Samuel 6 with the account of David bringing the ark of the covenant to Jerusalem.

The major source that scholars have identified is in 2 Samuel 9–20 and 1 Kings 1–2. Like other "sources" in the Bible, especially in the Pentateuch and the Deuteronomistic History, it is hypothetical—that is, it does not exist independently from its biblical context. This source is called the "**Succession Narrative**" because its purpose is to explain how Solomon became his father David's successor; some scholars also call it the "Court History of David." This narrative describes in detail the events that led to the birth of Solomon by Bathsheba, the death of

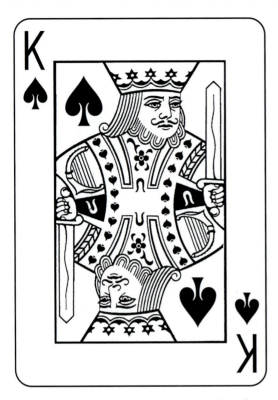

FIGURE 14.1   No contemporaneous portraits of David exist. In Western art he is frequently depicted with a sword and a lyre, as in this image from a deck of cards. The face cards were originally designed to teach ancient history; in addition to David, the king of spades, other characters from the Bible are Rachel and Judith, two of the queens.

to his daughter Merab. These final seven deaths demonstrate that the power of Saul's royal house resided not only with his lineal male heirs born to his wife, but extended to sons born to concubines and sons born to daughters.

The Succession Narrative

David and Bathsheba

Up to this point in the books of Samuel, the David we have come to know is a successful military commander and strategist. He is politically astute, methodically charting his path to greater and greater positions of power. We have also read repeatedly that Yahweh is with David. Moreover, while the house of Saul was neutralized, David's royal house

was fully established through a series of strategic marriages that resulted in numerous sons. It is at this peak of his power that the Succession Narrative begins, and one of its earliest and defining episodes is David's affair with Bathsheba. In this episode, we see David fail as military commander, politician, and servant of Yahweh, and we watch as David's actions plant the seeds for the nearly complete dismantling of his house.

His failure as a warrior is clear from the opening lines: "It was the springtime, the time when kings go forth to war . . . but David remained in Jerusalem" (2 Sam 11.1). If David had been acting as a king should, the implication is, he would have been on the battlefield with the ark and the army, not in his capital. While home in Jerusalem, David engages in a sexual affair with **Bathsheba**, the wife of one of his fighting men, and she becomes pregnant. David then attempts to use his political cunning to arrange for her husband Uriah to return from the battlefield so that the pregnancy can be attributed to him. However, when David repeatedly tries to get Uriah to go home, and, in the biblical euphemism, to wash his feet—that is, to have sexual intercourse with Bathsheba—Uriah refuses to enjoy luxury while the troops were camped in the open. This ploy having failed, David sends Uriah back to the front with a sealed message to Joab, the commander of the army, that was his own death warrant: "Set Uriah in the forefront of the hardest fighting, and then draw back from him, so that he may be struck down and die" (2 Sam 11.15). In this single episode, David commits adultery and murder by proxy, two sins that will define his family life until his death.

David was a sinner, but he proves himself capable of repentance. The prophet Nathan used a parable of a rich man's immoral expropriation of a poor man's single ewe lamb to elicit David's judgment that such a man deserves to die. Nathan then turned that judgment on David himself: "You are the man!" (2 Sam 12.7). David, in his reply, did not equivocate: "I have sinned against the LORD" (12.13). In divine retribution, David was punished through the fatal illness of his first child with Bathsheba, and Nathan pronounces an ominous prophecy that the sword would never depart from David's house.

Strife in David's House

Seventeen sons by various wives are attributed to David in the lists of 2 Samuel 3.2–5 and 5.13–16. Infant mortality was high in antiquity, and many children, like David and Bathsheba's first son, would not have lived very long, so it is not surprising that we know little about many of David's sons except their names. Because of its central theme—the question of succession—several of them figure prominently in the Succession Narrative: One after another, sons of David are killed or displaced, leading in 1 Kings 1 to the coronation, before his death, of Solomon, one of his youngest sons, as his successor.

The first son is Amnon, who as the oldest son would have succeeded his father. His calculating deception of his father and his rape of his half-sister Tamar in 2 Samuel 13 comes immediately after David's affair with Bathsheba: Like father, like son, the narrator implies. David's response was to do nothing to Amnon, "because he loved him, for he was his firstborn" (2 Sam 13.21). While Tamar is a mostly passive figure in this story, she does try to dissuade Amnon from the rape, and then after it she attempts to convince Amnon to marry her in order to save her from the shame of being a sexually used, unmarried woman. Our closing glimpse of her is brief, ending with the image of "a desolate woman, in her brother Absalom's house" (2 Sam 13.20). Then, in an equally calculating act, **Absalom**, Tamar's brother and Amnon's half-brother, killed Amnon. The house of David is riven by the sins of rape and murder, paralleling David's own acts with Bathsheba and Uriah.

Absalom was exiled for his fratricide. He was eventually allowed to return, and, perhaps having harbored resentment against David during his exile, immediately set on the course of action that culminated in a coup d'état. Absalom had many of his father's strengths, such as political savvy and personal charm, but ultimately he was no match for David, and he came to a disgraceful end.

Solomon, the second child of David and Bathsheba, has two names. At birth he was given the name Solomon, but the narrator tells us that Nathan, instructed by Yahweh, named him Jedidiah, "beloved of Yahweh," because "Yahweh loved him"

(2 Sam 12.24). Almost from the beginning of the drama its outcome is implied, which is Solomon's succession to the throne after his father.

While the struggle for succession within David's house is among sons, wives and daughters play crucial roles at key points in the narrative, sometimes as cunningly effective political actors and other times as unwitting victims. Royal wives and concubines constitute a special category. They could exercise power in their own right, while at the same time a man's control over them was a sign of his political power. Rizpah, Saul's concubine, is named and remembered through two events. First, her sons are considered potential heirs to the house of Saul, and as such are killed. Rizpah then risks royal displeasure to prevent the unburied bodies of her own two sons and the five sons of Saul's daughter Merab from being defiled. Her courageous action inspires David to give proper burial to the remains of Saul and Jonathan (2 Sam 21.1–14). Earlier, Saul's cousin Abner had claimed Rizpah as his own (2 Sam 3.7) in a move that Ishbaal viewed as usurping his power.

We see the same use of royal concubines as political tools in Absalom's taking possession "in the sight of all Israel" of the ten concubines whom David had left in Jerusalem (2 Sam 16.22), a public demonstration that David was no longer in charge. Finally, after David's death, his son Adonijah requested that he be given David's concubine Abishag (1 Kings 2.17), which Solomon immediately interpreted as a virtual coup and ordered Adonijah killed. David himself, we are told, had taken control of Saul's harem (2 Sam 12.8), part of his careful maneuvering to legitimate his rule. While these women are considered pawns in the power politics that surround them; the actions of Absalom and Adonijah are presented as sexual sins that mark David's house after his own adulterous affair with Bathsheba.

We find in the Succession Narrative an antiheroic portrait of David. He is presented as an overindulgent father, unwilling to punish either Amnon for the rape of Tamar or Absalom for his revolt. During the revolt itself, while continuing to demonstrate his shrewdness by having his advisor Hushai serve as a fifth column in the court of

FIGURE 14.3   Probable extent of David's kingdom.

Royal Administration

Second Samuel contains two lists of David's appointees, in 8.16–18 and 20.23–26. Although these could simply be variants stemming from different sources, their placement toward the beginning and the end of David's reign may be significant, reflecting changes that occurred as his rule continued. In either case, they appear to derive from official records probably dating to the time of David himself. The first list gives the following officials:

- Joab, son of Zeruiah (David's sister): over the army
- Jehoshaphat: "recorder" (perhaps the equivalent of a "prime minister," although the precise function of this office is unclear)
- Zadok and Abiathar (correcting the text's Ahimelech; see 2 Sam 20.25): priests
- Seraiah: "secretary" (or "scribe")
- Benaiah: over the Cherethites and Pelethites (the foreign mercenary component of the army that served as the palace guard)
- David's sons: priests

In managing his kingdom, David built on the foundations that had been laid by Saul, beginning with a professional army. The first official mentioned is Joab, David's nephew, who was in charge of the army; his position in the list reflects the importance of military actions at the beginning of David's reign. We see another military official, too: Benaiah, the head of the mercenaries. Shared military responsibilities would have served as a check on Joab's power.

This first list contains two sets of priests: Zadok and Abiathar, and David's sons (see page 218). As with the military, the presence of more than one priestly official would have enhanced royal control and diminished the status of the officeholder.

The second list is found in 2 Samuel 20.23–26:

- Joab: over the army
- Benaiah: over the Cherethites and Pelethites
- Adoram: over the forced labor
- Jehoshaphat: "recorder"
- Sheva: "secretary" (perhaps the same person as in the first list; his name has several spellings)
- Zadok and Abiathar: priests
- Ira the Jairite: David's priest

In this list is one new official, responsible for the "forced labor," apparently conscripts consisting of war captives, subjugated populations, and perhaps Israelites. He would have been responsible for public building projects such as the repairs of Jerusalem's

fortifications and the construction of David's palace (see Figure 14.2 on page 215).

Another telling monarchic innovation is the census (2 Sam 24). According to the narrative, its purpose was to ascertain the number of males able to be drafted into the army, although the figures given (v. 9) are impossibly high. The census also demonstrates a royal attempt to impose further centralization on the kingdom by assessing the population's resources for taxation and labor. As such, the census was opposed by some, including Joab, and for the Deuteronomistic Historians it was sinful, probably because it implied a lack of confidence in God, who should have been trusted to provide for Israel.

To what extent the increased complexity of administration of the kingdom affected ordinary life is difficult to say. It is important to keep in mind the scale. Israel proper was a relatively small entity (see further page 17), and Jerusalem under David had a population of only a few thousand. This makes the accounts of close personal relationships, such as those between Absalom and subjects seeking redress of grievances, plausible if historically unprovable.

Religion

David continued the pattern that began under Saul, increasing his control over religious institutions. At his initiative, the ark of the covenant, which appears to have been languishing in obscurity, was brought to the new capital, and once again was reportedly used as a protective divine symbol in battle. In the account of the ceremony in which the ark was brought to Jerusalem, David is the principal celebrant, wearing the ephod (a priestly vestment), offering sacrifices, and leading the ritual procession with dance and probably song as well (2 Sam 6.12–19). In fact, throughout the monarchy, kings continued to be identified and to act as priests, like their counterparts elsewhere in the ancient Near East.

Direct royal control of the priesthood is indicated by the presence of priests in the lists of David's officials. The first priests listed in 2 Samuel 8.16–18 are Zadok and Abiathar. Abiathar had been one of David's early supporters (1 Sam 22.20);

he was a great-grandson of Eli, who had been head priest at Shiloh (1 Samuel 1–2). Zadok's background is less clear. One suggestion is to connect Zadok with the line of Aaron; Abiathar and the entire Eli priesthood would have been in the line of Moses. Under this hypothesis, David's appointment of priests from different families was another strategic move, giving priests from both of the main priestly houses positions in the hierarchy of the new capital. An alternative is to connect Zadok with the indigenous priesthood of the Canaanite deity El in Jerusalem. The occurrence of the word "zedek" in the names of kings of pre-Israelite Jerusalem (Melchizedek, Gen 14.18; Adonizedek, Josh 10.1) is striking, especially since Melchizedek is also called a priest (see also Ps 110.4). Under this second hypothesis, the appointment of Zadok would have been strategic as well, incorporating the religious traditions of Jebusite Jerusalem and thus enhancing the allegiance of its inhabitants to David. Further down in the list is also the note that "David's sons were priests" (2 Sam 8.18).

Prophets continue to be depicted as functioning during the reign of David. Given the Deuteronomistic Historians' use of prophets as periodic commentators on events from the perspective of Deuteronomic law, it is unsure to what extent prophecy had emerged as a routinized office during the early monarchy. Two prophets appear in 2 Samuel, Nathan and Gad. Neither is given a formal introduction, presuming the audience's familiarity with them as well as with the institution of prophecy. Nathan appears in several roles. Like Samuel, he functions as king-maker. He announces the divine decree guaranteeing the dynasty of David (2 Sam 7.1–17), and he is central in the events that lead to Solomon's coronation (1 Kings 1), although this takes place without explicit mention of divine choice. Both Nathan and Gad, again like Samuel, transmit divine judgment to the king on his transgressions, Nathan in the matter of Bathsheba and Uriah (2 Sam 12.1–15) and Gad in the matter of the census (2 Sam 24.10–14). The presence of prophets in the royal court is consistent with accounts of prophets later in the monarchic period, when they were actively engaged with kings, both in the northern kingdom of Israel, such as Elijah and Elisha, and in the southern kingdom of Judah, such as Isaiah and Jeremiah.

The Deuteronomistic Ideology of Kingship

Reflecting their programmatic interest in the Davidic dynasty and in the Temple, the Deuteronomistic Historians insert into the narrative of David's reign an important passage that sets forth for the first time the ideology of kingship as they understood it. We will explore this ideology more fully in the next chapter; here we will examine its elaboration in 2 Samuel 7.1–17.

This chapter is placed immediately after the account of Jerusalem becoming the capital and the ark's transfer there. It opens with David expressing a desire to build a temple ("house") for Yahweh, since he himself already lives in a lavish palace ("a house of cedar"; see 2 Sam 5.11). The prophet Nathan expresses his approval, but Yahweh has another view, and Nathan receives an oracle to communicate to David: Yahweh does not want a temple, but he will guarantee the security of Israel and the dynasty ("house") of David unconditionally and in perpetuity, even if David's successor(s) act wrongly. Moreover, it is David's successor who will build a temple, and who will be the deity's son—to be punished like a child if he "commits iniquity," but never to lose the deity's "steadfast love," phrasing that suggests a covenant relationship.

The passage is complex, and it shows evidence of layering of traditions. Two stages can be detected. The first is a strong statement of divine opposition to building a temple at all (vv. 5–7), reminiscent of the opposition to the establishment of the monarchy in the first place in 1 Samuel. Then, somewhat awkwardly, in verse 13 we are told that David's successor "shall build a house" for Yahweh—despite Yahweh's just expressed negative view of such construction. This last part appears to be a second stage in the development of the passage, which in part contradicts the first.

In its final form, 2 Samuel 7 provides a further example of the Deuteronomistic Historians at work. They preserved inconsistent traditions, in part presumably because these traditions existed and were known and in part because they

Jerusalem in Biblical Times

The single most important place in the Bible is Jerusalem, the capital of ancient Israel and then Judah and Judea throughout the first millennium BCE. Because of its importance in the Bible, it has remained a holy city for Jews, as well as for Christians and Muslims. This section is intended to help readers visualize ancient Jerusalem and to illustrate its continuing importance. (See further Box 14.2 on page 214.)

PLATE 1: AERIAL VIEW OF JERUSALEM FROM THE SOUTH. (Compare Figure 15.1 on page 226.) In the center foreground is the city of David, which formed the nucleus of ancient Jerusalem. The large rectangular enclosure above it is the Muslim sanctuary built on the Temple mount, approximately the site of Solomon's Temple. Prominent in that enclosure is the Dome of the Rock, an octagonal shrine with a gold dome.

PLATE 2: A RECONSTRUCTION OF THE EXTERIOR OF SOLOMON'S TEMPLE. The horned altar of sacrifice (2 Chr 4.1) is on the right, and the great bronze sea (1 Kings 7.23–26) is on the left. (For plan, see Figure 15.2 on page 227.) This reconstruction, like that in Plate 3, is based on descriptions in the Bible and similar structures elsewhere in the Levant. (Reconstruction: © L. E. Stager; illustration: C. Evans)

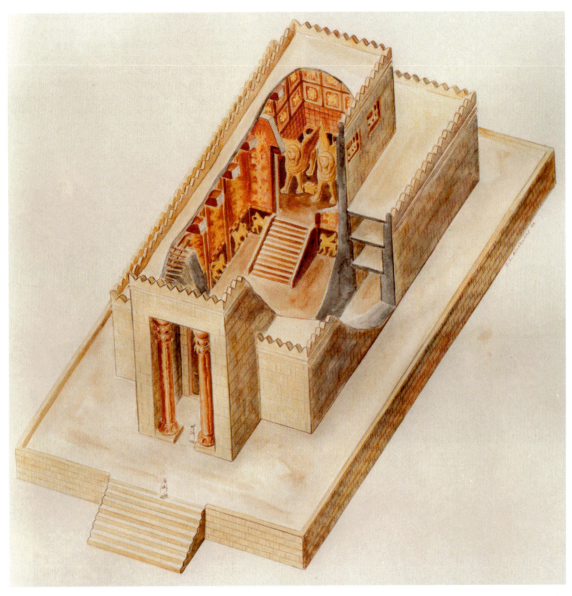

PLATE 3: Cutaway showing the interior of Solomon's Temple. The holy of holies, the innermost room that contained the cherubim and the ark, is at the top. (Reconstruction: © L. E. Stager; illustration: C. S. Alexander)

PLATE 4: A RITUAL STAND FROM TAANACH IN NORTHERN IS-RAEL. The stand is about 21 in (54 cm) high and dates to the tenth century BCE. Like the Temple of Solomon from the same period, it is decorated with a variety of motifs from ancient Near Eastern art, including, from the top, a bull calf between two styl-ized columns with a sun disk above it; two gazelles flanking a tree of life (compare Figure 3.3 on page 40), with a lion on either side; two sphinxes or cherubim; and a nude goddess, again with a lion on either side (compare Figure 3.4 on page 44).

PLATE 5: A BRONZE OFFERING STAND FROM CYPRUS. Dating to the eleventh century BCE, this stand was probably used for burn-ing incense and was wheeled, like the ten bronze stands in Solo-mon's Temple. This stand is about 12 in (30 cm) high, considerably smaller than those described in 1 Kings 7.27–37. The side shown depicts a seated woman playing a lyre (compare Figure 24.1 on page 387), with two musicians standing in front of her (see further pages 379–81).

PLATE 6: An ornate ivory panel depicting a cherub or sphinx. Dating to the eighth century BCE, it comes from Cyrus, is about 6.25 in (16 cm) high, and was originally attached to the side of a chair (compare Figure 17.3 on page 261). This miniature piece is a good illustration of the biblical cherubim that formed the throne on which Yahweh was invisibly seated. (See also Figures 8.3 on page 115 and 12.4 on page 188).

PLATE 7: Sphinx from the temple at Ain Dara in Syria. Carved in basalt, a dark volcanic stone, the sphinx is immediately to the right of the main entrance of this structure, as if to guard it. It is about 20 in (50 cm) high and dates to the early first millennium BCE. The temple's plan is similar to that of Solomon's Temple.

PLATE 8: Footprints at Ain Dara. Carved into the threshold stones of the Ain Dara temple are giant footsteps, over 3 ft (1 m) long, probably symbolizing the deity taking possession of the holy place.

PLATE 9: Depiction of Jerusalem in the late eighth century bce. This reconstruction, looking west, is based on details in the Bible and archaeological data, and shows the expansion of the city under King Hezekiah (see page 272). The Temple is in the upper right-hand corner. (Reconstruction: © L. E. Stager; illustration: C. S. Alexander)

PLATE 10: FORTIFICATION WALL OF JERUSALEM. The foundations of this wall are all that survive, but they are still about 10 ft (3 m) high and more than 23 ft (7 m) wide. The wall was constructed in the late eighth century BCE by King Hezekiah to incorporate the "Second Quarter" of the city within its defenses, in preparation for the invasion of the Assyrian king Sennacherib, which occurred in 701 BCE (see 2 Chr 32.5 and page 285). The Dome of the Rock, on the Temple mount, is at the top.

PLATE 11: VIEW OF JERUSALEM FROM THE WEST, LOOKING TOWARD THE MOUNT OF OLIVES IN THE BACKGROUND.   Three of the most sacred shrines of the three monotheistic religions are visible in this photograph. On the left is the large dome that forms part of the Church of the Holy Sepulcher, the traditional site of the burial of Jesus. In the center is the Dome of the Rock, the Muslim shrine covering the rock from which the prophet Muhammad is reported to have ascended to heaven. The Dome of the Rock is built on the platform on which stood the Jewish Temple destroyed by the Romans in 70 CE. A retaining wall of this platform, to the right and just below the Dome of the Rock, is known as the "Western Wall" or the "Wailing Wall," and for centuries it has been a place of prayer and pilgrimage for Jews.

implicitly recognized that history is not a neat progression of causes and effects. The composite result highlights the Deuteronomistic Historians' view of the centrality of the Temple, while preserving a more qualified and nuanced view that questions the Temple's legitimacy.

A LOOK BACK AND AHEAD

The Deuteronomistic Historians present a candid account of David's rule, drawing mostly on originally independent sources and only occasionally interrupting it with their own commentary and compositions. That account is informed by their conviction that, for all his flaws, David was the divinely designated ruler. In fact, in the rest of the books of Kings, all of his successors on the throne of Judah will be measured against the standard of David's unwavering fidelity to Yahweh, and few will meet it. Yet the Deuteronomistic Historians' portrait of David is far from uncritical, unlike that of the Chronicler. In the account of David's reign in Chronicles, which uses 2 Samuel as its principal source, the events in the Succession Narrative that cast David in a negative light are simply omitted, as they are in most of the rest of the Bible. On the other hand, as in 1 Samuel, where ambivalence toward the establishment of the monarchy was expressed by the juxtaposition of different sources, so too in the account of David's reign by the Deuteronomistic Historians, where their attitude toward David is decidedly mixed. This is true both in the composite 2 Samuel 7, with its conflicting views of the construction of the Temple, and especially in the Succession Narrative.

Thematic and linguistic connections between the Yahwist tradition (J) in Genesis and the Succession Narrative have led some scholars to suggest that they were written by the same author, or were even parts of a single work. For example, both J and the Succession Narrative have a tragic tale of fratricide—Cain and Abel, and Absalom and Amnon, respectively. Both also include narratives about women named Tamar (Gen 38; 2 Sam 13)—two of the only three women with this

name in the Bible (the third is Absalom's daughter, probably named for his sister; 2 Sam 14.27).

As we have seen, the boundaries of the land promised to Abraham in J (Gen 15.18–21) correspond to the idealized boundaries of the territory under the control of David and Solomon—and only during their reigns was this promise fulfilled. Moreover, in his choice as his first capital of Hebron, Abraham's burial place (see Gen 23; 25.9–10), David deliberately linked himself with Israel's ancestor to enhance his legitimacy as king.

The theme of exile from the Promised Land that is so prominent in Genesis—Abraham, Isaac, Jacob, Joseph, and finally Jacob's entire family all leave the land—is also found in the account of David's flight from Jerusalem during the revolt of Absalom. Yet like the ancestors of Israel, and, in the end, Israel itself, David returns to the land, and to Jerusalem.

Yet those connections, while tantalizing, are only suggestive. The most that can be inferred from them is that David's accession to the throne and the subsequent development of a dynastic monarchy that made extravagant claims for itself intrigued and even disturbed biblical writers. To put it somewhat differently, both the Succession Narrative and the apparent allusions to it in Genesis raise questions: To what extent could David's successes—and ultimately Israel's—be attributed to divine guidance rather than to David's own maneuvering, and, if David—and Israel—were in some sense chosen, then how could their failures be reconciled with their providential destiny?

The Deuteronomistic Historians offer no easy answers to these questions. The divine perspective is only rarely provided, and always through editorial note or prophetic mediation—Yahweh is not really a character in the narrative, as he was in earlier parts of the Deuteronomistic History and in the Pentateuch. Yet in the history of David's rule—however that rule was achieved, however troubling were its details, however immoral were David's own actions—the Deuteronomistic Historians see, even if ambiguously, the hand of God.

The final edition of the Deuteronomistic History was a product of the exilic period in the sixth century BCE, after Jerusalem had been captured and destroyed and the Davidic dynasty had come to an end. In the final Babylonian siege of Jerusalem in 586 BCE, the last descendant of David to rule, King Zedekiah, fled the city in disgrace, only to be captured and taken in chains to Babylon, never to return. David's flight from Jerusalem anticipates that of Zedekiah. But David did return from exile, and for the exilic audience of the Deuteronomistic History, that was a basis for hope in the darkest time in Israel's history.

IMPORTANT NAMES AND TERMS

Each name or term is defined briefly in the Glossary. Its first significant occurrence in this chapter appears in **boldface** type.

Absalom

Bathsheba

city of David

Jerusalem

Succession Narrative

United Monarchy

QUESTIONS FOR REVIEW

1. What is the cumulative portrait we get of David in 2 Samuel?

2. What are the themes of the Succession Narrative? What are its attitudes toward kingship? Are they similar to or different from the attitudes of other parts of 2 Samuel?

3. During the reigns of David and Solomon, Israel may have been the most important state in the Levant, a political prominence unequaled until the time of Herod the Great (40–4 BCE). What circumstances permitted this?

4. Give reasons why David benefited from the transfer of the ark of the covenant to Jerusalem.

BIBLIOGRAPHY

In addition to works by Hackett, Meyers, McKenzie, Baden, and Wright (see the bibliography to Chapter 13), see also P. Kyle McCarter, Jr., *II Samuel* (Garden City, NY: Doubleday, 1984); Steven L. McKenzie, "David," pp. 27–39 in *The New Interpreter's Dictionary of the Bible*, ed. K. D. Sakenfeld, vol. 1 (Nashville, TN: Abingdon, 2006); Jerome Murphy-O'Connor, "Jerusalem," pp. 246–59 in *The New Interpreter's Dictionary of the Bible*, vol. 2, ed. K. D. Sakenfeld (Nashville, TN: Abingdon, 2007); and John Barton, "Dating the 'Succession Narrative,'" pp. 95–106 in *In Search of Pre-exilic Israel: Proceedings of the Oxford Old Testament Seminar* (ed. John Day; London: T & T Clark International, 2004).

The Reign of Solomon

1 Kings 1–11 and Psalm 89

In this chapter we will consider the reign of **Solomon**, David's son and successor. Many of the themes of the Deuteronomistic History discussed in earlier chapters are elaborated further here, including the status of Jerusalem as the central place of worship, especially in the Temple that Solomon built. But like their presentation of David, the Deuteronomistic Historians give us a very mixed picture of Solomon's rule, including an account of his straying from one of the primary principles of the teaching of Moses, the exclusive worship of Yahweh.

coherent chronological narrative informed by their perspective: the Israelites' prosperity and even survival in the land is dependent on their observance of the law of Moses as found in the book of Deuteronomy, and especially in their obedience to the command to worship Yahweh alone, and only at the place that he has designated. Failure to do so, as prophets repeatedly warn throughout the books of Kings, will inevitably result in divine punishment, which for the Deuteronomistic Historians is ultimately exile from the Promised Land.

THE BOOKS OF KINGS

The books of Kings continue the narrative by the Deuteronomistic Historians of Israel's history in the Promised Land. The separation of the books of Kings from the books of Samuel and the later division of Kings into two books is artificial, as the continuities between them make clear. For example, 1 Kings 1–2 concludes the account of David's reign that begins in 2 Samuel, and 2 Kings 1 continues the story of the prophet Elijah that begins in 1 Kings 17.

As in the books of Samuel, the Deuteronomistic Historians have shaped various sources into a

1 KINGS 1–11

Contents and Structure

In compiling a narrative of Solomon's reign, the Deuteronomistic Historians incorporated a variety of originally independent sources:

- The conclusion of the Succession Narrative in 1 Kings 1–2, which reports how Solomon became king and eliminated his rivals and their supporters.
- Detailed descriptions of the Temple and its furnishings and of metal objects used in its rituals, in 1 Kings 6 and 7.

- Official records, such as "the Book of the Acts of Solomon" mentioned in 1 Kings 11.41. These include a list of royal officials and descriptions of the administrative districts into which the kingdom was divided (4.1–19) and the labor force for the building of the Temple, palace, and other royal projects (5.13–18; 9.15–24).
- Wisdom traditions, originating in the royal court, summarized in 1 Kings 4.32–33.
- Royal legends, such as the accounts of the Solomonic judgment concerning the two children of the prostitutes (3.16–28) and the visit of the queen of Sheba (10.1–13).

We also find Deuteronomistic compositions, including:

- Solomon's dream at Gibeon (1 Kings 3.3–15), where he prays for wisdom and is promised it as well as riches.
- The dedication of the Temple (1 Kings 8), with Solomon's lengthy prayer acknowledging that the people's sins may cause divine punishment in the form of military defeat, drought, famine, and exile, and requesting compassion when they pray for forgiveness at the sanctuary God has chosen.
- A concluding summary of Solomon's reign (1 Kings 11.1–40), in which it is predicted that Solomon's worship of other gods, blamed on his foreign wives, will result in the division of the kingdom.

The Narrative

These materials are combined into a complex narrative that both recognizes Solomon's accomplishments and points out the theological and political problems that his rule entailed. It is a selective narrative, as the reference to the "rest of the acts of Solomon . . . written in the Book of the Acts of Solomon" (1 Kings 11.41) indicates. Moreover, it is a narrative with a decidedly mixed view of Solomon. He succeeds David as king not as the result of explicit divine choice, but through palace intrigue. And his reign ends with a negative account of his worship of other gods. Yet Solomon is also portrayed as a wise and pious ruler.

The narrative opens with the conclusion of the Succession Narrative. David's sexual impotence leads his oldest surviving son Adonijah to attempt to have himself crowned as king, with the support of the army commander Joab and the priest Abiathar. But another faction in the court, led by the prophet Nathan and Solomon's mother Bathsheba and supported by the palace bodyguard, persuades the aging David to name Solomon as his successor, and in a hasty coronation Nathan and the priest Zadok anoint Solomon as king.

David gives final instructions to Solomon (1 Kings 2.2–9), which in Deuteronomistic style urge him to be faithful to the law of Moses. He also commands Solomon to kill both Joab for the murder of Abner and Amasa, and Shimei, a relative of Saul who had cursed David during Absalom's revolt. After a brief account of David's death and the chronology of his reign, the Succession Narrative concludes with Solomon systematically and ruthlessly disposing of his half-brother and rival Adonijah and his supporters, including Joab, as well as Shimei.

A series of unconnected episodes follows in 1 Kings 3–4, illustrating Solomon's piety, wisdom, and accomplishments. In the course of a sacrifice at Gibeon, Yahweh appears to Solomon in a dream and, in response to Solomon's request for wisdom in governing, grants him both wisdom and wealth. His wisdom is shown by the folk tale of his resolution of the case of the two prostitutes and their infants and by his international reputation, and his wealth is illustrated by a description of the kingdom's prosperity.

These incidental materials set the stage for the account of the building and dedication of the Temple, which is the centerpiece of the Deuteronomistic Historians' narrative of Solomon's reign. The account has three parts, the first dealing with the details of the construction of the Temple (1 Kings 5–6), and the second with the metalwork associated with it (7.13–51). Between these first two parts is a more perfunctory account (7.1–12) of the construction of the other buildings that comprised the palace complex, even though it took nearly twice as long as that of the Temple. The third part of the section devoted to the Temple is a lengthy account of its dedication (8.1–9.9).

The narrative of Solomon's reign continues with further accounts of his building projects and of his international relations (9.10–28; 10.13–29), into which is set an account of the visit of the queen of Sheba (10.1–13), an episode that illustrates both his wisdom and his international reputation.

A summary conclusion to the narrative concerning Solomon begins with a critique of his marriages with "foreign women," who, we are told, led him to worship other gods. For this apostasy, in the Deuteronomistic pattern of sin and punishment God decrees that after Solomon's death the kingdom will be divided (11.1–13). Then follows an account of opposition to Solomon both from such vassal states as Edom and Damascus and from Jeroboam, a northerner who is proclaimed by an anonymous prophet to be the instrument of divine punishment and the future ruler of what will become the northern kingdom of Israel after Solomon's death. The narrative ends with the chronology of Solomon's reign, his death, and the naming of his successor.

The Characters

Solomon

The main character is Solomon. But the sources used by the Deuteronomistic Historians, and their own compositions, rarely contain the vivid dialogue found in the narratives in 1 and 2 Samuel. We do find two exceptions. First, in 1 Kings 2.13–46, Solomon is an active participant in the elimination of his rival Adonijah and his supporters. Second, in resolving the dispute over the dead child (3.16–28), Solomon exhibits a shrewd practical wisdom. The rest of Solomon's reported speeches—in his dream at Gibeon (1 Kings 3.6–9), in his correspondence with Hiram (5.2–6), in his dedication of the Temple (8.12–21, 23–61)— are formulaic articulations of the Deuteronomistic Historians' views and reveal little of Solomon's personality.

Another facet of Solomon's character provided by the Deuteronomistic Historians is his penchant for luxurious living. Solomon had been raised in his father's court, and the peace accomplished by David had brought prosperity that increased during Solomon's reign. In the description of Solomon's court are included two striking catalogues of his lifestyle. The first is a record of the daily consumption at the court (1 Kings 4.22–23), and the second includes a description of the palace's furnishings (10.16–22).

It is a biblical cliché that wealth is a sign of divine favor, and this is one level of meaning here: The extraordinary riches of Solomon's palace confirmed that he was the divinely chosen ruler. But we may also detect both a hint of disapproval of the excess and a memory of a king who enjoyed a life of conspicuous consumption—well-fed, sitting on a lavish ivory throne, with exotic animals roaming freely in the palace garden, a garden of Eden, as it were. (See further Box 15.1.)

Other Characters

Only in the conclusion to the Succession Narrative (1 Kings 1–2) are other characters developed, as elsewhere in that source by means of dialogue. Nathan's adept exploitation of David's frailty succeeds in having David designate Solomon as his successor. Adonijah's efforts to gain the throne end in his murder. Joab challenges Solomon to violate the holiness of the altar where he has sought sanctuary, and he remains defiant until his death.

Bathsheba has emerged as an important power because of her alliance with the prophet Nathan and the priest Zadok, and, after Solomon's coronation, because of her position as queen mother (see further pages 242–43). She is the intermediary between King David and Nathan, acting as proxy for Solomon, and between King Solomon and Adonijah. Her role is reminiscent of that of the "wise women" earlier (2 Sam 14.2–20; 2 Sam 20.16–22).

Abishag, David's last concubine and the object of Adonijah's request, is a passive agent in the interplay of sex and politics that permeates the Succession Narrative. But by telling us of her presence when Bathsheba and Nathan go to David to advance Solomon's succession, the Deuteronomistic Historians invite readers to consider the feelings of both women.

Women also serve to reveal Solomon's character, as in his arbitration of the dispute between the prostitutes and in the visit of the queen of Sheba.

Box 15.1 SOLOMON IN LATER TRADITIONS

In the books of Chronicles, Solomon's role as builder of the Temple is subordinated to David's, who according to the Chronicler originated and carefully planned both the Temple and its worship. Yet like its source in 1 Kings, Chronicles devotes several chapters to the details of the Temple's construction.

Solomon's legendary wisdom is already evident in the books of Kings, in the narratives of the two prostitutes (1 Kings 3.16–28) and of the visit of the queen of Sheba (10.1–10), and in the summary of Solomon's compositions: "He composed three thousand proverbs, and his songs numbered a thousand and five. He would speak of trees, from the cedar that is in Lebanon to the hyssop that grows in the wall; he would speak of animals, and birds, and reptiles, and fish" (1 Kings 4.32–33). This passage explains the later attribution to Solomon of part of the book of Proverbs (see 1.1; 10.1; 25.1); of the book of Ecclesiastes, whose author pseudonymously identifies himself as "the son of David, king in Jerusalem" (Eccl 1.1); and of the book known as the Wisdom of Solomon. (For discussion of these books, see pages 385–88, 397–99, 425–26.) Attributing later writings to past worthies was a widespread practice in antiquity, as we have already seen with Moses and David.

Solomon is also credited with writing the Song of Solomon (1.1), a loosely linked series of love poems which most scholars date to the postexilic period (see pages 401–03). The tradition of Solomonic authorship is based in part on the repeated occurrence of Solomon's name in the text (1.5; 3.7, 9, 11; 8.11–12), but Solomon is not the male lover who speaks in the poems; rather, he is referred to by the speaker (see 8.12). An additional reason for attributing these love poems to Solomon may be the legendary size of Solomon's harem in 1 Kings 11.3. Later postbiblical tradition also reports a sexual relationship between the queen of Sheba and Solomon.

Despite his reputation as a prolific writer (see Sir 47.15–17), only two biblical psalms (72; 127) are attributed to Solomon; in postbiblical literature, however, such works as the Odes of Solomon and the Psalms of Solomon have Solomon as their supposed author.

The same is true of his wives. The size of Solomon's harem is extraordinary—seven hundred wives and three hundred concubines. It is not the size itself that the Deuteronomisitc Historians explicitly condemn, but the fact that many of these women were foreigners, who, with Solomon's support and even participation, continued to worship their native deities. Although many of Solomon's marriages, such as the one to the daughter of the king of Egypt (1 Kings 9.16), would have furthered his international diplomacy, that is of only passing interest to the Deuteronomistic Historians. For them, as in Deuteronomy 7.3–4, foreign women are a danger because they can cause apostasy.

HISTORY

As with David, we have no independent corroboration for Solomon's reign, and, apart from Hiram, the king of Tyre (see page 214–15), no individual or event mentioned in the biblical sources is attested in contemporaneous nonbiblical sources. A convergence of probabilities suggests that at least the broad outlines of Solomon's accomplishments are historically rooted and that his reign can be dated in the mid-tenth century BCE, approximately 968–928 (see further page 236). These dates allow for some coregency with David, indicated in the narrative by Solomon being anointed king before David's death.

Solomon is depicted as the ruler whose reign continued the era of peace and prosperity that David had inaugurated and who constructed the Temple in Jerusalem, where worship was carried out until its destruction by the Babylonians in 586 BCE. Because David's conquests had brought peace to the region (see Figure 14.3 on page 216), no military activities are reported during Solomon's reign until its end, when there were signs that Israel's control over its subject states was weakening and the northern part of the kingdom was becoming restive (1 Kings 11.14–40). That peace also enabled the extension of trade. Much of this trade was with the Phoenician city-state of Tyre, Israel's close ally to the north, which provided both raw materials and technical expertise for Solomon's building projects. Solomon is also reported to have joined Hiram, the king of Tyre, in exploiting the lucrative Red Sea trade route, with Hiram providing nautical expertise and Solomon the financing as well as the port of Ezion-geber in his own territory; this maritime venture was unusual for the ancient Israelites. The visit of the queen of Sheba, a region in southwestern Arabia, should be understood as related to this trade. Commerce in horses and chariots is also reported with Asia Minor (1 Kings 10.26–29).

This trade, along with the tribute from the vassal states that bordered Israel and taxes in kind collected internally, brought great wealth to the capital city and enabled Solomon to finance extensive building projects in Jerusalem and elsewhere. Principal among these public works was the construction of a royal quarter in Jerusalem. Solomon expanded the city of David to the north, doubling its size and constructing a royal quarter,

an elaborate complex that included residences for the king and his wives, administrative buildings, and the Temple (see Figure 15.1).

Archaeological evidence from the early first millennium BCE provides parallels not only for the plan of the **Temple of Solomon**, with its innermost chamber reserved for the deity and the priests, but also for its incorporation into a royal complex, which was considerably larger than the Temple. Other finds also illustrate many details of its construction (see Figure 15.2). The scale is important to keep in mind. The Temple's footprint was just 30 by 100 ft (9 by 30 m). Even with its expansion under Solomon, Jerusalem was a city of only about 25 acres (10 hectares) with some 5,000 inhabitants, and the population of the kingdom as a whole was probably less than 100,000. The grandiose descriptions, then, can give a misleading impression. Israel under Solomon was the most important of the several small states in the immediate region, controlling trade routes and neighboring kingdoms. This brought relatively great wealth into the city, but it was still a provincial backwater in comparison to the larger capitals of Egypt and Mesopotamia. And when these powers moved to reassert their control over the Levant, Israel was no match. This began soon after Solomon's death, when the Egyptian Pharaoh Shishak invaded Palestine (see page 236).

According to 1 Kings 9.15, Solomon built not only the Temple and his palace but also the wall of Jerusalem and the strategically situated cities of Hazor, Gezer, and Megiddo. Although the dates for the archaeological strata in question are disputed, a majority of scholars agree that gates and attached city walls with the same plan at the latter three sites were constructed in the tenth century BCE and can plausibly be interpreted as evidence of centralized planning by Solomon's administration. Other important cities were also fortified during the tenth century, further evidence for the centralization that occurred during the reigns of David and Solomon. The broad outline of the narrative, then, is historically correct, and many details in it are supported by archaeological data.

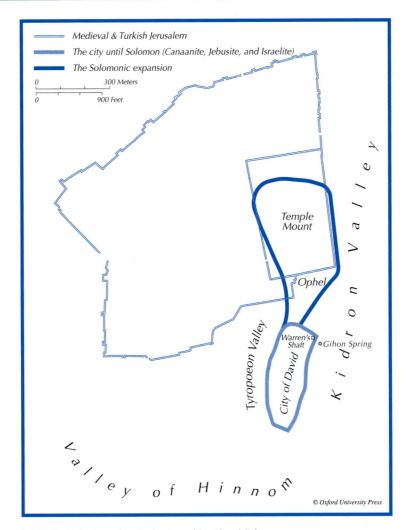

FIGURE 15.1   Jerusalem in the time of David and Solomon.

Institutions

Royal Administration

Comparing the list of Solomon's officials (1 Kings 4.1–6) with those of David (see pages 216–17) is instructive. The first position is that of the priest, reflecting the increased importance of the religious establishment when the Temple had been built. The chief priest is Azariah, the son of Zadok, whose father had been appointed by David and who had supported Solomon against Adonijah. The second position is held by "secretaries," probably because of the increased record-keeping required for the administration of the kingdom. Next comes the "recorder," Jehoshaphat, who had served in the same capacity under David. The position of army commander has moved from first to fourth position, perhaps because David's military successes over Israel's near neighbors had made the army less important. This position is held by Benaiah, who had supported Solomon's accession and who had been the head of David's bodyguards; he replaced Joab, who had sided with Adonijah and whom Solomon had had killed. Farther down the list are two sons of Nathan, one "over the officials" and another serving both as "priest and king's friend," the latter title

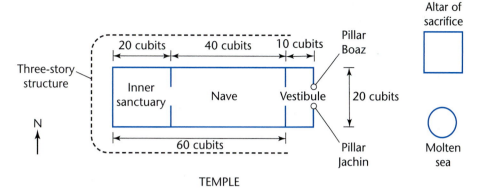

FIGURE 15.2   Plan of the Temple of Solomon as described in 1 Kings 6 (1 cubit = 1.5 ft [.45 m]).

probably meaning a close royal advisor; if their father is Nathan the prophet, this shows his continuing influence in the court, although he himself is not mentioned after the account of Solomon's coronation. Last is an official in charge of the palace and another in charge of the forced labor; the latter, Adoniram, is probably the same person as Adoram, who held this post under David and continued to do so under Solomon's successor Rehoboam (1 Kings 12.18). In this administrative structure, the king was the apex of authority, with political, military, and religious officials under his direct control.

According to 1 Kings 4.7–19, the kingdom was divided into twelve districts, excluding Judah, with an official appointed for each district to collect provisions for the royal court (see Figure 15.3 on page 228). Two of these district officials were married to daughters of Solomon, indicating the close ties between the officials and the king. The districts in the list only partially correspond to the old tribal boundaries, reflecting changes in the administration of the kingdom that replaced the old tribal divisions; now the economic resources of those districts were to be under direct royal control. The census undertaken by David may have been the first step in the creation of these districts. The omission of Judah from the list of districts may be significant: in the breakup of the kingdom that followed Solomon's death, the northern tribes claimed that their burden was excessive (1 Kings 12.4); Judah may have been administered separately, with an advantageous status.

Religion

Like his predecessors Saul and David, Solomon is described as personally offering sacrifices. This occurs first at "the principal high place" at Gibeon, not far to the northwest of Jerusalem (1 Kings 3.3–4). The worship at "high places" was generally unacceptable to the Deuteronomistic Historians, since it violated the principle of centralized worship in Jerusalem and often involved worship of other deities (see 1 Kings 11.7). It is probably not condemned in this case because the Temple had not yet been built.

The Temple

The prominence of the Temple in 1 Kings 5–8 reflects the Deuteronomistic insistence that there was only one legitimate place for the worship of Yahweh: the city that he had chosen, Jerusalem, and the Temple that he had commanded, or at least allowed, to be built. Its importance is indicated by the formal introduction to the account of the Temple's construction, which connects it with the Exodus: "In the four hundred eightieth year after the Israelites came out of the land of Egypt, in the fourth year of Solomon's reign over Israel . . . he began to build the house of the LORD" (1 Kings 6.1; the actual chronology is questionable). The importance of the Temple for the Deuteronomistic Historians is indicated further by the detailed descriptions of the Temple (1 Kings 6) and of its furnishings (1 Kings 7.13–51). Moreover, the descriptions are consistent with those found both in 2 Chronicles 3–4 (which, to be sure, uses

FIGURE 15.3   The dotted lines show the administrative districts of Solomon's kingdom (1 Kings 4.7–19).

1 Kings as a source, but did not copy it slavishly and has some independent details) and in Ezekiel 40–42, Ezekiel's plan for a restored Temple. We have, in other words, three separate witnesses to the particulars of the Temple, which served as the center of worship in Jerusalem for nearly four centuries.

We can thus be fairly sure what the Temple looked like. Many details of the building itself and of its furnishings are paralleled in archaeological discoveries from the Levant, just as much of the symbolism is derived from the Canaanite mythology that informed the ideology of the Davidic monarchy (see following), with few roots in older premonarchic tradition. Note especially the enormous "molten sea," a bronze basin some 15 feet (3.7 m) in diameter, which symbolized the primeval cosmic waters of chaos, and the twelve bronze bulls that supported the sea. These bulls, like the "lions, oxen, and cherubim" on the ten bronze stands (1 Kings 7.29), are inconsistent with the Decalogue's prohibition of the making of "graven images" (Ex 20.4). The live trees planted in the Temple's courtyard (see Pss 52.8; 92.12–13) and the architectural ornamentation representing palms and flowers (1 Kings 6.29) recalled the myth of the garden of Eden, the garden of God that was also a Canaanite tradition. The same is true of the cherubim, both those carved on the walls, doors, and stands and also the gigantic cherubim over the ark. Even if there were cherubim in some form associated with the ark in the premonarchic period, which some scholars question, those in the Temple were constructed specially for that purpose by Solomon. Made of solid wood and overlaid with gold, they were 15 ft (4.5 m) high and had a wingspan of the same distance and were certainly not portable. (For illustrations of the details of the Temple, see the color section following page 220.)

The priests and temple personnel were royal appointees, and maintenance of the Temple was a royal function. The king himself offered sacrifice at least occasionally. The Temple and its furnishings, then, were the manifestation of a state religion.

THE IDEOLOGY OF THE DAVIDIC MONARCHY

The influence of the Davidic monarchy on the formation of biblical traditions was considerable, not surprisingly given its more than four-hundred-year duration. A major part of this influence is what can be called the "**royal ideology**," a cluster of concepts that both derived from and supported and shaped the institution of the monarchy. Because of the complex nature of biblical traditions, we have no single explicit formulation of the royal ideology as such, but aspects of it are found throughout the Bible, especially in the historical books, the prophets, and the Psalms. Each of these sources has its own literary history, and so a synthesis runs the risk of collapsing what were often separate and even inconsistent perspectives. But because the royal ideology is so pervasive, it is appropriate to summarize its main features here.

The king was chosen by God, with whom he had a special relationship described by the metaphor of sonship. The divine oracle in 2 Samuel 7 speaks of David's successor in this way: "I will be his father, and he will be my son" (v. 14). The language of divine sonship is not to be understood literally; it represents an appropriation of the ancient Israelite and broader Near Eastern family structure in order to present the king as a divinely chosen heir. Using the familial metaphor expressed a special and mutual relationship of obligation between deity and monarch; as we have seen (page 102), the father-son metaphor is used to describe the relationship of suzerain to vassal.

The father-son metaphor also occurs in Psalm 2, whose genre is a coronation hymn. After a quotation of a divine proclamation—"I have set my king on Zion, my holy hill"—the king speaks:

> I will tell of the decree of Yahweh:
> He said to me, "You are my son;
>   today I have begotten you." (v. 7)

The "decree" is proclaimed on the day the king is crowned, the day that, by adoption as it were, the king becomes a son of God by virtue of his becoming king. The same idea probably also lies behind Isaiah 9.1–7, in which, again on the day of coronation, the members of the divine council celebrate the addition of a new member:

> For unto us a child is born,
>   unto us a son is given. (Isa 9.6 [KJV])

Another model used for the relationship between God and the king was that of covenant: In this contractual metaphor, God committed himself to the Davidic dynasty. This **Davidic covenant** was probably at first conditional:

> If your sons keep my covenant
>   and my decrees that I shall teach them,
> their sons also, forevermore,
>   shall sit on your throne. (Ps 132.12)

But soon the agreement came to be expressed in unconditional terms:

> When he commits iniquity, I will punish him with a rod such as mortals use, with blows inflicted by human beings. But I will not take my steadfast love from him, as I took it from Saul, whom I put away from before you. Your house and your kingdom shall be made sure forever before me; your throne shall be established forever. (2 Sam 7.14–16)

The covenant that guaranteed the dynasty became an "everlasting covenant" (2 Sam 23.5). Moreover, God had chosen Jerusalem as his home, as he had chosen the dynasty, and both would endure forever.

The language of sonship and of eternal covenant was nothing less than a revolution in ancient Israel's self-understanding, a deliberate effort to replace the premonarchic formulation of the relationship between Israel as a whole and its God. In the older system, Israel itself was God's son (Ex 4.22), and its relationship with God was direct; in the newer royal ideology, the king was the essential mediator between God and people. In Psalm 72, significantly one of only two biblical psalms attributed to Solomon, the prosperity of the nation and of its crops was linked with the king's rule, rather than with the conduct of the people as in the Ten Commandments (Ex 20.12) and in the blessings and curses associated with the Sinai covenant (Lev 26.3–45; Deut 28). This interposition of the

king between God and people was made concrete in the plan of Jerusalem in Solomon's expansion of the city: The palace complex was sited between the Temple and the city proper, where the populace lived (see Figure 15.1).

Moreover, the covenant between Israel and God was conditional: Israel's prosperity depended on continued obedience to the stipulations of the covenant (see Ex 19.5). But the Davidic covenant was unconditional: God guaranteed the continuation of the dynasty in perpetuity, without regard for the kings' conduct.

Symptomatic of the substitution by the Davidic covenant of the Sinai covenant is how in the royal ideology Mount **Zion**—a frequent poetic term for Jerusalem—replaces Mount Sinai as the locus of revelation:

> Out of Zion, the perfection of beauty,
>   God shines forth. . . .
> before him is a devouring fire,
>   and a mighty tempest all around him.
>   (Ps 50.2–3)

And, in a remarkable shift, it is from Zion, not Sinai, that "instruction" (*torah*) comes (Isa 2.3).

Given its importance in Pentateuchal traditions, it is also remarkable that Sinai (or Horeb, the alternate name of the mountain of the revelation to Moses) is mentioned only nine times outside the Pentateuch. Its disappearance from the literature concerning the period of the monarchy parallels that of the ark of the covenant. Bringing the ark to Jerusalem had served to legitimize David's kingship: Yahweh was with David (2 Sam 7.3) in a very real sense because David had brought the ark to the capital; the ark had been, so to speak, co-opted. And the ark, the visible sign of the divine presence, made the Temple Yahweh's home. But once installed in the innermost chamber of the Temple, the ark was virtually forgotten. In the Psalms, many of which were hymns used in worship at the Temple, the ark is referred to only once, in the account of its recovery by David (Ps 132.8). Nor is the ark mentioned in any of the prophets except in Jeremiah 3.16, which tellingly says: "It shall not come to mind, it shall not be remembered." Apart from the ark itself, the architecture, ornamentation, and rituals of the Jerusalem Temple had few links with earlier Israelite tradition.

A major purpose of the royal ideology was religious and political centralization. Premonarchic Israel had been decentralized, a loose confederation of tribes united by commitments to worship Yahweh alone and to mutual support. The unifying symbol of the confederation had been the ark of the covenant, a moveable object understood both as the footstool for the invisible god and as the container for the tablets of the covenant that expressed the tribes' commitments. The permanent installation of the ark in the Temple marked a shift from a decentralized to a centralized system of religious observance. Royal control of the rituals of the kingdom was part of the larger program of political centralization. The palace complex was the seat of government, and associated with it was a priesthood and an aristocracy, which often thrived by exploitation of those it ruled.

In the royal Judean ideology, then, deity, king, and city were linked; Yahweh proclaims: "I will defend this city to save it, for my own sake and for the sake of my servant David" (Isa 37.35). The plan of Jerusalem as expanded by Solomon reflected this ideology, as did many details of the Temple's design. The two pillars flanking the entrance to the Temple had the symbolic names of Jachin and Boaz: God had chosen to make his home in the dynastic Temple in Jerusalem, and he would establish it (Jachin) with his strength (Boaz) forever.

The ideology of the Davidic monarchy was a particular Israelite expression of a widespread Near Eastern understanding of kingship. The immediate source of the ideology can only be conjectured. One possibility is that it came from Tyre. The Phoenicians of Tyre were direct descendants of the second-millennium BCE Canaanites; their chief deities were originally Canaanite, and they inherited other aspects of religion and social and political concepts as well. The king of Tyre, Hiram, was an ally of both David and Solomon, and he supplied raw materials and specialists for the construction of the Temple. The plan of the Temple followed a typical Canaanite design and has close parallels from Syria. Many of the details of the Temple furnishings are also paralleled in Phoenician art. It is likely, then, that Phoenician—originally Canaanite—concepts and formulations lie behind the royal ideology of the Davidic monarchy.

Of interest in this connection is the identification in Psalm 48.2 of Mount Zion as "the heights of Zaphon," the home of the Canaanite storm-god Baal, which was located on the northern coast of Syria. The alternate translation of "the heights of Zaphon" as "in the far north" obscures the reference to Baal's home but also implies a Canaanite background, for Jerusalem is not a northern city in any ordinary geography.

Some influence may have come from the Canaanite sacred traditions of Jerusalem itself, which until its capture by David had not been part of Israel. One clue is the name of David's priest Zadok. His genealogy is inconsistently presented in different sources; apparently he was not from one of the main priestly families, although later writers did connect him with Aaron (see 1 Chr 6.1–8), which may be a legitimation after the fact. It is possible that Zadok was a priest of the Jebusite city (see pages 217–18) whom David appointed as one of his priests and whose family eventually became the most prominent of the groups of priests attached to the Temple. Under this hypothesis Zadok would have been one source for the royal ideology, which took hold so rapidly in the United Monarchy.

The most sustained treatment of the royal ideology is found in Psalm 89. In its final form, it dates either to the end of the monarchy or to the exilic period, but it incorporates much older traditions. It begins with an introduction (vv. 1–4) giving its main theme: praise of Yahweh, especially for his covenant with David. Then follows a section (vv. 5–18) praising Yahweh as the head of the council of the gods, the one who, like Marduk in *Enuma Elish* and Baal in Canaanite tradition (see pages 93–94 and 32–35), destroyed the primeval sea, and then, like Marduk, created the world.

The psalm continues the praise with a section describing the divine choice of David as ruler (vv. 19–37). David is guaranteed defeat of all his enemies, he is the firstborn son of Yahweh, and he shares the divine task of keeping the watery forces of chaos in check. Moreover, the king's rule is confirmed by an unconditional and eternal covenant.

This psalm is remarkable for what may be called its high mythology. Also remarkable is what is missing: No reference is made to any of

Box 15.2 THE ROYAL IDEOLOGY IN LATER TRADITIONS

Even after the end of the Davidic dynasty in 586 BCE, the royal ideology played an important role in later Jewish and Christian traditions. Both the Essenes, in the Dead Sea Scrolls (see Box 1.2 on page 6), and the earliest Christians, in the New Testament, applied the language of divine sonship to a future leader or messiah.

The term "**messiah**" itself is derived from royal titulature. In Israel, as elsewhere in the ancient Near East, objects and persons whose function or office brought them especially close to the divine were smeared with oil. Kings, priests, and at least occasionally prophets were anointed, and in the Hebrew Bible, the term "anointed one" (Hebr. *mashiah*, transliterated into English as "messiah") is used only of past or present leaders. Both Saul (1 Sam 24.6; 2 Sam 1.14) and David (2 Sam 19.21; 23.1) are called "the anointed of Yahweh," and the title is also used to refer to kings in general elsewhere.

In Hellenistic Judaism, the term "messiah" was applied to a future leader sent by God to restore autonomy to Israel, whose rule would inaugurate an era of peace and prosperity like that enjoyed under David. Earlier texts were reinterpreted to describe this future leader. So the anointed one, the "messiah," was to be a descendant of David, fulfilling the promise of an eternal dynasty to David in 2 Samuel 7.16, and like David, he would be born in Bethlehem (see Mic 5.2).

The early Christians believed that Jesus was this messiah. One of the titles used for him was "Christ," from the Greek word *christos*, which was originally simply a translation of Hebrew *mashiah*, "anointed one." They also made use of biblical traditions in their formulations of that belief. So Jesus was born in Bethlehem, David's home town, was called "son of David," and, like the Davidic kings, was "son of God."

The royal ideology also survives in the hope for a restored, or new, Jerusalem, in which the promises attached to the city would be fulfilled. In Western political theory, the concept of "the divine right of kings" is based in part on the biblical precedent of the Davidic monarchy.

---

the individuals or events of Israel's history—the ancestors, Moses, the Exodus, the Sinai covenant, the ark—that are so central in the Pentateuchal narratives. When the Israelites asked Samuel for a king, they requested a king "like all nations" (1 Sam 8.5), and that is what they got: a dynastic monarchy whose ideology was essentially Canaanite, only slightly connected with Israel's earlier traditions.

There was resistance to the royal ideology, although it is usually expressed subtly. Opposition

to the building of the Temple found in 2 Samuel 7.5–7 (see pages 217–18) may have prevented David from building the Temple himself. Noteworthy in that passage is Yahweh's expressed preference for a tent rather than a house of cedar: In Ugaritic myth, a house of cedar is built for Baal after his defeat of Sea and his installation as king of the gods. This implicitly criticizes overly close identification of Yahweh and Baal. Opposition to the royal ideology would be developed and expanded as time went on by several prophets.

Themes of the J tradition in the primeval history can be also read as implicit criticism of the royal ideology. In the tale of the garden of Eden (Gen 2–3), in the mythic fragment concerning the marriages of the sons of God and human women (6.1–4), and in the story of the tower of Babel (11.1–9), J stresses that an uncrossable boundary between the divine and the human exists and that any attempt to breach that boundary will be met with punishment. The tower of Babel narrative itself can be interpreted on one level as a condemnation of the building of the Temple.

The attitude of the Deuteronomistic Historians toward the royal ideology of the David monarchy is decidedly ambivalent. While the repeated theme of the book of Judges—"In those days there was no king in Israel: everyone did what was right in their own eyes"—has a kind of wistful nostalgia for an earlier time, the space devoted by the Deuteronomistic Historians to the rise of the monarchy in 1 Samuel and to its four-hundred-year history in 2 Samuel and 1 and 2 Kings reveals a much more complex understanding. On the one hand, under the monarchy the nation as a whole and particularly its rulers failed to live up to the primary requirement of the law given by God to Moses as the Deuteronomistic Historians understood it: exclusive worship of Yahweh. Yet the religious centralization introduced by David and Solomon and later renewed by King Hezekiah in the late eighth century BCE and King Josiah in the late seventh was in agreement with the insistence of the book of Deuteronomy on worship only at a central sanctuary. And the repeated praise of David, Hezekiah, and Josiah by the Deuteronomistic Historians indicates that for them not all kings were bad. Still, one of the unifying threads throughout Deuteronomy and the entire Deuteronomistic History from Joshua to the end of 2 Kings is a pattern of sin and punishment, a pattern that, especially from the perspective of the destruction of Jerusalem in 586 BCE, calls into question the claim of the Davidic monarchy to have an unconditional and eternal covenant. For the Deuteronomistic Historians, the Davidic monarchy was responsible for its own destruction, even if its claims to be divinely chosen had some merit. Thus, while recognizing the divine choice of the house of David, the Deuteronomistic Historians still maintained the priority of the Sinai covenant.

A LOOK BACK AND AHEAD

Like the entire Deuteronomistic History, the account of Solomon's reign is informed by the perspective of hindsight. This is especially evident in Solomon's final prayer at the dedication of the Temple, which refers to the Temple's destruction and to exile. Those events are interpreted by the latest stage of the Deuteronomistic History as fully deserved punishment for failure to observe the requirements of the law of Moses, a failure of which Solomon was especially guilty. Although he was the builder of the Temple, he "did not observe what the LORD had commanded" (1 Kings 11.10).

The book of Deuteronomy has only one passage dealing with kingship, the "law of the king," which states:

> [The king] must not acquire many horses for himself, or return the people to Egypt in order to acquire more horses, since the LORD has said to you, "You must never return that way again." And he must not acquire many wives for himself, or else his heart will turn away; also silver and gold he must not acquire in great quantity for himself.

The reign of Solomon as presented by the Deuteronomistic Historians is the principal example of failure to live up to this ideal; indeed, the prohibitions expressed in Deuteronomy seem to be based on Solomon's rule, which for the Deuteronomistic Historians was a moral disaster despite its accomplishments. Immediately after Solomon's death, the United Monarchy came to an end and was replaced by two separate kingdoms, Israel in the north and Judah in the south; the Deuteronomistic Historians understood this division as divine punishment.

IMPORTANT NAMES AND TERMS

Each name or term is defined briefly in the Glossary. Its first significant occurrence in this chapter appears in **boldface** type.

Davidic covenant

messiah

royal ideology

Solomon

Temple of Solomon

Zion

QUESTIONS FOR REVIEW

1. Discuss the ways in which religion and politics were intertwined in architecture and plan of Solomonic Jerusalem.

2. What were the strengths and weaknesses of Solomon's reign?

3. Describe the "royal ideology" and how it differed from the older, premonarchic views of the Israelite confederation.

BIBLIOGRAPHY

A good short commentary on 1 Kings is P. Kyle McCarter, Jr., "1 Kings," pp. 305–22 in *Harper's Bible Commentary* (ed. J. L. Mays; San Francisco: Harper & Row, 1988). For a longer commentary, see Mordechai Cogan, *1 Kings* (New York: Doubleday, 2000).

In addition to the essay by Meyers (see the bibliography to Chapter 13), for a summary of Solomon's career see Tomoo Ishida, "Solomon," pp. 105–13 in *Anchor Bible Dictionary*, Vol. 6 (ed. D. N. Freedman; New York: Doubleday, 1992).

For a summary of ancient Israel's views of kingship and monarchy in its ancient Near Eastern context, see

Marc Zvi Brettler, "King, Kingship," pp. 505–12 in *The New Interpreter's Dictionary of the Bible*, Vol. 3 (ed. K. D. Sakenfeld; Nashville, TN: Abingdon, 2008).

For a discussion of the Solomonic Temple and archaeological parallels to its features, see Elizabeth Bloch-Smith, " 'Who Is the King of Glory?' Solomon's Temple and Its Symbolism," pp. 18–31 in *Scripture and Other Artifacts: Essays on the Bible and Archaeology in Honor of Philip J. King* (ed. M. D. Coogan et al.; Louisville, KY: Westminster John Knox, 1994).

The Divided Kingdoms of Israel and Judah from the Late Tenth to the Early Eighth Centuries BCE

1 Kings 12–2 Kings 14
with an Introduction to Prophecy

As the book of Kings continues, the Deuteronomistic Historians narrate in varying degrees of detail the parallel histories of the two kingdoms that followed the United Monarchy that had flourished under David and Solomon. These were the **northern kingdom of Israel**, ruled by a succession of dynasties until its conquest by the Assyrians in 722 BCE, and the **southern kingdom of Judah**, ruled by the Davidic dynasty until its conquest by the Babylonians in 586 BCE. The Deuteronomistic Historians were writing in Judah after the fall of the northern kingdom, and their presentation of that kingdom is almost entirely negative. Moreover, their history of the divided kingdoms is highly selective. The reigns of some kings are treated only briefly, while considerable space is devoted to material that coincided with the ideological perspective of the Deuteronomistic Historians. In this chapter we will focus on the history of the divided kingdoms in the late tenth and ninth centuries BCE. The Deuteronomistic Historians also devoted considerable space to the activities of prophets, especially Elijah and Elisha, and in this chapter we will discuss the phenomenon of prophecy in detail.

HISTORY

Biblical Sources

The primary source for the history of Israel during the period of the Divided Monarchy is the Deuteronomistic Historians' account in the books of Kings. These historians in turn relied on earlier sources, including:

- *Royal annals*: In the concluding formulas for the reigns of almost all of the rulers of Israel and Judah, references are made to the "book of the days of the king of Israel [or: Judah]." The royal annals no longer survive, but they presumably resembled such chronicles known from other cultures, especially Assyria and Babylonia.

- *Prophetic legends*: Throughout the books of Kings, the Deuteronomistic Historians incorporate into their narrative folk tales concerning prophets, probably originally oral.

In organizing their narrative, the Deuteronomistic Historians used a dominant theme: the obligation of Israel to observe the requirements of the teaching of Moses, especially the worship of Yahweh alone. Failure to do so inevitably resulted in divinely imposed punishments, and that is how the Deuteronomistic Historians interpret internal and external events in the histories of the kings of Israel and Judah.

That interpretation of historical events as divinely controlled is often expressed in the books of Kings by prophets, and prophetic predictions of doom and their fulfillment punctuate the narrative, providing a running commentary on it. Most of the prophetic judgments have to do with the northern kingdom of Israel. From the perspective of the Deuteronomistic Historians, writing originally in Jerusalem, the capital of the southern kingdom of Judah, the northern kingdom was irrevocably contaminated by the "sins of Jeroboam," its first king, a phrase that is used more than a dozen times between 1 Kings 14.16 and 2 Kings 15.28. Closely related to this negative assessment of the northern kingdom are repeated positive statements about the Davidic dynasty in Jerusalem.

Nonbiblical Evidence

By the late tenth century BCE, direct correlations begin to occur between the Bible and other ancient Near Eastern texts. To some extent this is ominous: The more frequently Israel and Judah and their rulers are mentioned in nonbiblical records means that they were being more threatened by the great powers to their north and south, as well as by their more immediate neighbors. By the late tenth century BCE, the Assyrians in northern Mesopotamia had resumed their drive toward imperial conquest of the entire Near East, and Egypt also had regained some of its power. Israel and Judah were caught between the two.

The earliest direct correlation between biblical and nonbiblical sources concerns the invasion of Palestine and Transjordan by the Egyptian pharaoh Shishak (Shoshenq I) in the late tenth century BCE. According to 1 Kings 14.25, in the fifth year of Rehoboam, Solomon's successor as king of Judah,

Shishak "came up against Jerusalem . . . and took away the treasures of the house of the Lord and the treasures of the king's house." Second Chronicles 12.4 adds other details, including that Shishak captured the fortified cities of Judah. Shishak's own records list over 150 cities captured in an Asiatic campaign, including Gibeon, Mahanaim, Penuel, Taanach, and Megiddo. At Megiddo was found a fragment of a stela with Shishak's name on it, presumably part of a victory monument erected after his capture of the city. There is also archaeological evidence of the destruction of several cities in Judah in the late tenth century BCE. Why did Shishak invade Judah and Israel? Probably in an effort to reassert Egyptian sovereignty over them, taking advantage of the weakness of both immediately after their split following Solomon's death.

Shishak is the first Egyptian pharaoh named in the Bible. In narratives about earlier times, none of the pharaohs with whom Abraham, Joseph, the Israelites in Egypt, and Moses dealt is named. If the Deuteronomistic Historians had wanted to be vague here, they had ample precedent. But they are not, and so we have a direct correlation between the Bible and contemporaneous nonbiblical sources. Moreover, because our knowledge of Egyptian chronology is fairly secure, we also have an absolute date. Shishak died in 924 BCE. His Asiatic campaign is dated by the biblical historians to the fifth year of Rehoboam, who must therefore have assumed the throne no later than 928 BCE, a date that enables us to give an approximate chronology for his predecessors (see further page 203).

Three kings of Israel from the ninth and early eighth centuries BCE are named in the annals of Assyrian kings, generally as defeated or as paying tribute: Ahab, Jehu, and Jehoash. Moreover, two rulers of states neighboring Israel are mentioned both in the Bible and in nonbiblical records: Hazael, king of Aram-Damascus (2 Kings 8.15), and Mesha, king of Moab (2 Kings 3.4; see further pages 240–41).

These contemporaneous correlations and the chronological data they include confirm the historical accuracy of the broad outlines of the biblical narrative and provide a relatively secure chronology for the kings of Israel and Judah (see Box 16.1). In reconstructing the history of the Divided Monarchy, therefore, we have occasional corroborative evidence from outside the Bible, but our principal source is the Deuteronomistic Historians' narrative found in the books of Kings.

Synthesis of Biblical and Nonbiblical Sources

Much of the treatment in the books of Kings of the century and a half between the death of Solomon and the accession of Jeroboam II as king of Israel (788 BCE) is perfunctory, and so it is impossible to

Box 16.1 CHRONOLOGY OF THE LATE TENTH TO MID-EIGHTH CENTURIES BCE

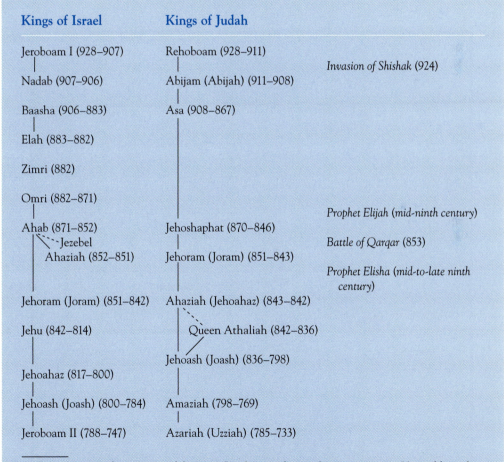

Kings of Israel	Kings of Judah	
Jeroboam I (928–907)	Rehoboam (928–911)	
		Invasion of Shishak (924)
Nadab (907–906)	Abijam (Abijah) (911–908)	
Baasha (906–883)	Asa (908–867)	
Elah (883–882)		
Zimri (882)		
Omri (882–871)		
		Prophet Elijah (mid-ninth century)
Ahab (871–852)	Jehoshaphat (870–846)	
Jezebel		*Battle of Qarqar (853)*
Ahaziah (852–851)	Jehoram (Joram) (851–843)	
		Prophet Elisha (mid-to-late ninth century)
Jehoram (Joram) (851–842)	Ahaziah (Jehoahaz) (843–842)	
Jehu (842–814)	Queen Athaliah (842–836)	
	Jehoash (Joash) (836–798)	
Jehoahaz (817–800)		
Jehoash (Joash) (800–784)	Amaziah (798–769)	
Jeroboam II (788–747)	Azariah (Uzziah) (785–733)	

Date ranges are for reigns, not life spans. Overlapping dates indicate coregencies. Vertical lines show genealogical connections. Dotted lines indicate marriage.

construct a detailed history of the events in this period. Furthermore, battles and encounters mentioned in Assyrian and other nonbiblical sources go unmentioned in the Bible, and likewise most events mentioned in the Bible are not documented elsewhere.

Following the death of Solomon, what had been a united monarchy immediately divided into two separate kingdoms, Judah in the south, ruled by Solomon's son **Rehoboam** (928–911 BCE), and Israel in the north, ruled by **Jeroboam I** (928–907 BCE), one of Solomon's officials who had rebelled against him. According to the biblical writers, the union between north and south had been fragile at best, and the fault line that divided the two opened again at Solomon's death. The reasons given by the Deuteronomistic Historians for the split are probably essentially correct. Solomon's construction of an oriental court in grand style had been paid for by high taxes and forced labor, and the northern tribes had paid more dearly than Judah. Resistance to Solomon's extravagance developed during his reign, and Rehoboam's refusal to promise reform made the break final.

From this point onward, Judah and Israel went their separate ways. Their relationship was generally one of rivals, although they were allies periodically.

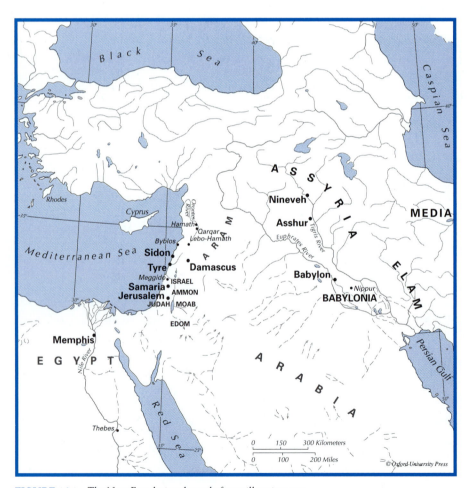

FIGURE 16.1   The Near East during the early first millennium BCE.

Israel was the larger, more populous, and more powerful of the two. Neither was able to maintain the allegiance of the neighboring kingdoms that had been under the control of David and Solomon, and these kingdoms, especially Aram-Damascus, grew in strength and made frequent incursions into Israel's territory.

The first ruler of the northern kingdom of Israel, Jeroboam I, moved quickly to solidify his control. Installed as king at the ancient tribal center of Shechem (see Box 11.1 on pages 171–72), he soon moved his capital to Penuel, another site associated with Israel's ancestral traditions (see Gen 32.30–31), and, perhaps after Shishak's withdrawal, to Tirzah, which remained the capital of the northern kingdom until Omri moved it to the city of Samaria.

Much of the space devoted by the Deuteronomistic Historians to Jeroboam's reign concerns his establishing two royal shrines, one at Bethel near the southern boundary of his kingdom and one at Dan near the northern boundary. The reason for this action is clearly stated: to discourage his subjects from worshiping in Jerusalem, the capital of the rival kingdom. It was Yahweh ("who brought you up out of the land of Egypt"—1 Kings 12.28) who was worshiped at the two shrines, enthroned on a calf following an ancient tradition. But for the Deuteronomistic Historians, this action violated the principle of a central sanctuary for all Israel and so they interpreted it as a form of idolatry. (For further discussion of the golden calf, see pages 117–19.)

Jeroboam's counterpart in Judah, Solomon's son Rehoboam, engaged in a systematic defensive buildup, fortifying major cities on his borders. This may have been in anticipation of the campaign of Shishak, and also because of repeated conflict with Jeroboam. Rehoboam was succeeded by his son Abijam (also called Abijah), and then by his grandson Asa. Asa's long reign is described in only a few verses. During it, conflict with Israel continued, and the king of Israel, Baasha, fortified the town of Ramah, just a few miles north of Jerusalem. To counter this threat, Asa formed an alliance with Ben-hadad, the king of Aram-Damascus on Israel's northeastern border. Baasha was forced to withdraw from Ramah when the Arameans attacked several cities in Israel.

The dynastic principle, that son succeeded father on the throne, which provided such stability to the southern kingdom of Judah, was never as established in the northern kingdom of Israel. In Israel, in the span of eighty-seven years from the accession of Jeroboam I (928 BCE) to that of Jehu (842 BCE), ten kings belonging to five different families ruled, and four of those ten were killed during coups (see Box 16.1 on page 237).

The dynasty of Omri, consisting of four kings during the mid-ninth century BCE, was one of the most powerful in the history of the northern kingdom. Omri moved the capital to **Samaria** (1 Kings 16.24), where he and his successor **Ahab** constructed a lavish royal city. Israel's political and economic power was enhanced by an alliance with the Phoenician kingdom of Tyre to the north, an alliance cemented by the marriage of Ahab to Jezebel, the daughter of Ethbaal, the king of Tyre. A similar marriage resulted in some Israelite control of Judah, when Athaliah, Ahab's daughter, married Jehoram, the crown prince of Judah.

During the mid-ninth century BCE, Israel and Judah were allies, often against Aram-Damascus, the northern kingdom's chief rival among the states of the region. The Deuteronomistic Historians introduce their account of the first attempt to regain control of the city of Ramoth-gilead in Transjordan with the statement "For three years Aram and Israel continued without war" (1 Kings 22.1), apparently an unusually long period of peace. According to the narrative in the books of Kings, at least ten major military encounters occurred between Israel and Aram from the reign of Ahab (871–852 BCE) to that of Jehoash (800–784 BCE), and in most of them the Arameans were victorious. During the long reign of the Aramean king Hazael (ca. 845–810 BCE) especially, the Arameans extended their control as far south as Philistia, and under the threat of a siege of Jerusalem, Jehoash the king of Judah was forced to pay tribute (2 Kings 12.17–18).

In 1993 and 1994, fragments of a stone monument with an Aramaic inscription were discovered

FIGURE 16.2 Fragments of an Aramaic inscription found at Tel Dan in northern Israel. In it, an unnamed ninth-century BCE king of Aram reports that he defeated a king of Israel and mentions the "house of David" (the highlighted words on the lower right). Carved in stone, it is 12.5 in (32 cm) high on the right.

at Dan, on Israel's northern border. (See Figure 16.2.) The inscription is dated to the mid- to late ninth century BCE and describes a defeat of Israel and Judah by an Aramean king whose name is missing, but who may be Hazael. The stela was erected at Dan as a victory monument. In it, the king attributes both his assumption of the throne and the victory to his national deity, the storm-god (Baal) Hadad, and mentions the "house of David"—the earliest nonbiblical reference to David and to the dynasty that he founded—and perhaps (the name is broken) King Ahaziah of Judah. The details of the conflict referred to in the stela do not match any biblical data.

When threatened from outside, however, the rival states of Israel and Aram could cooperate. Assyrian records describe a major battle in 853 BCE at Qarqar on the Orontes River in northern Syria between the Assyrian king Shalmaneser III and a coalition of southern forces, including contingents from Aram-Damascus and from Ahab,

king of Israel. That encounter was inconclusive, and the same coalition fought against Shalmaneser several more times. Not until 842 BCE could Shalmaneser claim victory, celebrated in the famous "Black Obelisk," which depicts Jehu, the king of Israel who had succeeded in ousting Omri's dynasty, bowing in submission as he paid tribute (see Figure 16.3). None of this is reported in the Bible; even Shalmaneser himself is unmentioned. Subsequently, payment of tribute is reported to the Assyrian king Adadnirari III (811–783 BCE) by Jehoash (Joash) of Israel; again, neither the tribute itself nor the Assyrian ruler is mentioned in the Bible.

The situation is somewhat different with an important Moabite text, the Mesha Stela, discovered in 1868 (see Figure 16.4). In it, King Mesha of Moab recounts, "Omri, king of Israel . . . oppressed Moab for many days, for Chemosh [the Moabite national deity] was angry at his land. And his son succeeded him, and also said, 'I will oppress Moab.' . . . But I triumphed over him and his house." The rest of the text describes Mesha's capture of seven thousand Israelites and of ritual objects. All of these he "devoted to destruction." The word used is the same as Hebrew *herem*, "ban" (see pages 170–72); here we see one of several close connections between Israelite and Moabite religious language and practice.

An account of the relationship between Moab and Israel in the late ninth century BCE from an Israelite perspective is found in 2 Kings 3. According to this narrative, which is part of the larger cycle of stories concerning the prophet Elisha (see pages 248–51), Ahab's son Jehoram joined forces with the king of Judah, Jehoshaphat, and the king of Edom in order to regain control over Moab from Mesha, who had stopped paying the annual tribute of 100,000 lambs and the wool of an equal number of sheep (see 2 Kings 1.1; 3.5). During the battle, the Moabites were on the verge of defeat when Mesha sacrificed his own son. "Great wrath came upon Israel," and the coalition was forced to retreat.

Both texts agree on the essentials: The northern kingdom of Israel controlled Moab for a time,

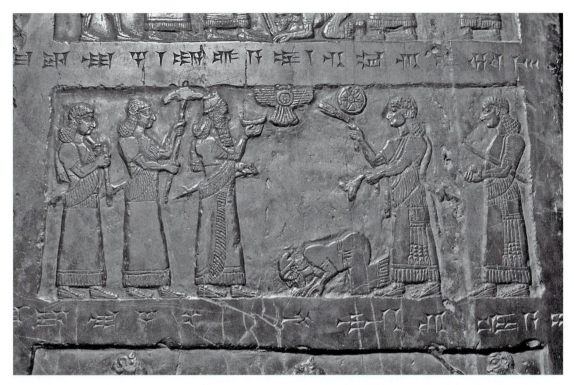

FIGURE 16.3   A panel from the "Black Obelisk" of King Shalmaneser III of Assyria, showing King Jehu of Israel bowing before Shalmaneser. Carved ca. 825 BCE, it is the only contemporaneous picture of an Israelite ruler.

but Moab successfully revolted and recovered its independence in the second half of the ninth century BCE. But it is difficult to correlate the details of the two texts, and they may be referring to different events in what must have been a lengthy struggle between Moab and Israel. Moreover, omissions remind us of the need to interpret both texts cautiously. Second Kings 3 does not mention either the capture of thousands of Israelites and much plunder or the loss of Israelite territory in Transjordan, all reported in the Mesha Stela. And the Mesha Stela does not mention either a near defeat of the Moabites or the human sacrifice that provoked the Israelites' rout.

The general picture that emerges from this spotty documentation is a time of intense rivalry and occasional cooperation between the smaller kingdoms of the southern Levant, all in the shadow of the Assyrian advance.

INSTITUTIONS AND SOCIETY

Because of the highly selective nature of the Deuteronomistic Historians' account of the history of Israel and Judah after the death of Solomon, we cannot construct a detailed picture of how primary institutions and society in general functioned during this period. Two categories, however, are worth noting.

The Army

From the very beginning of the monarchy, military leadership was often a path to political power. Both Saul and David became king in part because of their military successes, and in the northern kingdom of Israel several kings assumed power in military coups, no doubt because of their positions in

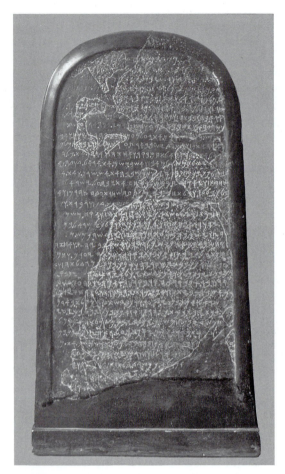

FIGURE 16.4   Stela erected by King Mesha of Moab to commemorate a victory over Israel in the mid-ninth century BCE. It is about 3.5 ft (1.1 m) high.

him. Although these appear to be round numbers and may be exaggerated, archaeological evidence confirms the importance of chariots in Israel in the ninth century BCE. At Megiddo, in a level dating to that period, excavators uncovered two complexes of pillared buildings with large open courtyards that have plausibly been identified as stables with attached chariot parks or exercise yards, with a capacity of about two hundred horses (see Figure 16.5). Similar structures are found elsewhere, and with two or three horses per chariot, Ahab could have had a chariot force numbering at least in the hundreds.

Queens and Queen Mothers

The book of Kings gives only a few glimpses of the roles of women in ancient Israel. They appear occasionally throughout the narrative, as daughters, wives, mothers, and widows. Because of the focus on kings and their deeds, the most prominent women are members of the royal families.

In the Davidic dynasty that ruled over Judah, the mother of almost every king from Rehoboam onward is named in the formulaic summary of the king's reign (see, for example, 1 Kings 14.31); by contrast, the mother's name of only one of the kings of Israel, Jeroboam I, is given. One of these women is explicitly called *gebira*, a title that literally means "powerful woman," and that is often translated as "queen mother." Concerning Maacah, the mother of King Asa of Judah, we are told that the king "removed his mother Maacah from being *gebira*, because she had made an abominable image for Asherah," the Canaanite goddess (1 Kings 15.13). This brief note suggests that the position had some status, and that the woman who held it could be removed from office.

Jezebel, the princess of Tyre who married Ahab, king of Israel, was one of the most powerful and notorious women of biblical times. As the king's consort she could manipulate local judicial processes, as in the episode of Naboth's vineyard, when she arranged for Naboth's execution on false charges (1 Kings 21.1–14). After Ahab's death, she remained a formidable power, as is clear in the account of Jehu's revolt. When Jehu approached the

the army. Thus, Baasha plotted against Jeroboam I's successor Nadab on the battlefield. His successor Elah was assassinated by Zimri, "commander of half his chariots" (1 Kings 16.9), and Zimri's seven-day rule ended when Omri, the commander of the army, was acclaimed as king on the battlefield and Zimri committed suicide (1 Kings 16.15–18). Likewise, both Jehu (2 Kings 9.5) and Pekah (2 Kings 15.25) were military officers who successfully conspired to oust the reigning king.

According to Shalmaneser III's account of the battle of Qarqar (see page 240), King Ahab of Israel contributed two thousand chariots and ten thousand infantry to the coalition that opposed

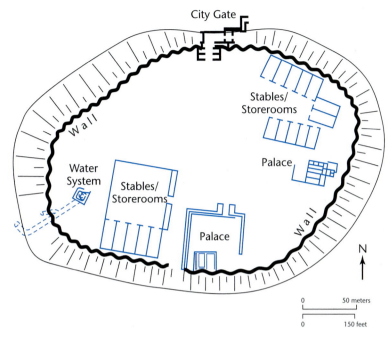

FIGURE 16.5 Plan of Megiddo during the ninth century BCE, showing two large complexes that were used as stables and probably also as storerooms.

royal residence in Jezreel, Jezebel prepared to meet him: "She painted her eyes, and adorned her head, and looked out of the window. As Jehu entered the gate, she said, 'Is it peace, Zimri, murderer of your master?'" (2 Kings 9.30–31). For the revolt to succeed, Jezebel had to be eliminated, and she was unceremoniously thrown from the window to her death. For the Deuteronomistic Historians, Jezebel is the quintessence of evil, but we may admire the courage and bravado of the queen who meets her death defiantly and in full regalia.

Another powerful woman of the monarchic period was Athaliah, a princess of the royal house of Israel (and perhaps Jezebel's daughter) who became the wife of the Judean king Jehoram and mother of his successor Ahaziah. When her son was killed during the revolt of Jehu, she assumed the throne, the only woman in Israelite history to have ruled on her own (see 2 Kings 11). She was queen over Judah for six years, but was killed during an uprising in which Jehosheba, Ahaziah's sister,

the wife of the high priest (2 Chr 22.11), and perhaps Athaliah's own daughter, played a crucial role.

Thus the king's wife and the king's mother could exercise considerable power in ancient Israel, as we have already seen in the case of Solomon's mother Bathsheba (see page 223).

PROPHETS AND PROPHECY

In most cultures from antiquity to the present, some men and women have been recognized as having the ability to interpret phenomena considered beyond ordinary human comprehension. In the ancient Near East, these phenomena included such natural occurrences as the movement of the heavenly bodies, the flight of birds, and the appearance of an animal's liver and other organs, as well as apparently random events like the casting of lots, dice, or arrows, as methods of divination.

Some of these persons also interpreted dreams or served as mediums between the living and the dead. Some had magical powers and the ability to heal and even to restore the dead to life. In most of these capacities, they functioned as intermediaries and channels of communication between the natural and the supernatural orders. Thus, random phenomena were interpreted as controlled by the gods and as containing a divinely revealed message. We see a spectrum of activities here, from the mundane to the most profound forms of communication with the divine. Such individuals are found throughout the ancient Near East, including Israel.

In one of the most widely attested forms of divination, lots were cast to give answers to questions that could be answered by either "Yes" or "No." This type of divination was used to decide on a course of action, to choose a leader, and to determine a guilty party when the material evidence was inconclusive. In ancient Israel, in addition to lots, sacred objects called the Urim and Thummim, and the ephod with which they were connected, functioned in a similar way, being thrown, perhaps like dice. They were part of priestly paraphernalia, indicating the divine role in the answer given.

Other forms of divination were also practiced in ancient Israel. The prophet Elisha, for example, instructs King Jehoash in the use of arrows as a kind of magical act to assure victory (2 Kings 13.15–19). Necromancy, the consultation of the dead, is also attested. When Saul consulted the woman of Endor, a medium, she was able to conjure up the spirit of the dead Samuel (1 Sam 28.14; see page 202). The practice of necromancy was apparently popular, as its repeated condemnation suggests.

At what we may call the high end of the spectrum of interpreters are the individuals known from the Bible as **prophets**. It is important to recognize at the outset that distinctions between prophets and other interpreters of divine will often were not sharply drawn—that is, the ancients had many ways of ascertaining the will of the god(s), and prophecy was one of them.

Like other forms of interpretation of the supernatural, prophecy is found throughout the ancient Near East. The evidence is incomplete because of the accidents of preservation and discovery, but prophets are known at Byblos in Phoenicia, at Hamath and Mari in Syria, and in Assyria, and span the period from the early second millennium to the mid-first millennium BCE. Biblical evidence also supports this picture of prophecy among Israel's neighbors. Thus, the Bible refers to "the four hundred fifty prophets of Baal and the four hundred prophets of Asherah" (1 Kings 18.19) who were part of the entourage of Jezebel, the Phoenician wife of King Ahab of Israel, and describes their activity simply as "prophesying." (The NRSV translation at 1 Kings 18.29, "they raved," is a pejorative mistranslation.)

One of the closest correlations between biblical and nonbiblical evidence concerns the prophet Balaam. According to Numbers 22, Balaam, the son of Beor, is a Syrian diviner hired by the king of Moab to curse Israel. But he is a true prophet who speaks the word that has been revealed to him, blessing for Israel and destruction of its enemies. He is one "who hears the words of El [NRSV: God], who sees the vision of Shadday [NRSV: the Almighty]" (Num 24.4). He receives his revelations in some sort of a trance, often at night, like the prophets Samuel (1 Sam 3.3) and Nathan (2 Sam 7.4). While the entire portrait of Balaam is colored by the biblical writers' experience of prophecy in Israel, the essential aspects of the depiction of Balaam in the Bible are also found in the eighth-century BCE Deir Alla texts. In them, the "seer" Balaam, the son of Beor as in the Bible, receives a vision from El at night that reveals a disaster decreed by the "Shaddayin," who are members of the divine council. (See further pages 143–44.)

Like similar specialists in other ancient and modern cultures, prophets could employ unusual techniques. One involves music. In 2 Kings 3, King Jehoram is leading a coalition against Moab, and on their march they are without water. Elisha is summoned, and he says, "Get me a musician." The text continues: "And then, while the musician was playing, the power of the Lord came on him" (2 Kings 3.15). The band of prophets with whom Saul has two encounters also uses music. When they "prophesy" (the NRSV translation "fell into a prophetic frenzy" is misleading), these prophets

Box 16.2 PROPHETS IN LATER TRADITIONS

Prophecy continued to be important in the later developments of the monotheistic traditions, especially in Christianity and Islam. Throughout the Gospels both John the Baptist and Jesus are identified as prophets, and in earliest Christianity prophecy was a recognized, and sometimes criticized, phenomenon. The book of Revelation, as its name implies, is the account of a vision by John while he "was in the spirit on the Lord's day" (Rev. 1.10). In subsequent Christian history, many individuals have identified themselves as recipients of divinely revealed messages. Notable examples are Nostradamus, Joseph Smith (the founder of The Church of Jesus Christ of Latter Day Saints [the Mormons]), and, since 1870, Roman Catholic popes.

In the Qur'an, the line of those with whom God communicated begins with Adam and continues through Noah, Abraham, Isaac and Ishmael, Jacob, David, Solomon, John the Baptist, and Jesus. This parade of messengers ends with Muhammad, the last and greatest of the prophets, who received his first revelation in a cave outside of Mecca during the "night of power." As in Judaism and Christianity, some branches of Islam believe in continuing revelation to specially designated individuals.

use "harp, tambourine, flute, and lyre playing" (1 Sam 10.5) to reach an ecstatic state, a state that is contagious: Both Saul, and later his messengers, also begin prophesying, and on the second occasion, Saul strips off his clothes (1 Sam 19.23–24). Another example of unusual behavior is attributed to the prophets of Baal, who, when they prophesied, "cried aloud and . . . cut themselves with swords and lances until the blood gushed out over them" (1 Kings 18.28); compare the similar practice of self-laceration by prophets of Yahweh in Zechariah 13.4–6. These accounts of ecstatic activity should probably be connected with the symbolic actions known as "prophetic gestures" attributed to some of the classical prophets, such as Ezekiel lying on his side for 430 days (Ezek 4.4–8).

Prophets in Ancient Israel

Terminology

Not surprisingly, given the diversity of their lives and activities, various terms are used to describe Israelite prophets. The English word "prophet" comes from Greek and literally means "spokesperson." It expresses the understanding that the prophets were delivering divinely sent messages. The primary content of these messages, as we have suggested, was interpretation of phenomena and events from a divine perspective. This notion of interpretation is implicit in the use of prophetic pronouncements by the Deuteronomistic Historians in the books of Samuel and Kings as a kind of running commentary on the historical narrative, and also in the canonical division of the Bible in Jewish tradition, which groups together as the "Prophets" both the historical books (Joshua, Judges, 1 and 2 Samuel, and 1 and 2 Kings) and the books named after individual prophets (the books of Isaiah through Malachi).

The most frequently used term in the Bible is the Hebrew word *nabi'*, usually translated as "prophet." Its etymology is not entirely clear, but the most likely origin is from a word meaning "to call"; a *nabi'* is thus someone called by the deity. Another frequently used title of prophets, "man of God," expresses the same idea. That designation is used of Moses, Samuel, Shemaiah, Elijah, and Elisha; of several anonymous prophets; and, significantly, of Yahweh's messenger who announces the conception and birth of Samson to Manoah and his wife (Judg 13.6–8). The prophets, in other words, had the same status as the divine messengers (later to be designated "angels"; see Box 25.2 on page 415) who appear in biblical tales: They were spokespersons for Yahweh himself.

Modes of Revelation

How did the prophets receive their messages? Such communication must be possible, but at the same time the deity's essential otherness must be preserved. One way of dealing with this paradox is the mythological device of messengers from the divine to the human. Another is to express the mode of revelation metaphorically. The two most common metaphors in the prophetic literature are those of speech and vision. The metaphor of speech draws on the understanding of the prophets as messengers, who transmit divine words they have received to individuals, to groups, to Israel as a whole, and sometimes to other nations. The metaphor of vision is found in another title used of the prophet, that of "seer" or visionary. A "seer" transmitted to the audience a vision, a dream, or the proceedings of the divine council. That the prophet as seer was endowed with preternatural vision is shown by the story of the nearly blind Ahijah who can recognize his disguised royal visitor (1 Kings 14.4–6); the paradoxical figure of the blind seer is attested elsewhere in world cultures. Sometimes the two metaphors are explicitly combined, as in Amos 1:1: "The words of Amos . . . which he saw concerning Israel."

Types of Prophets

The phenomenon of prophecy in ancient Israel is extraordinarily diverse. Some prophets, if not most, were trained professionals who earned their livelihood as prophets. The Bible mentions groups of prophets gathered around a leader, who can be called their "father," as were both Elijah (2 Kings 2.12) and Elisha (2 Kings 13.14), and perhaps others as well. These "sons of the prophet(s)" were presumably members of a kind of guild, presided over by a master prophet who instructed his apprentices. Samuel, who is a complex figure in his own right, also is described as the leader of such a group, and Isaiah may have been one as well.

How did prophets earn their living? Some were consulted to resolve specific problems by individuals who presumably paid a fee, like Saul visiting the "seer" Samuel when he was looking for his father's missing animals (1 Sam 9.6–10). Others functioned in a ritual capacity; to these "cultic" prophets we should attribute divine responses to prayer, such as those found in some of the psalms (see page 378). It is significant that at least two prophets, Jeremiah and Ezekiel, were also priests.

Alongside the professional prophets were also amateurs. The clearest example is Amos. When the priest at Bethel ordered Amos to return to his home in Judah, Amos replied: "I am no prophet, nor a son of a prophet; but I am a herdsman, and a dresser of sycamore trees, and the Lord took me from following the flock, and the Lord said to me, 'Go, prophesy to my people Israel'" (Am 7.14–15). Amos is saying, in effect, that he is not a professional: He is not a member of a prophetic school ("a son of a prophet"), and he has his own livelihood. But he is still a prophet because of the divine call that he received. (See further page 258.)

The Relationship of Prophets and Kings

As elsewhere in the ancient Near East, in Israel prophets were closely connected with kings. In addition to the prophets of Baal and Asherah in the court of Jezebel and Ahab, we find other individuals who belonged to the royal establishment, including Nathan, Gad, Isaiah, and Jeremiah.

The phenomenon of prophecy in ancient Israel largely overlaps with the period of the monarchy. References to prophecy are relatively rare in narratives of the premonarchic period. In the Pentateuch we find only five mentions of individual prophets. We also find two prophets in the book of Judges—Deborah (Judg 4.4) and an anonymous prophet (Judg 6.8). Then, beginning with the narrative of the establishment of the monarchy, prophecy becomes more frequent. The scarcity of such references in narratives set in earlier times shows the links between prophecy and kingship, as does the decline of prophecy after the end of the monarchy, in the exilic and postexilic periods.

One of the functions exercised by prophets was to designate the divinely chosen ruler, and as such, they are frequently described as participating in coronation rituals. Thus, Samuel anointed both Saul and David, and Nathan was a coparticipant in Solomon's coronation. Likewise, Ahijah appointed Jeroboam I as the first king of the northern kingdom of Israel, and Elisha appointed Hazael as king of Aram and sent one of his associates to anoint Jehu as king of Israel, in both cases carrying out a command given to his predecessor Elijah. It is also likely that it was a prophet who announced the divine choice of the king, as in Psalm 2.7–9 and Isaiah 9.2–7. (See further pages 229–30.) At the same time, however, according to the Deuteronomistic Historians the prophets functioned not just as king-makers but also as king-breakers, being actively involved in the process of succession by communicating divine rejection of a ruler. Moreover, many prophets, even some court prophets, are depicted as independent of the kings, and they could be harshly critical of individual kings and occasionally of the entire institution of monarchy.

Women Prophets

Although most of the named prophets are men, it is clear that women were also prophets. During the period of the monarchy, the best example is the prophet Huldah (2 Kings 22.14). Other named women prophets are Miriam (Ex 15.20), Deborah (Judg 4.4), and Noadiah (Neh 6.14). Further evidence for women as prophets includes the unnamed wife of Isaiah, herself identified as a prophet (Isa 8.3). When biblical authors mention women prophets, they do not emphasize their gender or suggest that the phenomenon of women prophets was unusual.

In his vision of the "day of Yahweh" (see Box 17.2 on page 262), the prophet Joel speaks of

Yahweh pouring out his spirit on the entire population:

> Your sons and your daughters shall prophesy,
> your old men shall dream dreams,
> and your young men shall see visions.
> Even on the male and female slaves,
> in those days, I will pour out my spirit.
> (Joel 2.28–29)

In this vision of restoration, the gift of prophecy—including dreams and visions—will be universal, rather than restricted to a narrow group or a specific socioeconomic class; again, the inclusion of women is apparently unremarkable.

Micaiah

The episode of Micaiah in 1 Kings 22 illustrates several aspects of the preceding discussion. In planning an attack on Aram for its taking of the Israelite city of Ramoth-gilead, the king of Israel, who is unnamed but is probably Ahab, asks Jehoshaphat, the king of Judah, to join him. Jehoshaphat agrees but suggests that they consult the prophets to inquire for the word of Yahweh. The king of Israel summons four hundred prophets, probably court prophets, and asks them: "Shall I go up against Ramoth-gilead, or shall I refrain?" (1 Kings 22.6). Prophets were often asked this sort of question: What was the divine view of a proposed course of action? The four hundred prophets, led by Zedekiah, replied: "Go up; for the Lord will give it into the hand of the king" (1 Kings 22.6). Suspicious at this unanimity, Jehoshaphat asks if there is any other prophet who might be consulted, and in due course Micaiah arrives on the scene. He is probably an independent prophet, not a court prophet, but one frequently consulted by the king. At first he agrees with the four hundred, but when pressed delivers an ominous oracle: "I saw all Israel scattered on the mountains, like sheep that have no shepherd; and the Lord said, 'These have no master; let each one go home in peace'" (1 Kings 22.17).

Micaiah goes on to explain how it was that the other prophets gave a false prophecy:

> Therefore hear the word of the Lord: I saw the LORD sitting on his throne, with all the host of heaven standing beside him to the right and to the left of

him. And the LORD said, "Who will entice Ahab, so that he may go up and fall at Ramoth-gilead?" Then one said one thing, and another said another, until a spirit came forward and stood before the LORD, saying, "I will entice him." "How?" the LORD asked him. He replied, "I will go out and be a lying spirit in the mouth of all his prophets." Then the LORD said, "You are to entice him, and you shall succeed; go out and do it." So you see, the LORD has put a lying spirit in the mouth of all these your prophets; the LORD has decreed disaster for you. (1 Kings 22.19–23)

Micaiah claims to have been a witness to the deliberations of the divine council, in which Yahweh decided to send his prophets a false communication. Other prophets make a similar claim. Isaiah also has a vision of the divine council as it deliberates:

> In the year that King Uzziah died, I saw the Lord sitting on a throne. . . . Seraphs were in attendance above him. . . . Then I heard the voice of the Lord saying, "Whom shall I send, and who will go for us?" And I said, "Here am I; send me!" (Isa 6.1–2, 8)

Likewise, Jeremiah attacks the false prophets, challenging the source of their message:

> Thus says the LORD of hosts: Do not listen to the words of the prophets who prophesy to you; they are deluding you. They speak visions of their own minds, not from the mouth of the LORD. . . . For who has stood in the council of the LORD so as to see and to hear his word? . . . I did not send the prophets, yet they ran; I did not speak to them, yet they prophesied. But if they had stood in my council, then they would have proclaimed my words to my people. (Jer 23.16, 18, 21–22)

But this is not the situation in 2 Kings 22, where Yahweh is deliberately deceiving his own prophets. As Deuteronomy 13.1–3 indicates (see pages 151–52), it was not always easy to decide whether a prophet's words were to be followed. But, as in Deuteronomy 18.22, the authenticity of Micaiah's revelation is shown by the outcome: The king of Israel is killed in the battle.

Finally, the Micaiah episode illustrates the chronological focuses of biblical prophecy. The prophets interpreted past, present, and immediately future events, but less frequently the distant future. To understand the prophets' messages, therefore, it is essential to understand the historical contexts in which they spoke.

THE LEGENDS OF ELIJAH AND ELISHA

Beginning in 1 Kings 17, the Deuteronomistic Historians have incorporated a large amount of originally independent material concerning the two northern prophets **Elijah** and **Elisha**. This material is interspersed in the ongoing narrative and lasts until the death of Elisha in 2 Kings 13.20. The independent origin of this material is evident in several ways. Elijah enters the narrative in 1 Kings 17.1 with minimal introduction, as though he were a character already well known to the Deuteronomistic Historians' audience. Also, many of the events described are miraculous, something not characteristic of the Deuteronomistic Historians.

Elijah was active during the reign of Ahab, ruler of the northern kingdom of Israel, and his wife Jezebel (see page 242). He condemned them for idolatry and for social injustice and was forced to flee for his life. On his return, at divine command, he anointed Elisha as his successor and then was taken up into heaven in a chariot. Elisha was active during the reign of Ahab's son Jehoram but participated in the revolt of Jehu by having him anointed as king while Jehoram was still alive. In the extended narratives about both prophets, miracle stories are interspersed with accounts of their social and political activities.

The careers of the two prophets are intertwined: Elisha is Elijah's divinely designated successor, and he completes the assignments given to Elijah at Mount Horeb (1 Kings 19.15–16; see 2 Kings 8.7–15; 9.1–13). Nevertheless, the cycles of stories about them were originally separate, as is suggested by the presence of doublets in which each prophet performs a similar action. Both raise a widow's son to life (1 Kings 17.17–24; 2 Kings 4.18–37), both multiply food (1 Kings 17.14–16; 2 Kings 4.1–7; 4.42–44), both prophesy the death of Jezebel (1 Kings 21.23–24; 2 Kings 9.10), both part the waters of the Jordan with their prophet's cloak (2 Kings 2.8, 14), and both are addressed as "My father, my father" at their deaths (2 Kings 2.12; 13.14).

Many folklore motifs are found here: the extraordinary transportation of the prophet from one place to another (1 Kings 18.12) and from this life to the next (2 Kings 2.11); the almost comic use of animals (2 Kings 2.23–25); and all sorts of miracles: some mundane, such as the recovery of an axe head from the Jordan River (2 Kings 6.1–7) and the neutralizing of poison in a stew (4.38–41), others less so, including healing the sick, restoring the dead to life, and calling fire from heaven.

This folklore has been reworked by the Deuteronomistic Historians, especially in the case of the Elijah narratives. In doing so, the Historians develop several themes. One is the presentation of Elijah as a new Moses: Like Moses, Elijah parted the water (2 Kings 2.8; compare Ex 14.21), built an altar to Yahweh (1 Kings 18.32; compare Ex 24.4), was instructed by God to appoint his successor (1 Kings 19.16; compare Num 27.12–23; Deut 31.23), and ended his life east of the Jordan River (2 Kings 2.9; compare Deut 34.5).

Like Moses, too, Elijah experienced a theophany on Mount Horeb (the alternate name of Mount Sinai). Fleeing from Jezebel, Elijah spent forty days and forty nights journeying to the same mountain where Moses also spent forty days and forty nights. Elijah returned to the same cave where Moses had seen God's back: The Hebrew says literally that Elijah came to "the cave" (1 Kings 19.9)—probably referring to the "cleft in the rock" where Moses had been covered by the divine hand as God passed by (Ex 33.22). But Elijah's experience of the divine presence was different from that of Moses. When God appeared to Moses on the mountain, he did so as a storm-god, with thunder and lightning, thick cloud, fire, smoke, and earthquake (Ex 19.18; Deut 4.11–12; 5.22). The same natural phenomena are present when Yahweh appears to Elijah, but they are not manifestations of the divine presence:

> Now there was a great wind, so strong that it was splitting mountains and breaking rocks in pieces before the LORD, but the LORD was not in the wind; and after the wind an earthquake, but the LORD was not in the earthquake; and after the earthquake a fire, but the LORD was not in the fire. (1 Kings 19.11–12)

After the fire, however, was "a sound of sheer silence" (1 Kings 19.12 [NRSV; the KJV is more allusive: "a still small voice"]). In this noteworthy passage, an important point is being made: No matter how Yahweh was said to have revealed himself in the remote past, in the experience of the prophet Elijah, and of the Israelites to whom he preached, the divine was not always so dramatically accessible. Although Yahweh still brought the rain that ended the drought (1 Kings 18.1, 41–45), he no longer appeared with the power and drama of a storm-god. Rather, Yahweh revealed himself as an almost hidden God.

A second theme in the Elijah stories is the insistence on the exclusive worship of Yahweh. In the northern kingdom especially, from the Deuteronomistic Historians' perspective, worship of other deities was widespread and would have disastrous consequences. Like Joshua at Shechem (Josh 24.15), in the contest with Baal's prophets on Mount Carmel Elijah offered the assembled people a choice: "If Yahweh is God, follow him; but if Baal, follow him" (1 Kings 18.21). Elijah was a prophet in the northern kingdom of Israel, but the Israel that he called upon was the full twelve-tribe confederacy, symbolized by the altar he constructed on Mount Carmel with twelve stones. He addressed the old, premonarchic Israel whose constitution was the Sinai covenant, which required that Yahweh alone be worshiped. Appropriately, Elijah's name means "My God is Yahweh."

We see an important development here. In Israel's earlier traditions, Yahweh was the preeminent deity (see Ex 15.11; Deut 32.8), more powerful than the other gods over whom he ruled. Now those gods, and Baal in particular, are shown to be powerless. The dramatic contest between Elijah and the prophets of Baal has a satiric dimension. He urges them: "Call with a loud voice! Surely he is a god; maybe he is in a meeting, or he is relieving himself, or he is on a journey, or perhaps he is asleep and must be awakened" (1 Kings 18.27). The prophets of Baal do call on their deity, but "there was no voice, no answer, no response" (1 Kings 18.29). The only god who answers is Yahweh, "the god of Elijah" (2 Kings 2.14), and the fire from heaven that he sends shows him to be the true god.

Box 16.3 ELIJAH IN LATER TRADITIONS

Because he was taken up to heaven without dying (like Enoch in Gen 5.24), Elijah became a major figure in later Jewish and Christian literature. The book of Malachi ends with an apocalyptic prediction of Elijah's return: "Lo, I will send you the prophet Elijah before the great and terrible day of the Lord comes. He will turn the hearts of parents to their children and the hearts of children to their parents, so that I will not come and strike the land with a curse" (Mal 4.5–6; see also Sir 48.10). In subsequent Jewish and Christian tradition, the return of Elijah is expected before the coming of the Messiah in the apocalyptic end of history, "the day of the Lord." At every Passover table, a cup of wine is poured for Elijah, and the door outside is opened to see if he is there, because according to Jewish tradition, it is at Passover that Elijah will announce the coming of the Messiah. Likewise, traditionally a chair is set out for Elijah at a boy's circumcision, so that he may witness the family's observance of the ritual.

Early Christian writers identified John the Baptist as Elijah, because he heralded the coming of the Messiah, fulfilling Malachi's prophecy (see Mt 11.10). Many of the miracle stories of Jesus's ministry also are based on the Elijah narratives, including healing the sick, raising the dead, multiplying food, calling fire from heaven, and ascending to heaven.

Presented in a folkloristic context, this is a movement toward monotheism: The only god with power is Yahweh, and he is implicitly the only god. Further evidence for this developing monotheism is also found in the divine instructions to Elijah at the end of the theophany. Elijah is told to anoint three persons: Hazael, Jehu, and Elisha (1 Kings 19.15–16). As it turns out, Elijah's successor Elisha will carry out the first two commands, designating Hazael as king of Aram (2 Kings 8.13) and sending one of his servants to anoint Jehu as king of Israel (2 Kings 9.1–10). As we have seen, a prophet's designation of a new ruler, even during the lifetime of a sitting king, has precedents (see 1 Sam 16.1–13; 1 Kings 1.38–39). But with the command to anoint a new king over Aram, we enter upon a new understanding of Yahweh's role in history. For the first time, a prophet is instructed to become involved in the internal politics of a nation outside Israel. If Yahweh is the only deity, then it follows that he plays a crucial role in what goes on throughout the world. Thus, conversion to the worship of Yahweh by non-Israelites can also occur, as in the case of Naaman, the Aramean court official whom Elisha healed (2 Kings 5). This understanding of Yahweh as the "lord of history" will become more explicit in pronouncements of subsequent prophets.

To the interwoven themes of incipient monotheism and of Yahweh's rule of the world is added another that will become characteristic of the preaching of many prophets, that of social justice. The episode of Naboth's vineyard (1 Kings 20) makes this point. The abuse of royal power by Jezebel to gain control of privately owned property desired by her husband, King Ahab, was, for the Deuteronomistic Historians, a telling example of the problems with the monarchy. Among the "ways of the king" against which the prophet Samuel had warned the people when they requested a king is that "he will take the best of your fields and vineyards and olive orchards" (1 Sam 8.14). Now, some two centuries later a king takes an Israelite's vineyard through proxies, and in doing so is guilty of violating not just the social order, in which property rights were essential, but also three of the Ten Commandments, by committing false witness, murder, and expropriation of property. For these sins, the prophet Elijah proclaims the divine judgment—the destruction of the dynasty and an ignominious death for Jezebel, which are in effect the curses attached to the violation of the covenant.

A LOOK BACK AND AHEAD

Having devoted considerable space to a detailed history of the early monarchy in 1–2 Samuel and 1 Kings 1–11, the Deuteronomistic Historians move briskly through the first century and a half of the Divided Monarchy, focusing on repeated prophetic interpretations of the failures of the northern kingdom especially to observe the requirements of the teaching of Moses. In so doing, they reinforce their view that the histories of Israel and Judah, and events beyond their borders as well, are ultimately controlled by Yahweh for his own purposes.

Those events include the repeated defeats of both kingdoms by neighboring states, and although the Assyrians will not be mentioned until 2 Kings 15.19, we know from nonbiblical sources that their imperialistic ambitions were beginning to have profound effects. This will become more apparent in the eighth century BCE, as we will see in the next chapter.

IMPORTANT NAMES AND TERMS

Each name or term is defined briefly in the Glossary. Its first significant occurrence in this chapter appears in **boldface** type.

Ahab

Elijah

Elisha

Jeroboam I

Jezebel

northern kingdom of Israel

prophet

Rehoboam

Samaria

southern kingdom of Judah

QUESTIONS FOR REVIEW

1. Discuss the importance of nonbiblical records for understanding the history of Israel and Judah.

2. Describe some of the ways in which prophets in the ancient Near East and in Israel functioned.

3. What was the relationship between prophecy and kingship?

BIBLIOGRAPHY

Excellent commentaries on the books of Kings are Mordechai Cogan, *I Kings* (New York: Doubleday, 2001); and Mordechai Cogan and Hayim Tadmor, *II Kings* (New York: Doubleday, 1988). A good summary of the history of this period is Edward F. Campbell, "A Land Divided: Judah and Israel from the Death of Solomon to the Fall of Samaria," Chap. 6 in *The Oxford History of the Biblical World* (ed. M. D. Coogan; New York: Oxford University Press, 1998; available in Oxford Biblical Studies Online).

For a collection of ancient Near Eastern texts about prophets, see Martti Nissinen, *Prophets and Prophecy in the Ancient Near East* (Atlanta, GA: Society of Biblical Literature, 2003).

For an introduction to prophecy in ancient Israel, see Joseph Blenkinsopp, *A History of Prophecy in Israel* (Louisville, KY: Westminster John Knox, rev. ed., 1996); and David L. Petersen, *The Prophetic Literature: An Introduction* (Louisville, KY: Westminster John Knox, 2002).

For a summary of interpretations about the prophets Elijah and Elisha, see Robert B. Coote, "Elijah" and "Elisha," pp. 241–43 and 245–46 in *The New Interpreter's Dictionary of the Bible*, vol. 2, ed. K. D. Sakenfeld (Nashville, TN: Abingdon, 2007).

CHAPTER 17

The Northern Kingdom of Israel in the Eighth Century BCE

2 Kings 14–17, Amos, and Hosea

The eighth century BCE was a period of turmoil and change. As the Assyrians moved toward Egypt in their ambition to control the entire Near East, the northern kingdom of Israel, like many other states in the region, was absorbed into the Assyrian empire, and the independence of the southern kingdom of Judah was curtailed severely. This is the context for the prophets Amos and Hosea, and also Isaiah and Micah, who will be treated in the next chapter. Here we will focus on the northern kingdom.

HISTORY

As in the ninth century BCE, the highly selective biblical account of the history of the northern kingdom of Israel in the eighth century is supplemented by nonbiblical sources, principally Assyrian texts. Payment of tribute to the Assyrian king Tiglath-pileser III (747–727 BCE; he is sometimes called Pul in the Bible) is reported by Jehoahaz (Ahaz) of Judah, and by Menahem, Pekah, and Hoshea, three of the last four kings of Israel. Tiglath-pileser also claims that he deposed and exiled King Pekah and installed Hoshea in his

place. Assyrian sources thus provide a secure chronology for the events of the period (see Box 17.1).

The advance of the Assyrians to their west and south paused at the end of the ninth century BCE, as the Assyrians dealt with problems in other regions of their empire, and also with plagues and internal revolts. As a result, during the first half of the eighth century BCE both Israel and Judah enjoyed considerable independence and prosperity. The threat to Israel from its Aramean neighbors to the northeast diminished because of conflict between the Aramean states of Damascus and Hamath, and Judah apparently was able to regain some control over the Edomites, Ammonites, and Philistines.

In the northern kingdom of Israel, the most important ruler of the period was Jeroboam II (788–747 BCE). The Deuteronomistic Historians give his long reign only scant attention, covering it in a mere seven verses (2 Kings 14.23–29); probably because of Assyrian preoccupation elsewhere, Jeroboam is not mentioned in Assyrian sources. According to 2 Kings 14.25, he restored Israelite territory in the north and east, in Aram and Transjordan. Moreover, it was during his reign that the prophets Amos and Hosea were active, and archaeological evidence confirms the picture they provide of prosperity.

Box 17.1 CHRONOLOGY OF THE EIGHTH CENTURY BCE

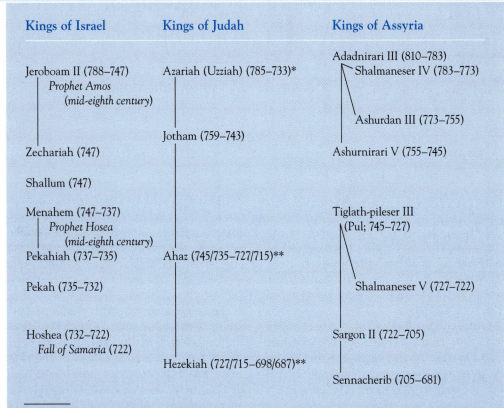

Kings of Israel	Kings of Judah	Kings of Assyria
		Adadnirari III (810–783)
Jeroboam II (788–747)	Azariah (Uzziah) (785–733)*	Shalmaneser IV (783–773)
Prophet Amos		
(mid-eighth century)		
		Ashurdan III (773–755)
	Jotham (759–743)	
Zechariah (747)		Ashurnirari V (755–745)
Shallum (747)		
Menahem (747–737)		Tiglath-pileser III
Prophet Hosea		(Pul; 745–727)
(mid-eighth century)		
Pekahiah (737–735)	Ahaz (745/735–727/715)**	
Pekah (735–732)		Shalmaneser V (727–722)
Hoshea (732–722)		Sargon II (722–705)
Fall of Samaria (722)		
	Hezekiah (727/715–698/687)**	
		Sennacherib (705–681)

Date ranges are for reigns, not life spans. Vertical lines show genealogical connections.

* During the last decades of Uzziah's reign he was quarantined because of serious illness, and his son Jotham and then his grandson Ahaz were corulers with him.

** The data are inconsistent for the chronology of the reigns of Ahaz and Hezekiah.

Illustrative are some remains from Samaria, the capital of the northern kingdom of Israel founded by Omri in the ninth century BCE, especially a collection of more than two hundred fragments of carved ivories that were used as a decorative veneer on walls and furniture (see Figure 17.3 on page 261). At Samaria we have only the ivories, not the walls or furniture, and although their precise archaeological context is no longer recoverable, evidence from elsewhere in the ancient Near East enables us to understand their function and to date them on art-historical grounds to the ninth and eighth centuries. Ornate architectural fragments also testify to the luxury that characterized Samaria.

All this changed in 745 BCE when a usurper, Tiglath-pileser III, assumed the throne of Assyria and swiftly resumed the Assyrian drive toward

FIGURE 17.1   Impression of a seal inscribed in Hebrew "Belonging to Shema, the servant of Jeroboam." The original seal, which was about 1 in (2.7 cm) high, was elegantly engraved and dates to the reign of Jeroboam II, king of the northern kingdom of Israel in the mid-eighth century BCE.

Egypt. As he moved south, he exacted tribute from many of the kings of the region, including Menahem of Israel, making them his vassals. He also continued the practice of his predecessors, going back to the thirteenth century BCE, deporting significant numbers of the populace of the conquered territories to multiple places within the empire and resettling the conquered territories with outsiders. This separated the conquered from their homelands and from each other, diminishing the likelihood of nationalistic uprisings, and provided a source of labor for royal building projects and for cultivating previously undeveloped regions.

In a futile attempt to block Tiglath-pileser, several of the small states in the region formed a coalition in 734 BCE. These included the king of Aram-Damascus, Rezin, and the king of Israel, Pekah, who tried to persuade Ahaz, king of Judah, to join them. He refused and became an Assyrian vassal, requesting assistance from Tiglath-pileser. (For further discussion of these events, called the Syro-Ephraimite War, see pages 278–80). Assyrian reprisal against the coalition was swift, and Damascus fell in 732. The Assyrians also occupied parts of the northern kingdom of Israel and helped Hoshea oust Pekah as its king. Following Tiglath-pileser's death in 727, Hoshea, who had been a loyal Assyrian vassal, took advantage of

this period of uncertainty and rebelled against Assyria. Once Tiglath-pileser's son and successor, Shalmaneser V, had secured power, however, he besieged Samaria, the capital of the northern kingdom of Israel, and captured it in 722. He and his successor, his brother Sargon II, made the northern kingdom an Assyrian province.

In the account of the fall of Samaria in 2 Kings 17, we have an especially clear example of the editorial work and the priorities of the Deuteronomistic Historians. Likely drawing on an annalistic source, the Deuteronomistic Historians devote only two verses to the three-year siege of Samaria, its subsequent conquest, and the deportation of its citizens to cities "in Halah, on the Habur, the river of Gozan," in northern Mesopotamia, and "in the cities of the Medes" to the east of the Tigris River (2 Kings 17.5-6). We then read, "This occurred because," which introduces fourteen verses in which the Deuteronomistic Historians provide their own theological interpretation of the events leading to the fall of Samaria. Writing from the perspective of the southern kingdom of Judah, they viewed the fall of the northern kingdom of Israel as the inevitable result of its continual apostasy. According to the Deuteronomistic Historians, the inhabitants of the northern kingdom had persisted in worshiping deities other than Yahweh from the time of Jeroboam I in the late tenth century BCE, despite repeated prophetic warnings. At the same time, the account includes historical details, like the location of the cities to which the Israelites were exiled. We are also told that the Assyrians transferred foreign peoples from elsewhere in their empire to the former northern kingdom. These newcomers continued to worship their own native deities, but apparently also worshiped Yahweh.

PROPHETIC BOOKS

Beginning in the eighth century BCE, the nature of the prophetic material that we have changes significantly. In addition to prophetic legends preserved in the Deuteronomistic History, like those about Elijah and Elisha, we also begin to have collections of material about and by individual prophets, which have been collected and edited in separate prophetic "books," known as the Latter Prophets in Jewish tradition.

In the Bible, these books are arranged in rough order of length, from the longest to the shortest. This arrangement by length of text is also found in other collections of religious texts, for example, the letters of Paul in the New Testament and the suras of the Qur'an. Thus, the Latter Prophets begins with the "Major Prophets," the long books of Isaiah (sixty-six chapters), Jeremiah (fifty-two chapters), and Ezekiel (forty-eight chapters). (In most Christian canons, the book of Daniel is placed next, but it is not a prophetic book, as Jewish tradition recognizes in placing it in the third section of its canon, the Writings; see further pages 5, 8.) Then comes a separate collection, the "Book of the Twelve" (see Sir 49.10) or the "Minor Prophets," shorter books ranging in length from Hosea and Zechariah, each with fourteen chapters, to Obadiah, only one chapter. Because of the amount of text that could conveniently fit on a single scroll, there were thus four scrolls of the prophets: Isaiah, Jeremiah, Ezekiel, and the Twelve.

Within the Book of the Twelve, the order was more fluid, as comparison of different manuscripts indicates. The arrangement found in current Bibles follows one ancient tradition and is roughly chronological. First come those prophets dated to the early Assyrian period: Hosea, Amos, Obadiah, Jonah, and Micah; Joel is undated, but it is placed before Amos because of links with it (see further page 362). These are followed by prophets that are set in the later Assyrian period: Nahum, Habakkuk, and Zephaniah. Last come those set in the Persian period: Haggai, Zechariah, and Malachi.

Each of the fifteen books of the Latter Prophets has its own literary and editorial history, which is often complicated, especially for the longer books. In general, the books include three types of materials:

- *Biographical materials about the prophet, in the third person.* These make it clear that the collection and editing of the prophetic books was completed by persons other than the prophets themselves.

- *Autobiographical materials, in the first person.* Some of these may go back to the prophet in question.

- *Oracles by the prophets.* The word "oracle" simply means a spoken word or speech, and in the prophets, it is most often associated with "an oracle of the LORD," through which the prophet announces the word of God, often introduced by the formula, "Thus says the LORD." The prophetic oracles are usually in poetic form, and draw on a wide variety of genres, including covenant lawsuit, oracle against the nations, judgment oracle, messenger speech, song, hymn, call narrative, lament, law, proverb, symbolic gesture, prayer, wisdom saying, and vision.

The prophetic books, then, are anthologies. Within each, there is often no clear principle of arrangement. For example, an account of the prophet's call is often put at the beginning of the book, as in Jeremiah, Ezekiel, and Hosea. Sometimes, however, it occurs elsewhere, as in Amos (7.15) and, according to some scholars, in Isaiah (chap. 6; see further page 276). As this illustrates, the material within each prophetic book is not necessarily arranged in chronological order.

Sometimes material is arranged by theme or by genre. A good example is the "**oracle against the nations.**" Many of the prophetic books include these prophetic pronouncements of divine judgments against nations other than Israel. Generally grouped together, they are found in Isaiah 13–23, Jeremiah 46–51, Ezekiel 25–32, Amos 1–2, Zephaniah 2.4–15, Zechariah 9.1–8, and Obadiah and Nahum in their entirety. The origins of this genre are obscure but may be related to oracles given in time of war. The first prophetic use of the oracles against the nations occurs in Amos, who may have originated the genre. As they now stand, these oracles vividly express the prophetic belief that Yahweh controlled the entire world. Other principles of arrangement will be apparent as we consider individual books, including the use of refrains and of catchwords, in which two originally independent passages are juxtaposed because both contain an identical or similar word.

The emergence of collections of written prophecies attributed to individual prophets is a significant development. Starting in the eighth century BCE, we have references to the writing down of prophetic oracles, notably in Isaiah (8.1–2, 16; 30.8), in Jeremiah (especially chap. 36), and in Ezekiel (for example, 43.11). This begins at the very time when evidence from ancient Hebrew inscriptions suggests a growing literate elite associated with temple and palace administration in both Israel and Judah. It is possible, then, that the emergence of this new type of literature, the collection of a prophet's oracles, was a result of this increasing literacy. Once written down, the collections were then edited and augmented by the prophets' disciples, in some cases by the Deuteronomic school, and perhaps even by the prophets themselves.

AMOS

The Book of Amos

Like most other prophetic books, the book of **Amos** is an anthology containing a variety of materials of different genres, some of which can be attributed to Amos himself:

- *Oracles against the nations* surrounding Israel and against Israel itself (1.3–2.16). This is the largest single unit in the book, occupying a prominent position and setting out themes that will be developed and alluded to in the following chapters.
- *Oracle concerning prophecy* (3.3–8).
- *Addresses to groups in Israel*, including the elite women of Samaria (4.1–3) and the wealthy in Samaria and Jerusalem (6.1–7; 8.4–8), *and to Israel as a whole* (3.1–2, 13–15; 4.4–12; 5.1–7; 5.10–17).
- *Visions*: In keeping with the identification of Amos as a "seer," there are five visions that express divine judgment on Israel. Four of them begin with the formula "This is what the LORD God showed me"—locusts (7.1–3), fire (7.4–6), a plumb line (7.7–9), and a basket of summer fruit (8.1–3)—and the fifth begins "I saw Yahweh standing beside the altar" (presumably at Bethel;

9.1–4). The vision of summer fruit requires explanation: The Hebrew words for "summer fruit" and for "end" (8.2) were near homonyms; the meaning of the vision is explained by the pun, a type of wordplay considered high art. These five visions have a climactic arrangement, in which Yahweh is first moved to mercy by the prophet's entreaties, yet then pronounces irrevocable doom. But the five visions are not found in an uninterrupted sequence. After the first three visions, which are first-person narratives, comes a third-person account of the confrontation at Bethel in 7.10–17. The visions resume in 8.1–3 with the basket of summer fruit, but then a collection of shorter judgment oracles intervenes (8.4–14) before the final vision in 9.1–4.

- *Confrontation at Bethel* (7.10–17), a third-person narrative describing how Amos's preaching at the royal sanctuary of Bethel was met by opposition from its priest.
- *Hymnic fragments*: Scattered throughout the book of Amos are several excerpts from hymns (4.13; 5.8–9; 9.5–6), resembling in language and theme some of the psalms and other hymns preserved in the Bible. These fragments share the refrain "Yahweh is his name" and emphasize the deity's actions as creator.

The arrangement of these parts is sometimes thematic, sometimes more superficial. One important organizing principle was the catchword. Thus, the placement of the hymnic fragment in 5.8–9 is probably due to the occurrence of the word "turn" in both 5.7 and 5.8. Another organizing principle is repetition, such as the phrase "Hear this word" (3.1; 4.1; 5.1) and the proclamation of "Woe" (NRSV "Alas"; 5.18; 6.1).

A majority of scholars think that not all of the material in Amos goes back to the prophet himself, but was added later by ancient editors of the book. Two examples of such later additions are:

- *The oracle against Judah* (2.4–5): Although it begins with the same formula and includes the same punishments as the preceding oracles against other nations, this oracle seems to be rhetorical prose rather than the poetry used in the others; it also contains Deuteronomistic clichés. Moreover, since the following oracle is directed against Israel in the sense of all Israel (see 2.9–10 and page 259), rather than just the northern kingdom, an oracle specifically directed against Judah alone would be inappropriate. This oracle may have been added after the destruction of the northern kingdom, to emphasize that the words of Amos applied to Judah as well.

- *The oracle of promise to David (9.11–15)*: The references to the "booth of David" that has "fallen" and is in "ruins," to "ruined cities" and a restored Israel, and to "the remnant of Edom" suggest that this epilogue to the book of Amos dates from a period later in the history of Judah, after the destruction of Jerusalem and of the Davidic dynasty in 586 BCE. Elsewhere, Amos is not concerned with the house of David (now merely a fragile "booth") as such, yet these verses predict its restoration along with abundant fertility in the Promised Land.

These likely later additions to the book show its continuing relevance for subsequent audiences and also provide glimpses of early interpretations of Amos's original words.

The Life of Amos

The superscription (the opening historical note) to the book of Amos dates the prophet's career to the reigns of Jeroboam II of Israel, who died in 747 BCE, and of Uzziah of Judah, who relinquished the throne in 759 because of illness (see 2 Kings 15.5) and died in 733. The superscription further dates Amos's preaching to "two years before the earthquake" (Am 1.1). This earthquake, also referred to in Amos 8.8, 9.1, and 9.5 and Zechariah 14.5, was a major catastrophe, as archaeological evidence at both Hazor and Samaria shows. None of this meager information enables us to date Amos's prophetic career precisely, but it took place around 750 and probably lasted no more than a decade.

The book of Amos gives us some information about the prophet. He was from Tekoa, in Judah, some 10 miles (16 km) south of Jerusalem. Most of his preaching was directed against the northern

kingdom and was delivered there. We know from ancient inscriptions that differences in dialect existed between the Hebrew of Judah and that of the northern kingdom of Israel. Amos's southern background, therefore, would have been obvious to his audience.

Amos was a sheep and cattle herder (1.1; 7.14–15). The word used to describe him in 1.1 means not just a shepherd but a wealthy owner of a large number of sheep. The same word is used in this sense in Ugaritic, and, in the Bible, of Mesha, the king of Moab, who is reported to have paid as an annual tribute to the king of Israel 100,000 lambs and the wool of an equal number of rams (2 Kings 3.4). Amos was also a farmer, raising sycamore figs (7.14). Although the sycamore fig is inferior to the true fig, it could be cultivated on a large scale. Thus, the older view that Amos sympathized with the needy because of his own impoverished background is no longer likely.

Amos claims to be a true prophet, one "taken" from his livelihood in response to a divine summons (7.15). He also insisted that he was not a professional prophet: "I am not a prophet nor a son of a prophet" (7.14). On one level, this denial indicates that Amos was not a member of a prophetic school and had not undergone extensive training (see further page 246). Given that this denial was directed at Amaziah, the priest of Jeroboam's royal sanctuary at Bethel, Amos was also indicating that, unlike Amaziah, his livelihood and therefore his prophetic word was not beholden to the crown.

The Message of Amos

The first major unit in the book of Amos is the series of oracles in which the nations surrounding Israel and then Israel itself are condemned for their violation of covenant (Am 1.3–2.16). The passage begins with six (or seven, if Judah is included) patterned condemnations of Damascus (Aram), Philistia, Tyre, Edom, Ammon, and Moab. For the first four we see an alternating geographical pattern: from northeast to southwest to northwest to southeast. Each of these nations is condemned for particular crimes: Aram and Ammon for their harsh occupation of Gilead, originally Israelite territory; Philistia and Tyre for what appears to be slave traffic with Edom; Edom for some vague aggression; and Moab for an offense against its southern neighbor Edom.

These six nations all bordered Israel and Judah, and also were either controlled by or allied with Israel during the reigns of David and Solomon in the tenth century BCE. Such control or alliance would have been expressed formally in terms of treaty or covenant, like that between Hiram, king of Tyre, and David and Solomon. In the oracle against Tyre, that Phoenician state is indicted "because they did not remember the covenant of brothers" (Am 1.7), language that recalls the formal parity treaty between Tyre and Israel (1 Kings 5.12) and the language used by Hiram to address Solomon, "my brother" (1 Kings 9.13). Likewise, Edom is condemned for mistreatment of "his brother" (Am 1.11), probably referring both to Israel as occasional covenant partner of Edom, and also to the traditional genealogical relationship between their ancestors, Jacob and Esau.

Even though the specific historical allusions in the oracles against the nations are often no longer recoverable, a good interpretation of them is that Yahweh as the deity who presided over the treaties or covenants that bound these nations to Israel is now, like the divine witnesses in Hittite and Assyrian treaties, enforcing the curses for violation of covenant. The punishment proclaimed in the divine speeches in Amos 1–2 is destruction of the capital and other cities of the nation being condemned, and often both exile of its inhabitants and annihilation of its ruling family.

These detailed predictions of impending military disasters are in themselves unremarkable. Assyrian policy for some time had been the systematic deportation of conquered populations and the destruction of their cities. (See Figure 17.2.) Although the Assyrians are not explicitly named in Amos as the agents of the disasters, in the mid-eighth century BCE it would not have taken divine revelation to anticipate the Assyrians resuming their conquest of the Levant. What is more significant is what is being claimed here: The disasters will be Yahweh's doing, for he controls all history for his own purposes, in these cases to punish nations that have violated the terms of covenants in which he was a principal deity.

One can only imagine the nationalistic enthusiasm that these divine judgments proclaimed by the prophet would have aroused in an Israelite audience, whose history since the late tenth century BCE had been largely one of losses to regional entities that they had once controlled. But the oracles against those foreign nations are only the prelude to the main focus of the divine wrath:

> For three sins of Israel,
>> and for four, I will not revoke the punishment. (2.6)

Initially, the meaning of "Israel" is ambiguous—it could mean just the northern kingdom. But the continuation of the oracle makes it clear that it refers to all Israel, the twelve-tribe entity, not divided into the northern kingdom of Israel and the southern kingdom of Judah:

> I brought you up out of the land of Egypt,
>> and led you forty years in the wilderness,
>> to possess the land of the Amorite. (2.10)

This interpretation is confirmed by the judgment speech that immediately follows the oracle against Israel:

> Hear this word that the LORD has spoken against you, O people of Israel, against the whole family that I brought up out of the land of Egypt:
>> You only have I known
>>> of all the families of the earth;
>> therefore I will punish you
>>> for all your iniquities. (3.1–2)

Israel is even more guilty of covenant violation than the other nations, for Israel had a unique relationship with Yahweh. The use of the verb "to know" ("You only have I known . . .") alludes to the Sinai covenant, both because of its connotation of sexual intimacy, recalling the marriage analogue for the covenant (see page 102), and also because the verb was a technical term in ancient treaties for mutual recognition by both parties of their obligations to each other.

The offenses of which Israel is accused are primarily social:

> They sell the righteous for silver,
>> and the needy for a pair of sandals—

they trample the head of the poor into the dust of
    the earth,
     and push the afflicted out of the way;
father and son go in to the same girl,
     so that my holy name is profaned;
they lay themselves down beside every altar
     on garments taken in pledge;
and in the house of their God they drink
     wine bought with fines they imposed. (2.6–8)

The details of these offenses are not always clear, but what is clear is that Israel is guilty of systemic injustice toward the innocent, the poor, and young women. The consequence is inevitable: Like the other nations, Israel will be punished, its army ineffective and scattered. What had been anticipated by the prophet's audience as a "day of Yahweh" in which Yahweh acting on Israel's behalf

FIGURE 17.2 Part of a relief of the Assyrian king Tiglath-pileser III, shown in his chariot in the lower panel. The upper panel shows a fortified city on the left, from which, on the right, captives and cattle are being taken. The cuneiform text between the two panels names the city, Astartu, probably biblical Ashtaroth in northern Transjordan, which the Assyrians captured in 732 BCE.

attacked its enemies would now be a day when Yahweh turned against Israel (see Box 17.2 on page 262).

As the initial oracle against Israel indicates, Amos is concerned principally with the Israel that Yahweh brought out of Egypt. Israel is guilty of breaking its primary contract with God, the Sinai covenant, and so the curses that were attached to that covenant will be executed. That covenant had two aspects: correct worship of Yahweh and of Yahweh alone (love of God) and just treatment of fellow Israelites (love of neighbor). Amos does refer to improper forms of worship, especially at the sanctuary at Bethel, and to profanation of the sabbath and other aspects of Israel's sacred life, but more attention is given to the second aspect of the covenant. In considerable detail, Amos emphasizes that Israel has failed in its primary obligation to provide for the powerless: The poor are trampled into the ground and deprived of justice. This exploitation of the poor is perpetrated by the wealthy elite, and Amos is ruthless in his denunciation of the ruling class:

> Woe to those who are at ease in Zion.
>   and to those who feel secure on Mount
>   Samaria. . . .
> Woe to those who lie on beds of ivory,
>   and lounge on their couches,
> and eat lambs from the flock,
>   and calves from the stall;
> who sing idle songs to the sound of the harp
>   and like David improvise on instruments of music;
> who drink wine from bowls,
>   and anoint themselves with the finest oils. . . .
> Therefore they shall now be the first to go into exile,
>   and the revelry of the loungers shall pass away.
>   (6.1, 4–7)

In this passage, Amos attacks the conspicuous consumption of the elite in the capital cities of Samaria and Jerusalem, whose wealth (see Figure 17.3) was acquired at the expense of the poor; even David is indirectly condemned. Amos also attacks the royal ideology, according to which the divine choice of the capital was a guarantee of security. That supposed guarantee is illusory: Like the elite of the capitals of Israel's neighbors, the elite of Samaria and Jerusalem will also be exiled. Israel's

special relationship with Yahweh is no guarantee of special treatment:

> Are you not like the Ethiopians to me,
>   O people of Israel? says the LORD.
> Did I not bring Israel up from the land of Egypt,
>   and the Philistines from Caphtor and the
>   Arameans from Kir?
> The eyes of the Lord GOD are upon the sinful
>   kingdom,
>   and I will destroy it from the face of the earth.
>   (9.7–8)

Israel must learn that Yahweh is the one who controls all of history, and that it is therefore not unique. If it fails to live up to its covenant obligations, he will treat it like any other "sinful kingdom."

The vehemence of Amos's attack on the establishment is the background for the confrontation between Amos and Amaziah, the royally appointed priest at Bethel, one of the principal sanctuaries of the northern kingdom (7.10–17).

FIGURE 17.3   One of the ivories from Samaria, dating to the reign of Jeroboam II in the mid-eighth century BCE. About 4 in (10 cm) high, it shows a sphinx in a lotus thicket. Ivories such as this were used as decorative inlays on furniture.

preceding biographical account. Some scholars have interpreted chapters 1 and 3 as referring to the prophet's relationships with two different women.

• Oracles of judgment against Israel, and especially against the northern kingdom, often called Ephraim (the dominant northern tribe, named after one of Jacob's two grandsons through Joseph), for its failure to live up to the requirements of its covenant with Yahweh by worshiping other gods and not carrying out the social requirements of the Ten Commandments. These oracles have been gathered into two separate collections, 4.1–12.1 and 12.2–14.9, each of which has a positive if vague assurance of restoration near its end.

The principles of arrangement of the two collections that form the latter part of the book are largely unclear. Sometimes catchwords are used, and sometimes the arrangement appears to be thematic. Because the oracles either lack specifics or allude to events not known from other sources, we cannot be sure if they are presented in some sort of chronological sequence.

As with Amos, we find evidence of later additions to the book of Hosea. Some of these are editorial, such as the superscription (Hos 1.1) and the conclusion (14.9), which is a generalization typical of wisdom literature (see further pages 383–84). Others concern Judah, although since Judah as well as the northern kingdom of Israel is the object of Hosea's attacks, particular cases are disputed. Most likely to be later additions are 1.7, 3.5, and 11.12, all of which speak positively about Judah or the Davidic dynasty, and 11.11, which describes a return from exile like homing pigeons or doves. As in Amos, these additions show that the prophet's message was considered relevant in later times.

The Life of Hosea

The career of Hosea is dated by the superscription (Hos 1.1) to the reign of Jeroboam II of Israel (788–747 BCE) and to the reigns of kings of Judah from Uzziah to Hezekiah, spanning most of the eighth century BCE. Such a long period is

historically unlikely, because the book shows no familiarity with the details of the fall of the northern kingdom to the Assyrians in 722. Most scholars, therefore, date Hosea's career to the third quarter of the eighth century, shortly after that of Amos.

Although the book tells us nothing of Hosea's background, the frequent references to places and events in the northern kingdom, along with peculiarities of language, indicate that Hosea himself was a northerner. According to the biographical narrative in chapter 1, Hosea's wife was named Gomer. Earlier interpretations that Gomer was a prostitute, or even a sacred prostitute, are now generally rejected: The word "prostitute" (Hebr. *zonah*) is never used directly of her, and the related word *zenunim* (Hos 1.2; 2.2) is better translated "promiscuity" rather than "harlotry" or "whoring" (NRSV), although when applied to Israel the sense of prostitution is not inappropriate: Israel has sold herself to her lovers for a prostitute's wages (9.1), and even hires them (8.9). Gomer and Hosea's three children are given symbolic names: Jezreel, which can be an ordinary name (as in 1 Chr 4.3), but here recalls Jehu's extermination of the dynasty of Omri at Jezreel (see 2 Kings 9–10); Not-loved; and Not-my-people. The autobiographical narrative in chapter 3 is probably an alternate version of the prophet's marriage, or a sequel to the preceding narrative.

That marriage was a stormy one, if chapters 1–3 describe what actually occurred. Because the prophet's marriage serves as an analogy for the relationship between Yahweh and Israel in these chapters, biographical details are difficult if not impossible to disentangle from their metaphorical use. If Hosea became aware of his wife's infidelity only after they had become married, that would parallel the relationship between Yahweh and Israel, which also started off well (see 2.15). If the prophet was aware that his wife was promiscuous before they married, then the analogy with Yahweh and Israel is less apt. We must keep in mind that the purpose of the two narratives is not to help us in a quest for the historical Hosea. Rather, they are a parable of sorts, an object lesson whose primary content is about Yahweh and Israel rather than Hosea and Gomer. (See Box 17.4 on page 267.)

The Message of Hosea

Hosea is best known for his extended use of the marriage metaphor to describe the relationship between Yahweh and Israel. This metaphor is implicit in the concept of covenant; the Hebrew word *berît*, traditionally translated "covenant," is used both of the relationship between Yahweh and Israel and of the marriage contract (as in Prov 2.17; Mal 2.14; see further page 102). Jeremiah and Ezekiel will also use this metaphor.

The use of the marriage metaphor has several dimensions. One is that Yahweh "loves" Israel, but the Hebrew word translated "love" can be understood in many ways. In its covenantal and marital sense, the meaning is likely "show exclusive allegiance to," rather than a more modern understanding of romantic love. When Yahweh announces his love for Israel, he signals that his attachment will endure, despite Israel's repeated infidelities by worshiping other gods. In Hosea's own case, his wife Gomer was unfaithful, yet he did not ultimately reject her. It must also be recognized how daring Hosea's use of this metaphor was. The Canaanite deity Baal, widely worshiped in the northern kingdom of Israel, was the storm-god who brought the winter rains that made agricultural produce and herds abundant. Baal was also closely associated with the goddess Asherah, another fertility-deity). By identifying Yahweh as Israel's husband, Hosea implicitly makes Yahweh a sexual deity, and also a god who provides fertility:

> She did not know
> > that it was I who gave her
> > the grain, the wine, and the oil. . . .
> Therefore I will take back
> > my grain in its time,
> > and my wine in its season;
> and I will take away my wool and my flax,
> > which were to cover her nakedness. (2.8–9)

Another metaphor used by Hosea for the relationship between Yahweh and Israel is that of parent and child:

> When Israel was a child, I loved him,
> > and out of Egypt I called my son. . . .

> Yet it was I who taught Ephraim to walk,
> > I took them up in my arms;
> > but they did not know that I healed them.
> I led them with cords of human kindness,
> > with bands of love.
> I was to them like those who lift infants to their
> > cheeks.
> > I bent down to them and fed them. (11.1–4)

Although some details of the translation of the Hebrew of these verses are uncertain, the imagery of God as parent is clear.

This metaphor is relatively rare in the Hebrew Bible. It is used in Exodus 4.23, where Yahweh calls Israel his "firstborn son." Like the metaphor of marriage, that of parent-child suggests not just familial intimacy but also a covenant relationship; note especially 2 Kings 16.7. Like a loving parent, God loves Israel, and this is reason for hope for the future of the relationship, as 14.4 indicates: "I will love them freely, for my anger has turned from them." Like a forgiving spouse or parent, God forgives Israel, because he loves it.

Both sections of the oracles of judgment (see page 264) begin with a "lawsuit" (NRSV: "indictment"). The Hebrew word used here is *rîb*, often used in the Bible in ordinary legal contexts. In several prophets, beginning with Hosea, the **"covenant lawsuit"** forms a distinct genre, in which Yahweh sues Israel for breach of contract, that is, for violation of the Sinai covenant. The first occurrence in Hosea sets the tone for what follows:

> Hear the word of the LORD, O people of Israel;
> > for the LORD has a lawsuit against the inhabitants
> > of the land.
> There is no faithfulness or loyalty,
> > and no knowledge of God in the land.
> Swearing, lying, and murder,
> > and stealing and adultery break out;
> > bloodshed follows bloodshed.
> Therefore the land mourns,
> > and all who live in it languish;
> together with the wild animals
> > and the birds of the air,
> > even the fish of the sea are perishing. (4.1–3)

The words for swearing, lying, murder, stealing, and adultery allude to the Ten Commandments, the text of Israel's primary contract or covenant with Yahweh. Israel has broken its contract, so the curses that formed part of the covenant genre are being implemented in the form of natural disasters. The same word *rîb* is also used at the beginning of the final section of the book:

> The LORD has a lawsuit against Israel [correction for "Judah"],
>   and will punish Jacob according to his ways,
>   and repay him according to his deeds. (12.2)

The theme of covenant is central in the book of Hosea and is a key to its interpretation. The Israelites have repeatedly "broken my covenant and transgressed my law" (8.1), worshiping other gods and denying social justice. Hosea focuses especially on forbidden worship: the worship of gods other than Yahweh and the making of graven images, such as the calves of Samaria and Bethel.

Another breach of covenant was making foreign alliances. These implied doubt in Yahweh's ability to act on Israel's behalf, and probably also involved swearing allegiance to or at least acknowledging the power of other gods in treaty-making ceremonies. For the last decade of its existence, the northern kingdom of Israel vacillated between loyalty to Assyria as its vassal and rebellion against it, sometimes in league with Egypt. The sketchy account in the book of Kings gives several specific examples of such policy shifts, and there must have been others. For Hosea, these foreign entanglements were another form of infidelity:

> They call upon Egypt, they go to Assyria. . . .
> Woe to them, for they have strayed from me!
>   Destruction to them, for they have rebelled
>   against me! (7.11, 13)

The result would be the same as for apostasy—divine punishment in the form of exile from the Promised Land, with a terrible ironic twist: "Ephraim shall return to Egypt, and in Assyria they shall eat unclean food" (9.3; see also 8.13; 11.5). The covenant curse of exile in a foreign land will be either a return to Egypt, reversing the Exodus, or a deportation to Assyria.

For Hosea, another example of lack of trust in Yahweh is the monarchy. Hosea takes a decidedly antimonarchical stance, at least toward the rulers of the northern kingdom of Israel. "They made kings, but not through me" (Hos 8.4): The kings' claim that they were divinely chosen is rejected. Part of the divine punishment will be a return to kingless rule (3.4), for "Samaria's king shall perish" (10.7).

Hosea refers repeatedly to traditions concerning Israel's ancestors; for example:

> The LORD has an indictment against Judah,
>   and will punish Jacob according to his ways,
>   and repay him according to his deeds.
> In the womb he tried to supplant his brother,
>   and in his manhood he strove with God.
> He strove with the angel and prevailed,
>   he wept and sought his favor;
>   he met him at Bethel,
>   and there he spoke with him. . . .
> Jacob fled to the land of Aram,
>   there Israel served for a wife,
>   and for a wife he guarded sheep. (12.2–4, 12)

These verses are connected with the narratives about Jacob found in Genesis, which, in a different order, recount his birth (Gen 25.19–26), his wrestling with God (Gen 32.22–32), his revelation at Bethel (28.10–21), and his service to Laban (Gen 29–31). We may also note in passing that the presence of these traditions in Hosea is evidence for their antiquity; an eighth-century Hosea is very familiar with the broad outlines of the Jacob narrative (see pages 76–77). The point of this historical retrospective is that Jacob (Israel) had shown questionable character from the beginning, cheating his brother and challenging God, and that this pattern continued in the history of Ephraim, Jacob's grandson and the poetic name for the northern kingdom, and of Judah (if this is the original reading), Jacob's son whose name was also that of the southern kingdom.

Hosea also refers to the Exodus:

> By a prophet the LORD brought Israel up from Egypt,
>   and by a prophet he was guarded. (12.13)

The prophet who brought Israel out of Egypt is Moses; in calling him a prophet, Hosea shows familiarity with other originally northern traditions, especially the Pentateuchal sources E and D. The prophet who "guarded" Israel may be Samuel or

Box 17.4 MARRIAGE IN ANCIENT ISRAEL

The book of Hosea provides important evidence concerning marriage in ancient Israel. It includes what may be an ancient Israelite wedding vow: "I will take you for my wife forever; I will take you for my wife in righteousness and in justice, in steadfast love, and in mercy. I will take you for my wife in faithfulness" (Hos 2.19–20). It also includes what may be a divorce formula: "She is not my wife, and I am not her husband" (2.2).

The relationship between husband and wife was one of unequal power, in which the husband initiated both marriage and divorce (see further Deut 24.1–4). The woman's family was also central: Her father, mother, and brothers could play key roles in setting the terms of her marriage and in negotiating the amount of bridewealth. Under this arrangement, the husband's family transferred wealth to the bride's family, and the bride moved into the husband's household (see page 130). We also see in Hosea's description of marriage an uncritical reference to a husband punishing his wife through physical deprivation ("I will kill her with thirst"), forced confinement ("I will build a wall against her"), public sexual shaming ("I will strip her naked and expose her"), and retaliation against the children ("Upon her children I will have no pity") (2.3–6). Within Hosea's view of marriage, all of these activities are appropriate if a wife is unfaithful. The fact that modern readers would characterize this as an abusive marriage is another reason to stress that the biblical understanding of marital "love" is different from our modern ideals (see further Box 20.2 on page 321).

The use of marriage as a metaphor for the exclusive relationship between Yahweh and Israel implies that a wife could have only one husband, and we find no examples of one wife with multiple husbands (polyandry) in the Bible. But the Bible contains many examples of men having more than one wife (polygyny), and until a relatively late period, monogamy was not required.

Elijah, but more likely is Moses as well, because of the poetic stylistic device known as synonymous parallelism (see further Box 23.2 on page 376). Both E and Deuteronomy emphasize the role of prophets as mediators of divine revelation, and the preeminent prophet in both is Moses, as in Hosea. Other references to the Exodus are scattered through the book of Hosea.

A close connection is found between Hosea and the Deuteronomic movement, which originated in the northern kingdom of Israel in the second half of the eighth century BCE (see pages 152–53). Like Deuteronomy, Hosea emphasizes the divinely given "torah" ("teaching"; see Hos 4.6; 8.1, 12; and Box 10.2 on page 154) and the covenant between Yahweh and Israel. Both Hosea and Deuteronomy stress the divine love for Israel and share an insistence on the exclusive worship of Yahweh. For Hosea, as in Deuteronomy, the penalty for violation of covenant is the fulfillment of the treaty curses. Hosea describes Yahweh metaphorically in the most gruesome terms: He is like maggots or a disease, eating away at Israel (5.12–13), he is Israel's predator (5.14; 13.7–8) and hunter (7.12).

Although Hosea is best known for his extended use of the marriage metaphor to describe the relationship between Yahweh and Israel, only a part of the book that bears his name is concerned with that analogy. Like his contemporary Amos, Hosea anticipated the conquest of the northern kingdom of Israel by the Assyrians, and he interpreted that imminent catastrophe as a deserved punishment carried out by Yahweh. This was a tumultuous period when Israel and Judah felt threatened by the far more powerful Assyria. Hosea captured the high emotions of the time by using tremendously versatile family metaphors. When he portrayed Yahweh as a wronged husband, Hosea was able to communicate both divine anger and the divine capacity for forgiveness and a renewed commitment to the covenantal relationship. Similarly, the depiction of Yahweh as the parent of an ungrateful and rebellious son communicates the righteousness of Yahweh's punishment of Israel as well as the inner turmoil that he feels in enacting that punishment: "How can I give you up, O Ephraim?" Through each metaphor, Hosea justified divine punishment and anticipated a restoration of the relationship between Yahweh and Israel.

A LOOK BACK AND AHEAD

Historically, the northern kingdom of Israel was doomed because it stood in the way of Assyria's imperial ambitions; the Assyrians would not allow that, and their conquest of Israel was predictable. But from the religious perspective of Amos and Hosea, as from that of the Deuteronomistic Historians, Israel was doomed because it had failed to live up to its covenant obligations with Yahweh, and it was he who was ultimately responsible for the Assyrian onslaught. Although neither Amos nor Hosea mentions the events of 722 BCE, when the Assyrians captured Samaria, the capital of the northern kingdom of Israel, and exiled many of its inhabitants, that end was consistent with their view of divine causality.

Although Judah escaped, it would not be for long, for it too stood in the way of the Assyrian advance. From 722 BCE onward, the focus of the biblical writers is on the southern kingdom of Judah, and the question that suffuses the literature of the next century and a half is: Would Judah learn from the mistakes of the northern kingdom?

IMPORTANT NAMES AND TERMS

Each name or term is defined briefly in the Glossary. Its first significant occurrence in this chapter appears in **boldface** type.

Amos	day of the Lord	oracle against the nations
covenant lawsuit	Hosea	

QUESTIONS FOR REVIEW

1. What is the nature of the books of the prophets, and how are they arranged?
2. How did Amos and Hosea interpret the impending Assyrian campaigns and conquests?
3. Discuss the uses that Amos and Hosea make of earlier biblical traditions.
4. Why do Amos and Hosea condemn the Israelites for lack of social justice?

BIBLIOGRAPHY

For the history of the period, see the work by Campbell cited in the bibliography to Chapter 16; for a commentary on 2 Kings, see the work by Cogan and Tadmor listed in the same place.

A good introduction to the prophetic books is Marvin A. Sweeney, *The Prophetic Literature* (Nashville, TN: Abingdon, 2005).

A good short commentary on Amos is Julia Myers O'Brien, "Amos," pp. 648–52 in *The HarperCollins Bible Commentary* (ed. J. L. Mays; San Francisco: Harper San-Francisco, 2000).

For an introduction to the book of Hosea, see Sharon Rose Moughtin-Mumby, pp. 367–78 in *The Oxford Encyclopedia of the Books of the Bible*, vol. 1, ed. M. D. Coogan (New York: Oxford University Press, 2011; available in Oxford Biblical Studies Online). A good short commentary on Hosea is John Day, "Hosea," pp. 571–78 in *The Oxford Bible Commentary* (ed. J. Barton and J. Muddiman; Oxford: Oxford University Press, 2001; available in Oxford Biblical Studies Online).

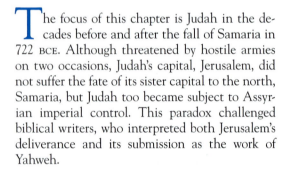

The Kingdom of Judah in the Eighth and Early Seventh Centuries BCE

*2 Kings 15–20, 2 Chronicles 29–32,
Isaiah 1–39, and Micah*

The focus of this chapter is Judah in the decades before and after the fall of Samaria in 722 BCE. Although threatened by hostile armies on two occasions, Judah's capital, Jerusalem, did not suffer the fate of its sister capital to the north, Samaria, but Judah too became subject to Assyrian imperial control. This paradox challenged biblical writers, who interpreted both Jerusalem's deliverance and its submission as the work of Yahweh.

HISTORY

The Assyrian campaigns that culminated in the conquest of the northern kingdom of Israel in 722 BCE also affected Judah. During the reign of the Assyrian king Tiglath-pileser III (745–727), Judah's king Ahaz (735–715) chose to be an Assyrian vassal rather than to join a coalition that opposed the Assyrian advance. This status as vassal continued for several decades, during the reigns of Tiglath-pileser's successors Shalmaneser V (727–722) and Sargon II (722–705). But when Sargon died, Ahaz's son, the Judean king Hezekiah (715–687), asserted his independence. Sargon's successor

Sennacherib (705–681) responded by attacking in force, and Judah had no choice but to resubmit to Assyrian rule.

Judah was only one of Assyria's concerns, however. A major preoccupation was with Babylon, Assyria's powerful neighbor to the south. Babylon had been taken over by Tiglath-pileser III earlier in the seventh century BCE, but Assyria's hold on Babylon remained tenuous. For a decade during the reign of Sargon, in fact, Assyria lost control of southern Mesopotamia to the Babylonian ruler Marduk-apla-iddina, known in the Bible as Merodach-baladan. But a series of campaigns by Sargon and Sennacherib culminated in the capture of Babylon itself in 689 BCE.

For these events in the last third of the eighth century BCE we have several different sources. The Bible has contradictory perspectives on the events, especially those affecting Judah. Assyrian sources are also abundant for the period, recording the payment of tribute in 734 BCE to Tiglath-pileser by Ahaz, and, as we have seen, describing the capture of Samaria in 722. For the next two decades, Assyrian records make no mention of Judah, but Sennacherib's lengthy account of his campaign to the west in 701 includes a long section on the devastation of Judah and the siege of

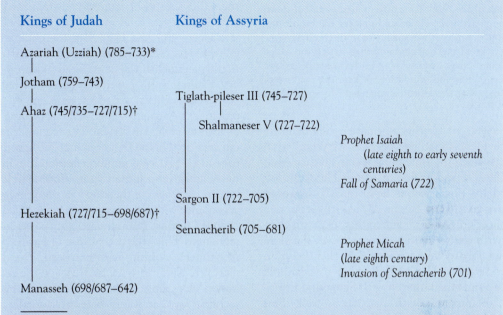

Box 18.1 CHRONOLOGY OF THE EIGHTH AND SEVENTH CENTURIES BCE

Kings of Judah	Kings of Assyria	
Azariah (Uzziah) (785–733)*		
Jotham (759–743)		
Ahaz (745/735–727/715)†	Tiglath-pileser III (745–727)	
	Shalmaneser V (727–722)	
		Prophet Isaiah (late eighth to early seventh centuries)
		Fall of Samaria (722)
	Sargon II (722–705)	
Hezekiah (727/715–698/687)†	Sennacherib (705–681)	
		Prophet Micah (late eighth century)
		Invasion of Sennacherib (701)
Manasseh (698/687–642)		

Date ranges are for reigns, not life spans. Overlapping dates indicate coregencies. Vertical lines show genealogical connections.

* Azariah (Uzziah) was apparently quarantined for much of his reign with a skin disease, and Jotham and Ahaz ruled while he was still alive.

† The data are inconsistent for the chronology of the reigns of Ahaz and Hezekiah.

Jerusalem in that year. Supplementing this account is a series of reliefs from Sennacherib's palace at Nineveh depicting in vivid detail the capture and destruction of Lachish, one of the principal Judean cities. Archaeological evidence supplements these sources. Excavations at Lachish have confirmed the essential accuracy of the Assyrian reliefs, and, as we will see, discoveries in Jerusalem can also be connected with Sennacherib's campaign. The king of Judah during most of this period was Hezekiah, who ruled for nearly thirty years.

The Reign of Hezekiah

Hezekiah came to the throne either in 727 BCE, just before the Assyrian conquest of the northern kingdom of Israel, or, more likely, in 715, soon after that event, and he ruled until either 698 or, more likely, 687. The dates given in the Bible for his reign are inconsistent.

For the Deuteronomistic Historians, Hezekiah was one of the most important kings of Judah; they state that "there was no one like him among all the kings of Judah after him, or among those who were before him" (2 Kings 18.5). From their ideological perspective, this was because of Hezekiah's fidelity to the Deuteronomic Code concerning exclusive and pure worship of Yahweh:

> He did what was right in the sight of the LORD just as his ancestor David had done. He removed the high places, broke down the pillars, and cut down the sacred pole. He broke in pieces the bronze serpent that Moses had made, for until those days the people of Israel had made offerings to it; it was called Nehushtan. . . . He held fast to the LORD; he did not depart from following him but kept the commandments that the LORD commanded Moses. (2 Kings 18.3–4, 6)

Other reasons for this affirmative judgment are also evident. Judah had been an Assyrian vassal at least since the time of Hezekiah's father Ahaz in 734 BCE, and at first, it seems, Hezekiah followed his predecessor's lead. In 705, however, the Assyrian king Sargon II died in battle, and the most pressing problem for his successor Sennacherib was to maintain control over Babylon. Presumably to take advantage of this Assyrian preoccupation, Hezekiah decided to withhold tribute and allied himself with Egypt and Ethiopia, and probably with Babylon as well. This amounted to a declaration of independence from Assyrian sovereignty.

Hezekiah's rebellion had disastrous consequences. Sennacherib attacked Judah with devastating force, creating economic and social catastrophe. Hezekiah avoided the destruction of the capital, Jerusalem, only by abject submission and payment of enormous tribute. For the rest of his reign, and during the reign of his son and successor Manasseh (687 [698]–642 BCE), Judah was a loyal Assyrian vassal. Not until Assyria itself came under attack in the late seventh century BCE would Judah regain any real independence.

Both in Kings (2 Kings 18–20) and in Chronicles (2 Chr 29–32), a disproportionate amount of space is given to Hezekiah, and so we are better informed about his reign than about those of most other Israelite kings. What emerges from these sources is a picture of a daring nationalist. The Assyrian conquest of the northern kingdom apparently resulted in an influx of refugees into Judah

(see 2 Chr 30.25) and especially into its capital, Jerusalem. It is estimated that by the end of the eighth century BCE both the size and the population of Jerusalem were four times larger than they had been during Solomon's reign in the mid-tenth century, from some 25 acres (10 hectares) to more than 100 acres (40 hectares) and from five thousand inhabitants to as many as twenty thousand (see Figure 18.1 and Plate 9 in the color section following page 220). Hezekiah exploited this situation to reestablish the centralized Judean monarchy, extending his control to parts of what had been the northern kingdom (now an Assyrian province). Accompanying and supporting this policy was a religious revival. The originally northern traditions of the Deuteronomic movement (see pages 152–53), were reinterpreted and revised in Judah and given a Judean slant. Worship in Jerusalem and throughout the kingdom was reformed in accordance with Deuteronomic regulations. These changes further strengthened the power of the monarchy. Thus, the destruction of locales where illegitimate worship was practiced, the "high places" (2 Kings 18.4; 2 Chr 31.1), and the centralization of worship in Jerusalem, meant that the sacrificial system was now entirely under royal control.

The Deuteronomists and the monarchy have been kindred spirits, each using the other to their own advantage. That is the implication of the scholarly hypothesis that the first edition of the Deuteronomistic History was produced under Hezekiah (see further page 162). Inspired by the king's commitment to the principles of their movement, the Deuteronomists compiled an ideologically informed history of Israel, according to which the separation of north and south was a disaster, and the divine choice of the Davidic monarchy, and its current ruler, were emphasized.

The length of the accounts of Hezekiah's reign may skew our view of his importance. More likely, however, is that the attention given to Hezekiah in biblical and in Assyrian sources is recognition that his reign was pivotal. An important contemporary of Hezekiah was the prophet **Isaiah**.

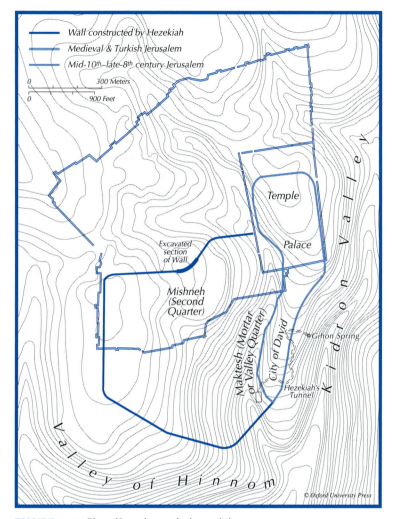

FIGURE 18.1   Plan of Jerusalem in the late eighth century BCE.

ISAIAH

The Book of Isaiah

With its sixty-six chapters, the book of Isaiah is one of the longest books in the Bible. Until the late nineteenth century, the entire book was generally considered the work of the prophet whose name is found at its beginning, Isaiah son of Amoz, who lived in Jerusalem in the late eighth and early seventh centuries BCE. Some premodern scholars

recognized some problems with this assumption, and further work in the eighteenth and nineteenth centuries culminated in the commentary on Isaiah by the German scholar Bernhard Duhm in 1892. Duhm found three principal parts in the book: **First Isaiah**, chapters 1–39, the bulk of which could be dated to the time of Isaiah of Jerusalem; Second (or Deutero-) Isaiah, chapters 40–55, dating to the sixth century BCE; and Third (or Trito-) Isaiah, chapters 56–66, a century or more later. Most modern scholars agree with this view.

This analysis of the book of Isaiah shares several presuppositions and conclusions with the critical analysis of the Pentateuch (see pages 46–51). It assumes that an eighth-century BCE prophet in Jerusalem could not have known about details of sixth-century history, such as the fall of Jerusalem to the Babylonians in 586 BCE, repeatedly mentioned in Isaiah 40–55; the rise to power of the Persian king Cyrus the Great in 559, mentioned in Isaiah 44.28 and 45.1; and his defeat of Babylon in 539, mentioned in Isaiah 47 and 48.14. Such specific historical references show that parts of the book were written after those events. This critical judgment does not allow for the possibility that the prophets could, under divine inspiration, know of events in the distant future. That is more in the realm of theology, but at least it may be said that the rise of a king in Persia who would conquer Babylon would have made little sense to an eighth-century Judean audience, for whom Persia was unknown and Babylon no threat at all.

The book of Isaiah is thus the result of a lengthy process of formation, which began with the collection of oracles of Isaiah of Jerusalem. To this nucleus later writings were attached, and many additions were made to its early parts. The entire anthology shares a common vocabulary, frequently referring to Yahweh as "the holy One of Israel" and making repeated mention of "justice" and "righteousness," and is pervaded by the view that Jerusalem/Zion is central to Yahweh's plans.

Beginning in the latter part of the twentieth century, some scholars have focused more on the final form of the book of Isaiah than on its hypothetical literary history. This type of criticism, often called "canonical criticism," accepts the idea of multiple authors and editors but resists atomizing or fragmenting a biblical book like Isaiah into a collection of competing voices, dated to successive time periods. Rather than search for original authors or editors, canonical criticism emphasizes the received form of the book and its unifying themes. It recognizes that communities of faith from the late biblical period onward viewed the book of Isaiah as a single work containing a coherent and divinely inspired message. This approach also stresses that the processes that led to the final form of the book were not just mechanical editing, using scissors and paste as it were, but the result of a living intellectual tradition.

The School of Isaiah

First Isaiah contains several references to the writing down of the prophet's words. Typical is Isaiah 30.8:

> Go now, write it before them on a tablet,
>   and inscribe it on a scroll,
> so that it may be for the time to come
>   as a witness forever.

The prophet's words are recorded and preserved, so that their truth may be confirmed by subsequent events. The same process is found in 8.1–3, the prediction of the birth of Maher-shalal-hash-baz, and in 8.16: "Bind up the testimony, seal the teaching among my disciples"—the prophetic message, having been written on papyrus, is rolled up, tied with string, and sealed, to be opened at a later time to prove its accuracy. Moreover, the message is entrusted to the prophet's "disciples," presumably those responsible for collecting and preserving the prophet's oracles.

Isaiah and his disciples, who were something like the "sons of the prophet" (see page 246), were the nucleus of a school of thought, like the Deuteronomic School that we have identified earlier (see pages 154–55). We should also note the close connections between Isaiah and the Deuteronomists: Isaiah is the only one of the "Latter Prophets" with any prominence in the Deuteronomistic History, in 2 Kings 19–20, and those chapters were incorporated into the developing book of Isaiah.

It was this Isaianic school that scholars think was responsible for the composition and addition of new material to the original collection of narratives and oracles of the eighth-century BCE prophet Isaiah of Jerusalem. Like schools of Greek philosophy, these disciples continued the style and viewpoint of their founder for several centuries. This Isaianic school not only added material to the earlier prophet's work, but also constantly revised it, an indication that later generations considered

Isaiah's original words as relevant for them. (We will discuss on pages 336–42 and 354–55 the parts of the book of Isaiah called Second Isaiah and Third Isaiah.)

First Isaiah (Isaiah 1–39): Contents

Within the book of Isaiah as a whole, First Isaiah is also an anthology. Note first its overlaps with other biblical books:

- Isaiah 2.2–4 = Micah 4.1–5, with slight variations
- Isaiah 15–16 = Jeremiah 48
- Isaiah 36–39 = 2 Kings 18.13–20.19

Moreover, the principles of arrangement in First Isaiah are neither self-evident nor chronological. For example, what originally was a poem with several stanzas and a common refrain ("For all this his anger has not turned away, and his hand is stretched out still") has been divided. The refrain occurs first in 5.25, and then again in 9.12, 17, 21; and 10.4. The first stanza has been separated from the body of the oracle by the material in 6.1–9.7.

The outline of the contents of First Isaiah shows its diversity of arrangement; within each of these larger divisions is evidence of later additions.

- *Chapters 1–12*: A series of oracles, primarily against Israel, interspersed with autobiographical and biographical narratives. The material found in these chapters refers to events throughout the late eighth and early seventh centuries BCE. These include a vision of the prophet in the year of the death of King Uzziah (most likely 733 BCE), found in 6.1–13; the account of the attack on Jerusalem by the combined forces of Israel and Aram in 734 (chaps. 7–8); references to the Assyrian conquest of the northern kingdom of Israel in 722 (9.8–21; 10.11); a coronation hymn, probably for Hezekiah's accession to the throne in 715 (9.2–7); and references to the invasion of Sennacherib in 701 (1.7–9; 10.5–11). At the same time, this material has been reworked as part of the lengthy process of the book's formation.

Chapter 1 can plausibly be viewed as a kind of overture to the book of Isaiah as a whole, setting forth themes and introducing vocabulary that will recur throughout the book. The opening chapters of Isaiah also contain material that is later than the eighth century, such as the visions of a glorious future in chapters 2 and 11 (significantly, chap. 2 has its own introductory note) and the concluding hymnic interludes in chapter 12.

- *Chapters 13–23*: Oracles against foreign nations. These oracles are an extended elaboration of the genre first found in Amos 1–2 (see page XXX). This section includes oracles against Babylon (chap. 13) and its king (14.3–21). A late eighth-century BCE oracle against Babylon by Isaiah of Jerusalem is not inconceivable, given the diplomatic contact between Hezekiah and the Babylonian king Merodach-baladan, as both rebelled against Assyrian control (see page 256 and 2 Kings 20.12 [= Isa 39.1]). In Isaiah 13.17–22, however, mention is made of the Medes, who were located in the region east of Mesopotamia (modern Iran) and were involved in the overthrow of the Babylonians in the mid-sixth century BCE; reference is also made to Babylon's fall. In part, then, if not in its entirety, the oracle against Babylon is to be dated to the sixth century, no earlier than the Babylonian conquest of Judah.

- *Chapters 24–27*: The "Isaiah Apocalypse," a highly mythological account of the divine judgment of the end-time, perhaps written in the fifth century BCE (see further page 361).

- *Chapters 28–33*: Miscellaneous oracles, generally concerned with Judah and Ephraim and their relationships with Egypt.

- *Chapters 34–35*: More postexilic additions, consisting of an attack on Edom, which was an ally of Babylon during the attack on Jerusalem in 586 BCE, and a description of the return of the exiles from Babylon through a transformed wilderness, anticipating the fuller treatment of this theme in Second Isaiah (see page 338).

- *Chapters 36–39*: The narrative of the Deuteronomistic Historians, borrowed from 2 Kings.

The Life of Isaiah

The book of Isaiah gives us some information about the prophet himself. According to the superscription, the opening historical note, his prophetic career occurred during the reigns of the kings of Judah from Uzziah to Hezekiah, that is, in the second half of the eighth and the beginning of the seventh centuries BCE. He was married to a woman the text also identifies as "a prophet," using the feminine form of this noun (Isa. 8.3). Interpretations that suggest her title is derivative of his office, "Mrs. Prophet" as it were, are unconvincing (see page 247). They had several children, who, like those of the prophet Hosea and his wife Gomer (see page 264), had symbolic names: "I and the children whom the LORD has given me are signs and portents from the LORD of Hosts, who dwells on Mount Zion" (8.18). These children are Shear-jashub ("A remnant will return"; 7.3; see 10.21–22), Maher-shalal-hash-baz ("Quickly the plunder, hastily the spoils"; 8.1–3), and probably Immanuel ("God is with us"; 7.14; see further Box 18.2 on page 279); all three names have both positive and negative significance in the book. The prophet also had "disciples" (8.16), who constitute the beginning of the school of Isaiah discussed on page 274.

Judging from the frequent encounters between Isaiah and the kings Ahaz and Hezekiah, it is plausible that Isaiah was a court prophet. As such, he may have been involved in the coronation of Hezekiah as Ahaz's successor, as Nathan was with Solomon (1 Kings 1.45); see further below. Like Nathan, too, Isaiah was an independent voice, criticizing as well as supporting the political and religious establishment in Jerusalem. The prominence of Isaiah both in the book that bears his name and in 2 Kings suggests that he was a major figure in the history of Judah during the late eighth century BCE.

The Message of Isaiah

The superscription to the book of Isaiah describes its contents as "the vision . . . which he saw" (1.1). Unlike the books of Jeremiah and Ezekiel, however, the book of Isaiah does not open with an account of the call of the prophet. What has sometimes been identified as an inaugural vision or call comes later in the book, in chapter 6. The account of the vision begins with the first precisely dated historical reference in the book (6.1: "the year that King Uzziah died," probably 733 BCE) and is in the first person, so that although it draws heavily on traditional themes and genres, it presents itself as autobiographical by the prophet, even if it is not actually so. According to the chronology used in this book, the vision would have occurred after the events described in the subsequent chapters, and thus it is not an inaugural vision or call. To the vision have been added references to later events, including Sennacherib's devastation of Judah in 701 (6.11) and probably to the Babylonian deportations of the early sixth century BCE (6.12–13).

In the vision, Isaiah describes himself as present for a meeting of the divine council, like Micaiah (1 Kings 22.19–23) and later Jeremiah (Jer 23.18, 22). That meeting occurs in the Temple, which was the earthly manifestation of the divine home, and whose location in Jerusalem was part of the royal ideology. Addressing the council, Yahweh asks: "Whom shall I send, and who will go for us?" (Isa 6.8). Unlike Moses (Ex 3–4) and Jeremiah (1.6), Isaiah is not a reluctant prophet; he volunteers to be the council's emissary: "Here I am; send me!" (6.8). The task he is given, however, dampens his enthusiasm. He is instructed to deliver a message to "this people" (not "my people") that they will reject, and, in words often found in petitions and laments (see further page XXX), he plaintively asks, "How long, Lord?" The answer is no more comforting:

> Until cities lie waste
>> without inhabitant,
> and houses without people,
>> and the land is utterly desolate. (Isa 6.11)

The message of Isaiah, then, like that of other prophets, includes dire pronouncements of divine judgment.

Juxtaposed with the proclamations of doom, however, are lyrical passages, such as Isaiah 9.2–7. In that oracle, which later Christian interpretation understood as a messianic prophecy, the prophet proclaims the decree of the divine council on the occasion of a coronation, probably that of Hezekiah:

> For a child has been born for us,
>   a son given to us;
> authority rests upon his shoulders;
>   and he is named
> Wonderful Counselor, Mighty God,
>   Everlasting Father, Prince of Peace.
> His authority shall grow continually,
>   and there shall be endless peace
>   for the throne of David and his kingdom.
> He will establish and uphold it
>   with justice and with righteousness
>   from this time onward and forevermore. (9.6–7)

Adopted as a divine son (see pages 299–30), the newly crowned king is given throne names that describe the deity's enduring support of the dynasty founded by David.

The royal ideology that proclaimed an eternal divine guarantee both for the dynasty and for its capital city is a significant theme in Isaiah. That divine guarantee, however, did not mean that the royal establishment was free to ignore the obligations of social justice. The prophet did not hesitate to condemn the monarchy and the Jerusalem establishment for their social inequities:

> The LORD rises to argue his lawsuit;
>   he stands to judge the peoples.
> The LORD enters into judgment
>   with the elders and princes of his people:
> "It is you who have devoured the vineyard;
>   the spoils of the poor are in your houses.
> What do you mean by crushing my people,
>   by grinding the face of the poor?"
>   says the Lord GOD of hosts. (3.13–15)

Here Isaiah employs the metaphor of the lawsuit (Hebr. *rîb*) for breach of contract, which first appears in Hosea (see pages 265–66). But the party sued by Yahweh is now the leadership of the community—"the elders and princes," who are guilty of the same kinds of social injustice for which Hosea and Amos had condemned the nation as a whole.

Thus, although Jerusalem (Zion) is a central component of the divine plan, it will be punished because its leaders accept bribes and no longer give the least powerful, orphans and widows, their legal rights. Nevertheless, after the divine judgment, Zion will once again be called "the city of righteousness, the faithful city" (1.26; compare 1.21).

Even the most lyrical passages can also express divine judgment, as in the "Song of the Vineyard" in Isaiah 5.1–7. Drawing on what may have been a popular love song, the passage makes it a parable of Yahweh's unrequited love for Israel. Using a frequent biblical metaphor, the song identifies Israel as Yahweh's beloved, his vineyard, which he had carefully tended. Yet after all that Yahweh had done for Israel, it failed to fulfill his requirements. The prophet concludes with a play on words:

> He expected justice [Hebr. *mishpat*],
>   but there was only bloodshed [*mishpah*];
> righteousness [*sedaqa*],
>   but there was only a cry [*se'aqa*]! (5.7)

Isaiah's insistence on social justice echoes the views of Amos and Hosea (see Box 17.3 on page 263), insisting that religious ritual is not the primary obligation:

> When you stretch out your hands,
>   I will hide my eyes from you;
> even though you make many prayers,
>   I will not listen;
>   your hands are full of blood.
> Wash yourselves; make yourselves clean;
>   remove the evil of your doings
>   from before my eyes;
> cease to do evil,
>   learn to do good;
> seek justice,
>   rescue the oppressed,
> defend the orphan,
>   plead for the widow. (1.15–17)

Failure to "seek justice" inevitably will bring upon Israel the divinely caused curses resulting from covenant disobedience. For Isaiah, those curses will take the form of Assyrian invasion. In texts that can be connected with the events of 734 and 701 BCE, the prophet has a distinct attitude toward Assyria, expressed most clearly in 10.5–7:

> Ah, Assyria, the rod of my anger—
>   the club in their hands is my fury!

Against a godless nation I send him,
    and against the people of my wrath I command him,
to take spoils and seize plunder,
    and to tread them down like the mire of the
        streets.
But this is not what he intends,
    nor does he have this in mind;
but it is in his heart to destroy,
    and to cut off nations not a few.

In the prophetic view, it is Yahweh who is ultimately responsible for historical events. Whatever the Assyrians' intentions, ultimately they are simply an instrument in the divine hands, a weapon used in the punishment of Judah.

We can view what happened to the kingdoms of Israel and Judah historically, as part of the Assyrian imperial drive toward dominance of the entire ancient Near East, but according to the prophets all was part of a divine plan. This theological perspective, shared by the Deuteronomic school (see pages 154–55), understands historical events as the working out of divine justice, or theodicy, in which Yahweh is punishing the nation for its failure to trust in him and to observe his commandments.

The prophet Isaiah's intimate involvement in the events of his own times is evident in the sieges of Jerusalem in 734 and 701 BCE.

THE SIEGE OF JERUSALEM IN 734 BCE

Reconstructing the events of the late 730s BCE requires synthesis of several different sources, including the fragmentary records of the Assyrian king Tiglath-pileser III and, in the Bible, the telescoped and occasionally inconsistent accounts found in 2 Kings 16, 2 Chronicles 28, and the book of Isaiah, especially chapters 7–8. Here is a likely scenario, one accepted by most scholars.

In 734 BCE, as Tiglath-pileser moved to reestablish Assyrian control over the smaller kingdoms of the Levant, several of them, including Aram of Damascus (Syria) and the northern kingdom of Israel (often called Ephraim in prophetic texts),

and probably Tyre, Ashkelon, and Edom, formed a coalition in an attempt to block the Assyrian king's advance. Judah must have refused to join this coalition. To force it to do so, the kings of Aram and Israel, Rezin and Pekah, laid siege to Jerusalem, in what is called the **Syro-Ephraimite War**. The siege may have been accompanied by devastation of the kingdom of Judah outside the capital, as suggested in 2 Chronicles 28.5–7. The intention of the kings of Aram and Israel was to depose the newly crowned king, Ahaz, and to replace him with "the son of Tabeel," who would join their anti-Assyria coalition. "The son of Tabeel" cannot be further identified, but he probably was a member of the Judean ruling family and thus a descendant of David.

Ahaz was only twenty years old, and he had just become king. With Jerusalem under siege, he made a strategic decision. To remove the threat to his throne and to his capital, he requested assistance from Tiglath-pileser. According to the Deuteronomistic Historians, that request was couched in the formal language of submission as a vassal: "I am your servant and your son. Come up, and rescue me from the hand of the king of Aram and from the hand of the king of Israel, who are attacking me" (2 Kings 16.7). Ahaz's submission to Tiglath-pileser is confirmed by the mention in Assyrian sources of his paying tribute in 734 BCE. All three biblical sources present Ahaz's submission to Assyria as a lack of trust in Yahweh.

In interrelated passages in chapters 7–8, the book of Isaiah deals with the crisis of 734 BCE. The first, 7.1–17, is a third-person narrative of two encounters between Ahaz and Isaiah, including the prophet's proclamation of a "sign": the birth of a boy named Immanuel and the return of peace and prosperity to Judah in that child's early years. Then we find in 7.18–25 what appear to be several oracles expanding the themes of the preceding passage while also referring to later events, such as the fall of Samaria in 722 and the invasion of Sennacherib in 701. Chapter 8, which is entirely in the first person, like chapter 6, opens with a prediction of the birth of another boy. This is followed by condemnation of Judah for its alliance with Assyria and by three shorter units, having to do with confidence in Yahweh, preservation of the prophet's word, and condemnation of those who prefer to consult the dead.

In the first of the two encounters (Isa 7.3–9), the prophet advises the king not to panic because of the attack by the kings of Aram and Israel. His message is "Be quiet, do not fear" (7.4)—that is, do not do anything, but trust in Yahweh. To reinforce this advice, in a second encounter (7.10–17) the prophet gives the king a sign: The child of a pregnant woman apparently present at the scene will be a son, who will be given the symbolic name **Immanuel** ("God is with us") (see Box 18.2). The guarantee that that name implied will be evident soon: Within a few years after the birth of the child ("by the time he knows how to refuse the

evil and choose the good"), "he shall eat curds and honey"—that is, the land will enjoy almost mythical abundance and return to the peace and prosperity that had characterized the United Monarchy in the tenth century BCE, before "Ephraim departed from Judah." A variation on that message is found in the account of the conception, birth, and symbolic naming of the prophet's son Maher-shalal-hash-baz in 8.1–4.

King Ahaz rejected the prophet's advice, and it is here that we can place the account in 2 Kings 16.5–9 of Ahaz's request to Tiglath-pileser for help and his submission to him as a vassal. Soon thereafter, Isaiah went back to the king with a different interpretation of the original sign, the name Immanuel. Because Ahaz had rejected the divine

Box 18.2 THE IDENTIFICATION OF IMMANUEL

Because of its use in the New Testament, Isaiah 7.14 is one of the most discussed verses in the Hebrew Bible. The identities of the pregnant woman and of her future son, whom the prophet names Immanuel, are not given in the text, nor are they essential for understanding the "sign" that the child's birth, naming, and early life communicate.

Modern scholars generally identify the child either as a son of King Ahaz, probably his successor Hezekiah (see 2 Kings 18.1), or as a son of the prophet Isaiah and his wife, also a prophet. Hezekiah is prominent in the book of Isaiah, as is the divine guarantee of the Davidic dynasty, and he may indeed be the child who is the sign. But the chronology of Hezekiah's reign is confused. According to 2 Kings 18.1, he was twenty-five years old when he assumed the throne; whether that was in 727 BCE (following 2 Kings 18.1) or 715 (following 2 Kings 18.13, the chronology preferred here), he would have been born several years before the events of 734.

It is more likely, then, that Immanuel was the son of Isaiah and his wife, like Maher-shalal-hash-baz in 8.1–3. The parallels between 7.14 and 8.3 are instructive: In both, a pregnant woman is to give birth to a son with a symbolic name.

In the gospel of Matthew (1.22–23), in part because of the translation into Greek of the Hebrew word for young woman, *almah*, as *parthenos* ("virgin"), Immanuel is identified as Jesus, and the young woman as his mother Mary. The Hebrew of Isaiah 7.14 does not use the technical term for "virgin," but rather a more general word, and also uses the past tense: "The young woman has (already) conceived." Matthew thus uses a mistranslation of the text of Isaiah as a vehicle to express early Christian belief in the divine origin of Jesus and thus in his mother's virginity.

assurance and had sought help from Assyria, Yahweh would give them Assyria. Using a dire metaphor, because they had rejected the divinely given water supply of Jerusalem—"the waters of Shiloah that flow gently" (8.6)—Yahweh would send them the waters of the Euphrates River, in the Assyrian heartland:

> Therefore, the Lord is bringing up against it the mighty flood waters of the River, the king of Assyria and all his glory; it will rise above all its channels and overflow all its banks; it will sweep on into Judah as a flood, and, pouring over, it will reach up to the neck; and its outspread wings will fill the breadth of your land, O Immanuel. (Isa 8.7–8)

The name of the child had originally been a positive sign: God is with us, to save and protect us. Now it becomes ominous: God is with us, but to punish, at the hands of the Assyrians. That would occur in 701 BCE.

THE ASSYRIAN INVASION OF JUDAH IN 701 BCE

In 701 BCE, Sennacherib invaded Judah. For this campaign, we have several sources. Each must be interpreted, for none is an objective account of the events, and synthesizing them is a classic exercise in interpretation. Let us begin with the sources themselves.

Assyrian Sources

In the Bassam Cylinder, now in the British Museum, Sennacherib gives his own account (see Box 18.3). In it, he describes a whirlwind campaign south through the Levant, in which he accepted submission and accompanying tribute from a majority of the kings of the states of the region

---

BOX 18.3 SENNACHERIB'S ATTACK ON JERUSALEM (701 BCE) ACCORDING TO THE ASSYRIAN ANNALS

In my third campaign, I marched to Hatti [northern Syria]. The awesome splendor of my lordship overwhelmed Luli, king of Sidon, and he fled overseas far-off. The terrifying nature of the weapon of the god Ashur my lord overwhelmed his strong cities, Greater Sidon, Little Sidon, Bit-zitti, Zarephath, . . . Achzib, Acco, . . . and they bowed in submission at my feet. I installed Tubalu on his royal throne over them and imposed upon him tribute and dues for my lordship payable annually without interruption.

The kings of Amurru, all of them—Minuhimmu of Samsimuruna, Tubalu of Sidon, Abdiliti of Arvad, Urumilki of Byblos, Mitinti of Ashdod, Puduilu of Beth-Ammon, Chemosh-nadbi of Moab, Ayarammu of Edom—brought me sumptuous presents as their abundant audience-gift, fourfold, and kissed my feet.

As for Sidqa, king of Ashkelon, who had not submitted to my yoke—his family gods, he himself, his wife, his sons, his daughters, his brothers, and all the rest of his descendants, I deported and brought him to Assyria. I set Sharru-lu-dari, son of Rukibi, their former king, over the people of Ashkelon and imposed upon him payment of tribute and presents to my lordship; he now bears my yoke. In the course of my campaign, I surrounded and conquered . . . cities belonging to Sidqa, who did not submit quickly, and I carried off their spoils.

The officials, the nobles, and the people of Ekron who had thrown Padi, their king, who was under oath and obligation to Assyria, into iron fetters and handed him over in a hostile manner to Hezekiah, the Judean, took fright because of the offense they had committed. The kings of Egypt, and the bowmen, chariot corps, and cavalry of the king of Cush, assembled a countless force and came to their [the Ekronites'] aid. . . . Trusting in the god Ashur, my lord, I fought with them and inflicted a defeat upon them. The Egyptian charioteers and princes, together with the charioteers of the Cushites, I personally took alive in the midst of the battle. I besieged and conquered Eltekeh and Timnah and carried off their spoils. I advanced to Ekron and slew its officials and nobles who had stirred up rebellion and hung their bodies on watchtowers all about the city. The citizens who committed sinful acts I counted as spoils, and I ordered the release of the rest of them, who had not sinned. I freed Padi, their king, from Jerusalem, and set him on the throne as king over them, and imposed tribute for my lordship over him.

As for Hezekiah, the Judean, I besieged 46 of his fortified walled cities and surrounding smaller towns, which were without number. Using packed-down ramps and applying battering rams, infantry attacks by mines, breaches, and siege machines, I conquered them. I took out 200,150 people, young and old, male and female, horses, mules, donkeys, camels, cattle, and sheep, without number, and counted them as spoils. He himself I locked up within Jerusalem, his royal city, like a bird in a cage. I surrounded him with armed posts, and made it unthinkable for him to exit by the city gate. His cities which I had despoiled I cut off from his land and gave them to Mitinti, king of Ashdod, Padi, king of Ekron, and Silli-Bel, king of Gaza, and thus diminished his land. I imposed dues and gifts for my lordship upon him, in addition to the former tribute, their yearly payment.

He, Hezekiah, was overwhelmed by the awesome splendor of my lordship, and he sent me after my departure to Nineveh, my royal city, his elite troops and his best soldiers, which he had brought in as reinforcements to strengthen Jerusalem, his royal city, with 30 talents of gold, 800 talents of silver, choice antimony, large blocks of carnelian, beds inlaid with ivory, armchairs inlaid with ivory, elephant hides, ivory, ebony-wood, boxwood, multicolored garments, garments of linen, wool dyed red-purple and blue-purple, vessels of copper, iron, bronze and tin, chariots, siege shields, lances, armor, daggers for the belt, bows and arrows, countless trappings and implements of war, together with his daughters, his palace women, his male and female singers. He also dispatched his messenger to deliver the tribute and to do obeisance.*

---

* Translation adapted from M. Cogan, pp. 112–15 in *The Raging Torrent: Historical Inscriptions from Assyria and Babylonia Relating to Ancient Israel* (Jerusalem: Carta, 2008).

and punished those who did not submit (see Figure 18.2). Among the latter was Hezekiah, king of Judah, whose territory was brutally taken over and whose capital, Jerusalem, was besieged. According to Sennacherib, these measures compelled Hezekiah to surrender, and also to pay an enormous tribute.

In addition to this text, we have a vivid depiction of the siege and capture of one of the main fortified cities of Judah, Lachish, in reliefs that decorated a large room in Sennacherib's palace at Nineveh. Curiously, the Assyrian text does not mention Lachish, although the city on the reliefs is identified in a kind of caption (see Figure 18.3).

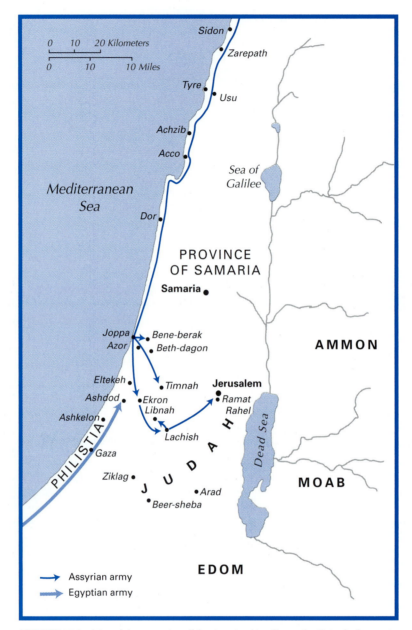

FIGURE 18.2   Map of the campaign of the Assyrian king Sennacherib in the Levant in 701 BCE.

2 Kings 18–20

Scholars have identified two different sources in the Deuteronomistic Historians' account of Hezekiah's reign in 2 Kings. The first is a matter-of-fact, annalistic account of Sennacherib's invasion:

> In the fourteenth year of King Hezekiah, King Sennacherib of Assyria came up against all the fortified

FIGURE 18.3 The Assyrian king Sennacherib at the Judean city of Lachish, from reliefs in his palace at Nineveh. The cuneiform inscription at the upper left reads "Sennacherib, king of the world, king of Assyria, sitting on his throne and reviewing the spoils from Lachish." The king's face has been mutilated, perhaps during the capture of Nineveh by the Babylonians in 612 BCE.

cities of Judah and captured them. King Hezekiah of Judah sent to the king of Assyria at Lachish, saying, "I have done wrong; withdraw from me; whatever you impose on me I will bear." The king of Assyria demanded of King Hezekiah of Judah three hundred talents of silver and thirty talents of gold. Hezekiah gave him all the silver that was found in the house of the LORD and in the treasuries of the king's house. At that time Hezekiah stripped the gold from the doors of the temple of the LORD, and from the doorposts that King Hezekiah of Judah had overlaid and gave it to the king of Assyria. (2 Kings 18.13–16)

This brief account, often called the A-source, corresponds closely to that of Sennacherib himself,

although the Assyrian version gives many more details.

The A-source is followed by a very different set of narratives. Called the B-source, it actually consists of two parallel accounts of communications between Sennacherib and Hezekiah and the latter's reactions. The first (B¹) is 2 Kings 18.17–19.9a, and probably concludes with 19.36–37; the second (B²) is 2 Kings 19.9b–35. In the first, a delegation of Assyrian officials appears before the walls of Jerusalem and, addressing first Hezekiah's representatives and then the city's inhabitants directly, challenges Hezekiah's trust in Yahweh. Although the speech is part of an invented dialogue, it is noteworthy for its detailed attack on Hezekiah's policy of centralization of worship. How can Hezekiah rely on Yahweh if it is his shrines that the king destroyed? Reflecting the prophetic view that Yahweh controlled historical events, the speech goes on to observe that if the Assyrians are present, it must be because Yahweh has sent them; resistance is therefore futile. Although the king is disheartened, the prophet Isaiah gives him assurance: "Do not be afraid. . . . I will cause him [the king of Assyria] to fall by the sword in his own land" (2 Kings 19.6–7).

In the second encounter, Sennacherib sends Hezekiah a letter after the conquest of Lachish. Again, Sennacherib challenges the people's trust in Yahweh: "Do not let your God on whom you rely deceive you by promising that Jerusalem will not be given into the hand of the king of Assyria" (2 Kings 19.10). And, as he had earlier, he refers to the Assyrian victories over all other lands and the weakness of their gods. Because the letter repeats much of the speech of the Assyrian envoy (the Rabshakeh) in the previous episode, most scholars interpret the two as variations (hence, B¹ and B²). Hezekiah's response to this communication is a pious prayer for Yahweh's help, and in response, the prophet Isaiah delivers an oracle of deliverance. The B-source concludes with a direct divine intervention: "That very night the angel of the LORD set out and struck down one hundred eighty-five thousand in the camp of the Assyrians; when morning dawned, they were all dead bodies" (2 Kings 19.35).

This composite B-source has the character of prophetic legends, like those found earlier in the Deuteronomistic History. In it, the prophet Isaiah is a central figure, advising Hezekiah to trust in Yahweh. And, according to this source, Hezekiah does so; his piety contrasts with that of his predecessor Ahaz, who had trusted in Assyria rather than in Yahweh.

So different in tone and in detail are the A- and B-sources that some conservative scholars have argued, because the biblical account should be taken at face value, that there must have been two campaigns of Sennacherib: one in 701 BCE, described in the A-source and in Sennacherib's annals, ending in an Assyrian victory; and another, recounted in the B-source but not in any surviving Assyrian record, ending in an Assyrian defeat. Most contemporary scholars, however, have rejected this "two-campaign hypothesis," recognizing that the biblical tradition here, as elsewhere, simply juxtaposes two different accounts of the same event.

2 Chronicles 32

Although largely reproducing its source in 2 Kings, the Chronicler's narrative of the events of 701 BCE provides details not found elsewhere, especially concerning Hezekiah's preparations for the attack. We are told that Hezekiah repaired and added to Jerusalem's fortifications (2 Chr 32.5), and also that he redirected the waters of the Gihon Spring to the west of the city of David (2 Chr 32.30). This expands on the statement in 2 Kings, which reports more briefly that "he made the pool and the conduit and brought water into the city" (2 Kings 20.20).

Isaiah

References to Sennacherib's invasion are found throughout First Isaiah, beginning in the first chapter:

Your country lies desolate,
    your cities are burned with fire;
in your very presence
    aliens devour your land;
    it is desolate, as overthrown by foreigners.
And daughter Zion is left
    like a booth in a vineyard,
like a shelter in a cucumber field,
    like a besieged city.
If the LORD of hosts
    had not left us a few survivors,
we would have been like Sodom,
    and become like Gomorrah. (1.7–9)

This passage poetically describes the devastation that accompanied the Assyrian onslaught. All the cities outside Jerusalem were burned, and Jerusalem itself was left standing like a ramshackle guard's hut in a vineyard or field.

The book of Isaiah also reproduces 2 Kings 18–20 in Isaiah 36–39, with one notable omission: The Isaiah version omits the account in 2 Kings 18.14–16 (the A-source described earlier) of Hezekiah's surrender and payment of tribute, making it appear that Sennacherib's arrogant assault on Yahweh's home was punished by the deity himself. It also adds another prayer of Hezekiah during his illness, in the sequel to the B-source (Isa 38.9–20). The result is a consistent narrative that emphasizes Hezekiah's piety.

Archaeological Evidence

At many Judean sites, a massive destruction layer has been connected convincingly with Sennacherib's campaign in 701 BCE, which, according to both Assyrian and biblical sources, devastated Judah. Excavations at Lachish have uncovered such a destruction layer, and also have confirmed details of the depiction of Lachish in the reliefs from Nineveh, especially the fortifications and the Assyrian siege ramp (see Figure 18.4).

Discoveries in Jerusalem contribute further to our understanding of the events of the late eighth century BCE. Considerable evidence exists for an eighth-century expansion of the city beyond the fortified limits of the city of David, especially to its west. Some of this expansion can be attributed to an influx of refugees from the northern kingdom of Israel, especially after its destruction by the Assyrians in 722 BCE. This expanded area, called the "Second Quarter" (2 Kings 22.14; Zeph 1.10), was fortified by Hezekiah, and parts of these fortifications have been discovered (see Plate 10 in the color section following page 220). Also connected with Hezekiah's defensive preparations for the anticipated Assyrian attack on his capital was the construction of a water tunnel (see Box 18.4 on page 286).

Synthesis

Recognizing that each source needs to be interpreted, it is possible to synthesize them. Having neutralized the unrest in Babylon, Sennacherib briefly turned his attention to his western frontier, and in a swift campaign subdued the coastal cities,

FIGURE 18.4 Another detail from the reliefs in Sennacherib's palace at Nineveh, showing the city of Lachish under siege. At the left, an Assyrian battering ram attacks the city's gate as the defenders send down arrows, torches, and stones. At the lower right, captives leave the gate, headed for exile.

and then the rebellious kingdom of Judah, whose king, Hezekiah, had withheld the required tribute and fomented unrest among other states in the region.

The campaign against Judah had several stages. First, the fortified cities of the kingdom were captured—forty-six in all, according to Sennacherib's count. Then Sennacherib laid siege to and captured the major southern Judean city of Lachish, where he established his headquarters. Finally, having devastated the Judean countryside, he turned his attention to Jerusalem, some 20 miles (32 km) northeast of Lachish. With his kingdom decimated and his capital under siege and cut off from food supplies, Hezekiah soon surrendered, and later sent a heavy tribute to the Assyrian capital at Nineveh.

As this event was retold, however, the survival of Jerusalem came to be interpreted as divinely

Box 18.4 HEZEKIAH'S TUNNEL

One of the earliest modern discoveries in Jerusalem was the underground water conduit known as "Hezekiah's Tunnel" or the "Siloam Tunnel." This construction, which is over 1,700 ft (500 m) long, was a feat of ancient engineering. Its purpose was to divert the city's main source of water, the Gihon Spring in the Kidron Valley on the lower northeastern slopes of the city of David, to the Siloam Pool on the southwest, which was enclosed by the newly constructed fortifications. The city's water supply would therefore have been protected from enemy attack or poisoning.

On the wall of the tunnel itself, near its southern end, an inscription was found in 1880 carved in elegant Hebrew script, one of very few monumental texts from the monarchic period. Now incomplete, it describes how the teams of workers, starting from opposite sides, finally met:

. . . the piercing. And this is the account of the piercing. While . . . were still . . . the ax, each man toward his neighbor, and while

FIGURE 18.5 The interior of Hezekiah's Tunnel, constructed in preparation for the Assyrian attack of 701 BCE. Marks left by the picks of the ancient workers are visible on the sides and roof of the tunnel.

there were still three cubits to the piercing, [there was hear]d the voice of a man calling to his neighbor, because there was a crack in the rock, on the right and on the left. And on the day of the piercing, the hewers struck, each man toward his neighbor, ax against ax, and the waters flowed from the source to the pool, one thousand two hundred cubits, and one hundred cubits was the rock above the heads of the hewers.

accomplished. After all, if Yahweh was responsible for the Assyrian onslaught, as the Deuteronomistic and prophetic interpreters had argued, then he was also responsible for the failure of the Assyrians to capture and destroy Jerusalem. Most other cities in the Levant that had not submitted to Assyrian rule, including Samaria, had been destroyed, but not Jerusalem. So the deliverance of Jerusalem came to be understood as a miracle that demonstrated the divine guarantee of the city itself and of the Davidic dynasty whose capital it was.

MICAH

The Book of Micah

The book named for Isaiah's contemporary, the prophet **Micah**, consists of oracles of judgment against Judah interspersed with oracles of restoration, as the following outline shows:

1.1	Superscription
1.2–2.11	Oracles of judgment
2.12–13	Oracle of restoration
3.1–12	Oracles of judgment
4.1–5.15	Oracles of restoration
6.1–7.6	Oracles of judgment
7.7–20	Oracles of restoration

Like other prophetic books, the book of Micah was expanded in later times, as its message continued to be thought relevant. For example, many scholars understand 7.8–10 to refer to the destruction of Jerusalem in 586 BCE, and the mention of the rebuilding of Jerusalem's walls in 7.11 to refer to the activity of Nehemiah in the fifth century BCE. In this editorial process, material from other sources was added to the collection, including 4.1–4, which as noted earlier is almost identical to Isaiah 2.2–4.

The Life of Micah

Micah's career is dated by the book's editorial introduction to the reigns of Jotham, Ahaz, and Hezekiah, approximately the second half of the eighth century BCE, dating that is confirmed in the book itself by references to the fall of Samaria in 722 BCE (1.6) and to the Assyrian attack on Jerusalem in 701 (1.8–16). He was therefore a contemporary of his fellow Judean Isaiah. But while Isaiah was from Jerusalem, Micah was from the smaller town of Moresheth-gath in southern Judah and was considerably more hostile toward the capital than was Isaiah. The book gives no other details about the prophet's life.

The Message of Micah

Even though it is a relatively short book, Micah uses a variety of genres, including lament (1.8–16; 7.8–10), theophany (1.3–4), and hymnic prayer of petition and confidence (7.14–20). Like Hosea and Isaiah, Micah also includes an example of the covenant lawsuit (see pages 265–66), in which Yahweh sues Israel for breach of contract (6.1–8). The lawsuit begins with an address to the mountains and hills, reminiscent of the "olden gods" in the lists of divine witnesses of the suzerainty treaties (see further page 101). It continues with a summary of what Yahweh had done for Israel from the Exodus to the entry into the Promised Land, recalling the historical prologue of the treaties. It concludes with the requirement of justice and "kindness," that is, covenant fidelity, rather than sacrifice (see further Box 17.3 on page 263).

One indication of the importance of Micah's message is its being referred to in Jeremiah 26.18, written over a century later. Micah's judgment on Jerusalem (Mic 3.12) is quoted in Jeremiah's defense by some of his contemporaries:

> Micah of Moresheth, who prophesied during the days of King Hezekiah of Judah, said to all the people of Judah:
> "Thus says the LORD of hosts,
>   Zion shall be plowed as a field;
>   Jerusalem shall become a heap of ruins,
>   and the mountain of the house a wooded height."
> Did King Hezekiah of Judah and all Judah actually put him to death? (Jer 26.18–19)

Just as Hezekiah did not sentence Micah to death for his prophecy of doom, the argument goes, neither should King Jehoiakim sentence Jeremiah to death for his prediction of Jerusalem's destruction. This is a rare instance of one biblical book explicitly quoting another.

A LOOK BACK AND AHEAD

In the last four decades of the eighth century BCE, Jerusalem had been under siege twice and had not fallen. The royal ideology was apparently true: Yahweh had chosen Jerusalem as his home and the Davidic dynasty as his designated rulers. Quoting the prophet Isaiah speaking in the name of Yahweh, the Deuteronomistic Historians put it this way: "I will defend this city to save it, for my own sake and for the sake of my servant David" (2 Kings 19.34 = Isa 37.35). Moreover, unlike Ahaz, Hezekiah had trusted in Yahweh rather than in Assyria and had also been faithful to the Deuteronomic program of reform, and Yahweh had rewarded him with deliverance.

Yet Hezekiah's revolt against Assyria and the subsequent invasion of Sennacherib inaugurated a dark age in the history of Judah. The kingdom would not recover for many decades, although the message of the prophets, especially of Isaiah, was preserved. That message linked continuing divine protection to observance of the covenant, and especially to social justice. Would Judah continue to heed the prophetic warnings and learn from the experience of the northern kingdom of Israel? That question would not be answered for another century.

IMPORTANT NAMES AND TERMS

Each name or term is defined briefly in the Glossary. Its first significant occurrence in this chapter appears in **boldface** type.

Ahaz

First Isaiah

Hezekiah

Immanuel

Isaiah

Micah

Sennacherib

Syro-Ephraimite War

QUESTIONS FOR REVIEW

1. Why is Hezekiah given such high praise in the book of Kings?

2. Describe the interactions between the prophet Isaiah and the kings of Judah.

3. How do the various biblical and nonbiblical accounts of the siege of Jerusalem by Sennacherib differ from each other, and what is the significance of those differences?

BIBLIOGRAPHY

For good summaries of the history of the period, see the concluding pages of the essay by Edward F. Campbell cited in the bibliography to Chapter 16 and the opening sections of Mordechai Cogan, "Into Exile: From the Assyrian Conquest of Israel to the Fall of Babylon," Chap. 7 in *The Oxford History of the Biblical World* (ed. M. D. Coogan; New York: Oxford University Press, 1998; available in Oxford Biblical Studies Online).

An excellent summary and synthesis of the various sources for Sennacherib's campaign is found in Cogan and Tadmor, *II Kings* (New York: Doubleday, 1988), pp. 246–51. For a minority view, which takes the biblical narrative more literally as describing two separate events, see A. Kirk Grayson, "Sennacherib," pp. 1088–89 in *Anchor Bible Dictionary*, Vol. 5 (ed. D. N. Freedman; New York: Doubleday, 1992).

For an introduction to the interpretation of the book of Isaiah, see Richard J. Clifford, "Isaiah, Book of," pp. 75–91 in *The New Interpreter's Dictionary of the Bible*, Vol. 3 (ed. K. D. Sakenfeld; Nashville, TN: Abingdon, 2008).

A good introduction to the book of Micah is Carolyn J. Sharp, "Micah," pp. 78–85 in *The Oxford Encyclopedia of the Books of the Bible*, vol. 2, ed. M. D. Coogan (New York: Oxford University Press, 2011; available in Oxford Biblical Studies Online).

chapter 19

Judah in the Seventh and Early Sixth Centuries BCE: The End of Assyrian Domination and the Fall of Jerusalem

2 Kings 21–25, 2 Chronicles 33–36, Zephaniah, Nahum, Habakkuk, and Jeremiah

At the beginning of the seventh century BCE, the Assyrian empire was approaching the pinnacle of its power, but by the end of the century the Assyrians had disappeared from the scene. In the jockeying that attended the empire's collapse, Judah was caught between a resurgent Egypt and a rising Babylon, and would inevitably be the loser. This was the era of two important Judean kings, Manasseh, Hezekiah's son and successor, a loyal Assyrian vassal, and Josiah, Manasseh's grandson, who took advantage of Assyrian weakness to again assert Judah's independence and to carry out a religious reform.

But the momentum of the forces leading to Judah's destruction increased. Just over two decades after the untimely death in 609 BCE of King Josiah, in whom so much hope had been placed, the dynasty founded by David over four hundred years earlier came to an end and Jerusalem and its Temple were destroyed, all at the hands of the Babylonians. Because these events were so significant, it is not surprising that the Bible preserves a number of perspectives on them, not just in 2 Kings and 2 Chronicles, but also in the books of Jeremiah and Ezekiel, both of whom were participants in the events, and elsewhere throughout biblical tradition, for example,

in the book of Lamentations and some of the Psalms. In the next several chapters, we will examine the events themselves and the varied reactions and responses to them.

HISTORY

Having disposed of the irritation posed by the rebellious Judean king Hezekiah and having regained control of Babylon, the Assyrians continued their drive toward imperial control of the entire Near East. They achieved this goal in 663 BCE when the Assyrian army captured the Egyptian capital of Thebes in Upper (southern) Egypt. Under the kings Esarhaddon (681–669) and Ashurbanipal (669–627), the Assyrian empire was at its peak. But, overextended, by the last quarter of the seventh century BCE, its decline was rapid.

Egypt declared its independence from Assyria under Psammetichus I in 655 BCE, although relations between the two powers continued to be friendly. From the mid-seventh century BCE on, outbreaks of unrest occurred in Babylon, Assyria's powerful southern subject. A catalyst for Assyria's demise was probably the death of Ashurbanipal in 627. Because of internal struggles in the succession to Ashurbanipal, Assyrian central power was weak. Taking advantage of this, Nabopolassar, a general who had assumed the throne of Babylon in 626, had taken charge of all of Babylonia by 620. Meanwhile, the Medes, from the region east of the Tigris River, invaded central Assyria and soon allied themselves with Babylon. In 612, their combined forces attacked and looted Nineveh, the Assyrian capital.

Fearing a decrease in their own independence if the Babylonians succeeded in eliminating the now weakened Assyrians, the Egyptians intervened several times on the Assyrian side, but to no avail. All that remained was to complete the takeover of Assyrian territory, which the Babylonians accomplished in 609 BCE; we find no mention of Assyria as an imperial power after 608. In 605, the Egyptians, now fighting alone and probably seeking to extend their own sphere of control northward, challenged the Babylonians in Syria, but they were defeated soundly. The Assyrian empire became the Neo-Babylonian empire, ruled first by Nabopolassar and then by his son and successor **Nebuchadrezzar** II (in the Bible also called Nebuchadnezzar; 605–562).

In Judah, Hezekiah's son Manasseh ruled for nearly five decades and was a loyal vassal of the Assyrian kings. Assyria's preoccupations elsewhere meant that after the mid-seventh century BCE, Judah was essentially on its own. Following the brief reign of Amon, Josiah came to the throne and eventually, following the example of his great-grandfather Hezekiah in the previous century, decided to take advantage of Assyrian weakness and effectively declared his independence.

When the Egyptian army under Neco II was heading north, both to assist the tottering Assyrians and to extend Egyptian control over the Levant, Josiah tried to block the advancing Egyptian army and was killed in a battle at Megiddo in 609 BCE. Josiah's son Jehoahaz succeeded him, but after only three months Neco replaced him as king of Judah with another of Josiah's sons, Jehoiakim (Eliakim), who in effect became an Egyptian vassal.

It is symptomatic of the selective nature of our sources that the two great biblical histories of the Israelite monarchy, the books of Kings and Chronicles, make no mention of the great Assyrian king Ashurbanipal and that Assyrian and Egyptian records make no mention of Josiah. In fact, Assyrian sources become spotty as the empire disintegrates, and they make no mention of Judah after 643 BCE.

With the final defeat of the Assyrians and their Egyptian allies in the battle of Carchemish in 605, the Babylonians under Nebuchadrezzar moved quickly to contain Egypt, which was attempting to regain control over the Levant. From this point onward, Egypt was neutralized and largely restricted to its own borders, although unlike the Assyrians, the Babylonians never succeeded in conquering Egypt.

In Judah, the three-month reign of Josiah's successor Jehoahaz ended when the Egyptian pharaoh Neco replaced him with his brother, Eliakim (608–598), whose throne name was Jehoiakim. Jehoiakim was at first a loyal vassal of Egypt, but when the Babylonians attacked the Egyptian frontier, Jehoiakim became a vassal of Babylon. When the Babylonians withdrew, however, Jehoiakim rebelled against the king of Babylon, refusing to pay the required tribute. As Nebuchadrezzar was preparing to reassert his control over Judah, Jehoiakim died and was succeeded by his son Jehoiachin, a confusingly similar-sounding name.

Jehoiachin was king in 597, during the first Babylonian siege of Jerusalem, which ended with his surrender and subsequent exile to Babylon along with, we are told, several thousand of the elite. The Babylonians ransacked the Temple and royal treasuries but did not destroy the city, and Nebuchadrezzar appointed another son of Josiah, Mattaniah, as king, renaming him Zedekiah.

Like Hezekiah and Josiah with Assyria, and his more immediate predecessor Jehoiakim, Zedekiah asserted his independence from Babylon, probably around 590. Babylonian reprisal was swift. In 587, Nebuchadrezzar's army laid siege to Jerusalem again. The Babylonian attack on the city was joined by vassal states of Babylon in the Levant, including Aram, Moab, Ammon, and Edom. In the summer of 586, weakened by famine, the city fell. The king was captured as he fled, and was taken as a prisoner to Babylon. The royal quarter was razed, and more of the elite were deported.

Box 19.1 CHRONOLOGY OF THE SEVENTH AND EARLY SIXTH CENTURIES BCE

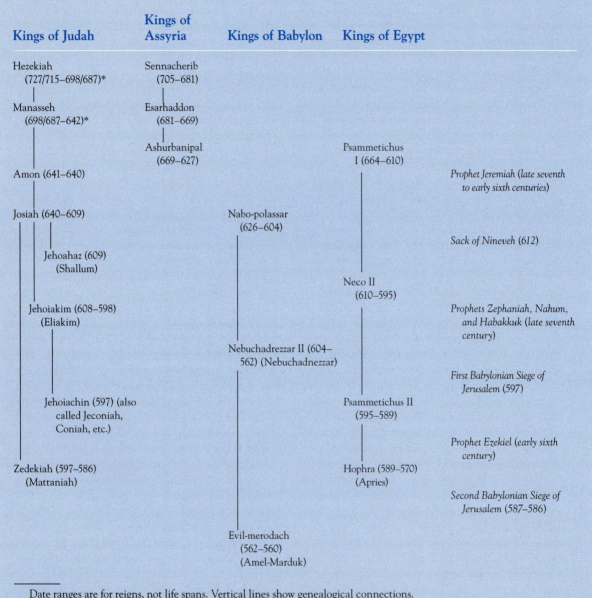

Kings of Judah	Kings of Assyria	Kings of Babylon	Kings of Egypt	
Hezekiah (727/715–698/687)*	Sennacherib (705–681)			
Manasseh (698/687–642)*	Esarhaddon (681–669)			
	Ashurbanipal (669–627)		Psammetichus I (664–610)	Prophet Jeremiah (late seventh to early sixth centuries)
Amon (641–640)				
Josiah (640–609)		Nabo-polassar (626–604)		Sack of Nineveh (612)
Jehoahaz (609) (Shallum)			Neco II (610–595)	
Jehoiakim (608–598) (Eliakim)				Prophets Zephaniah, Nahum, and Habakkuk (late seventh century)
		Nebuchadrezzar II (604–562) (Nebuchadnezzar)		First Babylonian Siege of Jerusalem (597)
Jehoiachin (597) (also called Jeconiah, Coniah, etc.)			Psammetichus II (595–589)	
				Prophet Ezekiel (early sixth century)
Zedekiah (597–586) (Mattaniah)			Hophra (589–570) (Apries)	Second Babylonian Siege of Jerusalem (587–586)
		Evil-merodach (562–560) (Amel-Marduk)		

Date ranges are for reigns, not life spans. Vertical lines show genealogical connections.

*   The data are inconsistent for Hezekiah's reign and the beginning of Manasseh's reign.

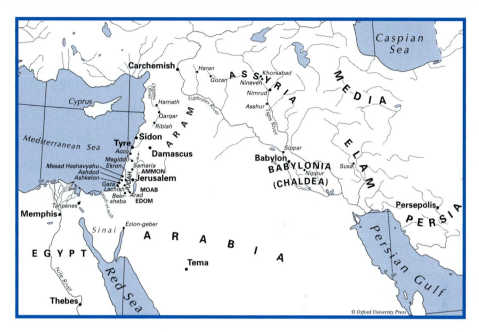

FIGURE 19.1   Map of the Neo-Babylonian empire.

For the history of the last few kings of Judah our primary sources are biblical, especially the Deuteronomistic History in the book of Kings, and the book of Jeremiah, both of which we will examine in detail in this chapter; further information is provided by the books of Ezekiel and Chronicles. Nonbiblical textual sources are scant and fragmentary. The most important is the "Babylonian Chronicles," cuneiform tablets that summarize the reigns of Babylonian rulers in the late seventh and sixth centuries BCE. The relevant tablet dealing with the reign of Nebuchadrezzar describes his attack on Jerusalem in 597:

> Year 7: The king . . . encamped against the city of Judah, and on the second of Adar, he captured the city and he seized its king. A king of his choice he appointed there; he took heavy tribute and carried it off to Babylon.

The corresponding section dealing with the second attack on Jerusalem in 587–586 is missing. Finally, broken tablets found in the ruins of Nebuchadrezzar's palace in Babylon list rations delivered to captives under a kind of house arrest, including Jehoiachin, who is called "king of Judah," and his five sons.

Excavated sites also provide considerable evidence for the events of this period. Nebuchadrezzar's campaign to the south in 604 caused massive destruction levels at important coastal cities. Excavations at Lachish show a refortification of the city ruined by the Assyrian king Sennacherib in 701; this city (called Level II) was destroyed in the Babylonian campaign of 587–586. Among the ruins of the gate of this level were nearly two dozen inscribed potsherds, or ostraca, known as the Lachish letters. One of them contains this message sent to the Judean garrison at Lachish from an unnamed location:

> May my lord know that we are watching for the firesignals of Lachish, according to all the signs which my lord has arranged, for we can no longer see (the signals of) Azekah.

This correlates with Jeremiah 34.6–7, which describes the situation shortly before the letter was sent:

> Then the prophet Jeremiah spoke all these words to Zedekiah king of Judah, in Jerusalem, when the army of the king of Babylon was fighting against Jerusalem and against all the cities of Judah that were left, Lachish and Azekah; for these were the only fortified cities of Judah that remained.

Jerusalem, too, shows evidence of destruction in 586, including a widespread layer of ashes among which were found arrowheads both of the Judean defenders of the city and of its attackers (see Figure 19.2).

The Reign of Manasseh

Manasseh was king of Judah for nearly half a century, longer than any other ruler in the Davidic dynasty, yet for that long reign we have little documentation. The Deuteronomistic Historians dispose of it in a mere eighteen verses consisting largely of Deuteronomistic clichés (2 Kings 21.1–18), and their interest is almost entirely in condemning Manasseh's religious apostasy. From the Deuteronomistic perspective, Manasseh was the worst of the kings of Judah, contrasting sharply with both his predecessor Hezekiah and his successor Josiah. Surprisingly, however, we find no prophetic perspective on Manasseh.

To this stereotypical and negative portrait of Manasseh, the book of Chronicles provides some modification. According to it, Manasseh was arrested by the king of Assyria (2 Chr 33.11). While in prison, he repented of his apostasy and was returned to his throne by divine intervention; from this point onward, the Chronicler asserts, Manasseh was a pious and model ruler (2 Chr 33.12–19). This story may have a historical basis; evidence can be found of other kings having been summoned to Assyria. For the Chronicler, however, this episode serves as an implicit explanation of Manasseh's long reign, which must have been the result of divine favor. The place of Manasseh's imprisonment was Babylon, and although that

FIGURE 19.2   A layer of ashes from the Babylonian destruction of Jerusalem in 586 BCE (see 2 Kings 25.9). These remains, found adjacent to the city's fortifications, include arrowheads of two types: one used by the attackers of the city on the upper left and three of local origin, used in vain by the city's defenders.

Box 19.2 ASHURBANIPAL'S LIBRARY

The great Assyrian king Ashurbanipal had a fascination with the past, and during his forty-two-year reign, he sponsored the collection and copying of older texts for his library at Nineveh. His aggressive acquisitions policy resulted in a carefully catalogued library of as many as twenty thousand tablets consisting of more than fifteen hundred different works. The collection included myths, such as *Enuma Elish* and *Gilgamesh*; hymns; prayers; and medical, mathematical, ritual, divinatory, and astrological texts alongside all sorts of administrative documents, letters, and contracts. The discovery of these tablets in the mid-nineteenth century by Hormuzd Rassam, and their decipherment soon after, provided the modern world its first detailed glimpse of the languages and literature of ancient Mesopotamia, and their connections with biblical traditions soon became apparent.

city was then under Assyrian control, its mention seems historically questionable. In Chronicles, Manasseh's detention in Babylon, his repentance, and his restoration to Judah are a kind of prototype for the experience of the nation as a whole in the sixth century BCE.

It was during Manasseh's reign that Assyria's power was at its height, and he is twice mentioned in Assyrian sources as providing materials for the construction of a palace in the Assyrian capital at Nineveh and troops for the capture of the Egyptian capital at Thebes. Assyrian dominance over Judah is illustrated by the presence of Assyrian forts on the kingdom's southern boundary.

Given the tendentious and limited character of the sources, it is difficult to know exactly what Manasseh's policies were. For the most part, he seems to have been a loyal Assyrian vassal. He also seems to have reversed many aspects of his father Hezekiah's religious reform, a reversal that may have been popular with his subjects. Most significant perhaps is his survival: During his long reign, we know of no attacks on Judah, and the dynasty remained secure. The era of Manasseh, then, was a period of relative calm, even if Judah's power was limited.

Manasseh was succeeded on the throne by his son Amon, whose brief two-year reign was cut short by a palace coup. According to the Deuteronomistic Historians, the conspirators themselves were killed by "the people of the land," who installed Amon's son Josiah on the throne (2 Kings 21.23–24).

The Reign of Josiah

Josiah became king at the age of eight, in 640 BCE, and he ruled for some three decades. The account of Josiah's reign in the Deuteronomistic History (2 Kings 22.1–23.30) is almost entirely devoted to his religious reform, which it dates to the eighteenth year of his reign.

According to 2 Kings 22, during repairs to the Temple, a "book"—more correctly, a scroll—was found in the Temple archives. This "book of the law" (2 Kings 22.8) inspired the king to begin a comprehensive reform. He restricted the worship of Yahweh to Jerusalem and purged the kingdom and especially the capital of the worship of gods other than Yahweh. The royal zeal extended into the territory of the former northern kingdom, the Assyrian province of Samaria (2 Kings 23.15–20). The reform was capped with a national celebration of the Passover.

Since the early nineteenth century, following the suggestion of the German scholar Wilhelm de

Wette, the scroll found in the Temple has been identified as some form of the biblical book of Deuteronomy, a suggestion that had been made earlier by some medieval scholars. As we have seen (on pages 148–49), Deuteronomy has its own complicated history, but its origins lie in northern Israel, and an early form of the book probably was brought to Jerusalem with the refugees from the Assyrian destruction of the northern kingdom in 722 BCE. There it served as the inspiration for the reform of Josiah's predecessor Hezekiah (see pages 271–72), and it may be that having been deposited in the Temple library, it was forgotten or neglected during the period of Assyrian domination, the first three quarters of the seventh century BCE. We should note, however, that elsewhere in the ancient world, the discovery of a supposedly ancient text is often used to justify royal activity. Having been "discovered," whether by accident or by design, it reportedly inspired Josiah to undertake a reform; when hearing it read to him, he tore his clothes in the traditional sign of mourning, an appropriate reaction to the dire curses and punishments found in Deuteronomy.

Our primary source for Josiah's reform is 2 Kings 22–23, hardly an objective account. The books of Kings are part of the Deuteronomistic History, a product of the Deuteronomic school that interpreted Israel's history in the land in light of the principles laid down in Deuteronomy. Thus, in Deuteronomy, Moses commanded the Israelites to "do what is right in the eyes of the LORD" (Deut 13.18), and neither they nor their kings should "turn to the right or to the left" (Deut 5.32). Throughout the books of Kings, when they are measured against this standard, most rulers of both Israel and Judah fall short. A few kings of Judah are given qualified approval: These did "what was right in the eyes of Yahweh," but failed to remove the "high places" where illicit worship was carried out. Only two kings, Hezekiah and Josiah, are given unqualified approval by the Deuteronomistic Historians. As we have seen on pages XXX–XX and XXX–XX, it is likely that the first edition of the Deuteronomistic History was produced during Hezekiah's reign. A second edition was produced during the reign of Josiah. For

the Deuteronomistic Historians, like some of his predecessors, Josiah "did what was right in the eyes of the LORD" (2 Kings 22.2). But only of Josiah is it said that "he walked in all the way of his father David; he did not turn aside to the right or to the left" (2 Kings 22.2). Moreover, unlike most of his predecessors, Josiah destroyed the high places, in accord with Deuteronomic law.

For the Deuteronomists of Josiah's time, his reign was a climax. During it, Israel returned to the ideals of the teaching of Moses as promulgated in Deuteronomy. The Deuteronomistic Historians present a paragon of fidelity to the teaching of Moses in King Josiah, "who turned to the LORD with all his heart, with all his soul, and with all his might" (2 Kings 23.25). According to the Deuteronomistic Historians, Josiah's coming had been foreseen by a prophet centuries before in an attack against the newly established sanctuary at Bethel: "O altar, altar, thus says the LORD: 'A son shall be born to the house of David, Josiah by name; and he shall sacrifice on you the priests of the high places who offer incense on you, and human bones shall be burned on you'" (1 Kings 13.2). This prophetic pronouncement is a major clue to the purpose and date of the Josianic edition of the Deuteronomistic History: It was written in support of Josiah's reform. It is thus a kind of propaganda, with a distinct theological bias. At the same time, as we have continually seen, the authors of the Deuteronomistic History are no mere ideologues: They are also historians, who often include information from sources that is inconsistent with their own perspective.

In this reform, we are told, the king had the support of the Temple priesthood, who may even have initiated the reform in an effort to centralize their own power. Support also came from the prophet Huldah, who predicted that because of his repentance, the king would, in due course, die in peace (2 Kings 22.20). Her prediction proved wrong, and surprisingly was not revised in the light of Josiah's untimely end in battle against the Egyptian pharaoh Neco at Megiddo.

It is difficult to assess the actual historical importance of Josiah, since the primary textual source we have is the Deuteronomistic History. Archaeological data provide some further clues. We see evidence of extensive building or refortifying key sites throughout Judah from the mid-seventh century BCE onward, suggesting that as Assyrian control diminished, the Judean monarchy began to extend its reach. This activity is especially evident on the kingdom's eastern and southern borders, where it was threatened by states taking advantage of Assyrian weakness to expand their territories. A reasonable conclusion, then, is that although the Deuteronomistic Historians' account of Josiah's reign is exaggerated by their ideological program and perhaps shaped by memories of Hezekiah's earlier reform, it has some historical basis: Josiah took advantage of the brief interlude between Assyrian and Babylonian domination to extend Judah's control beyond the restricted borders that had been established early in the seventh century after the invasion of the Assyrian king Sennacherib.

Josiah's reign ended in disaster. When the Egyptian pharaoh Neco headed north, Josiah attempted to block his advance at the famous site of Megiddo (see Box 19.3), and in the battle he was killed, notwithstanding Huldah's prophecy.

The Last Kings of Judah

Three of the last four kings of Judah were sons of Josiah; the other, Jehoiachin, was his grandson. The first, Jehoahaz (also called Shallum), was deposed after a rule of only three months by Pharaoh Neco, who replaced him with his brother Jehoiakim (originally Eliakim). Jehoiakim was first a vassal of Egypt, but after 604 BCE, he switched his allegiance to Babylon. When he tried to assert his independence, Nebuchadrezzar prepared to retaliate, but before he actually attacked, Jehoiakim died. Although the book of Kings devotes only a few verses to Jehoiakim's reign, it receives more attention in the book of Jeremiah. There he is depicted as a king

who builds his house by unrighteousness,
    and his upper rooms by injustice;
who makes his neighbors work for nothing,
    and does not give them their wages,

who says, "I will build myself a spacious house
    with large upper rooms,"
and who cuts out windows for it,
    paneling it with cedar,
    and painting it with vermilion. (Jer 22.13–14)

Jehoiakim's character is further revealed in a passage in Jeremiah, according to which the king systematically burned the papyrus scroll on which Baruch, Jeremiah's scribe, had written down the prophet's words. The contrast between Jehoiakim's reaction to hearing a scroll read and that of his father Josiah is striking. When Josiah "heard the words of the book of the law, he tore his clothes" (2 Kings 22.11); in the case of Jehoiakim, however, "neither the king, nor any of his servants who heard all these words, was alarmed, nor did they tear their clothes" (Jer 36.24).

Jehoiakim died in 598 and was succeeded by his son and Josiah's grandson **Jehoiachin**. During Jehoiachin's brief reign of three months in 597, Nebuchadrezzar launched his first attack on Judah proper, laying siege to Jerusalem and taking captive to Babylon the king, the queen mother, and a significant part of the royal establishment, some ten thousand persons in all (2 Kings 24.12, 14; somewhat different numbers are given in 2 Kings 24.15–16 and in Jer 52.28). Among the priests who were deported was the prophet Ezekiel (see pages 320–22). The resources of the Temple treasury were also used to pay tribute. In place of Jehoiachin, Nebuchadrezzar installed his uncle, Josiah's son Mattaniah, as king, and gave him the throne name Zedekiah.

Zedekiah was the last of the Davidic dynasty to rule, and his reign lasted for eleven years. His status as king may have been compromised by the presence of his nephew and predecessor in Babylon. The Deuteronomistic Historians end their account of Israel's history in the Promised Land not with Zedekiah, but with this surprising note:

In the thirty-seventh year of the exile of King Jehoiachin of Judah, in the twelfth month, on the twenty-seventh day of the month, King Evil-merodach of Babylon, in the year that he began to reign, released King Jehoiachin of Judah from prison; he spoke

Box 19.3 MEGIDDO AND ARMAGEDDON

Josiah's attempt to block the Egyptian advance in 609 BCE took place at **Megiddo**, a site that defended a major pass from the coastal road to the interior. Because of its strategic location, many battles took place at Megiddo from ancient to modern times. In the mid-fifteenth century BCE, the Egyptian pharaoh Thutmoses III defeated a coalition of Canaanite kings there, and, according to Judges 5.19, it was at "the waters of Megiddo" that Israelites led by Deborah defeated "the kings of Canaan." More recently, Megiddo was the site of a decisive battle between British and Turkish forces for control of Palestine in 1918.

Because of the many battles fought there, in the book of Revelation Megiddo, rendered as Armageddon (from the Hebr. *har Megiddo*, "mountain of Megiddo"), is identified as the site of the future final battle between the forces of good and evil (Rev 16.16).

FIGURE 19.3   Aerial view, looking west, of the impressive site of Megiddo, showing its strategic location.

kindly to him, and gave him a seat above the other seats of the kings who were with him in Babylon. So Jehoiachin put aside his prison clothes. Every day of his life he dined regularly in the king's presence. For his allowance, a regular allowance was given him by the king, a portion every day, as long as he lived. (2 Kings 25.27–30)

Ezekiel, too, dates his inaugural vision with reference to "the fifth year of the exile of King Jehoiachin" (Ezek 1.2). Ezekiel's prophetic ministry took place entirely in Babylon, and so it is possible that Jehoiachin continued to be thought of as the legitimate ruler among the exiles in Babylon, and perhaps also by some in Judah. Zedekiah, then, may not have had full support from his subjects.

At first Zedekiah was a loyal vassal of the Babylonians, but around 590, with the support of the neighboring states of Edom, Moab, Ammon, Tyre, and Sidon, he stopped paying tribute to Nebuchadrezzar. Neither he nor his advisors had learned from the failed rebellion of his predecessor Jehoiakim, or from the earlier rebellion of Hezekiah against the Assyrians. The Babylonians retaliated with a full-scale attack on Jerusalem. After a lengthy siege, the city was captured and burned, and Zedekiah was taken prisoner and sent to Babylon. That was the end of the Davidic dynasty.

The Fall of Jerusalem

The fullest version of the Deuteronomistic Historians' account of the fall of Jerusalem is in Jeremiah 52. It opens with a formulaic summary of the reign of Zedekiah and the judgment of the Deuteronomistic Historians on him:

> He did what was evil in the sight of the LORD, just as Jehoiakim had done. Indeed, Jerusalem and Judah so angered the LORD that he expelled them from his presence. (Jer 52.2–3 = 2 Kings 24.19–20)

From the perspective of the Deuteronomistic Historians, the fall of Jerusalem was a deserved punishment for the sins of the king and of the nation as a whole. But exactly how did Yahweh punish them? The account continues with a straightforward narrative of the city's siege, capture, and destruction, which begins with a succinct statement of the proximate cause: "Zedekiah rebelled against the king of Babylon" (Jer 52.3 = 2 Kings 24.20).

The siege of Jerusalem lasted a year and a half. Finally, with the city suffering from famine, the army and the king fled, heading east toward Jericho and the fords of the Jordan River, probably intending to take refuge in Transjordan. The Deuteronomistic History begins with the Israelites under Joshua's leadership crossing the Jordan from the east and with divine help conquering Jericho. Now the Deuteronomistic Historians, in a literary irony, depict Zedekiah, the last ruler of the

Davidic dynasty, moving in the opposite direction, and captured by the Babylonians in the vicinity of Jericho.

At Nebuchadrezzar's headquarters in southern Syria, Zedekiah's sons were executed. Like their imperial predecessors the Assyrians, the Babylonians must have been aware of the propaganda of the Davidic dynasty; elimination of the heirs to the throne would end the notion of divinely granted eternal rule. Then Zedekiah was blinded, so that the last sight of the last descendant of David to sit on the throne was the execution of his own sons. Finally he was taken in chains to Babylon.

The plundering of the Temple and its furnishings by the Babylonians is described in considerable detail, poignantly recalling the lengthy account of their construction and manufacture during Solomon's reign (1 Kings 6–7). Much of Jerusalem's population was also taken to Babylon, joining those who had been deported in 597. Some were allowed to remain in Judah, however, and tension between them and the Babylonian exiles would become a significant problem in subsequent decades.

The Deuteronomistic History ends on an ambiguous note. On one hand, Jerusalem and its Temple had been destroyed. Yet, we are told, one of the descendants of David, Jehoiachin, was released from captivity and, although still in Babylon, was called "king" (2 Kings 25.27). It is unclear if we are to interpret this as a faint expression of hope for the survival of the Davidic monarchy from the final editors of the Deuteronomistic History or if it is simply an endnote.

THE BOOK OF ZEPHANIAH

According to its editorial heading (1.1), the superscription, the prophet **Zephaniah** was active during the reign of Josiah. In his genealogy, one of his ancestors was named Hezekiah, but whether this was the king of Judah with that name is not stated. Otherwise we know nothing about the prophet.

The book of Zephaniah, one of the Minor Prophets, consists of a series of divine pronouncements of judgment on Judah and Jerusalem and on other nations, including Assyria. Like many of the prophetic books, Zephaniah concludes with a message of hope, when Zion's fortunes will be restored.

The book of Zephaniah makes use of earlier prophetic themes and genres, including oracles against the nations (see page 257) and a call to repentance. Zephaniah also contains a fully developed form of the motif of the "day of the LORD" (1.7, 14–18; see further Box 17.2 on page 262). That day will be a day of doom, primarily for Judah, but also for nations surrounding it, and, in fact, for the whole world. This is because Yahweh is the only god with power, and he will be universally recognized as such:

> The LORD . . . will shrivel all the gods of the earth,
>   and to him shall bow down,
>   each from its place,
>   all the islands of the nations. (2.11)

While this is not yet a fully developed monotheism, it continues the viewpoint of earlier prophets that Yahweh's domain extends beyond Israel to the entire world.

The judgment on Judah is based on earlier prophetic critiques of false worship and social injustice. But this judgment is linked by its placement with that on the rest of the world; the oracles against the nations (2.4–15) are sandwiched between two condemnations of Judah and Jerusalem (1.4–2.3; 3.1–8). Especially shocking is the juxtaposition of Nineveh, Assyria's capital, with Jerusalem, Judah's capital. Both will be made desolate, for both rebelled against Yahweh's authority.

Zephaniah mentions prohibited practices—worship of Baal and other deities (1.4–6)—and more obscure rituals—"leaping over the threshold" (1.9). Although such apostasy and syncretism were supposedly abolished during Josiah's reform—hence the activity of Zephaniah could be dated to early in Josiah's reign—practices like these continued, as their condemnation in Jeremiah and Ezekiel makes clear. At best, therefore, we can conclude that the substance of Zephaniah's oracles dates to the last few decades of the seventh century BCE. The absence of mention of Babylon, which by the end of the century was a major power, suggests earlier rather than later in that period.

The experience of the Babylonian exile occasioned a reapplication of the original message of the prophet to a new context, and the conclusion to the book of Zephaniah, a later addition, has close affinities with the literature of the late sixth century BCE, celebrating Jerusalem's restoration and the return of its exiles (see further Chapter 21).

THE BOOK OF NAHUM

The book of **Nahum**, some forty-eight verses in length, is one of the shortest of the Minor Prophets, and nothing is known about the prophet himself. As its title, "an oracle concerning Nineveh," suggests, it is devoted entirely to an attack on Assyria and especially its capital city, Nineveh, and is an expanded example of the oracle against the nations. It dates originally to the late seventh century BCE: It refers to the destruction of Nineveh, which occurred at the hands of the Medes and Babylonians in 612.

Adopting the general prophetic view that Yahweh is responsible for all events in history, the book opens with hymnic praise of Yahweh as the divine warrior whose dramatic theophany affects the entire cosmos (1.2–8). Then follow a confusing group of pronouncements, some of which are directed against Assyria (1.9–2.2). The dominant section of the book is the detailed description of the sack of Nineveh (2.3–3.19). It captures in vivid detail the horror of ancient warfare, as in this free translation in the NRSV:

> The crack of whip and rumble of wheel,
>   galloping horse and bounding chariot!
> Horsemen charging,
>   flashing sword and glittering spear,
> piles of dead,
>   heaps of corpses,
> dead bodies without end—
>   they stumble over the bodies! (Nah 3.2–3)

The book of Nahum is a celebration of the fall of Assyria, a message of comfort for Israel, Judah, and others who had experienced the "endless cruelty" (3.19) of the Assyrians. It is thus a sustained and unrelieved expression of intense nationalism, without any ethical nuances. In Nahum, as in many of the psalms, we find an intense hatred of the enemy, by which the audience is to be "comforted," which is the meaning of Nahum's name.

THE BOOK OF HABAKKUK

The short book of **Habakkuk** is one of the books of the Minor Prophets, placed between Nahum and Zephaniah, a location that along with later traditions suggests a date during the early Babylonian period. This is a hypothesis because, unlike most other prophetic books, Habakkuk has no superscription providing information about the prophet and when he lived. But Habakkuk 1.6 does refer to the rise of Chaldeans, another name for the Babylonians. Since the book makes no explicit mention of the attacks on Jerusalem or the exile of its inhabitants to Babylon in 597 and 586 BCE, it probably dates to the Babylonian campaign at the end of the seventh century BCE.

The book is formally divided into two parts, "the oracle that the prophet Habakkuk saw" in chapters 1–2 and "a prayer of the prophet Habakkuk" in chapter 3. The first part is a dialogue between the prophet and Yahweh, in which prophetic laments about the violence being done to the righteous alternate with divine responses. These conclude with five curses on the Babylonians, who are apparently responsible for the suffering that has occurred, although they are not explicitly named.

The third chapter of the book is a hymn describing in mythological language the triumph of Yahweh as the divine warrior. It is reminiscent of such earlier Israelite poems as Exodus 15, Judges 5, and Psalm 18, but whether it is a truly ancient poem added to the "oracle of Habakkuk" or a late monarchical imitation of archaic poetry is disputed. The hymn celebrates the awe-inspiring divine appearance, which causes upheaval in nature; from it the author takes heart, for even in the midst of disaster, God provides ultimate victory.

Nothing is known about the prophet Habakkuk himself, but later legends developed about him. In the apocryphal addition to the book of Daniel called "Bel and the Dragon" (see page 420), the prophet Habakkuk was miraculously transported from Judea to bring a bowl of stew to Daniel, who was in the lions' den in Babylon (Bel 33–39), and in a first-century CE writing called "The Lives of the Prophets," Habakkuk's journey to and return from Babylon is interpreted as a sign of the return of the exiles.

JEREMIAH

The Book of Jeremiah

Placed after the book of Isaiah, probably because the three longest prophetic books are arranged in chronological order, the book of **Jeremiah** also shows evidence of a complicated literary history. We find repetitions (see, for example, Jer 7.1–15 and 26.1–9, and Jer 39 and 52) as well as a bewildering variation among ancient texts, almost as if Jeremiah were a work in progress to which later generations gave their own touches, adding new and rearranging existing material. A significant difference in length and in arrangement is seen between the traditional Hebrew text (the Masoretic Text) and the ancient Greek translation (the Septuagint). The Greek is one-eighth shorter than the Masoretic Text, and the second half of the book has a very different arrangement in the two textual traditions. These differences are also found in fragments of different Hebrew manuscripts of Jeremiah among the Dead Sea Scrolls. The complicated literary history of the book may be an indirect reflection of the chaos of the time, but it also reveals a kind of open-ended understanding of a "book." Rather than being a finished composition, it was a work in progress that subsequent authors and editors felt free to revise and to

PART FIVE

EXILE AND RETURN

After the Fall: Judeans in Judah and Babylon

Lamentations, Psalm 137, Obadiah, and Ezekiel

Beginning with the first exile of Judeans to Babylon in 597 BCE, ancient Judeans entered a new historical period with profound implications for their religious practices and beliefs, their national identity, and their text preservation and production. One of the first changes we see involves terminology. With the destruction of the Jerusalem temple, the religion of ancient Israel and Judah had to adapt and within that adaptation away from temple-centered worship, we see practices emerge that mark the beginnings of Judaism. In terms of national identity, the forcible deportation of Judeans away from their homeland meant that for the first time, the term "Judean" did not necessarily imply a geographical location. A Judean could be a person who lived in Judah or a person whose family had once come from Judah but now lived in exile. The Hebrew does not mark this transition with a change in terminology, but some scholars begin translating the term for Judeans as Jews in order to signal that this group we had once tied to the land of Judah was now dispersed across multiple lands; in the chapters that follow we will use the term "Judean." Finally, the crisis of conquest and exile, and the fact that the literate elite were among the first to experience exile, led to a sustained program of preserving and editing ancient Israel's sacred

texts. What had been a collection of national histories and sacred stories gradually developed into authoritative scripture.

HISTORY

Our knowledge of Judeans in both Judah and Babylon in the decades after the fall of Jerusalem is fragmentary at best, and our only written source is the account of the Deuteronomistic Historians in Jeremiah 40–41, summarized in 2 Kings 25.22–26. In Judah, the Babylonian ruler Nebuchadrezzar put one of the nobility, Gedaliah, in charge. His headquarters were at Mizpah, an important pre-monarchic center 8 miles (13 km) north of Jerusalem, because Jerusalem itself had been destroyed. Among his supporters was the prophet Jeremiah. After only a few months, however, a group led by Ishmael, a member of the royal family, assassinated Gedaliah and his entourage. This was followed by a countercoup which caused Ishmael to flee to Ammon. The subsequent deportation of more Judeans by the Babylonians in 582 BCE, mentioned in Jeremiah 52.30, may have been a reprisal for this short-lived revolt.

According to the Deuteronomistic Historians, in the conquest of Jerusalem in 586 BCE the Babylonian "captain of the guard" carried away into exile "all the people who were left in the city" leaving only "the poorest people of the land to be vinedressers and tillers of the soil" (2 Kings 25.10–12.) It is difficult to give precise numbers for how many Judeans stayed in the land and how many went into exile. While some major cities, especially those that served as fortresses, notably Jerusalem and Lachish, had been at least partially destroyed, others continued to be occupied, and some of the destroyed cities were resettled by those Judeans who remained. Jeremiah and Ezekiel considered "the poorest of the land" who remained in Judah as squatters rather than rightful owners of the land (Jer 40.7; 52.16; Ezek 11.15.)

This largely rural population would form the nucleus of a restored Judean community, whose claims to the land would come into conflict with the eventual returnees from Babylonian exile. Some exiles, among them the prophet Ezekiel, considered themselves to be the true Israel, with whom Yahweh himself had gone into exile, while those left in the land were among the guilty. The exiles seem to have created the notion of an "empty land," a land without inhabitants, which some modern scholars have adopted. Archaeological evidence, however, suggests a more nuanced view. Although much of the population of Judah, and especially the elite from Jerusalem, had been taken into captivity in Babylon, a significant portion of the population would have remained in Judah. To these Judean survivors we should attribute some of the literature of this period, including the book of Lamentations and the final edition of the Deuteronomistic History, as well as, perhaps, the editing of several prophetic books, including Jeremiah.

THE BOOK OF LAMENTATIONS

The book of Lamentations is a collection of detailed and sustained reactions to the fall of Jerusalem in 586 BCE, in which one or more poets lament the destruction of the city. According to ancient postbiblical tradition, the book was written by Jeremiah, perhaps on the basis of such passages as 2 Chronicles 35.25, in which laments for the dead King Josiah are said to have been composed by the prophet, and Jeremiah 9.1, in which the prophet expresses his grief for Israel's fate. This traditional view accounts for the placement of Lamentations after Jeremiah in the Christian canon; in the Jewish canon it is one of the "Five Scrolls," grouped with the Song of Songs, Ruth, Ecclesiastes, and Esther (see further Chapter 1). Modern critical scholars, however, generally have concluded that the prophet was not its author.

Using the funeral dirge as a genre, the book expresses grief for the ruined city of Jerusalem in a series of five separate and perhaps originally independent poems, the first four of which are acrostics (see Box 20.1).

We have examples of dirges for deceased individuals in David's laments for Saul and Jonathan (2 Sam 1.17–27) and for Abner (2 Sam 3.33–34). In Lamentations, the poet (or poets, for it is difficult to determine if the five separate poems in the book had more than one anonymous author) grieves for Jerusalem, personified as a dead woman, or sometimes as one who has been bereaved. As in the funeral dirge, the former beauty and strength of the personified city are contrasted with her present appearance and state.

The destruction of cities was a frequent phenomenon in the ancient world, and we have examples of the lament for a destroyed city from the ancient Near East, mainly from Sumerian literature originally written in the late third and early second millennia BCE, but which continued to be copied for many hundreds of years. As in the Sumerian laments, the dirges in Lamentations have a theological dimension: The destruction of the city is attributed to the action of the city's deity, who was angry at it:

> The Lord has become like an enemy,
>   he has destroyed Israel. (Lam 2.5)
> The Lord gave full vent to his wrath;
>   he poured out his hot anger,

and kindled a fire in Zion
    that consumed its foundations. . . .
It was for the sins of her prophets
    and the iniquities of her priests,
who shed the blood of the righteous
    in the midst of her. (Lam 4.11, 13)

The punishment that Yahweh inflicted on Jerusalem is vividly described. Drawing on the same language of sexual violence and shaming that we saw in Hosea's marriage metaphor, Jerusalem is depicted as a dead woman and as a widow and mother who has been stripped naked and publically exposed. (See further Box 20.2 on page 321.)

In general, Lamentations reflects the dominant biblical view that what had happened to Jerusalem was a deserved punishment. But it is expressed with considerable poignancy, contrasting the royal ideology's claim that the city was invincible with its present state in ruins.

The book concludes on an ambiguous note:

But you, O LORD, reign forever;
    your throne endures to all generations.
Why have you forgotten us completely?
    Why have you forsaken us these many days?

Restore us to yourself, O LORD, that we may be
    restored;
    renew our days as of old—
unless you have utterly rejected us,
    and are angry with us beyond measure.
    (Lam 5.19–22)

In other ancient cultures, the defeat of a nation meant that its deities were less powerful than those of the conqueror, and so the logical reaction was to worship the conqueror's gods. The end of the book of Lamentations wrestles with this dilemma. Even in the midst of the trauma of Jerusalem's fall, the poet expresses faith in Yahweh's supremacy but is at a loss to explain how that can be reconciled with what has occurred.

Although no specific details enable precise dating of the poems that comprise the book of Lamentations, most scholars reasonably assume that they were written in Judah not long after the fall of Jerusalem in 586 BCE. A different perspective on the fall of the city, that of the exiles in Babylon, is found in Psalm 137 and also in Ezekiel.

BOX 20.1 ACROSTIC POEMS

An **acrostic** is a poem in which the first letters of successive lines form a word or pattern. Such acrostics were favorites in antiquity, and those found in the Bible are alphabetic acrostics. Each is divided into verses or stanzas, and each verse or stanza begins with a successive letter of the twenty-two letters of the Hebrew alphabet. The alphabetic structure of such a poem served to aid the reciter's memory, and also perhaps to indicate that in the poem, the author attempted to cover the entire range of what could be said on any given topic—from A to Z, as it were.

The book of Lamentations contains four alphabetic acrostics in its first four chapters, and chapter 5, although not an acrostic, also has twenty-two verses. The most elaborate acrostic in Lamentations is chapter 3, in which each stanza has three lines and each line begins with the same letter. Other alphabetic acrostic poems in the Bible are Psalms 9–10, 25, 34, 37, 111, 112, 119, and 145; Proverbs 31.10–31; Nahum 1.2–8; and Sirach 51.13–30. The most elaborate is Psalm 119, which is also the longest chapter in the Bible.

THE JUDEANS IN BABYLONIA

Other than passing reference in fragmentary Babylonian records to the exiled King Jehoiachin and his sons (see page 293), our only source for the status of the Judeans in Babylonia in the sixth century BCE is the Bible. That the community eventually flourished there we know from the fifth-century BCE records of the commercial house of Murashu in Nippur, a city near Babylon. Among the many principals and witnesses in documents recording loans, leases, and other transactions were Judeans, who were full participants in the commercial life of the city, illustrating how Babylonia became one of the major centers of Jewish life and learning for centuries to come.

About ancient Babylonia we know much more. Babylon and other cities under the patronage of the Babylonian kings were carefully planned and lavish urban centers, unlike anything the Judeans had ever seen (see Figure 20.1). But their amazement would have been tempered by grief at what they had left behind.

FIGURE 20.1   One of the gates of the city of Babylon excavated in the late nineteenth century is the "Ishtar Gate." Made of multicolored glazed bricks showing dragons, bulls, and other mythological creatures, it is a sample of Babylon's magnificence in the sixth century BCE and of artistic sources that informed the prophet Ezekiel's visions. This reconstruction in the Berlin Museum contains some of the original bricks, but the structure itself is only an approximation.

PSALM 137

Most of the psalms are difficult to date, for they usually articulate individual or communal piety in general terms without reference to specific historical events or contexts (see further page 379). One of the few exceptions is Psalm 137, which tells us in its opening words that its author had been one of the exiles "by the rivers of Babylon." These rivers are probably the irrigation canals that dispersed water from the Euphrates and Tigris rivers for agriculture. The poet recalls the situation of the exiles in Babylonia, overpowered by grief when remembering Jerusalem. To add to the grief, their Babylonian captors taunted the Judeans, urging them to sing "one of the songs of Zion" (Ps 137.3). "O you Judeans," we can imagine the Babylonians saying, "sing us one of your psalms, which tells how Jerusalem is an impregnable city, never to be captured or destroyed, protected by Yahweh as his own home, the city of God" (see, for example, Pss 46; 48).

The response to this taunting is the plaintive question: "How can we sing the Lord's song in a foreign land?" (Ps 137.4). How could they continue to worship the god of their homeland, Yahweh, who they believed resided within the now destroyed Temple in Jerusalem? How could they continue to worship Yahweh when he had failed to protect his city and its inhabitants? The ultimate answer to these questions is the transformation of the religion of Israel into Judaism, which is the focus of this and subsequent chapters. The poet's answer to the crisis of exile is to stress the importance of memory: "If I forget you, O Jerusalem." He then utters a curse against himself: May his hand that strums the strings of the lyre and his tongue that sings the words become crippled and useless if he does not continue to make Jerusalem, Yahweh's home, the center of his life. So, in exile, the Judeans in Babylon committed themselves to remember Zion, and one of the ways they accomplished this was through copying and editing their sacred texts, preserving the Torah of Moses. After a few decades, as we will see, the exiles were given the opportunity to return to Zion, and some did

return. Still, many chose to remain in Babylonia, and these members of the **Diaspora** established houses of prayer, community centers that came to be called **synagogues**. One of the activities associated with synagogues was the study and interpretation of the Torah. Since ancient times, synagogues have been designed so that when the worshipers pray they are facing in the direction of Jerusalem: One way to continue to sing the songs of Zion was to make it a focus of worship and remembrance.

The psalm ends with a violent plea for divine vengeance on the Babylonians and their vassals the Edomites for the destruction of Jerusalem in 586 BCE.

THE BOOK OF OBADIAH

The book of Obadiah shares the unrelieved hostility of the singer of Psalm 137 toward Edom. **Obadiah** is the shortest book in the Hebrew Bible, and its mere twenty-one verses are entirely devoted to a single topic, the divine judgment on Edom, Judah's longtime rival and neighbor to the southeast. It is thus a freestanding example of the oracle against a foreign nation (see page XXX), like Nahum's attack on Assyria. The book concludes with a report of the forthcoming "day of Yahweh" (see Box 17.2 on page 256), when Edom will be punished for its participation in the destruction of Jerusalem. The judgment on Edom, the book anticipates, will be carried out by an Israel returned from exile and restored to its ancient borders. The mood is one of vindictiveness, along with glee at the reversal of fortunes, when the once-defeated Israelites will be victorious and the once-powerful Edomites brought low.

From the perspective of the otherwise unknown author of Obadiah, the hostility between Israel and Edom had a long history, going back to the sibling rivalry between their respective ancestors Jacob and Esau. That hostility is also evident in the repeated attacks on Edom elsewhere in prophetic literature. We have already noted the close connection between the book of Obadiah and the oracle against Edom in Jeremiah 49 (see page 302). Clearly a literary relationship existed between the two, but the precise nature of that relationship is uncertain: Did one borrow from the other, or do both share a common source?

Although the book of Obadiah contains few specific details, most scholars date its nucleus to the sixth century BCE, not long after the fall of Jerusalem in 586 BCE, although a date in the next century is also possible.

EZEKIEL

The prophet **Ezekiel** was a priest who had been exiled to Babylon along with other Judean elite in 597 BCE. The book attributed to him is the most unusual of the prophetic books, as rabbinic tradition recognized when it debated whether or not the book should be admitted to the canon of scripture. It contains elaborate and sometimes fantastic visions, yet its arrangement is more orderly than prophetic books of comparable length. Ezekiel has been called a surrealist, and he was that. He was also, in the end, a profound theologian who reshaped Judean religious beliefs, making Yahweh present to his exilic community and investing that community with the hope of a restored Israel.

The Book of Ezekiel

Unlike the other long prophetic books that precede it, Isaiah and Jeremiah, the book of Ezekiel is mostly prose, not poetry. Also unlike those books, it is arranged in a strict chronological order, as the dates throughout the book indicate. The book opens with the prophet's inaugural vision in 593 BCE ("the fifth year of the exile of King Jehoiachin," 1.2) and concludes with the vision of the restored Jerusalem in 573 ("in the twenty-fifth year of our exile," 40.1). The only disruption of this order is 29.17, dated to 571.

The book is cast almost entirely in the first person and presents itself as an autobiographical narrative; only 1.2–3, a kind of editorial note, is in the third person. That note indicates that the book has been shaped by editorial activity, although less so than other prophetic books.

The book of Ezekiel has a clear structure, as the following outline shows:

Chapters 1–3   The call of the prophet
      4–24   Oracles of judgment against Judah and Jerusalem
      25–32   Oracles against the nations
      33–39   Oracles of restoration, including a second oracle against Edom (35) and two against Gog of Magog (38–39)
      40–48   Vision of the restored Temple and the return to the land

Previous generations of scholars often attributed much of the book to a series of disciples and editors, rather than to the prophet himself; one influential study in the early twentieth century proposed that less than one-seventh of the book could be traced back to Ezekiel. Many scholars today, however, are less radical and attribute most of the book's contents to the prophet himself.

The Life of Ezekiel

Most contemporary scholars accept the autobiographical form of the book at face value, that is, as the work of Ezekiel himself, who in it tells us a great deal about himself and is often idiosyncratic in thought and phrasing. It is unnecessarily skeptical to attribute the book to some anonymous author who constructed around a little known figure a detailed fictional autobiography. The chronology of the book is consistent with the view that Ezekiel himself was its primary author. We find no references to datable events or persons after the reign of Nebuchadrezzar, which ended in 562 BCE.

According to the book, Ezekiel was exiled to Babylonia during the first deportation by Nebuchadrezzar in 597 BCE. This makes him a contemporary of the prophet Jeremiah, although while Jeremiah preached in Judah, Ezekiel's prophetic career took place entirely in Babylonia. As with

Jeremiah, however, the historical context of his life shaped his message. That context included not only exile, but also the fall of Jerusalem and the destruction of the Temple in which Ezekiel had served as a priest.

In the fifth year of his exile, he experienced his first prophetic revelation, "by the river Chebar" (1.1–2), to the south of Babylon, and the audience for Ezekiel's words is clearly his fellow exiles. In his call Ezekiel is presented with a scroll containing the message he is to deliver, "and written on it were words of lamentation and mourning and woe" (2.10). He is instructed to eat the scroll, and he found that although the words he was given to deliver were terrible, the scroll itself was sweet. The eating of the scroll is a metaphor: The prophet has internalized the divine message. At the same time, it is also a guarantee that, unlike what happened to Jeremiah's scroll (Jer 36.23), this scroll cannot be destroyed.

The eating of the scroll is the first of many prophetic gestures by Ezekiel that can only be termed bizarre. These include speechlessness, lying on his side for lengthy periods, shaving his head (an especially unusual action for a priest), and eating while trembling. Others are more reminiscent of the symbolic actions of other prophets, like packing a bag and pretending to go into exile and not mourning for his deceased wife. Behaviors such as these have led to diagnosis of the prophet's physical or mental condition as epilepsy or catatonic schizophrenia. Since socially abnormal and ecstatic behaviors were part of prophetic activity throughout the Near East (see pages 244–45), it goes beyond the evidence to give Ezekiel's condition a specific diagnosis. It is also possible that he was engaged in a kind of performance art, in which he expressed his message by means of dramatic actions and attitudes. In any case, whether the prophet's gestures were physiologically or psychologically caused, or

Box 20.2 YAHWEH AS VIOLENT HUSBAND

Ezekiel 16 and 23 are an extended elaboration of the metaphor of Jerusalem (and Samaria, the capital of the northern kingdom of Israel) as Yahweh's unfaithful wife, a metaphor also used by Hosea and Jeremiah. These chapters are troubling if not offensive to many modern readers. In them, the prophet describes almost pornographically how Yahweh found Jerusalem as an abandoned infant, raised her, and when she had reached sexual maturity, married her. But she proved unfaithful, and, more than a whore, was nymphomaniacal in her pursuit of other lovers, whom she paid for their sexual favors. As a consequence, she will be punished in the presence of her lovers, stripped naked in public and then given a stoning and slashed with swords, her children killed and her houses destroyed. The same punishment had been given to her equally promiscuous sister Samaria to the north, and the message is that Jerusalem should have learned from Samaria's fate.

These two chapters, together with other examples of the marriage metaphor in Hosea, Jeremiah, and Lamentations, develop in lurid detail the covenant analogy of Yahweh as husband and Israel as wife. They show the physical and economic power that a husband had over his wives. If a wife engaged in adulterous behavior, a husband could subject her to physical and sexual violence, public shaming, and even death. Passages such as these raise questions about the status of the Bible as an authoritative guide for family values.

man" (NRSV: "mortal"). This means simply "a human being," contrasting the prophet with the transcendent deity; only later, as in the book of Daniel, does the term develop an apocalyptic connotation (see Box 25.3 on page 416). The message he is given is one of divine judgment on the "rebellious house" of Israel—"words of lamentation and mourning and woe" (2.5–10).

The Sins and Punishment of Israel

In Ezekiel's repeated pronouncements of the divine judgment upon Israel, the primary offenses of which the nation is guilty have to do with idolatry and ritual impurity. The Israelites have worshiped idols throughout the land and have defiled the sanctuary of Yahweh with forbidden forms of worship in the Temple in Jerusalem. These are described in explicit detail: images of "creeping things and loathsome animals" (8.10); "women . . . weeping for Tammuz" (8.14), the ancient dying and rising god of Mesopotamia; and worship of the sun (8.16). The priests are especially guilty, for they have failed to maintain the boundaries between sacred and profane, between clean and unclean.

Ezekiel places less emphasis on issues of social justice than his prophetic predecessors, and when he does so, it is usually in general terms. Nevertheless, as in the Sinai covenant as interpreted by Priestly tradition, an individual's obligations to God and to his neighbor are linked:

> If a man is righteous and does what is lawful and right—if he does not eat upon the mountains or lift up his eyes to the idols of the house of Israel, does not defile his neighbor's wife or approach a woman during her menstrual period, does not oppress anyone, but restores to the debtor his pledge, commits no robbery, gives his bread to the hungry and covers the naked with a garment, does not take advance or accrued interest, withholds his hand from iniquity, executes true justice between contending parties, follows my statutes, and is careful to observe my ordinances, acting faithfully—such a one is righteous; he shall surely live, says the LORD God. (18.5–9; see also 22.6–12)

Ezekiel takes several received traditions of his time and transforms, even reverses some, in order

to speak a new word to his time and to the context of a people in exile. We have already noted how his visions gave mobility to Yahweh and brought him to Babylon. Another of his theological innovations involves the concept of collective family guilt. The Ten Commandments speak of Yahweh as one who "punishes children for the iniquity of parents to the third and fourth generation" (Ex 20.5; 34.7; Deut 5.9). Ezekiel acknowledges this belief as part of his received tradition but then dares to upend it: "What do you mean by repeating this proverb . . . 'The parents have eaten sour grapes and the children's teeth are set on edge?' As I live, says the Lord God, this proverb shall no more be used by you in Israel . . . it is only the person who sins that shall die." (Ezek 18.2–3)

This reversal of the idea of generational sin is then applied in two directions. First, concerning Jerusalem's situation at the time of the Babylonian conquest; the city is understood to be so pervasively sinful that even if three of the legendary righteous individuals of antiquity lived in it—Noah, Danel (a hero of Ugaritic epic, not the hero of the book of Daniel; see Box 5.4 on page 72), and Job—their righteousness could not save the city (14.14; contrast Gen 18.22–33). Ezekiel thus interprets the exile to Babylon and the destruction of Jerusalem as deserved punishments for the sins of those who themselves committed them. Once we turn to the generation of exiles that were born in Babylonia, however, Ezekiel's rejection of generational sin would be a source of hope. If the exiles turned away from the sinful ways of their parents, the punishment of exile might come to an end. In other words, divine justice is absolutely equitable; it is not "the way of the LORD that is unfair" but the ways of Israel (18.25, 29).

Ezekiel and Jeremiah

The prophets Jeremiah and Ezekiel were contemporaries. Both were deeply affected by the deportations of Judeans to Babylonia and the destruction of Jerusalem by the Babylonians in 586 BCE, but from different vantage points. Until his emigration to Egypt in the late 580s, Jeremiah was in Judah, witnessing the catastrophe personally, while Ezekiel had been taken to Babylonia in the first deportation of 597 and learned of Jerusalem's destruction only secondhand. References to letters sent between Jerusalem and Babylon by Jeremiah and others indicate that communication existed between the Judeans and the exiles in Babylonia, as do Jeremiah's familiarity with events there and the report of Jerusalem's fall brought to Ezekiel. Thus, although Jeremiah and Ezekiel were in different locations, it is reasonable to assume that they had some knowledge of each other's prophecies.

That assumption is confirmed by the many connections between the two books. These connections include references in both books to the word that the prophet was given by Yahweh to deliver being put in his mouth, the image of the prophet as sentinel, and the metaphor of the northern and southern kingdoms as sisters. Both prophets agree that because of its sins, Jerusalem's doom was inevitable and deserved. Jeremiah also quotes and rejects the proverb about generational guilt (Jer 31.29; Ezek 18.2). Both attack false prophets who predicted peace. Both envision a restoration of divine love for Israel after its punishment, speaking of a renewed covenant in which Yahweh will again say, "You shall be my people, and I will be your God" (Jer 30.22; Ezek 36.28). Finally, both Jeremiah and Ezekiel announce that Yahweh himself will remove the corrupt shepherds of his flock and will shepherd them himself, although both books also allow for the restoration of the Davidic dynasty.

As we have seen in the previous chapter, the book of Jeremiah has a complex literary history, whereas Ezekiel is for the most part the work of a single individual. It is therefore hazardous to try to determine in which direction the influence from one to the other went. At the very least, however, it is clear that there was compatibility between them that was recognized, if not by the prophets themselves, then by those who edited their books.

Ezekiel and Priestly Traditions

Since he was a priest in the Temple in Jerusalem, it is not surprising that we find connections between Ezekiel and priestly tradition, even though Ezekiel condemned the corruption of the Jerusalem priesthood of his day. Scholars have long observed an overlap of language and themes between Ezekiel and the P(riestly) source of the Pentateuch (see pages 49–50). Thus, a characteristic phrase of P, "be fruitful and multiply," in Ezekiel occurs in reverse order, "multiply and be fruitful" (Ezek 36.11). Similarly, in P's Exodus narrative, a reason given for the signs and wonders is so that both the Israelites and the Egyptians may "know that I am Yahweh" (for example, Ex 6.7), and the same phrase is used more than sixty times in Ezekiel. A final example is the phrase "eternal [NRSV: "everlasting"] covenant," which occurs eight times in P, of the covenants made by God with Noah, Abraham, Isaac, the Israelites, and Aaron and Phinehas and their descendants, and in Ezekiel 16.60 and 37.26, both times of the restored relationship between Yahweh and Israel.

Some broader themes of the P tradition are also found in Ezekiel. One is the special status given to the descendants of Aaron through Zadok, a chief priest under David and the sole holder of that office under Solomon, as opposed to the Levites. The Levites, as in P, are demoted to the status of lesser clergy. This hierarchy is reflected in the distribution of the land, where the Temple and its immediate environs are restricted to the Zadokite priests, and an adjacent area is given to the Levites, farther removed from the Temple itself (see page 329).

We also find important connections of theme and vocabulary between Ezekiel and the Holiness Code (Lev 17–26; see pages 126–29). So close are the Holiness Code and some passages in Ezekiel that some scholars have suggested that Ezekiel himself was the author of the Holiness Code. This is less likely than that both Ezekiel and the Holiness Code drew on the same body of laws, collected and preserved by the Jerusalem priesthood and eventually codified into the Holiness Code.

Given the lack of consensus among scholars concerning the dates of both P and the Holiness Code, it is impossible to determine whether the prophet Ezekiel knew them in more or less their present form. But even if in their final form both are to be dated later than Ezekiel (see pages 50 and 128), they are derived from older traditions with which Ezekiel the priest would have been familiar,

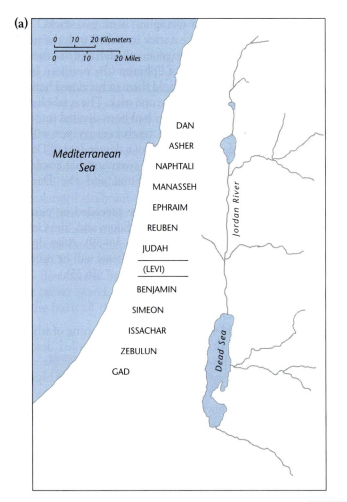

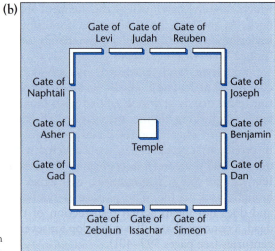

FIGURE 20.4   Schematic representations of Ezekiel's conception of the geography of a restored Israel (a) and a restored Jerusalem (b).

LORD entered the temple by the gate facing east, the spirit lifted me up, and brought me into the inner court; and the glory of the Lord filled the temple. (Ezek 43.2–5)

Just as Ezekiel had felt the presence of Yahweh with him in exile, he imagined the return of Yahweh from Babylonia with his people, when Yahweh would take up residence in a restored Temple, as he had at the dedication of the Temple built by Solomon (1 Kings 8.10).

Ezekiel's detailed vision of a restored home for Yahweh shows his understanding of the Temple as an earthly facsimile of the divine home on the cosmic mountain. These mythological elements are found at the beginning, where we are told that the Temple is set on a very high mountain (40.2), and at the end (47.1–12), where a healing, fertile river flows from the base of the Temple. As this river moves eastward, it becomes progressively deeper, and on its banks are trees that supply fruit and medicinal leaves year-round. When the river reaches the Dead Sea, it will render that barren body of water fresh, so that fish will thrive in it as they do in the Mediterranean. This theme will be reused in later Jewish and Christian apocalyptic literature (see Zech 14.8; Rev 22.1–2).

The Land Restored

To the priests is assigned the land immediately surrounding the sanctuary. Part of this district, but farther from the Temple, is given to the Levites; unlike the historical situation, in which the Levites were a landless tribe (see pages 165–67 and 187), in Ezekiel's vision they too have a territorial allotment. Next is land for the prince, on the west and the east, and then the allotments for the twelve tribes, in a roughly symmetrical arrangement. In contrast to the actual historical geography, however, the tribes are distributed on both sides of the Holy City, with Judah and six tribes to the north, and Benjamin and four other tribes to the south. Judah and Benjamin, which had been part of the kingdom of Judah, are thus set immediately adjacent to the sacred and royal

territories, although their actual geography is reversed, with Judah now north of Jerusalem and Benjamin to its south. Moreover, tribal holdings are restricted to the land west of the Jordan, in contrast both to the division of the land according to the book of Joshua and to the actual historical situation, in which tribes such as Reuben, Manasseh, and Gilead claimed territory east of the Jordan.

The geography has a practical dimension as well: Parts of the holy city are set aside for ordinary uses, for houses, and as agricultural land (48.15–20). For the most part, however, the description is idealized. The land is to be divided equally among the twelve tribes, with Jerusalem in its center. The city has twelve gates, one for each of the tribes, symbolizing the unity of the restored community. Finally, the city is given a new name, signifying the return of the divine presence: "Yahweh is there" (48.35).

A LOOK BACK AND AHEAD

In Ezekiel's vision, exile is not a permanent condition, for Yahweh will lead his people from Babylon back to the Promised Land. This theme of a new Exodus will be elaborated in the lyrical poetry of Second Isaiah (see page 338). But alongside the optimism with which the book of Ezekiel ends is evidence of developing tensions over the ownership of the Promised Land, and especially over the identity of the true Israel. Ezekiel and Jeremiah were in agreement: Those who had not been exiled were bad figs, so bad that they had to be destroyed; the exiles are the good figs, whom Yahweh will restore to the land (Jer 24). Those who remained in the land, however, felt differently. When some of the exiles returned, later in the sixth century, these conflicting views would have to be addressed; from their resolution would emerge facets of what we can now call early Judaism.

identified as the Torah, the first five books of the Bible, which according to the Documentary Hypothesis was given its definitive form by P. Even if, as some scholars argue, the book that Ezra brought back to Judah was not identical with the final form of the Torah, it was a substantial and authoritative stage in its formation.

One of the themes of P is that of exile and return, under divine guidance, to the land promised to Abraham, Isaac, and Jacob. That theme is introduced in the narratives of the primeval history and recurs in the ancestral narratives in Genesis 12–50. The plot of the rest of the Pentateuch is essentially the extended narrative of the journey home from Egypt. The eventual return of the exiles from Babylon is thus anticipated in the return of other individuals and groups to the Promised Land.

The cumulative evidence indicates, then, that one moment in the crystallization of traditions that comprise P was the time of the exile in Babylon, the sixth century BCE. For the exiles, P's message was one of hope and optimism, coupled with insistence on faithful observance of the laws given to Moses.

THE EXILIC EDITION OF THE DEUTERONOMISTIC HISTORY

Another school active in the exilic period was that of the Deuteronomists, who produced another revision of the book of Deuteronomy, as well as of their major work, the Deuteronomistic History (see pages 154–55 and 161–63). In their account of the history of Israel in the Promised Land, from the time of the conquest under Joshua to the destruction of Jerusalem, the Deuteronomistic Historians used as principal themes the requirement of strict fidelity to the teaching of Moses, and especially that of worshiping Yahweh alone. The failure of the people to do so inevitably resulted in their punishment by Yahweh.

Thus, the explanation of the Deuteronomistic Historians for the disasters that befell both the northern kingdom of Israel in 722 BCE and the southern kingdom of Judah in 586 was the classic one of divine justice, or theodicy. According to the theological explanation of the events of 586, "Jerusalem and Judah so angered Yahweh that he cast them from his presence" (2 Kings 24.20), and they were exiled and the Temple in Jerusalem was destroyed. The nation had failed to live up to the requirements of the teaching of Moses, and in consequence, the covenant curses, which included exile, had come upon them.

Even though their primary focus was the past, the Deuteronomists were also concerned with the future. Sprinkled throughout the exilic edition of the book of Deuteronomy and the Deuteronomistic History are passages that urge repentance and express hope in divine forgiveness (for example, Deut 4.25–31; 30.1–10; 1 Kings 8.46–51). Such optimism would soon become a reality, when Cyrus the Great conquered Babylon in 539 BCE. The most exuberant reaction to that event is found in Isaiah 40–55.

ISAIAH 40–55

One of the most important conclusions of eighteenth- and nineteenth-century historical-critical scholarship was that the biblical book of Isaiah is not a single work dating from the time of the prophet Isaiah of Jerusalem in the late eighth and early seventh centuries BCE, but rather is composed of writings from several different periods. In addition to the material going back to Isaiah of Jerusalem, known as First Isaiah and found in much of Isaiah 1–39 (see page 275), scholars identified two other major parts of the book, **Second Isaiah** (also called Deutero-Isaiah; Isa 40–55), and Third Isaiah (Trito-Isaiah; Isa 56–66). In this chapter, we will deal with Second Isaiah.

Several factors show that Second Isaiah is later than First Isaiah. The historical context is entirely different. In First Isaiah, the principal enemy was Assyria; in Second Isaiah, it is Babylon, which in the late seventh century BCE replaced Assyria as the dominant power in the Near East. In First Isaiah, Jerusalem was under siege but never was destroyed; in Second Isaiah, the city has been destroyed and will be restored, and the exile to Babylon has taken place. Finally, Second Isaiah (but not First Isaiah) twice mentions Cyrus, the king of Persia, and describes him in glowing terms usually reserved for Israel's own leaders: He is the "anointed" of Yahweh, his "shepherd," chosen by Yahweh to destroy Babylon and to rebuild the Temple (Isa 44.28–45.1). Another significant difference is that in First Isaiah, the prophet is named and is a major character in both autobiographical and biographical accounts, but in Isaiah 40–66 the prophet is unnamed and we are given no details about his life or his family. The historical references suggest a mid-sixth-century date for Second Isaiah.

In Third Isaiah the historical context has changed again. Despite some links in style with the previous chapters of Second Isaiah, Third Isaiah does not make use of Second Isaiah's frequent description of an imminent return from exile in Babylon as a second Exodus. By the time of Third Isaiah, the return has already taken place, and the audience is situated in Judah rather than in Babylonia. The Temple has been rebuilt, and worship is taking place there. A majority of modern scholars have therefore concluded that Isaiah 56–66 dates somewhat later than Second Isaiah, in the late sixth or early fifth century BCE; we will consider these chapters in more detail on pages 354–55.

Despite general scholarly agreement that chapters 40–66 of the book of Isaiah were not written by the eighth-century BCE prophet, more recent scholarship has also observed that since very ancient times, the parts of Isaiah were viewed as one book and that they have many links of vocabulary and theme. One prominent example is the designation of Yahweh as "the holy one of Israel," which occurs over thirty times in Isaiah but only infrequently elsewhere in the Bible. A repeated phrase that connects the parts of the book is "do not fear," as also does the presence of "signs." Other unifying elements are a focus on Jerusalem (Zion), and the concepts of justice and righteousness. One explanation of these links is that there was something like a "school of Isaiah," a kind of intellectual movement that was active for several centuries (see further pages 274–75). This

school not only would have preserved and edited the original oracles of the eighth-century prophet, but also would have continued after his death and written new compositions in his style, applying his original message to new situations. This resulted in additions to the original collection, including not only Second Isaiah (chaps. 40–55) and Third Isaiah (chaps. 56–66), but also chapters 24–27, 34–35, and 36–39 (taken from the Deuteronomistic History in 2 Kings 18–20). The chapters that form Second Isaiah are thus the product of the school of the prophet Isaiah, comparable to the schools or movements that produced the Priestly source and the Deuteronomistic History.

Closely connected with Second Isaiah are two sections in the earlier part of the book of Isaiah: chapters 24–27, often called "the Isaiah Apocalypse" (see further page 361), and chapters 34–35, comprising an oracle against Edom and an account of the return from exile. The latter has several verbal parallels with chapters 40–55.

Because Second Isaiah is anonymous, it is difficult to know exactly when and where it was written. The majority of scholars think that the author of Second Isaiah was writing in Babylonia like his predecessor Ezekiel, probably around 540 BCE, shortly before or after the city's capture by Cyrus. The author was familiar with Babylonian ritual and religious traditions, but no specifics make the Babylonian option certain. An alternative is that it was composed in Judah, perhaps in Jerusalem itself. But little attention is given to the situation in Judah, and so the primary audience was most likely the exiles themselves.

While it is difficult to discern the logic governing the arrangement of materials in Second Isaiah, the author made use of a variety of genres. In doing so, the author freely adapted and transformed them, like a composer's variations on a theme. To put it somewhat differently, we might consider Second Isaiah as an interlocking series of oracles with an overall thematic unity but without rhetorical design or strictly logical development.

We will examine three principal themes of Second Isaiah: its description of the return from exile as a new Exodus, its presentation of the "servant of Yahweh," and its explicit monotheism.

A New Exodus

The central theme of Second Isaiah, its unifying thread as it were, is that of the imminent return from Babylon as a new Exodus. The author imagines this return as a ritual procession to Zion led by Yahweh himself. The importance of this theme is indicated by its strategic placement at the beginning (Isa 40.3–5) and the end (55.12–13) of the book.

The return to Zion is linked repeatedly with Israel's earlier journey under divine guidance from Egypt to Canaan. When Yahweh brought the Israelites out of Egypt, he was their shepherd, guiding "his people . . . in the wilderness like a flock" (Ps 78.52). Now, according to Second Isaiah, reprising an image already used by Jeremiah and Ezekiel, he will lead his flock once again (Isa 40.11).

Yet, while resembling the earlier journey from Egypt to Canaan, the return from exile will be qualitatively different: It will be something "new" (Isa 42.9; 43.19). Thus, whereas in the original Exodus, the participants left "in great haste" (Ex 12.11; Deut 16.3), the participants in this journey will "not go out in haste" (Isa 52.12). The region through which the Israelites had passed on their journey from Egypt to Canaan had been a "great and terrible wilderness, an arid wasteland" (Deut 8.15). In this new Exodus, the vast desert between Mesopotamia and the Promised Land will be transformed into an Edenic paradise, forested and in bloom, with the trees clapping their hands for joy as the procession passes. The returnees will travel on a level road, with every valley filled and every hill made low. In the first Exodus, water was divinely provided but scarce. This time it will be everywhere: There will be rivers in the desert, with springs in abundance and the wilderness itself a pool of water.

Making use of mythology, Second Isaiah links this new Exodus with Yahweh's earlier acts, especially his defeat of the waters of chaos before his creation of the world. In Isaiah 51.9–11, the poet addresses Yahweh's powerful arm (see Deut 4.34), urging it to rouse itself for battle as it had in the days of old, when he defeated the primeval waters, here called Rahab (as in Ps 89.10) and "the dragon" (see Isa 27.1). In a telescoping of chronology characteristic of mythological language, the poet combines the primeval battle with two reflexes of the same event, the escape of the Israelites from Egypt through the Reed Sea and the return from Babylon:

> Was it not you who cut Rahab in pieces,
>   who pierced the dragon?
> Was it not you who dried up the sea,
>   the waters of the great deep;
> who made the depths of the sea a way
>   for the redeemed to cross over?
> So the ransomed of the LORD shall return,
>   and come to Zion with singing;
> everlasting joy shall be upon their heads;
>   they shall obtain joy and gladness,
>   and sorrow and sighing shall flee away.
>   (Isa 51.9–11)

We thus see a consistency in the divine action, and at the same time something new. While repeatedly alluding to the earlier Exodus, in a lovely paradox the poet exhorts his listeners: "Do not remember the former things, or consider the things of old" (Isa 43.18).

The Servant of Yahweh

In 1892, the German scholar Bernhard Duhm isolated four passages as distinct, the "**servant songs**" or the "songs of the servant of Yahweh." In the first (Isa 42.1–4), the servant is called the chosen one, to whom Yahweh has given his spirit, as he did to the judges of old, to "establish justice" throughout the world, but in a nonviolent way. In the second (49.1–6), the servant himself speaks to the entire world, and identifies himself as one called by God before birth. In the third (50.4–11), the servant speaks again, and, in words reminiscent of the "confessions" of Jeremiah (see page 306), declares his confidence in divine help even in the face of persecution. Finally, the fourth (52.13–53.12) continues this theme of the suffering of the servant, relating how despite his innocence the servant was oppressed "like a lamb that is led to the slaughter," but his suffering is vicarious—he is like the scapegoat (Lev 16; see page 126), bearing the guilt of the people. Duhm hypothesized that these poems had been composed by another author and added to Second Isaiah at a later stage. Modern scholars are less inclined to view them as independent compositions, and some question whether "song" is the best label, but Duhm's characterization has framed subsequent interpretation.

The identification of the servant is the most challenging issue in the interpretation of Second Isaiah. Two principal approaches have been taken. In the first, the servant is an individual, and several candidates have been proposed. From Israel's more distant past, these include Moses; from the late eighth and early seventh century BCE, Hezekiah the king of Judah; from the sixth century, Jehoiachin the king of Judah, Jeremiah the prophet, Cyrus the king of Persia, Zerubbabel, and the anonymous prophet who wrote Second Isaiah himself. In Jewish tradition, the servant was sometimes identified as a messianic figure of the future. In the New Testament Jesus is explicitly identified as the "suffering servant" (a phrase that does not actually occur in the Bible) of the last "song" (see Mt 8.17; Acts 8.26–35).

In other parts of the Bible, the title "servant of the Lord" is used of important individuals in Israel's history, including Abraham, Moses, Joshua, David, Job, and even the Babylonian king Nebuchadrezzar. The term "servant" as applied to one divinely chosen is thus not unusual, and the description of the servant draws on preexisting biblical tradition, but none of the persons already mentioned is a suitable identification for the servant in Second Isaiah because in it the servant is more a figure of the present and the immediate future than of the past.

A second line of interpretation is to see the servant as a kind of literary figure, a personification of the nation of Israel, regarded as an individual as often elsewhere in the Bible. This identification is supported by the text itself:

And he said to me, "You are my servant,
   Israel, in whom I will be glorified." (Isa 49.3)

But the occurrence of "Israel" in this verse is puzzling, since in the following verses, the servant is commissioned by the deity

to bring Jacob back to him,
   and that Israel might be gathered to him . . .
to raise up the tribes of Jacob
   and to restore the survivors of Israel. (Isa 49.5–6)

Because of this inconsistency, some scholars have argued that the reference to Israel in verse 3 should be deleted. Throughout Second Isaiah, however, Israel is explicitly identified as the servant of the Lord several times. Thus, if we consider the "servant songs" as an integral part of the entire work rather than later additions, the best identification of the "servant" is Israel itself, personified as a kind of prophet; as Jeremiah had been called from before birth to be "a prophet to the nations" (Jer 1.5), so now Israel also has been destined to be a "light to the nations" (Isa 42.6; 49.6; 51.4), that is, a prophet to the rest of the world.

The poet uses the personification of Israel as a prophetic servant of Yahweh fluidly, and at times the servant does seem to be distinct from Israel. Perhaps the prophet was incorporating his own experience, so that some of the passages describing the servant are autobiographical, or perhaps the poet had in mind not all Israel, but a restored Israel, the "remnant" of First Isaiah (10.20–22; 46.3). In this interpretation, the suffering of the innocent during the catastrophe of 586 BCE and its aftermath was the "punishment that made us whole" (53.5).

The variety of possible interpretations makes clear that there is no certain identification of the servant, and we should also allow for the possibility that the ambiguity is deliberate. On one level, the servant can be understood as an individual, or a group within Israel; on another, the servant can refer to Israel itself, understood both collectively and as an individual. As such, having experienced a kind of redemptive suffering, the servant has been divinely commissioned to bring all nations to acknowledge the only God.

Monotheism

In Second Isaiah, for the first time in biblical literature, we get a clear statement of **monotheism**, the belief that the only god is Yahweh, the god of Israel. This is not expressed in abstract philosophical terms, for Second Isaiah is poetry rather than treatise. Moreover, the monotheistic principle is not entirely new; rather, it had been developing for some time (see Box 21.2 on page 340).

Box 21.2 THE DEVELOPMENT OF MONOTHEISM

In Israel's early legal system, as expressed in the Decalogue, the text of its contract or covenant with Yahweh, the Israelites were commanded not to worship other gods, but no unequivocal statement was made about Yahweh being the only god (Ex 20.3; Deut 5.7; see page 104). Rather, in bringing Israel out of Egypt, he had shown his superiority to other gods, as he also had in defeating the forces of chaos and creating the world.

In the preexilic prophets, the "oracles against the nations" (see page 256) implied Yahweh's rule over the entire world. One stimulus for this development was the increasingly frequent attacks on and ultimately the conquest of both the northern kingdom of Israel and the southern kingdom of Judah by the Assyrians and the Babylonians. The prophets interpreted these attacks not as the result of Yahweh's inferiority to the more powerful gods of other nations, but as his use of those nations to punish Israel and Judah for having violated their covenant with him.

In Second Isaiah, the concept of Yahweh's superiority is taken to its logical conclusion: If Yahweh was responsible for what happened to Israel, if Assyria, and then Babylon, and finally Cyrus, were all instruments in the divine hand, if Yahweh was directing history for his own purposes, then not only was he more powerful than other gods, but other gods in fact did not exist, as Second Isaiah repeatedly proclaims. The development of explicit monotheism thus can be understood as a further response to the catastrophe of the destruction of Jerusalem in 586 BCE.

Monotheism became the defining characteristic of Judaism, followed by Christianity and Islam. The ancient words of the Shema were reinterpreted as a monotheistic declaration—"The LORD our God, the LORD is one" (Deut 6.4; see further Box 10.1 on page 149), reiterated in the pronouncement of Paul—"for us there is one God, the Father, from whom are all things and for whom we exist" (1 Cor 8.6), and in the Muslim profession of faith—"There is no god except God."

The concept of monotheism is clearly expressed in Isaiah 44.6:

I am the first and I am the last;
    besides me there is no god. (See also 43.11; 44.8; 45.5, 21.)

Monotheism is developed in Isaiah 44.9–20, a satire on the making and worship of idols. In it, the foolishness of idolaters is elaborated, such as the carpenter who carves an idol from a tree and worships it, and then with the rest of the wood makes a fire and cooks himself a meal. The satirical depiction of idolaters, also found in Jeremiah and Psalm 115, became a favorite motif of later biblical and postbiblical writers.

Genesis 1 alludes to *Enuma Elish*, the Babylonian account of creation by the god Marduk after his defeat of Tiamat, implicitly offering a monotheistic alternative to the Mesopotamian myth: As the sole deity, it was Yahweh who defeated the primeval forces of chaos and created the world (see further pages 35–37). Second Isaiah makes this explicit. In the Babylonian new year festival at which *Enuma Elish* was recited, the statue of Marduk along with that of his son Nabu (biblical Nebo) was carried in procession to his temple. Referring to Marduk by his title Bel, Second Isaiah asserts that this need to be carried "on weary animals" (Isa 46.1) demonstrates Marduk's powerlessness:

> [The statue] cannot move from its place.
> If one cries out to it, it does not answer,
>   or save anyone from trouble. (Isa 46.7)

By way of contrast, in the procession of the returnees to Zion, Yahweh is not carried; rather, he carries Israel, after having given birth to it (46.3) (see Box 21.3).

According to Second Isaiah, it was Yahweh, not Marduk, who defeated primeval chaos, the "great deep" (Isa 51.10); it was Yahweh, not Marduk, who created the world (40.12), who formed light and created darkness (45.7). Moreover, unlike Marduk, he did this alone, without the assistance of other deities (44.24); unlike Marduk, Yahweh is neither the offspring of other gods nor did he father any (43.10). Yahweh's supreme power is demonstrated both in his exacting punishment against Israel and in his enacting Israel's restoration, which at this

historical moment also involved designating Cyrus as his anointed agent of the return of the exiles to Zion (Isa 45.1), part of a divine plan that reaches back to creation:

> For I am God, and there is no other;
>   I am God, and there is no one like me,
> declaring the end from the beginning
>   and from ancient times things not yet done.
>   (Isa 46.9–10)

At the same time, Second Isaiah sometimes seems to suggest that other deities exist. In an imaginary courtroom, Yahweh summons the Babylonian deities to trial, but, when he questions them, they are silent (Isa 41), like Baal in Elijah's contest on Mount Carmel (1 Kings 18.20–29; see page 249). Many scholars have also recognized in the plural imperatives of Isaiah 40.1–2 ("Comfort ye . . .") an address by Yahweh to the divine council, the assembly of the gods over which Yahweh presided; at this council meeting, as in 1 Kings 22.20–22, members of the council speak (Isa 40.3, 6). Given

Box 21.3 FEMALE IMAGES OF GOD

Yahweh, the god of Israel, is generally described in the Bible as a male deity. The grammatical forms used for him are always masculine, and he is frequently depicted in predominantly male images, for example as a king, a warrior, a husband, and a father. Scattered throughout the Bible, however, are also female images of Yahweh, and such images are clustered in Second and Third Isaiah. In his speeches, Yahweh compares himself to a woman in labor whose long wait is over (Isa 42.14), as one who not only fathered but also gave birth to his children (Isa 45.9–12; compare Num 11.12). The metaphor is most explicit in Isaiah 49.14–15:

> Zion said, "Yahweh has forsaken me,
>   my Lord has forgotten me."
> Can a woman forget her nursing infant,
>   or show no compassion for the child of her belly?

Third Isaiah gives an example of another feminine image of God, that of the midwife (66.9; compare Ps 22.9–10).

Although the depiction of Yahweh as mother and midwife is relatively infrequent, it reminds us that all language used of the divine is metaphorical.

Second Isaiah's explicit monotheism, however, all of these references to other gods, like P's allusion to the divine council in its account of creation (Gen 1.26), are literary convention rather than an expression of polytheistic belief.

A LOOK BACK AND AHEAD

From its opening words commanding comfort for Jerusalem to its closing statement guaranteeing that the divine purpose will be fulfilled, Second Isaiah has an exuberant optimism. Babylon will be defeated by Cyrus, the exiles will return, and Jerusalem will be restored to a place of "joy and gladness" (Isa 51.3).

One of the leaders of the returning exiles was Zerubbabel, a grandson of King Jehoiachin and thus a descendant of David. Some of the returnees, may have expected that part of the divine plan was that the Davidic dynasty would be restored. A permanent Temple had been part of Israel's life since it had been built by Solomon in the mid-tenth century BCE, but the reconstruction of the Temple is mentioned only once in Second Isaiah (44.28). Moreover, although P gives elaborate descriptions of the tabernacle and its rituals, in P's narrative of the journey from Egypt to Canaan that tabernacle is a portable structure suitable for a people on the move. But in Ezra 1, rebuilding the Temple is a primary concern of the returnees, and it becomes an important focus of the literature of the late sixth century.

When the exiles did return, the expectation of a restoration of the monarchy, along with Second Isaiah's optimism and P's careful program for reestablishing worship, all met the cold realities of the actual situation in Judah. Tensions also developed among several groups—the returning exiles, those who had remained in the land, and those who remained in exile, both in Babylon and elsewhere—and, despite the promise of Persian support, rebuilding the Temple proved difficult. In the next chapter, we will examine the literature concerned with the decades immediately following the return from Babylon.

IMPORTANT NAMES AND TERMS

Each name or term is defined briefly in the Glossary. Its first significant occurrence in this chapter appears in **boldface** type.

Cyrus

monotheism

Nabonidus

Second Isaiah

servant songs

Zerubbabel

QUESTIONS FOR REVIEW

1. How did the policies of the Persians toward conquered peoples differ from those of the Babylonians?

2. How does the Pentateuchal source P deal with the problems raised by the destruction of Jerusalem and the exile in Babylon?

3. How did the Deuteronomistic Historians revise their work in light of the exile?

4. How does Second Isaiah reinterpret earlier biblical traditions in response to the events of the sixth century BCE?

5. Why did monotheism become important in the sixth century BCE?

BIBLIOGRAPHY

A good summary of the Persian period is Mary Joan Winn Leith, "Israel among the Nations: The Persian Period," Chapter 8 in *The Oxford History of the Biblical World* (ed. M. D. Coogan; New York: Oxford University Press, 1998; pb 2001; available in Oxford Biblical Studies Online).

For commentaries on Ezra, see the bibliography to Chapter 22.

For commentaries on Second Isaiah, see Richard J. Clifford, *Fair Spoken and Persuading: An Interpretation of Second Isaiah* (New York: Paulist, 1984; rp. Academic Renewal, 2002); and Christopher R. Seitz, "The Book of Isaiah 40–66," pp. 307–551 in *The New Interpreter's Bible*, Vol. 6 (ed. L. E. Keck; Nashville, TN: Abingdon, 2001).

For a sketch of the development of monotheism, see Baruch Halpern, "Monotheism," pp. 524–27 in *The Oxford Companion to the Bible* (ed. B. M. Metzger and M. D. Coogan; New York: Oxford University Press, 1993; available in Oxford Biblical Studies Online); and for its significance in Second Isaiah, see "Monotheism in Isaiah 40–55," pp. 179–94 in Mark S. Smith, *The Origins of Biblical Monotheism: Israel's Polytheistic Background and the Ugaritic Texts* (New York: Oxford University Press, 2001).

On feminine imagery used of God, see Carol Meyers, "Female Images of God in the Hebrew Bible," pp. 525–28 in *Women in Scripture* (ed. Carol Meyers; Boston: Houghton Mifflin, 2000).

PART SIX

RECONSTRUCTION, CONSOLIDATION, AND CHALLENGE

The Restoration: Judah in the Late Sixth and Fifth Centuries BCE

Ezra 3–10, Nehemiah, Haggai, Zechariah, Isaiah 24–27 and 56–66, Joel, and Malachi

The Jews in exile in Babylonia were allowed to return to their homeland after Cyrus the Great's capture of Babylon in 539 BCE. What the returnees encountered, however, was not nearly as glorious as Second Isaiah had proclaimed. The community in Judea was divided, and Jerusalem was in shambles. The reconstruction of the Temple would take several decades, and that of the city nearly a century. There were struggles over leadership, and tensions existed between the returnees and those who had remained in Judah, between the returnees and neighboring peoples, and among the returnees themselves. In this chapter, we will look first at the history of the return and the early restoration, including the rebuilding of the Temple in the late sixth century BCE.

Then we will consider events in Judah in the fifth century BCE and writings from that period included among the prophets, many of which belong to an early stage of a genre called "apocalyptic literature." The restored community in Jerusalem continued to experience difficulties and internal disputes, and in part because of this, hope focused more and more on the distant future.

HISTORY

Cyrus the Great, the king of Persia who had captured Babylon and allowed those of the Judean exiles who wished to return to do so, died in battle in 530 BCE and was succeeded by his son Cambyses, who completed the imperial designs of his father by capturing Egypt. Cambyses died under mysterious circumstances in 522 on his way back from Egypt and was succeeded by a distant cousin and commander in his army, Darius I, who ruled until 486.

During his long reign, Darius I consolidated Persian control over regions already conquered and sought to extend it to the north and east. Darius's successor, his son Xerxes, moved to expand the empire farther to the west. This meant a confrontation with the city-states of Greece, especially Athens and Sparta. Both sides won a number of battles, but neither side was able to defeat the other decisively, and the conflict continued for another century and a half.

These events have left few traces in biblical literature, which does not contain a continuous historical narrative. Instead, for information about

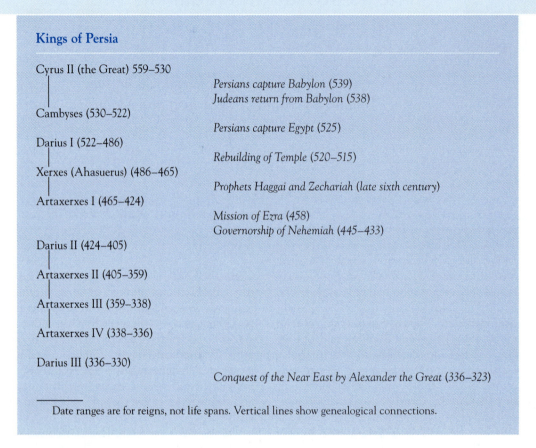

Box 22.1 CHRONOLOGY OF THE MID-SIXTH TO THE FOURTH CENTURIES BCE

Kings of Persia

Cyrus II (the Great) 559–530

                     Persians capture Babylon (539)
                     Judeans return from Babylon (538)

Cambyses (530–522)

                     Persians capture Egypt (525)

Darius I (522–486)

                     Rebuilding of Temple (520–515)

Xerxes (Ahasuerus) (486–465)

                     Prophets Haggai and Zechariah (late sixth century)

Artaxerxes I (465–424)

                     Mission of Ezra (458)
                     Governorship of Nehemiah (445–433)

Darius II (424–405)

Artaxerxes II (405–359)

Artaxerxes III (359–338)

Artaxerxes IV (338–336)

Darius III (336–330)

                     Conquest of the Near East by Alexander the Great (336–323)

Date ranges are for reigns, not life spans. Vertical lines show genealogical connections.

Jewish communities both in the Diaspora and in Judah, we are dependent on incomplete and sometimes inconsistent sources, and reconstructing what may have occurred is necessarily tentative.

The return described at the beginning of the book of Ezra seems to have been of a small group. According to Ezra 3, as soon as they arrived in Jerusalem, the returnees built an altar to reestablish the regular sacrifices to Yahweh. Then, "in the second year after their arrival" (Ezra 3.8), with appropriate ceremonies, they started the reconstruction of the Temple, to replace the Temple that had been built by Solomon in the mid-tenth century BCE and destroyed by the Babylonians in 586 BCE. But when the foundation of the Temple was laid, those present had mixed emotions:

> Many of the priests and Levites and heads of families, old people who had seen the first house on its foundations, wept with a loud voice when they saw this house, though many shouted aloud for joy, so that the people could not distinguish the sound of the joyful shout from the sound of the people's weeping. (Ezra 3.12–13)

Clearly the new Temple's foundations were not nearly as magnificent as those of the first. Work on the reconstruction was half-hearted at best, if it did not come to a complete halt. Some of the returnees were preoccupied with their own resettlement needs and had little time for work on the Temple. There was also local opposition. It is difficult to describe the parties and politics of Judah in this period and in the subsequent century because our sources are incomplete, but one important group was the returnees, who claimed that the reconstruction had the support of Cyrus and Cambyses. Another group identified as "the adversaries of Judah and Benjamin" (Ezra 4.1) offered their assistance, asserting that they too were worshipers of Yahweh, although they had been settled in the former northern kingdom of Israel by the Assyrians; their offer was rebuffed. A third group was the "people of the land," a phrase that in this period probably means Judeans who had not been taken into exile. They seem to have tried to use their influence with the Persian court to disrupt the reconstruction. New and differently used labels for groups of people suggest that old labels like "Judean" and "Israelite" no longer fit and were inadequate to describe the groups living in Jerusalem with conflicting goals.

Early in the reign of Darius I, about 520 BCE, work on the rebuilding of the Temple resumed under dual leadership. Political authority lay with Zerubbabel, who, like Sheshbazzar, the leader of the returnees in 538, had the title of "governor," a designation of the top official in a province in the Persian imperial system. Also like Sheshbazzar, Zerubbabel was a descendant of Jehoiachin (Jeconiah), the king of Judah who had been exiled to Babylon in 597. Religious authority lay with the high priest Jeshua (also called Joshua, a variant form of the same name). This shared leadership and their efforts to reconstruct the Temple had the support of two prophets, Haggai and Zechariah.

According to the book of Ezra, Persian imperial support for the restoration was confirmed by Darius, in response to a query from Tattenai, the governor of the province of "Beyond the River," that is, the province west of the Euphrates River, roughly the Levant. Apart from the Persian kings themselves, Tattenai is the only individual in the biblical sources for this period mentioned in a contemporaneous nonbiblical text. That support was not just political, but also financial, according to the book of Ezra: Tattenai was to pay for the cost of the reconstruction and also to supply materials for sacrifices. This account is consistent with Persian policy elsewhere: In Babylon, Cyrus restored the proper worship of Marduk, its principal deity, and in Egypt, Cambyses and Darius sponsored the reestablishment of local sanctuaries and priestly schools. As in Judah, the Persian kings thus both gained the support of local authorities and at the same time exercised imperial control over them.

FIGURE 22.1   The Persian king Darius I seated on his throne, with his son Xerxes behind him, on a relief at the royal palace in Persepolis.

The reconstruction now proceeded relatively swiftly, and in 515 BCE the Temple was dedicated. The rebuilt Temple is often called the "**Second Temple**," and the "Second Temple period" in Jewish history lasts from the late sixth century BCE to 70 CE, when Jerusalem was captured by the Romans and the Temple (which had been rebuilt again in the late first century BCE by Herod the Great) was destroyed. In the restored Temple, rituals resumed, in conformity with "the book of Moses" (Ezra 6.18). Immediately thereafter, the Passover was celebrated by the returnees, along with "all who had joined with them and separated themselves from the pollutions of the nations of the land" (Ezra 6.21). The latter group were probably those who had remained in the land, but who were willing to accept the religious authority of the leaders, especially as it related to qualifications for membership in the community.

At this point, a hiatus occurs in the biblical sources until the mid-fifth century BCE. We have no further information about Zerubbabel and Jeshua, nor, as previously, is there any mention in Persian sources of the tiny province of Judah (also called Yehud). From the Persian perspective, Judah was a relatively unimportant part of their empire; scholars estimate that the entire population of Judah at this time was no more than ten thousand persons, and that of Jerusalem fewer than a thousand.

EZRA 3–6

Ezra and Nehemiah lived in the fifth century BCE, and we will discuss them and the structure of the books that have their names on pages 355–59. Here we will focus on Ezra 3–6, a narrative history of the events of the late sixth century, from the return from Babylon to the dedication of the restored Temple in Jerusalem.

The chronology of this section of the book of Ezra is confused. For example, Ezra 6.22 mentions the king of Assyria, either a deliberate anachronism or simply a mistake, for Assyrian rule had ended in the previous century. Also, the account of the reconstruction of the Temple moves abruptly from the reign of Darius to that of his successor Ahasuerus (Xerxes) in Ezra 4.6, then quotes correspondence of the next Persian king, Artaxerxes I, in 4.7–23, only to return to the time of Darius in 4.24. (For a chronology, see Box 22.1 on page 348.) The correspondence has to do with opposition to Nehemiah in the mid-fifth century BCE, as he undertook to rebuild Jerusalem's fortifications (see further pages 356–57).

Moreover, at Ezra 4.8, the language of the text switches from Hebrew to Aramaic (see Box 22.2), only to return to Hebrew in Ezra 6.19. Another Aramaic section, also quoting a royal letter, appears in Ezra 7.12–26.

Box 22.2 ARAMAIC

A few small parts of the Jewish scriptures are not written in Hebrew (and thus the term "Hebrew Bible" is not strictly accurate), but in a related language called **Aramaic**. These are Ezra 4.8–6.18 and 7.12–26, Daniel 2.4b–7.28, Jeremiah 10.11, and two words in Genesis 31.47.

Aramaic is one of the Semitic languages, originally spoken in Aram, roughly the same as modern Syria. During the first half of the first millennium BCE, Aramaic came to be used as a kind of lingua franca, an international language of diplomacy and commerce. This was in part a result of the Assyrian practice of deporting the elite of conquered regions, so that Aramaic speakers from Syria came to be spread throughout the Assyrian empire. Thus, during the siege of Jerusalem in 701 BCE (see pages 280–87), the representatives of the Judean king Hezekiah asked the representative of the king of Assyria: "Please speak to your servants in the Aramaic language, for we understand it; do not speak to us in the language of Judah within the hearing of the people who are on the wall" (2 Kings 18.26). The implication is that the aristocrats spoke Aramaic, as did the Assyrian envoy, but ordinary people in Jerusalem could not understand it.

Gradually the use of Aramaic spread. During the Persian period, it is widely attested in inscriptions from throughout the Persian empire, as far east as India and as far west as Asia Minor, and especially in Egypt, where the climate allowed hundreds of papyri written in Aramaic to be preserved. The use of Aramaic for official Persian documents in the book of Ezra is thus historically accurate, although many scholars question whether the documents themselves are authentic.

It was during the Persian period in the fifth and fourth centuries BCE and the subsequent Hellenistic period that Aramaic slowly replaced Hebrew as the ordinary spoken language of Palestine. It remained so well into the Common Era, although, as the result of the conquests of Alexander the Great and the rule of his successors (see page 406), Greek replaced Aramaic as the lingua franca of the region, a status it maintained until the Arab conquest in the seventh century CE.

Thus, Aramaic was the ordinary spoken language of Galilee in the first century CE, and the Gospels, which were written in Greek, quote Jesus speaking Aramaic on several occasions. Many of the Dead Sea Scrolls were also written in Aramaic, including the earliest known "targums," or translations of the scriptures from Hebrew into Aramaic. So dominant was the use of Aramaic that texts of the Hebrew Bible came to be written with Aramaic characters, and the Aramaic script remains the usual way of printing Hebrew.

Later in the Roman period, Aramaic developed into Syriac and other dialects, and small communities in Syria and Iran still speak a form of Aramaic.

An important theme of the narrative sections of Ezra 3–6 is the reestablishment of proper worship and the reconstruction of the Temple. The first step was the building of the altar, on which the prescribed sacrifices were then regularly offered as the principal holy days were observed. Then, under priestly supervision, the Temple was built. Like its predecessor the Temple of Solomon, this Temple was reportedly constructed using imported cedars from Lebanon. Paralleling the account of the building of the altar and the laying of the foundation (Ezra 3.1–13) is the account of the dedication ceremony when the rebuilding was complete (6.16–22). The priesthood was installed, and the Passover was celebrated with joy. For the author of Ezra, this was truly a restoration.

THE BOOK OF HAGGAI

Among the leaders mentioned by the book of Ezra are the prophets **Haggai** and Zechariah (Ezra 5.1; 6.14), both of whom actively supported the reconstruction of the Temple under Zerubbabel and Jeshua. Two of the twelve books of the Minor Prophets are named for them.

The book of Haggai is one of the shortest of the prophetic books. It consists of a third-person narrative that contains four oracles delivered by the prophet during the last few months of 520 BCE, the second year of the reign of Darius I. The book gives no other biographical details about Haggai.

As the book opens, in the late summer of 520, the Temple has not been rebuilt, although the houses of the leaders, the governor Zerubbabel and the high priest Joshua (as Jeshua is called in this book), are luxurious enough. As a result, the community has not fared well, for Yahweh has caused a drought. Inspired by the prophet's words, the reconstruction starts, and Haggai continues to encourage the leaders, assuring them that "the latter splendor of this house shall be greater than the former" (Hag 2.9).

When the Temple's foundation is being laid, the prophet pronounces Yahweh's blessing on the community and, in an extravagant conclusion, on its leader:

> Speak to Zerubbabel, governor of Judah, saying, I am about to shake the heavens and the earth, and to overthrow the throne of kingdoms; I am about to destroy the strength of the kingdoms of the nations, and overthrow the chariots and their riders; and the horses and their riders shall fall, every one by the sword of a comrade. On that day, says the LORD of hosts, I will take you, O Zerubbabel my servant, son of Shealtiel, says the LORD, and make you like a signet ring; for I have chosen you, says the LORD of hosts. (Hag 2.21–23)

The language recalls that of the "day of Yahweh" (see Box 17.2 on page 262) and is an example of early apocalyptic imagery that we will explore on pages 459–61. With these concluding words, the book of Haggai seems to support the hopes for a reestablishment of the Davidic monarchy. Jeremiah had spoken of Jehoiachin, the king who had been exiled to Babylon in 597 BCE, as a rejected signet ring (Jer 22.24). The book of Kings ends with the mention of the release of Jehoiachin from prison. Zerubbabel was a grandson of King Jehoiachin, and thus a descendant of David. Now he was the "governor of Judah" who, like David, had been chosen by Yahweh. Zerubbabel is addressed by Yahweh as "my servant," just as David had been, and he is called a signet ring, like Jehoiachin. Thus, Haggai strongly implies, but does not explicitly state, that Zerubbabel would preside over a restored Davidic kingdom under divine protection.

In the book of Haggai, then, we get a detailed look at one brief period in the early restoration, and also at one particular viewpoint.

ZECHARIAH 1–8

As with the book of Isaiah, modern scholars have detected distinct hands at work in the book of Zechariah. Chapters 1–8 of the book deal with the late sixth century BCE, especially the issues of leadership in the restored community in Judah and the reconstruction of the Temple. Chapters 9–14, on the other hand, are different in style and content and come from a later period. Here we will consider Zechariah 1–8, often called "First Zechariah"; for Zechariah 9–14 ("Second Zechariah"), see pages 361–62.

According to the chronology given at the beginning of the book, **Zechariah** and Haggai were contemporaries; like Haggai, Zechariah's prophetic career began in 520 BCE, and according to subsequent dates given in the book it continued for at least two more years. Little else is known about the prophet. The book opens with an introductory oracle (1.2–6) in which the prophet urges his listeners not to follow the rebellious pattern of their ancestors in disobeying divine commands. Then follow eight visions (1.7–6.15), and First Zechariah concludes with oracles about fasting (7.1–14; 8.18–19) and about Jerusalem (8.1–17, 20–23).

The most unusual part of Zechariah 1–8 is the eight visions in the first six chapters. These visions are interlocking, with recurring themes and imagery. Like the visions of Amos they are symbolic, and like those of Ezekiel they are revealed by a divinely sent messenger. But their elaborate symbolism marks a new stage in the development of prophetic discourse and anticipates apocalyptic literature, in which the divine plan for the future, sometimes even the distant future, is revealed by a messenger using elaborate and even fantastic images (see further pages 359–60).

The first vision (Zech 1.7–17), like that in chapter 4, takes place at night, a frequent time for revelations to prophets. The prophet sees a man riding a red horse, among some myrtle shrubs, perhaps a natural corral, among which are three more horses of different colors. The prophet's interpreter, the divinely sent messenger, explains that the task of the horsemen, like that of the "*satan*" in the book of Job (Job 1.7; 2.2; see further Zech 3.1–2 and Box 24.1 on page 391), is to "patrol the earth." They report that the earth is at peace. The messenger then addresses Yahweh directly, asking when Jerusalem will be restored, and Yahweh replies with the comforting promise that the Temple will be rebuilt and prosperity will return. The same images recur in the eighth vision (6.1–8): Horses of different colors, in this case pulling chariots, represent the four winds, which also patrol the earth.

The second vision (Zech 1.18–21) is of four horns, representing the nations that scattered the Jews, principally the Babylonians. They will be destroyed by four metalsmiths, also agents of Yahweh. Horns are symbols of power, and the use of horns to represent nations will recur in the book of Daniel (7.7–8, 24; 8.6–8, 20–21). Yahweh then proclaims again that he will punish the nations that destroyed Jerusalem.

In the third vision (2.1–5), the prophet sees another divine messenger, who has a measuring line to determine the dimensions of the restored Jerusalem. This is reminiscent of Ezekiel's vision of a messenger who measures the restored Temple (Ezek 40–42).

The fourth (chap. 3) and fifth (chap. 4) visions use symbolic language to affirm the divine choice of Joshua (as Jeshua is called in this book) and of Zerubbabel. The prophet is assured that Zerubbabel, who began the reconstruction of the Temple, will see it to completion and that Joshua has been vindicated in the divine council, declared ritually pure, and given the appropriate priestly attire.

The sixth vision (Zech 5.1–4) also alludes to Ezekiel. Like Ezekiel (Ezek 2.9–10), the prophet sees a scroll, but this time it is an enormous flying scroll containing curses on thieves and on those who swear falsely. The dimensions of the scroll, 20 cubits by 10 cubits, are identical to those of the vestibule of the Temple of Solomon (1 Kings 6.3), suggesting the importance of the Temple for Zechariah.

The seventh vision (5.5–11) is of a woman named "Wickedness," who is taken in a covered container from Judah to Babylon (called Shinar), like an evil genie confined in a jar.

The cumulative message of the visions is of a divine plan being carried out: Babylon destroyed, Jerusalem and the Temple restored, and divinely chosen leaders ruling the community. The shared nature of that leadership from the prophet's perspective is clear. Both Zerubbabel and Joshua are called "sons of oil" (Zech 4.14), an unusual phrase implying that they had been anointed, as were both kings and priests in preexilic Israel (see Box 15.2 on page 232). But the prophet uses a careful circumlocution (the NRSV translation "anointed ones" is misleading), perhaps to avoid explicitly claiming royal status for Zerubbabel, whose official Persian title was "governor." Zerubbabel is also called "the Branch" (3.8; 6.12), a title that may mean that in him the Davidic monarchy had been restored. His restoration of the Temple would also have been appropriate for a royal figure, since throughout the ancient Near East, temple building was a demonstration both of a king's power and of divine favor.

Zechariah 7–8, dated to the fourth year of Darius (518 BCE), consists of several loosely connected oracles. They contrast Jerusalem's deserved punishment with its restored state:

> Jerusalem shall be called the faithful city, and the mountain of the LORD of hosts shall be called the holy mountain. Thus says the LORD of hosts: Old men and old women shall again sit in the streets of Jerusalem, each with staff in hand because of their great age. And the streets of the city shall be full of boys and girls playing in its streets. . . . They shall be my people and I will be their God, in faithfulness and in righteousness. (Zech 8.3–5, 8)

The last phrases echo the marriage formula in Hosea (2.19–20).

According to Zechariah, people from all over the world will come to this restored Jerusalem to worship Yahweh (Zech 8.20–23). This reiterates a theme found in Second Isaiah, and may be a counter to the narrower understanding of the community found in Ezekiel 44.9 and in the book of Ezra. First Zechariah, thus, is essentially an elaboration of themes in the book of Haggai, with a broad view of membership in the restored community.

ISAIAH 56–66

As we have already mentioned (see pages 273 and 336), chapters 56–66 of the book of Isaiah are from a different era than either First Isaiah or Second Isaiah. Since the late nineteenth century, this section has been called "**Third Isaiah.**" As in Second Isaiah, Jerusalem has been destroyed, and there is a promise that the exiles will return, but there are also passages in which the Temple has been restored and is functioning. Third Isaiah thus is a work of the early postexilic period, rather than of the preceding exilic period, the time of Second Isaiah. A date in the late sixth century BCE, after the completion of the Temple in 515 BCE, is likely, although sometime in the fifth century is also possible. The absence of specific historical references makes dating difficult. Third Isaiah does not mention the hope of some Judeans for a restoration of the Davidic monarchy, nor does it mention Zerubbabel.

Third Isaiah is also difficult to date and to interpret because of its frequent quotations of and allusions to earlier biblical materials. The author (or authors) of Third Isaiah make use of Hosea, Jeremiah, First Isaiah, and especially Second Isaiah. This use of quotations and allusions contributes to a lack of structure in Third Isaiah. Like some other postexilic writings, it is a kind of collage of originally independent units that are connected only loosely. Some of its themes and vocabulary link it with the entire book of Isaiah, such as the centrality of Jerusalem/Zion (named in over a dozen verses), the phrase "holy one of Israel" (60.9, 14), and the presence of a sign (66.19). For this reason, the oracles in Third Isaiah, or at least their editing, can be attributed to the school of Isaiah.

The viewpoints of Third Isaiah are at times different from those of Haggai and Zechariah. One oracle seems to express opposition to the rebuilding of the Temple:

> Thus says the LORD:
> Heaven is my throne
>   and the earth is my footstool;
> what is the house that you would build for me,
>   and what is my resting place? (Isa 66.1)

This is reminiscent of Yahweh's refusal to allow David to build him a Temple (2 Sam 7.5–7; see pages 217–18). It is also inconsistent with other passages in Third Isaiah that describe the Temple and the offerings there more positively, such as Isaiah 60.7, which describes the Temple as Yahweh's "glorious house," and 56.7, which calls it a "house of prayer" where sacrifices will be accepted. Such inconsistency is doubtless due to the composite nature of Third Isaiah.

In some of the oracles in Third Isaiah, we find an inclusive view of the restored community. It is to be one in which foreigners from all nations are to be welcomed, a point of view that will become a major issue of contention in the fifth century BCE. One group of foreigners, however, is singled out for divine vengeance: the Edomites, whose participation in the Babylonian destruction of Jerusalem in 586 BCE had been condemned earlier in Psalm 137 and the book of Obadiah (see page 319). In Isaiah 63.1–6, Yahweh describes himself returning from battle with his garments stained by Edomite blood, as if he had been treading grapes to extract their juice for wine; in the famous paraphrase of Julia Ward Howe, he has been "trampling out the vintage where the grapes of wrath are stored."

Like some of its prophetic predecessors (see Box 17.3 on page 263), Third Isaiah also emphasizes the importance of social justice over ritual observance:

> Is not this the fast that I choose:
>   to loose the bonds of injustice,
>   to undo the thongs of the yoke,
> to let the oppressed go free,
>   and to break every yoke?
> Is it not to share your bread with the hungry,
>   and bring the homeless poor into your house;
> when you see the naked, to cover them,
>   and not to hide yourself from your own kin?
> Then your light shall break forth like the dawn,
>   and your healing shall spring up quickly;
> your vindicator shall go before you,
>   the glory of the LORD shall be your rear guard.
> Then you shall call, and the LORD will answer;
>   you shall cry for help, and he will say, Here I
>   am. (Isa 58.6–9)

The conclusion of this passage also illustrates Third Isaiah's optimism about the restored community in

Jerusalem, the center of "the new heavens and the new earth" that Yahweh will create (Isa 65.17; 66.22).

THE BOOKS OF EZRA AND NEHEMIAH

After the rebuilding of the Temple in the late sixth century BCE, we know little about life in Judah until the mid-fifth century, which is when most scholars date the activity of Ezra and Nehemiah.

In the Hebrew Bible, the books of Ezra and Nehemiah form one unit; in Christian Bibles since late antiquity, they usually have been divided into two books. Most modern scholars consider these books to be a single work. The two parts get their names from their principal characters, Ezra and Nehemiah, both of whom are vividly portrayed. The entire work probably was written in the late fifth or early fourth century BCE. The contents can be outlined as follows:

Ezra 1–2: The return from exile (see pages 332–34)

Ezra 3–6: The early restoration (see pages 350–51)

Ezra 7–10: The mission of Ezra, including a first-person memoir (7.27–9.15)

Nehemiah 1.1–7.5: Nehemiah memoir

Nehemiah 7.6–73: List of returnees (almost identical to that in Ezra 2)

Nehemiah 8.1–12.26: Ceremonies of renewal, to which are added a census of Jerusalem residents and other lists

Nehemiah 12.27–13.31: Resumption of Nehemiah memoir

As this outline indicates, Ezra-Nehemiah is a composite work, compiled from different sources, a conclusion supported by the use of Aramaic rather than Hebrew in Ezra 4.8–6.18 and 7.12–26 (see Box 22.2 on pages 350–51). We also find frequent shifts from third-person narrative to apparently autobiographical accounts. The latter are more likely a kind of fictional autobiography, like the first-person narratives in some of the prophets, although they

may be derived from actual writings of Ezra and Nehemiah themselves. Because the opening verses of the book of Ezra duplicate the concluding verses of 2 Chronicles, many scholars have concluded that there was a literary relationship, perhaps even the same author, for the books of Chronicles, Ezra, and Nehemiah. We will return to this issue on page 369.

The work covers a considerable period, beginning in the second half of the sixth century BCE and continuing well into the fifth. But the two parts of the work overlap, and chronological problems exist. A major issue is the dates of the missions of Ezra and Nehemiah and their relationship. Nehemiah's first mission is dated from the twentieth to the thirty-second year of Artaxerxes (Neh 5.14). Nearly all modern scholars agree that this was Artaxerxes I, which would date Nehemiah's activity in Jerusalem from 445 to 433 BCE; some unspecified time after that he returned from the Persian capital to Jerusalem for a second mission (Neh 13.6). Ezra's mission is dated to the seventh year of Artaxerxes (Ezra 7.7), but there were several Persian kings with that name (see Box 22.1 on page 348). It cannot be Artaxerxes IV, whose reign lasted only two years. A majority of modern scholars, following the sequence in the books themselves, place the mission of Ezra earlier than that of Nehemiah, in the reign of Artaxerxes I in 458, and that is the position taken here. A minority of scholars have placed the mission of Ezra during the reign of Artaxerxes II, in 398, and consider the references to Ezra and Nehemiah as contemporaries (Neh 8.9; 12.26) to be later additions.

Although Nehemiah, like Zerubbabel in the sixth century BCE, has the official title of "governor," like both Zerubbabel and Jeshua neither Nehemiah nor Ezra is mentioned in any contemporaneous nonbiblical sources.

The Mission of Ezra

According to the introduction to the account of his mission, **Ezra** was a member of a priestly family and "a scribe skilled in the *torah* of Moses" (Ezra 7.6). With the Persian king's sanction, Ezra traveled to Jerusalem with a sizable entourage of "leaders from Israel" (7.28) to impose the requirements of the

FIGURE 22.2   A relief of the Persian king Darius I at Behistun, in Iran, from about 520 BCE. The king, shown life-size, is the largest figure, facing defeated enemies. Above, the symbol of the Persian deity Ahura Mazda blesses the king. Surrounding the picture, which is cut into a cliff face several hundred feet above ground level, are inscriptions in three languages: Persian, Elamite, and Babylonian. The discovery of these texts in 1835 enabled the decipherment of Babylonian cuneiform in the 1850s.

divinely given commandments, especially those concerning marriage with "foreign" women. Apparently such intermarriage was frequent, for it took several months to identify all the men who had done so. The ending of the book of Ezra is abrupt, and its last few words obscure, but an ancient tradition interprets them to mean that the "foreign" women and their children were sent away or at least ostracized from the community.

Ezra is mentioned again in Nehemiah 10 as the leader of a lengthy ceremony of renewal, at which the "book of the *torah* of Moses" was read, and during which the fall festival of Booths was celebrated. The ceremony concluded with a commitment by all "to walk in God's *torah*, which was given by Moses the servant of God, and to observe and do all the commandments of the LORD" (Neh 10.29). Three particulars are mentioned: no intermarriage, sabbath observance, and support of the Temple personnel with tithes of agricultural produce and an annual tax.

Although the details of the renewal are not entirely consistent with the prescriptions of the Torah in its present form, it is likely that the text that Ezra brought from Babylonia and that served as the basis for the renewal was some form of P's edition of the Torah, the first five books of the Bible (see pages 334–36).

Ezra's mission, which seems to have lasted for several years, was thus primarily religious, although it had important social components. Authority lay not with those who had earlier returned to Jerusalem and Judah, or had never left, but with the leaders of the Diaspora in Babylonia. Especially important is the issue of intermarriage, to which we will return.

The Missions of Nehemiah

According to the sequence of events in the books of Ezra and Nehemiah, Ezra's moves toward religious revival and conformity were encouraged by

Nehemiah in two missions, the first as governor of Judah for twelve years, and then during a brief return sometime later. According to the highly embellished first-person memoir, Nehemiah had held the important position of king's cupbearer, and at his own initiative sought royal approval to go to Jerusalem and rebuild it. On his arrival, an inspection tour revealed how dire the situation was: All of the city's defenses were in ruins. The description of Nehemiah's tour by night of the walls and the city gates cannot be fully correlated with archaeological data from Jerusalem, but the picture we get is of a relatively small city, with a population of only a few thousand.

Nehemiah began the reconstruction of the city's walls, but immediately faced opposition. Some was internal and led by prophets, one of whom, Noadiah, was a woman (Neh 6.14). Presumably they and others in Jerusalem resented the imported authority of Nehemiah, and probably also that of Ezra. More opposition came from the leaders of neighboring provinces, Tobiah the Ammonite, Geshem the Arab, and Sanballat the Horonite. The last of these is also mentioned in a contemporaneous nonbiblical source, the Elephantine papyri (see Box 22.3), in which he is identified as the governor of Samaria. Nehemiah skillfully foiled their plots, and the walls were rebuilt.

Why would the Persians have permitted and even encouraged the refortification of Jerusalem? From 460 to 454 BCE, a revolt against Persian rule took place in Egypt, a revolt supported by Persia's rival Athens. For the Persians, it would have made strategic sense to strengthen Jerusalem, a city not far to the north of Egypt. Why was there such opposition from Judah's neighbors? They may have been suspicious that the leaders of a revived Jerusalem would attempt to extend their control over the surrounding region.

That control was not just political but religious and social. Close relationships had existed between the Judeans and their neighbors, many of whom were worshipers of Yahweh. In the time of Zerubbabel, the Samarians had wanted to assist in the reconstruction of the Temple, for they too were worshipers of Yahweh, but they were rebuffed.

Tobiah, who may also have had the title "governor," was a Yahwist, as his name, which means "Good is Yah(weh)," indicates, and further evidence of his status and his piety is his having a special room in the Temple precinct (Neh 13.7). Two of Sanballat's sons mentioned in a papyrus from Elephantine, Delaiah and Shelemiah, also had Yahwistic names. Moreover, both Tobiah and Sanballat were linked with important Judean families: Tobiah's wife was the daughter of Shecaniah, who belonged to an important priestly family; Tobiah's son was married to the daughter of Meshullam, one of Nehemiah's supporters; and Sanballat's daughter was married to a son of the high priest.

The Issue of Intermarriage

Although the Jewish community had been challenged by the events of 586 BCE, it had managed not only to survive, but also to redefine itself and to restore its Temple. For some, the only way to maintain their identity was to insist on ethnic and religious purity. Exogamy, marriage outside one's group, inevitably weakens a group's identity. The children of Judeans who had married Ammonite, Moabite, and Ashdodite women, we are told, "could not speak the language of Judah, but spoke the languages of various peoples" (Neh 13.24). So the insistence of Ezra and Nehemiah that their version of Yahwism was the only legitimate one was reasonably motivated, a defense against assimilation.

Part of that defense was the strict prohibition of intermarriage outside the group that defined itself as the true Israel. That prohibition had strong precedents in the sacred traditions that had been collected, edited, and shaped in Babylon. Nehemiah 13.26 refers to the apostasy that resulted from Solomon's marriages with foreign women, and aversion to intermarriage is a recurring theme throughout Genesis and the Deuteronomistic History. So, because "the book of Moses" excluded Ammonites and Moabites from the "assembly of God" (Deut 23.3, quoted in Neh 13.1), all those of foreign background were separated from Israel. The need to determine who belonged to Israel and who was "foreign" is one

Box 22.3 THE ELEPHANTINE PAPYRI

The Murashu texts give us a glimpse of Judeans in Babylonia in the fifth century BCE (see page 318). We get a similar picture of life in the Diaspora from another collection of texts, several dozen contracts and letters from Elephantine in southern Egypt, where a colony of Judean mercenaries and their families had lived for several centuries. The texts were written on papyrus in Aramaic, which had become the lingua franca of the Persian empire (see Box 22.2 on pages 350–51), and date mostly to the second half of the fifth century BCE. From them we get a picture of generally observant Jews, worshipers of Yahweh, who had built a temple in which animals were sacrificed, who kept the sabbath and celebrated Passover, and who consulted with their fellow Jews in Judah and Samaria for advice and support. Their brand of Judaism differed from that of the Jerusalem establishment, however, since they also worshiped other deities alongside Yahweh, or at least intermarried with non-Jews who worshiped them.

FIGURE 22.3   A papyrus document from Elephantine, tied with string and sealed with a clay seal.

explanation of the censuses and other lists of persons in the books of Ezra and Nehemiah.

The issue of intermarriage reveals a community deeply divided on questions of identity and on where authority lay. To some extent these are a continuation of earlier tensions. After the first deportation in 597 BCE, Jeremiah referred to the exiles as "good figs" and those who remained in the land as "bad figs" (Jer 24). Yet those in the land claimed that because they had not been taken to Babylon, they had not been punished by God; it was the exiles who were the guilty ones. Ezekiel, himself an exile, emphatically rejected that view. After the decree of Cyrus in 538 BCE, Judeans returning from Babylon established a shared religious and political leadership under

Jeshua and Zerubbabel. Now, in a similar diarchy, Ezra and Nehemiah came from Mesopotamia to impose standards on those in the Promised Land.

In the books of Ezra and Nehemiah, we have mainly the perspective of one side, that of leaders from the Diaspora who sought to impose their views on those living in Judah, including some who must have descended from the first returnees. As we have seen, there was opposition to this insistence on religious and ethnic purity. Some opposition came from those whose motives may have been mixed, like Sanballat and Tobiah, who although worshipers of Yahweh, were vying for power with Nehemiah. Other opposition came from some prophets. And more opposition must have come from those directly affected by the prohibition against intermarriage, who were told that they had to separate from their wives and children.

The books of Ezra and Nehemiah represent only one perspective on the issue of intermarriage. We find examples of a different view in the book of Ruth, in which Ruth the Moabite became the great-grandmother of King David (see pages 407–08), and in the book of Esther, whose marriage to the king of Persia seems not to have bothered the original writer of her story (see further pages 409–11).

APOCALYPTIC LITERATURE

Beginning in the postexilic period and continuing into the Common Era, there developed a genre of literature known as "**apocalyptic**," from a Greek word meaning "to uncover, to reveal." The Hebrew Bible contains a few examples of this genre, which have been incorporated into larger books; another is the book of Revelation in the New Testament; and many more occur in postbiblical Jewish and Christian literatures.

Grouped together, these works have several common elements, although not all of them occur in every work:

- Revelation to a designated human by a heavenly messenger or in a vision or dream. The messenger may be either an angel, or someone who, like

Enoch (Gen 5.24) and Elijah (2 Kings 2.11), was taken into heaven before death and is now returning with a communication from God concerning the end-time.

- Detailed explication of the past and present, often in coded language.

- Description of the end-time, along with a chronology indicating when it will occur, often thought to be in the near future.

- Dualistic language, contrasting good and evil, light and darkness, life and death, and present and future.

- Pessimism about the present, but optimism for the future based on the expectation of an ultimate divine victory and the subsequent transformation of the cosmos—"new heavens and a new earth" (Isa 65.17; 66.22; Rev 21.1).

- Incorporation of mythic traditions in which the end-time resembles the beginnings of the cosmos, especially the battle between the creator deity and the primeval forces of chaos. In a terrible final battle, the deity will be ultimately victorious, as he was in battle before creation.

- Imagery that is surreal, even fantastic, rather than realistic.

Many scholars think that apocalyptic literature developed out of prophecy. It is significant that, except for the book of Daniel (see pages 411–14), all of the apocalyptic passages in the Hebrew Bible are found in books of the prophets. Moreover, although most of the writings of the preexilic prophets are concerned with interpreting the past, the present, and the immediate future from a divine perspective, most of them also contain passages that describe a more remote and glorious future, a restoration of divine favor after judgment. Such passages often occur at the end of prophetic books, and many are later additions. Nevertheless, their incorporation into the prophetic books is evidence of a commonality between prophecy and apocalyptic literature.

Many of the features of apocalyptic literature listed above are also found in earlier prophetic literature. A clear line of development can be traced from oracles in Amos, Hosea, First Isaiah, and

Jeremiah concerning imminent punishment, and occasionally forgiveness, by Yahweh to the more elaborate revelation by a heavenly messenger of a restored Jerusalem in Ezekiel 40–48, and finally to the fully worked-out examples of apocalyptic literature in Daniel 7–12 and the book of Revelation.

Prophecy and apocalyptic literature also share ways of expressing the concept of revelation. Several prophets claim that they are messengers from the divine council, and especially its presiding deity, to their audiences. This is closely related to the idea of a heavenly messenger, an image widely attested in the ancient Near East and in biblical literature. In sixth-century BCE prophecy, the heavenly messenger becomes a frequent medium of revelation, as in Ezekiel 40–48, in which he discloses to the prophet the details of the new Jerusalem and its restored Temple, and Zechariah 1–6, in which the prophet's visions are accompanied by and interpreted by such a messenger. The same kind of revelation is found frequently in apocalyptic literature.

Another link between prophecy and apocalyptic literature is revelation through visions and dreams. Examples of prophetic visions are found in Amos, Isaiah, and Jeremiah (Jer 1.11–13) and in more developed form in Ezekiel and Zechariah. As with the prophets Nathan and Zechariah, revelations could occur at night, presumably in dreams. Both visions and dreams become frequent modes of revelation in apocalyptic literature, and, like the dreams of ordinary persons, those of apocalyptic writers often blend realism and fantasy. The meanings of these visions and dreams are provided by the heavenly interpreter.

Among the sources that apocalyptic writers used were a variety of biblical genres and ancient Near Eastern mythology. The concept of the "day of the Lord" (see Box 17.2 on page 262), used in earlier prophets to describe divine judgment on Israel and Judah in the near term because of their failure to observe divine commands, was transformed by apocalyptic writers into a more remote day of universal judgment not just on Israel but on the entire world. As apocalyptic literature developed, its writers drew on other sources, especially the literature of a Persian religious movement

known as Zoroastrianism, in which a far-reaching dualism was expressed by contrasting war and peace, light and darkness, and good and evil. During the Hellenistic period beginning in the late fourth century BCE, Greek ideas were also incorporated into apocalyptic vocabulary.

The origins of apocalyptic literature, then, are to be found in preexilic biblical prophecy. In literature of the sixth century BCE, especially in Ezekiel, Isaiah 40–55, Isaiah 56–66, Haggai 2, and Zechariah 1–8, we are in a transition phase between prophecy and apocalyptic literature, and this literature has been called "protoapocalyptic." By the fifth century BCE, some literature that looks more like the later apocalyptic literature found in the books of Daniel and Revelation has developed; this literature is sometimes called "early apocalyptic," and we will look at it in detail later in this chapter.

The fall of Jerusalem in 586 BCE and the Babylonian exile were traumatic for those who experienced them, and many scholars have seen such moments of crisis as the setting for apocalyptic movements. Imaginative hope for a better future would have been natural for those whose present was apparently hopeless. This explanation does fit some early apocalyptic literature, and some later as well, notably the book of Daniel during the persecution of Antiochus IV in the early second century BCE, and perhaps also the book of Revelation during persecutions of Christians during the late first century CE. Not all apocalyptic literature, however, can be so precisely dated, and it is likely that having developed as a genre, it was used by writers of various times and places even if they were not alienated from their immediate circumstances.

Finally, we should note that apocalyptic literature has had a fascination for readers of later eras, who have often attempted to read it literally and to see especially in its detailed chronologies a divinely revealed timetable for the end of the present world in their own lifetimes. None of these precise interpretations, however, has (so far) been accurate.

In Chapter 24, we will examine the only example of fully developed apocalyptic literature in the Hebrew Bible, Daniel 7–12. In the rest of this chapter, we will examine some early apocalyptic literature included in books of the prophets. Scholars have dated many of these works to the fifth century BCE, largely on indirect evidence, since none of them mentions either Ezra or Nehemiah or any of the activities and events connected with them.

THE "ISAIAH APOCALYPSE" (ISA 24–27)

The book of Isaiah in its final form includes four chapters (Isa 24–27) that most scholars identify as an early example of apocalyptic literature. Written for the most part in poetry, this "**Isaiah Apocalypse**" vividly describes the end-time, when all creation will be under the divine judgment: the earth withered, the heavens languishing, and human society disordered, with no distinctions between priests and laity, owners and slaves, lenders and debtors. "On that day"—the day of the LORD—Yahweh will finally defeat his primeval adversary "Leviathan the fleeing serpent, Leviathan the twisting serpent, and he will kill the dragon that is in the sea" (27.1; see further Box 24.3 on page 394). At the sound of a great war-trumpet, the scattered Israelites will be gathered from their lands of exile and return to Jerusalem to worship Yahweh on his holy mountain. There they will enjoy a lavish feast, while an unnamed "city of chaos" (24.10) will be in ruins. In this new age, Death, the god of the underworld, who in Ugaritic myth swallowed the storm-god Baal, will himself be swallowed up (25.8), and Yahweh's people who had died will be restored to life (26.19), perhaps the earliest biblical example of belief in the resurrection of the dead (see further pages 399–401).

Although it contains several features typical of apocalyptic literature, Isaiah 24–27 is not a fully developed apocalypse. Unlike later apocalyptic literature, the chapters lack a systematic chronology, and events occur almost at random rather than in a narrative sequence. Thus, Isaiah 24–27 appears to be a collection of originally independent shorter poems, linked by the theme of the end-time, but haphazardly arranged. Confirming this interpretation is the presence of excerpts from hymns that are interspersed in the chapters.

These poems have been incorporated into the book of Isaiah; they share themes and vocabulary both with the preceding chapters and with Second Isaiah. Taken as a whole, the chapters comprise too short a unit to say with certainty that this is another product of the school of Isaiah. Perhaps its author or authors, familiar with Isaiah, composed some variations in apocalyptic mode on the themes of Isaiah; this naturally would have led later editors to incorporate it into the final canonical book of Isaiah. In contrast to both First Isaiah and Second Isaiah, however, Isaiah 24–27 lacks precise historical references. This makes Isaiah 24–27 difficult to date, although sometime in the early postexilic period, perhaps in the fifth century BCE, is likely.

ZECHARIAH 9–14

The second part of the book of Zechariah (chaps. 9–14, often called "Second Zechariah" (or "Deutero-Zechariah"), has a different character than the first (chaps. 1–8; "First Zechariah"). As with the book of Isaiah, materials written in more than one era have been combined into the book of Zechariah. First Zechariah (see pages 352–53) is internally dated to the late sixth century BCE. Second Zechariah has no specific datable references to events or individuals, but a majority of scholars date it to the fifth century BCE.

Second Zechariah has two parts, each with the heading "oracle" (9–11; 12–14). Taking their lead from these headings, some scholars have further divided Zechariah 9–14 into Second and Third Zechariah. The last book in the Minor Prophets, the book of Malachi, also has the heading "oracle," perhaps indicating that an ancient editor linked the end of the book of Zechariah with Malachi, despite their different contents.

The two oracles in Second Zechariah are loosely connected by a common theme, the "day of the LORD." This theme is developed, however, in a variety of genres in small units, some in prose and others in poetry. In general, the first oracle describes how Yahweh will defeat Israel's neighboring nations and bring back the exiled Israelites, but to an as yet uncertain future because of corrupt and ineffective leadership. The second oracle principally concerns restoration: Jerusalem will be cleansed and "the LORD my God will come, and all the holy ones with him" (Zech 14.5). The land will be transformed into a level plain, with no night, and Jerusalem will be the seat of the divine rule over all the earth. As in the mythologies of other ancient Near Eastern deities, living waters will flow from Yahweh's sacred mountain year-round, not just in the rainy season. All nations will come to Jerusalem to observe the festival of Booths. As this summary indicates, much of Second Zechariah is concerned with the future and has many apocalyptic features.

This summary necessarily glosses over the many obscurities in Second Zechariah. One of the reasons that Second Zechariah is so difficult to date and to interpret is its frequent quotation of and allusions to earlier prophetic traditions, as in Third Isaiah (see page 354). Using the genre of the oracle against the nations (see page 256), the book describes Yahweh's devastation of the nations surrounding Jerusalem; this material is closely related to Amos 1–2. As a result, political entities, such as Assyria and the northern kingdom of Israel, are mentioned, even though they were no longer important in the fifth century BCE, when the book was probably written. There is also a reference to Ionia, the Greek cities on the western coast of Asia Minor, which became important only after the fall of Assyria in the late seventh century BCE. Some scholars have seen in the mention of Ionia evidence for an even later date, in the Hellenistic period that began in the late fourth century, but the same region is mentioned in Ezekiel 27.19, and the Greek colonies in Ionia unsuccessfully revolted against Persian rule in the early fifth century BCE. The reference to Ionia, then, is not specific enough to require dating Second Zechariah later than the fifth century.

Like other early apocalyptic literature of the exilic and postexilic periods, Second Zechariah anticipates a new era. Yahweh will defeat the enemies of his people, restore them to their land, and establish peace and prosperity. In this new era, as also in Ezekiel 34, the worthless shepherds will be removed. Jerusalem is urged to rejoice, and the writer goes on to speak of a new leader, who like the ideal Israelite king of old, will have a universal rule. Some continued to hope that the Davidic dynasty would be restored, a hope that had not been fulfilled in the person of Zerubbabel in the late sixth century BCE, nor in the fifth century BCE, despite prophets who asserted, "There is a king in Judah!" (Neh 6.7). In part because of these disappointments, the restoration of the monarchy in the person of a future king was included in the apocalyptic account of the end-time and became important in the development of the concept of the Messiah in postbiblical Judaism and in Christianity (see Box 15.2 on page 232).

The book of Zechariah ends with the mysterious phrase: "There will be no Canaanite in the house of the LORD of hosts on that day" (Zech 14.21). This may refer to the exclusion of non-Israelites from the recently restored community, also a concern of the book of Ezra. The Temple, and in fact all of Jerusalem, will be sacred to Yahweh, and foreigners will be barred from it.

Second Zechariah thus describes a definitive divine defeat of Israel's traditional enemies, a glorious restoration of the monarchy, and Jerusalem restored to its status as center of the world in an Edenic landscape.

THE BOOK OF JOEL

The short book of **Joel**, one of the Minor Prophets, is located between the books of Hosea and Amos, perhaps because parts of a verse near the end of Joel (3.16) and one near the beginning of Amos (1.2) are identical. Another apparent quotation from Amos is Joel 3.18 (see Am 9.13), and both Amos (7.1–3; see also 4.9) and Joel describe a plague of locusts.

The book of Joel falls naturally into two parts:

- 1.2–2.27: A vivid lament occasioned by an infestation of locusts, interpreted as a form of divine punishment that can be stopped by a communal ritual of repentance, and concluding with an assurance of divine deliverance.
- 2.28–3.21: An apocalyptic description of the end-time in which Judah's enemies will be punished and its land restored to a paradisiacal abundance.

Scholars disagree on whether these two parts were originally a unity, or whether two separate compositions, Joel and Deutero-Joel as it were, have been combined; with a book as short as Joel (seventy-three verses in all), it is difficult to decide. The two parts are linked sequentially in the sense that part one presents a locust plague as a divine judgment against God's people, and part two follows by imagining a future time when that same divine anger will be directed against Judah's enemies.

In both parts of the book, Joel uses the phrase the "day of the LORD" first introduced by Amos. Both the locusts and the ultimate vindication of God's people are understood as a manifestation of the terrible power of God. In the second part of the book, in a style that anticipates later apocalyptic literature, on that day nature will be convulsed, the enemies of God's people will be defeated, and then Judah will be restored.

Neither the superscription (Joel 1.1) nor any historical references in the book give any specific information about its date or about the prophet for whom it is named. Indirect evidence, however, supports the scholarly consensus that the book is a product of the Persian period, in the fifth or fourth century BCE. There is mention of priests and elders, and the Temple is functioning, but there is no mention of a king. Together with a reference to the exile, these suggest a postexilic date, some time after the rebuilding of the Temple in the late sixth century. Moreover, Joel quotes or alludes to several other biblical books, and so must be later than they are. In addition to the quotations from Amos mentioned earlier, note especially the marked quotation in 2.32, apparently

referring to Obadiah 17; the description of the day of Yahweh in 2.1–2, which borrows phrases from Zephaniah 1.14–15; and in 3.10 the reversal of Isaiah 2.4 (= Mic 4.3).

Later apocalyptic literature will make use of themes from Joel. The image of locusts is elaborated vividly in Revelation 9.3–11, and Christian tradition will see the promise of outpouring of the divine "spirit" to everyone in Joel 2.28–29 (see also Num 11.29) fulfilled in the new age by the coming of the "holy spirit" (Acts 2.16–21).

THE BOOK OF MALACHI

The short book of **Malachi** is one of the latest of the prophetic books, and the last of the twelve Minor Prophets. In the Jewish canon, it thus concludes the first two sections of the Bible, the Law and the Prophets, appropriately ending with mention of Moses, the giver of the law, and Elijah the prophet (Mal 4.4–5). In the arrangement of the Christian canon, it is the last of the books of the Old Testament, and the concluding reference to the return of Elijah before the "day of the LORD" (Mal 4.5) has traditionally been understood by Christians as referring to John the Baptist, who is explicitly identified as the messenger who prepares the way of the Lord (Mal 3.1, quoted in Mt 11.10 and Mk 1.2, although in Mark erroneously attributed to Isaiah).

The entire book is essentially one unit, as the heading "an oracle" suggests. As we have seen, the latter part of the book of Zechariah, which immediately precedes Malachi, contains two units with the same heading (Zech 9.1; 12.1), suggesting a link between these two final books of the prophets. The opening verse also gives the prophet's name as Malachi, but no such individual is known from other sources. The name is probably not a person's name at all; rather, it means "My messenger" and was taken from 3.1: "I am sending my messenger to prepare the way before me." If this is the case, then we know nothing about the author of the book, not even his name.

The book contains no specific historical references, but a date in the fifth century BCE is likely.

The Temple has been rebuilt and a sacrificial system is in place. We find no mention of a king, but the term "governor" (Mal 1.8) is the usual title of the administrator of the Persian province of Judah. Finally, several of the issues addressed in the book, including marriages between Judeans and foreigners, divorce, and tithing, were concerns during the time of Ezra and Nehemiah in the mid-fifth century.

The structure of the book is understood best as a set of loosely connected divine accusations against the people in general and the priests in particular, with an introduction (Mal 1.1) and two brief concluding appendixes (4.4, 5). Throughout, the language is starkly antithetical. The LORD has loved Jacob, but hated Esau (1.2–3); the priests who give blessings will be cursed and the dung of the sacrificial animals smeared on their faces (2.2–3); anyone who has married "the daughter of a foreign god" (probably meaning a non-Israelite woman) will be cut off from Jacob (2.11–12); all the evildoers will be burned like stubble, but for "those who revere my name the sun of righteousness shall rise, with healing in its wings" (4.1–2).

Within this general framework are many obscurities. What is the relative status of the priests and the Levites (Mal 2.1–9; 3.3)? Who is "the messenger of the covenant" (3.1)? Although the second appendix (4.5) implicitly identifies him with Elijah, that may be a later editor's attempt at clarification; other possibilities are that it refers to the prophet himself, or to a divine messenger. When does the writer expect the day of the LORD (3.2; 4.1) to occur? Is the book of remembrance (3.16) a reference to an actual document, or to a future metaphorical "book of life," as in later apocalyptic literature? Finally, although one of the central concerns of the writer, who may himself have been a priest or a Levite, is the careful carrying out of ritual prescriptions, at the same time we see a distancing from the Temple: "For from the rising of the sun to its setting my name is great among the nations, and in every place incense is offered to my name, and a pure offering; for my name is great among the nations, says the LORD of hosts" (1.11). Does this suggest that since Yahweh was worshiped throughout the Diaspora with incense rather than animal sacrifice, animal sacrifice was not essential? Or does it, as in Second Isaiah, anticipate a time when Yahweh will be worshiped by all people? That a book of only fifty-five verses can raise so many questions is a reminder of how incomplete our knowledge is and how difficult to interpret many biblical texts are.

The first of the concluding appendixes (Mal 4.4) stresses fidelity to the teaching (Hebr. *torah*) of Moses, using language that is derived from Deuteronomy. The second (Mal 4.5) promises the return of Elijah (see further Box 16.3 on page 250) before "the great and terrible day of the LORD." The book of Malachi concludes with a reference to the end-time, when the righteous will be rewarded and the wicked suffer a terrible punishment, a motif also found in the book of Joel and in Zechariah 9–14.

A LOOK BACK AND AHEAD

More exiles had returned, and the Temple had been rebuilt under the leadership of the Persian-appointed governor Zerubbabel and the high priest Jeshua, with the support of the prophets Haggai and Zechariah. In some circles hope existed that the Davidic monarchy would be restored, perhaps even in the person of Zerubbabel. But that hope was disappointed, and Zerubbabel disappears from the scene. The appearance of a future Davidic ruler, a messiah, would be postponed to a more remote future. Moreover, despite the rebuilding of the Temple, the situation in Judah was unstable. The physical restoration of Jerusalem and the social restoration of the community would need to continue, and questions about the composition of that community would have to be resolved. These issues became pressing in the mid-fifth century BCE.

In the fifth century BCE, the restoration of the Jewish community in Judah continued. But because the reality of the restoration failed to live up to the hopes of many, in apocalyptic literature the final restoration of the ideal community was deferred to a remote divine intervention.

Collection, revision, and quotation of earlier material are characteristic of much of the biblical literature from the postexilic period. In part this is the result of the process of the formation of what will become "sacred scripture," the identification of some writings as authoritative. At the same time, it implicitly recognizes that those writings need to be adapted for new circumstances. In the next chapter we will see further examples of such activity.

IMPORTANT NAMES AND TERMS

Each name or term is defined briefly in the Glossary. Its first significant occurrence in this chapter appears in **boldface** type.

apocalyptic

Aramaic

Ezra

Haggai

Joel

Malachi

Nehemiah

Second Temple

Third Isaiah

Zechariah

QUESTIONS FOR REVIEW

1. Discuss the tensions among various Jewish communities during the Persian period.

2. Why was it important for the Temple to be rebuilt?

3. What was the nature of leadership in the restored community in Judah? What is the significance of Zerubbabel's ancestry?

4. What are the characteristics of apocalyptic literature? Under what circumstances did it develop?

BIBLIOGRAPHY

For a summary of the history of the period, see the bibliography to Chapter 21.

A good commentary on Ezra-Nehemiah is by H. G. M. Williamson, *Ezra/Nehemiah* (Waco, TX: Word, 1985). For a shorter commentary, see Tamara Cohn Eskenazi, "Ezra-Nehemiah," pp. 192–200 in *Women's Bible Commentary*, ed. C. A. Newsom, S. H. Ringe, and J. E. Lapsley (Louisville, KY: Westminster John Knox, 3d ed., 2012).

For an introduction to Haggai, see Stephen L. Cook, "Haggai," pp. 357–61 in *The Oxford Encyclopedia of the Books of the Bible*, vol. 1, ed. M. D. Coogan (New York: Oxford University Press, 2011; available in Oxford Biblical Studies Online). For Zechariah, see Stephen L. Cook, "Zechariah," pp. 465–71 in *The Oxford Encyclopedia of the Books of the Bible*, vol. 2, ed. M. D. Coogan (New York: Oxford University Press, 2011; available in Oxford Biblical Studies Online). Two good longer commentaries on Haggai and Zechariah are Carol L. Meyers and Eric M. Meyers, *Haggai, Zechariah 1–8* (Anchor Bible; New York: Doubleday, 1987), and *Zechariah 9–14* (New York: Doubleday, 1993); and David L. Petersen, *Haggai and Zechariah 1–8: A Commentary* (Philadelphia: Westminster, 1984), and *Zechariah 9–14 and Malachi* (Louisville, KY: Westminster John Knox, 1995).

For Third Isaiah, see the commentary by Christopher R. Seitz listed in the bibliography to Chapter 21, and for Isaiah 24–27, see the bibliography to Chapter 18.

A selection of the Elephantine texts has been translated by Bezalel Porten in *The Context of Scripture*, Vol. 3: *Archival Documents from the Ancient World* (ed. W. W. Hallo; Leiden: Brill, 2003), pp. 116–32, 141–98.

For an introduction to apocalyptic literature, see John J. Collins, *The Apocalyptic Imagination: An Introduction to Jewish Apocalyptic Literature* (Grand Rapids, MI: Eerdmans, 2d ed., 1998). During the Hellenistic and Roman periods, Jewish writers produced many apocalyptic works, some of which have been translated and collected in James H. Charlesworth, ed., *The Old Testament Pseudepigrapha* (New York: Doubleday, 2 vols., 1983, 1985).

For an introduction to the book of Joel, see Theodore Hiebert, "Joel, The Book of," pp. 873–80 in *Anchor Bible Dictionary* (ed. D. N. Freedman; New York: Doubleday, 1992), Vol. 5.

Two good short introductions to Malachi are David L. Petersen, "Malachi," pp. 209–11 in *The Prophetic Literature: An Introduction* (Louisville, KY: Westminster John Knox, 2002), and Stephen L. Cook, "Malachi," pp. 34–41 in *The Oxford Encyclopedia of the Books of the Bible*, vol. 2, ed. M. D. Coogan (New York: Oxford University Press, 2011; available in Oxford Biblical Studies Online).

CHAPTER 23

Retelling the Story of David

1–2 Chronicles and Psalms

The restoration of the Jewish community in Judah, beginning in the late sixth century BCE with the reconstruction of the Temple and continuing in the fifth century under Ezra and Nehemiah, was apparently complete by the fourth century BCE. During this period new books were written and older literary traditions were collected and edited; this process would eventually culminate in the formation of the Hebrew Bible. In the arrangement of the books of the Bible in Jewish tradition, the third part is known as the "Writings," and it is a mixed bag, containing a variety of genres. The books that comprise the Writings were either written or edited relatively later than the first two parts, the Law or Torah and the Prophets. (See further Chapter 1.)

In this chapter we will examine the two longest books in the Writings—Chronicles and Psalms, both of which are connected in significant ways to the figure of David. Chronicles is an interpretive history of Israel with a vast chronological scope, extending from Adam to the Persian period. While Chronicles retells, often verbatim, the history contained in 1 Samuel–2 Kings, it presents David in a considerably more positive light through elimination of some stories and additions to others. We will focus here on the distinctive features of this late Persian-period history. The book of Psalms is a collection of hymns from a relatively broad chronological range that gives us a window into the personal and communal piety of ancient Israel over many centuries. Eventually, the entire book is credited to David, again adding a pious, prayerful dimension to David's character.

THE BOOKS OF CHRONICLES

The books of Chronicles, like those of Samuel and Kings, originally were a single book. Its Hebrew title is "The (book of) the events of the days," a generic term that also occurs repeatedly in the books of Kings as part of the title of sources used by the Deuteronomistic Historians. In its ancient Greek translation, Chronicles was called "The things omitted," meaning what had been left out in the books of Samuel and Kings. Neither title is especially descriptive. Since late antiquity the book has been called "Chronicles," also a somewhat vague name.

In Jewish tradition, the books of Chronicles are often placed last in the Writings, after Ezra-Nehemiah; in this position they thus are the final book of the Hebrew Bible. In Christian canons, the books of Chronicles come immediately after the books of Kings, and they are followed by Ezra-Nehemiah, which fits the narrative chronology.

Contents

The contents of the books of Chronicles are as follows:

1 Chronicles 1–9	Genealogies, from Adam to the fifth century BCE
10	The death of Saul
11–29	The reign of David
2 Chronicles 1–9	The reign of Solomon
10.1–36.21	The history of Judah from Rehoboam to the fall of Jerusalem
36.22–23	The decree of Cyrus allowing the exiles to return

As this outline makes clear, the overall chronological framework of Chronicles is sweeping. Within this framework, however, the history is selective. Most of the focus is on the kingdom of Judah from David to the fall of Jerusalem in 586 BCE. Even though **the Chronicler**, a frequently used term for the author of Chronicles, was familiar with earlier Israelite traditions as they had been collected by his time into the Pentateuch and the Deuteronomistic History (see following), he omits, or barely mentions, the principal events described in the first five books of the Bible as well as those in the books of Joshua, Judges, and 1 Samuel. Even the covenant at Sinai is mentioned just in passing, when the Chronicler explains the origins of the two tablets in the ark installed in the Temple (2 Chr 5.10). Only intermittent attention is given to the history of the northern kingdom of Israel, mainly when it relates to that of the southern kingdom of Judah; the Chronicler does not mention the Assyrian capture of Samaria, the capital of the northern kingdom, in 722 BCE. Nor, despite the Chronicler's considerable interest in prophecy, does he mention the activity of Elijah and Elisha, whose activity was confined exclusively to the northern kingdom. He does include the story of Micaiah (2 Chr 18 = 1 Kings 22), but that is because the king of Judah, Jehoshaphat, is part of that story.

Sources

The principal source of the author of Chronicles is the Deuteronomistic History, especially the books of 2 Samuel and 1–2 Kings. Paragraph after paragraph, sometimes chapter after chapter, is taken from this earlier work, either verbatim or with slight alteration. This is a practice we have already observed, that of one author to use freely the work of another; ancient views on such issues as originality and plagiarism were different from our own. By studying ways in which the Chronicler deviated from his principal source, we can learn something of the author's intent.

The Chronicler also uses other biblical sources. The Pentateuch, in relatively final form as compiled by P, was familiar to him, and considered authoritative. Details in the genealogies in 1 Chronicles 1–9 are dependent upon the Pentateuch, along with Joshua and other books. There are frequent quotations from the book of Psalms, which had probably also been collected by this time (see further page 375), and occasional quotations from or allusions to the books of Isaiah, Jeremiah, and Ezekiel. Moreover, the ending verses of 2 Chronicles are the same as the opening verses of the book of Ezra.

In addition to biblical sources, like the Deuteronomistic Historians the Chronicler cites other works that we no longer have. Some of these are not named by the Deuteronomistic Historians, principally writings attributed to the prophets Samuel, Nathan, Gad, Isaiah, and more than half a dozen other, less familiar prophets. Typical of such references is 2 Chronicles 9.29: "Now the rest of the acts of Solomon, from first to last, are they not written in the history of the prophet Nathan, and in the prophecy of Ahijah the Shilonite, and in the visions of the seer Iddo concerning Jeroboam son of Nebat?" (2 Chr 9.29). The citation of these prophetic sources is significant, because for the Chronicler, as for the Deuteronomistic Historians, the prophets functioned as primary transmitters of divine messages.

In using these and other sources, the Chronicler often provides details that are not found elsewhere in the Bible. Some of these have been confirmed by ancient nonbiblical texts and archaeological data, such as the account of Shishak's campaign in the late tenth century BCE (2 Chr 12.2–4; see page 236) and the description of Hezekiah's protection of Jerusalem's water supply in preparation for the Assyrian attack in the late eighth century BCE (2 Chr 32.2–4, 30; see pages 284–85). Chronicles is thus not just a revision of the already existing Deuteronomistic History, but a genuinely independent work, with its own perspective on Israel's past.

Date

No conclusive internal evidence enables us to set a precise date for the writing of Chronicles. It is clearly a product of the postexilic period, since it concludes with the decree of Cyrus in 538 BCE allowing the exiles to return. Other details support this. First Chronicles 29.7 mentions the "daric," a Persian coin named for Darius I (522–486 BCE) and first issued early in his reign, and 2 Chronicles 16.9 alludes to Zechariah 4.10, itself written no earlier than the late sixth century BCE. Moreover, the genealogy of David in 1 Chronicles 3 gives seven generations beyond Zerubbabel, the governor of Judah in the late sixth century BCE; this takes us well into the fifth century BCE. On the other hand, no evidence suggests that the author was influenced by Greek thought, and so Chronicles was probably written before Hellenization made a significant impact on Judaism, beginning in the late fourth century BCE (see further page 406). A majority of contemporary scholars date Chronicles to the late fifth or the fourth century BCE, during the latter part of the Persian period. Some prefer an earlier date, in the late sixth or early fifth century, or suggest a series of editions of the work, the earliest of which would have been in the late sixth century.

As we have observed in previous chapters, our knowledge of the history of Judah during the Persian period is spotty, and by the fourth century BCE, the preferred date for Chronicles, it becomes virtually nonexistent. Because Chronicles is concerned with events that occurred some time before it was written, little direct evidence in the book enables us to determine the social and historical context of its author, or of events that might have had an impact on him.

The Relationship between Chronicles and Ezra-Nehemiah

There are close connections between the books of Chronicles and the books of Ezra and Nehemiah. This is shown by the overlap between them: The last verses of Chronicles (2 Chr 36.22–23), relating the decree of Cyrus the Great allowing the exiles to return to Judah, are identical to the opening verses of Ezra (1.1–3). There are also thematic links, including the importance of the "torah of Moses" (for example, Ezra 3.2; 2 Chr 23.18), the Temple, and the Temple's rituals and personnel.

Because of these connections, until recently scholars generally assumed a common authorship for the books of Chronicles, Ezra, and Nehemiah and referred to the author of all of them as "the Chronicler." Now, however, a consensus has developed that the books of Chronicles did not have the same author as those of Ezra and Nehemiah, and they use "the Chronicler" only for the author of Chronicles, as we do in this book. Among the reasons for this scholarly judgment are differences in language, style, and content. For example, the Chronicler is not as concerned with intermarriage by Jews as is the author of Ezra-Nehemiah. Also, the attitude of the Chronicler toward the former northern kingdom of Israel is much less antagonistic than that of Ezra-Nehemiah (see Box 23.1).

The Genealogies

The Chronicler begins his history by setting it in a universal context, drawing directly on the already formed Pentateuch. Thus, 1 Chronicles 1.1–4 condenses the genealogy from Adam to Noah in Genesis 5, and 1 Chronicles 1.5–27 moves from Noah to Abraham, closely following Genesis 10.1–29 and 11.10–26. The Chronicler

Box 23.1 SAMARIA AND THE SAMARITANS

Throughout the history of Israel in the preexilic period, tensions existed between north and south, tensions expressed in Genesis in narratives about the rivalries among the twelve sons of Jacob. David and Solomon were able to unite the two regions during the tenth century BCE, but at Solomon's death, they became separate entities, the northern kingdom of Israel with its capital for most of its history in Samaria and the southern kingdom of Judah with its capital in Jerusalem. From the perspective of the Deuteronomistic Historians, writing in Judah, the north was a sinful kingdom and was divinely punished for its idolatry by being conquered by the Assyrians in 722 BCE. Subsequently, we are told, the Assyrians colonized what had become the Assyrian province of Samaria with foreigners who worshiped other gods alongside Yahweh.

These tensions continued in the postexilic period. According to the books of Ezra and Nehemiah, antagonism existed between the northerners and the leaders of the restored community in Judah. One of the major differences between the books of Chronicles and Ezra-Nehemiah is that while Ezra-Nehemiah is hostile toward its northern neighbors, as well as to others in the region except for the "true Israel," that is, the returned exiles, Chronicles is more inclusive. For the Chronicler, the ideal is of one Israel, all twelve tribes. Thus, according to the Chronicler, all Israel, north and south, participated in the national festivals inaugurated by David and reinstituted by Hezekiah and Josiah.

At the same time, the Chronicler was aware that there were tensions between the two regions. When Hezekiah invited all Israel "from Dan to Beersheba" to Jerusalem to celebrate the Passover, only a small number of northerners came; the others responded to Hezekiah's messengers with scorn (2 Chr 30.10–11). The Chronicler's emphasis on Judah, and virtual ignoring of the northern kingdom of Israel, which had become the Persian province of Samaria, may be evidence of continuing conflict and rivalry.

Over time, the division became acute, for reasons that are not entirely clear. Ben Sira, writing in Jerusalem in the early second century BCE, refers to the Samaritans as "the foolish nation of Shechem" who are "not even a people" (Sir 50.25–26), and links them with Israel's ancient enemies, the Edomites and the Philistines. Eventually, a complete break developed between the Samaritans and the Jerusalem establishment, each with its own Temple, and each claiming to be authentic Judaism and to possess the only authoritative version of the Torah. This schism had its roots in the history summarized here, but has left few traces in the Jewish scriptures; it is more prominent in the New Testament, in the first-century CE Jewish historian Josephus, and in rabbinic literature.

then summarizes the ancestral narratives, moving from Abraham to Isaac and Ishmael, from Isaac to Jacob and Esau, and from Jacob to his twelve sons (1 Chr 1.28–2.2). This material, then, is prologue, but it links what follows with Israel's past, a past apparently familiar to its audience, who do not need to be told who such individuals as Adam or Noah were.

Then the Chronicler slows the pace and focuses on the sons of Jacob, the ancestors of the tribes of Israel. The sons of Jacob are not given in birth order or by their various mothers (see Figure 5.3 on page 76), but rather by the importance to the Chronicler of the tribes named for them, in a roughly geographical order. In a careful arrangement, the genealogies of Judah and Benjamin, the most important tribes from the Chronicler's perspective, frame the genealogies of the others and are given in more detail. Included in the genealogy of Judah is a lengthy genealogy of the descendants of David (see page 372).

In central place in the genealogies (1 Chr 6) is an extended list of members of the tribe of Levi, the priestly tribe responsible for Israel's rituals. The Levites have a major role in Chronicles, with several lists of Levites and their sacred functions inserted by the Chronicler into his narrative. So important are the Levites in Chronicles that some scholars have conjectured that the Chronicler himself was a Levite. This is supported by the remarkable statement that in the time of Hezekiah "the Levites were more upright in heart than the priests in sanctifying themselves" (2 Chr 29.34). At the very least, and as in the book of Deuteronomy (see pages 149–50), the Chronicler is giving an alternative to the subordinate position given to the Levites in P (see pages 136–37). But the Chronicler cannot change the assignment of the most sacred ritual functions to the priests, the branch of the tribe of Levi that had Aaron as their ancestor.

Chapter 9 updates the genealogies already presented, giving the names of those who returned from Babylon; it is closely related to Nehemiah 11.3–19 and 1 Chronicles 8.28–38. The postexilic community is thus directly linked with its past. Again, the Levites have the dominant position in this list. The genealogies conclude with a repetition of the lineage of Saul, providing a transition to the account of the death of Saul that follows in 1 Chronicles 10.

David

We get a good sample of the Chronicler's methods by comparing his presentation of David with that of the Deuteronomistic Historians (1 Sam 16–31; 2 Sam; 1 Kings 1–2). Omitting all of the material in 1 Samuel except for the account of Saul's death in battle against the Philistines in 1 Chronicles 10 (= 1 Sam 31), the Chronicler begins his narrative about David with an account of his being anointed as king over all Israel (1 Chr 11.1–3). Although the Chronicler is aware that David ruled first at Hebron and then in Jerusalem (1 Chr 3.4), he does not mention that at Hebron David was king initially only of Judah and not of the ten northern tribes (see 2 Sam 2.1–7; 5.5). For the Chronicler, Israel was always a unified entity.

The Chronicler includes lists of David's heroes (1 Chr 11.10–47; compare 2 Sam 23.8–39), and adds to them another list of David's companions while he was on the run from Saul, along with a census of his army, drawn from all twelve tribes (1 Chr 12). Then, according to the Chronicler, having consulted with all Israel, David summoned the priests and Levites to Jerusalem and arranged for the ark to be brought there (1 Chr 13.1–4; 15.1–24). The actual discovery and transfer of the ark closely follow the version in 2 Samuel 6, but adding new material in 1 Chronicles 16, the Chronicler describes David as ordering the singing of praises, and a collage of psalms follows (1 Chr 16.4–42). David then arranges for the regular activities of the priests and the sacred singers and musicians. At this point, the Chronicler returns to his source, closely following 2 Samuel 7–8 and 10, omitting only the material concerning Mephibosheth (2 Sam 9.1–13). The battle for Rabbah, the capital of the Ammonites, is taken from 2 Samuel 11.1, 12.26, and 12.30–31. But here is the Chronicler's most telling omission: None of the narrative in 2 Samuel concerning David and Bathsheba, the arranged death of her husband Uriah, the rape of Tamar, the revolt of Absalom, and the machinations that led to Solomon becoming king is incorporated into the Chronicler's account. In other words, the Chronicler omits the Succession Narrative (2 Sam 9–20; 1 Kings 1–2; see pages 209–10) almost in its entirety. The result is a one-dimensional portrayal of David different from that with which we (and the audience of Chronicles) are familiar. For the Chronicler, David is an ideal king, without flaws.

The Chronicler then moves to an account of David's census, which leads to his purchase of the site of the future Temple. At this point, the Chronicler abandons his source in 2 Samuel entirely and describes in detail how David made preparations for building "the house of the LORD God" (2 Chr 22.1), the Temple. David, of course, did not build the Temple himself, and the Chronicler knows this, but he makes David the virtual designer of the Temple and the founder of its worship because, we are told, Solomon was "young and inexperienced" (1 Chr 22.5). Thus, all of 1 Chronicles 22–29 is the Chronicler's own material, much of it concerned with the duties of the various families of the priests and Levites. Finally, the Chronicler succinctly recounts David's death and Solomon's orderly succession.

Like the Deuteronomistic Historians, the Chronicler devotes a disproportionate amount of space to David. For both, David was the ideal king of Israel, the standard against whom subsequent kings were judged. Moreover, according to the Chronicler, David was the founder of the Temple and its worship, which had been restored and were functioning, a powerful symbol of continuity between preexilic and postexilic Israel. This is also suggested in the genealogy of David (1 Chr 3), which lists the descendants of David several generations beyond Zerubbabel, that is, well into the fifth century BCE. But the Davidic dynasty had not been reestablished, despite the hope of some that it would be. By giving such prominence to David, the Chronicler may also be hinting at support for the return of a Davidic king, if not in his own time, then at some future date.

Other Kings

The kings that the Chronicler treats positively in the rest of his history resemble David in several ways. Highest praise is given to those who were both pious and who ruled over all Israel. The first of these is Solomon.

In his account of Solomon's reign, the Chronicler reproduces much of the material in 1 Kings 1–11, including the actual construction of the Temple, the manufacture of its furnishings, and its dedication. He makes some telling changes and omissions, however. The Chronicler does not mention Solomon building the royal palace and associated structures (see 1 Kings 7.1–12). Also, according to 1 Kings 9.11, Solomon gave Hiram, the king of Tyre, twenty cities in the Galilee in payment for the raw materials used in the construction of the Temple and palace complex. According to the Chronicler, however, the cities were given by Huram (as Hiram is called) to Solomon (2 Chr 8.2); the territorial integrity of Israel was not only preserved but increased. Finally, the Chronicler's summary of the end of Solomon's reign omits most of 1 Kings 11, the account of Solomon's foreign marriages and the apostasy that resulted from them.

Another king for whose reign the Chronicler gives considerable detail is Hezekiah, who ruled in the late eighth and early seventh centuries BCE. A lengthy addition to the material concerning Hezekiah found in 2 Kings narrates how Hezekiah restored the Temple and its worship according to the system established by David (2 Chr 29.3–36; 31.2–21). He also invited the northern tribes to come to Jerusalem for the celebration of Passover (2 Chr 30). Typical of the Chronicler's approach is his treatment of the invasion of the Assyrian king Sennacherib in 701 BCE: He omits the account of Hezekiah paying tribute to Sennacherib, perhaps because one source of that tribute was the treasury of the Temple and its ornamentation (2 Kings 18.14–16).

The treatment of Hezekiah's successor Manasseh is another example of the Chronicler at work. For the Deuteronomistic Historians, Manasseh was the worst of the kings of Judah. According to the Chronicler, however, Manasseh was taken as a prisoner to Babylon, where he repented of his worship of other gods, and then returned to Jerusalem and became a model ruler (2 Chr 33.11–16). The historicity of this episode is debated, and the mention of Babylon is especially suspicious, anticipating the Judeans' exile to and return from there in the sixth century BCE. Perhaps for the Chronicler the length of Manasseh's reign, which implied divine protection and reward, needed some justification, so he constructed a story of Manasseh's repenting of his earlier apostasy.

In his accounts of these and other kings, the Chronicler can be tagged a revisionist historian, editing and adding to his sources in support of his ideological program, in which a unified Israel was best led by pious rulers in the line of David who were faithful to the commandments given by God through Moses and worshiped at the Temple in Jerusalem. For the Chronicler, history provided a compelling model for the restored community of his day.

THE BOOK OF PSALMS

The book of Psalms is the longest in the Bible, with 150 chapters in the traditional numbering. It is an anthology of the hymns of ancient Israel, collected and edited into relatively final form probably in the fifth or fourth century BCE. Its title in Hebrew, *tehillim*, means "praises," a vague term that does not take into account the different types of hymns found in the book. Praise is certainly an important element in the book, and the word *tehillim* is related to the phrase *halleluyah* ("Praise Yah[weh]"), which occurs more than twenty times at the beginning or end, or both, of psalms in the last part of the book. The English title of the book, "Psalms," is derived from a Greek word for a stringed instrument (*psalterion*), indicating the musical character of the book's contents.

The book of Psalms is divided into five parts, probably a deliberate parallel to the five books of the Torah. This is also suggested by the content of Psalm 1, a wisdom psalm that describes divine reward for those who observe the Torah and punishment for those who fail to do so. The five parts are Psalms 1–41, 42–72, 73–89, 90–106, and 107–150. Each of the first four of these divisions ends with a blessing (Pss 41.13; 72.18–19; 89.52; 106.48), and the last psalm in the collection, Psalm 150, is a conclusion to the fifth division, as well as to the book of Psalms as a whole.

This structure was the culmination of a long process of collecting and editing, and the book of Psalms contains much evidence of earlier stages in the process. Thus, Psalm 72 ends with the note

"The prayers of David son of Jesse are ended"; apparently a collection of prayers attributed to David was incorporated into the book of Psalms at some early stage, although after Psalm 72, eighteen more psalms are attributed to David, indicating that "the prayers of David" was not a definitive edition. Within the book of Psalms there are other collections as well. For example, each of the psalms from 120 to 134 includes in its title the phrase "A Song of Ascents," probably because pilgrims used these psalms as they went up to Jerusalem; because of the city's geographical situation and elevation, traveling from almost any direction to Jerusalem, and especially to the Temple mount, meant going uphill. We should note, however, that these fifteen psalms include different genres or forms, according to the form-critical analysis to be discussed later in this chapter.

Another collection is indicated by the title "of the sons of Korah," which is found in Psalms 42–49 and 84, 85, 87, and 88. Korah was the ancestor of one of the principal priestly families in the Temple in Jerusalem, which according to 2 Chronicles 20.19 led the people in song. Among the sons of Korah were Asaph and Heman. To Asaph are attributed Psalms 50 and 73–83, and to Heman Psalm 88. According to 1 Chronicles 6.31–43, Asaph and Heman were "in charge of the service of song" in the Temple. They also played cymbals (1 Chr 15.19), and their sons, along with those of Jeduthun, to whom three psalms (39; 62; 77) are also attributed, prophesied "with lyres, harps, and cymbals" (1 Chr 25.1). We have already noted the connection between prophecy and music (see pages 244–45); it is possible that members of these priestly families also functioned as prophets, giving worshipers a divine oracle or response to prayer. (See Figure 23.1.)

Another indication of earlier collections that have been incorporated into the book is the close proximity of psalms that deal with divine kingship (93–99) and psalms that have the opening or closing "*halleluyah*" ("Praise Yah[weh]") (Pss 104–106; 111–113; 135; 146–150; these are sometimes called "Hallel" psalms).

Further evidence that the book of Psalms is an anthology, or perhaps more properly an anthology of anthologies, is the repetition within the book. Thus, Psalms 14 and 53 are identical, except for the

FIGURE 23.1   Musicians on a ceramic stand from Ashdod, dating to the early tenth century BCE. Each figure is about 2 in (5 cm) high. From the left, the instruments being played are a double flute, a lyre, and probably a hand drum. (For another depiction of a lyre player, see Figure 24.1 on p. 387.)

shift of the divine name from Yahweh to Elohim; Psalm 40.13–17 = Psalm 70; and Psalm 108 is a combination of Psalms 57.7–11 and 60.5–12.

In addition to the collections marked in the text itself, scholars also have identified another major collection, Psalms 42–83, called the "Elohistic Psalter" because in it, the divine name *Elohim* ("God") is used about five times more frequently than *Yahweh* ("The LORD"), whereas in the rest of the book, *Yahweh* is used about ninety-five percent of the time. This preference for *Elohim* has plausibly been suggested as evidence that some of these psalms originated in the northern kingdom of Israel, as did the Elohist (E) source in the Pentateuch, in which *Elohim* is also used in Genesis instead of Yahweh (see further pages 48–49). It should be noted, however, that two of the hymns in this collection are hymns in praise of Zion (Jerusalem), which complicates the matter, since Jerusalem was the capital of the southern kingdom of Judah. This "Elohistic Psalter" also spans the second and third of the five divisions of the book of Psalms noted

earlier, further indicating that the arrangement of the collection into five "books" took place at a later stage.

In recent years some scholars have attempted to discover more detailed principles of arrangement, in which psalms were grouped together because of shared themes and vocabulary. These efforts, although instructive, have not yet won consensus.

The book of Psalms is therefore the result of a long process of compilation and editing. Each sanctuary or place of worship, preeminently but not exclusively Jerusalem, and each priestly family, would have had its own collection of hymns, and these different collections were gradually combined into the book we now know as Psalms.

Titles to the Psalms

We have already mentioned the "titles" that precede the text of most of the psalms; most of the psalms have these introductory notes, which were added by ancient editors. Sometimes the titles are brief, as in Psalm 98, but occasionally they are lengthy, as in Psalm 18. The single most common title is "Of David," used in seventy-three psalms. An ambiguous Hebrew preposition is generally interpreted to mean that David was considered the author of the psalm in question; the same preposition is used, for example, in Proverbs 24.23: "These also are by the wise." The titles of thirteen psalms have historical notes connecting them with events in the life of David.

David's reputation as a poet and a musician is well attested (see Box 14.1 on page 210), so it is not surprising that many hymns are attributed to him, especially since in Chronicles he is presented as the originator of the Temple's elaborate system of worship. Thus, David becomes the presumed author of many of the psalms, just as Moses is presented as the human author of Israel's legal traditions and David's son Solomon as the author of writings about wisdom (see page 385) and love (see page 401). It is unlikely, however, that David wrote most of the psalms attributed to him. Some, such as Psalms 68 and 122, refer to the Temple in Jerusalem, built by Solomon in the mid-tenth century BCE after David's death, and others, such as Psalm 69.35–36, mention the Babylonian destruction of Jerusalem in 586 BCE.

Only two psalms are attributed to Solomon, Psalms 72 and 127. Psalm 72 is a royal psalm, which also mentions Sheba, whose queen is reported to have visited Solomon (1 Kings 10.1), and Psalm 127 refers to Yahweh building the house (v. 1) and to "his beloved" (v. 2; Hebr. *ye-dido*), which recall Solomon's construction of the Temple and the name Jedidiah (Hebr. *yedidyah*; 2 Sam 12.25) given him by the prophet Nathan.

Others to whom psalms are attributed include Moses (Ps 90) and several priestly figures (see earlier in this chapter). Some psalms have more than one attribution (Pss 39; 62; 77; 88), making the accuracy of the ancient identification of authorship even less likely.

In addition to indicating authorship, some titles of the psalms include mysterious rubrics, including "to the leader" (fifty-five times), and references to musical instruments and melodies (see further later in this chapter). What appear to be ancient categories of psalms, such as "miktam," "maskil," "mizmor, "song," "prayer," and others, also occur. In some cases, two or more of these terms are applied to the same psalm, which makes their exact meaning elusive at best.

Dating the Psalms

The book of Psalms in more or less its present shape was probably formed before the end of the Persian period in the late fourth century BCE. We find no examples of Greek influence or vocabulary, as occur in writings from the succeeding Hellenistic period. Moreover, the Septuagint, the translation of the Hebrew Bible into Greek that dates from the third century BCE, includes an additional psalm after Psalm 150, known as Psalm 151 (and considered part of the Bible by some Orthodox Christian churches); the title to this psalm describes it as "outside the number" of the already closed collection of 150.

Many psalms are from the time of the monarchy, with their repeated references to the king and the Temple. Others are from the exilic period, including Psalm 137 and some that describe a community without a Temple, either in Judah before the Temple was rebuilt or in exile without access to the restored Temple.

Several psalms also incorporate already developed Pentateuchal traditions (see further pages 48–50), such as Psalm 78 with its echoes of Exodus 15, and Psalm 105's account of the ancestral period and the covenant between Yahweh and Abraham, Isaac, and Jacob, but such allusions provide only a relative chronology. The book of Psalms, then, as an anthology, contains poems from several periods in Israel's history, but most individual psalms are impossible to date precisely.

Ancient Near Eastern Parallels

Among the hundreds of thousands of texts recovered from the ancient Near East are personal and communal hymns and prayers similar to those found in the book of Psalms. Babylonian petitions, for example, have a structure close to that of the biblical petitions, and Psalm 104 is close even in precise details to the Egyptian Hymn to the Sun-disc (Aten) in its praise of the divine creator. While no direct links between the biblical and the nonbiblical texts can be proved or need even be assumed, these parallels are reminders that Israel did not exist in a vacuum, but was part of a cultural continuum, and that throughout the Near East similar genres and vocabulary were used in human communication with the divine.

As in the Bible, most of these ancient Near Eastern texts are poetic, and many also employ the poetic phenomenon of parallelism (see Box 23.2). The texts include hymns and prayers to various deities in genres like those identified for the biblical psalms, such as petitions and hymns of praise and thanksgiving.

Form Criticism of the Psalms

The most significant modern study of the psalms is by the German scholar Hermann Gunkel, who was also a pioneer in the study of the Pentateuch and prophets. Beginning with a study of selected psalms in 1904 and culminating in his commentary on the book of Psalms in 1926 and his introduction to the psalms published in 1933, shortly after his death, Gunkel applied the discipline of form criticism (see pages 69–72) that he had developed to the psalms.

This method of analysis groups the psalms by genre, and sometimes by content. The main categories identified by Gunkel are individual and communal laments (which we will call "petitions"), songs of thanksgiving, royal psalms, and hymns. Although subsequent scholars have refined his analysis, Gunkel's categorization of the psalms by form or genre has been followed widely. Categories often overlap, in mixed types.

Box 23.2 PARALLELISM

Like most biblical poetry, the psalms feature as their primary poetic device a phenomenon called **parallelism**. This technique, also found in Ugaritic and Mesopotamian poetry, is a kind of thought rhyme, in which an idea is developed by the use of repetition, synonyms, or opposites. In this example of synonymous parallelism, the two lines express essentially the same idea:

> The LORD is my light and my salvation;
>   whom shall I fear?
> The LORD is the stronghold of my life;
>   of whom shall I be afraid? (Ps 27.1)

In antithetic parallelism, opposites are used:

> The LORD watches over the way of the righteous,
>   but the way of the wicked will perish. (Ps 1.6)

Another type of parallelism is called climatic:

> Behold, your enemies, O Yahweh,
>   behold, your enemies shall perish;
>   all evildoers shall be scattered. (Ps 92.9)

The following is a summary, with examples, of the principal forms and subforms.

Petitions

Petitions are appeals for divine help in distress, and are subdivided into two principal categories:

- *Individual petitions:* This is the most frequently occurring type in the book, with more than forty psalms belonging to this genre (for example, Ps 3). The speaker of the psalm is an individual who speaks in the first person. Royal petitions, in which the king is the speaker, overlap with this category (see page 378). The following elements are found in the petitions, although the order in which they occur varies, and not all elements are always included:

  Address to God.

  Description of the distress from which the individual wishes to be relieved. The language used is often metaphorical and can be hyperbolic.

  Prayer for divine help and deliverance.

  Cursing of the enemies the individual considers responsible for his situation.

  Expression of confidence that God will hear the individual's prayer.

  Protestation of innocence or confession of guilt.

  A vow anticipating a positive divine response, in which the psalmist promises to thank God for it.

  A song of thanksgiving, which follows naturally from the vow.

- *Communal petitions:* These have the same elements as individual petitions, but the speakers are plural, presumably the entire community. The distress is usually communal, such as famine, plague, or attack by enemies. In these petitions (such as Ps 44), the expression of confidence is often replaced by an appeal to God to continue to act on behalf of the community as he has in the past, including frequent references to the history of Israel.

Many of the other genres or forms used are expansions of one or more of the elements of the petitions.

Songs of Trust

These psalms consist largely of the expression of confidence in divine assistance (for example, Ps 23).

Songs of Thanksgiving

These psalms express gratitude for divine assistance that has been granted and may be either individual or communal, in the latter case as for a military victory or a plentiful harvest (for example, Ps 65).

Hymns

This category consists of songs of praise of Yahweh under several aspects:

- *Hymns of divine kingship:* In these hymns, Yahweh's rule over heaven and earth is celebrated, often in highly mythological language. Examples include Psalm 29, in which the entire assembly of the gods is called on to praise Yahweh for his powers as the storm-god who defeated the primeval watery chaos.

  Three psalms in this category, which occur in close proximity, open with the phrase "Yahweh is king" (Pss 93.1; 97.1; 99.1; see also 47.8; 96.10). The Hebrew (*Yahweh malak*) can also be translated "Yahweh has become king." Some scholars have conjectured that the Israelites held an annual celebration of the divine enthronement, similar to the Babylonian new year festival, in which Marduk's accession to rule over the gods was celebrated (see pages 32–35 and 340). In the ritual reenactment of myth, the primeval cosmic acts of the deity are in a sense repeated annually. Like Marduk and the Canaanite storm-god Baal, Yahweh became king when he defeated the forces of chaos, and that event would have been celebrated in a festival of divine enthronement. A close parallel in Jewish tradition is the reenactment of the Exodus in the annual celebration of the Passover and in Christian tradition in the celebration of Easter, during which the congregation proclaims: "Christ is risen!"

As attractive as this theory is, however, apart from the psalms and similar hymns, we find no evidence for such a festival of divine enthronement in ancient Israel, and so it remains hypothetical.

- *Creation hymns:* Closely related to the hymns of divine kingship are hymns that describe divine activity in creation; these hymns often also use mythological language (for example, Ps 104).
- *Hymns celebrating divine actions in Israel's history:* These celebrate Yahweh's actions on behalf of Israel, such as Psalms 105 and 106.

Some of the hymns, notably Psalms 135 and 136, connect the themes of creation and Exodus, as indeed does the narrative of the Pentateuch.

Liturgies

Some psalms have been identified as "liturgies" because their contents suggest that they were used during public worship. Some of them have internal indications of the ritual setting where they were used, including a procession (Ps 24) and a pilgrimage (for example, Ps 122; see following).

Several of these psalms have a question-and-answer format, such as Psalms 15 and 24. Of interest here is the identity of the responder to the worshiper's question. One probability is that the response was given by the priest, or perhaps by a prophet.

Other psalms that include a liturgical element are responsorial psalms, like 136, in which a leader would give the verse and the worshipers would reply with a repeated refrain; this alternation is known as antiphony. The ceremonies at which such psalms could have been used include the renewal of the covenant; such covenant renewal ceremonies are described in Deuteronomy 27, Joshua 24, and 2 Kings 23.

Royal Psalms and Hymns Concerning the Davidic Covenant

Several psalms have the ruling king as their speaker, and others deal principally with the king.

These include a royal wedding hymn (Ps 45); three that are probably coronation hymns (Pss 2; 72; 110); petitions (Pss 89; 101; 144.1–11); prayer for victory (Ps 20); and thanksgiving for victory (Pss 18; 21). A related category is that called "hymns concerning the Davidic covenant" (Pss 78; 89; 132) in which the king is not the speaker, but the royal ideology (see further pages 229–33) is a principal subject. Although a specific king is not named in any of these psalms, they can be presumed to come from the time of the monarchy, except for Psalm 89 in its final form, which seems to speak of the fall of the dynasty.

Zion Hymns

Another small group of psalms, overlapping in content with the royal psalms, is those that have as their subject Jerusalem and especially God's choice and protection of it and hence its invincibility. Examples include Psalms 46, 48, and 87.

Pilgrimage Hymns

A small number of psalms may have been written for use by pilgrims to a sacred place, specified as Jerusalem in Psalms 84 and 122.

Wisdom Psalms

A few psalms belong to the category of "wisdom literature," to be discussed later in this chapter, because they deal with issues of human existence and use the same vocabulary as in such books as Proverbs and Job. An example is Psalm 37, which, since it is also an acrostic (see Box 20.1 on page 317), lacks a clear development, being an almost random assortment of proverbs expressing traditional views of divine justice.

Torah Psalms

Closely related to the wisdom psalms are three psalms that focus on the *torah* (see Box 10.2 on page 154), the divine law or teaching, observance of which guarantees divine reward. These are Psalms 1, 19 (especially vv. 7–14), and 119. All are probably relatively late, which means that *torah* may refer to the first five books of the Bible. That is suggested by the placement of Psalm 1 as the introduction to the entire collection of psalms, which, as we have seen, is also divided into five parts.

The form-critical analysis of the psalms has been extraordinarily productive; yet as the previous summary makes clear, the form-critical categories are not mutually exclusive, nor do they necessarily correspond to ancient understandings of genre. Moreover, some psalms, notably Psalm 68, do not seem to belong to any single category. The fluidity of the psalms, especially in the overlapping classifications noted here, cautions us against making these form-critical categories too rigid; rather, they should be taken as a starting point for interpretation.

The Psalms as Prayers

As we have seen, for the most part the psalms lack specifics and are thus difficult to date and to categorize. One reason for the preservation of these hymnic prayers, and not of others that must have existed in ancient Israel, may be this very lack of specificity, or, more positively, their universality. The absence of references in the psalms to the specific festivals and rituals of Israel is striking: We find no allusion to the Passover, the feast of Weeks, the feast of Tabernacles, or even the sabbath (except in the title of Ps 92), nor to the various types of rituals described in such detail in biblical legislation and narrative.

This generality explains the continuing appeal of the psalms, for they can be appropriated relatively easily in times and circumstances other than when they were written. They are by and large concerned with fundamental aspects of the human condition, with individuals and communities who are, or feel, ill, threatened, and persecuted, or happy, grateful, and trusting. These prayers, through which ancient Israelites expressed and sustained their beliefs, are thus profound religious expressions. They have continued to be used by Jews and Christians in ceremonies of worship and have been sources of inspiration and expressions of piety for individuals throughout the ages.

MUSIC IN ANCIENT ISRAEL

Readers of the Bible, especially the book of Psalms, encounter a bewildering array of references to music and dance. The frequency of these references makes it clear that these arts were a major feature of life in ancient Israel, as in the rest of the ancient world, but they are an aspect that we can barely recover. With the destruction of the Second Temple in 70 CE by the Romans, most of Israel's liturgical music was lost or deliberately abandoned. The reconstruction of Israel's musical traditions is thus a difficult task, and it relies on often obscure references in the Bible, occasional archaeological discoveries, and illustrations of musical instruments from the ancient Near East (see Figures 23.1, 23.2, and 23.3).

The most frequently mentioned biblical form of music is the song, used to celebrate major events in the life cycle and the liturgical year. We also find many references to funeral dirges, sung by both men and women, and passing references

FIGURE 23.2   A flute player. Detail of a relief from the palace of the Assyrian king Ashurbanipal at Nineveh, dating to the seventh century BCE.

FIGURE 23.3 Ceramic figurine of a woman playing a drum, about 8 in (20 cm) high, from the first half of the first millennium BCE.

to harvest songs, wedding songs, and music at banquets.

The prophets frequently made use of music in delivering their message. The "band of prophets" who meet Saul after his anointing by Samuel are accompanied by "harp, tambourine, flute, and lyre" as they prophesy (1 Sam 10.5), and the Chronicler mentions those who "prophesy with lyres, harps, and cymbals" (1 Chr 25.1).

Many of the most famous biblical poems are songs, including the textured love lyrics of the Song of Solomon (see pages 401–03) and the hymns celebrating the victories of God and Israel attributed to Miriam (Ex 15.21) and to Deborah and Barak (Judg 5.1). These and other references indicate that women were not just participants but on some occasions also leaders in music-making in ancient Israel. Mixed choruses performed both the

secular music of the court and the hymnody of the Temple.

The music most in evidence in the Bible is sacred music. We find frequent references to music and dance in the detailed descriptions of the performers of sacred music and in the psalms themselves. Many of the psalms are called "songs," and many more make use of the verb "to sing." The psalms also refer to musical instruments, which fall into three groups: percussion, including tambourines, drums, cymbals, and bells; stringed instruments, such as the lyre and the harp; and winds, including the trumpet, the horn, the ram's horn, and the flute. The exact translation of the names of the more than twenty instruments named in the Bible is often a guess, based on related words in other languages, ancient interpretations and translations, depictions of instruments in ancient art, and chance archaeological finds. Excavators in Jerusalem, for example, uncovered part of a flute made from a cow's hind leg bone, with six finger holes. Some of the titles to the psalms also seem to refer to musical directions, including well-known melodies, as in such evocative phrases as "The Doe of the Dawn" (Ps 22), "The Dove on Far-off Terebinths" (Ps 56), and "The Lily of the Covenant" (Ps 60), and to musical notations, such as "the eighth" (Hebr. *sheminit*, Pss 6; 12), which may refer either to an eight-stringed instrument or to an octave.

Another mysterious term that may have musical significance is "selah," which occurs seventy-one times in the book of Psalms, and only three times elsewhere in the Bible, all in the "Psalm of Habakkuk" (Hab 3). It is placed either at the end of a psalm or at the end of what appears to be an ancient division into a stanza or strophe, but its precise function and meaning are unknown.

All of this detail is immensely frustrating. It is as if we had only the libretto and some of the orchestral instruments for a Verdi opera whose score was lost. We must therefore use our imagination in thinking about the poetry of ancient Israel, most of which, as elsewhere in the ancient world, was set to music, and in re-creating in our minds the sights and sounds of dancers and musicians, as in the final hymn of the book of Psalms

(Ps 150.3–5), a virtual catalogue of ancient Israelite instruments, and in the liturgical procession mentioned in Psalm 68.25:

> the singers in front, the musicians last,
> between them girls playing tambourines.

A LOOK BACK AND AHEAD

The books of Chronicles are a rewritten history, highly selective and ideologically driven. We may also view it, however, as a creative reinterpretation, in which familiar history and new details are combined to provide a model for a new generation of Israelites living in a new situation.

The collection and reshaping of older traditions is also evident in the book of Psalms, ancient Israel's hymnbook as it were. In their final form, both Chronicles and Psalms illustrate the paradigmatic role of King David in postexilic Israel.

In the next chapter, we will consider another example of how older traditions were collected in the book of Proverbs, and also how the dominant biblical view of a just God who rewards the good and punishes the wicked is challenged in the books of Ecclesiastes and Job.

IMPORTANT NAMES AND TERMS

Each name or term is defined briefly in the Glossary. Its first significant occurrence in this chapter appears in **boldface** type.

the Chronicler   parallelism

QUESTIONS FOR REVIEW

1. What are the sources used by the author of the books of Chronicles, and how does he use them?

2. In what ways does the presentation of the history of Israel and Judah in Chronicles differ from that in the Deuteronomistic History? What do these differences indicate about the Chronicler's own views?

3. How would you describe the book of Psalms, and what are its principal genres?

4. Discuss the various ways in which psalms were used in ancient Israel. How do these uses contribute to the preservation of the psalms?

BIBLIOGRAPHY

For a brief introduction to the books of Chronicles, see Gary N. Knoppers, "Chronicles, First and Second Books of," pp. 622–31 in *The New Interpreter's Dictionary of the Bible,* ed. K. D. Sakenfeld, vol. 1 (Nashville, TN: Abingdon, 2006).

An important commentary is by Sara Japhet, *I & II Chronicles: A Commentary* (Louisville, KY: Westminster/John Knox, 1993).

For a summary of the evidence concerning the Samaritans, see James D. Purvis, "Samaritans," pp. 911–14 in *The HarperCollins Bible Dictionary* (ed. M. A. Powell; New York: HarperOne, 3d ed., 2011).

A good introduction to the book of Psalms is Stephen A. Geller, "Psalms," pp. 193–212 in *The Oxford Encyclopedia of the Books of the Bible,* vol. 2, ed. M. D. Coogan (New York: Oxford University Press, 2011; available in Oxford Biblical Studies Online). For a short commentary, see C. S. Rodd, in *The Oxford Bible Commentary* (Oxford: Oxford University Press, 2001; available in Oxford Biblical Studies Online), 355–405.

For an introduction to music and musical instruments in ancient Israel, see Philip J. King and Lawrence E. Stager, *Life in Biblical Israel* (Louisville, KY: Westminster John Knox, 2001), 285–300. A complete discussion is found in Joachim Braun, *Music in Ancient Israel/Palestine: Archaeological, Written, and Comparative Sources* (Grand Rapids, MI: Eerdmans, 2002).

CHAPTER 24

The Wisdom of the Sages: Preservation and Challenge

Proverbs, Job, Ecclesiastes, and the Song of Solomon with an Introduction to Wisdom Literature

Throughout the ancient Near East we find writings that scholars call "wisdom literature," texts that deal with the vagaries of human existence on various levels. In this chapter, we will consider books of the Bible that belong to this category. The book of Proverbs is a collection of instructions about how to succeed in life and how to please God. The books of Job and Ecclesiastes take positions opposed to the dominant biblical view of theodicy, found in the book of Proverbs as well as in the Deuteronomistic History and the prophets, according to which there is a divine justice operative in the history of nations and in the lives of individuals as well. But experience suggests otherwise, the authors of Job and Ecclesiastes argue. In their dissent, they join similar voices found in other ancient Near Eastern literatures. We will also look at the Song of Solomon, a series of love poems whose erotic language prompted debate about whether this book should be in the Bible at all. Its attribution to Solomon, who was known as both a wise king and a lover of women, may account for its inclusion in the canon.

WISDOM LITERATURE

Throughout the ancient Near East, from the third millennium BCE into the early Common Era, and from Egypt to southern Mesopotamia, there flourished a type of writing that has been called **"wisdom literature."** This literature is concerned with the realities of human experience, from the mundane to the sublime, and with the relationship between that experience and the divine.

Wisdom literature is remarkably similar in different eras and different places, and so it can appropriately be called universal. In some ways, it is analogous to philosophy, as developed by the Greeks, but it is not as abstract or as systematic. Rather, it is consistently rooted in the everyday, although from that perspective it also can deal with such profound issues as suffering, death, and divine justice.

The very word for "wisdom" (Hebr. *hokmah*, with related words in other Semitic languages) expresses the range of the literature. A "wise" person is one who has knowledge of some sort. Smiths, carpenters, and other artisans are therefore "wise" because they have technical expertise. Those who know how to succeed in life are also wise, as are, ultimately, those who know the ways of the divine.

Wisdom literature was an international phenomenon, with the same or similar genres, such as proverbs, instructions, dialogues, and fables, attested throughout the ancient Near East in most periods and places. Much of this literature consists of collections made by scribes, often under royal auspices; since ancient Near Eastern literature in general is a literature of the elite, this is not surprising. The specifics of cross-fertilization among regions are unclear, although there is evidence that in centers of power such as royal courts, scribes were familiar with the work of their colleagues elsewhere.

The **proverb**, a short saying that pithily expresses insight into experience, is the most widely attested genre of wisdom literature. In Mesopotamia, collections of proverbs are known from as early as the third millennium BCE in Sumer, and the latest examples date to the third century BCE. Egyptian proverbs have a similar chronological span, continuing into the Common Era. From both regions, and from many other locales, thousands of proverbs have been found, similar in form and sometimes in content to those in the Bible. Because they often deal with ordinary life, borrowing is difficult to identify, but the compilers or authors of the biblical book of Proverbs clearly were familiar with the Egyptian *Instruction of Amenemope*, from the late second millennium BCE.

The preface to that work provides a rationale for making an anthology of proverbs:

> The beginning of the instruction about life,
>   the guide for well-being,
> all the principles of official procedure,
>   the duties of the courtiers . . .
> Written by the superintendent of the land,
>   experienced in his office,
>   the offspring of a scribe of the Beloved Land . . .
> for his son, the youngest of his children,
>   the least of his family. (1.1–2.11)*

The frequent designation of the son as addressee of the maxims taught by his father suggests that some originated in a familial setting. Throughout the ancient Near East, proverbs often reflect what we may call a kind of folk wisdom, and thus, although they were ultimately collected and preserved in the royal courts, many probably come from a wider societal background. But the instruction of the son need not have been restricted to one who was to inherit his father's occupation and status, as with Amenemope, or to any male offspring. The father-son metaphor could also be used of a teacher-student or master-apprentice relationship, as with the "sons of the prophet" who addressed their leader as "father" (see page 246).

Learning and copying the proverbs was part of the curriculum of courtiers and of younger scribes in training for the civil service. Through the proverbs they learned how to succeed—in the mundane sense (through proverbs about table manners and court protocol), in human relationships, and in a more profound way: how to live a life pleasing to the gods. In a similar way, in American education in the nineteenth century, the copying of proverbs and maxims taught penmanship and needlework, as well as inculcating social and religious principles.

Wisdom Literature in the Bible

Although examples of wisdom literature occur throughout the Bible, it is mostly found in the third division of the Jewish canon, the Writings, in the books of Proverbs, Job, and Ecclesiastes. The Roman Catholic and Orthodox canons, in the division that consists of poetical books, add to these other wisdom writings, notably the Wisdom of Solomon, and Ben Sira ("The Wisdom of Jesus, Son of Sirach," or "Sirach" for short), which is also known as Ecclesiasticus (see further Chapter 1).

The books of Proverbs, Job, and Ecclesiastes share a concern with the present and are largely focused on the human condition as it is actually

---

* Translation by W. K. Simpson in *The Literature of Ancient Egypt*, pp. 224–25.

experienced. These books are noteworthy for their lack of explicit reference to the main events and personalities of Israel's history. We find no mention of Israel's ancestors, the Exodus, Moses, the covenant at Sinai, or Joshua and the conquest of the land of Israel. None of the prophets are mentioned. The kings David, Solomon, and Hezekiah are named only in occasional editorial notes. This literature, then, is essentially ahistorical, and this is consistent with the universal aspect of wisdom literature throughout the ancient Near East. Only in the later books of Sirach and the Wisdom of Solomon, probably compiled in the second and first centuries BCE, respectively, are the familiar personalities and the events of Israel's history combined with the wisdom tradition. (See pages 425–26.)

Much of this literature is attributed to Solomon. Just as his father David was credited with authorship of many of the psalms, Solomon became the favorite pseudonymous author of all sorts of wisdom literature, including not only collections of proverbs but also the book of Ecclesiastes and the Song of Solomon (see following), and the later apocryphal book the Wisdom of Solomon. In part this is because of Solomon's reputation as the quintessentially wise ruler, evidenced in several passages in 1 Kings, including the Solomonic judgment concerning the disputed child (1 Kings 3.16–28) and the visit of the queen of Sheba (1 Kings 10.1–10), and in this summary:

> God gave Solomon very great wisdom, discernment, and breadth of understanding as vast as the sand on the seashore, so that Solomon's wisdom surpassed the wisdom of all the people of the east, and all the wisdom of Egypt. . . . He composed three thousand proverbs, and his songs numbered a thousand and five. He would speak of trees, from the cedar that is in the Lebanon to the hyssop that grows in the wall; he would speak of animals, and birds, and reptiles, and fish. (1 Kings 4.29–33; see also Box 15.1 on page 224)

Apart from the wisdom books themselves, elements of wisdom tradition are found throughout the Bible. As we saw in the previous chapter, scholars have identified some psalms as belonging to the category of wisdom literature (see page 378). Popular proverbs are found in many biblical books,

some widely known, as is shown by occurrence of the same proverb—"The fathers have eaten sour grapes, and the children's teeth are set on edge"— in both Jeremiah (31.29) and Ezekiel (18.2).

We find frequent references in biblical literature to wise women and wise men, such as the wise women of Tekoa and of Abel Beth-maacah (2 Sam 14.2; 20.16), and the wise men of the Judean court (Isa 29.14; Jer 8.8–9; 9.23; 18.18), government officials who would have been involved in the editing and copying of wisdom traditions. Scholars also have identified wisdom elements in the Joseph story (Gen 37–50), in the book of Deuteronomy, in some of the prophets, and, in fact, in almost every book of the Bible, although not all such identifications are equally compelling.

THE BOOK OF PROVERBS

Like the book of Psalms, which it follows in the Bible, the book of Proverbs is an anthology or, more accurately, an anthology of anthologies. This is clear from the headings provided in the book itself:

1.1	The proverbs of Solomon son of David, king of Israel.
10.1	The proverbs of Solomon.
22.17	The words of the wise.
24.23	These also are by the wise.
25.1	These are other proverbs of Solomon that the officials of King Hezekiah of Judah copied.
30.1	The words of Agur son of Jakeh, of Massa.
31.1	The words of Lemuel, king of Massa, that his mother taught him.

Although the attribution to Solomon of three of these collections is probably not accurate, taken together with the note that one collection of Solomon's proverbs was copied in the court of Hezekiah, the king of Judah in the late eighth and early seventh century BCE, and the attribution of other proverbs at the end of the book to King

Lemuel, it is clear that in Israel as elsewhere in the ancient Near East one locale for the production of this type of literature was the royal court. The last two headings are more obscure. About Lemuel and Agur we know nothing, and about their land of origin, Massa, only that it is in northern Arabia; wisdom is often associated with the regions east and southeast of Israel.

Within the collections of proverbs the principle of arrangement is often random. Sometimes proverbs with a common theme or vocabulary are grouped together, and proverbs with a similar form, such as numerical sayings (Prov 30.15–31), also occur in proximity, but a deliberate arrangement for the book as a whole has eluded scholars. As in the book of Psalms, which is also an anthology, we find repetitions. For example, the same proverb occurs in both 21.9 and 25.24, with a variant in 21.19.

Because the book of Proverbs is an anthology, and because the proverbs do not refer to specific historical events or circumstances, the individual proverbs are impossible to date with precision, although those having to do with kings probably come from the time of the monarchy, which roughly corroborates the attribution of the collections to Solomon and the "men of Hezekiah." We find little evidence of Greek influence in vocabulary or thought, so that the consensus of scholars is that the collection itself was compiled before the Hellenistic period, probably in the fifth or fourth century BCE.

The proverbs fall into two general categories: those that express, in memorable language, some insights about human experience—like *Poor Richard's Almanac*—and those that have a religious dimension. A close parallel is the Analects of Confucius, in which a successful life and a pious life are related. Yet the two categories are not entirely separate. Proverbs having to do with Yahweh are interspersed with those concerning ordinary life throughout the book, although those with a more explicitly religious dimension occur more frequently in its first nine chapters, perhaps to set a tone for the anthology as a whole.

The religious dimension is for the most part one of an absolute divine justice: Yahweh looks with favor on the righteous and punishes the wicked. Just as the sacred and the secular cannot be separated, neither can the material and what we might call the spiritual. Attention to divine instructions was as important as to those of parents and rulers.

We should note that the authors of the book of Proverbs, like the ancient Israelites in general, did not have a fully developed belief in life after death, especially not in an afterlife where there was bliss for some and damnation for others (see further pages 399–401). The reward for "fear of Yahweh" was thus "riches and honor and [long] life" (Prov 22.4) in the present rather than in some postmortem future.

The Social Worlds of Proverbs

Proverbs contain simple insights into human life expressed in pithy aphorisms and metaphors. Some proverbs may have originated in the life of agrarian towns and villages, as references to seasonal agricultural activities such as plowing, planting, and harvest suggest. Most of the proverbs, however, depict the lives of the wealthy elite, in an urban setting, and especially in the royal court. Many have as their general theme the way to advancement, from correct table manners to a discreet tactfulness; this is unsurprising in view of the role of the royal bureaucracy in the collection and editing of the proverbs. We also find sly critiques of monarchic excesses, as in the numerical saying in 30.29–31 and elsewhere (for example, 29.4, 14; 30.24–28).

While generally conventional in its values, the book of Proverbs testifies to some of the ideals of ancient Israelite law and of the teachings of the prophets concerning social justice. Special attention is repeatedly given to the poor and the needy, whose rights are to be respected even though they are not described entirely sympathetically, and who can even be blamed for their own condition (10.4). The rights of widows and orphans are also to be protected. Resident aliens, on the other hand, are less equitably treated than elsewhere in the Bible, and some proverbs are xenophobic, expressing prejudice and hostility toward outsiders.

The social world of the book of Proverbs is essentially patriarchal, although as in the commandment to honor father and mother (Ex 20.12), the mother's status in the family is acknowledged (for example, Prov 1.8; 10.1). The book of Proverbs ends with an acrostic poem (see Box 20.1 on page 317) celebrating the qualities of an ideal Israelite woman. But the values of the authors of the book of Proverbs are for the most part conventional and male-dominated. The addressee of the book is also male, as is indicated by nearly two dozen explicit addresses to "my son" and by the advice to stay away from the "strange woman."

The Strange Woman

Over and over in the book of Proverbs the young man to whom the proverbs are addressed is warned about a sexual relationship with a "foreign" or "strange" woman. In some passages, such as 7.16–20, she is described in detail, as a woman already married to someone else, who entices the young man to her house. The young man is repeatedly warned that yielding to the seductive overtures of such a woman is a recipe for disaster. On one level, this is practical advice; on another, the designation of the woman as "foreign" or "strange" (that is, a stranger, a non-Israelite) recalls the frequent biblical insistence on marriage within the community.

Yet the passages advising against a relationship with such a woman (and she is always singular) are interspersed among those that advise the young man rather to seek after Woman Wisdom, and so on another, almost allegorical level, the "foreign" woman is a foil, a counterpart, to Wisdom and can be interpreted symbolically, as her alternate designation, "foolish woman" (9.13; 14.1), suggests. To understand this metaphorical meaning, we must look at the figure of Wisdom.

Woman Wisdom

In Proverbs 1–9, and implicitly elsewhere in the book, we find reference to Wisdom as a female figure who speaks to the young man and invites him into her house, and also who accompanies the deity. This "**Woman Wisdom**" speaks frequently in the first person (1.20–33; 8.1–36; 9.1–6) and

identifies herself not just as the divine companion, but also as the source of order in society and success in life (8.15–21).

The same language is found in other wisdom literature, such as Job 28, Wisdom of Solomon 7–9, and Sirach 24. In these texts, "Wisdom" is depicted as a divine being, but scholars are in disagreement about her exact status. For many, she is a hypostasis, a divinized personification of an abstract quality, like Victory or Justice. For others, she has qualities that imply that she is depicted as a goddess. In support of this interpretation, we should note the remarkable hymn in Proverbs 8.22–30, in which Wisdom speaks of herself as having been created before anything else and as Yahweh's companion and even assistant at the creation of the ordered world. The language of this poem is highly mythological, and it also has sexual overtones, a daring appropriation of the common ancient Near Eastern view that every male deity had a female consort.

Drawing, then, on ancient mythology, and likely reflecting the diversity of Israelite practice

FIGURE 24.1 Drawing of one of the graffiti found on a large storage jar at Kuntillet Ajrud in the northern Sinai and dating to the eighth century BCE. The Hebrew inscription mentions "Yahweh of Samaria and his Asherah," who may be the two figures beneath the inscription, with Yahweh on the left and the goddess Asherah on the right. If so, then this is a rare if crude depiction of Yahweh and an expression of popular belief that he had a divine wife.

as well, the authors of the book of Proverbs may be offering an acceptable alternative to goddess worship in the figure of Woman Wisdom, a tree of life more valuable than silver, gold, or jewels (3.13–18).

The praise of the "woman of power" that ends the book has plausibly been interpreted as a continuation of the symbolic depiction of Wisdom, who, somewhat domesticated, is the perfect life companion for an Israelite male (a similar sentiment is expressed in Wis 8.2; Sir 15.2).

THE BOOK OF JOB

"Ye have heard of the patience of Job" (Jas 5.11), says the author of the letter of James in the New Testament, in the famous phrasing of the King James Version. In the book of Job, Job himself begins by demonstrating his proverbial "patience," but he soon becomes angry, passionately protesting his innocence and demanding to know why he has suffered unjustly at the hands of God. Was Job patient or not? Was God just or not? These questions lie at the heart of the interpretation of the book of Job, one of the most difficult and most challenging books in the Bible.

The biblical book of Job is only one chapter in the history of the legend of **Job**, an innocent man who suffered. Although Job is not mentioned in any prebiblical ancient Near Eastern sources, Ezekiel refers to Job as a well-known character in folklore. Speaking of Jerusalem, which is so wicked that, in contrast to Sodom, the presence of good people in the city could not save it, the prophet declares that "even if Noah, Danel, and Job, these three, were in it, they would save only their own lives by their righteousness" (Ezek 14.14). (Danel is not the hero of the biblical book of Daniel, discussed in the next chapter, but the Canaanite hero known also from Ugaritic texts; see Box 5.4 on page 72.) As far as we can tell from this brief reference, the authors of the book of Job made use of an earlier Job legend about as a quintessentially good person in order to explore the problem of innocent suffering.

Structure

The book of Job at first glance has a relatively simple structure, as the following summary shows:

Chapters 1–2	Prologue
3.1–42.6	Dialogues, between Job and his friends, and then between Yahweh and Job
42.7–14	Epilogue

The prologue and epilogue, which are in prose, frame the dialogues, which are in poetry. The first set of dialogues consists of alternating speeches between Job and his three friends, Eliphaz, Bildad, and Zophar, in what originally was three cycles:

I	Job	Chapters 3
	Eliphaz	4–5
	Job	6–7
	Bildad	8
	Job	9–10
	Zophar	11
II	Job	12–14
	Eliphaz	15
	Job	16–17
	Bildad	18
	Job	19
	Zophar	20
III	Job	21
	Eliphaz	22
	Job	23–24
	Bildad	25.1–5
	Job	26; 27–28; 29–31

As is clear from this outline, toward the end of the third cycle, the pattern is disrupted. Bildad's final speech is uncharacteristically short, only five verses long, and Zophar has no third speech. Moreover, rather than being continuous, the final speeches of Job to his friends are interrupted by repetitive introductions (27.1; 29.1; compare 26.1), and in these speeches Job sometimes expresses views more appropriate in the mouth of one of his friends.

A majority of scholars conclude that the book has suffered some dislocation beginning in chapter 25. They differ, however, on the details. Many assign 26.13–23 to Zophar, and also consider chapter 28, a hymn to Wisdom (see pages 387–88) that stresses her inaccessibility, to be a later addition.

Following the last words of Job (see 31.40), a new character appears on the scene, a young man named Elihu. For several chapters (32–37) he attempts to provide a better argument than Eliphaz, Zophar, and Bildad have. Elihu has little new to say, however, and many scholars consider these chapters to be another later addition, especially since Elihu is not mentioned in either chapter 2 or chapter 42.

The conclusion that the present form of the book of Job shows evidence of additions by later hands is not supported by any independent textual data, and recently some scholars have attempted a more holistic reading of the book, in which the inner contradictions somehow make sense. But no consensus exists on these issues.

After Elihu's speeches comes a dialogue between Yahweh and Job. Yahweh answers Job out of the storm and speaks at some length (chaps. 38–39; 40.6–41.34); Job's replies are limited to a few verses (40.4–5; 42.2–6).

Authorship and Date

The author of Job is anonymous, although later rabbinic tradition attributed it to Moses. The time frame of the book is Israel's ancestral period; although we find no mention of any specific figures from Genesis, there are many echoes of Genesis 12–50 in language and setting. Postbiblical Jewish tradition recognized this when it identified Job's unnamed wife as Jacob's daughter Dinah.

Since it belongs to the broader category of wisdom literature, and thus is universal, it is not surprising that the book of Job contains no references to specific historical events or persons that would help date it. As a result, scholars disagree on when it was written; proposed dates range from the tenth to the third centuries BCE, with many preferring a date sometime in the exilic period, perhaps as early as the sixth century.

In that context, the book of Job can be interpreted as a consideration not just of the general problem of **theodicy**, divine justice, but of the issues raised by the destruction of Jerusalem in 586 BCE. This conjecture is supported by verbal connections between Job and the literature of the sixth century BCE, especially Jeremiah, Lamentations, and Isaiah 40–55.

Ancient Near Eastern Parallels

Several ancient Near Eastern texts are often cited as antecedents and parallels to Job. These include:

- "I Will Praise the Lord of Wisdom": A Babylonian poem dating to the second half of the second millennium BCE, this is a thanksgiving hymn to the Babylonian god Marduk. In it, a man who has suffered social, physical, and emotional distress relates how when he called to his gods for help, they did not respond, despite his life of piety:

> Prayer to me was the natural recourse, sacrifice my rule.
> The day for reverencing the god was a joy to my heart.

Puzzled by the discrepancy, the sufferer muses:

> Who can learn the will of the gods in heaven?
> Who understands the intentions of the gods of the underworld?
> Where have human beings learned the way of a god?

Finally, in a dream, a luminous young man sent by Marduk caused the man's health to return:

> The Lord took hold of me,
> The Lord set me on my feet,
> The Lord revived me . . .*

and all of Babylon praised Marduk.

---

* Translation adapted from B. R. Foster (trans.), *From Distant Days*, pp. 304–5, 311.

- "The Babylonian Theodicy": A text dating to ca. 1000 BCE. Like the book of Job, this lengthy poem is in dialogue form. In it, a sufferer, seeking an explanation of his anguish, consults with a friend, pointing out, as does Job, that those who lack piety often prosper and those who pray can become destitute. The friend replies that the intentions of the gods are inscrutable, but in the end, the wicked will be punished. The poem ends with a prayer by the sufferer for pity from the gods. It is also an acrostic (see Box 20.1 on page 317).
- "The Protestation of Guiltlessness": From the Egyptian Book of the Dead (second and first millennia BCE). This lengthy collection of assertions of innocence formed part of the Egyptian burial traditions. In them, individuals were provided with a formulaic catalogue of sins that they had not committed, to be recited as their souls were weighed and judged by Osiris, the divine ruler of the underworld. Job's recitation of what he had not done (Job 31) is often compared to this catalogue. The Egyptian text concludes with positive assertions of piety and goodness, for example:

> I have contented the god with that which he loves. I have given bread to the hungry, water to the thirsty, clothing to the naked, and a boat to the boatless. I have made divine offerings for the gods, invocation-offerings for the blessed dead. Save me, then. Protect me, then.[†]

Scholars have found no direct connection between the book of Job and these and similar texts. They do illustrate the use of the dialogue form, and also how in pondering the problem of the suffering of the innocent, traditional views were often questioned and the nature of divine justice and of the human condition probed, as in the book of Job.

Interpretation

Since translation is one form of interpretation, the ancient translation of the Hebrew Bible into Greek, the Septuagint, dating from the third century BCE, is one of the earliest interpretations we have of the book of Job. But in it, the book looks significantly different from that found in the traditional Hebrew text. The Septuagint text of Job is about one-sixth shorter than the Hebrew, and missing verses are more frequent in later parts of the book. But we also see additions, notably an expansion of the only speech of Job's wife (after 2.9; see Box 24.4 on page 396) and a supplement to the epilogue (after 42.17). Other differences reduce divine responsibility for Job's misfortunes and make Job less angry and more pious. It is possible that the Septuagint translators produced a thoroughgoing revision of Job rather than just a literal translation, but that is less likely than that they were carefully translating the Hebrew text they had, a text significantly different from the traditional Hebrew text. Complicating the picture is another early but fragmentary text, a targum or translation into Aramaic, found among the Dead Sea Scrolls. In this version, the book ends at 42.11, six verses earlier than the Hebrew text.

Several factors may have contributed to cause these variants. First, as with Jeremiah and a few other books, the final form of the text was not fixed; rather, Job was something like a work in progress revised by writers and translators at different times. Second, traditions about Job other than those found in the biblical book certainly existed, and these too may have influenced some of the changes. Finally, some of the changes may have been motivated by theological concerns; in some of the ancient translations, verses that attribute Job's problems directly to God are softened or omitted. It should also be noted that the Hebrew text of Job is among the most difficult of any book of the Bible. More than a hundred words in Job occur nowhere else in the Bible, and many verses are simply unintelligible.

Even with these early variants and linguistic problems, however, the central issue of Job remains clear. As the prologue informs us, Job is a blameless person "who feared God and turned away from evil" (1.1), and in accord with the retributive justice of biblical tradition, he has been

---

[†]   R. K. Ritner, trans., in *The Literature of Ancient Egypt* (ed. W. K. Simpson), p. 274.

amply rewarded. As the result of a challenge from Yahweh to one of the sons of God, "the *satan*" (see Box 24.1), Job suffers a series of disasters, culminating in the deaths of his seven sons and three daughters and in his being afflicted with a loathsome skin disease. Throughout these troubles, Job exhibits his proverbial patience, and despite his wife's advice to the contrary, continues to bless Yahweh. His piety, then, is not dependent on divine favor. To put the problem somewhat differently, Job is an innocent person who suffers at Yahweh's hands. This is the central issue of the book: Presuming divine causation for all aspects of life, why do the innocent suffer? This question, established in the prologue, is the subject of probing in the dialogues, first between Job and his friends, and then between Yahweh and Job.

The dialogues begin with an outburst by Job against God. In it, and throughout the dialogues with his friends, Job is anything but patient, as this vivid paraphrase by Stephen Mitchell shows:

> God damn the day I was born
>   and the night that forced me from the womb.
> On that day—let there be darkness;
>   let it never have been created;
>   let it sink back into the void. . . .
> My worst fears have happened;
>   my nightmares have come to life.
> Silence and peace have abandoned me,
>   and anguish camps in my heart. (Job 3.3–4, 25–26)

This passage begins the dialogues with high intensity, and it is difficult to see any development in Job's emotional state. It is also difficult to ascertain any development in the arguments of his

Box 24.1 THE SATAN

In Job 1–2 appears a figure called "the *satan*," which means something like "the accuser," or, following the forensic metaphors that are employed throughout the book, "the prosecutor." He is a member of the divine council, "the sons of God," who appear periodically before Yahweh (see Box 4.3 on page 54). The word *satan* occurs in four contexts in the Hebrew Bible of an adversary who is greater than human: Job 1–2; Numbers 22.22, 32, of the divine messenger sent to block the prophet Balaam's way; Zechariah 3.1, in a scene of the divine council resembling that in Job 1–2; and 1 Chronicles 21.1, explaining why David was motivated to conduct a census of Israel.

The last example is especially enlightening, for it points to the development of the figure of Satan. In 2 Samuel 24.1, the source for 1 Chronicles 21.1, it was Yahweh himself who incited David to take the census. In revising his source, apparently troubled by this attribution of temptation and sin to the deity, the author of Chronicles transferred the blame to "a *satan*." Only in later Jewish and in Christian tradition would this shadowy figure develop into the familiar devil, with attributes taken from other biblical narratives, such as the serpent in the garden of Eden (Gen 3) and the daystar who fell from heaven (Isa 14.12–15).

Although the *satan* is an important character in the prologue of the book of Job, he is absent in the dialogues and in the epilogue (42.7–17). For Job, for his friends, and for the narrator, it is ultimately Yahweh himself who is responsible for Job's suffering. Yahweh himself says to the *satan*, "You incited me against him, to destroy him for no reason" (2.3). The later development of Satan as a theological explanation for the problem of evil in monotheism is not the view of the book of Job.

friends. These arguments are those of mainstream wisdom tradition:

> Think now, who that was innocent ever perished?
>   Or where were the upright cut off?
> As I have seen, those who plow iniquity
>   and sow trouble reap the same.
> By the breath of God they perish,
>   and by the blast of his anger they are consumed.
>   (Job 4.7–9)
> Do you not know this from of old,
>   ever since mortals were placed on earth,
> that the exulting of the wicked is short,
>   and the joy of the impious is but for a moment?
>   (20.4–5)

The point of these arguments is clear: Since God always punishes the wicked, Job is suffering because he too has sinned. Job has only to confess his guilt, and Yahweh will look with favor upon him once again.

In his replies, Job unequivocally rejects these arguments and challenges the wisdom of his interlocutors concerning divine justice. He observes that he can find no consistent correlation between goodness and the prosperity that indicates divine favor or between wickedness and the misfortunes that result from divine disfavor:

> How often is the lamp of the wicked put out?
>   How often does calamity come upon them?
>   How often does God distribute pains in his anger?
> How often are they like straw before the wind,
>   and like chaff that the storm carries away? . . .
> How then will you comfort me with empty nothings?
>   There is nothing left of your answers but
>   falsehood. (21.17–18, 34)

In expressing his views, Job even employs parody. The pious amazement of the author of Psalm 8,

> When I look at your heavens, the work of your fingers,
>   the moon and the stars that you have established;
> what are human beings that you are mindful of them,
>   mortals that you care for them? (Ps 8.3–4)

is turned by Job into a bitter complaint about excessive divine attention to mere mortals:

> What are human beings, that you make so much of them,
>   that you set your mind on them,
> visit them every morning,
>   test them every moment?

> Will you not look away from me for a while,
>   let me alone until I swallow my spittle?
>   (Job 7.17–19)

Job rejects the trite clichés of his friends and insists on a better explanation from God himself:

> I would speak to Shaddai,
>   and I insist on arguing my case with God. (13.3)

Moreover, Job knows, as do we, the readers, that he is in fact innocent (see also Box 24.2):

> As long as my breath is in me
>   and the spirit of God is in my nostrils,
> my lips will not speak falsehood,
>   and my tongue will not utter deceit.
> Far be it from me to say that you are right;
>   until I die I will not renounce my integrity.
> I hold fast my righteousness, and will not let it go
>   my heart does not reproach me for any of my
>   days. (27.3–6)

And Job catalogues his innocence, stating the highest values of Israelite ethics:

> I delivered the poor who cried,
>   and the orphan who had no helper.
> The blessing of the wretched came upon me,
>   and I caused the widow's heart to sing for joy.
> I put on righteousness, and it clothed me;
>   my justice was like a robe and a turban.
> I was eyes to the blind,
>   and feet to the lame.
> I was a father to the needy,
>   and I championed the cause of the stranger.
> I broke the jaws of the unrighteous,
>   and made them drop their prey from their teeth.
>   (29.12–17)

Job concludes with a subpoena to God himself:

> O that I had one to hear me!
>   Here is my signature! Let Shaddai answer me!
>   (31.35)

From chapter 3 to chapter 31, the discussion and debate has been entirely human; Job and his friends grope and fight to come to a clearer understanding of how God works in the human realm. It is they who make the connection between Job's suffering and God's implied punishment. At no point in the dialogues do Job and his friends hear the word of God. Then, after the interruption of the speeches of Elihu, Yahweh does answer Job.

Box 24.2 "I KNOW THAT MY REDEEMER LIVETH"

One of the most famous passages in the book of Job is 19.25–26. In the King James Version, made famous by its use in the libretto of Handel's *Messiah*, it is translated:

> For I know that my redeemer liveth,
>   and that he shall stand at the latter day upon the earth:
> And though after my skin worms destroy this body,
>   yet in my flesh shall I see God.

In Christian tradition, this has been interpreted as an anticipation of the resurrection of Jesus (the "redeemer") and of the dead.

The verses are among the most difficult in the book of Job. The Hebrew literally means:

> But as for me, I know that my vindicator lives,
>   and that he will at last stand forth upon the dust.
> This will happen after my skin has been stripped off,
>   but from my flesh I would see God.

The "vindicator" is the *goel*, in biblical law the next of kin who is obligated to avenge or to assume the duties of a person, usually someone who has died. Job seems to be saying that he is confident that after he has died, the truth of his case will be demonstrated by his *goel*, but he would rather it happen during his lifetime.

Nowhere else in the book does Job express any belief in a personal, bodily resurrection; that concept does not develop until near the end of the biblical era. Nor does he view the afterlife as a time when his innocence will be ultimately rewarded by God: Throughout the book, he insists on an answer from God in his present life. (On the development of views concerning life after death, see pages XXX–XX.) Just as the book of Job repurposes earlier written traditions, sometimes even inverting their meanings, so too have Christian interpreters reshaped the received text of Job to express Christian concerns and beliefs.

For many interpreters, the very fact of the divine answer is significant. God is neither absent nor silent. His response, however, further complicates the issue. It consists of a magnificent catalogue of the marvels of the created cosmos, in some of the most lyrical, and also most highly mythological, poetry in the Bible. (See Box 24.3.) Yet Yahweh does not give a direct answer to Job's passionate query about why he has suffered.

The world described by the creator is one in which nature is often violent and in which humans play a limited role. Most important, in his speeches Yahweh completely ignores Job's pleas for an explanation of the divine purpose. Job had anticipated this reaction:

> If I summoned him and he answered me,
>   I do not believe that he would listen to my voice.
> For he would crush me with a storm. (9.16–17)

Nevertheless, when Job is finally given the divine response, he apparently returns to the piety and humility that he had shown at the beginning

Box 24.3 BEHEMOTH AND LEVIATHAN

Yahweh concludes his poetic catalogue of the wonders of creation with lengthy descriptions of Behemoth (Job 40.15–24) and Leviathan (41.1–34). Since ancient times, commentators have often identified them as the hippopotamus and the crocodile, while recognizing that their descriptions have a fantastic quality, perhaps because of the unfamiliarity of an Israelite writer with these animals from the Nile valley in Egypt. More recently, many scholars have understood both beasts as forms of the chaos deity destroyed by the storm-god in the battle that preceded creation (see pages 32–37).

Leviathan in particular is a term used for this adversary, in both Ugaritic and Hebrew. Leviathan is a seven-headed serpent, a prototypical dragon, which is how the primeval sea-goddess Tiamat is depicted in Mesopotamian art. In the Bible, Leviathan is identified with the primeval sea (Job 3.8; Ps 74.13) and, in apocalyptic literature (see pages 359–61) describing the end-time, when that adversary of the deity before creation will be finally defeated (Isa 27.1; see also Rev 12.3). In the Bible, Behemoth occurs only in Job 40, which describes it as "the first of God's creations." Ancient postbiblical tradition paired Behemoth with Leviathan, and Behemoth is probably another form of the primeval sea-monster.

In the divine speeches in Job, Behemoth and Leviathan are composite mythical creatures with enormous strength, which humans like Job could not hope to control. But both are reduced to the status of divine pets, with rings through their noses and Leviathan on a leash.

FIGURE 24.2   A Sumerian depiction of combat between a seven-headed dragon and a god, dating to the mid-third millennium BCE. Both in Canaanite myth and in the Bible, Leviathan is described as a seven-headed serpent who is defeated by the storm-god, either Baal or Yahweh, respectively.

of the book. In both of his replies to the divine speeches (40.4–5; 42.2–6), he is docile and submissive, more like the Job of the prologue than the one who had argued so passionately with his friends. His last response to Yahweh (42.1–6) is hard to interpret, and it illustrates the difficulties in understanding the book as a whole. He begins his brief statement with apparently total submission:

> I know that you can do all things,
> and that no purpose of yours can be thwarted.
> (42.2)

He then repeats, although not verbatim, what Yahweh had said to him:

> "Who is this that hides counsel without knowledge?"
> (42.3; see 38.2)

and replies, again with submission:

> Therefore I have spoken, but did not understand;
> things too wonderful for me, which I did not know.
> (42.3)

Then follows a second quotation of Yahweh's discourse:

> "I will question you, and you inform me" (42.4; see 38.3; 40.7),

and then Job's final words in the book:

> I had heard of you by the hearing of the ear;
> but now my eye sees you;
> Therefore I despise myself,
> and repent in dust and ashes. (42.6)

The Hebrew of the last verse is especially difficult and has been understood in very different ways. One is to see this final verse as consistent with those immediately preceding and to understand Job as piously submitting to the divine revelation he has just received. His experience—his vision—was an almost mystical one, in which, enlightened by Yahweh, he no longer felt it necessary to question the divine purpose. Confronted with the wonders of creation as recited by Yahweh, and face to face with Yahweh himself, his perspective shifted dramatically. He recognized that he was insignificant in the divine scheme, being only "dust and ashes" (see Gen 18.27), yet, almost

paradoxically, his vision of Yahweh had in a sense vindicated him. According to this interpretation, experience cannot be reduced to a simple formula, and human reason cannot comprehend the mysterious ways of God. All that is possible is for humans to submit in faith to God's providence, like Job.

Several modern scholars give a very different reading: Job's reasonable question about why he, an innocent man, has suffered, is not answered. Instead, Yahweh, speaking from the overwhelming power of the storm, recites for Job the wonders of creation but ignores Job's immediate concern. Job's response to this blustering tyrant is to say whatever it takes to make him stop talking, so he acquiesces, tongue in cheek.

Despite its presence in the Bible and its allusions to other biblical literature, Job is a book without explicit references to the great events and personalities of Israel's history. We find no promise to the ancestors here, no covenant with Abraham or with Israel, no explication of the divine guidance of the history of Israel and of all nations. The problem of innocent suffering that is the book's focus is universal. Neither Job nor his friends are Jewish, and in the dialogues they rarely if ever refer to the deity by his proper name Yahweh, using more often Elohim ("God"), and especially El and Shadday, the name of the god of the ancestors of Israel and of the Canaanites as well (see further pages 77–79). But the author of Job is Jewish, and uses the name Yahweh in narrative sections throughout the book. Thus, it is Yahweh who answers Job from the storm, revealing himself not as one who acts in history but as the sovereign defeater of the forces of chaos and the establisher of order in the cosmos as whole. This deity is neither loving nor just, but he is all-powerful, and the best mere humans can do is to accept him on his own terms.

Job's reply to Yahweh is not the end of the book. The narrator resumes the old folktale, telling us that Job's fortune is restored, now doubled, and that he receives a new set of children though the means of their arrival is not specified (see Box 24.4). Finally, having lived to a ripe old age, like Israel's ancestors, he dies, "sated and full of days" (Job 42.17; see Gen 25.8; 35.29).

Box 24.4 JOB'S WIFE AND DAUGHTERS

Women occur only incidentally in the book of Job. Job's wife is typical: In the framework narrative, she is mentioned only in 2.9–10 and not at all in the epilogue, and in the dialogues, she is referred to twice, in passing (19.17; 31.10). In the biblical book of Job, she is nameless. In the ancient Greek translation of the Hebrew scriptures, the Septuagint, she is named Dinah, and her brief speech in 2.9 is expanded as follows:

> How long will you persist and say, "Look, I will hang on a little longer, while I wait for the hope of my deliverance?" For look, your legacy has vanished from the earth—sons and daughters, my womb's birth pangs and labors, for whom I wearied myself with hardships in vain. And you? You sit in the refuse of worms as you spend the night in the open air. As for me, I am one that wanders about and a hired servant—from place to place and house to house, waiting for when the sun will set, so I can rest from the distresses and griefs that now beset me. Now say some word to the Lord, and die!*

As the story of Job is subsequently retold, his wife's role becomes more complex; in the postbiblical work *The Testament of Job* she is a major character.

Most other women are given equally cursory treatment in the biblical book. Thus, Job refers in passing to his mother, and to his brothers and sisters, and in his protestation of innocence, he insists that he has never looked on a virgin with desire (31.1) or committed adultery (31.9).

Job's daughters, however, are given unusual attention. The epilogue tells us that Job had seven sons and three daughters, to replace those who had died. While the sons are not named, the three daughters are: Jemimah (which means "dove"), Keziah ("cinnamon"), and Keren-happuch ("horn of eye-makeup") (42.14). As is typical in folklore, the daughters are the most beautiful women in the land (42.15). Moreover, contrary to the usual pattern of inheritance laws, the daughters are given a share of their father's estate. No precedent is found in biblical literature for this arrangement, although in Ugaritic, the daughters of Kirta (see page 72) are to be given the rights of a firstborn son.

---

* Trans. Claude E. Cox, in *A New English Translation of the Septuagint* (ed. A. Pietersma and B. G. Wright; New York: Oxford University Press, 2007), p. 671.

So, the book of Job has an apparently happy ending, but many interpreters find it unsatisfactory. Job has indeed been rewarded for his endurance, and in the end, God has shown himself to be just. But why did all of Job's suffering have to happen, and why, in the service of theodicy, did his children have to die? Job had complained that his sufferings were "without cause" (9.17); in the epilogue, Yahweh affirms that it was Job, not his friends, who spoke the truth (42.7). Perhaps the ambiguity of Job's final reply to Yahweh, and of the book as a whole, is deliberate: No easy answer exists to the problem of suffering, no formula that can adequately explain the justice of God.

time; moreover he has put a sense of past and future into their minds, yet they cannot find out what God has done from the beginning to the end. (3.9–11)

There are—there must be—divinely decided times for various events in life, but humans are unable to know what those times are and hence are also unable to affect the course of the events. Given their woeful ignorance of divine intentions, the best that humans can do is to enjoy life—"to eat, and to drink, and to be merry," in the famous phrase of 8.15 as translated in the King James Version.

The author asks more questions than he provides answers. His conclusion is that even wisdom itself is elusive. The sole certainty in life is death, which is the same for all, regardless of how they have lived their lives:

Everything that confronts them is vanity, since the same fate comes to all, to the righteous and the wicked, to the good and the evil, to the clean and the unclean, to those who sacrifice and those who do not sacrifice. As are the good, so are the sinners; those who swear are like those who shun an oath. This is an evil in all that happens under the sun, that the same fate comes to everyone. (9.1–3)

The subversive character of this idiosyncratic book was evident to the ancients too. Only its presumed authorship by Solomon enabled it to be included in the canon of scripture in the first century CE; even earlier, a pious scribe had added a cautionary epilogue:

The sayings of the wise are like goads, and like nails firmly fixed are the collected sayings that are given by one shepherd. Of anything beyond these, my child, beware. Of making many books there is no end, and much study is a weariness of the flesh. The end of the matter; all has been heard. Fear God, and keep his commandments; for that is the whole duty of everyone. For God will bring every deed into judgment, including every secret thing, whether good or evil. (12.11–14)

Whatever Qoheleth had written, this scribe asserts, is only the idle speculation of intellectuals, those who write books. Rather, the tried and true wisdom of the ancients—as found in collections of proverbs—is sufficient. And the message of that proverbial wisdom is clear: In the end, all that matters is fear of God, because there is a divine justice. But Qoheleth had emphatically disagreed.

THE DEVELOPMENT OF BELIEFS IN LIFE AFTER DEATH IN ANCIENT ISRAEL

The ancient Israelite view of life after death was complex, and it is better to speak of several views. In general, there seems to have been popular belief in some sort of survival for the dead. Standard idioms used for the death of individuals are that they "sleep with their fathers" (for example, Deut 31.16; 1 Kings 2.10; 11.43) or are "gathered to their kin" (Gen 49.29; Num 20.24; Judg 2.10); these can be interpreted both literally, as a reference to the deposit of a corpse in a family tomb, and symbolically, implying that the dead members of a family continued to have some existence.

The most common term for the underworld in the Bible is "Sheol." Like the grave itself, it is a dark, damp, and dirty place, and one descends to it, as one is lowered into a grave or pit; the latter is a frequent synonym for Sheol. It is the land of no return, with gates and bars to keep its inhabitants from getting out. At the same time, like Hades in early Greek mythology, Sheol is a place where the dead do survive, although in a miserable and powerless state. Grave goods are found in many Israelite tombs from the Iron Age (ca. 1200–586 BCE), including jewelry, tools, weapons, combs, mirrors, and amulets, along with jars, bowls, and juglets that would have held food and perfumes for the use of the deceased after death (see Figure 24.3). It must be observed, however, that these funerary offerings are sparse compared to the much more elaborate contents of ancient Egyptian tombs of the wealthy. The Hebrew word *nephesh*, which is often erroneously translated "soul," usually refers to the whole person, or to the essence of the person, and it is the *nephesh* that goes down to Sheol.

FIGURE 24.3   Close-up of a bone repository in a rock-cut tomb in Jerusalem dating to the ninth to seventh centuries BCE. In family tombs like this, which could be used for many generations, the bodies of the deceased were placed on benches until the flesh had decayed. Then the bones, and often the grave goods, were collected and transferred into the repository below the bench. Tombs like this illustrate the biblical idiom that when individuals died, they were "gathered to their fathers" (Judg 2.10).

Sheol is a place where all are equal, whether kings or slaves (Job 3.13–19), but there they cannot do anything. This is the view of Ecclesiastes, for whom death is irrevocable and life after death is devoid of content: "[T]he dead know nothing . . . for there is no work or thought or knowledge or wisdom in Sheol" (Eccl 9.5, 10). As the psalms repeatedly note, appealing to the divine self-interest, for God to allow a person to die, to go down to Sheol, would mean that that person would no longer be able to praise God (for example, Pss 6.5; 30.9); a different view is also found (Ps 22.29). At the same time, as the supreme deity, Yahweh has control over Sheol, just as his Canaanite counterpart Baal was able to defeat Death.

Judging from the prohibitions and condemnations of necromancy, the consultation of the dead, in biblical law and in the prophets, the view that one could have contact with the dead was widespread. The most detailed example is that of the raising of the spirit of the dead prophet Samuel by the woman of Endor (1 Sam 28); surprisingly, the narrative only implicitly condemns the practice. Saul, the king at whose request the medium summoned Samuel, had forbidden it, but the medium is successful and Samuel, called a "god," does come up from the "earth," which here, as often, means the underworld. There is also evidence that in popular religion some form of ancestor worship was practiced in ancient Israel as it was elsewhere in the ancient Near East.

These views parallel those of early Greek writers, who in general thought that all the dead were together in the underworld. Only in the fifth century BCE do we begin to hear of some souls surviving elsewhere, in "the upper regions," and slightly later there developed the notion that the spirit or "soul" (Grk. *psyche*) of the person was distinct from the body. In the dualism of the Greek philosopher Plato and his followers, while the physical part of the person ceased to exist, the soul lived on.

Under the influence of Greek thought, this belief is found in Jewish writings of the Hellenistic period. The soul, some believed, survived after death and at the moment of death was either rewarded or punished for the life that the person had led.

The idea of bodily resurrection developed separately and was not universally held. According both to the first-century CE Jewish historian Josephus and to the New Testament, the Pharisees believed that the bodies of the dead would be raised and reunited with their souls, but the Sadducees did not. The earliest text that unequivocally affirms the bodily resurrection of at least some of the dead and the rewards and punishments that will await them in the life to come is Daniel 12.2–3. This was written in the context of one of the darkest moments in early Jewish history, during the forced Hellenization and persecution by the successors of Alexander the Great in Palestine, especially the infamous Antiochus IV Epiphanes in the early second century BCE. It is ironic that this development was possible in part because of the influx of Hellenistic ideas, many of which had been so strenuously opposed by those who resisted Antiochus. (See further page 406.) In developing the idea of bodily resurrection, Jewish thinkers were able to synthesize Greek views of body-soul dualism with earlier biblical texts that speak of Yahweh's control over Sheol and of his ability to give life as well as to take it away.

THE SONG OF SOLOMON

The short biblical book known as the "Song of Solomon" is also called "the Song of Songs," which is a superlative that means "the best of all songs" (compare "king of kings" or "holy of holies"). In the Jewish canon it is one of the Writings and is generally placed as the first of the Five Scrolls, between the books of Job and Ruth. In Christian Bibles it usually follows Proverbs and Ecclesiastes, so that texts traditionally attributed to Solomon are grouped together.

The book consists of poetic speeches, mainly by two young lovers, with other occasional speakers, the woman's companions ("the daughters of Jerusalem," 1.8; 5.9; 6.1) and her brothers (8.8–9). As its title indicates, the book was attributed to King Solomon, in part because of his reputation as a writer of songs (see 1 Kings 4.32 and Box 15.1 on page 224), and also perhaps because of his sizeable harem, which consisted of "seven hundred princesses and three hundred concubines" (1 Kings 11.3). Although Solomon is mentioned half a dozen times in the Song, he is not its original author, nor is he the imagined lover. Instead, Solomon and his palatial surroundings figure into the fantasies of the lovers. In one passage, the male speaker may be comparing his lover to Solomon's harem and finding her superior:

> There are sixty queens and eighty concubines,
>   and maidens without number,
> My dove, my perfect one is the only one,
>   the darling of her mother,
>   flawless to her that bore her.
> The maidens saw her and called her happy;
>   the queens and concubines also, and they praised
>   her. (Song 6.8-9)

Furthermore, some of the vocabulary of the Song is much later than that of the tenth century BCE when Solomon lived. The consensus of scholars, based on a few words of Persian and possibly Greek origin, is that in its present form it dates to the postexilic period.

The genre of the book is also unclear. Since late antiquity, many interpreters have viewed the Song as a dramatic dialogue consisting of speeches by the two lovers with occasional choral interludes. But the dialogue is not very clearly structured or developed, and verses are often repeated in no evident pattern. The closest ancient Near Eastern parallels are several collections of love poems from Egypt, mostly dating to the late second millennium BCE. As in the Song of Solomon, these poems use lush imagery, and the apparently unmarried young lovers refer to each other as "brother" and "sister." Like the collections in which the Egyptian love poems occur, the Song of Solomon can also be understood as an anthology of love poems, perhaps from several periods, finally collected in the fourth or third century BCE. It is possible that the poems may have functioned as wedding songs, but they were not necessarily written for that purpose.

Metaphors from nature suffuse the book, with frequent references to gardens and vineyards, birds and animals, and fruits, flowers, and perfumes. We find detailed descriptions of the physical beauty of the two lovers, often using culturally distinctive images: The woman describes herself as "black and beautiful" (1.5, a more accurate translation than the older "black but beautiful"); her hair is "like a flock of goats, moving down the slopes of Gilead" (4.1); her nose is like "a tower of Lebanon, overlooking Damascus" (7.4); her teeth are "like a flock of shorn ewes that have come up

from the washing" (4.2); her breasts are like "two fawns . . . feeding among the lilies" (4.5). The man's "eyes are like doves beside springs of water" (5.12); "his lips are lilies, distilling liquid myrrh" (5.13). The sensuous eroticism of the book is also striking, a characteristic sometimes obscured or softened in translation.

So erotic is the Song that since early in the Common Era many Jewish and Christian commentators have interpreted it allegorically, as a description of God's love for Israel or of Christ's love for the church, and this, along with the attribution to Solomon, may have contributed to the book's inclusion in the canon of scripture. The consensus of recent scholars, however, is that the book is originally secular, a conclusion supported by the absence of any reference in it to God and by a remark of Rabbi Akiba (late

FIGURE 24.4   A priestess and her husband, depicted in their tomb in Saqqara, Egypt, dating to about 2400 BCE. Her right hand is resting on his shoulder.

first–early second century CE) that it was sung in taverns.

In the end, we can only marvel at the presence in the Bible of this lyrical celebration of a "love as strong as death" (8.6), set in the springtime when

the flowers appear on the earth;
    the time of singing has come,
and the voice of the turtledove
    is heard in our land. (2.12)

A LOOK BACK AND AHEAD

The book of Proverbs presents a worldview that is predictable and governed by divine justice. With proper study and a devotion to wisdom, humans can discern the ways of God, and parents can teach those ways to their children. The book of Proverbs has a perspective that is essentially the same as that of the Deuteronomists, describing God as one who rewards the righteous and punishes the wicked in this life. In response to this worldview, both Job and Ecclesiastes leave the troubling issue of theodicy, of divine justice, unresolved. The author of Job lets God speak for himself, but in his speeches, God has nothing to say about the problem of the innocent Job's suffering. Ecclesiastes expresses a kind of agnosticism: God exists, but we can never fathom his intentions. It is a measure of the complexity and even the strength of biblical tradition that these books are included in the Bible, where the dominant view is emphatically that there is a divine justice, that God rewards goodness and punishes wickedness. Despite what the Deuteronomistic Historians and the prophets claim, Job and Ecclesiastes remind readers that there are no easy answers, only questions.

The Song of Songs seems to operate on a wholly different plane. While it is in conversation with an existing Solomonic tradition, it is mostly a celebration of the erotic love between an unnamed woman and her lover. If we accept the allegorical reading of this book as one of the reasons for its admission into the canon, then the Song presents Israel as a beautiful woman who longs to be united with her God.

Together, the books within the wisdom corpus present a God who can be known through diligent study (Proverbs), a God whose justice is unpredictable and whose creative powers leave a mere human with his hands covering his mouth (Job), a God whose ways are out of human reach such that no matter how much one toils, "no one can find out what is happening under the sun" (Ecclesiastes), and finally a God who is like a lover whom one longs to find and be joined to (Song of Songs).

In the next chapter we will return to the issues faced by Judeans in the Diaspora. One historical romance, the book of Esther, deals with Judeans in Persia itself. By the end of the fourth century BCE, the Persians had been replaced as rulers of the Near East by the Greeks, and the Hellenistic culture that the Greeks brought would pose further challenges to emergent Judaism. Those challenges will be considered in the next chapter, especially in the book of Daniel.

IMPORTANT NAMES AND TERMS

Each name or term is defined briefly in the Glossary. Its first significant occurrence in this chapter appears in **boldface** type.

Ecclesiastes

Job

Leviathan

proverb

theodicy

wisdom literature

Woman Wisdom

QUESTIONS FOR REVIEW

1. What is wisdom literature? How do biblical examples of wisdom literature resemble others from the ancient Near East?

2. What functions would proverbs have had in ancient Israel?

3. What is the central issue of the book of Job? How is the issue resolved?

4. What is the central issue of the book of Ecclesiastes? How is the issue resolved?

5. Discuss how both the book of Job and the book of Ecclesiastes differ from other biblical traditions.

6. Why has the Song of Songs been interpreted in several different ways?

BIBLIOGRAPHY

For an introduction to wisdom literature, see Richard J. Clifford, *The Wisdom Literature* (Nashville, TN: Abingdon, 1998). Samples of Mesopotamian and Egyptian wisdom literature are found in James B. Pritchard, ed., *Ancient Near Eastern Texts Relating to the Old* Testament (Princeton, NJ: Princeton University Press, 3d ed., 1969); William W. Hallo, *The Context of Scripture*, Vol. 1, *Canonical Inscriptions from the Biblical World* (Leiden: Brill, 1997); Benjamin R. Foster, *From Distant Days: Myths, Tales, and Poetry of Ancient Mesopotamia* (Bethesda, MD: CDL, 1995); Miriam Lichtheim, *Ancient Egyptian Literature: A Book of Readings* (Berkeley: University of California Press, 1973–1980; 2006); and from William Kelly Simpson, ed., *The Literature of Ancient Egypt: An Anthology of Stories, Instructions, and Poetry* (New Haven, CT, and London: Yale University Press, 3d ed., 2003), 224–25.

A good introduction to the book of Proverbs is Katharine J. Dell, "Proverbs," pp. 183–92 in *The Oxford Encyclopedia of the Books of the Bible*, vol. 2, ed. M. D. Coogan (New York: Oxford University Press, 2011; available in Oxford Biblical Studies Online. For a short commentary, see Carole R. Fontaine in *The HarperCollins Bible Commentary* (ed. J. L. Mays; San Francisco: HarperSanFrancisco, 2000), 447–65.

The best short commentary on Job is by Carol A. Newsom, in *The New Interpreter's Bible* (ed. L. A. Keck et al.; Nashville, TN: Abingdon, 1996), 4.319–637. A starting point on the history of the interpretation of Job is the collection of essays edited by Leo G. Perdue and W. Clark Gilpin, *The Voice from the Whirlwind: Interpreting the Book of Job* (Nashville, TN: Abingdon, 1992). The translation by Stephen Mitchell quoted on page 391 is from his work *The Book of Job* (San Francisco: North Point, 1987). For an imaginative modern reading, see Elie Wiesel, "Job Our Contemporary," pp. 211–35 in *Messengers of God: Biblical Portraits and Legends* (New York: Random House, 1976).

For a summary of the evidence concerning Satan, see C. Breytenbach and P. L. Day, "Satan", pp. 726–32 in *Dictionary of Deities and Demons in the Bible* (ed. K. van der Toorn et al.; Leiden: Brill, 2d ed., 1999).

A good introduction to the book of Ecclesiastes is by James L. Crenshaw, "Ecclesiastes, Book of," in *Anchor Bible Dictionary* (ed. D. N. Freedman; New York: Doubleday, 1992), 2.271–80.

A good summary of the evidence concerning life after death in ancient Israel is T. J. Lewis, "Dead, Abode of the," in *Anchor Bible Dictionary* (ed. D. N. Freedman; New York: Doubleday, 1992) 2.101–5; see also "Death, Burial, and Afterlife," pp. 363–81 in P. J. King and L. E. Stager, *Life in Biblical Israel* (Louisville, KY: Westminster John Knox, 2001).

For a good summary of scholarly views about the Song of Solomon, see Roland E. Murphy, "Song of Songs, Book of," in *Anchor Bible Dictionary* (ed. D. N. Freedman;

New York: Doubleday, 1992), 6.150–155. A fuller treatment that emphasizes the erotic dimension of the song is Carey Ellen Walsh, *Exquisite Desire: Religion, the Erotic, and the Song of Songs* (Minneapolis, MN: Fortress, 2000), as does the commentary by Cheryl Exum, *Song of Songs* (Louisville, KY: Westminster John Knox, 2005); a somewhat different view is found in Richard S. Hess, *Song of Songs* (Grand Rapids, MI: Baker Academic, 2005).

Heroes in Foreign Lands: Postexilic Literature and Diasporic Identity

Ruth, Jonah, Esther, and Daniel

After the Babylonian conquest of Judah in 586 BCE, both Judeans in exile and those who remained in the Promised Land found themselves under foreign rule. Babylonian imperial control of the Near East passed to the Persians in the mid-sixth century, and then to the Greeks under the leadership of Alexander the Great in the late fourth. This marks the beginning of what is called the Hellenistic period, which lasted until the Hellenistic empire was taken over by the Romans in the first century BCE. In the Persian and Hellenistic periods, we see the developments of Judaism as a religion of the Diaspora, and so we can begin to refer to the Judean people as Jews. The struggle between the Persians and the Greeks had little direct impact on Jews, whether in Judah itself or in the Diaspora, and it is barely mentioned in the Bible. But the conquests of Alexander had a profound effect—the Greeks brought with them their language, their culture, and their philosophy, irrevocably transforming the entire Near East, a process known as Hellenization, from the Greek word for Greece, *Hellas.*

This flood of Greek ideas inevitably contributed to the development of Judaism, although many Jews fiercely resisted Hellenism both intellectually and even at times militarily, viewing it as a threat to Jewish identity and tradition. During the Persian and Hellenistic periods, new genres of literature appeared. These include prophetic satire, the short story or novella, and a more fully developed apocalypse. Self-contained biblical books like Ruth, Jonah, Esther, and Daniel narrated the stories of heroes living outside their homeland while managing to model steadfast faithfulness to Yahweh and to the Jewish people. Three of these novellas, Ruth, Esther, and Daniel 1–6, can be considered under the rubric of historical romance, featuring a hero who demonstrates loyalty to the Jewish people and to the religion of their ancestors in the often-difficult circumstances of foreign rule. The apocalyptic chapters of Daniel 7–12 address the fears of Jews living under foreign domination and assert the power of Yahweh over the course of history. Finally, the story of Jonah uses humor and satire to communicate the expanding international sphere of influence for the Israelite god Yahweh.

Like the Joseph story in Genesis that is their ultimate model, these romances are short works of fiction. Each has a historical setting, although many of the details are inaccurate. Some scholars have suggested that these inaccuracies are deliberate, signaling to readers that these works are to be understood as fiction. The characters usually are drawn broadly, and women are often major protagonists.

Recurring motifs in these novellas are threats to the protagonists because they are Jewish, ironic reversals of plot in which their persecutors are punished with the same means they had planned to use on the Jews, and satisfying resolutions and happy endings. They seem to have been written both to entertain and to instruct Jews on how to remain faithful to their traditions and to each other under foreign rule. Many also would have provided comfort for those experiencing severe persecution. Perhaps because it was too dangerous to criticize the ruling powers directly, these narratives of resistance and fidelity were deliberately set in earlier periods.

THE BOOK OF RUTH

In the Jewish canon (see Chapter 1), the book of Ruth is one of the Writings. In the Christian canon, Ruth comes between Judges and 1 Samuel because of its setting "in the days when the judges ruled" (1.1). In this position it interrupts the Deuteronomistic History, to which it does not belong. Like the books of Esther and Judith, the book of Ruth is historical fiction, with a woman as protagonist. Unlike Esther and Daniel, the hero of this book is a foreigner, the Moabite Ruth, and she is the one who lives in Diaspora among the Judeans. Although Jewish tradition attributed its authorship to the prophet Samuel, modern scholars are divided over the date of the book, for which almost every period from the tenth to the fourth centuries BCE has been proposed; in any case, it was written some time after the events that it narrates.

The purpose of the book is also unclear. If its genealogical conclusion, which makes Ruth the great-grandmother of King David, is original, the tale may have originated as an explanation of David's mixed ancestry. According to Deuteronomic law, "no . . . Moabite shall be admitted to the assembly of the LORD . . . to the tenth generation" (Deut 23.3); David's connection with Moab must have been something of an embarrassment. By presenting Ruth as a model proselyte and by making Naomi the surrogate mother of David's

ancestor, the embarrassment is mitigated. If the book dates to the postexilic period, it may be intended to counter a limitation of membership in the community to those of pure lineage (see, for example, Neh 13.1–3).

Whatever its origins and purpose, the tale of Ruth "amid the alien corn" (Keats, "Ode to a Nightingale") is a masterpiece of Israelite narrative. The German Romantic writer Goethe called it "the loveliest little whole" of antiquity. As one Israelite writer's view of the premonarchic period, it is noteworthy on several counts. Most of the action of the book advances by dialogue, which accounts for nearly two-thirds of the text, a higher proportion than in any other book in the Hebrew Bible. Moreover, it is principally a story of two women, Naomi, a Judean widow, returning to Bethlehem from Moab, and her Moabite daughter-in-law **Ruth**, also widowed. Together they plot to have Ruth marry Boaz, a wealthy relative of Naomi, so that both women acquire a male protector. The son born to Boaz and Ruth, Obed, serves as a continuation of Naomi and Ruth's dead husbands' lineage and also ensures that both women will be cared for in their old age.

These two women dominate the narrative, which gives us a glimpse not only of how ancient Israelite village society functioned but also of the roles available to women in it. In that society, women were dependent on their male relatives, in this case husbands and sons. When both Naomi and Ruth are left childless widows, they take the initiative to get a distant relative, Boaz, to marry Ruth, and from the male offspring of this union, both women are fulfilled. The legal transaction is conducted at the town's gate, the ordinary place of commerce, judicial proceedings, and informal gatherings, and the women are not present. But their maneuverings have secured the eventual resolution: Boaz's assumption of a nearer kinsman's obligation to Ruth as the widow of a member of the clan.

Often called "**levirate marriage,**" this legal tradition is also attested in Genesis 38 and Deuteronomy 25.5–10. It provides a specific example of the role of the "redeemer" (Hebr. *goel*), the kinsman whose responsibility was to assume the position of male protector when the primary head of household had died. Another example of how legal traditions functioned is the practice of gleaning, in which fields and vineyards would not be completely harvested, leaving the residue for the benefit of the marginalized in Israelite society—the poor, widows, orphans, and resident aliens (see Lev 19.9–10; 23.22; Deut 24.19–22). Less clear is the procedure involving the sandal in Ruth 4.7; even for the narrator it was a custom no longer in use.

Taken as a whole, the book of Ruth is an intimate portrait of rural life in ancient Israel, with its scenes of famine and harvest, and of women's lives in that context. The bond between Naomi and the Moabite Ruth is without precedent. Ruth's fidelity to Naomi and to the Judean people and to Yahweh mark her as a hero who unites with Naomi in order to manipulate the patriarchal system to their mutual advantage. From such stock, the narrator concludes, Israel's greatest king was born.

THE BOOK OF JONAH

In the mid-eighth century BCE, according to the Deuteronomistic History, Jeroboam II, the ruler of the northern kingdom of Israel, "restored the border of Israel . . . according to the word of the LORD, the god of Israel, which he spoke by his servant Jonah son of Amittai, the prophet" (2 Kings 14.25). This obscure prophet is the protagonist of the short book that bears his name, and because he was a prophet, that book is included in the collection of the twelve Minor Prophets. But unlike the books that surround it in the Bible, it contains few of the prophet's own words. Rather, it is a fictional narrative about the prophet **Jonah**, probably written in the early postexilic period, between the sixth and the fourth centuries BCE, which uses satire and irony to convey several messages.

The four chapters of the book of Jonah present four successive scenes. In the first, the prophet receives a divine call, commissioning him to proclaim divine judgment directly to the wicked city of Nineveh, the capital of Assyria, the primary enemy of Israel and Judah from the ninth through the seventh centuries BCE. Jonah is, perhaps understandably, reluctant to undertake this task, and boards a ship headed in the opposite direction from Nineveh. Yahweh will have none of this, and sends a storm that threatens to sink the ship. More pious than the prophet, who is snoring in the ship's hold, the non-Israelite sailors pray to their gods for help. When Jonah reveals that the storm is a divinely imposed punishment on him, they refuse to throw him overboard until they have no choice, another indication of their righteousness. The chapter ends with Jonah being swallowed by a "great fish" (not a whale), a widespread folklore motif.

Chapter 2 is presented as Jonah's prayer for divine aid from the belly of the fish, but it is actually an individual song of thanksgiving (see page 377), probably an independent composition not entirely appropriate to Jonah's specific setting but incorporated into the narrative secondarily. Finally, after three days, the fish vomits Jonah onto the shore, and, realizing the futility of refusal, he heads for Nineveh.

In the third scene, Jonah is in Nineveh. There, in a display of prophetic efficacy and success that is unmatched by any prophet who prophesied to the Israelites, Jonah's message is heeded by the Ninevites. All the city's inhabitants fast and repent, starting with the king himself, and its animals too: Again, the pagans are models of piety. In response, God also repents of the evil he had planned to bring on Nineveh.

Finally, in chapter 4, we see Jonah outside the city, waiting for his prophetic word to be fulfilled. The divine mercy infuriates him, and, quoting an ancient Israelite formula, he complains: "That is why I fled to Tarshish at the beginning; for I knew that you are a gracious God and merciful, slow to anger, and abounding in steadfast love, and ready to relent from punishing" (Jon 4.2; see Ex 34.6). Using a quick-growing plant as a parable, Yahweh reminds Jonah that he has concern for all, even the cattle of Nineveh.

The book has a comical side, but it is also puzzling. It can be understood as a statement of divine freedom, an elaboration of Jeremiah 18.7–8: "At one moment I may declare concerning a nation or a kingdom, that I will pluck up and break down and destroy it, but if that nation, concerning which I have spoken, turns from its evil, I will change my mind about the disaster that I intended to bring on it." The prophets repeatedly pronounced divine judgment on the Assyrians, for their destruction of the northern kingdom of Israel in the eighth century BCE and their attack on Jerusalem in 701 BCE, and the book of Nahum is entirely devoted to an oracle against the Assyrian capital of Nineveh (see pages 300–1). Is the book of Jonah rejecting the intense nationalism of such attacks, suggesting, like Second Isaiah (see Isa 45.12–14; 51.4–5), that Yahweh controls history for good as well as for woe, that Yahweh has a message for all, and that it is the obligation of the Israelites—typified in their prophet Jonah—to proclaim him to the entire world? Or is the central message of the book one of divine forgiveness as a response to repentance, of divine mercy trumping divine justice? With the Promised Land under foreign control and Jews dispersed all over the Near East, the book of Jonah seems to be a creative attempt to understand what this new context means for Jewish identity and the understanding of God's purposes for the entire world. The book ends with God posing a question to Jonah: Should he not have concern for the inhabitants of Nineveh, both human and animal? The question is not answered and therefore leaves open several possible interpretations. The book as a whole seems to use humor to invite the reader to reflect on the ever-expanding sphere of divine activity.

THE BOOK OF ESTHER

The book of Esther is one of the Five Scrolls, which form part of the Writings, the third division of the canon in Jewish tradition; in Christian Bibles it is usually included among the historical books. It is a gripping tale of palace intrigue, in which the Jewish queen of Persia, Esther, for whom the book is named, saves her people from destruction. It is also a puzzling book, for although it shares some plot elements with other short fictions of the postexilic period, it is essentially a secular book, in which God is not mentioned and in which Jewish identity is a matter of ethnicity rather than of religious observance.

The book of Esther is set in the early fifth century BCE during the reign of the Persian king Ahasuerus (Xerxes; 486–465 BCE), but it was probably written in the following century, in the late Persian or early Hellenistic period. Many details in the book concerning the Persian court and the workings of the imperial bureaucracy appear to be accurate, but there is no independent evidence that Esther, Mordecai, Haman, or Vashti ever existed. The book also has a major chronological

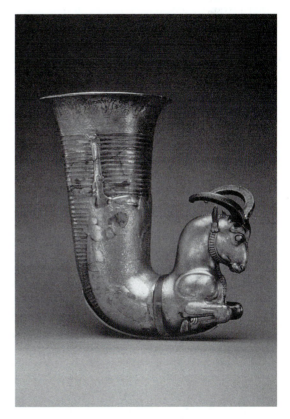

FIGURE 25.1 An ornate Persian drinking cup on a ram, from the fifth century BCE. Made of silver, it is about 8 in (20 cm) high and is the kind of vessel that might have been used at a banquet like that described in Esther 1.5–8.

error: Mordecai is described as one of the exiles deported from Jerusalem in 597 (Esth 2.6; the NRSV emends the text here), which would have made him well over a hundred years old when the events described in the book took place. It is thus the consensus of modern scholars that the book is fictional, a kind of historical novella written partly to provide an etiology, a narrative explanation, for the Jewish festival of Purim.

The story begins with the refusal by the chief wife of Ahasuerus, Queen Vashti, to obey a royal summons to attend a banquet where her beauty would be paraded before the guests, and with her being banished for her rebelliousness. She was replaced by the beautiful **Esther**, the cousin of Mordecai, a Jewish exile from Judah. The king, however, was unaware of Esther's Jewish identity. After Esther became queen, Mordecai uncovered a plot to assassinate the king, which Esther passed on to her royal husband.

The king had appointed a man named Haman as the second highest person in the kingdom, and all except Mordecai acknowledged his status by bowing in his presence. Infuriated, Haman plotted to kill Mordecai and all the Jews in the kingdom, and informed the king that they refused to obey his edicts. The day for their execution, the

thirteenth day of the month of Adar, the twelfth month, was chosen by lot.

Mordecai instructed Esther to intervene with the king to save her people. Violating court protocol, she approached the king and invited him and Haman to dine in her quarters on the following day. Meanwhile, Haman prepared a gallows for Mordecai. That night, suffering from insomnia, the king read reports of how Mordecai had saved his life and asked Haman: "What shall be done for the man whom the king wishes to honor?" (Esth 6.6). Thinking that the king was speaking of him, Haman suggested lavish public acclaim, but the king instructed him to arrange it for Mordecai. Then, at the banquet, Esther revealed Haman's intentions. The king ordered him executed on the gallows he had prepared for Mordecai and gave Mordecai royal authority. Mordecai issued edicts in the king's name protecting the Jews, and on the same day that the Jews were to be killed, they attacked and massacred their enemies. The next day, the fourteenth of Adar, was declared an annual holiday for feasting and rejoicing, called Purim.

In the story of Mordecai, we have a variant of that of Joseph (Gen 39–41), the Jew who although falsely accused becomes the most powerful royal

Box 25.1 THE FESTIVAL OF PURIM

In Esther 3.7, Haman cast a lot (Hebr. *pur*) to determine the day of the Jews' destruction, and when "the wicked plot that he had devised against the Jews" came "upon his own head," these days of **Purim** ("lots") were to be observed as a Jewish holiday (Esth 9.25–26). The word *pur* occurs in the Bible only in the book of Esther and is probably Babylonian in origin. The festival may have been incorporated into Jewish tradition during the exile in Babylonia, with the book of Esther providing an explanatory narrative or etiology that rationalized the adoption of an originally non-Jewish feast; no nonbiblical parallels to the feast are known, however. The earliest mention of Purim in other sources is in 2 Maccabees 15.36, as "Mordecai's day." In Jewish tradition since late antiquity, it has often been celebrated in a boisterous carnival-like atmosphere, with costumed participants booing Haman and cheering Mordecai as the book of Esther is read.

functionary in a Gentile land; the same plot is also found in the book of Daniel (see pages 412–13). Ironically, Mordecai received the honors that his persecutor Haman had desired, and Haman suffers the punishment that he had planned for Mordecai. We also see other ironic reversals. Ahasuerus, "who ruled over one hundred twenty-seven provinces from India to Ethiopia" (Esth 1.1), is easily manipulated by his wives and courtiers. Esther is installed in the royal harem at Mordecai's initiative and initially follows his instructions, but as the plot develops she takes matters into her own hands and even instructs Mordecai. The ultimate reversal is the victory of the Jews over their enemies and their being granted "peace and security" in all the provinces of the Persian empire (9.30).

The secular character of the book of Esther has been observed since ancient times. It never refers to such primary components of Jewish tradition as Abraham, Moses, Torah, covenant, or Jerusalem. For the author of the book, being Jewish has to do with ethnic identity rather than piety. Esther is married to a non-Jew and does not seem to be concerned about dietary purity. The book of Esther never even mentions God. This secular character will be altered in the version of Esther preserved in the ancient Greek translation (see page 419). The primary purpose of the book of Esther, then, seems to be entertainment rather than religious edification, like the holiday of Purim for which the book provides a narrative explanation (see Box 25.1).

THE BOOK OF DANIEL

The book of Daniel has had a significance disproportionate to its relatively short length since it was written in the second century BCE. On a mundane level, the book's scene of Daniel in the lions' den (6.16–24) is well known, and the phrases "feet of clay" (see 2.42) and "the writing on the wall" (see 5.1–9) have become proverbial in English. Moreover, Daniel's fantastic visions have been taken as detailed predictions of the

end of the world since antiquity, and early Christian writers made use of them in their interpretations of Jesus, especially the account of the "son of man" in Daniel 7. But the nature of the book of Daniel is far from agreed upon. In Jewish tradition, it is placed among the Writings, the third part of the Hebrew Bible, in part because of its relatively late date. In the Christian arrangement of the books of the Bible, it is placed among the prophets, after Ezekiel, because the second half of the book appears to consist of predictions. But the book of Daniel is unlike other prophetic books, such as Amos, Isaiah, and Jeremiah, and Daniel is never called a prophet in the book itself, although he was identified as such within little more than a century after the book's composition.

In fact, the book of Daniel is not prophecy, but comprises two distinct genres. Chapters 1–6 are tales of heroic fiction in which Daniel is the protagonist, containing plot motifs like those we have seen in the book of Esther; chapters 7–12 are apocalyptic literature, giving detailed if encrypted interpretations of history and vague predictions of the future. Despite their different content, however, the two parts of the book are linked not just by the figure of Daniel himself, but also by a shared view both of the ultimate supremacy of God and of the progression of empires.

The book of Daniel has another unusual feature: Like the book of Ezra, part of it is not in Hebrew but in Aramaic (see Box 22.2 on page 350). The shift to Aramaic begins in the middle of a conversation between the Babylonian king Nebuchadnezzar (as Nebuchadrezzar is called in this book) and his dream interpreters in Daniel 2.4b, and continues to the end of chapter 7; from chapter 8 to the end of the book, the language is Hebrew. The Aramaic sections thus do not correspond to the two-part structure of the book, and the shifts from Hebrew to Aramaic and back to Hebrew are difficult to explain, except that in general, the book itself is a composite, drawn from different sources, some of which may have been in Aramaic. In this connection, we should also note the additions made to the book in its Greek version (see pages 419–20).

Daniel 1–6

The first six chapters are a collection of interrelated tales concerning a legendary hero named **Daniel**. He is probably not the same "Daniel" (more correctly "Danel") mentioned in the book of Ezekiel (14.14, 20; 28.3), who should be identified with the Danel known from Ugaritic epic (see Box 5.4 on page 72); Ezekiel links this Danel with Noah and Job as legendary ancient righteous individuals, who also happen to be non-Jewish.

The main character of the book of Daniel is a Jew in the Babylonian Diaspora. Faithful to Jewish beliefs and practices, he refuses to worship any god other than Yahweh, the god of Israel, observes the dietary laws, and prays frequently. Like Joseph, he is a divinely endowed interpreter of dreams, and like Joseph and Mordecai, although falsely accused, he eventually rises to a position of prominence in the court of a foreign ruler. Daniel thus serves both as a model of how Jews are to act under foreign rule and as an example of how God will protect his faithful followers. The tales in these chapters also include numerous miraculous details.

In Daniel 1, Daniel and his companions, Hananiah, Mishael, and Azariah, are in training in the court of Nebuchadnezzar and are given Babylonian names, Belteshazzar, Shadrach, Meshach, and Abednego, respectively. At Daniel's initiative, they refuse to eat the food provided for them because it is impure, but after ten days on a diet of only vegetables and water, they are healthier than those who had eaten the assigned rations. When their training is complete, they are recognized as superior to their fellow trainees because God had endowed them with wisdom. They are better than all the other magicians and enchanters in Nebuchadnezzar's kingdom; the Hebrew word for magicians used here occurs elsewhere in the Bible only in the stories of Joseph and Moses, both of whom were superior to the magicians of the Egyptian kings of their times.

Daniel 2 is devoted to a dream that troubled Nebuchadnezzar; he summoned his interpreters, ordering them not only to interpret the dream, but first to tell what he had dreamt. When they were unable to do so, Daniel received a revelation, and after praying to God, went to the king and told him the dream. In it, there was a statue made of different materials, a head of gold, torso and arms of silver, abdomen and thighs of bronze, legs of iron, and feet of iron and clay. A stone smashed the statue and was transformed into a great mountain. The four materials are, Daniel explained, four kingdoms, that of Nebuchadnezzar and three successive kingdoms, each weaker than the previous. The stone is a new kingdom established by God and therefore one that will endure forever.

In Daniel 3, Nebuchadnezzar erects a huge gold statue and orders all to worship it on pain of death by being thrown into a blazing furnace. Shadrach, Meshach, and Abednego, being pious Jews, refuse to do so and are thrown into the furnace. The flames are so hot that they kill those who throw them in, but the young men are protected by an angel. The king then issues a decree promoting them and acknowledging the power of their god.

Daniel 4 contains another royal dream, of a great tree that was cut down by divine command. The tree, Daniel explains, is the king, who will be cast out from his kingdom and become like an animal. As we have seen (on page 331), this probably refers to the mysterious absence from Babylon of Nabonidus, Nebuchadnezzar's successor, rather than to Nebuchadnezzar. The prediction proves true, and when the king recovers, he again recognizes the greatness of God.

In Daniel 5, during a banquet given by King Belshazzar (misidentified as Nebuchadnezzar's son and successor) at which the guests drank from goblets looted from the Temple in Jerusalem in 586 BCE, disembodied fingers mysteriously appear and write on the wall the words "Mene, mene, tekel upharsin." No one at the banquet is able to decipher the words, except Daniel. He decodes the words, which literally refer to units of weight (a mina, a mina, a shekel, and two paras [half-shekels]), by their etymology: God has numbered (Aramaic mena) the days of Belshazzar's kingdom, he has weighed it out (teqal), and it will be divided (perisat) between the Medes and the Persians. That night, the king is murdered, and his kingdom given to an otherwise unknown ruler, Darius the Mede.

FIGURE 25.2 Daniel in the lions' den, in an eleventh-century Spanish codex.

Daniel 6 is a variation on chapter 3. Darius is about to appoint Daniel as head of his governors, when they plot against him "in connection with the law of his God" (6.5). They persuade Darius to decree that only he is to be worshiped, and anyone who refuses to do so will be thrown into a lions' den. Daniel, a pious Jew who prays only to God, and facing Jerusalem, is accordingly thrown to the lions, to the king's regret, but an angel saves him. The next day, the king is relieved to discover that Daniel is unharmed, orders his accusers to be thrown to the lions themselves along with their wives and children, and recognizes the power of the god of Daniel, as "the living god, enduring forever" (6.26).

These narratives are relatively freestanding, set in the reigns of three different kings. They probably formed part of a cycle of tales about Daniel that circulated widely in the Hellenistic period but originated as early as the Persian period. The tales were collected and modified by the author of the book of Daniel in the second century BCE. As in the other narrative fictions that are the focus of this chapter,

the history and chronology are confused. Thus, Nebuchadnezzar assumed the throne in 605 BCE, and the first exile from Judah took place in 597, the seventh year of his reign (see Jer 52.28), but his dream, interpreted by Daniel, one of the exiles, is dated to the second year of his reign (Dan 2.1). The successors of Nebuchadnezzar were Amel-Marduk (Evil-merodach, 2 Kings 25.27) and Nabonidus, not Belshazzar, as Daniel 5.2 states; Belshazzar was Nabonidus's son and coregent (see further page 331). Darius the Mede is unknown and is probably a confusion with the Persian king Darius, who succeeded Cyrus in 522. These errors suggest that the book was written a considerable time after the events described, or they may be deliberate indications that it is not to be understood as historical.

Daniel 7–12

In contrast to the first half of the book, which is a third-person narrative about Daniel, beginning in chapter 7 almost all of the rest of the book is a first-person account supposedly by Daniel himself. But the character of Daniel is very different. Whereas in the first half of the book, Daniel was the consummate interpreter of the dreams of others, in the second half, he himself has dreams and visions and can interpret them only with the assistance of the angel Gabriel. These chapters also exhibit a developed angelology (see Box 25.2). The presence of the messenger from heaven is an important characteristic of apocalyptic literature, a genre for which Daniel 7–12 provides the most developed example in the Hebrew Bible. (For a fuller discussion of apocalyptic literature, see pages 359–61.)

Like other apocalyptic literature, these chapters are mythological in tone and draw heavily on earlier biblical material, as the vision in Daniel 7 illustrates. The four creatures come from "the great sea," which as we have often seen is the primeval force of chaos needing to be controlled by a storm-god. The deity appears as the "Ancient of Days," a title reminiscent of epithets of the god El, "the father of years" in Ugaritic texts and "the eternal one" in Genesis. This white-robed and white-haired "Ancient of Days" is seated on a fiery wheeled throne (compare Ezek 1.13–28) and surrounded by innumerable attendants (as in Deut 33.2; Ps 68.17). A meeting of the divine council is taking place, at which Daniel is an observer, like the prophets of old (see 1 Kings 22.19; Isa 6.1; Jer 23.18; see further pages 247–48). At the meeting "the court sat in judgment, and the books were opened" (Dan 7.10). The last most terrifying of the four beasts was destroyed, and then Daniel saw a figure "like a son of man," coming with the clouds of heaven and given supreme power (see Box 25.3).

The interlocking visions of Daniel 2 and 7–12 describe in symbolic language the succession of imperial powers in the ancient Near East from the sixth to the second century BCE; see Box 25.4. The four empires are those of Babylonia (609–539 BCE), Media (originally independent, but united with Persia in the mid-sixth BCE century by Cyrus the Great), Persia (539–332), and Greece under Alexander the Great (336–323). After Alexander's death, his empire was divided and there was a succession of rulers, whose reigns are presented in the narrative

chronology of the book as revelations to Daniel concerning the future. The later the ruler, the more detailed is the description in Daniel, and the last ruler referred to in the book is Antiochus IV Epiphanes, whose edicts provoked the revolt of the Maccabees in 167 BCE.

The prominence of Antiochus IV is obvious and also important. In the visions, he will replace the prescribed offerings in the Temple in Jerusalem with an "abomination that makes desolate" (Dan 11.31; 12.11) and will persecute the "people who are loyal to their god" (11.32). This shift from vagueness to precision is the principal reason for the scholarly consensus that the book was written during the difficult years immediately preceding the revolt of the Maccabees in 167 BCE. The book is thus a work of propaganda, arguing in often symbolic and extravagant language that God will ultimately prevail for his people over the forces of evil, of which Antiochus is the latest manifestation.

That deliverance has not yet happened at the end of the book, but is only promised. When will it happen? Here the book is again vague: In "a time, two times, and half a time" (12.7; see also 7.25), perhaps meaning that the persecution will end after three and a half years (the 1,290 days of 12.11). The book concludes with a message of hope for Daniel himself, who according to the book's narrative chronology, lived centuries before the events that are presented as prediction: "But you, go your way, and rest; you shall rise for your reward at the end of the days" (12.13). Daniel himself, as one of the wise, will be raised from the dead, and with them "shine like the brightness of the sky . . . like the stars forever" (12.2–3); the concept of the resurrection of the dead (see further pages 399–401) is first mentioned in the Hebrew Bible here.

A LOOK BACK AND AHEAD

The Greek takeover of the Near East had a profound impact on emergent Judaism. For some, the arrival of the Greeks was an opportunity; for others, it was a threat to their beliefs and practices, and even their survival. The books of Esther

Box 25.2 ANGELS AND DEMONS

In the book of Daniel, we find unnamed angels in 3.28 and 6.22, and two named angels, Gabriel, God's principal messenger (Dan 9.21), and Michael, the warrior angel (10.13). Both angels and demons appear frequently in literature of the Second Temple period.

The English word "**angel**" comes from the Greek *aggelos*, which means "messenger" (as does the Hebrew word *mal'ak*, for which *aggelos* is the ordinary translation) and refers to both human and divine messengers. Although most English translations use the term "angel" for this word in the Hebrew Bible, only in its latest books does it come to mean the benevolent semidivine beings familiar from later mythology and art. In earlier biblical literature, the term simply means a messenger sent by God, probably to be understood as one of the lesser members of the divine council presided over by Yahweh. Thus, Jacob dreams of a staircase between heaven and earth, on which messengers are going up and down (Gen 28.12), and these divine messengers often appear to human beings to announce divine protection and assistance. In the postexilic period, with the development of explicit monotheism (see Box 21.2 on page 340), these divine beings—the "sons of God" who were members of the divine council (see further Box 4.3 on page 54)—were in effect demoted to what are now known as "angels," understood as finite beings created by God, but immortal and thus superior to humans. Corresponding to the angels are malevolent entities, or demons, understood as "fallen" angels.

Later Jewish and Christian traditions will develop elaborate systems of angelology and demonology, often based on reinterpretations of earlier biblical passages. There are various ranks or "choirs" of angels, among which are included the cherubim and seraphim of biblical tradition. The demons are headed by Satan, identified in postbiblical Jewish and Christian writings as the snake in the garden of Eden (Gen 3.1). He is also called Lucifer (Isa 14.12; see also Lk 10.18), Belial, and Beelzebul, and his lineage can be traced back to the sea-monster of ancient Near Eastern myth. In Christian apocalyptic, he is identified as "the great dragon . . . that ancient serpent, who is called the Devil and Satan, the deceiver of the whole world" (Rev 12.9); see further Box 24.1 on page 391.

The dualism implicit in the conception of angels and demons is heavily influenced by the ancient Persian religious tradition of Zoroastrianism, which viewed the world as a battleground between forces of good and forces of evil, between light and darkness, imagery found in many subsequent Jewish and Christian writings, especially apocalyptic literature (see further pages 359–61).

and Daniel present fictional models of how to survive under foreign rule. As the Jewish community in Judea faced more and more difficulties under the Greeks and then the Romans, the issue of divine justice, of theodicy, would become as pressing as it had been in the aftermath of the destruction of Jerusalem in 586. Alongside these weighty questions are more practical concerns: How does a Jew live in a foreign land? What does she eat? To whom does he pray?

The book of Daniel is the latest of the books of the Hebrew Bible, the canon of Judaism; in some

Box 25.3 "SON OF MAN"

Mainly because of its use in the New Testament, the term **"son of man"** has been the subject of considerable discussion. It is used in a general sense in the Bible to mean "human being," often in contrast to a divine being. The prophet Ezekiel is repeatedly addressed as "son of man" (Ezek 2.1; etc.), as is Daniel himself (Dan 8.17), in both cases emphasizing their status as mere mortals, inferior to the one making a revelation to them. (In all of the occurrences of the term in the Hebrew Bible, the NRSV paraphrases it with "human being," "mortal," and the like.) "Son of man" is also frequently used by Jesus in the Gospels as a way of referring to himself.

In Daniel, the term is used once of one "like a son of man coming with the clouds of heaven" who was presented to the Ancient of Days and given universal rule (Dan 7.13). Here we have a figure who looks human but is clearly more than human. The precise identification of the figure is debated. One possibility is that it refers to the angel Michael, who elsewhere in the book of Daniel is a leader, together with Gabriel, of divine forces against Persia and Greece, and who is also the protector of the Jewish people. If Michael is the "one like a son of man," then he is given supreme power on earth. A second possibility is that the figure "like a son of man" is the faithful people of Israel personified, "the holy ones of the Most High," who also are given an "everlasting kingdom" (7.27). A third identification, made in Jewish writings as early as the first century CE, is as a Messianic figure. This is also found in the New Testament, which, as part of its understanding of Jesus as the Messiah, speaks of his return "in clouds with great power and glory" (Mk 13.26) to gather the elect and to punish the wicked.

Box 25.4 OUTLINE OF THE VISIONS OF SUCCESSIVE KINGDOMS IN THE BOOK OF DANIEL

Empire	Daniel 2	Daniel 7	Daniel 8
Babylon	Head of gold	First beast (lion)	————
Media	Torso and arms of silver	Second beast (bear)	First horn of ram
Persia	Belly and thighs of bronze	Third beast (leopard)	Second horn of ram
Greece	Legs of iron	Fourth beast (horns)	Great horn of goat
Alexander's successors	Feet of iron and clay	Ten horns	Four horns of goat
Antiochus IV	————	Little horn	Little horn of goat

Christian canons, there are slightly later works. For both religious communities the ending of the canon is somewhat arbitrary, for the history of Judaism has continued, as have the religions derived from it, Christianity and Islam. The last books of the Hebrew Bible (and of the Old Testament) to be written are thus not a conclusion, but a stage in an ongoing process. That process continues in other Jewish writings of the Hellenistic and Roman periods, and, after the fall of Jerusalem to the Romans in 70 CE, ultimately in rabbinic literature. It also continues in a different line in the New Testament and, later, in the Qur'an.

All of these writings exhibit not just the creativity but also the diversity that characterize the books of the Hebrew Bible. This diversity creates a tension that is not negative, but rather productive; each generation in effect rethinks the fundamentals of tradition for itself, or, to put it somewhat differently, the process of interpreting scriptural texts begins in those texts themselves and continues beyond them. We have seen this process at work, for example, in Deuteronomy's alternate collection of laws, in the revision of the history of the monarchy found in 1 and 2 Chronicles, and in innumerable smaller ways in almost every book of the Old Testament. The process of interpretation does not end with the close of the canon of texts regarded as scripture, but has continued to the present, as each community of faith for which the texts are in some sense authoritative reconsiders how they are relevant to its changing circumstances. In that sense, the Bible is an open-ended book, inviting, even authorizing, its readers to continue the task of interpretation. Moreover, interpretation is found not only in explicitly religious texts and commentaries, but also in literature, art, and music that uses biblical themes. For all of these reasons, the Bible is one of the most important, most challenging, and most rewarding books to study.

IMPORTANT NAMES AND TERMS

Each name or term is defined briefly in the Glossary. Its first significant occurrence in this chapter appears in **boldface** type.

angel	Jonah	Ruth
Daniel	levirate marriage	son of man
Esther	Purim	

QUESTIONS FOR REVIEW

1. How is the heroism of the Moabite Ruth different from that displayed by Esther and Daniel?

2. What role does humor and satire play in the book of Jonah?

3. How do the stories of Esther and Daniel address the difficulties of Jews living in Diaspora?

4. Why do most scholars date the book of Daniel to the second century BCE rather than to the sixth century BCE when Daniel is reported to have lived?

5. What aspects of apocalyptic literature like that found in Dan 7–12 would prove helpful to Judeans living under oppressive foreign rule?

BIBLIOGRAPHY

For the history of the period, see Leonard J. Greenspoon, "Between Alexandria and Antioch: Jews and Judaism in the Hellenistic Period," chap. 9 in *The Oxford History of the Biblical World* (ed. M. D. Coogan; New York: Oxford University Press, 1998; pb 2001; available in Oxford Biblical Studies Online).

For an introduction to the book of Ruth, see Mary Joan Winn Leith, "Ruth," pp. 279–82 in *The Oxford Encyclopedia of the Books of the Bible*, vol. 2, ed. M. D. Coogan (New York: Oxford University Press, 2011; available in Oxford Biblical Studies Online). One of the best commentaries on Ruth is Edward F. Campbell, *Ruth* (Garden City, NY: Doubleday, 1975).

A good short commentary on the book of Jonah is by Sidnie White Crawford, "Jonah," in *The Harper-Collins Bible Commentary* (ed. J. L. Mays; San Francisco: HarperSanFrancisco, rev. ed., 2000), 656–59. The same scholar also has a good short commentary on Esther in *Women's Bible Commentary* (ed. C. A. Newsom, and S. H. Ringe, and J. E. Lapsley; Louisville, KY: Westminster John Knox, 3d. ed., 2012), 201–7. An excellent fuller commentary on Esther is by Jon D. Levenson, *Esther: A Commentary* (Louisville, KY: Westminster John Knox, 1997).

For Daniel, an excellent introduction is Carol A. Newsom, "Daniel and the Additions to Daniel, pp. 159–73 in *The Oxford Encyclopedia of the Books of the Bible*, vol. 1, ed. M. D. Coogan (New York: Oxford University Press, 2011; available in Oxford Biblical Studies Online). See also her *Daniel: A Commentary* (Louisville, KY: Westminster John Knox, 2014).

The Apocryphal/Deuterocanonical Books

In Chapter 1 we saw that some important Jewish religious writings of the late biblical period are considered part of the canon of scripture by the Roman Catholic and Orthodox churches, but not by Jews and Protestants. These works are known as the Apocryphal or Deuterocanonical books, and they contain many of the genres found elsewhere in the Bible: historical narrative, short works of fiction, wisdom literature, hymns, and apocalyptic. In this appendix we will briefly examine them and their relationship to other biblical literature.

REVISIONS OF AND ADDITIONS TO BIBLICAL BOOKS

In antiquity, the concept of a literary work was more fluid than it is today, and later writers often changed or added to earlier compositions. Several books of the Bible that were modified in this way are included in the Apocrypha in their revised form.

Additions to the Book of Esther

The ancient Greek translation of the Hebrew Bible, the Septuagint, has a revised and expanded version of the traditional Hebrew text of the book of Esther (see pages 409–411). One motivation for many of the changes was to make an apparently secular book more explicitly religious. In some modern Bibles the entire Greek text of Esther is presented with the additions inserted where they occur; reading this version in comparison to the shorter Hebrew text shows the differences between the two books.

The Greek version of the book of Esther adds repeated references to God guiding events and includes lengthy prayers by Mordecai and Esther, making both more pious than they are in the Hebrew version. Esther now hates that she sleeps with someone who is uncircumcised and apparently observes Jewish dietary laws. These additions were incorporated at different times, probably before the end of the second century BCE.

Additions to the Book of Daniel

The Septuagint includes several additions to the book of Daniel (see pages 411–417). But unlike those to the book of Esther, which amount to a rewriting of the book, each of the three additions to Daniel is relatively self-contained, elaborating on or providing additional narratives in the style of Daniel 1–6. They are preserved only in Greek, but at least some of them were originally written

419

in Hebrew or Aramaic, probably in the late Persian or early Hellenistic period.

The Prayer of Azariah and the Song of the Three Jews

The first addition occurs between Daniel 3.23 and 3.24, right after Shadrach, Meshach, and Abednego have been thrown into the fiery furnace. The addition states that they sang hymns and prayed, and two prayers follow. The first (vv. 3–22) is attributed to Abednego (called by his Hebrew name Azariah); like some psalms found in other biblical narratives, it was an independent work only secondarily inserted into the text. It is a communal petition (see page 377), acknowledging the community's failure to obey divine commandments and praying for divine deliverance. Since the three have been thrown into the fire because they refused to bow down to the golden statue that Nebuchadnezzar had made, the psalm scarcely fits their situation.

The addition continues with a prose interlude (vv. 23–27), in which the Chaldeans (the Babylonians) make the fire so hot that they themselves are burned, but inside the furnace, it is cool because of the presence of an angel of the Lord. A lengthy hymn follows (vv. 29–68), in which variations of a responsive refrain are repeated. The hymn is a communal praise of God, especially for the wonders of creation, and, except for the final verses, which refer to the three in the furnace, seems also to have been an originally independent composition.

Susanna

The second addition is usually added to the book as an appendix, although it takes place early in Daniel's life in Babylon. It is a classic tale of false witnesses exposed by a clever interrogator, and has been called the first detective story.

Two lecherous old judges, who are hearing cases in the house of a wealthy man, attempt to force his beautiful and virtuous wife, Susanna, to sleep with them. When she screams for help, they accuse her of having committed adultery with a young man, and because of their standing in the community, they are believed. Sentenced to death, Susanna

prays to God. Just before she is to be executed, "a young man named Daniel," not previously introduced, states that he will not participate in the communal execution, for the trial has been improperly conducted. The execution is postponed, and Daniel questions the witnesses separately. When details of their testimony are inconsistent, he accuses them of perjury and perversion of justice, and they are executed instead of Susanna. The story concludes with a note that this was the beginning of Daniel's reputation, presumably for wisdom.

Although set in the Diaspora, the tale is entirely an intra-Jewish narrative; the villains are Judeans, as are the heroes, Susanna and Daniel. The somewhat simplistic moral of the story is that obedience to the law of Moses will be rewarded by God, and the innocent will be vindicated.

Bel and the Dragon

The third addition is a two-part narrative based on the frequently occurring postexilic motif of a satire against the worshipers of false gods. The tale is set in the mid-sixth century BCE, in the time of Cyrus, the king of Persia who captured Babylon. Cyrus questions Daniel about his failure to worship the Babylonian deity Bel (another name of Marduk), who consumes large quantities of food every day. Daniel proves that it is Bel's priests and their families who are eating the food rather than Bel himself, and Bel's temple is destroyed and the priests killed.

In the second part, Daniel poisons a great dragon or serpent also worshiped by the Babylonians, proving that the serpent is not divine. Pressure from the Babylonians forces the king to throw Daniel into the lions' den (a variation on Dan 6.16–24). But the lions, despite having been starved, leave Daniel unharmed, and Daniel himself is miraculously fed by the prophet Habakkuk. Once again, the king recognizes that Daniel's god is the true God, and his accusers are thrown to the lions and immediately devoured.

The moral of this composite narrative is clear: Judeans in the Diaspora should recognize that only God, the creator of all, is to be worshiped. As in the tales in Daniel 1–6, Daniel is able to outwit the pagans, and the truth of monotheism is affirmed.

1 Esdras

There are two books of Esdras, the Greek rendering of the Hebrew name Ezra. The book of 1 Esdras (also sometimes called 3 Esdras) is a composite work, consisting of excerpts from the books of 2 Chronicles, Ezra, and Nehemiah in a somewhat different order and with minor variants and additions:

- 1 Esdras 1   = 2 Chronicles 35.1–36.21
- 1 Esdras 2.1–15   = Ezra 1.1–11
- 1 Esdras 2.16–30 = Ezra 4.6–24
- 1 Esdras 5.7–46   = Ezra 2
- 1 Esdras 5.47–73 = Ezra 3.1–4.5
- 1 Esdras 6–7   = Ezra 4.24–6.22
- 1 Esdras 8.1–9.36 = Ezra 7–10
- 1 Esdras 9.37–55 = Nehemiah 7.73–8.12

This use of earlier texts is an example of how many ancient writers worked, freely quoting, abridging, rearranging, and supplementing their sources. The book probably dates to the second century BCE.

The principal addition is 1 Esdras 3.1–5.6, a charming tale whose basis is a riddle: What is the strongest force in the world? Three members of the personal bodyguard of the Persian king Darius argue in turn that wine, the king, and women are the strongest force. The third guard adds that truth is the strongest force of all because it is a manifestation of God. This third speaker is identified as Zerubbabel, and the king offers to give him whatever he wants. Zerubbabel replies that he wants the king to fulfill his promise to assist the reconstruction of the Temple in Jerusalem. The king agrees and gives orders to that effect. Thus a popular tale has been revised to make its hero the leader of the reconstruction (see page 349).

Several other postbiblical writings have Ezra's name attached to them; one of them, 2 Esdras, is discussed on pages 426–27.

HISTORIOGRAPHIC LITERATURE

In addition to the reworked account in 1 Esdras, the Apocrypha include other historical narratives.

1 Maccabees

The principal account of the period from 185 to 135 BCE, and especially of the Judean revolt in 168 BCE against the religiously offensive policies of Antiochus IV (see further pages 401), is found in the book known as 1 Maccabees, originally written in the late second or early first century BCE in Hebrew; ironically, this chronicle of resistance to Hellenization is preserved only in Greek. Although not part of the Jewish canon, it is a significant writing for Jews, containing among other things an account of the origins of the festival of Hanukkah.

First Maccabees has a hybrid style, combining both Hellenistic and biblical models. Throughout the book, the principal characters give speeches, as in Greek historical writings, but the author also incorporates poetic petitions and hymns reminiscent of biblical prototypes. While it uses authentic sources in its pragmatic account of the victories of the Maccabees, it is a partisan account, written to legitimate their rule.

2 Maccabees

The book of 2 Maccabees is another account of the Maccabean revolt, paralleling 1 Maccabees but covering a shorter period, from 175 to 161 BCE. It was written in Greek, perhaps in Egypt, in the late second or early first century BCE.

There are many differences between 1 and 2 Maccabees. Second Maccabees omits some details found in 1 Maccabees, and we also find inconsistencies of chronology, most notably concerning the order of events. The geography of 2 Maccabees is confused at points and lacks the precision of 1 Maccabees, suggesting that the author (or his source) was not personally familiar with locations in Judea.

Second Maccabees is infused with the stylistic conventions of Greek historiography, such as addresses to the reader by the author, quotations of official records, and frequent speeches by the principal characters. Yet while 1 Maccabees has a decidedly secular character, 2 Maccabees is more explicitly religious. The book mentions God repeatedly, and we see several examples of direct divine intervention, some of which have an apocalyptic character.

Second Maccabees ends with the defeat of Nicanor, the general of Demetrius I, in 161 BCE (see 1 Macc 7.26–50). The decisive victory over one of the persecutors of the Jews became a national holiday, the "Day of Nicanor" on the day before Purim, now no longer observed. Despite its very biblical flavor, 2 Maccabees also shows the effects of Hellenization, including its having been written in Greek.

4 Maccabees

The book called 4 Maccabees is not part of the canon of any religious community, although since ancient times it has often been included in editions of the Bible because it includes a retelling of events described in 2 Maccabees. It was probably written, in Greek, during the same general period as the Wisdom of Solomon (first century BCE to first century CE; see pages 425–26) and shares with it a philosophical tone and belief in the immortality of the soul. In the introductory chapters, the author, whose identity and place of origin are unknown, gives examples of virtue from Jewish history and practice, and then moves to a summary of the crisis that led to the revolt of the Maccabees. Most of the book, however, is devoted to the parallel stories of Eleazar and of seven sons of a devout "Hebrew mother," who suffered horrible deaths because they would not stop observing Jewish dietary laws, but were given a reward in heaven.

HISTORICAL FICTION

Two books of the Apocrypha are a kind of historical fiction, in the form of a novella, like the book of Esther (see further pages 409–11).

Tobit

The book of Tobit is a tale illustrating how Judeans are to live under foreign rule, emphasizing individual piety. The book was probably originally written in Aramaic, or perhaps in Hebrew; the book is best preserved in its Greek translation, however, and in that version, it was included in the Christian canon until the Reformation. It probably dates to the early Hellenistic period, the fourth or third century BCE, before the persecutions of the early second century BCE.

The narrative setting of the book is the Diaspora among the exiles deported by the Assyrians from the northern kingdom of Israel in the late eighth century BCE, although the book is confused about Assyrian history, chronology, and geography. There are two interlocking plots. The first concerns the hero for whom the book is named, Tobit, a pious Jew living in the Assyrian capital of Nineveh. Although originally a favored courtier of the Assyrian king Shalmaneser, Tobit fell into disfavor with Shalmaneser's successor Sennacherib. Tobit's property was confiscated and he was forced to flee, but when the evil king Sennacherib died, Tobit was reinstated because his nephew Ahiqar was a court official. His troubles had not ended, however, for while he was piously burying the dead, a sparrow dropped its dung on him and he was blinded. Tobit's wife Anna was forced to work, while he asked that God take away his life.

At this point the scene shifts far to the east at Ecbatana in Media, where a distant relative of Tobit, Sarah, was also praying that she be allowed to die, for she had been afflicted by a demon who had killed in succession seven of her husbands before their marriages had been consummated. In response to both Tobit's and Sarah's prayers, the angel Raphael was sent to rectify their situations.

Tobias, Tobit's son, and Raphael, disguised as a man, made their way to Media. On the journey, a large fish jumped out of the Tigris River, and following Raphael's directive, Tobias killed it, kept its inner organs as medicine, and roasted and salted the rest. When they reached their destination, Raphael arranged a marriage between Tobias and the hapless Sarah, his distant cousin. Following Raphael's instructions, on the wedding night Tobias put the liver and heart of the fish on the incense that was burning in the bridal chamber, and the stench forced the demon to flee all the way to Egypt. The successful nuptials were celebrated for another two weeks. Finally, Tobias and Sarah went back to Nineveh and Tobias smeared the bile of the fish on Tobit's eyes, healing his blindness.

With its intricate plot and well-developed characters, the book of Tobit is highly entertaining, but it is also a religious text, providing instruction for Jews about how to survive in the Diaspora as a community of believers.

Judith

The book of Judith is named for its heroine, a fictional character who uses sexual wiles to save her people. The name Judith literally means "the woman of Judah" or "the Jewess," suggesting that Judith is a model of the ideal Jewish woman and of Judaism itself. The book's setting is Judea, as Judah came to be called in the Hellenistic and subsequent periods. It was probably written during the second century BCE, not long after the Maccabean revolt. It is known only in Greek, although it may have been translated from a Hebrew or Aramaic original.

As in other Jewish novellas of the late biblical period, some historical details in the book of Judith are inaccurate. The opening verse introduces Nebuchadnezzar as king of the Assyrians in Nineveh. But Nebuchadnezzar was a Babylonian, not an Assyrian, and the Assyrian capital of Nineveh was destroyed eight years before he assumed the throne in 605 BCE. Later in the book, Nebuchadnezzar is described as ruling after the return of the Judeans from exile and the rebuilding of the Temple, events that took place several decades after his death in 562. Much of the geography of the book is also confused.

The book has two parts. The first (chaps. 1–7) describes how Nebuchadnezzar, preparing to wage war on the king of the Medes, summoned military support from the western provinces of his empire. They refused, and, after his defeat of the Medean king, Nebuchadnezzar sent his general Holofernes to punish them. The Israelites, however, concerned about what would happen to the Temple in Jerusalem, which had just been rebuilt, fortified the strategic passes that led from the Mediterranean coast to the Judean heartland. In retaliation the Assyrians laid siege to the Israelite city of Bethulia. Cut off from water and food, the Israelites soon were ready to surrender.

In the second part of the book (chaps. 8–16), Judith, a pious and beautiful widow, managed to gain admittance to the Assyrian camp and into the tent of Holofernes, who was captivated by her beauty and her wisdom. At a private dinner with Judith, Holofernes became intoxicated and passed out, and she cut off his head and returned to her compatriots in Bethulia. In the morning, the Assyrians mustered to attack them, but when they discovered Holofernes's headless corpse, they panicked and were easy prey for the Israelites, who routed them and looted their camp. The book ends with a victory celebration led by the women of Israel.

Drawing on older biblical models, the book of Judith is a dramatic adventure story of a woman defeating a powerful enemy single-handedly. The tale is intended as an inspiration for Jews in the most trying times, and Judith herself personifies the ideal Jew, pious but not passive.

3 Maccabees

The book of 3 Maccabees has a misleading title, since it is not about the second-century BCE fighters with that name who are the subject of 1 and 2 Maccabees. Rather, it is set in Egypt in the preceding century, during the reign of Ptolemy IV Philopator (221–204 BCE). Written in Greek, probably during the first century BCE, the book is included in the canon of many Eastern Orthodox churches.

In its account of royal persecution thwarted by Jewish solidarity and divine intervention, 3 Maccabees is similar to the books of Esther, Tobit, and Judith. Like them, it also features lengthy prayers in the course of the narrative, and it especially resembles the book of Esther in its narrative explanation of a festival celebrating deliverance. Such a festival in Egypt is also mentioned by the first-century CE Jewish historian Josephus.

Few of the details of the book seem to be historical. Rather, 3 Maccabees uses historical fiction to exemplify how steadfast piety in the face of persecution is rewarded by God.

WISDOM LITERATURE

Two of the apocryphal books belong to the category of wisdom literature (see pages 383–385), the Wisdom of Jesus, Son of Sirach, and the Wisdom of Solomon. Unlike earlier works of this type in the Hebrew Bible, which tend to be universal, these two books include recapitulations of the history of Israel as a basis for comfort in the contexts of the late Hellenistic and Roman periods in which they were written. Despite the resistance to Hellenization shown in the revolt of the Maccabees, these books contain Greek ideas and vocabulary.

The Wisdom of Jesus, Son of Sirach (also known as Ben Sira and Ecclesiasticus)

Although most wisdom literature is anonymous, the book of Ben Sira is named after its author, "Jesus, son of Eleazar son of Sira of Jerusalem" (Sir 50.27). The author's name "Jesus" is a Greek rendering of Hebrew "Yeshua" (an alternate form of "Joshua"), a common name among Jews of the Hellenistic and Roman periods; the name "Sira" is obscure. The author is generally referred to as Ben Sira ("son of Sira") or as Sirach, a Greek form of the name, to distinguish him from Jesus of Nazareth. The Latin title of the book, "Ecclesiasticus" (not to be confused with Ecclesiastes [Qoheleth], discussed on pages 397–399), meaning "the church book," is a frequently used alternate title.

Ben Sira's grandson, who translated the book from Hebrew into Greek, says in the prologue that he began the translation after he came to Egypt in the thirty-eighth year of Euergetes, that is, in 132 BCE, during the long reign of Ptolemy VIII Euergetes (170–116), and implies that he completed it after that ruler's death. The book speaks in the past tense of the high priest Simon II, son of Onias II, who held that office from 219 to 196, but makes no mention of the oppression under Antiochus IV and the revolt of the Maccabees that occurred in 167–164. The book was therefore written in the early second century BCE.

The informative prologue also tells us that the book was originally written in Hebrew. The most complete surviving form of the book is its Greek version, but several incomplete Hebrew manuscripts have also been found. Much of the book is a collection of wisdom sayings in the form of proverbs (see pages 383–385), like those in the book of Proverbs, many of which Ben Sira repeats or modifies. Like the book of Proverbs, the book of Ben Sira deals with human existence on all levels. The proverbs are often grouped together by topic or theme, but without logical order or structure. The difficulties in determining the structure of the book are ancient; the Hebrew and Greek manuscripts include several headings, but they are not placed consistently. In addition to proverbial sayings, the book also includes other genres, such as hymns of praise, blessings, prayers, and a lengthy catalogue of the major figures of biblical history.

From the prologue, the autobiographical note in Sirach 50.27, and other details in the book, we can conclude that Ben Sira lived in Jerusalem during the late second and early first centuries BCE. He had devoted himself to studying the Jewish scriptures, although he was also familiar with Greek literature. Intellectually and emotionally attached to the Jerusalem Temple and to its rituals, he was probably associated with the priestly establishment, perhaps as a scribe, an authority on the interpretation of Jewish tradition and especially of the Torah, the Law.

The centrality of the Law in Ben Sira's understanding is especially evident in his treatment of the figure of Woman Wisdom. In Proverbs 8.22–31, Job 28, and the Wisdom of Solomon, Wisdom is a divine figure (see pages 387–388), and Ben Sira alludes to this view. But Ben Sira demythologizes Woman Wisdom; for him, she is

> the book of the covenant of the Most High God,
> the law that Moses commanded us. (Sir 24.23)

The centrality of Jerusalem and the rituals in the Temple are especially evident in the most unified section of the book, the "hymn in honor of our ancestors" in chapters 44–50, a poetic catalogue of the major personalities of the Bible. The passage begins, in the familiar wording of the King

James Version, "Let us now praise famous men" (44.1). One theme that connects several of the encomiums is the role that leaders such as Aaron, David, and Zerubbabel and Jeshua played in the founding and restoring of the Temple rituals. The passage concludes with an extravagant eulogy for the high priest Simon.

Ben Sira's views are conventional, as is apparent in his treatment of women, a subject that he addresses repeatedly. The dominant attitude is that women are dangerous, which is why men need to control them strictly. In Ben Sira's treatment of women, only mothers (always parallel to fathers) are portrayed entirely positively.

The Wisdom of Ben Sira is representative of one strand in Judaism as it encountered Greek ideas and culture. Although inevitably affected by Hellenism, Ben Sira was a conservative, maintaining a resolute attachment to Jewish tradition especially as found in the scriptures.

The Wisdom of Solomon

The book called the Wisdom of Solomon (or sometimes just Wisdom) dates to the late first century BCE or the early first century CE. Although it belongs to the category of wisdom literature, the book has a very different flavor from other biblical books of that category. Not only was it written in elegant Greek, but it is permeated by Greek philosophical concepts. Scholars have suggested that the book was written in Alexandria in Egypt, a center of Hellenism in general and of Hellenistic Jewish learning as well.

The book presents itself as a speech given by Solomon to other kings. It is loosely based on the information concerning Solomon found in 1 Kings 3–4, which tells how Solomon prayed for and was granted wisdom by God. The historical Solomon was not the actual author of the book, since among other things, he would not have known Greek; rather, the persona of Solomon is adopted by the author as a vehicle to present his own ideas. Those ideas are presented in a carefully structured meditative discourse, using a highly developed rhetorical style that imitates the parallelism of biblical poetry but with complex sentences and a sometimes striking lyricism.

The audience of the book must have been Jewish, for its negative portrayal of the Egyptians makes it unlikely to have been written to persuade non-Jews to become monotheists. Rather, it is a learned discourse combining earlier biblical traditions with Greek philosophy and other Hellenistic sources to demonstrate the superiority of Judaism and to persuade Jews who may have abandoned their religion to return to it.

The book consists of three interrelated sections, with the figure of Wisdom (see pages 386–87) and God's protection of those who cultivate wisdom as unifying elements:

- *Chapters 1–6*   A discussion of the fate of the righteous and the wicked, concluding with an appeal to the reader to cherish Wisdom
- *Chapters 7–10*   An elaboration of Wisdom, including Solomon's prayer to be given her, and her role in the history of the Jewish people
- *Chapters 11–19*   A retelling of the story of the Exodus from Egypt, contrasting the fates of the foolish idol-worshiping Egyptians and of God's people the Israelites

The Wisdom of Solomon draws heavily on Greek philosophy. Wisdom herself, in the original Greek *sophia*, is also an important philosophical concept. She teaches her devotees self-control or temperance, prudence, justice, and courage (8.7), the four so-called cardinal virtues, as defined especially by the Stoic philosophers of the Hellenistic period. Moreover, the catalogue of Wisdom's qualities in 7.22–23 contains twenty-one terms, a number symbolizing perfection (the product of seven times three); many of the terms also are technical philosophical vocabulary.

The first section of the Wisdom of Solomon deals with the issue of theodicy, of divine justice, especially the problem of the suffering of the innocent. The author has adopted the Greek view that the soul survives death. This solves the problem of divine justice in this life: God will reward the good in the life to come. The way to achieve this eternal life is through the pursuit of wisdom.

Wisdom, however, is not just an abstraction; as in Proverbs 8, Job 28, and Sirach 24, she is presented as a woman, even a goddess. Solomon's attachment to her is romantic, almost sexual. As an image of the invisible and transcendent deity, Wisdom was directly involved in human history, and especially in the history of Israel. This is illustrated by a summary retelling of how Wisdom rescued the principal heroes of Israel's history, from Adam to Joseph, and then Israel itself under the leadership of Moses.

The final section of the book is an interpretive retelling of the narrative of the Exodus from Egypt, contrasting the idolatrous Egyptians and the faithful Israelites and God's appropriate treatment of both. The series of contrasts is interrupted by a lengthy digression on idol worship (Wis 11.15–15.19).

The author of the Wisdom of Solomon offered to Hellenized Jews in Egypt an exhortation to remain faithful because Jewish tradition is superior to Hellenistic philosophy and mythology: True wisdom is derived from God. To prove these assertions, the author reinterprets biblical sources, providing an example of the creativity of biblical interpretation during the Hellenistic and Roman periods.

OTHER COMPOSITIONS

Baruch

Although the short book of Baruch was probably originally written in Hebrew, it survives only in its Greek translation. Its purported author is Baruch, the scribe of the prophet Jeremiah, and the book dates itself to 582 BCE, the fifth year after the Babylonian conquest of Jerusalem. The actual author of the book, however, lived long after that event, perhaps in the second century BCE, and it contains a number of historical errors.

Following the introduction, the book has three parts, each with a primary source in biblical literature. The first part (Bar 1.15–3.8) is a communal admission of guilt and plea for divine mercy, derived from Daniel 9.4–19 and supplemented by phrases taken from other biblical texts, including Leviticus, Deuteronomy, and Jeremiah. The second part (3.9–4.4) is a hymn to wisdom, based largely on Job 28; like Sirach 24.23 (see page 424), this hymn identifies wisdom with the Torah. The third part (4.5–5.9) is a poem of consolation, largely made up of phrases from Isaiah 40–66, in which Zion (Jerusalem) both speaks and is spoken to. The book thus appears to be a composite, in which three unrelated texts, each essentially a collage of biblical quotations, were combined under the supposed authorship of Baruch.

The Letter of Jeremiah

Drawing on the tradition that Jeremiah wrote letters, such as that to the exiles in Babylon (Jeremiah 29), this brief work, probably written in the third or second century BCE, is a highly stylized polemic against the worship of idols: "They are not gods, so do not fear them" is a refrain that with variations occurs eight times in the book. The Letter of Jeremiah draws on passages such as Jeremiah 10.2–15 and Isaiah 44.9–20 and incidentally contains the only biblical reference to cats (v. 22). It is included in the Roman Catholic canon as chapter 6 of the book of Baruch, but many modern Bibles print it separately.

2 Esdras

Among several postbiblical works ascribed to or featuring Ezra is the book of 2 Esdras, also known as the Apocalypse of Ezra and 4 Ezra. Although 2 Esdras was sometimes included in manuscripts of the Bible as a kind of appendix and is frequently included in modern study Bibles, it is considered canonical only by some Orthodox churches.

The book contains three originally independent compositions in the apocalyptic genre; in the first two Esdras (the Greek form of Ezra's name) is the principal character. The three parts are as follows:

- 2 Esdras 1–2: Also known as 5 Ezra, these chapters are a Christian apocalypse probably dating to the early second century CE.

- 2 Esdras 3–14: Also known as 4 Ezra, this is a Jewish apocalypse originally written in Hebrew or Aramaic in the late first century CE. In it, Esdras receives revelations concerning the significance of the destruction of the Second Temple by the Romans in 70 CE and the eventual destruction of the Roman Empire itself.
- 2 Esdras 15–16: Also known as 6 Ezra, this is another Christian apocalypse, probably dating to the third century CE.

The Prayer of Manasseh

The additions in Chronicles to the account of Manasseh's reign (2 Chr 33.10–13; see also 33.18) are the basis for "The Prayer of Manasseh," an individual petition (see page 377) composed late in the biblical period, and probably originally written in Greek. It is included in the canon of most Eastern Orthodox churches.

Psalm 151

Some ancient manuscripts include an additional psalm after Psalm 150, known as Psalm 151, which is part of the canon of some Eastern Orthodox churches. The title to this psalm describes it as "outside the number" of the 150 psalms. Originally written in Hebrew in the fourth or third century BCE, it is a narrative poem attributed to King David, in which he recounts his early life.

BIBLIOGRAPHY

For an introduction to the Apocrypha, see David A. DeSilva, *Introducing the Apocrypha: Message, Content, and Significance* (Grand Rapids, MI: Baker Academic, 2002); and Daniel J. Harrington, *Invitation to the Apocrypha* (Grand Rapids, MI: Eerdmans, 1999).

During the Hellenistic and Roman periods, Jewish writers produced many other fictional expansions of biblical narrative; many are conveniently translated and collected in James H. Charlesworth, ed., *The Old Testament Pseudepigrapha* (New York: Doubleday, 2 vols., 1983, 1985); Richard Bauckham, James R. Davila, and Alexander Panayotov, eds., *Old Testament Pseudepigrapha: More Noncanonical Scriptures*, Vol. 1 (Grand Rapids, MI: Eerdmans, 2013); Louis H. Feldman, James L. Kugel, and Lawrence H. Schiffman, eds., *Outside the Bible: Ancient Jewish Writings Related to Scripture* (3 vols.; Philadelphia: Jewish Publication Society, 2013); and Lawrence E. Wills, *Ancient Jewish Novels: An Anthology* (New York: Oxford University Press, 2002).

Chronology

Dates	Period	Canaan	Syria
ca. 3300–2000 BCE	**Early Bronze Age**	Under Egyptian influence and control	Under Mesopotamian influence and control
ca. 2300–2000			
ca. 2000–1550 ca. 1650–1550	**Middle Bronze Age**		
			Rise of Hittites
ca. 1550–1200	**Late Bronze Age**		Under Hittite influence and control
		Israelite Exodus from Egypt (?)	
ca. 1200–586	**Iron Age**	*Arrival of the Philistines in Canaan*	
		The Israelite judges (ca. 1150–1025)	

————Emergence of independent states————

Israel

Saul (1025–1005)

David (1005–965)
|
Solomon (968–928)

Israel	Judah
Jeroboam I (928–907)	Rehoboam (928–911)
Nadab (907–906)	Abijam (Abijah) (911–908)
Baasha (906–883)	Asa (908–867)
Elah (883–882)	
Zimri (882)	

Date ranges for rulers are for reigns, not life spans. Overlapping dates indicate coregencies. Vertical lines show genealogical connections. Important events are in italics.

Egypt	Mesopotamia	Persia	Greece
Early Dynastic Period and Old Kingdom	Sumerian city-states		
First Intermediate Period			
Middle Kingdom Second Intermediate (Hyksos) Period	Rise of Babylon Hammurapi (1792–1750)		
New Kingdom Seti I (1294–1279) | Rameses II (1279–1213) | Merneptah (1213–1203)			

Invasion of Shishak (924)

Dates	Period	Israel	Judah	Syria
ca. 1200–586	**Iron Age**	Omri (882–871)		
		Ahab (871–852)	Jehoshaphat (870–846)	*Battle of Qarqar (853)*
		Jezebel		
		Ahaziah (852–851)		
		Prophet Elijah (mid-ninth century)		
		Jehoram (Joram) (851–842)	Jehoram (Joram) (851–843)	
		Prophet Elisha (mid-to-late ninth century)		
		Jehu (842–814)	Ahaziah (Jehoahaz) (843–842)	
			Queen Athaliah (842–836)	
			Jehoash (Joash) (836–798)	
		Jehoahaz (817–800)		
		Jehoash (Joash) (800–784)	Amaziah (798–769)	
		Jeroboam II (788–747)	Azariah (Uzziah) (785–733)	
		Prophet Amos (mid-eighth century)	Jotham (759–743)	
		Zechariah (747)		
		Shallum (747)		
		Menahem (747–737)	Ahaz (745/735–727/715)*	
		Prophet Hosea (mid-to-late eighth century)		
		Pekahiah (737–735)		
			Prophet Isaiah (late eighth to early seventh century)	
		Pekah (735–732)		
		Hoshea (732–722)		
		Fall of Samaria (722)		
			Hezekiah (727/715–698/687)*	
			Prophet Micah (late eighth century)	
			Invasion of Sennacherib (701)	
			Manasseh (698/687–642)*	
			Amon (641–640)	

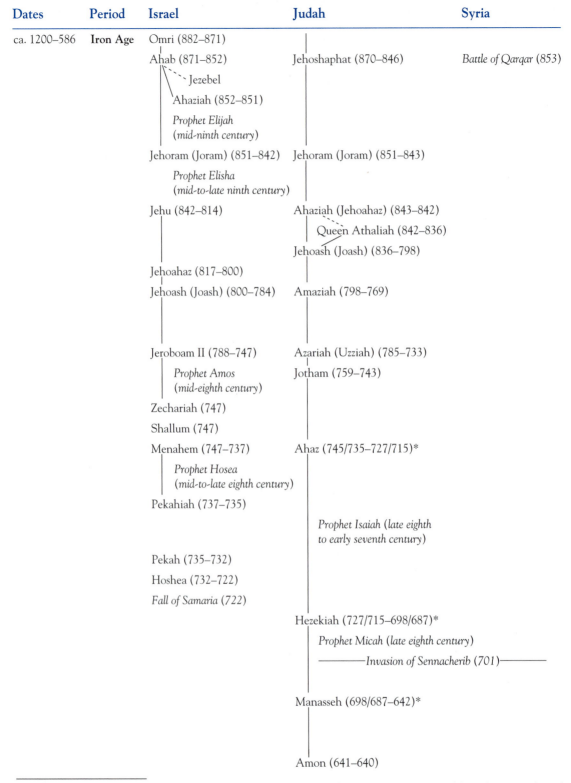

Date ranges for rulers are for reigns, not life spans. Overlapping dates indicate coregencies. Vertical lines show genealogical connections. Dotted lines indicate marriage. Important events are in italics.

*   The data are inconsistent for the reigns of Ahaz, Hezekiah, and Manasseh.

Egypt	Mesopotamia	Persia	Greece

Kings of Assyria

Adad-nirari III (810–783)

Shalmaneser IV (783–773)

Ashur-dan III (773–755)

Ashur-nirari V (775–745)

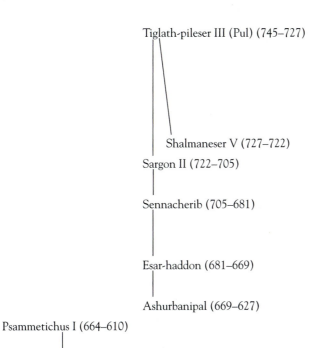

Tiglath-pileser III (Pul) (745–727)

Shalmaneser V (727–722)

Sargon II (722–705)

Sennacherib (705–681)

Esar-haddon (681–669)

Ashurbanipal (669–627)

Psammetichus I (664–610)

Dates	Period	Judah
ca. 1200–586	**Iron Age**	Josiah (640–609)
		Prophet Jeremiah (late seventh to early sixth centuries)
		Prophets Zephaniah, Nahum, and Habakkuk (late seventh century)
		Jehoahaz (Shallum) (609)
ca. 600–539	**Neo-Babylonian Period**	Jehoiakim (608–598) (Eliakim)
		Jehoiachin (also called Jeconiah, Coniah, etc.) (597)
		First Babylonian Siege of Jerusalem (597)
		Zedekiah (Mattaniah) (597–586)
		Prophet Ezekiel (early sixth century)
		Babylonian Capture of Jerusalem (586)
ca. 539–332	**Persian Period**	
		Jews return from Babylon (538)
		Reconstruction of the Temple (520–515)
		Prophets Haggai and Zechariah (late sixth century)
		Mission of Ezra (458)
		Governorship of Nehemiah (445–433)
ca. 332–63 BCE	**Hellenistic Period**	*Revolt of the Maccabees (167–164)*
ca. 63 BCE–330 CE	**Roman Period**	*Fall of Jerusalem and destruction of the Second Temple (70 CE)*

Date ranges for rulers are for reigns, not life spans. Overlapping dates indicate coregencies. Vertical lines show genealogical connections. Important events are in italics.

Egypt	Mesopotamia	Persia	Greece

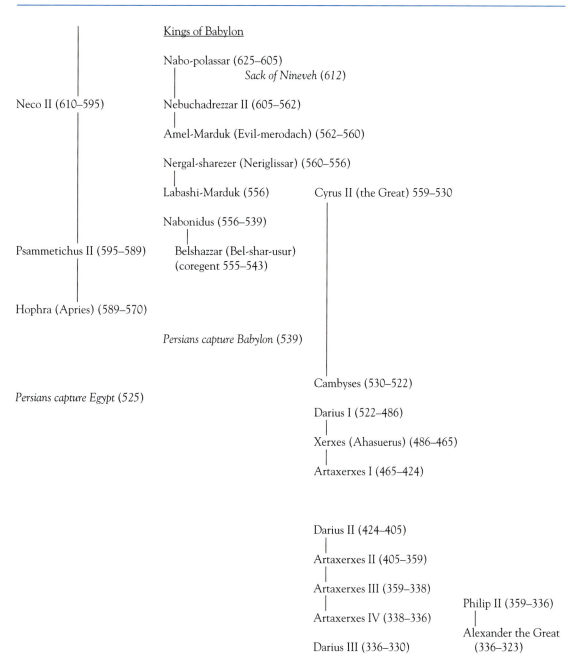

Egypt

Neco II (610–595)

Psammetichus II (595–589)

Hophra (Apries) (589–570)

Persians capture Egypt (525)

Mesopotamia

<u>Kings of Babylon</u>

Nabo-polassar (625–605)
   Sack of Nineveh (612)

Nebuchadrezzar II (605–562)

Amel-Marduk (Evil-merodach) (562–560)

Nergal-sharezer (Neriglissar) (560–556)

Labashi-Marduk (556)

Nabonidus (556–539)

Belshazzar (Bel-shar-usur)
(coregent 555–543)

Persians capture Babylon (539)

Persia

Cyrus II (the Great) 559–530

Cambyses (530–522)

Darius I (522–486)

Xerxes (Ahasuerus) (486–465)

Artaxerxes I (465–424)

Darius II (424–405)

Artaxerxes II (405–359)

Artaxerxes III (359–338)

Artaxerxes IV (338–336)

Darius III (336–330)

Greece

Philip II (359–336)

Alexander the Great
(336–323)

Brown, R. E., et al., eds. *The New Jerome Biblical Commentary*. Englewood Cliffs, NJ: Prentice-Hall, 1990.

Dunn, J. D. G., and J. W. Rogerson, eds. *Eerdmans Commentary on the Bible*. Grand Rapids, MI: Eerdmans, 2003.

Keck, L. A., et al., eds. *The New Interpreter's Bible*. 12 vols. and index. Nashville, TN: Abingdon, 1994–2004.

Mays, J. L., ed. *The HarperCollins Bible Commentary*. San Francisco: HarperSanFrancisco, 2000.

Newsom, C. A., S. H. Ringe, and J. E. Lapsley, eds. *Women's Bible Commentary*, 3d ed. Louisville, KY: Westminster John Knox, 2012.

Yee, G. A., H. R. Page, Jr., and M. J. M. Coomber, eds. *Fortress Commentary on the Bible: The Old Testament and Apocrypha*. Minneapolis, MN: Fortress, 2014.

History of Ancient Israel

Coogan, M. D., ed. *The Oxford History of the Biblical World*. New York: Oxford University Press, 1998 (pb ed. 2001; available in Oxford Biblical Studies Online).

Isserlin, B. S. J. *The Israelites*. Minneapolis: Fortress, 2001.

Miller, J. M., and J. H. Hayes. *A History of Israel and Judah*. Louisville, KY: Westminster John Knox, 2d ed., 2006.

Nelson, R. D. *Historical Roots of the Old Testament (1200–63 BCE)*. Atlanta: SBL Press, 2014.

Ancient Near Eastern and Other Nonbiblical Texts

Aḥituv, S. *Echoes from the Past: Hebrew and Cognate Inscriptions from the Biblical Periods*. Jerusalem: Carta, 2008.

Bauckham, R., et al., eds. *Old Testament Pseudepigrapha: More Noncanonical Scriptures*. Vol. 1. Grand Rapids, MUI: Eerdmans, 2013.

Charlesworth, J. H., ed. *The Old Testament Pseudepigrapha*. 2 vols. New York: Doubleday, 1983, 1985.

Chavalas, M. W. *The Ancient Near East: Historical Sources in Translation*. Malden, MA: Blackwell, 2006.

Cogan, M. *The Raging Torrent: Historical Inscriptions from Assyria and Babylonia Relating to Ancient Israel*. Jerusalem: Carta, 2008

Coogan, M. D. *A Reader of Ancient Near Eastern Texts: Sources for the Study of the Old Testament*. New York: Oxford University Press, 2012.

Coogan, M. D., and M. S. Smith, ed. and trans. *Stories from Ancient Canaan*, 2d ed. Louisville, KY: Westminster John Knox, 2012.

Feldman, L.H., J. L. Kugel, and L.H. Schiffman. *Outside the Bible: Ancient Jewish Writings Related to Scripture*. 3 vols. Philadelphia: Jewish Publication Society, 2013.

Hallo, W. W., and K. L. Younger, eds. *The Context of Scripture*. 3 vols. Leiden: Brill, 1997–2002.

Pritchard, J. B., ed. *Ancient Near Eastern Texts Relating to the Old Testament*, 3d ed. Princeton, NJ: Princeton University Press, 1969.

Vermes, G. *The Complete Dead Sea Scrolls in English*. New York: Penguin, 7th ed., 2012.

Archaeology of Ancient Israel and the Near East

Ben-Tor, A., ed. *The Archaeology of Ancient Israel*. New Haven, CT: Yale University Press, 1991.

King, P. J., and L. E. Stager. *Life in Biblical Israel*. Louisville, KY: Westminster John Knox, 2001.

Magness, J. *The Archaeology of the Holy Land: From the Destruction of Solomon's Temple to the Muslim Conquest*. New York: Cambridge University Press, 2012.

Master, D., ed. *The Oxford Encyclopedia of the Bible and Archaeology*. 2 vols. New York: Oxford University Press, 2013 (available in Oxford Biblical Studies Online).

Mazar, A. *Archaeology of the Land of the Bible: 10,000–586 B.C.E.* New York: Doubleday, 1990.

Meyers, E. M., ed. *The Oxford Encyclopedia of Archaeology in the Near East*. 5 vols. New York: Oxford University Press, 1997 (available in Oxford Biblical Studies Online).

Meyers, E. M., and M. A. Chancey. *Alexander to Constantine: Archaeology of the Land of the Bible*, Vol. 3. New Haven, CT: Yale University Press. 2012.

Stern, E. *Archaeology of the Land of the Bible*, Vol. 2: *The Assyrian, Babylonian, and Persian Periods (732–332 B.C.E.)*. New York: Doubleday, 2001.

———, ed. *The New Encyclopedia of Archaeological Excavations in the Holy Land*. 5 vols. New York: Simon and Schuster, 1993; Jerusalem: Israel Exploration Society, 2008.

Theology of the Old Testament

Birch, B. C., et al. *A Theological Introduction to the Old Testament*. Nashville, TN: Abingdon, 2d ed., 2005.

Levenson, J. D. *The Hebrew Bible, the Old Testament, and Historical Criticism: Jews and Christians in Biblical Studies*. Louisville, KY: Westminster John Knox, 1993.

Rad, G. von. *Old Testament Theology*. 2 vols. New York: Harper & Row, 1962–65.

Rendtorff, R. *The Canonical Hebrew Bible: A Theology of the Old Testament*. Leiden: Deo, 2005.

History of the Religion of Ancient Israel

Albertz, R. *A History of Israelite Religion in the Old Testament Period*. 2 vols. Louisville, KY: Westminster John Knox, 1994.

Bodel, J., and S. M. Olyan, eds. *Household and Family Religion in Antiquity*. Malden, MA: Blackwell, 2008.

Cross, F. M. *Canaanite Myth and Hebrew Epic: Essays in the History of the Religion of Israel*. Cambridge, MA: Harvard University Press, 1972.

———. *From Epic to Canon: History and Literature in Ancient Israel*. Baltimore: The Johns Hopkins University Press, 1998.

Eilberg-Schwartz, H. *The Savage in Judaism: An Anthropology of Israelite Religion and Ancient Judaism*. Bloomington: Indiana University Press, 1990.

Kaufmann, Y. *The Religion of Israel from Its Beginnings to the Babylonian Exile*. Trans. and abridged by M. Greenberg. Chicago: University of Chicago, 1960.

Miller, P. D. *The Religion of Ancient Israel*. Louisville, KY: Westminster John Knox, 2000.

Niditch, S. *Ancient Israelite Religion*. New York: Oxford University Press, 1997.

Smith, M. S. *The Memoirs of God: History, Memory, and the Experience of the Divine in Ancient Israel*. Minneapolis: Fortress, 2004.

Vaux, R. de. *Ancient Israel: Its Life and Institutions*. New York: McGraw-Hill, 1965.

Weber, M. *Ancient Judaism*. New York: Free Press, 1952.

Dictionaries and Encyclopedias

Brawley, R. L., ed. *The Oxford Encyclopedia of the Bible and Ethics*. 2 vols. New York: Oxford University Press, 2014 (available in Oxford Biblical Studies Online).

Coggins, R. J., and J. L. Houlden, eds. *A Dictionary of Biblical Interpretation*. Philadelphia: Trinity, 1990.

Coogan, M. D., ed. *The Oxford Encyclopedia of the Books of the Bible*. 2 vols. New York: Oxford University Press, 2011 (available in Oxford Biblical Studies Online).

Freedman, D. N., ed. *The Anchor Bible Dictionary*. 6 vols. New York: Doubleday, 1992.

———. *Eerdmans Dictionary of the Bible*. Grand Rapids, MI: Eerdmans, 2000.

Hayes, J. H., ed. *Dictionary of Biblical Interpretation*. 2 vols. Nashville, TN: Abingdon, 1999.

McKenzie, S. L., ed. *The Oxford Encyclopedia of Biblical Interpretation*. 2 vols. New York: Oxford University Press, 2013 (available in Oxford Biblical Studies Online).

Metzger, B. M., and M. D. Coogan, eds. *The Oxford Companion to the Bible*. New York: Oxford University Press, 1993 (available in Oxford Biblical Studies Online).

Meyers, C., T. Craven, R. S. Kraemer ed. *Women in Scripture: A Dictionary of Named and Unnamed Women in the Hebrew Bible, the Apocryphal/Deuterocanonical Books, and the New Testament*. Boston: Houghton Mifflin, 2000.

O'Brien, J., ed. *The Oxford Encyclopedia of the Bible and Gender Studies*. 2 vols. New York: Oxford University Press, 2014 (available in Oxford Biblical Studies Online).

Powell, M. A., ed. *The HarperCollins Bible Dictionary*. New York: HarperOne, 3d ed., 2011.

Sakenfeld, K. D., ed. *The New Interpreter's Dictionary of the Bible*. 5 vols. Nashville, TN: Abingdon, 2006–2009.

Strawn, B., ed. *The Oxford Encyclopedia of the Bible and Law*. 2 vols. New York: Oxford University Press, 2014.

Toorn, K. van der, et al., eds. *Dictionary of Deities and Demons in the Bible*, 2d ed. Leiden: Brill, 1999.

Glossary

This glossary provides brief definitions of the "Important Names and Terms" printed in boldface in the text and listed at the end of each chapter. In the glossary itself, internal cross-references are also in **bold**. For information about other people, places, events, institutions, realities, and concepts in the Bible, students should consult the Index, as well as a concordance and one of the dictionaries or encyclopedias listed in the Bibliography on pages 435–437.

Aaron: Brother of **Moses** and Israel's first priest.

Abel: Second son of **Adam** and **Eve**, who was killed by his older brother **Cain**.

Abraham (Abram): An ancestor of Israel. He was the father of **Ishmael**, by **Hagar**, and of **Isaac**, by **Sarah**. God promised him many descendants and the land of Canaan (*see* **Promised Land**), and required that he and all of his male offspring be **circumcised**.

Absalom: Son of **David** who killed his half-brother Amnon, who had raped Absalom's sister Tamar. Later he led a revolt against his father's rule but was defeated and killed by David's men.

acrostic: A text in which the opening letters of successive lines form a word, phrase, or pattern. The acrostics in the Bible are poems in which the first letters of successive lines or stanzas are the letters of the Hebrew alphabet in order.

Adam: The first human, whose name comes from the word for soil, from which he was made. In the **garden of Eden** he and his wife **Eve** were punished for having eaten from the fruit of the **tree of the knowledge of good and evil**. Father of **Cain** and **Abel**.

Ahab: king of **Israel** (871–852), and husband of **Jezebel**.

Ahaz: King of **Judah** (735–715 BCE) who became an **Assyrian** vassal despite the advice of the prophet **Isaiah**.

Ammonites: **Israel**'s neighbors east of the Jordan River. The Ammonites are the "sons of Ammon," who according to Genesis 19 was the son of Lot by one of his daughters. Their name is preserved in the modern city of Amman, Jordan.

Amos: Prophet in Israel in the mid-eighth century BCE; also the book named for him.

angel: A word of Greek origin originally meaning messenger. In the Bible, these are supernatural beings sent by God to humans.

anthropomorphic (anthropomorphism): The attribution of human characteristics to a nonhuman being, such as a deity.

apocalyptic: A genre of literature in which details concerning the end-time are revealed by a heavenly messenger or **angel**.

Apocrypha: Jewish religious writings of the Hellenistic and Roman periods that are not considered part of the Bible by Jews and Protestants, but are part of the **canons** of Roman Catholic and Orthodox churches, who also call them the Deuterocanonical books.

apodictic law: A type of law characterized by absolute or general commands or prohibitions, as in the **Ten Commandments**. It is often contrasted with **casuistic law**.

Aramaic: A language originating in ancient Syria that in the second half of the first millennium BCE became used widely throughout the Near East. Parts of the books of **Daniel** and **Ezra** are written in Aramaic.

ark of the covenant: The religious symbol of the premonarchic confederation of the twelve tribes of **Israel**, later installed in the **Temple** in **Jerusalem** by **Solomon** in the tenth century BCE. It formed the footstool for the **cherubim** throne on which **Yahweh** was thought to be invisibly seated.

Assyria: Kingdom in northern **Mesopotamia** that ruled much of the Near East during the first millennium BCE. The Assyrians captured the **northern kingdom of Israel** in 722 BCE and laid siege to **Jerusalem** in 701 BCE.

avenger of blood: (Hebr. *goel*) The closest male relative who is legally responsible for his kin, usually in matters relating to vengeance or property. The word is often translated "redeemer."

Baal: The Canaanite storm-god, who in **Ugaritic** myth defeats Sea and Death. In the Bible, worship of Baal is condemned.

Babylon: The capital city of Babylonia, a kingdom in southern **Mesopotamia** that ruled much of the Near East in the late seventh and sixth centuries BCE. The Babylonians laid siege to **Jerusalem** in 597 and destroyed it in 586, exiling many of its inhabitants to Babylonia.

Balaam: A non-Israelite **prophet** who was hired by the king of **Moab** to curse the Israelites on their way to the **Promised Land** after the Exodus but, inspired by God, blessed them instead.

ban: (Hebr. *herem*) Something dedicated to a deity and restricted for the deity's use, such as the spoils of war, including captured people.

Bathsheba: Wife of Uriah the Hittite, one of King **David's** warriors. David committed adultery with her and had her husband killed. Later she became the mother of **Solomon**.

Cain: Oldest son of **Adam** and **Eve**, who killed his brother Abel.

Canaan: The name of the **Promised Land** before the Israelite conquest. In second-millennium BCE Egyptian sources, Canaan refers to the entire southern **Levant**. According to Genesis 9, the Canaanites, the inhabitants of the land of Canaan, were descendants of **Noah's** grandson Canaan.

canon: A list of the books considered scripture by a religious group.

casuistic law: Case law, often in the form of a conditional sentence, in which specific situations are addressed. It is often contrasted with **apodictic law**.

cherubim: Composite supernatural beings who function as guardians of the entrance to the **garden of Eden** in Genesis 3.24 and whose outstretched wings over the **ark of the covenant** supported the throne of **Yahweh**.

Chronicler: In modern scholarship, the term used for the author(s) of the books of Chronicles and, according to some scholars, of the books of **Ezra** and **Nehemiah**.

circumcision: The removal of the foreskin. According to Genesis 17.9–14, it is the sign of the **covenant** between God and **Abraham** and is to be performed on all of Abraham's male descendants on the eighth day after birth.

cities of refuge: In the Bible, six cities set aside as places where someone accused of murder could find asylum until the case was decided.

city of David: Another name for **Jerusalem**, especially the ancient pre-Israelite city that King **David** captured and made his capital in the early tenth century BCE. In later tradition, it is also used of Bethlehem, David's birthplace.

Code of Hammurapi: An ancient collection of laws issued by the **Babylonian** king Hammurapi (also spelled Hammurabi) in the mid-eighteenth century BCE.

confessions of Jeremiah: In modern scholarship, those parts of the book of **Jeremiah** in which he laments to God the difficulties he experienced as a **prophet**. The confessions are in Jeremiah 11.18–12.6, 15.10–21, 17.14–18, 18.18–23, and 20.7–18.

cosmology: An account of the origins of the world; in the ancient Near East, cosmologies are usually creation **myth**s.

covenant: (Hebr. *berît*)A term originally meaning "contract," used in the Bible of marriage, slavery, and international treaties and used metaphorically to characterize the relationship between God and the Israelites and between God and individuals such as **Abraham**, **Aaron**, and **David**.

Covenant Code: In modern scholarship, the collection of laws found in Exodus 20.22–23.19, identified as "the book of the covenant" (Ex 24.7). It is one of the oldest collections of laws in the Bible.

covenant lawsuit: A genre used by the **prophets** in which **Israel** is put on trial by **Yahweh** for having violated its **covenant** with him.

Cyrus: King of **Persia** (559–530 BCE) who captured **Babylon** and allowed the Judean exiles there to return to **Judah**.

D: The Deuteronomic source according to the **Documentary Hypothesis**, which is found almost exclusively in the book of Deuteronomy.

Daniel: The hero of the book named for him, in which he is a courtier in the court of kings of **Babylon** and **Persia** and receives revelations concerning the history and the future of the Jews.

David: Son of Jesse, from Bethlehem. As a young man he served in **Saul's** army and killed the Philistine champion **Goliath**. Although he was a close friend of Saul's son **Jonathan** and had married Saul's daughter **Michal**, he and Saul became enemies. When Saul died, David succeeded him as king of **Israel** about 1000 BCE and soon moved his capital to **Jerusalem**. He was succeeded by his son **Solomon**, whose mother was **Bathsheba**.

Davidic covenant: The **covenant** between **Yahweh** and **David**, which guaranteed the divine protection of the dynasty that David founded and of **Jerusalem**, its capital city.

Day of Atonement: A fall ritual of purification, described in Leviticus 16, later known as Yom Kippur. *See also* **scapegoat**.

day of the LORD: A phrase used by the **prophets** to describe **Yahweh**'s fighting against his enemies. In **apocalyptic** literature it is used of the final battle between good and evil.

Dead Sea: A large body of water in the Rift Valley into which the Jordan River flows. Due to evaporation, it has a high mineral content and no life is found in it, hence its name.

Dead Sea Scrolls: Ancient manuscripts found in caves on the western side of the **Dead Sea** beginning in 1948. Some of them are the oldest surviving manuscripts of books of the Bible, dating as early as the third century BCE.

Deborah: One of the **judges** who led a coalition of **Israelite** tribes against **Canaanite** adversaries in the twelfth century BCE, celebrated in the Song of Deborah named for her.

Decalogue: A word of Greek origin that means "ten words"; another name for the **Ten Commandments**.

Delilah: Woman who betrayed **Samson** to the **Philistines** by revealing that the secret of his strength was his uncut hair.

Deuterocanonical books: *See* **Apocrypha**.

Deuteronomic Code: According to modern scholars, the core of the book of Deuteronomy in chapters 12–26, a collection of ancient laws that differ in many details from those found in the books of Exodus and Leviticus.

Deuteronomic school: A group of writers who over several centuries produced the book of Deuteronomy and the **Deuteronomistic History**.

Deuteronomistic History: According to modern scholars, the books of Joshua, Judges, 1 and 2 Samuel, and 1 and 2 Kings, which form a narrative history of **Israel** in the **Promised Land**. It was produced in several editions from the late eighth to the sixth centuries BCE by the Deuteronomistic Historians, who were informed by the principles of the book of Deuteronomy.

Diaspora: Literally, scattering or dispersion, used to refer to exiles from **Judah** to **Babylonia** in the early sixth century BCE, and subsequently for any Jews living outside of **Israel**.

divine council: The assembly of gods, over which the high god presides. In the Bible, **Yahweh** is described as the head of the divine council, and **prophets** claim to have witnessed or participated in its meetings.

Documentary Hypothesis: The theory classically formulated by Julius **Wellhausen** in 1878, which explains the repetitions and inconsistencies in the first five books of the Bible, the **Pentateuch**, as the result of originally independent sources or documents having been combined over several centuries. The principal hypothetical sources are **J, E, D,** and **P**.

E: The Elohist source according to the **Documentary Hypothesis**, found in the books of Genesis through Numbers.

Ecclesiastes: The pseudonym of the author of the book named for him, in which he explores the meaning of life. Also known as Qoheleth.

El: Head of the Canaanite pantheon and the creator deity in **Ugaritic** texts, who presides over the **divine council**; also a title for the god of Israel.

Elijah: A **prophet** in the **northern kingdom of Israel** in the mid-ninth century BCE.

Elisha: A **prophet** in the **northern kingdom of Israel** in the mid- to late ninth century BCE; successor of **Elijah**.

elohim: The Hebrew word for god or gods, which, although plural in form, is often used as a title for **Yahweh** and is translated "God."

endogamy: The custom of marrying within one's ethnic or religious group.

Enkidu: In the epic of *Gilgamesh*, the wild man created by the gods to distract Gilgamesh from his destructive behavior. Gilgamesh and Enkidu became friends, and Enkidu's death motivated Gilgamesh to seek immortality.

Enuma Elish: Also called the Babylonian Creation Epic, this is a work on seven tablets in praise of the patron god of **Babylon, Marduk**. It describes how Marduk defeated the primeval sea-goddess **Tiamat** and then created the world and humans. Its title is its opening words, which mean "when above."

Esau: Son of **Isaac** and older twin brother of **Jacob**; ancestor of the Edomites.

Esther: Judean exile and heroine of the book named for her, according to which she became queen of **Persia** and saved her people. *See also* **Purim**.

etiology: A narrative that explains the origin of a custom, ritual, geographical feature, name, or other phenomenon.

Eve: The first woman, who ate from the **tree of the knowledge of good and evil** in the garden of **Eden** and gave its fruit to her husband **Adam**. Her name means "life." She was the mother of **Cain, Abel**, and Seth.

Ezekiel: A **prophet** among the exiles in **Babylonia** in the early sixth century BCE; also the book named for him.

Ezra: A scribe expert in the **Torah**, a priest, and a leader of exiles returning to **Judah** from **Babylon** in the mid-fifth century BCE, and the book named for him.

Fertile Crescent: The arable area of land from southern **Mesopotamia** northward and then westward and southward through the **Levant**.

First Isaiah: In modern scholarship, the parts of Isaiah 1–39 that are associated with the eighth-century BCE **prophet Isaiah**.

form criticism: The study of relatively short literary units in literature and in folklore with regard to their forms or genres, their original settings (German *Sitz im Leben*), and their social, religious, and political functions. It was developed by Herman **Gunkel**.

Former Prophets: In Jewish tradition, the first division of the **Prophets**, comprising the books of Joshua, Judges, 1 and 2 Samuel, and 1 and 2 Kings.

garden of Eden: The garden of God in which **Adam** and **Eve** lived until they ate from the tree **of the knowledge of good and evil**. Its location is unknown.

genealogy: A family history in the form of a list of descendants.

Gilgamesh/*Gilgamesh*: The hero of the Mesopotamian epic named for him, who with **Enkidu** travels widely and ultimately meets **Utnapishtim**.

glory of Yahweh: The visible sign of the presence of the invisible God, depicted as a light-filled cloud, characteristic of both **P** and **Ezekiel**.

golden calf: The statue of a calf that the Israelites worshiped at Mount **Sinai** according to Exodus 32, and also similar statues at the shrines of Bethel and Dan in the **northern kingdom of Israel**.

Goliath: A **Philistine** champion killed by **David**.

Gunkel, Hermann (1862–1932): The German scholar whose commentaries on Genesis and Psalms applied **form criticism** to the Bible.

Habakkuk: A **prophet** in **Judah** in the late seventh century BCE; also the book named for him.

Hagar: Secondary wife of **Abraham** with whom she had **Ishmael**.

Haggai: A **prophet** in the late sixth century BCE who urged the rebuilding of the **Temple**; also the book named for him.

Hannah: Wife of Elkanah and mother of **Samuel**.

Hebrew Bible: The **Tanakh**. Its contents are the same as in the Old Testament in the Protestant **canon**, but the order of the books differs.

Hezekiah: King of **Judah** (715–687 BCE) during whose reign the **Assyrian** king **Sennacherib** attacked **Jerusalem**. He was advised by the prophet **Isaiah**.

Holiness Code: In modern scholarship, chapters 17–26 of the book of Leviticus, an originally independent source whose principal theme is the holiness of **Yahweh** and of his people.

Hosea: A **prophet** in the **northern kingdom of Israel** in the mid-eighth century BCE; also the book named for him.

Immanuel: The child whose birth and early life were signs from God to **Ahaz**, king of **Judah**, during the Syro-Ephraimite War (Isa 7.14). He was probably the child of the **prophet Isaiah** and his wife, who was also a **prophet**.

Isaac: Son of **Abraham** and **Sarah**, who inherited the divine promise rather than his older half-brother **Ishmael**.

Isaiah: A **prophet** in **Judah** in the late eighth and early seventh centuries BCE who advised **Ahaz** and **Hezekiah**; also the book named for him. *See also* **First Isaiah; Second Isaiah; Third Isaiah**.

Ishmael: Son of **Hagar** and **Abraham**, and older half-brother of **Isaac**.

Israel: This name is used in several senses. First, it is the new name given to the patriarch **Jacob** in Genesis 32.28; Jacob's twelve sons then become the ancestors of the tribes of **Israel**. Second, it designates the people and later the geopolitical entity formed from the twelve tribes. Third, it is used as the name of the **northern kingdom of Israel**, as opposed to the **southern kingdom of Judah**.

J: The Yahwist (or Jahwist) source according to the **Documentary Hypothesis**, found in the books of Genesis through Numbers.

Jacob: Son of **Isaac** and **Rebekah** who inherited the divine promise rather than his older twin brother **Esau**. Father of twelve sons through **Leah**, **Rachel**, Bilhah, and Zilpah; they became the ancestors of the twelve tribes of **Israel**.

Jephthah's daughter: Jephthah was one of the **judges** who before a battle vowed to sacrifice to God whatever first came out of his house if he returned victorious. His daughter, who is not named, came out, and he fulfilled his vow with her agreement.

Jeremiah: A **prophet** in **Judah** in the late seventh and early sixth centuries BCE who interpreted the destruction of **Jerusalem** as divine punishment; also the book named for him.

Jeroboam I: First king of the **northern kingdom of Israel** in the late tenth century BCE, who made golden calves for worship at Bethel and Dan.

Jerusalem: Capital city of **Israel** and later **Judah**; also called Zion.

Jezebel: Daughter of the king of Tyre who was the wife of King Ahab of Israel in the mid-ninth century BCE, whom the prophets Elijah and Elisha condemned.

Job: Hero of the biblical book named for him, in which he challenges God to explain why disasters have overcome him even though he is blameless.

Joel: A **prophet** and the book named for him, which probably dates to the fifth or fourth century BCE.

Jonah: Hero of the book named for him, in which he is described as a **prophet** who reluctantly goes to the **Assyrian** capital of Nineveh. On the way there he is swallowed by a great fish.

Jonathan: Son of **Saul** and close friend of **David**.

Joseph: Oldest son of **Jacob** and **Rachel**. He was sold into slavery and in Egypt became an important official. Father of Ephraim and Manasseh.

Joshua: **Moses's** successor, and the book named for him, according to which he led the Israelites in their conquest of the **Promised Land**.

Josiah: King of **Judah** (ruled 640–609 BCE) who conducted a reform of worship inspired by a version of the book of Deuteronomy.

Judah: The name of one of **Jacob's** sons, the ancestor of the tribe of Judah. This tribe dominated southern **Israel** and became the **southern kingdom of Judah**. Later the same region was called Judea.

judge: A ruler or a military leader, as well as someone who presided over legal hearings.

Kadesh(-barnea): Site in northern **Sinai** where the Israelites stayed for some time during their journey from **Egypt** to the **Promised Land**.

King James Version: The most important translation of the Bible into English, first published in 1611. Also known as the Authorized Version.

Kirta: The hero of the **Ugaritic** epic that is named for him; the epic has many connections with biblical literature. Also called Keret.

Latter Prophets: In Jewish tradition, the second part of the **Prophets**, comprising the books of **Isaiah**, **Jeremiah**, and **Ezekiel** and the Book of the Twelve (**Minor Prophets**).

Leah: Sister of **Rachel**, first wife of **Jacob**, and mother of six of his sons.

Levant: A term used for the western part of the Near East, comprising the modern countries of Syria, Lebanon, Israel, Palestine, and Jordan.

Leviathan: A primeval watery adversary of God, often depicted as a dragon. *See also* **Behemoth**, **Rahab** (monster).

Levites: The priestly tribe, named for **Jacob's** son Levi, whose primary responsibilities were ritual.

Major Prophets: In modern scholarship, the books of **Isaiah**, **Jeremiah**, and **Ezekiel**, so called because of their relative length compared to the shorter books of the **Minor Prophets**. In Christian tradition, the books of Lamentations and **Daniel** have often been included under this heading.

Malachi: A **prophet**; also the book named for him, which probably dates to the fifth century BCE.

Manasseh: King of **Judah** (ruled 687–642 BCE), often described as an evil king.

manna: The divinely given "bread from heaven" (Ex 16.4) that fed the Israelites in the wilderness after the Exodus from Egypt.

Marduk: The chief god of **Babylon**, the storm-god who defeated **Tiamat**, as recounted in *Enuma Elish*.

Megiddo: A major city in northern **Israel** that because of its strategic location was the site of many battles. In **apocalyptic** literature, it can be called Armageddon and will be the site of the final battle between the forces of good and evil.

Mesopotamia: A word of Greek origin meaning "(the land) in the middle of the rivers." It refers to the fertile floodplain between the Tigris and the Euphrates rivers and comprises much of modern Iraq and northern Syria.

messiah: Derived from the Hebrew word *mashiah*, meaning "anointed one," this term is used in the Hebrew Bible to refer to past and present kings and priests who had been anointed. In later Jewish and in Christian traditions, it is used of a future leader to be sent by God.

Micah: A prophet in **Judah** in the late eighth century BCE; also the book named for him.

Michal: Daughter of **Saul** and wife of **David**.

Midian: Home of the Midianites, who were adversaries of Israel during their Exodus from Egypt and during the period of the **judges**. Zipporah, the wife of **Moses**, was a Midianite. Midian is located in northwestern Arabia, which may be the location of Mount **Sinai**.

Minor Prophets: In modern scholarship, the twelve shorter prophetic books, from **Hosea** through **Malachi**.

Miriam: Sister of **Aaron** and **Moses** who led the Israelites in a victory hymn after the Exodus and later, with Aaron, challenged Moses's leadership.

Moabites: Israel's neighbors east of the Dead Sea. The Moabites are the "sons of Moab," who according to Genesis 19 was the son of Lot by one of his daughters.

monotheism: The belief that there is only one god.

Moses: Leader of the Exodus from Egypt to whom God gave his laws on Mount **Sinai**. Brother of **Aaron** and **Miriam**.

myth: A traditional narrative about the remote past in which gods and goddess are often principal characters.

Nabonidus: Last king of **Babylon** (ruled 556–539 BCE), famous for having lived in Arabia for an extended period.

Nahum: Prophet in **Judah** in the late seventh century BCE; also the book named for him.

Nebuchadnezzar: *See* **Nebuchadrezzar**.

Nebuchadrezzar: King of **Babylon** (ruled 605–562 BCE) who captured **Jerusalem** in 586 and exiled many of those living there to Babylon. Also spelled Nebuchadnezzar.

Nehemiah: Governor of **Judah** appointed by the **Persians** in the mid-fifth century BCE, who rebuilt the walls of **Jerusalem** and led religious reforms.

Noah: Hero of the biblical Flood story.

northern kingdom of Israel: The territory that split from **Judah** after the death of **Solomon** in the late tenth century BCE and was an independent kingdom with its capital in **Samaria** until the **Assyrians** conquered it in 722 BCE.

Obadiah: A sixth- or fifth-century BCE **prophet** who attacked Edom; also the book named for him.

Old Testament: In Christian tradition, the name for the first part of the Bible, which comprises the Hebrew scriptures.

oracle against the nations: A genre used by the **prophets** and in **apocalyptic** literature to describe **Yahweh**'s judgment on foreign nations.

P: The Priestly source according to the **Documentary Hypothesis**, found in the books of Genesis through Numbers and at the end of the book of Deuteronomy.

parallelism: A feature of biblical and other ancient Near Eastern poetry, in which one phrase or line is followed by another that is synonymous, contrasting, or climactic.

Passover: The spring festival commemorating the Exodus from Egypt.

Pentateuch: A word of Greek origin, meaning "five books," used by modern scholars to refer to the first five books of the Bible. *See also* **Torah**.

Persia: Kingdom in modern Iran that ruled the Near East from the late sixth to the late fourth centuries BCE. *See also* **Cyrus**.

Philistines: One group of the Sea Peoples. In the late second millennium BCE, having failed to conquer the Egyptians, they settled on the southeast coast of the Mediterranean where they vied with **Israel** for the control of **Canaan**. The term "Palestine" is derived from their name.

Promised Land: The land promised by God to **Abraham** and his descendants. Its boundaries vary in the Bible, but it corresponds roughly to the territory comprising modern Israel and Palestine.

prophet: A word of Greek origin meaning "spokesperson." The prophets were believed to be recipients of direct communications from God. Sayings of and stories about many of the prophets are found in the part of the Bible known as the **Prophets**.

Prophets: In Jewish tradition, the second of the three parts of the **Hebrew Bible**, comprising the books of **Joshua** to 2 Kings and **Isaiah** to **Malachi**. *See also* **Former Prophets; Latter Prophets; Major Prophets; Minor Prophets; Torah; Writings**.

proverb: A short pithy saying, often in poetry.

Purim: The festival commemorating the deliverance of the Judeans from the plot of the Persian official Haman by **Esther** and Mordecai.

Rachel: Sister of **Leah**, second wife of **Jacob**, and mother of **Joseph** and Benjamin.

Rahab: Prostitute in Jericho who helped spies sent by **Joshua** to escape. She and her family became part of **Israel**.

Rebekah: Wife of **Isaac** and mother of **Esau** and Jacob.

redaction criticism: In modern scholarship, the study of the processes of redacting or editing, by which such larger works as the **Pentateuch** and the book of Isaiah were given their final forms.

Reed Sea: The body of water that the Israelites crossed in their **Exodus** from Egypt. Although later identified as the Red Sea, it is more likely one of several smaller bodies of water or wetlands east of the Nile Delta.

Rehoboam: The first king of the **southern kingdom of Judah** (ruled 928–911 BCE) after the death of his father **Solomon**.

Ritual Decalogue: In modern scholarship, the replacement copy of the **Ten Commandments** that **Moses** received from God after he had broken the first set because of his anger at the **golden calf** incident. Found in Exodus 34.10–26, it is exclusively concerned with worship, hence its name.

royal ideology: In modern scholarship, the term for the complex of ideas associated with the Davidic monarchy, including the **Davidic covenant**.

Ruth: Heroine of the book named for her, in which, although a **Moabite**, she becomes the mother of Obed and thus the great-grandmother of **David**.

sabbath: The day of rest, the seventh day of the week. The term can also be used for longer periods of time, as in a "sabbatical year."

Samaria: The capital of the **northern kingdom of Israel** from the early ninth century to 722 BCE, when it fell to the **Assyrians**. Subsequently, Samaria was used as the name of the region in which the city was located.

Samson: A **judge** known for his great strength, involvement with **Delilah**, and killing **Philistines**.

Samuel: A **prophet**, priest, and **judge** in eleventh-century BCE Israel. He anointed both **Saul** and **David** as Israel's first kings. The books of Samuel are named for him.

Sarah (Sarai): Wife of **Abraham** and mother of **Isaac**.

Saul: First king of **Israel**, in the late eleventh century BCE. Father of **Jonathan**, **Michal**, and Ishbaal (Ishbosheth). After his death in battle with the **Philistines**, he was succeeded by **David**.

scapegoat: A goat "for Azazel" (Lev 16.10), who was probably originally a desert demon, to which the sins of the community are symbolically transferred on the **Day of Atonement**.

Second Isaiah: In modern scholarship, chapters 40–55 of the book of **Isaiah**, dated to the mid-sixth century BCE. Also called Deutero-Isaiah.

Second Temple: The Temple completed in 515 BCE to replace the **Temple of Solomon**, which had been destroyed by the **Babylonians** in 586.

Sennacherib: King of **Assyria** (705–681 BCE) under whom the Assyrians laid siege to **Jerusalem** in 701.

servant songs: In **Second Isaiah**, a group of four poems that speak of a servant of **Yahweh**. They are Isaiah 42.1–4, 49.1–6, 50.4–11, and 52.13–53.12.

Shema: In Jewish tradition, three excerpts from the books of Deuteronomy and Numbers that are recited daily and, written on small scrolls, attached to the body during prayer and to the door of a house. The term means "Hear," from the opening word of Deuteronomy 6.4.

Sinai: The mountain from which God gave the Israelites his laws after their **Exodus** from Egypt. Its location is disputed. Also called Horeb. The Sinai Peninsula is named for the mountain.

Solomon: Son of **David** and **Bathsheba** who succeeded his father as king of Israel in the mid-tenth century BCE and built the **Temple** in **Jerusalem**.

son of man: A phrase that in the Hebrew Bible means human being. In Daniel 7.13, it is used of someone who is given universal rule; the identity of this person is disputed.

southern kingdom of Judah: The kingdom that after the death of **Solomon** in the late tenth century BCE continued to be ruled by the Davidic dynasty with its capital in **Jerusalem**, until it was captured by the **Babylonians** in 586 BCE. *See also* **Judah**.

Succession Narrative: In modern scholarship, an originally independent source incorporated into the **Deuteronomistic History** that relates how **Solomon** eventually succeeded **David** on the throne. It is found in 2 Samuel 9–20 and 1 Kings 1–2. Also called the Court History of David.

suzerainty treaty: In modern scholarship, a binding agreement between a king or suzerain and a lesser king, the suzerain's vassal. Elements of suzerainty treaties are used by the biblical writers in their presentation of the **covenant** between God and **Israel**.

synagogue: A word of Greek origin meaning "gathering together," used of religious assemblies of Jews and the buildings in which such assemblies took place.

Syro-Ephraimite War: The attack on **Judah** and **Jerusalem** by the **northern kingdom of Israel** and Aram in 734 BCE, in an attempt to force the king of Judah, **Ahaz**, to join an anti-**Assyrian** alliance.

tabernacle: The movable shrine that housed the Israelite deity and served as a sacred center of the wandering Israelite community after the Exodus from Egypt, described in detail in **Exodus** 26. Also called the "tent of meeting."

Tanakh: An acronym used for the three parts of the **Hebrew Bible** in Jewish tradition, formed from the first letter of each of its three parts: the **Torah**, the Neviim (the **Prophets**), and the Ketuvim (the **Writings**).

tell: An artificial mound formed from the stratified accumulated debris of successive human occupations.

Temple of Solomon: The Temple in **Jerusalem** built by King **Solomon** in the mid-tenth century and destroyed by the **Babylonians** in 586 BCE. It is also known as the First Temple.

Ten Commandments: The text of the contract or **covenant** between God and **Israel** made on Mount **Sinai**. *See also* **Decalogue**.

textual criticism: The study of manuscripts to determine an original text.

theodicy: A word of Greek origin meaning "divine justice," used with reference to literature that deals with the problem of human suffering, especially the suffering of the innocent.

theophany: A word of Greek origin meaning the appearance of a god, used by modern scholars to refer to the appearance of a deity to humans, usually with appropriate manifestations of divine power.

Third Isaiah: In modern scholarship, chapters 56–66 of the book of **Isaiah**, dating to the late sixth or early fifth century BCE. Also called Trito-Isaiah.

Tiamat: The goddess of the primeval salt water who in *Enuma Elish* is defeated by the storm-god **Marduk**.

Tiglath-pileser III: King of **Assyria** (745–727 BCE) who extended Assyrian control over the Near East.

tithe: A religious offering of one-tenth of the value of produce, livestock, or other commodities.

Torah/*torah*: In Jewish tradition, the Torah is the first of three parts of the **Hebrew Bible**, comprising the five books of Moses from Genesis to Deuteronomy. The word *torah* literally means "teaching" or "instruction" and is often translated "law." *See also* **Prophets**; **Writings**.

Tower of Babel: The tower built after the Flood in an attempt to reach the heavens. God punished the builders by scattering them and confusing their languages.

tree of life: The tree in the **garden of Eden** whose fruit provided immortality.

tree of the knowledge of good and evil: The tree in the **garden of Eden** whose fruit was forbidden.

Ugaritic: A Semitic language closely related to Hebrew used in second-millennium BCE texts from the site of Ugarit on the Mediterranean coast of Syria. The Ugaritic texts include a number of **myths** and epics that shed light on **Canaanite** religion.

United Monarchy: During the tenth century BCE, the ten northern tribes of **Israel** and the southern tribe of **Judah** were united under the rule of **David** and his son **Solomon**, both of whom are called "king of **Israel**." When Solomon died in 928 BCE, the united kingdom of **Israel** was split into the **northern kingdom of Israel** and the **southern kingdom of Judah**.

Utnapishtim: In the *Gilgamesh* epic, the hero of the story of the Flood.

Wellhausen, Julius (1844–1918): A German scholar who wrote *A History of Israel* (1878), which is the classic formulation of the **Documentary Hypothesis**.

wisdom literature: A type of writing whose focus is human existence and often its relationship to the divine. It employs a variety of forms, such as proverbs, dialogues, and fables. Wisdom literature was used widely in the ancient Near East and is found throughout the Bible, especially in the books of Job, Proverbs, and Ecclesiastes, and in Sirach and the Wisdom of Solomon in the **Apocrypha**.

Woman Wisdom: The depiction of the concept of wisdom as a goddess who is the companion of **Yahweh**.

Writings: In Jewish tradition, the third of three parts of the **Hebrew Bible**, comprising the books of Psalms, Proverbs, Job, Song of Solomon, Ruth, Lamentations, Ecclesiastes, Esther, Daniel, Ezra, Nehemiah, and 1 and 2 Chronicles. *See also* **Prophets**; **Torah**.

Yahweh: The personal name of the God of **Israel**.

Zechariah: A **prophet** in **Judah** in the late sixth century BCE; also the book named for him.

Zedekiah: Last king of **Judah** (ruled 597–586 BCE), during whose reign **Jerusalem** was destroyed by the **Babylonians**.

Zephaniah: A **prophet** in **Judah** in the late seventh century BCE; also the book named for him.

Zerubbabel: One of the leaders of the return to **Judah** from exile in **Babylon** in 538 BCE

Zion: A name of **Jerusalem**, used especially in poetic texts.

Weights and Measures

The modern equivalents for weights and measures in the Old Testament are presented in the following tables.

WEIGHTS

Hebrew	NRSV	Equivalence	U.S. Avoirdupois	Metric Units
kikkar	talent	60 minas	75.558 pounds	34.3 kilograms
maneh	mina	50 shekels	20.148 ounces	571.2 grams
sheqel	shekel	2 bekas	176.29 grains	11.42 grams
pim (or payim)	pim	.667 shekel	117.52 grains	7.61 grams
beqa'	beka, half a shekel	10 gerahs	88.14 grains	5.71 grams
gerah	gerah		8.81 grains	.57 gram

The practice of weighing unmarked ingots of metal used in commercial transactions prior to the invention of money explains why the names of the units of weight were used later as indications of value, and as names for monetary standards. There is, however, no direct relation between the shekel-weight and the weight of a shekel piece.

MEASURES OF LENGTH

Hebrew	NRSV	Equivalence	U.S. Measures	Metric Units
'ammah	cubit	2 spans	17.49 inches	.443 meter
zeret	span	3 handbreadths	8.745 inches	.221 meter
ṭopaḥ, ṭepaḥ	handbreadth	4 fingers	2.915 inches	.074 meter
'etsba'	finger		0.728 inch	.019 meter

The cubit described in Ezekiel 40.5; 43.13 is equal to seven (not six) handbreadths, namely 20.405 inches.

HEBREW MEASURES OF CAPACITY: LIQUID MEASURES

Hebrew	NRSV	Equivalence	U.S. Measures	Metric Units
kor	measure, cor	10 baths	60.738 gallons	230 liters
bat	bath	6 hins	6.073 gallons	23 liters
hin	hin	3 kabs	1.012 gallons	3.829 liters
qab	kab	4 logs	1.4349 quarts	1.276 liters
log	log		0.674 pint	.32 liter

MEASURES OF CAPACITY: DRY MEASURES

Hebrew	NRSV	Equivalence	U.S. Measures	Metric Units
ḥomer	homer	2 lethechs	6.524 bushels	229.7 liters
kor	measure, cor	2 lethechs	6.524 bushels	229.7 liters
letek	lethech, measure	5 ephahs	3.262 bushels	114.8 liters
'epah	ephah, measure	3 seahs	20.878 quarts	22.9 liters
se'ah	measure	3.33 omers	6.959 quarts	7.7 liters
'omer	omer	1.8 kabs	2.087 quarts	2.3 liters
'issaron	tenth part (of ephah)			
qab	kab		1.159 quarts	1.3 liters

Index

Bold page numbers indicate material in figures.